REPUBLICAN
ROME

H.L.HAVELL

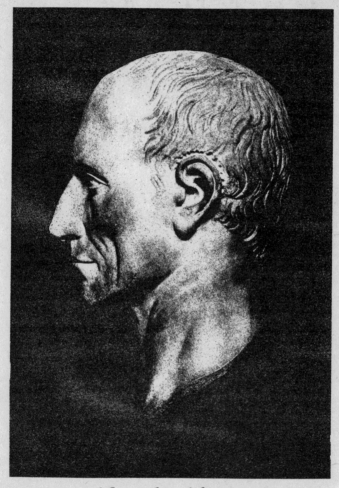

Caius Julius Caesar

REPUBLICAN
ROME

H.L.HAVELL

ORACLE

Republican Rome

First published in 1914 by George G. Harrap & Co. Ltd.,
London

This edition published in 1996 by Oracle Publishing Ltd.,
2A Kingsway, Royston, Hertfordshire,
SE8 5EG, England.

ISBN 1 86196 005 0

Printed and bound in Guernsey by
The Guernsey Press Co. Ltd

PREFACE

SHORTLY after the manuscript of this book was completed Mr. Havell, when on a visit to England from Halle, where he lectured in the University, met with a fatal accident while cycling.

This lamentable termination of a busy and honoured life removed from the book in its progress through the press the assistance which would in ordinary circumstances be rendered by the author. Fortunately Mr. Havell was extremely careful in finishing his manuscripts. But his work upon the selection of the illustrations was not very far advanced, and only some notes concerning the maps were found to be serviceable. It was therefore necessary to begin this part of the work afresh, and Mr. H. B. Cotterill was good enough to undertake the selection of the illustrations and to write the explanatory Notes upon them. We are also greatly indebted to him for valuable advice and assistance in the compilation of the maps.

Mr. Cotterill desires that acknowledgment should be made here of the kind assistance given him in the selection of the coins by Mr. J. Allan, of the Department of Coins and Medals, British Museum.

THE PUBLISHERS

CONTENTS

vii

REPUBLICAN ROME

LIST OF PLATES

To illustrate the history of Republican Rome fully and attractively is very much more difficult than to find interesting pictures illustrative of early Greek history, where one has not only a great number of Cretan, Trojan, Mycenaean, and Dipylon antiquities, but also many magnificent temples and a large choice of statues. In the case of Rome most of the great works of architecture are of a date somewhat too late for one's purpose, and of early Roman sculpture and bronzes (mostly the work of Greek or Etruscan artists) very little has survived. One is, therefore, compelled to give *sites*, such as those here given of Carthage, Corinth, Syracuse, Caere, Veii, Lake Trasimenus, and so on, or pictures of somewhat shapeless ruins, such as that of the Servian *Agger*, or of what are not strictly Roman antiquities, such as Etruscan walls and Etruscan tombs, seeing that Etruscan civilization and Etruscan art existed at a time when Rome produced little that interests the art-lover or the archaeologist. H. B. COTTERILL

The names of those to whom the compiler is indebted for permission to use copyright photographs are printed in italic.

patchwork. The bronze seems to have been in existence
(that is, not lost) ever since the days of Cicero. In the
Middle Ages (*e.g.* during Alberico's domination of Rome,
c. 930) it stood in a hall of the Lateran palace (the *Aula
ad lupam*) and was known popularly as the 'Mater
Romanorum.' The twins are of sixteenth-century workmanship and of Michelangelesque type. *Photo Alinari.*

3. 'THE WALLS OF ROMULUS'

On the slope of the Cermalus, not far to the south of the
great Domus Tiberiana on the Palatine, below the
precinct of the Magna Mater and above the stairs of
Cacus the Giant, in a quarter where the 'Lupercal'
may have been (the place where the twins were believed
to have been suckled by the she-wolf) and where the
Tugurium Faustuli or Casa Romuli stood—*i.e.* the cottage
of Faustulus the shepherd, or of Romulus, in later times
the central sanctuary of Rome—there were excavated
in 1907 very ancient tufa blocks that may possibly be
relics of the walls of 'Roma quadrata,' which are
attributed by tradition to Romulus. A huge pit for
offerings to the infernal deities (*mundus*) has lately
been found, dating from the foundation of the city.
This pit was already forgotten in Republican times, and
was built over by the palaces of the Caesars. *Photo
Alinari.*

4. 'TOMB OF HORATII AND CURIATII'

A monument on the road between Albano and Ariccia. Also
formerly called 'Tomb of Aruns Tarquinius.' Criticism
now holds it to date from late Republican, or even late
Imperial, times, and to be merely an imitation of the
ancient Etruscan style. But it certainly reminds one
forcibly of the tomb of Porsenna as described by Varro,
and may surely be a restoration of some old Etruscan
original; and that this original was *not* the tomb of Aruns
or of the Curiatii, who can prove ? *Photo Anderson.*

5. THE LAST RELICS OF THE PONS SUBLICIUS

See p. 13. The oldest and for a long time the only Roman
bridge, built on wooden piles (*sublicae*), which were
renewed from age to age: traditionally the bridge
defended by Horatius Cocles. It was reconstructed in
stone by the triumvir Lepidus, but was ruined by a
flood. This picture, taken in 1871, shows the relics
of the piles, which were demolished when the Tiber was
canalized and 'regulated.' *Photo Alinari.*

6. THE TIBER AND THE CLOACA MAXIMA

An old view taken before the Lungo Tevere was constructed.
In background the Round Temple (Plate 54) and the
fine Campanile of Sta. Maria in Cosmedin. See pp. 14, 18.
Livy (i. 38) and Pliny seem to attribute the building of
the great Cloaca to Tarquinius Priscus. It was one of

LIST OF PLATES

REPUBLICAN ROME

The three animals (*sus, ovis, taurus*) which were sacrificed on occasions of 'lustration'—*e.g.* the atonement or purification connected with the quinquennial census, or with the setting forth of an army on a campaign, or the foundation of a temple. The animals were led round the assembly, or the place, that was to be purified, and then slaughtered. The custom is mentioned by Livy (i. 44) in connexion with the census rites instituted by Servius Tullius. This fine relief is post-Republican. It forms a side of one of the splendid marble parapets erected by Trajan on the Rostra. They were discovered (1872) in course of the excavations of the Forum, in a building that had been walled up. *Photo Anderson.*

Looking up-stream from near the Ponte Rotto (the ancient Pons Aemilius). The view was taken before considerable 'improvements' altered the Cestian Bridge and the buildings on the island. To the right one sees the Pons Fabricius (Plate 57) by which one crosses the left arm of the river (for some years dry, during 'regulation' of the Tiber). The island, the form of which was compared to that of a ship, contained the temple of Aesculapius. In 293 B.C. the ravages of a plague induced the Romans to "fetch the god Aesculapius" from Epidaurus. They brought him to Rome in the form of a large snake, and when the ship arrived near this island, says the legend, the snake escaped to it and hid himself there. The present church of S. Bartolomeo probably stands on the site of the old temple. The Cestian Bridge, built by Augustus, very much restored, joins the island with Trastevere. *Photo Alinari.*

Porta dell' Arco or 'dei Capi,' so called from the massive arch supported on Etruscan masonry, and from the two ancient heads. For Volterra see Plate 10. *Photo Brogi.*

Naples, Mus. Naz. Found at Herculaneum. Only the edge of helmet restored. The Macedonian helm, the kingly scarf and the oak-garland (a special attribute of his) make it almost certain that it is meant for Pyrrhus (319–272 B.C.). The workmanship is of the Lysippus style, and denotes a date during or shortly after the life of Pyrrhus. *Photo F. Bruckmann, Munich.*

Found in the Atrium Vestae, and now in the Thermae Museum. Probably of later workmanship, but doubtless gives the ancient costume (*stola* and *pallium*) of the Vestal Virgins. The hood (*suffibulum*), that has a curious

REPUBLICAN ROME

LIST OF PLATES

LIST OF PLATES

REPUBLICAN ROME

MAPS AND PLANS

CHAPTER I

FROM THE FOUNDATION OF ROME TO THE EXPULSION OF THE KINGS

AMONG all the strange things that may be brought to light by a diligent explorer in the vast lumber-room of history, few, perhaps, are stranger than the imposing family tree which was set up by the learned Greek Dionysius as a tribute of admiration to the imperial people of Rome. The Greeks, as is well known, branded all nations of non-Greek descent as barbarians; and they reserved a peculiar mark of infamy for their Roman masters, taunting them as the descendants of freebooters and vagabonds. Dionysius, who had a deep and sincere admiration for Roman greatness, was much concerned at this petulant spirit in his countrymen, and in the first book of his *Roman Antiquities* he makes an elaborate attempt to provide a pedigree for the despised foundling among the great family of nations. The Greeks, he argues, may well bear their yoke with patience, for their conquerors are of the same race as themselves, descended in a direct line from the most ancient cradle of Greek civilization. The inquiry is pursued with infinite minuteness and carried to a prodigious length, but its main results may be briefly summed up as follows:

Legendary Origin of the Romans

In the beginning the Aborigines [1] came from Arcadia to Italy, drove out the Sicels, and settled in Latium. These were followed by the Pelasgians from Thessaly, who were welcomed as kinsmen and given a share in the conquered

---

[1] Pronounce Aborigĭnes—no connexion with *origo*.

territory. Then came a second colony of Arcadians from Pallantium, with their king Evander, and occupied a hill by the Tiber, which they called the Palatine in memory of their native seat. The fourth infusion of Greek blood was brought by Heracles, who is gravely exhibited by Dionysius as a great warrior and statesman, carrying the blessings of civilization to the remotest confines of Europe. In his beneficent progress he visited Italy, and some of his followers were incorporated among the previous settlers in Latium. These, it seems, were mostly Epeans from Elis, and they made their abode on the hill afterwards called the Capitoline. Last of all came Aeneas with his Trojans; and he also, we are assured, was a Greek, a true scion, like Achilles himself, of the Olympian Zeus, and the ancestor of the mighty Julian line.

Such was the wonderful patent of nobility worked out with enormous prolixity by the pious zeal of the Greek antiquarian, from a desire to soothe the injured pride of his countrymen by convincing them that the Romans were even more Greek than themselves. The process of falsifying history, which here reaches its climax, had been going on for nearly three centuries, from the time when the Romans began to make themselves felt as one of the great powers of Europe; and the result of all this solemn trifling was the sorry patchwork with which the Romans were taught to conceal the noble simplicity of their origin.

If we scrutinize carefully the huge heap of rubbish which Dionysius has piled up at the threshold of his subject, we may be rewarded by a few particles of genuine fact. The Sicels, for instance, have a real place in history, and they are recognized by Thucydides [1] as among the original inhabitants of Italy. The Aborigines, again, are probably to be identified with the Aurunci, and these are no other than the Oscans, an early offshoot of the great Umbro-Sabellian stock, and closely related to the Latins. And underlying the legend of the Greek settlements in Latium there is an important germ of truth, for between Greek and Roman there was a close ethnic affinity.

FOUNDATION OF ROME

The Latins

When the Latins first appear in history they are confined to a few square miles of territory in the northern part of the extensive district which afterwards formed one political unit under the name of Latium. They were a hardy race of farmers and shepherds, living in open hamlets, each of which had its own walled stronghold, to serve as a common place of meeting, and as a refuge in times of danger. By degrees these rude forts would develop into towns, thirty of which are mentioned as being united at a very early date in a sort of federal league, under the presidency of Alba Longa, the earliest of the Latin settlements. For ages after the political centre had been transferred to Rome the Latin Festival continued to be held every year on the Alban Mount, as the oldest centre of national union.

Foundation of Rome

Alba, then, was the mother-city of all the old Latin townships ; and the youngest of her children was Rome. According to the generally received chronology, about the middle of the eighth century B.C. a band of colonists, led by the young princes Romulus and Remus, set out from Alba, and planted a settlement on the northern frontier of Latium, choosing as the site of their new home the central height in a group of hills on the left bank of the Tiber, about fifteen miles from the river-mouth.

The foundation of Rome belongs to a time when all the more fertile and attractive sites in Old Latium were already occupied, and this explains that part of the tradition which describes the young colonists as a band of needy adventurers. It was necessity, remarks Strabo,[1] rather than choice which directed the ancestors of the imperial people to that barren and unhealthy spot. But when once the colony was planted the immense political and military advantages of the place led to a rapid and steady development.

[1] v. 3, 2.

REPUBLICAN ROME

Romulus and Remus

Romulus and Remus are of course no more to be regarded as historical characters than Hengist and Horsa. But the story of their birth is a true national growth, full of beauty and meaning, and a most interesting example of the manner in which history is manufactured out of legend. It would appear that the original names were Romus [1] and Romulus, and these are the titles of the Lares, or tutelary spirits, of Rome. [2] Faustulus, or Faunus, their foster-father, is an old pastoral god, and his wife, Acca Laurentia, who rears the children, is one of the many incarnations of the goddess of agriculture, the genial power who quickens the seed-corn in the furrow, and takes charge of a more costly seed, when we consign our beloved dead to their mother earth. The wild creatures of nature minister to the first wants of the helpless babes. The woodpecker, the sacred bird of Mars, brings them morsels of food, and the she-wolf gives them suck. This is plainly no imported myth, but the genuine coinage of a stalwart race of fighting peasants, whose hand was equally ready for the sword and the plough, and who owed all their virtues to the grand primeval industry of agriculture. In after-ages, when the Romans were sunk deep in corruption, Virgil and Horace exerted all the magic of their genius to revive the antique beauty of that nobler life; and four generations later the fierce heart of Juvenal finds utterance in a great and bitter cry, calling upon the spirits of the mighty dead to arrest the wild iniquity of the time. [3]

The same pastoral character meets us at every step in the early days of Rome. The name of the hill [4] which formed the central stronghold of the young colony; the feast of Pales, an ancient deity, worshipped as the guardian of flocks and

---

[1] Dionysius constantly uses the form Romus, of which Romulus is clearly the diminutive.

[2] Seeley, introduction to first book of Livy.

[3] Virgil, *Georgics*, *passim*; Horace, *Odes*, iii. 6, *Epodes*, ii.; Juvenal, *Satires*, ii.

[4] Palatine, like Pales, connected with *pasco*, ' to feed ' (of flocks or herds).

4

PLATE II. THE SHE-WOLF OF THE CAPITOL 4

PLATE III. THE WALLS OF ROMULUS.'

herds; the Porta Mugionis, or 'Gate of Lowing,' through which the herdsmen drove their cattle for safe-keeping in times of danger, all point to the same fact. The line of the defending wall was marked by a plough drawn by a heifer and a bull, and the dance of the Luperci, or priests of Faunus, continued until the latest times to commemorate the original limits of the city.

ROMAN SHEPHERD

DEVELOPMENT OF THE CITY

Mention has been made of the natural advantages which led to the unparalleled development of Rome, and raised her by successive stages from an obscure colony of Alba to the position of metropolis of Latium, the queen of Italy and the centre of a world-wide empire. Before proceeding with the scanty annals of the kings it will be well to examine this point a little more closely. The original city was confined to the Palatine Mount, and from thence it advanced steadily, taking in hill after hill, until it covered the whole of the surrounding heights. Each of these settlements would for some time assume the character of an independent community, and this would lead to a collision of interests, training the inhabitants in the elements of international law. Next we have to notice the central position of Rome, at the junction of the three great racial divisions of Italy, the Sabine, the Etruscan, and the Latin. Then, again, the barrenness of the soil and the unhealthiness of the surrounding country both served to protect and foster the growth of the young state. Here were none of the perilous attractions which drew horde after horde of invaders to the neighbouring land of Campania and made that favoured province the battle-ground of Italy. On the other hand, the poverty of their own fields would stimulate the energies of a warlike people and guide them into the path of aggression and conquest. Nor must we overlook the situation of Rome on a

5

navigable river, at some distance from its mouth, which gave the city at once the advantages of an inland and a maritime position. This happy circumstance was a source of manifold benefits. It placed Rome beyond the reach of sudden raids from the Tuscan pirates; it made intercourse with foreign states easy, thus bringing her into contact with

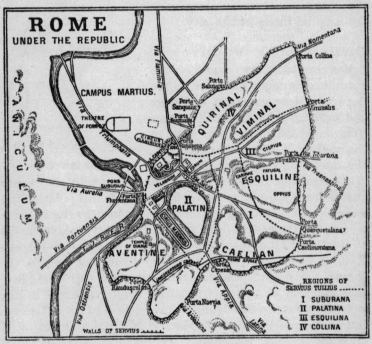

more developed forms of civilization and preserving her from the stagnation into which a more isolated power such as Sparta is liable to fall; and at the same time it kept her free from those corrupting influences which are the curse of great maritime cities.[1]

Already, within thirty-seven years from the foundation of Rome (753–717 B.C.), the period assigned by tradition to the reign of Romulus, the Pomoerium, or sacred circle of the city,

---

[1] See the beautiful passage in Cicero, *De Rep.* ii. 4.

had been extended so as to take in the neighbouring spurs
of the Esquiline and the Caelian, and the Capitol and Quirinal
had been occupied by new settlers. The last-named sites
were peopled by a swarm of Sabines, who according to the
generally received account made war on the Romans, and after
a severe struggle were admitted to the full rights of citizenship.
The name Quirites, which afterwards came to be applied to the
Romans in their civil capacity, is a word of Sabine origin,
signifying 'spearmen.' We hear also of a war with Veii, a
powerful city of Southern Etruria, whose jealousy may well
have been excited by the rapid rise of a Latin colony so near its
borders. Romulus, we are told, gained a great victory over
the Veientines, and wrested from them the whole of the land
skirting the right bank of the Tiber from Rome to the sea, as
well as the valuable salt-works at the river's mouth. Whatever
may be the amount of truth contained in this account, it is
certain that from a very early date the Romans were in possession of this district.   The Arval Brethren,[1] a primitive religious
brotherhood, whose ritual chant is the most ancient monument
of the Latin language now extant, had the chief seat of their
worship on this side of the Tiber, about four miles from Rome.

NUMA POMPILIUS

In the second year after the death of Romulus a Sabine
named Numa Pompilius, who enjoyed a high reputation for
wisdom and sanctity, was chosen king, and he reigned for
more than forty years. Numa has even less claim than
Romulus to be regarded as historical. He represents the
religious aspect of the Roman character, as Romulus represents
its warlike and political aspect. Both names illustrate the
tendency to ascribe the institutions of a people, which are the
slow growth of ages, to the creative genius of a single legislator,
a tendency which is found in all early attempts at historical
writing, and has only disappeared in quite modern times,
with the rise of a more critical method.   The reign of Numa, so
runs the legend, was a time of golden peace and leisure, when

[1] See Mommsen, vol. i. ch. iv.

every man sat under his vine and his fig-tree, and the sound of arms was never heard in the land. This pleasing fiction may be dismissed without ceremony ; the main business of a young people is fighting, and we may be quite sure that during so many years there were hard knocks enough exchanged between the fierce inmates of the 'wolf's den' and their jealous neighbours. But in the total silence of history the reign of Numa remains a blank, and it will be convenient to fill up the interval by giving some account of Roman religion in its general features, and of its organization for domestic and public purposes, which is associated by tradition with the name of the Sabine sage.

Roman Religion

The Romans, like the English, were a practical race, and in their dealings with the gods we constantly discern their hard and businesslike character. They were averse to all high and abstract speculation, and cared nothing for that form of religion which leads man to forget himself in mystical communion with the Godhead. They were profoundly convinced that the affairs of men were guided and governed by divine power, and this earnest faith continued to maintain its ground until the age of their decline. But the shrewd farmers, the politic statesmen, and the ambitious warriors who were bred on the soil of Latium were trained to regard the supernatural forces chiefly as a means of promoting their own worldly advantage. In their anxiety to appropriate every particle of the divine essence to their own practical ends, they were led into an infinite multiplication of the objects of worship, until every process in nature, every incident in daily life, every thought, word, and deed, received its shadowy counterpart in the spiritual world. The meaning of this statement will be made plain by a single illustration. Just before the capture of Rome by the Gauls a mysterious voice was heard at dead of night in the very heart of the city, warning the people of the coming danger. No one paid heed at the time, but after the departure of the Gauls an altar was dedicated to

FOUNDATION OF ROME

Aius Locutius, ' the God of the Warning Voice.' There was
no limit to this minute specialization. Every kind of influence,
good or evil, had to be recognized and propitiated, so that there
was a god of sowing, a god of garnering, a god of fermentation,
and a god of blight.[1]

Thus the old Latin religion was a true image of the unspoilt
mind of Rome, in its native simplicity and its rustic humour.
And as the nation grew in moral stature and became conscious
of its high destiny these rural gods put on a new dignity which
was all their own. Jupiter, who sat enthroned on the Capitol,
looking down on the grave debates of the Senate and the keen
rivalries of the Forum, if he lacked the cosmic magnificence
of his brother on Olympus, had yet a sober civic majesty
which well befitted the divine president of a people born to
rule the world. Ceres, the giver of bread and the kind mother
of the poor, was also the lawgiver and the guardian of social
order. And the fierce Mars himself, who rejoices in the roar
of battle, is transfigured by the light of history into the incarnate
spirit of progress, carrying the banner of civilization in the van
of the conquering legions.

Very interesting also are those forms of worship which
illustrate the Roman character on its gentler and more human
side. For under the iron surface of Roman manners there
was a true vein of tenderness and sweetness and a passionate
love of home, which find their best expression in the poetry of
Virgil and Catullus. The eternal fire of Vesta, which no doubt
had its origin in a simple practical need, assumed a deep
spiritual significance as the symbol of domestic purity, the
source of national health and strength. The Lares and
Penates, the spirits of the home, stood in a still more intimate
relation with the sanctities of family life, watching over the
Roman mother as she went about her daily tasks, fostering the
growth of the children, and taking their share in all the joys and
sorrows of the little circle which sat at meat under their shrine.

To complete this slight sketch of Roman religion something
must be said of the auspices, the various signs by which the

[1] Mommsen, *loc. cit.*

9

gods made known their will to men, and the science of augury, which was applied to the interpretation of those signs. Every act of human life was controlled by a host of invisible beings,

who gave token of their purpose in various ways, by the flight and voice of birds, by the message flashed from the thunder-cloud, by certain occult marks on the internal organs of slaughtered animals, and by the manner in which the sacred chickens took their food. To interpret these signs correctly was a difficult matter, requiring a long training and special gifts ; and hence arose the science of augury, which was worked out in great detail by a body of men who gave their lives to this study, and formed a close corporation, with peculiar honours and privileges. Also, all the chief gods of Rome had their colleges of priests, who sought their favour in due form by

PRIEST PRESENTING
INCENSE-BOX

sacrifice and prayer. But in the exercise of their religious functions both priests and augurs were rigidly excluded from all direct influence on politics. The same restriction was maintained in the private life of Rome. Every Roman was a priest so far as his personal affairs were concerned, and though he might seek the advice of a religious expert in cases of difficulty, he would submit to no dictation from his spiritual adviser. By this wise limitation the Romans were preserved from that priestly interference which has crept like a palsy into the life of some nations.

Tullus Hostilius

The long slumber of Numa's reign is broken at last, and the warlike Tullus Hostilius, of true Roman birth, ascends the throne. A succession of border forays soon led to an open rupture with Alba, and in the shrewd device of Tullus,[1] by which he contrived to throw the burden of offence on the

[1] Livy, i. 22 ; Dionysius, iii. 3.

Albans, we may recognize the beginnings of Roman statecraft. The rival armies took the field, and a battle was about to begin, when it was proposed that the quarrel should be decided by the prowess of three Roman and three Alban warriors. These were the sons of two Alban women, one of whom was wedded to the Roman Horatius, the other to the Alban Curiatius, and by a miraculous coincidence they were all born on the same day. The strange conflict ended in favour of the Romans, and according to the terms of the compact the metropolitan rights of Alba passed to Rome. But the Alban general, Mettius Fufetius, broke faith with Tullus, and this led to the total destruction of Alba, whose citizens were transported in a body to Rome and settled on the Caelian Mount. By this forced migration the population of Rome was doubled. With true kingly wisdom Tullus made no distinction between conquerors and conquered. The leading nobles of Alba were enrolled among the senators, and the bravest of her warriors went to swell the number of the knights.[1] Thus the seat of empire was transferred to Rome ; and among the great houses which afterwards became famous in history by far the most illustrious was the Alban house of Julius. Tullus provided a new home for the augmented Senate, the venerable Curia Hostilia, where the Alban Fathers [2] now sat side by side with the elders of Rome.

A famous story is told in connexion with the struggle between Rome and Alba, which gives a legendary sanction to the most cherished privilege of Roman citizens, the right of appeal to the people in capital cases. Horatius, as he returns from the battlefield, carrying the spoils of the fallen Curiatii, is met by his sister, who breaks out into loud lamentations on learning the fate of her cousins, to one of whom she was betrothed. In sudden anger Horatius strikes her dead, and being brought to trial for the murder, he is acquitted by the voice of the people, who are constituted final arbiters in the case by the authority of the king. From the manner in

---

[1] Young men of rank and wealth, who served as horsemen.
[2] Virgil, *Aeneid*, i. 7.

which the incident is related we are led to infer that the right of appeal to the people was not derived from immemorial custom, but from a deliberate surrender of the royal prerogative.

ANCUS MARTIUS

Tullus was succeeded by Ancus Martius, grandson of Numa, who seemed likely to walk in the footsteps of his grandfather. But when the Latins, presuming on his peaceful disposition, began to plunder the outlying farms of the Romans he proved himself no sluggard. It is on this occasion that we first hear of the sacred college of Fetiales,[1] who had charge of all the ceremonies connected with the declaration of war and the conclusion of peace, and were the official guardians of international law. With due observance of these religious forms the Latins were called upon to give satisfaction for the violation of Roman territory, and on their refusal to comply, the king, after taking the advice of the Senate, solemnly declared war. Then one of the Fetiales took a spear, pointed with iron, or hardened with fire and dipped in blood, and, going to the hostile frontier, in the presence of not less than three witnesses announced the decision of the king and Senate and flung the spear across the border.

The wars of Ancus resulted in an extension of Roman territory on the left bank of the Tiber. Three cities were destroyed in this district, and their population was removed to Rome, finding a dwelling-place on the Aventine. The Latins then concentrated all their forces at Medullia, a powerful city near the Sabine border, and after an obstinate struggle Ancus was once more victorious, and returned to Rome with a vast spoil and many thousand prisoners, whom he settled in the ' Myrtle Valley,'[2] between the Aventine and Palatine.

'Still more important was the occupation of the Janiculum, an outlying hill on the right bank of the Tiber, which was fortified as an outpost against Etruria, and connected with

[1] Livy, i. 32. According to Dionysius (ii. 72), they were instituted by Numa.
[2] Vallis Murcia.

PLATE IV. 'TOMB OF HORATII AND CURIATII'

12

PLATE V. THE LAST RELICS OF THE PONS SUBLICIUS

the city by a bridge constructed entirely of wood, called the Pons Sublicius. And by the foundation of Ostia, a harbour-town at the mouth of the Tiber, which also was a work of Ancus, Rome first assumed the character of a maritime power.[1]

GROWTH OF THE STATE

The last century of the monarchy at Rome was an age of rapid progress both at home and abroad. Important conquests led to a wide extension of territory, including the whole of Old Latium and a considerable part of Southern Etruria. Then were begun, and for the most part completed, those vast engineering and architectural works which remained the wonder of posterity even in the time of the Empire. Under the second of these powerful and politic princes, too, the people were organized on a new basis, which served as a foundation for the Republican constitution.

The thick veil of legend which surrounds the name of the Tarquins makes it impossible to reconstruct the history of this period in authentic detail; but it is at least a highly probable conjecture that for more than three generations Rome was under the rule of the Etruscans, who were then by far the greatest power in Italy. The fifth and seventh kings of Rome are admitted to have been of Etruscan descent, and according to one account the sixth king, Servius Tullius, was also an immigrant from Etruria.

TARQUINIUS PRISCUS

In the narrative of Livy and Dionysius, Tarquinius Priscus is described as the son of a Greek exile from Corinth, a certain Demaratus, who settled at Tarquinii, the chief city of Etruria, married a lady of high Etruscan birth, and became the father of two sons. The younger of these died just before his father, and the elder, whose original name was Lucumo, was thus left sole heir to a vast estate. Being discontented with his position at Tarquinii, he migrated to Rome with his family, changed

---

[1] Dionysius, iii. 44.

REPUBLICAN ROME

his name to Lucius Tarquinius, and, gaining the friendship of
Ancus, was appointed guardian of his two sons by the royal
will. After the death of Ancus he sent the young princes
away on a hunting expedition, and by exerting all his influence contrived to be elected in due form as the lawful
king of Rome.[1] In order to strengthen his position he added
a hundred new members, chosen from his own partisans,[2]
to the Senate, thus raising the number to three hundred.

The reign of the first Tarquin was long and glorious. He
conquered many of the cities of Old Latium, defeated a great
coalition of Sabines, Latins, and Etruscans, and received the
symbols of sovereignty, which were brought him in token of
submission by a deputation from the states of Southern
Etruria.[3] These outward signs of royalty were the crown of
gold, the ivory chain, the eagle-headed sceptre, a purple tunic
worked with gold, a purple embroidered robe, and the twelve
axes, enclosed in bundles of rods, which were carried by the
lictors when the king appeared in public.

Far more enduring, however, were those works of embel-
lishment or utility which were begun by this king, and continued by his successors. Of these the most important were
the wonderful system of *cloacae*, or underground canals, lined
with solid masonry, which were designed to drain the low-lying
district between the Quirinal, the Capitoline, and the Palatine
hills, and the laying of a solid substructure to support the
foundations of the great temple of Jupiter on the Capitoline,
a work of vast labour and difficulty, which occupied the closing
years of Tarquin's reign. The great stone wall, taking in the
whole circuit of the seven hills, which bears the name of Servius
Tullius was also planned and in part carried out by the elder
Tarquin.

SERVIUS TULLIUS

In the midst of these important designs Tarquin was
murdered by the contrivance of a party headed by the sons

[1] It should be remembered that the kingship at Rome was elective, and not
hereditary.   [2] *Factio regis* (Livy, i. 35).   [3] Dionysius, iv. 12.

14

of Ancus. But the conspirators were prevented from reaping the fruits of their treason by a man far abler than themselves. This was Servius Tullius, a favourite of Tarquin, who had grown up in the king's palace and married one of the king's daughters. Soon after his elevation to the throne, which he owed to the influence of the new senators created by Tarquin, Tullius prepared to carry out the constitutional reforms which had been planned and in part executed by his father-in-law.

Nearly two centuries had now elapsed since the foundation of Rome, and during this period there had been a steady increase of the population from outside, either by voluntary settlement for purposes of trade or by enforced migration from the conquered cities of Latium. Some of these new settlers were enrolled in the list of the old burghers, as happened in the case of Alba, but a large proportion remained in the position of resident foreigners, excluded from all political privileges, though in many cases they may have become wealthy men and have bequeathed large estates to their descendants. Roman citizenship was confined, with few exceptions, to a small inner circle, composed of those who could trace their descent from the original founders of Rome. These were divided into three tribes, the Ramnes, Tities, and Luceres, and there was a further division into thirty Curies, or wards, forming together the Comitia Curiata, the primitive Parliament of Roman citizens.

PATRICIANS AND PLEBEIANS

Such was probably the origin of the famous distinction between Patricians and Plebeians. A patrician, like the Spanish hidalgo, was ' somebody's son,' and he alone, with his peers, was a true child of Rome and a member of the Populus Romanus. The plebeian [1] was an outsider, the son of nobody, for all political purposes a mere cipher. The great reform of Servius led in the end to the removal of this invidious

[1] Literally, ' one who helps to *fill up* ' a certain number, or, as we might say, a make-weight.

15

distinction, and placed the patrician and plebeian on a footing of
equality ; but nearly three centuries elapsed before this result
was finally perfected, and the immediate effect of the change
was an increase of burdens for the plebeians without any
increase of privilege. Before the time of Servius the whole
weight of the public duties fell on the patricians ; they alone
served in the army, and they alone were charged with the
tributum, or war-tax. The constitution of Servius was designed
to remove this anomaly and to distribute the public burdens
among the whole body of Roman residents in proportion to
their wealth. In this new organization the three old tribal
divisions were set aside, and four fresh tribes were created,
including the whole free population of Rome. These divisions
were purely local, being named after the four city districts,
the Palatine, the Esquiline, the Suburan, and the Colline ; and
it seems probable, though the point is somewhat doubtful,
that the inhabitants of the country districts were enrolled in
the four city tribes,[1] which were intended to serve as a basis
for a complete registration of property.

MILITARY ORGANIZATION

More important was the division into classes and centuries,
which after the fall of the kings became the free Parliament of
Rome. But in its original intention this was a purely military organization, arranged on the principle that the duty of
defending the State ought to fall heaviest on those who have
most to defend. The infantry of Rome, which at this time
fought in a solid mass, like the Greek phalanx, was marshalled
by Servius in five classes. The first class, numbering eighty
centuries, was composed of those whose fortune amounted to
not less than a hundred thousand *asses*, or pounds of copper ; [2]
these formed the front ranks, clothed in complete armour,
after the Greek fashion. Next to them stood the twenty
centuries of the second class, with a fortune of not less than

[1] According to another account, the rural population was distributed by
Tullius into twenty-six country tribes.

[2] The valuation in money belongs to a later date ; the original computation
was probably in cattle and slaves. See p. 533.

seventy-five thousand *asses*, and to these were added two centuries of *fabri*, or engineers. The third class consisted of those whose fortune was not less than fifty thousand *asses*, and these also numbered twenty centuries. The same number of centuries, with two additional centuries of musicians, made up the fourth class, with a fortune of not less than twenty-five thousand *asses*; and for the fifth class, composed of thirty centuries, the standard was fixed at not less than twelve thousand five hundred *asses*. In each of the five classes the number of centuries was equally divided into two groups, one of Seniors, composed of men above the age of forty-six, and one of Juniors, whose age was between seventeen and forty-six. The juniors were employed in active military service, and the seniors served for home defence. For the four centuries of engineers and musicians there was no fixed standard of fortune.

AS OF THE CITY OF TUDER

Outside the five classes stood, at one end, the eighteen centuries of Equites, or cavalry, and, at the other, one century of those who, having little or no fortune, were counted by the head, and hence called *capite censi*. The scale of equipment was gradually reduced according to the amount of property in the several classes, the fourth and fifth being without any defensive armour, and serving as light-armed troops, furnished with javelins and slings.

It must be observed that the term 'century' is merely nominal, the number contained in each century being in some cases less and in other cases far more than a hundred.

When this military organization, which was called the Comitia Centuriata, came to be used for political purposes, the voting was conducted, not by heads, but by centuries, and consequently the eighty centuries of the first class, with the eighteen centuries of cavalry, if they held together, formed a standing majority, with power to control the whole machinery of government.

REPUBLICAN ROME

By this great reform Servius prepared the way for the unification of the Populus, which was worked out by slow degrees, in the course of a long and bitter struggle. And that the people might have an abiding dwelling-place, secure against all assault, he included the seven hills of Rome in one system of fortification, enclosing an area about equal to that of ancient Athens.[1] On the north-eastern side, which was most exposed to attack, he raised a huge earthwork, faced with stone, and defended in front by a broad and deep moat.

To complete this series of peaceful triumphs, Servius entered into a close league with the Latins, and the temple of Diana, which was erected on the Aventine by the joint labour of the Latins and Romans, became the visible symbol of Roman supremacy in Latium.[2]

TARQUINIUS SUPERBUS

After reigning for forty-three years Servius was murdered by Lucius Tarquinius, his son-in-law, and a grandson of the elder Tarquin. The career of the last king of Rome, who bears the significant title of Superbus, is marked by all the familiar features which meet us in the story of the Greek tyrants. He is a usurper, who has gained possession of the throne by violence and rules in open defiance of the law. He lives in jealous seclusion from his subjects, and is surrounded day and night by a strong bodyguard. He grows rich on the spoils of the murdered nobles, and crushes the people by enforced labour. After enduring his tyranny for twenty-four years, high and low make common cause against him, and he and his sons are driven into exile.

Like his two immediate predecessors, the second Tarquin was a great builder. To him is ascribed the construction of the Cloaca Maxima, part of which still serves its original purpose, after the lapse of twenty-four centuries ; and during his reign the temple of Jupiter on the Capitol, which had been planned by his grandfather, was begun and carried almost to completion. Nor was his energy less conspicuous in his dealings with the

[1] Dionysius, iv. 13. [2] Livy, i. 45.

18

PLATE VI. THE TIBER AND THE CLOACA MAXIMA

Plate VII. Agger of Servius Tullius

neighbours and rivals of Rome.. He put down a conspiracy of the Latins, and from him dates the long series of wars with the Volscians, which lasted, with interruptions, for two hundred years.[1] With Tarquin also, if we may trust our authorities, began that system of military colonies which is so characteristic of Roman policy.

THE FIRST TWO CENTURIES

We may now look back for a moment and trace in outline the growth of Rome during the two centuries and a half which elapsed between the foundation of the city and the expulsion of the kings. Beginning, like the other towns of Latium, as a rude shepherd stronghold, the little settlement on the Palatine steadily expands, until it takes in the whole circle of the seven hills, which are enclosed in one strong rampart by the wisest of the Roman kings. Step by step with this internal growth, the frontier of Rome is pushed forward by a succession of conquests, so that at the close of the regal period she commands both banks of the Tiber as far as the sea, and holds in a strong grasp all Latium, from Ostia to Circeii, and from the Sabine border to the Volscian highlands. A liberal policy encourages free intercourse with the outer world, and a constant influx of new settlers brings an increase of strength and intelligence to the growing community. The presence of this younger population, outside the privileged circle of the old Populus, will in time give rise to many problems, which will tax the genius and prudence of the Romans to the utmost, and train them to become the teachers of all mankind as legislators and statesmen. Already the means of constitutional development have been placed in their hands by the far-seeing policy of Servius Tullius ; and after an interval of arbitrary rule the sovereign power, which has been so grossly abused, returns to its original source,[2] and thus, without any violent severance of the old traditions, we pass from the Rome of the kings to the free Rome of the Republic.

[1] Livy, i. 53.   [2] *I.e.* the people ; *cf.* Dionysius, iv. 34.

CHAPTER II
GENERAL REVIEW OF EARLY
ROMAN HISTORY

THE later annals of the kings are peculiarly rich in legend, shedding the light of romance on the fall of the monarchy and the birth of the Republic. But these beautiful stories, if they are to be told with effect, must be given with an amount of detail which would be out of all proportion to the limits of the present volume. We must therefore ask leave to assume that Brutus the idiot has become Brutus the hero, has avenged Lucretia's wrongs and died on the field of battle, that Horatius has kept the bridge and that Clodia has swum the Tiber, that the battle of Lake Regillus has been fought and won, and that the Romans, stripped of a great part of their territory, but free and safe within their own walls, are left face to face with their destiny.

But before taking up our narrative at this point it will be useful to make a general review of these remote times, and to put together, however imperfectly, such scattered fragments of tradition as have come down to us from the wrecks of the past. We have already, in the previous chapter, sketched the gradual growth of the city from its foundation by Romulus to the expulsion of the second Tarquin. Our present task must be to fill in the outline which has there been given of Roman manners and institutions under the kings, and to ascertain as far as possible the origin of that wonderful Roman spirit which outlived for ages the mould in which it was cast, which penetrated like a leaven into the hearts of savage nations, and which still survives as a vital formative principle among the states of modern Europe. Something must also be said

20

EARLY HISTORY

of the other races which peopled the great Italian peninsula, all destined, more or less, to contribute their part in the formation of Roman character and the development of Roman power. And, finally, we shall have to bestow a brief glance on the remote shores of the Mediterranean, on Carthage, on Greece, and on the East, and thus obtain a connected view of the stage on which the great historical drama is to be enacted.

The Sabellians

To the east of Latium,[1] round the upper waters of the Aternus, the Apennines attain their greatest elevation, forming a rugged knot of mountains which, geographically and in some sense historically, is the core of Italy. For here was bred the great Sabellian race, to whom the Romans owed the best part of their character—the stern simplicity of their manners, their dauntless valour, their piety, and their reverence for the sanctities of home. From their original seat the Sabellians sent out offshoots which gradually occupied the whole mountain district from the borders of Umbria to the strait of Messina. Of these the most important for early Roman history were the Sabines, who dwelt between the Anio and the Tiber, and a section of whom, as we have already seen, became incorporated with the primitive population of Rome. The further extension of the Sabellian stock will have to be noticed presently.

The Oscans

Closely allied to the Sabellians, and probably identical with them in origin, were the Oscans, whose name, under the various disguises of Opici, Opsci, Aurunci, and Ausones, occurs constantly in the annals of ancient Italy. The name Osci or Opsci means ' labourers,' and the Oscans appear to have been that branch of the Sabellian race who at some remote period came down from their mountain homes and

[1] This account of the Latins is closely modelled on that of Duruy, which has at least the merit of being intelligible.

21

took up their abode in the lowland districts by the western
sea. Probably there were several migrations, occurring at
different intervals of time, for we find other branches of the
Oscan race in the Volscian mountains, and on the western
spurs of the Apennines, where the Aequians lived in their
strongholds among the hills, and these retained their original
highland character.

One group of these Oscan wanderers made their home in the
northern plain of Latium, and, uniting with the old inhabitants,
the Sicels or Pelasgians, became the ancestors of the Prisci
Latini, or Ancient Latins, who founded thirty towns, and were
combined in a loose federal league, with a common centre of
worship on the Alban Mount. A parallel case is afforded
in Greek history by the Ionians, who would seem to have
sprung from a blending of Achaean and Pelasgic blood.[1]

If this theory is correct, it will account for the singular
union of flexibility and strength which enabled the Roman
State to bear the strain of almost indefinite expansion. All
authorities agree in commending the liberal policy of the
Romans, who from the earliest times opened their gates to
the stranger, gradually admitting the new members to the
full rights of citizenship, and thus ensuring a constant renewal
of vigour by infusions of new blood from without. The
lesson is pointed by a contrast with the narrow policy of the
Spartans, who by jealously excluding all foreign admixture
sowed the seeds of early decrepitude and decay. On the
purely intellectual side, this singular receptivity of mind
explains the peculiar character of Roman literature, in which
the germs of native genius were destroyed in the bud, so that
the barren stock produced neither flowers nor fruit until
quickened by the genial influence of the Greek. It must be
added that this policy of amalgamation, which was the cause
of Rome's political greatness, became in later times the source
of national corruption. Writing in the second century of our
era, Juvenal, the last of the great poets whose verses breathe
the true Roman spirit, tells us how the waters of Syrian

[1] Leaf, *Companion to the Iliad.*

Orontes have mingled with the Tiber, bringing all the pollutions of the East to defile the City of the Seven Hills.

THE ROMAN CHARACTER

The Roman character, then, as exhibited to us in the full light of history, is a highly complex production, combining elements drawn from all the shores of the Mediterranean, and we must exercise some care if we would grasp its essential features in their original grandeur and simplicity. It must be remembered also that for the first five centuries after the foundation of Rome we are left almost entirely without contemporary documents ; and this was the true period of Roman greatness, to which the poets and historians of the Empire looked back with fond regret. Nevertheless, if we examine our authorities with discrimination, we may hope to recover some faint picture of that great, silent age.

In the vigorous youth of their nation the Romans knew how to combine the advantages of city and country life. The mere farmer, who spends all his days in tilling the soil, is generally a dull and half-savage creature, cut off from the higher wants and the higher instincts of civilized man. The mere citizen, whose life is a perpetual violation of all natural laws, inevitably becomes stunted and deformed alike in body and in mind. The primitive Roman avoided both of these extremes, and thus achieved a harmonious development in both directions. He looked to the land for his support, and spent most of his time in the free air and wholesome activities of the fields. But he was also a citizen, who from the earliest times had some voice at least in the national affairs; and after the establishment of the Republic he might rise to the command of armies and the highest offices of State. Unlike the Greeks, who were in the main a seafaring people, the Romans never took kindly to the sea, and they thus escaped that fickle and restless character which ultimately made the more gifted race a byword to their sterner kinsmen. They remained faithful to the land, and from the land they drew their living and their homely virtues. The elder Cato, who lived as a monument of antique virtue in an age when Roman manners were already on the decline, was an enthusiastic farmer, and wrote a treatise on agriculture, which still survives. "To our ancestors," he says in his introduction, "a good man meant a good farmer. Those who are engaged in agriculture make the bravest and most active soldiers, and the

profits obtained from land are the most constant, the most virtuous, and the least exposed to suspicion. Furthermore, the hardy life of a farmer leaves little room for evil thoughts." And whatever we may think of the famous stories which tell us how the farmer was called from his plough to be dictator, and the dictator went back to his plough when he had saved his country, such legends, if legends they be, could only have arisen among a people whose chief pursuit was agriculture.

A FARMER'S CALENDAR
(of about 29 B.C.)

But a state of agriculture in those early times was also a state of war, and the farmer might be called upon at any moment to become a soldier. To the Latin peasant, surrounded on three sides by fierce highland tribes—the Aequian, the Sabine, and the Volscian—cattle-raids and incursions into his corn-lands must have been incidents as familiar as they were in later times to the thrifty denizens of the Scottish border. Such a life, divided between the toils of the field and the perils of war and of the chase, was eminently adapted to develop every robust and manly quality. And the means of a more liberal culture were always at hand, in the vigorous civic community which every year went on spreading from hill to hill on the banks of the Tiber.

From hunter to nomad, from nomad to farmer, from farmer to citizen—these are the successive stages by which man slowly

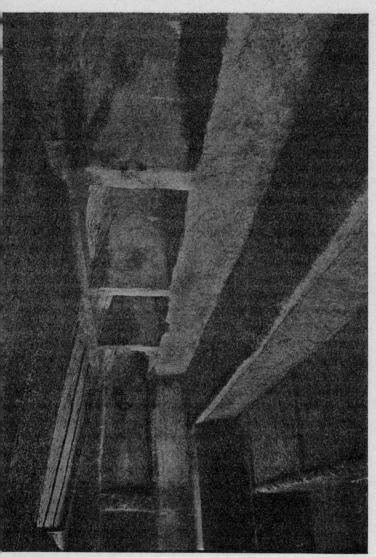

PLATE VIII. 'SEPULCHRE OF THE TARQUINS'

24

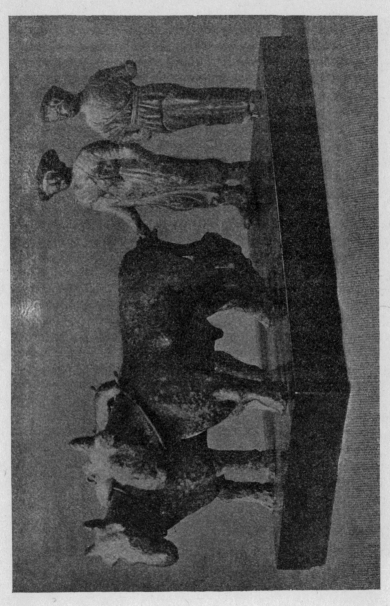

PLATE IX. ANCIENT ETRUSCAN BRONZE

emerges from barbarism to civilization. The operations of agriculture, to be successful, imply a fixed hearth and a settled abode. And this brings us to another feature in the unspoilt Roman character, its intense feeling for home. The attachment of the Greek was to his city. The ties of home, in the narrower sense of the word, had, comparatively speaking, but a weak hold on his affections : his home was the market-place, the gymnasium, the theatre ; and the degradation of women, especially among the Ionians, was a fatal obstacle to the growth of a high domestic ideal. But with the Romans, as with ourselves, home was a sacred name, hallowed by the worship of the Lares and Penates, and affording a theme, in later times, to some of their most gifted poets. Nor was the tie broken by death, for the spirits of the beloved dead still hovered round the familiar hearth, watching with affectionate care over those who remained, shielding them from every evil influence, and receiving a grateful recompense in the prayers and thank-offerings of the survivors. And thus the name of home received a spiritual significance, which raised it far above the grosser associations of mere bodily wants.

Where there is a house there must be a head, and though in a more artificial state of society domestic relations are often strangely inverted, the natural head of the house is the father, the bread-winner, to whom all the inmates look for their means of living, and from whom some of them derive their very existence. Now the Romans, like their descendants, the Latin races of modern Europe, were hard and stern logicians, and they pushed the principle here asserted to its utmost limits. The noble idea of fatherhood runs through all their institutions, political, religious, and domestic. The king is the father of his people, and the father is a king in his own household. The heads of the chief houses, enrolled as senators, first by the king, then by the consul, and afterwards by the censor, bear the collective title of Conscript Fathers. The same principle was invoked to give a religious sanction to the relation between patron and client   And the proudest boast of the great patriot Cicero was the title of Parent and Father, conferred on him by the Senate after he had crushed the conspiracy of Catiline.

THE ROMAN AS FATHER

In his own household the Roman ruled with an almost despotic sway. By his own authority, and without having recourse to any form of law, a father might punish his son with stripes, imprisonment, or death. The relation of a son to a father was, formally speaking, in all respects that of a slave, who was the creature, the chattel, of his master, and might be sold like any other piece of movable property. Indeed, the son was in a state of even more abject dependence than the slave, for the slave who had once been sold and had subsequently been set free by his new owner became a free man, while in the case of a son this process had to be repeated three times before he became his own master. The right of summary execution, which sheds a doubtful lustre [1] on the name of the first Brutus, was exercised by Manlius Torquatus, and by many other Roman fathers,[2] down to the last century of the Republic, and was not formally abrogated until the fourth century after Christ.

MARRIAGE LAW

The same system of iron discipline and unchecked command governed the relations between man and wife. The most primitive form of marriage among the Romans was a sacrament, and the tie thus formed was regarded as indissoluble. When the consecrated bread, which gave its name to the ceremony,[3] had been broken and the solemn words had been uttered the woman passed completely and for the rest of her life into the power of her husband. From that moment she existed only in him and for him. He was her lord, her master, and her judge, and if she rebelled against his authority it was for him to appoint and carry out the penalty. For graver transgressions the punishment was death, and among these were reckoned

[1] Virgil, *Aeneid*, vi. 822.   [2] Dionysius, viii. 79.   [3] *Confarreatio.*

26

intemperance [1] and the breach of the marriage vow, as altogether heinous and unpardonable.

So stern were the laws by which these old Romans sought to guard the sanctity of marriage, regarding this as the source of all public and private good, which must at any cost be secured against contamination. And so effectual were the safeguards thus provided that for more than five centuries divorce was unknown among them. The sacramental marriage was confined to the patricians ; among the plebeians a mere civil contract was held sufficient, and in later times this looser tie was extended to both orders. As the mode of life became softer and more luxurious the standard of domestic purity sank lower and lower, and a general licence ensued, which defied all the efforts of legislators and all the declamations of moralists. [2]

FEMININE STATUS

The women of Rome, then, under the original polity, remained in a state of perpetual pupilage. For a woman, according to the ancient theory of jurisprudence, was a child, to be guided, guarded, and governed for her own good. That a woman should play a part in public affairs or appear unattended in the haunts of men was in the estimation of a Roman something monstrous and unnatural. The epitaph of an antique Roman matron, the crowning record of a well-spent life, was comprised in these pithy words : " She sat at home and span." Not until Imperial times, when the very fibre of the national mind was warped and rotted, do we find the names of women who figured conspicuously in the arena of public life. Yet even while the old system remained unshaken these iron fetters were not always found sufficient to check the female will. On more than one occasion the women of Rome broke out of bounds, and caused serious uneasiness and alarm to the authorities.

---

[1] Dionysius (ii. 25) simply says, " if she drank wine " ; but probably this is not to be interpreted too literally.
[2] See especially Horace, *Odes*, iii. 6 ; Juvenal, *Satires*, vi.

REPUBLICAN ROME

Such, then, in its austere and rigid outline, was the domestic life of the early Romans. We must not be over-hasty in judging it, or decry it as something altogether merciless and inhuman. That it worked on the whole for good is seen by the result. It was a bridle of iron, which curbed the wild impulses of fierce and unruly natures and compelled them to become good servants of the State. It taught the Romans, first, to govern themselves, and afterwards to govern others, and helped to make them the conquerors and lawgivers of the ancient world.

Public Opinion

We must not suppose, however, that the powers entrusted to a Roman father were altogether without restraint. There was, first, the strong force of public opinion, which always imposed a check on the wanton abuse of authority. That tendency to self-isolation so strongly marked in the Teutonic races, which finds expression in our own proverb " An Englishman's house is his castle," was unknown to the nations of ancient Italy. The Roman lived in the light of publicity, and individual caprice was kept within bounds by a highly organized and sensitive public conscience. The feeling that every man owes a duty to society and that no important step ought to be taken without consulting the opinion of others was a deeply rooted conviction in the Roman mind, which no one could defy with impunity. Before inflicting any severe punishment on an erring member of his household the Roman was under the obligation of summoning a family council, and though the ultimate decision lay with him the opinion of the assembled relatives could not lightly be disregarded. Moreover, private rights always had to give way to public rights. Any son who held the office of magistrate was for the time being emancipated from his father's control. A striking example of this is given by Livy in his twenty-fourth book.[1] Fabius, the consul, is encamped at Suessula, and

[1] xxiv. 44. I owe this reference to Mr. Greenidge, *Roman Public Life*, p. 23, n. 4.

hearing that his father, who is acting under him as his subordinate, is approaching the camp, he goes out to meet him, preceded by his twelve lictors. The old man, who is on horseback, rides slowly up, without making any sign of obeisance to his superior officer. He passes eleven of the lictors, who refrain from stopping him out of reverence for his age and rank. When he reaches the last lictor, Fabius calls on the man to be ready, and commands his father to dismount. The father instantly obeys, remarking, as he sets foot on the ground, "I only wished, my son, to try your spirit, and to see whether you had a proper sense of your dignity as consul."

GENTLER INFLUENCES

There were other influences at work which tended to mitigate the severity of this iron code. Under all disguises and in spite of all restraints human nature is the same, and the gentle ministrations and sweet intimacies of home life will go far to soften the most rugged natures. But, apart from this, there is not wanting direct evidence of a very pure and tender relation between father and son, husband and wife, in the Roman household. We learn from Plutarch [1] that the stern Cato, in whose character we shall presently have to notice certain very harsh and repulsive features, was kind and indulgent to his family. "The man who beats his wife or children," said this grim pattern of Roman virtue, "is guilty of sacrilege against the holiest of things." The truth is that only the strong are capable of true tenderness, and what seems to us hard and cruel in the domestic discipline of the Romans is only the reverse side of a profound and religious reverence for the most precious things of life. The higher their value, the more relentless we must be in guarding our treasures from violation. The terrible satirist of Imperial Rome, who lashes the vices of his age with so pitiless a scourge, melts into more than womanly tenderness at the sight of childish helplessness and innocence. "Fathers," says this

[1] *Marcus Cato*, c. 20.

great poet in an impressive passage, "remember that the *greatest reverence* is due to a little child." And a curious remark of Plutarch's, that Cato never bathed in the presence of his son, shows a fine and rare delicacy, careful in all things not to tarnish the bloom of a virgin mind. The exhibition of nudity, which was so general among the Greeks and contributed so largely to the development of the plastic arts, was condemned by the stern decorum of old Roman manners.[1]

DEBTOR AND CREDITOR

In Rome, as in Athens, under the old *régime*, the laws regulating the relations of creditor and debtor were extremely severe. A certain period of grace was allowed after the debt had become due, and if the claims of the creditor were not satisfied before that term expired he could seize the person of his debtor, keep him in bonds, and compel him to perform task-work, or sell him into slavery beyond the Tiber. If there were several creditors, they could cut the debtor into pieces, and divide the fragments of his body among them. There is, indeed, no case on record in which this last penalty of the law was exacted, but Livy gives instances of fearful outrages committed on the persons of insolvent debtors, and the poems of Solon, describing the miseries of the poor under the old Attic law, illustrate the state of things which prevailed among his Roman contemporaries.

This griping avarice and indifference to the claims of humanity, which lie on the dark side of the Roman character, are thrown into strong relief by a passage in Cato's treatise on agriculture, written, it must be remembered, in a later and milder age. With a rare touch of dramatic vividness, contrasting strangely with his usual dry, sententious brevity, Cato describes the return of the master to his farm after a visit to Rome. On entering the house he makes a gesture of reverence to the Lar Familiaris,[2] like a modern Roman Catholic saluting the image of his patron saint. Then he goes the round of his farm, noting with a vigilant eye any signs of neglect or

---

[1] *Cf.* Dionysius, vii. 72.   [2] The tutelary spirit of the home.

carelessness; for he knows, as Cato remarks with quaint pleasantry in another passage, that his servants have more respect for his face than for his back. This duty performed, he sends for his bailiff, and calls him to a strict account of all outgoings and incomings, and of the manner in which the time has been employed during his absence. When he has satisfied himself on all these points, he concludes the interview with this pithy collect of a farmer's morality : " Make money out of everything : whatever is not wanted in the house, whatever is past its work—old oxen, sick cattle, wool, hides, worn-out implements, old or invalid slaves—must be sold. For Pater Familias must be a seller, and not a buyer." For this sordid and miserly spirit he is severely censured by his biographer Plutarch, who speaks on this occasion with a noble humanity worthy of a Christian sage.

If they were thus severe in their own households, it may well be believed that the Romans did not err on the side of lenity in dealing with public offenders. Here and there in the earlier books of Livy we catch a genuine echo from the remote past, interrupting the mellifluous flow of the great stylist with a note of jarring dissonance. Such is the fragment of the old law of treason quoted in connexion with the case of Horatius : " Let two judges try the case of treason : if he appeal against their judgment, let the appeal be tried : if the judgment be confirmed, let him be hanged by a cord to the accursed tree ; [1] let him be scourged, within or without the city bounds."

With these words ' of awful import' we may fitly conclude our brief survey of the public and private discipline of the Romans. It was an ordeal of fire, deliberately imposed on itself by a young society in order to purge away its grosser elements and brand into the public conscience the great lessons of obedience, honour, purity, and self-denial. For nations, like individuals, can only learn by suffering ; and that the lesson was well learnt is shown by the fact that long after the original Roman stock had fallen into decay the type

[1] The cross.

of character thus created lived on among alien races and in distant lands.

RELIGION AND POLITICS

The general features of Roman religion have already been sketched in the last chapter, but something must be added as to its influence on the political life of the Romans and on their career as a conquering people. In one aspect it was a gross superstition, which filled the hours of daylight with portents and peopled the black spaces of the night with dread. For a long period the privileged classes were enabled, by working on the terrors of the vulgar, to keep the reins of government in their own hands ; nor can we fail to admire the policy which wrought out of this crude mass of superstition an engine to serve great public ends. But this Roman religion, this binding constraint on the conscience, has another and a higher aspect. Under the coarse husk of pagan credulity there lay concealed a genuine and earnest faith—a faith in themselves, in the favour of heaven and in the conquering destiny of Rome.

THE PILLARS OF SOCIETY

Those who have followed as far as this point will be led to the conclusion that the three pillars of Roman society were piety, domestic purity, and devotion to agriculture. After the foundation of the Empire this truth was clearly grasped by Augustus, and by his adviser Maecenas, who invoked the Muse of epic and lyric poetry to revive the traditions of a simpler and better age. The same moral intention is seen in Livy, and three generations later in Tacitus, whose description of Germany is full of an implied satire on the manners of contemporary Rome. But all the efforts of legislators and all the eloquence of poets could not avail to people the deserted fields of Italy, to rekindle the true spirit of worship, or to restore the old ideals.

THE ETRUSCANS

It remains to speak of the other races of Italy, and to take a brief glance at the great world outside. The most powerful

32

nation of Italy at the close of the sixth century before Christ
were the Etruscans, a mysterious people, resembling no other
race in language or manners, whose origin remains a riddle
at the present day. Descending probably at some remote
period through the central passes of the Alps, where they left

traces of their presence in the district of Rhaetia,[1] they overran the
whole plain of the Po, founding
mighty cities, and subduing the
Umbrians, a people akin to the
Sabellians, who had settled in the
northern region of Italy at a still
earlier date. Then, crossing the
Apennines, they poured into the
rich upland province of Etruria,
which they found occupied by a
mixed Umbrian, Pelasgian, and
Ligurian population. At the time
which we have reached they
were still undisputed masters of

AN ETRUSCAN SIDEBOARD

Etruria, and their influence extended to the coast districts
of Latium, and to the favoured land of Campania, where they
held several important cities, the chief of which was Capua. In
the great northern plain of Italy [2] their dominion was now
curtailed by the irruption of the Gauls. In the age of their
greatness the Etruscans were a vigorous, intelligent, and
industrious people, who left the marks of a strong material
civilization wherever they went. Under their rule the fine
natural resources of Etruria were sedulously developed, and
the province reached a height of prosperity which was
remembered in after-ages with poignant regret by the noble
spirit of Tiberius Gracchus.[3] Marshes were drained, strong

[1] Perhaps derived from Rasena, the ancient name of the Etruscans.
Rhaetia included the modern Grisons, Tyrol, and part of Tuscany. *Cf.*
Livy, v. 33, fin.

[2] It should be explained that though we use the term ' Italy ' here for
convenience, the name was not extended to the whole peninsula south of
the Alps until the time of Augustus.

[3] Plutarch, *Tib. Gracchus*, c. 8.

fortified cities, connected by well-kept roads, were founded, and mining, agriculture, pottery, and woollen industries brought great wealth into the country. The painted vases of Etruria rivalled those of Greece, and her workers in metal produced masterpieces which still form the chief ornaments of many a collection. Their ports on the western coast gave them the command of the Tuscan sea, which was called after them, and the name of the treacherous and stormy gulf which divides Italy from the Balkan peninsula still preserves the renown of the harbour-town of Adria, early founded by the Etruscans between the Po and the Adige. An overland trade brought to this town the amber of the Baltic, which is alluded to in the legend of Phaethon's sisters, who wept crystal tears at their brother's tragic end.

In primitive times trade and piracy went hand in hand, and the pirates of Tuscany are mentioned already in the Homeric Hymns.[1] Their constant depredations brought them into collision with the Greek settlers of Italy and Sicily, and "the wild hordes of Tuscany"[2] at length sustained a crushing defeat off Cumae, which broke their naval power. Carthage also, who had for a time been their ally, was at last excited by commercial jealousy to turn her arms against them. Later still they were thrust out of their possessions in Campania by the Samnites, and when the final struggle for the possession of Italy begins we find them restricted to the province which bears their name.

From Etruria came the sombre and gloomy element which cast a shadow over the brighter and purer worship of the old Sabine and Latin religion, and the science of augury, destined to play so important a part in the political life of the Romans. To the Etruscans also the Romans owed the beginnings of their art, and the gigantic structures of the later kings were planned and executed by the skill of Etruscan architects and engineers. Etruscan also in origin were the gladiatorial shows, which can be traced back to the practice of self-immolation at a great man's funeral; and we have

[1] Hymn to Dionysus, l. 8; Apollodorus, iii. 3, 1.   [2] Pindar, *Pyth*. i. 71.

PLATE X. ETRUSCAN WALLS OF VOLTERRA

34

PLATE XI.   ETRUSCAN SARCOPHAGUS   35

already noticed that the insignia of royalty, which were afterwards assumed by the consuls, came from Etruria. In all the arts of civilization the Etruscans were at this time, and until a much later date, far in advance of the Romans. We have the authority of Livy for the statement that it was the custom to send young Romans of noble birth to complete their education in Etruria, as in Cicero's days they were sent to Athens. But with all their gifts and accomplishments the Etruscans were a gross people, wanting in all higher spiritual qualities ; and a fragment of the historian Theopompus, preserved by Athenaeus,[1] gives a frightful picture of the debauchery which prevailed among them in the fourth century before Christ.

THE LIGURIANS

In the rude and barren region between the north-western corner of Etruria and the Alps dwelt the Ligurians, a hardy race of mountaineers, who made a stubborn fight for their liberty, and were not finally subdued until after the fall of the Roman Republic.

THE VER SACRUM

Mention has been made of the Samnites, who were an offshoot of the Sabellian stock, and who are said to have originated as a people [2] from a curious custom often mentioned as peculiar to the Sabellians and kindred Italian races. At times of scarcity or peril a propitiatory offering to the gods was made of all children who should be born in the following spring— hence called a *Ver Sacrum*, or Sacred Spring (see p. 228). The firstlings of the tribal flocks and herds were included in the offering. Originally, doubtless, the children were actually sacrificed with the animals, but in later times they were allowed to reach maturity, when they were conducted to the border and wandered forth to find a new home. The Samnites grew into a powerful nation, and of all the Italians

[1] xii. 14.   [2] Strabo, c. 250.

they were Rome's most dreaded enemies, until they were finally extirpated by Sulla.

GREEK COLONIES IN ITALY

Of the Greek colonies which dotted the coast of central and south-western Italy and the shores of the southern gulf, the oldest was Cumae, said to have been founded about 1050 B.C. Cumae in its turn established colonies, the most important of which was Neapolis, or Naples, the ' New City.' All this district of Campania, which in Strabo's time was gay with the gardens and villas of wealthy Romans, all the coast of Latium as far as Circeii, and the adjacent islands, were saturated with Greek influence, and every name calls up some famous legend. Under the bold promontory which still bears her name was the cave of the mighty Circe, in which were confined the human victims of her magic, disguised in brutish form, whose wild cries affrighted the hearts of Aeneas and his Trojans as they crept past the headland, shunning that abode of fear.[1] In the narrow strip of coastland which stretches southward from Circeii dwelt the Aurunci, of Oscan race, whose huge frames and savage manners caused them to figure in Latin poetry as the descendants of the Laestrygones,[2] a fierce tribe of cannibal giants mentioned in the *Odyssey*. Three rocky islands off Cape Misenum were named after the Sirens, who sang their last song when the *Argo* passed that way. But the centre of religious awe and dread was in the neighbourhood of Cumae, where the Sibyl chanted her dark oracles in her solemn cave by the black and silent waters of Avernus ; and near at hand, in the depths of a haunted wood, were the mysterious portals of the Underworld.

As we go southward through the coastlands of Lucania and Bruttium our path is strewn with records of that people whose brief career of power and prosperity gave to this part of Italy the name of Greater Greece. The waters of the Silarus form a swamp where they wander through the rich plain that was once bright with the rose-gardens of Paestum. A few

---

[1] Virgil, *Aeneid*, vii. 10.   [2] Duruy ; see also Dionysius, vi. 32.

broken fragments mark the spot where stood the birthplace of Parmenides,[1] and a river conceals the site of Sybaris, once the wealthiest and most powerful city of southern Italy. The rapid rise and decline of these brilliant Greek colonies is one of the most curious and instructive chapters in ancient history. Situated in the most favoured parts of the peninsula, they soon became engulfed in the advancing tide of barbarism, or fell, as in the case of Tarentum, into effeminacy and sloth; while Rome, founded on a ring of barren hills surrounding a morass, rose by steady degrees to be mistress of the world. Yet wherever the Greeks settled they left ineffaceable marks of their peculiar genius. The names of Parmenides and Pythagoras will live as long as men retain an interest in the deepest problems of thought and life; and the temples of Paestum yet stand, a monument of fallen greatness, and a witness to that grander and purer influence which can never pass away.

THE OUTER WORLD

Looking at the political map of the ancient world at the time when the Tarquins were banished from Rome, we see little which might help us to forecast the course of events during the next three centuries. The Romans are restricted to their own walls and to a narrow belt of land in northern Latium. Etruria is still by far the mightiest power in Italy. The great Sabellian race, who have contributed so important an element to the original population of Rome, now stand aloof from their kinsmen, whom they far surpass in numbers and extent of territory. In the vast region watered by the Po the Gauls are steadily gaining ground, and they will presently spread terror and havoc through half the peninsula. In Sicily and southern Italy the Greeks are still supreme, and it is Syracuse, not Rome, which within the next generation will have to face the first shock of invasion from the opposing shores of Africa.[2] Founded about a century before her rival on the Tiber, Carthage was now rising rapidly to a great height of prosperity and power. In western Sicily, in Corsica,

[1] Elea, or Velia.   [2] Virgil, *Aeneid*, iv. 628.

REPUBLICAN ROME

and in Sardinia she had planted her factories, and after
Phoenicia had fallen under the influence of Persia she was
the greatest naval power in the Mediterranean.

The mention of Phoenicia may lead us to turn our eyes
to the East, where great events had been happening during
the reigns of the last two kings of Rome. In the course of
some forty years a new empire has arisen on the ruins of
Assyria, Media, and Lydia, Egypt has been conquered, and the
Persians have carried their victorious arms to the northern
frontiers of Greece. The young democracy of Athens, just
emerged from the evil days of tyranny, will soon have to put
out all its strength to beat back the hosts of Darius and of
Xerxes.

A Greek of that age, if he had heard of the Romans at all,
must have despised them as an obscure and barbarous community, without arts, without literature, destitute of all that
gives grace and beauty and dignity to life. And to all appearance he would have been right in his opinion. For the Greeks
had a glorious past behind them, which gave promise of a yet
more glorious future ; the Romans were still learning the
rudiments of civilization, and at this moment even their
material power could hardly command respect. Yet these
rude Romans had qualities in them against which all the
genius of Greece and all the resources of Asia were to contend
in vain.

CHAPTER III

PLEBS AND POPULUS

A GENERAL view of the changes in the Roman constitution which were effected during the first two centuries after the fall of the kings shows us how the regal power was gradually distributed among a multitude of subordinate officials, who tended more and more to become the servants of the Senate. Then follows the long and glorious administration of that illustrious body, under which Rome became the mistress of Italy and extended her conquests from the Euphrates to the Atlantic. When we enter upon the last scene we find the " assembly of kings " degenerated into a gathering of triflers and profligates, and after a fearful struggle the spoils of empire, gained at the cost of so much national effort, fall into the hands of a single ambitious soldier.

PRAETORS AND CONSULS

The banishment of the Tarquins left Rome without a head ; but this want was immediately supplied by the election of two co-ordinate magistrates, with the title of Praetors, afterwards changed to Consuls, as the direct successors to the regal power. This power, however, was restrained by a threefold limitation. First, the consuls held office only for one year, and were consequently responsible to the community, and subject to impeachment at the end of their term of office if they abused the powers entrusted to them. Secondly, by a principle which runs through the whole of Roman constitutional law, each of the consuls had the right of interfering with the acts of his colleague, and by exercising that right could render his proceedings null and void. A third check was supplied by the right of appeal in capital cases against the sentence of the consul, the final decision being thus reserved to the votes of the sovereign people. At the same time two officers called Quaestors were appointed, encroaching on the consular powers in another direction, the department of finance (see p. 60).

One of the earliest acts of the first consuls was the restoration of the Senate, whose numbers had been greatly reduced during the tyrannical reign of the last Tarquin. Its ranks were filled up by the promotion of wealthy citizens belonging to the Equestrian Order, and the full complement of three hundred was thus re-established. But the supreme ascendancy of the Senate in State affairs belongs to a later date. For the present the chief powers of government are wielded by the consuls. They are always chosen from the patricians, and act in the interests of their own class. When the struggle between the orders begins, the first efforts of the reformers are aimed at the diminution of consular power.

It will be remembered that from the time of Servius Tullius Rome possessed two Parliaments, the old Parliament of the Curies, or wards, in which, though plebeians were not excluded, the patricians, with their clients, always maintained a dominant influence, and the Parliament of the Centuries, organized on a basis of property, in such a manner as to secure a standing majority for the rich.[1] In its original intention the assembly of the centuries was purely military, and down to the latest times this fact was never forgotten. It was convoked by the sound of the trumpet in the Field of Mars, and could be dismissed by the striking of a red flag on the Janiculum. Its political importance begins from the first days of the Republic, and from this time the curiate assembly falls more and more into the background. The most important duties of the centuriate assembly were the election of consuls and the trying of cases of appeal.

[1] The word ' Parliament ' is used for convenience. It must be clearly understood that membership of these bodies did not confer the right of speaking, but only that of voting.

PLEBS AND POPULUS

REX SACRIFICULUS

The conservative character of the Roman mind is shown
by the perpetuation of certain priestly functions which had
belonged to the king in the person of a new official, created for
that special purpose. He was called the Rex Sacrificulus,
and held his office for life. But he was jealously excluded
from all participation in public affairs, and his very title [1]
conveys an impression of contempt.

THE DICTATOR

It is obvious that in times of crisis and peril the dual character
of the consulship, with its system of balance and check, might,
by paralysing the whole machinery of government, produce
the most ruinous consequences to the State. The inventive
genius of these primitive Roman statesmen saw the danger,
and provided a means of meeting it. In any sudden emergency
a decree of the Senate empowered one of the consuls to appoint
a dictator, who was to rule with absolute power, within and
without the city, for a period not exceeding six months. With
the dictator was associated another officer, appointed by him,
and acting under his commands, who bore the title of Magister
Equitum, or Master of the Horse. All the other magistrates
were subject to the dictator's authority, and while he remained
in office the right of appeal was suspended. Moreover, the
dictator was not responsible for his acts, and therefore could
not be called to account when his term of office had expired.
The appointment of a dictator was thus a temporary reversion
to kingly rule, or, as Dionysius has it, the dictatorship was
a brief despotism, voluntarily submitted to by the citizens.
Armed with supreme control, the dictator was invested with
something of the pomp of sovereignty. Twenty-four lictors
marched before him, showing that the powers of both consuls
were combined in his person, and the axe, symbolizing the
power over life and death, was displayed in the bundle of

---

[1] Perhaps originally a mere nickname.

rods carried by each lictor even when the dictator made his appearance in the city.

In most cases a dictator was appointed to meet some formidable attack aimed at Rome from without, and the first dictator, we are told, led the Roman army which crushed the coalition of the Latins, and thus destroyed the last effort of the Tarquins to restore the kingship in Rome.[1] But after the struggle between patricians and plebeians had begun the dictatorship was often used by the privileged class as an instrument to overawe the refractory commons.

THE TWO ORDERS

The peaceful revolution which ended at last in the complete amalgamation of the two orders extended altogether over a period of more than two centuries. In this chapter we shall confine ourselves to those changes which were brought about in the century which elapsed between the First Secession of the Plebs and the sack of Rome by the Gauls (494–390 B.C.). At the beginning of that epoch the old nobility of Rome formed a solid phalanx, armed with an almost entire monopoly of political power. They were masters of the whole mystery of statecraft, acquired by the experience of many generations ; the three hundred seats in the Senate were filled chiefly, if not solely, from their ranks ; the consuls, wielding at present an almost regal authority, were the chosen champions of their order ; and in the newly created dictatorship they had always a potent weapon in reserve, which could be brought forth at any moment if the clamours of the unprivileged grew too loud. Moreover, they controlled the whole machinery of State religion, and their pontiffs and their augurs were trained in the art of working on the superstitious terrors of the multitude. The control of religion meant the control of the law, which until the time of the decemvirs was preserved by oral tradition, leaving a large scope to the arbitrary discretion of the presiding magistrate.

[1] According to other accounts, the first dictator was appointed in 501 B.C., five years before the battle of Lake Regillus (Livy, ii. 18).

42

PLEBS AND POPULUS

It will easily be understood that on the social side the gulf between the privileged and unprivileged classes was still wider. Apart from the natural prestige attaching to rank and wealth, many of the plebeians were kept down by a sense of personal obligation to the great patrician houses, and if this check was wanting low-born presumption was held at bay by direct intimidation. No marriage could be contracted between a patrician and a plebeian, and it follows from this that the offspring of any irregular unions was illegitimate.

To complete this side of the picture we must add that the patricians, by their wealth, commanded a majority in the centuriate assembly, that they were the natural leaders of the people in war, and that they were generally superior in personal valour and prowess, being better armed and better nourished, and possessing ample leisure for the practice of martial exercises.

Confronting this formidable array of rank, wealth, knowledge, and power, we see the great mass of the people, a needy multitude of mixed descent, with no bond of union but their common wants, without leaders, untrained in all the arts of public life, with no concerted plan of action, destitute of political ideals, and even of political ambition. Far from demanding any share in the government, they will be satisfied if they are allowed to live as free men. Despair drives them into revolt, and they obtain what they want, a recognized head. Then, feeling their way at first timidly, but gradually with more confidence, they advance step by step, opposing craft to craft and violence to violence and learning the business of politics as they proceed, until the barriers of patrician privilege fall one by one before them and they obtain an equal share in the most coveted honours of the State. Finally, after seven generations of bitter contest, the inward discord which once threatened the very life of the nation is brought to an end, and we see the Plebs merged in the Populus, marching side by side with their old enemies to the goal of conquest and empire. We have now to relate the earlier stages in the process

43

which led to this great achievement, the most wonderful, perhaps, of its kind which history affords.

THE FLOGGED CENTURION

There are moments in the annals of these remote times when the thick cloud which hides from us the realities of a distant past is rolled aside and we obtain a fleeting glimpse into the life of a young nation. Such is the incident which is recorded by Livy [1] as occurring in the fourteenth year after the foundation of the Republic. It was a time when the distress of the plebeians, who were impoverished by the long wars and loaded with debt, had reached a climax. In the embittered state of feeling consequent upon these conditions a report reached Rome that the Volscians were in arms and preparing to invade the Roman territory. The consuls called for a levy, and the Forum was soon filled with an excited multitude, loudly protesting against the iniquity of the patricians who demanded this service from their oppressed and injured fellow-citizens. " They have stripped us of our farms," was the cry, " they have carried our brethren into bondage, and now they call upon us to fight their battles. Why should we fight for them, who have made us houseless and homeless? They are our worst enemies, and we are safer in the hands of the Volscians than in Rome." While they were thus clamouring, and tales of wrong and outrage multiplied from lip to lip, suddenly all eyes were turned upon a new-comer, who rushed with wild cries into the middle of the Forum. He was a man advanced in years, whose wasted features and haggard eyes were half hidden by a shaggy beard and a mass of rough hair. His body, scantily clothed with a ragged and filthy garment, was seamed with the marks of brutal ill-usage. Yet, disfigured as he was, his identity was soon revealed, and murmurs of pity and horror went up from the bystanders as they recognized in this image of misery one of Rome's bravest soldiers. Then a great hush fell upon the people as he took his stand on a raised platform and began his sad story. " Fellow-citizens," he

[1] ii. 23 ; Dionysius, vi. 26.

said, baring his breast, "look at these scars. They were gained in the service of my country. I have fought in many battles, and I can see some among you who have served under me as their centurion. And now behold my reward!" Thereupon he stripped off his tunic to the waist and displayed his back, still bleeding from recent stripes. He went on to tell how his farm had been wasted, his cattle driven off, and his house burnt in a war with the Sabines, and how he had been compelled to pledge first his land and afterwards his liberty to procure the means to live. His creditor, a hard, cruel man, had loaded him with chains and kept him with a gang of similar wretches in virtual slavery until he was utterly broken by toil, blows, and starvation.

His faltering tones, wasted figure, and lamentable tale raised the popular indignation to the point of fury, and the whole city became a scene of tumult and uproar. Hundreds of debtors who had been brought to a similar condition escaped from their confinement and paraded the streets, crying for protection against their oppressors. Bands of rioters roved through the city, insulting any patricians whom they met. The Senate House was beset by an angry mob, and even the consuls themselves hardly escaped from violence. Presently the news arrived that the Volscians were advancing to attack the city. "Let them come," said the boldest of the mutineers; "we will not raise a hand against them. Let the patricians fight their own battles. As for us, we have nothing left to fight for." At length, after a promise had been given that the laws of debt should be temporarily suspended, order was restored, the appeased plebeians gave in their names for enlistment, and in the battle which ensued the Volscians were repulsed with great loss.

But when the danger was over the plebeians found that their position was no better than before. Debtors who had been released from their bonds to serve in the army were sent back to the dungeons of their creditors, and all the old scenes were enacted over again. A new attack from the Volscians extorted new promises of relief from the government; the enemy

were beaten, and the promises were broken as before. At
length, in the sixteenth year of the Republic (494 B.C.), twelve
months after the story of the old centurion had so enraged
the people, matters were brought to a crisis. Once more the
citizens had been called upon to enlist for a campaign against
their inveterate enemies, the Volscians, and on their refusal
the patricians had played their last card and had appointed
a dictator. The choice fell on Valerius, a name dear to the
plebeians, for he belonged to a house always distinguished
by its regard for the poor and oppressed. Having extracted
new pledges from the Senate, Valerius induced the plebeians
to give in their names for enrolment in the legions ; but on
his return from a successful campaign he found the patricians
as obdurate as ever against any proposal for lasting reform.
Accordingly he laid down his dictatorship, and left his infatuated
fellow-nobles to settle their differences with the plebeians as
best they could.

First Secession of the Plebs

The danger was indeed imminent, for the plebeians had
for some time past adopted the practice of holding informal
meetings on the Aventine and elsewhere for the discussion of
their grievances, and if the victorious legions were disbanded,
their feelings, exasperated by so many disappointments, might
drive them to take some desperate step. To avert a catastrophe
an order was issued, under a pretext that the Aequians had
taken the field, that the legions were to remain under arms.
Then at length the storm broke, and as soon as they had passed
the city gates the soldiers abandoned their generals and,
plucking up their standards, marched off in a body and pitched
their camp on a hill beyond the Anio, distant about three miles
from Rome, and from that time known in history as the
Sacred Mount. Their design was to found a new city and
leave the old walls, which for them had been but the walls
of a prison, to the patricians. This desperate scheme was soon
found to be impracticable, however. The wives and families
of the seceders were at the mercy of their opponents, and they

themselves were dependent on casual supplies brought into the camp by sympathizers from the surrounding districts. We may easily imagine that hunger and homesickness soon began to do their work, and when the patricians, who were now seriously alarmed, sent deputies to propose terms of accommodation the way was already prepared for a peaceful adjustment of the feud. We need hardly refer to the foolish legend of Menenius Agrippa with his fable of the limbs and the belly, evidently the invention of some literary dotard who desired to invest the ancient Romans with a character of childlike innocence and simplicity. These wronged and suffering men, we may be sure, were not to be cozened like children by nursery tales, and it was very different language which induced them to relinquish their purpose.

THE TRIBUNATE

The root of the mischief which had divided the two orders lay in the defencelessness of the plebeians. All existing magistracies were in the interests of the patricians, and since the institution of the dictatorship the plebeians might be deprived at any moment of their sole resource, the right of appeal.[1] To remedy this evil it was finally resolved to appoint two officers, chosen from the plebeians, who were to be called Tribunes, and whose business it was to protect those of their own class against the arbitrary jurisdiction of the consuls. Whether their right of interference extended to the dictator remained a disputed question. They were to hold office for one year, and their authority was confined to the city and the district lying immediately outside it, to a distance of one mile from the sacred enclosure.[2] To ensure freedom of access, their doors were to be kept open day and night, and they were forbidden to sleep outside the city except on the occasion of the Latin Festival.

In its original intention the tribunate was designed to remove an economic grievance, and to relieve a particular section of the plebeians, the class of small farmers, who were

---

[1] Dionysius, vi. 58.   [2] The Pomoerium.

crushed under a burden of debt and threatened with ruin. The powers of the tribunes were at first purely negative. They had the right of veto ; that is to say, they were allowed to interfere with the action of the consuls in administering the harsh laws of debt. But the change could not stop here. From the moment of its birth the tribunate struck into other paths, which carried it far from the purpose for which it was created, and led in the end to the establishment of monarchy. How this came about will be seen later. At present we are only concerned with the wonderful political development which resulted immediately from the vague powers embodied in the new office. First, however, we must observe that the mischief which it was designed to remove, the ruin of the peasant proprietor, went steadily on, and agriculture fell more and more into decay. This was partly due to the selfishness of the nobles, who clung with fierce tenacity to their most cherished privilege, the monopoly of land, and partly to the pressure of constant warfare, which compelled the farmer to exchange the plough for the sword. Some partial remedy was afforded, as time went on, by the foundation of military colonies. But the restless life of a soldier tends more and more to render him unfit for the slow and monotonous operations of tillage, and so the evil went on apace, and the problem of restoring the balance between civic and rural life, which was essayed by one Roman patriot after another, remained unsolved. Bearing this in mind, we may now proceed to trace the progress of the plebeians under their new leaders.

The first step had been taken ; the great disorganized mass of unprivileged citizens, like a trunk without brain or hands, had at last found a head and a voice. But the head must be protected from violence, and to ensure this the persons of the tribunes were declared sacred, and anyone who assailed them or hindered them in the performance of their duty was laid under a curse and might be slain with impunity as an outlaw. But this reform was not enough : the power of interfering on behalf of plebeians was seconded by the power to impeach those who had offended them. This claim was bitterly

48

contested by the patricians, who held that a plebeian magistrate had no jurisdiction outside his own class. We see this strongly brought out in the story of Coriolanus, which, overlaid as it is by legend and distorted by the inventions of patrician pride, contains a valuable germ of historic truth and illustrates the kind of party warfare which was constantly going on in the city-states of Greece and Italy. The proud patrician was broken by the storm of popular fury and driven into exile. And in the years which followed his fate was shared by the most distinguished members of his class, great soldiers and powerful statesmen, who were condemned by the popular tribunal to banishment, confiscation, or death. If we had before us a full and faithful history of these times, we should probably know with certainty that among the Romans, as among the Greeks, there was always a class of political exiles, watching every turn of events from a distance, and ready to seize the first opportunity of turning the tables on their opponents. Such is in all likelihood the true explanation of the story of Coriolanus, and of the later attempt made by Appius Herdonius, the forerunner of Catiline,[1] who fifty years after the fall of the kings placed himself at the head of a band of exiles, clients, and runaway slaves, and got possession of the Capitol, from which he was only expelled after a desperate struggle.

Two points of capital importance, the inviolability of the tribunes and their right to impeach, were thus established. The next step was to organize the mixed multitude of plebeians into an independent body, which might act with promptitude and effect under its lawful leaders. This brings us to one of the most obscure and doubtful questions in Roman constitutional history. According to the view now generally held, the plebeians had hitherto been mustered in curies, and the first tribunes are said to have been elected by them. But the old curiate assembly was subject to the influence of the patricians,[2] and they, with their dependents, were often able to secure the election of tribunes favourable to themselves.

[1] Mommsen. [2] Livy, ii. 56.

To meet this objection it was proposed to employ the tribal
unit for the reconstruction of the plebeian assembly, and in
spite of the furious outcry of Appius Claudius, the great
champion of patrician arrogance, the measure was carried.
Henceforth the plebeians met and voted, not by curies, but
by tribes, which were now twenty-one in number, and in this
way a third Parliament was added to the complicated political
machinery of Rome.

A New Constitution

Thus within the course of one generation a new constitution
had grown up side by side with the old. It was a state within
a state, with its own magistrates, its own assembly, and its
own methods of procedure. The tribunate developed on
parallel lines with the consulship, encroaching, as it advanced,
on the functions of the supreme patrician magistrate. It was
a wedge inserted into the compact structure of time-honoured
privilege, and driven farther and farther home by successive
blows, until it rent the whole solid fabric asunder. After the
union of the orders the office of tribune changed its character
altogether, and became a convenient party instrument for
controlling the turbulent mob of Rome. But this change
belongs to a much later date.

It must not be supposed that the patricians remained
passive spectators of this momentous revolution. Every art
of political chicanery and every mode of intimidation, cajolery,
and corruption was employed to check the progress of democratic aggression. Sometimes the meetings of the plebeians
were broken up by bands of riotous young nobles, who mingled
with the crowd, insulted the speakers, and often went the
length of open violence. At other times subtler methods were
employed, and the patricians abused the advantages given
them by rank and wealth to work upon the weakness or the
necessities of their opponents. And on one occasion at least
they did not shrink from using the weapon of assassination.
Twenty years after the first secession of the plebeians a
tribune named Genucius, who had tried to carry an obnoxious

50

measure, was found murdered in his bed. The peculiar character which belonged to all the Roman magistracies placed another means of obstruction in their hands. For the tribunes if they were to carry any project to a successful issue, were obliged to act unanimously, as the dissent of one member of their college was sufficient to quash the whole proceeding. And when their numbers were successively raised from two to five and from five to ten it became easy for the patricians to win over one or more of the members to their side.

On the other hand, the tribunes had the power, by interposing the veto, of causing serious embarrassment to the executive. When danger threatened from without they could stop the levies, and thus leave Rome exposed to the attacks of her enemies. Lastly, the haughtiest patrician knew by repeated examples that if he went too far he would incur the risk of impeachment, and pay for his presumption by the loss of his property, his country, or his life.

Thus the strange conflict swayed to and fro for many generations, but at the end of each crisis the plebeians always gained some new concession. There were doubtless cases of injustice and of actual outrage on both sides ; on the whole, however, this long constitutional struggle was singularly free from the cruelty and ferocity which mark the later history of Republican Rome.

TENURE OF THE LAND

It has already been explained that the tribunate owed its origin to the depressed condition of the small farmers, and we must now go back a little and speak more at large of a question which came up again and again down to the last century of the Republic, the question of the tenure of land. The welfare of Rome depended greatly on the maintenance of a numerous, a prosperous, and a contented rural population ; but all efforts to secure the permanence of this condition were thwarted by the selfish greed of the nobles. A certain portion of the Roman territory, varying in extent, was owned by the State, and this was either allotted in small parcels to needy plebeians, rented for pasture, or assigned for regular occupation at an easy rent. In the case last mentioned the State never relinquished its hold on the land—the tenant never became, in the eyes of the law, a freeholder. But as a matter of practice lands thus rented from the State were treated in all respects as private property, passed from father to son, or changed hands by ordinary process of sale. The whole admini-stration of these public lands lay, of course, with the patricians, and this gave ample scope for that sort of jobbery which in all ages marks the transactions of privileged corporations.

SPURIUS CASSIUS

Among the great nobles who stood at the head of affairs there was always a small minority, consisting of those who are designated by an eminent modern historian [1] Reform Lords, men of large and liberal views, who sympathized with the wrongs of the plebeians, and wished to conciliate them by yielding to all righteous claims. One of the most distinguished of these was Spurius Cassius, whose true nobility of character has received tardy recognition after centuries of calumny. The tribunate, as we have seen, had failed in its primary object, the relief of the poorer agriculturists. Cassius, while holding the office of consul (486 B.C.), proposed a measure which was designed to cope with the old grievance. Certain new territories, recently acquired by conquest, were to be parcelled out in freehold lots to indigent plebeians. If Cassius had stopped here he might have succeeded. But he went farther, and tried to meddle with those parts of the public lands which had long been regarded by the patricians as their own private possessions ; and, not content with this, he pro-posed to give the Latin allies of Rome a share in the new distribution of territory. By attempting too much he wrecked his whole scheme and brought ruin on himself. The patricians were enraged by his interference with their monopoly, and the plebeians viewed with jealousy the proposed admission of the Latins to a share of the coveted prize. This feeling was

[1] Ihne.

craftily fanned by the patricians, and they raised the ominous cry, which proved fatal to many a Roman patriot, " He would make himself a king." All classes were thus united against Cassius, and at the end of his year of office he was prosecuted as a public enemy and condemned to die the death of a traitor. In the last age of the Republic his name was still branded with infamy, and Cicero mentions him among those who suffered the just penalty of a criminal ambition.

MYSTERY OF THE LAW

A new stage in the long contest between patricians and plebeians is marked by the proposal of the tribune Terentilius to appoint a commission to draw up a code of laws with the object of defining and restricting the judicial powers of the consuls (462 B.C.). Up to this time the law had been a mystery, the knowledge of which was preserved by oral tradition in the colleges of priests, who acted as legal advisers to the patrician magistrates. This would naturally lead to all sorts of manipulation and sharp practice, and as the people had no written standard for testing the administration of the law by its official interpreters, they were left at the mercy of those who had every motive for abusing their trust. But the times were not yet ripe for so important a reform, and a ten years' struggle ensued, during which every feature which marks the long war between the orders was renewed—on the side of the plebeians refusal to enlist, insubordination in the field, and an unscrupulous use of the weapon of impeachment, and intrigue, corruption, and open violence on the part of the patricians. One incident may be singled out for special mention as illustrating the manners of the time. A young noble, Kaeso Quintius, son of the famous Cincinnatus, had made himself conspicuous in a riot which was raised by him and a band of kindred spirits, to break up a meeting of the popular assembly. He was summoned to stand his trial, and in the course of the proceedings a witness came forward with a story of lawless outrage which made his conviction certain. The witness, a former tribune, stated that some

53

time before, when a pestilence was raging in Rome, he had met
the young Quintius, with others of his own class, in the Subura,
a populous district in the heart of the city, where they were
behaving in a disorderly manner and molesting the passers-by.
A brawl arose, and the witness's own brother, an elderly man,
was so brutally beaten by Quintius that he died soon afterwards.
" Year after year," concluded the ex-tribune significantly,
" I applied to the consuls for redress, but they refused to
listen to my case." The charge was afterwards proved to be
false, but the case, like that of Virginia, is doubtless typical
of the social tyranny which was practised by the patricians,
aggravating the strife of parties, and inflaming the feelings of
the plebeians by a sense of private wrong. Ages later, in the
days of Juvenal,[1] the street-bully was still a familiar figure
in the most frequented parts of Rome. It must be added
that the calumny served its immediate purpose, for Quintius
was sentenced to pay a heavy fine, and his father, Cincinnatus,
was reduced to poverty by defraying the charge.

THE DECEMVIRATE

The tribunes, whose number had now been raised to ten,
held fast to their purpose, and at length the patricians, whose
obstinacy was shaken by the constant terror of impeachment,
consented to adopt some measure of legislative reform. The
proposal of Terentilius, which aimed merely at limiting the
consular jurisdiction, was now laid aside, and it was resolved
to carry out a complete revision and codification of public and
private law. As a preliminary step, commissioners were sent to
examine the existing codes in the chief cities of Greece, and on
their return a board of ten was appointed, whose members were
to hold supreme authority for one year, superseding all other
magistrates, and devoting themselves to the task of settling
for all time a fixed standard of justice. The new magistrates
bore the title of Decemvirs, and the leading spirit among them
was Appius Claudius,[2] who had dropped his former character
of an uncompromising oligarch and seemed to live only by

---

[1] *Satires*, iii. and xvi.　　　[2] Nephew of the Claudius mentioned above.

PLATE XII. L. JUNIUS BRUTUS (?)   54

Plate XIII. Etruscan Bronze: Head of
a Youth   55

the breath of popular favour.[1] Each of the decemvirs took his turn to administer justice for one day, attended, on that occasion only, by twelve lictors, with their bundles of rods.

THE TWELVE TABLES

Everything went smoothly during the first year of the decemvirate, and ten tables of the law were drawn up and exhibited for the inspection and criticism of all comers. In due course the new code was ratified by the votes of the centuriate assembly, and henceforth remained as the fountain of public and private right. At the end of the year it was found that two tables were still wanting to complete the code, and Appius, whose assumption of disinterested patriotism had been merely a cloak to hide his real purpose, now showed himself in his true character. Having contrived by unworthy arts to get himself elected on the new board, he filled up its numbers with his own creatures, all men of little mark, and three of them plebeians. Then he gave rein to his natural propensities, and the second year of the decemvirate was rendered infamous by every species of wrong and violence. All the familiar incidents of a Greek tyranny were now enacted within the walls of Rome, aggravated by the circumstance that in Rome there were ten tyrants instead of one. And every day the Romans could see their new masters parading the Forum, attended by a hundred and twenty lictors, who carried their axes within the sacred precinct, as a visible symbol that the sovereign rights of the people had passed to their oppressors.

The year drew toward its close, and the two remaining tables were completed and published. No exception was taken to their contents, and they were afterwards formally sanctioned and added to the Roman Corpus Juris. But when it became evident that Appius and his gang intended to remain in office and rivet the chains of tyranny on their countrymen the spirit of the nation was roused to resistance. Two famous instances of injustice, the murder of the brave centurion Dentatus and the outrage attempted against Virginia, a

[1] Livy, iii. 32.

beautiful plebeian maiden, at length drove the people to open revolt, and the second decemvirate was overthrown. The detested Appius escaped the axe of the executioner by a voluntary death, and the partners of his crimes were driven into exile.

We have passed lightly over these famous events, partly because they are too well known to be recounted in detail and partly because the real history of these times is involved in impenetrable obscurity. What were the true motives of Appius, whether, as Livy would have us believe, he was a hypocrite who courted the popular favour with the design of making himself a tyrant, or whether, as Ihne asserts, he was a genuine patriot, whose merits were buried under a heap of calumny by those of his own order, cannot now be determined. It will be more profitable to bestow a glance on the remaining fragments of the Twelve Tables and see what they can teach us respecting the life and manners of the Romans under the old Republic. It should perhaps be observed that these curious remnants cannot be regarded as genuine monuments of early Latin, having been repeatedly edited and modernized by the writers who preserved them. In substance, however, they are undoubtedly genuine.

DEBTOR LAW

The most valuable of the extracts are those relating to debtor and creditor, and by putting them together we are enabled to obtain some vivid glimpses of primitive society in Rome. Once more the veil is rent which hides from us a remote antiquity, and we follow the Roman Shylock as he goes on the track of his unhappy victim. The time of grace is past, a summons has been served on the debtor, and he has neglected to obey the call. Then forth issues the angry creditor determined to pursue his claim to the utmost limit allowed by the law. He finds his man in the Forum, or in the busy hive of the Subura, and calls upon a passer-by to bear witness that he is compelled to use force in asserting his right. Permission being granted, he plucks him by the ear,[1] and utters the

---

[1] Horace, *Satires*, I, ix. 76.

word " Remember ! " to signify that he will call him to give evidence in case of necessity. After these preliminaries he proceeds to the formal act of arrest, and the debtor, seeing his intention, tries to trip him up,[1] but he is overpowered and dragged off to the court. Or it may be that the debtor is bedridden with age or sickness, and in that case the creditor is required by law to provide a vehicle, and if he is more than usually humane he may even spread a pallet in the cart to save the bones of the unfortunate wretch ; this, however, was not insisted on. But, sick or sound, old or young, the insolvent debtor is now within the clutches of the law, and has to stand his trial.

Every precaution was taken to give litigants the full benefit of the statute and guard against unseemly haste. If judge, plaintiff, or defendant was detained elsewhere by important business, or completely disabled by sickness, or if any witness was not forthcoming when required, the case was adjourned. The missing witness was summoned by going to his house and shouting his name aloud before the door. After all forms had been satisfied and the case had been fairly heard the judge proceeded to pass sentence, and if the fact of the loan was clearly established thirty days were still allowed for payment. At the end of this time, if the money had not been paid, the defaulter was once more brought before the judge, and unless some responsible person offered bail he was assigned to his creditor, who carried him to his house and kept him in bonds, providing him, if necessary, with food, at the rate of a pound of meal a day. The debtor remained in durance for sixty days, and the creditor was obliged to produce him in court on the last three market-days falling within that period, to give opportunity for his friends or relations to redeem him. Then at last, if no one intervened to save him, the bond was declared forfeit, and his person was handed over to the absolute discretion of his creditor. Or if there were more than one creditor they might cut him in pieces and divide the portions among them. " And if any creditor," adds the

[1] I venture to suggest this version of *pedem struit* (*Bein stellen*), the meaning of which has been much disputed.

law with grim precision, "should cut more than his share, it shall not be reckoned against him."

Such was the law of debt in ancient Rome, as stated in a code which was drawn up specially to meet the demands of plebeians ; and as no complaint was raised against it on the ground of undue harshness we must conclude that all classes acquiesced in this iron standard of civil obligation.

SCOPE OF THE TWELVE TABLES

The laws of the Twelve Tables cover the whole field of public and private life, entering with minute precision into every circumstance which could give occasion for dispute. In cases of severe bodily injury the old barbarous law of retaliation, "An eye for an eye, and a tooth for a tooth," was clearly affirmed. The penalties against witchcraft remind us of the savage statutes which formerly disgraced the penal code of England. In the laws regulating the conduct of funerals we recognize the stern gravity of the Roman character, which condemned every form of idle ostentation and all violent display of emotion. Women are forbidden to tear their cheeks or cry the *lessus* over their dead. No gold is to be buried with a corpse, except that which is used in dentistry. With this very human touch, which seems for a moment to bring these antique people near to ourselves, we may conclude our brief notice of the earliest monument of Roman jurisprudence.

VALERIO-HORATIAN LAWS

The first consuls appointed after the fall of the decemvirs were Valerius and Horatius, who gave their name to certain important measures passed immediately afterwards in favour of the plebeians. The first of these declared that henceforth all resolutions carried in the plebeian assembly were to be binding on the whole people. Such resolutions, however, must have been confined for a long time after to matters only affecting the plebeians, and the law was not intended to give to the tribal assembly the general right of initiating legislation. The second forbade the creation of any magistrate without the right of appeal, and the third confirmed, with full legal sanction, the inviolability of all plebeian magistrates.

CONSULAR TRIBUNES

Fortified by these new statutes, and led by their tribunes, who now for the first time obtained a bench at the door of the Senate House, the plebeians resumed with fresh vigour the fight for full political and social equality. Two years later (445 B.C.) a tribune, Canuleius, brought in a bill for removing the obnoxious barrier between the two orders by legalizing marriages between patricians and plebeians. At the same time the demand was put forward that the consulship should be thrown open to plebeian candidates. With regard to the former of these proposals, it must be remarked that the patricians claimed to be the sole interpreters of the divine will, ascertained by means of the auspices, and it was argued that a blending of the two orders would cut off the whole people from the favour of heaven. This objection, however, was overruled, and the bill of Canuleius became law. After this great victory it seemed as if the plebeian aspirant had only to put out his hand and seize the most coveted prize of political ambition. But by a series of skilful manœuvres the patricians contrived to delay the final issue for nearly eighty years. They began by proposing a new title for the supreme magistrates, that of Military Tribunes with Consular Power, who were to be chosen from both orders. This change was not intended to be permanent, and its object was to cool the ambition of plebeian candidates by lowering the dignity of the office. For the new magistracy, in spite of its name, was but a shadow of the consulship, and those who held it were cut off from several valued distinctions, such as the right of celebrating a triumph, the privilege of setting up waxen images of themselves in their houses (a sort of title of nobility), and the attainment of consular rank, which gave the right to speak in the Senate. But the leaders of the plebeians accepted the proposal, and for the greater part of a century consular tribunes continued to be appointed, in numbers varying from three to six. The

REPUBLICAN ROME

consulship, however, was not suspended, and during all this period consuls were appointed from time to time. Greatly inferior as it was in splendour, the newly created office remained in the hands of the patricians, and more than forty years elapsed before the first plebeian consular tribune was elected.

CENSORS

Two years later the patricians, in pursuance of the same policy, curtailed the power of the consuls in another direction, by taking from them the duty of holding the census and the control of finance. These departments were now assigned to two magistrates, appointed for the purpose, who were called Censors, and held office for five years, though this term was soon afterwards reduced to a year and a half. The powers of the censors gradually increased until they extended to a sort of inquisitorial jurisdiction over the lives and manners of Roman citizens, corresponding in this respect to the Council of Areopagus at Athens. The office thus became invested with peculiar dignity, so that it was regarded as the crowning honour of a public career.[1] For the present, however, its functions were strictly limited, and for three generations the censors remained true to the traditions of their order as the jealous watch-dogs of patrician privilege.

QUAESTORS AND AEDILES

One or two points of detail must be added to complete this brief outline of Roman constitutional history during the first century of the Republic. As we have already seen, at the foundation of the consulship two officers called Quaestors were appointed, with duties connected with the administration of public money. Originally they were nominated by the consuls. On the analogy of this office two plebeian magistrates, called Aediles, were appointed when the tribunate was instituted, and these, under the tribunes, had special charge of the tables on which were inscribed the laws passed in the popular assemblies and the decrees of the Senate. This was a measure of precau-

[1] Plutarch, *Cato Major*, c. 16.

PLEBS AND POPULUS

tion to guard these important documents against the risk
of falsification at the hands of patricians. The number of
the quaestors was subsequently raised to four, two of whom
remained in the city, while the other two followed the consul
in the field. At some time before this their appointment had
been taken out of the hands of the consuls and transferred
to the people ; and at the close of the first century of the
Republic we find the office occupied by a plebeian on three
occasions in the same year.

Spurius Maelius

While the plebeians were thus steadily advancing toward
their goal, the old grievance which had given the first
impulse to reform remained unabated. The experience of
ages has shown that it is useless to apply a political remedy
to an economic evil, and though all the barriers between class
and class might be thrown down this could not check the
rapacity of the rich or relieve the wants of the poor. Rich
plebeian capitalists joined hands with the patricians in keeping
a monopoly of the public lands and in opposing all measures
for an equitable division, and the struggling farmer, driven
by his necessities to borrow, saw himself threatened with
bonds, slavery, and death. How bitterly the moneyed class
resented any sign of sympathy with the suffering poor is seen
in the case of Spurius Maelius, a wealthy knight, who in a time
of scarcity gave a largess of corn to his hungry fellow-citizens.
He was accused of aiming at the kingly power, and to meet
the pretended crisis Cincinnatus was appointed dictator,
with Servilius Ahala as his master of the horse. Next day
Maelius, as he was walking in the Forum, received a summons
to appear before the dictator and answer the charges against
him, and when he demurred he was stabbed to death by Ahala
before the eyes of the people. Spurius Cassius, Spurius Maelius,
and the Gracchi are classed together by Cicero as traitors to
their country, while Ahala takes rank in the eyes of the same
writer with the " honourable men " who dyed their hands
with the blood of Caesar.

61

CHAPTER IV

EXTERNAL AFFAIRS DOWN TO THE
SACK OF ROME BY THE GAULS

BETWEEN the expulsion of the kings and the disaster
of the Allia a period of a hundred and twenty years
elapsed, during which the Romans were engaged in
continual fighting, first for their existence as a nation,
and afterwards for the mastery in Latium and southern
Etruria. Two years after the banishment of the Tarquins
they were threatened with extinction by a formidable attack
from the Etruscans, led by Lars Porsena of Clusium. That
danger past, they were occupied for some time in irregular
warfare with the Sabines. Then, seven years after the attempt
of Porsena, they had to meet a coalition formed by thirty
cities of Latium to restore the tyranny at Rome. So far the
struggle had been for life and death ; but when the last effort of
the Tarquins had been broken, and when the league between
Rome and the Latins had been renewed on a fresh basis,
affairs began slowly to assume a different aspect, and the
Romans saw gradually opening before them the path which,
after centuries of warfare, led them to universal dominion.
Down to the middle of the fifth century progress was slow,
and the young Republic drew its breath in the midst of perils.
For the State was torn by faction, and the anxious watchers
on the city walls, with the roar of the Forum in their ears,
could see the smoke of burning farmsteads and armed bands of
Aequians and Volscians harrying the fields outside. But after
the fall of the decemvirs, and the legislative reforms which
followed, civil feud, though not yet silenced, lost much of its
bitterness, and a milder spirit began to prevail between the

62

rival orders. The effect was seen in the successes gained by the Roman arms during the next half-century, in the course of which they steadily advanced toward the supremacy of Latium and achieved their first great success against a foreign power by the capture of Veii. But this brilliant triumph was followed by an overwhelming disaster, for the Gauls swept down like a tempest from Etruria and Rome was burnt and her people were scattered. How the city rose again from its ashes and the Romans took up again the broken thread of their destiny will be told in the next chapter. We now proceed to relate more in detail the events which have thus been indicated in outline.

LARS PORSENA

We have already observed that the Etruscans at the close of the sixth century were by far the greatest power in Italy. It is true that in the great northern plain between the Alps and the Apennines the Gauls had for some time been encroaching on their territory. But they still held command of the two seas which wash the eastern and western shores of the peninsula, and their possessions in Campania were as yet untouched. It is difficult, therefore, to avoid the conclusion that the expedition of Lars Porsena, which is commonly attributed to friendship for the Tarquins, was a deliberate attempt to fill up the awkward gap in the Etruscan dominions by effecting the conquest of Latium, thus uniting the whole western district of Italy, from the Arno to Vesuvius, in one solid system of empire. For we know that Rome was actually conquered by Porsena, who compelled the Romans to relinquish all their lands on the right bank of the Tiber, and to give up the use of iron except for purposes of agriculture. Yet in spite of this signal victory the Tarquins were not restored ; and we may set aside without hesitation the sentimental reasons which were afterwards invented by Roman annalists to account for this singular forbearance. Our knowledge of the facts is not sufficient to enable us to explain the sudden withdrawal of Porsena from Rome But we read of the

crushing defeat sustained under the wall of Aricia by his son
Arruns, who had been sent to carry the war farther into
Latium. After this the attempts of the Etruscans to extend
their conquests south of the Tiber appear to have ceased.

THE FABII

Twelve miles to the north of Rome, on an eminence between
two affluents of the Tiber, was situated the wealthy and
populous city of Veii, one of the heads of the ancient Etruscan
league and the most important political centre in southern
Etruria. Between Veii and Rome there was an ancient feud,
dating from the earliest times of the kings, and we read of wars
undertaken by Romulus and Tullus Hostilius for the possession
of Fidenae, a town with a mixed Latin and Etruscan population,
commanding the bridge over the Tiber. Some twenty years
after the retreat of Porsena, at a time when they were constantly harassed by raids of the Aequians and Volscians, the
Romans found themselves involved in a war with their ancient
enemy. It lasted nine years, and with it is connected the
famous legend of the Fabii. This illustrious house, which
traced its descent from Hercules, was long the staunchest
pillar of patrician privilege, and for seven successive years a
Fabius was elected to the consulship. The persistent opposition of the Fabii to all proposals for agrarian reform excited
the bitter enmity of the plebeians, which rose to such a pitch
that on one occasion when with much difficulty an army had
been raised for carrying on the war against Veii the soldiers
serving under Kaeso Fabius refused to follow up a flying enemy,
grudging their general the honour of a triumph.[1] Two years
later, however, we find a total change in the policy of the
Fabii, and the same Kaeso who had been betrayed in the field,
being again elected consul, urged the Senate to carry out the
proposals of Spurius Cassius. His advice was rejected, and
the Fabii, finding that they had become unpopular with
their own class, resolved to leave Rome and maintain the war
against Veii by holding a fortified post in the enemy's country.

[1] Livy, ii. 43.

EXTERNAL AFFAIRS

Having obtained permission, all the fighting men of the Fabian house, three hundred and six in number, marched out of Rome and took up their station on a steep hill overlooking the Cremera, a little river formed by the junction of the two streams which skirt the walls of Veii. Here they raised a fortified camp, and for two years they held their own against all the assaults of the enemy, and inflicted much damage on the Veientine territory. But at length they were drawn into an ambush and cut off to a man. Only one boy who had been left behind in Rome remained to carry on the Fabian line, and from him was descended that renowned Fabius, surnamed Cunctator, whose iron firmness broke the fiery genius of Hannibal, "and by delay restored the State." [1]

After the destruction of the Fabii the Etruscans again assumed the offensive, and succeeded in lodging an armed force on the Janiculum, a hill which formed a sort of outlying citadel on the right bank of the Tiber, just opposite to Rome. They thus retaliated on the Romans the hardships which they themselves had endured from the garrison on the Cremera. But from this position they were shortly afterwards expelled, and in the next year, being joined by an army of the Sabines, they and their allies suffered a severe defeat under the walls of Veii. After this there was a cessation of hostilities on the side of Etruria for nearly forty years (474–438 B.C.).

West versus East

During the whole of the fifth century the Etruscan power was steadily on the decline. Already, seven years before the beginning of that epoch, they had been foiled in their attempt to effect the conquest of Latium ; and in the same year which saw the conclusion of peace between Rome and Veii their naval power was utterly broken by Hiero, tyrant of Syracuse, in a great sea-fight off Cumae. Two other events must be mentioned in this connexion, as forming parts in one great historical series. The first is the defeat of the Persians at Salamis, followed in the next year by the destruction of their

[1] Virgil, *Aeneid*, vi. 846 (from Ennius).

army at Plataea, and the second is the great victory gained by Gelo of Syracuse over an immense host of Carthaginians at Himera, in northern Sicily. It is almost certain that the last-named expedition was undertaken in direct understanding with Xerxes, whose influence was then paramount in Phoenicia, the mother-country of Carthage. But, setting this aside, the battles of Salamis, Plataea, Himera, and Cumae are all parts of one historical drama, on the issue of which depended the question whether Oriental or Western ideals were to shape the destinies of Europe. For, whatever may have been their origin, the Etruscans, in spite of their geographical position, were Orientals in character and the enemies of liberty and progress ; and the Romans, though in some respects they were still barbarians, were united, all unconsciously, in the same cause with the Greeks. Whether Eastern despotism, with all its degrading consequences, or Roman law and Greek enlighten-ment were to prevail in Europe—these were the momentous issues at stake when the Greeks raised their war-cry at Plataea and Himera or charged the galleys of Tuscany and Phoenicia. And therefore these events have still a living interest for us, for in them were involved those higher principles in which and by which we live.

The Sabine War

We have now to speak of Rome's dealings with her imme-diate neighbours in the district lying between the Tiber and the Liris. These were the Sabines, who dwelt in the region skirting the left bank of the Tiber, with a southern frontier somewhat vaguely defined by the lower valley of the Anio ; the Latins, in the plain of Latium and the Alban hills ; the Aequians, who had gradually descended from their ancient seat about Lake Fucinus to the hills above Praeneste and Tibur ; the Hernicans, connected by blood with the Sabines, and most critically situated in the upland region between the valleys of the Liris and the Trerus ; and the fierce Volscians, whose home lay in the rugged group of mountains reaching down from the valley of the Trerus to the sea at

EXTERNAL AFFAIRS

Tarracina. It was with the first of these, the Sabines, whose capital was Cures, that the Romans had to try their strength, three years after the retreat of Porsena. We hear something of victories gained by the famous brothers Publius and Marcus Valerius Publicola, and the contest was ended for the time by a decisive battle fought at Cures, in which, if we may trust our authorities, ten thousand of the Sabines were slain.[1] Spurius Cassius, under whose command the victory was won, obtained a triumph, and the Sabines were forced to sue for peace.

In the second year of this war (504 B.C.), when the Sabines were mustering all their forces for a decisive blow, an event occurred which brought an accession of strength to the Romans from a totally unexpected source. A certain Attius Clausus, one of the most powerful of the Sabine nobles, who had roused the anger of his countrymen by his vigorous opposition to the war, migrated with all his family and dependents to Rome, where he received full patrician rank, and a grant of lands beyond the Anio. According to Dionysius, his followers, counting only those capable of bearing arms, numbered not less than five thousand. After his migration he took the name of Appius Claudius Sabinus, and became the founder of the famous Claudian line, which was distinguished by its furious antagonism to the plebeians, and in after-times gave more than one emperor to Rome.

TREATY WITH THE LATINS

Under the rule of the Tarquins Rome had held an acknowledged position as the head of Latium, and the marauding tribes who constantly threatened the lowland districts were successfully held in check. But with the fall of the monarchy this state of things came to an end, and a century and a half of fighting was required to recover what had been lost. The Latins held that their allegiance was cancelled by the expulsion of the Tarquins, and after the Sabine war had been brought to a conclusion the Romans had to face a powerful

[1] Dionysius, v. 49.

coalition of the revolted Latin cities, formed to procure the restoration of the exiled princes. The league of the Latins was broken up by the battle of Lake Regillus, and the Tarquins went into perpetual banishment. It is obvious that sooner or later community of interests was sure to bring the Romans and Latins together. For, besides the fact that they were closely connected by ties of blood and common worship, both Romans and Latins were lowlanders, devoted to agriculture, and constantly exposed to loss and danger from the raids of the mountain tribes by whom they were surrounded. Accordingly, in the year following the first secession of the plebeians and the creation of the tribunate (493 B.C.) a solemn treaty was made between the Romans and Latins, the terms of which are thus given by Dionysius : [1] " Let there be peace between the Roman and Latin cities, as long as heaven and earth remain steadfast in their appointed places. Let them neither make war against each other, nor countenance any such war made by others, nor give to each other's enemies a passage through their own land. Let them lend aid to each other against all attacks, and share equally whatever spoils or booty are won by their common arms. Let all private suits be settled within ten days, and let all such cases be tried in whatsoever town the affair giving rise to the suit may have occurred." The chief mover in this important transaction was the same Spurius Cassius who had triumphed over the Sabines, and who afterwards fell a victim to his zeal for agrarian reform. Seven years later, just before the proposal of his last fatal measure, Cassius earned a new title to the gratitude of his fellow-citizens by concluding a second treaty, on the same terms, with the Hernicans. The position of these hardy and valiant mountaineers made their alliance peculiarly valuable, for they interposed a living barrier between the Aequians on the north and the Volscians on the south, diminishing the danger of combined action on the part of these two peoples, and securing to the Romans early information of any movement preparing on either side against them.

[1] vi. 95.

68

PLATE XIV. ETRUSCAN WALL, FAESULAE (FIESOLE)

PLATE XV.   COLUMNS AND ANCIENT WALL, CORA

69

EXTERNAL AFFAIRS

Cassius had, indeed, performed an inestimable service, and probably saved his countrymen from utter ruin, by the conclusion of these two treaties. For during the next forty years Rome was plunged in civil strife and weakened by repeated visitations of pestilence, and if the Latins and Hernicans had joined her other enemies it is hardly possible that she could have made head against them. As it was, the dual compact was faithfully observed throughout that troubled period, though the Latins especially suffered terribly from the incessant assaults of the Aequians and Volscians, and in the course of the long struggle with these fierce tribes no less than thirteen of their cities were destroyed.

AEQUIAN AND VOLSCIAN WARS

It would only weary the reader and would serve no useful purpose to give a list of the countless campaigns against the Aequians and Volscians which are recorded with all historical gravity by Livy and Dionysius. The details of time, place, addresses to the soldiers, and numbers slain are doubtless for the most part pure invention. It will be sufficient, therefore, to mark the main features of these weary contests. The Aequians directed their attacks chiefly to the district lying on the northern side of the Alban hills, and gained a footing on Mount Algidus, from which position they made repeated descents on the fields of the Latins. The Volscians held their outposts on the southern side of the same mountain group, and, sometimes acting by themselves, sometimes in concert with the Aequians, spread fire and havoc almost to the gates of Rome. For a whole generation following the conclusion of the Latin treaty little progress was made against them, and at one time Tusculum was the sole stronghold left to the Latins by the Aequian invaders. But from the middle of the fifth century onward there was a marked improvement, and at last the Romans, Latins, and Hernicans, fighting under a dictator, gained a great victory over the combined forces of the Aequians and Volscians at Mount Algidus (431 B.C.). After the Gallic invasion we hear little more of the Aequians, but the Volscians were not finally subdued until half a century later. Then at length this rude warrior people earned the last wages of the sword and met the fate which they had brought on themselves by centuries of rapine. Their country was turned into a desert, and from this time their name disappears from history.

Military Colonies

It is in connexion with the Aequian and Volscian wars that we first hear of the system of military colonies which formed so important a part of the Roman policy, and was the chief means of saving Italy in the terrible crisis of the Second Punic War. As the Roman frontier advanced, some place of strategic importance was chosen, and a colony of Roman citizens was sent to occupy it, each man receiving a fixed portion of land. In some cases colonies were formed with mixed bodies of Romans and Latins. If possible, some captured town was selected for the settlement, but, failing that, a new city was founded. The earliest colonies were planted on the Aequian and Volscian frontiers, and in several instances they were taken by the enemy, and subsequently recovered. The full development of this system belongs, of course, to a later period, but its early adoption marks the first step in the career of the Romans as a conquering and civilizing people. Besides their military importance, these colonies served the useful purpose of providing a livelihood for the poorer citizens and diverting attention from the ever-recurring question of agrarian reform, which caused so much bad blood between the two orders.

Quarrels in Camp

A few incidents may be singled out from the narrative of these wars as being true at least in character and throwing light on the manners of the times. We have seen that the patrician generals who commanded the armies of Rome were repeatedly thwarted and hindered in their conduct of a campaign by the mutinous behaviour of the plebeians

70

serving in the ranks. But by acting thus the plebeians exposed themselves to great perils. In Rome low-born petulance might riot unchecked, having a perpetual refuge in its authorized champions, the tribunes. But when once the legions had taken the field such barriers were removed, and the plebeian soldier was left at the mercy of his aristocratic commander. Thus Appius Claudius, the second of the name, being embittered by a political defeat, sought to revenge himself upon the plebeians by a gross abuse of his military authority. While conducting a campaign against the Volscians he gave free rein to the natural violence of his temper, and tried the patience of his troops to the utmost by persistent harshness and cruelty. This behaviour produced its natural consequences. Whenever he made his rounds in the camp he was met by fierce looks and muttered curses, until even his savage mind was shaken by these unmistakable signs of the general abhorrence, and he shut himself up in his tent, transacting all business through his subordinates. But even then he gave vent to his spleen in bitter taunts, declaring that the soldiers had been corrupted by their centurions, whom he nicknamed 'Voleros,' after a peculiarly obnoxious tribune. These insults, following their ill-treatment, exasperated the soldiers to such a pitch that when they were brought face to face with the enemy they threw down their arms and fled to their camp. Nothing remained to Appius but to draw off his troops, and as soon as he had got beyond the reach of pursuit he pitched his camp and held a court-martial for the punishment of the mutineers. The soldiers who were found without their arms, the standard-bearers who had deserted their ensigns, and any centurion who had left his post were beaten with rods and beheaded. Then lots were cast among the main body of the army, and every tenth man was clubbed to death.[1]

At a much later date (414 B.C.), when the rage of party warfare had to a large extent subsided, we hear of another case of insubordination, ending in the violent death of an

---

[1] This was a common form of military punishment among the Romans, and was called *fustuarium*. See Livy, ii. 59, and Epitome.

unpopular general. A certain Postumius, while commanding an army as consular tribune, gave great offence to his men by defrauding them of their just share of the booty after the sack of the town of Bola. Being summoned from the camp to quell some civil disturbance in Rome, he excited general disgust among the citizens by an indecent expression which he let fall at a meeting summoned to decide what was to be done with the recently conquered land. When one of the tribunes proposed that the fields should be divided among the soldiers who had won them by their valour, Postumius exclaimed in the style of a vulgar bully : " I advise my men to keep quiet, or they'll come by the worse." This was a common phrase, conveying a threat of a beating, employed by masters to cow a refractory slave, and on hearing of the incident the men broke into open mutiny. Postumius hurried back from Rome to restore order, but on his appearance he was surrounded by a yelling mob and stoned to death.[1]

CORIOLANUS

Two famous stories which belong to this period are too characteristic to be passed over in silence. Proudest among the proud aristocracy of Rome was the young Caius Marcius, who, when little more than a boy, had gained great honour by his valiant feats at the battle of Lake Regillus. His greatest achievement, however, was performed some years later, in a war with the Volscians, when he succeeded, almost single-handed, in taking the town of Corioli, thus earning the title of Coriolanus. But his haughty manners and contempt of all meaner men turned the people against him, and when he appeared as a candidate for the consulship he was rejected. Provoked by this failure, he became more violent in his opposition to the plebeians than ever, and in a year of scarcity, when it was proposed to sell the corn in the public granaries at a low price, he spoke strongly against the measure, and denounced the insolence of the populace, who since the institution of the tribunate had risen, he said, to greater and greater

---

[1] Livy, iv. 49–50.

heights of sedition. " Let there be an end," he concluded, " of these weak concessions. The more we give way, the more they will encroach, until the State is reduced to anarchy. If you will be guided by me, you will meet their clamours with this answer : No tribunes, or no corn ! " This audacious attack on their sole means of defence so enraged the plebeians that Marcius narrowly escaped being torn to pieces on his way home from the Senate House. The storm, moreover, did not abate until the Senate agreed that he should stand his trial before the tribal assembly, which then for the first time assumed the functions of a judicial body. Marcius escaped sentence by going into voluntary exile, and retired to Antium, where he was hospitably entertained by Attius Tullus, a man of great influence among the Volscians. By the advice of Tullus he was appointed to the supreme command of the Volscian army, and his heart exulted when he saw the means of vengeance thus placed in his hands. First he led the Volscians against the coast-lands of Latium, from Circeii to Lavinium, sacking town after town, and leaving ruin and desolation in his track. Then he marched through the region north of the Alban Mount, and after taking five cities he pitched his camp within five miles of Rome.

Meanwhile among the Romans all was panic and dismay. There was no thought of resistance ; their sole hope lay in moving the compassion of their enemy. Five envoys, the eldest and most venerable among the patricians, were sent to sue for peace. But Coriolanus sent them back, saying that he would listen to no terms unless the Romans would consent to restore all the lands and cities taken in war from the Volscians and make them citizens of Rome. Then the priests and augurs, arrayed in their robes and carrying their sacred vessels, moved in solemn procession from Rome to the Volscian camp. But Coriolanus remained unmoved, and they brought back no message of peace. In this extremity Rome was saved by the instinct of a woman. For Juno, says the story, put a wise thought into the mind of Valeria, a noble lady, while she was praying in the temple of the goddess, and a voice whispered

73

in her ear : " He cares not for the elders, he heeds not the priests, but he will reverence his mother and his wife." So Valeria went to Volumnia, the wife of Coriolanus, and to his mother Veturia, and said : " Take your little ones by the hand and go together to this proud man, and throw yourselves at his feet, and ask mercy for Rome and for yourselves." The women arose and went to Coriolanus ; and when he saw their mourning garments and their faces wasted by fasting and sorrow his heart melted at last, and he said : " Mother, thou hast prevailed ; but in saving Rome thou hast ruined thy son." Then without delay he led off his forces, and the danger which had hung over Rome passed away. But the Volscians could not forgive Coriolanus for letting slip the chance of humbling their old enemy to the dust, and they put him to death as a traitor.

CINCINNATUS

In the story of Coriolanus we see exhibited the struggle between public duty and private resentment ; that of Cincinnatus, the date of which falls a generation later (458 B.C.), illustrates another side of the Roman character, its antique simplicity and contempt of all pomp and ostentation. After a short interval of peace the Aequians had taken the field again, and, having pitched their camp on Mount Algidus, were plundering the fields of Tusculum and Labici. Envoys were sent from Rome to protest against the violation of a truce which had been made a year before, and they found the Aequian general, Cloelius Gracchus, sitting before his tent under the shade of a venerable oak. He heard their complaints with a contemptuous smile, and answered, pointing to the spreading boughs of the oak : " Talk to that tree : I have other business in hand." One of the envoys caught up his word, and uttered a solemn prayer to the guardian genius of the wood, and to all the other heavenly powers, invoking speedy vengeance on those who had broken their sworn covenant and had violated the law of nations. The gods heard his prayer, but delayed its fulfilment. For the consul Minucius, who was appointed to lead the Roman army against the Aequians, acted imprudently, and allowed himself to be caught in a deep valley, shut in by steep cliffs, and barred at both ends by the soldiers of Gracchus. A few horsemen, however, contrived to break through the enemy's lines, and brought news to Rome of the consul's sore strait. Now Cincinnatus at this time was living on his little farm beyond the Tiber, and one day as he was digging in a field messengers came to him from the Senate and told him that he had been appointed dictator, that he might save Minucius and his army from destruction. Bidding his wife farewell, he went with the messengers to Rome. On the following day he proclaimed that all business was to be suspended in the city, and that every man of military age was to go armed to the Field of Mars, taking with him food for five days and twelve wooden stakes. By evening all was ready, and such was their dispatch that the army reached Mount Algidus at midnight, and soon after came to the place where Minucius had now been blockaded for three days. Having examined the position, Cincinnatus drew out his forces so as completely to surround the Aequian army, and as each man reached his post he planted his stakes and began to dig a trench. Thus the besiegers became the besieged, and suddenly a great shout from beyond the Aequian lines told the men of Minucius that succour was at hand. Being thus caught in a trap, Gracchus was compelled to make what terms he could, and he and his army were passed under the yoke.[1]

Thus did Cincinnatus save a Roman army from ruin and disgrace, and within sixteen days he was once more on his estate, ploughing and digging his fields like a simple farmer.

War with Veii

The last half-century of this epoch is marked by two events of capital importance, one the most brilliant success hitherto achieved by Roman arms, the other a crushing defeat, which

---

[1] A ceremony in which a defeated army was compelled to march unarmed, in token of subjection, under an arrangement of two upright spears with a third bound across the top.

seemed for a moment to threaten the young state with total extinction. These were the capture of Veii and the disaster of the Allia. The long peace between Rome and Veii was broken after the lapse of a whole generation, and once more the Romans might boast that they were drawing the sword in a righteous cause. For Lars Tolumnius, the Veientine king, had been guilty of a gross act of perfidy, having instigated the people of Fidenae to murder certain Roman envoys who had been sent to check a movement of revolt among the Etruscan portion of the inhabitants. In the war which followed Cornelius Cossus obtained great renown by slaying King Tolumnius with his own hand, thus winning the *spolia opima*, ' the splendid spoils ' which fell to a Roman commander who had overthrown the enemy's general in battle.[1] In spite of this severe blow, repeated outbreaks occurred during the next twelve years, ending with the total subjugation of Fidenae and the acceptance of a twenty years' truce by the Veientines. When the final struggle between Rome and Veii began, the other states of Etruria were too weak to lend any effectual aid. The great empire which once seemed likely to extend its dominions over the whole Italian peninsula was now rapidly falling to pieces. The Gauls were fast gaining ground in the northern plain, and the Syracusans were steadily building up a maritime power, which, after the failure of the great Athenian expedition (415–413 B.C.), was extended to the eastern and western coasts of Italy, while within two years of the truce concluded between Rome and Veii the Samnites came pouring into Campania, took Capua and Cumae, and tore from the Etruscans their fairest province.

The story of the last war with Veii is the Roman *Iliad*, and in the loose popular narrative the siege, like that of Troy, lasted for ten years. The actual investment of the place, however, was not completed until after two years of irregular warfare, for the Romans were still occupied in a war with the Volscians, and help came to the besieged from the Etruscan

[1] It was a question whether Cossus was entitled to this distinction, as he seems only to have held a subordinate command. See Livy, iv. 20.

cities of Capena and Falerii, whose troops broke through the Roman lines and opened communication with the surrounding country.

It was during the Volscian war just mentioned, at a time when a Roman army was engaged in the siege of Anxur, that a change, momentous in its consequences, was introduced into the Roman military system. Hitherto the Roman foot-soldier had served without pay, being called from his farm for a campaign which lasted for a few weeks, and returning to his labour when the fighting was over. But in the year in which the war with Veii began (406 B.C.) the Senate passed a decree that the soldiers should receive pay from the public treasury. A further step in the same direction was taken when the army besieging Veii passed their first winter in the field. Thus began that fatal severance between civil and military life which went on unchecked until an impassable gulf was created between citizen and soldier and Rome was left at the mercy of her defenders.

The fall of Veii as narrated in the Roman annals is surrounded by a halo of romance, and every circumstance is added which could enhance the contrast between this great achievement and the overwhelming catastrophe which followed. As the end drew near rumours of strange portents went abroad, but these were generally little regarded, as there were no Etruscan seers at hand to interpret their meaning. One of these signs was too startling, however, and too serious in its immediate effects to be left unheeded. This was the miraculous overflow of the Alban crater-lake, which in a season remarkable for drought rose suddenly above the level of the steep cliffs which enclosed it and poured in torrents over the surrounding fields. Then the Romans sent messengers to Delphi to inquire the meaning of this prodigy ; and while they were gone an old Etruscan who had been taken captive at Veii told them that they must drain off the waters and not suffer them to flow into the sea, for otherwise Veii could never be taken. And presently the messengers came back from Delphi, and brought these words from the god : " Suffer ye not that the waters of Alba reach the sea, but divide them by many channels for the watering of your fields." So the Romans sent workmen and skilled engineers and made a long and deep tunnel piercing the rocky side of the crater, and the waters were drawn off. After that the doom of Veii was sealed.

CAMILLUS

In the last scene of the war a new character appears prominently on the stage of Roman history, where he remains the central figure for the next thirty years This was Marcus Furius Camillus, the most famous general in the early annals of Rome. He had first gained distinction in the battle of Mount Algidus, where he fought with great valour against the Aequians and Volscians,[1] and he had subsequently filled the office of censor. Knowing his ability and disgusted by the incompetence of their other commanders, who had brought the army at Veii to the verge of ruin, the Senate resolved to recall them and appoint Camillus dictator. Whereupon the Veientines were so alarmed that they sent ambassadors to sue for peace. And one of these, finding that they had come on a vain errand, turned as he was going and said : " O men proud and froward of heart, doubtless ye deem it a fair deed to level a great city with the ground and enslave her children. But be sure that, when ye have done this thing, it shall not be long ere ye are yourselves made homeless."

FALL OF VEII

Camillus fully justified the confidence reposed in him, and being in command of a powerful army, composed of Latins Hernicans, and Romans, he pressed the siege with vigour and gave the Veientines no rest. The city ultimately fell by the same means as had been used to subdue the waters of the Alban Lake. For Camillus caused a tunnel to be dug, which was carried under the walls and so guided that it should issue within the temple of Juno, which stood on the citadel of Veii. The work went on apace, for the men dug day and night.

---

[1] Plutarch, *Camillus*, c. 2.

PLATE XVI. NEAR VEIO (VEII)

PLATE XVII. MATER MATUTA 79

EXTERNAL AFFAIRS

One day when but a few more strokes of the pick were wanted to bring them to the surface it chanced that the king of Veii was offering sacrifice in the temple, little dreaming of the stealthy foe who were creeping on, inch by inch, beneath his feet. He had just taken the vessel with the meat-offering into his hand when the priest said : " The victory is for him who shall complete this sacrifice." His prophecy was fulfilled, but not as he meant it. For the Romans who were in the mine heard his words, and, breaking through the last barrier, they rushed into the temple, seized the offering, and gave it to Camillus. So the sacrifice was completed by the hands of a Roman, and the soldiers came thronging up through the tunnel and made themselves masters of the citadel. Then some of them broke down the city gates, letting in the main army, and Veii was given up to pillage and slaughter.

This signal victory was followed by a rapid advance of the Roman arms, which carried them beyond the wild mountain region known as the Ciminian Forest and placed the towns of Falerii, Sutrium, and Nepete in their hands. But, says the chronicle, so swift a rise of fortune excited the envy of heaven, already incensed against the Romans by their arrogant repulse of the humble petition which had been brought to them from Veii. The first to feel the stroke of divine vengeance was Camillus, now raised to the height of glory by the conquest of a city as large and populous as Rome itself. For he had celebrated his triumph in a manner exceeding the modesty not merely of a citizen, but of a man. Entering the city in a chariot drawn by four white horses, he had driven to the Capitol as if he were aping the majesty of Jove himself. So the people murmured against him, and when he was brought to trial by one of the tribunes on a charge of concealing part of the spoils of Veii for his own use they condemned him to pay a heavy fine. His friends and clients offered to raise the whole amount out of their own purses, but he refused their aid and went into exile, after praying, like Achilles,[1] that the Romans might soon be brought into such a strait as would

[1] *Iliad*, i. 240.

cause them to long for the champion whom they had so wantonly cast out.

THE GAULS

His prayer was soon fulfilled. Within a year after he had retired from Rome the Gauls were encamped amid the smoking ruins of the city and laying close siege to the Capitol. Before we explain how this came about, however, it will be well to say something as to the character and previous history of this strange people, whose very name remained a terror to the Romans for ages after. The Gauls were the first of the Indo-Germanic peoples to reach the western ocean, and from their earliest seats in the country now called France they spread to the British Isles, to Spain, to the lands of the Upper Danube, and even to Asia Minor. Wherever we find them they exhibit the same characteristic qualities—a fickle, restless disposition, impatient of fixed abode or steady industry, lively talents, inclining them especially to the cultivation of eloquence, and an impetuous valour, appalling at the first onset, but soon dying out, like a fire in stubble. Their most splendid endowment was a high and soaring imagination, to which we owe, in great part, the noblest creations of modern poetry. But with all their · brilliant and attractive gifts, generous, gay, and debonair, the Gauls were singularly deficient in those virtues which are the source of true greatness in states. They were vain and capricious as children, jealous of all control, eager to take up an adventure, quick to abandon it on the first hint of difficulty. Their courage was all founded on personal vanity, and very different from that sober, enduring valour which rests on a sense of civic obligation. Hence it was that their multitudinous armies, after sweeping down like some elemental force which leaves havoc and devastation behind it, spent all their energies in one tremendous blow and achieved no lasting conquests.

Like all savage races, the Gauls were lazy and self-indulgent, and whatever truth there may be in the story that they were first attracted to Italy by the report of the

rich wines produced in that peninsula, it shows the light in
which they appeared to the civilized nations of antiquity.
The physical character universally ascribed by ancient writers
to the Gauls—their light hair and blue eyes, their huge frames,
strong only for a sudden effort [1]—have perplexed modern
ethnologists from Niebuhr downward.

At what time the Gauls first crossed the Alps and entered
the rich district now known as the plain of Lombardy is
uncertain ; but the movement had doubtless been carried
on from generation to generation, one horde of invaders
pressing upon another, and thrusting out the Umbrians and
Etruscans, the earlier occupants of the soil. The last to arrive
were the Senones, who, finding all the more fertile regions
already taken, were forced to content themselves with the
narrow and barren strip of coastland which lies between
Ravenna and Ancona. But they knew that a rich and favoured
land lay within a few days' march beyond the mountains,
and a year after the fall of Veii they crossed the passes of
the Apennines and pitched their camp before the walls of
Clusium. Their numbers, their savage cries, and their ferocious
appearance filled the people of Clusium with dismay, and by
a strange reversal of fortune the same city which, four generations back, had achieved the conquest of Rome now sent a
humble petition for help to her ancient enemy. Three Roman
envoys were dispatched in answer to this message, and on
their arrival at Clusium they addressed a civil remonstrance
to Brennus, the Gaulish leader, warning him not to meddle
with " the friends and allies " of the Roman people. The
haughty chieftain returned a disdainful answer, and the
conference being broken up both sides prepared for battle.
Then the envoys, who all belonged to the illustrious house of
the Fabii, forgetting the peaceful character of their mission,
openly took part with the men of Clusium, and one of them
slew a Gaulish captain with his own hand. Their persons

---

[1] *Magna corpora, tantum ad impetum valida,* says Tacitus in his account
of the Germans. But the description applies at least equally to the ancient
Gauls.

and their conspicuous valour caused them to be easily distinguished from the Etruscans, and Brennus, incensed by this act of perfidy, at once drew off his forces and sent an embassy to Rome demanding that those who had thus violated the law of nations should be given up for punishment. Far from giving the required satisfaction, the Romans elected the three Fabii as consular tribunes for the ensuing year.

DESCENT OF THE GAULS ON ROME

This crowning insult inflamed the anger of the Gauls to the highest pitch, and, breaking up their camp at Clusium, they marched with all speed to take vengeance on the offending Romans. As they advanced, covering a wide extent of country with horse and foot, the people forsook their fields, and in every town they passed they saw the gates barred and the walls thronged with armed men. But these precautions were needless, for without pausing to attack any place of strength they swept impetuously on, shouting, "To Rome! To Rome!"[1]

Meanwhile the Romans were lulled in a sense of false security, and no extraordinary precautions were taken to meet the approaching crisis. Orders, indeed, were issued for a levy of troops, but the consular tribunes by whose guilt the State had been brought into this peril proceeded carelessly with their duty, as if they hardly believed that they would be called upon to fight at all. But they were rudely awakened from their apathy when hurrying messengers arrived, one after another, with the news that a vast host of Gauls was pouring swiftly down the valley of the Tiber. Then, as if wild haste could atone for blind indifference, they led out their forces, ill-disciplined and ill-prepared, and took up a position on the banks of the Allia, a little stream which flows into the Tiber eleven miles from Rome. They saw the hills on the opposite bank thronged with a multitude of Gauls, whose wild cries and savage war-songs made the valley ring from side to side.

[1] Livy, v. 37.

EXTERNAL AFFAIRS

BATTLE OF THE ALLIA

The Roman line extended along the southern bank of the
Allia, with its left toward the Tiber, and its right posted on
some hilly ground and protected on the flank by the broken
and wooded country beyond. It was on this latter point
that Brennus directed his chief attack, and here the soldiers,
who were mostly raw recruits, gave way at the first onset
and fled along the bank of the river, carrying disorder and
panic into the centre and left. Never was a victory more
complete or more easily won; for the Romans were, indeed,
beaten in spirit [1] before a blow was struck, and so rapid was
their flight that the number slain was comparatively small.
The greater part escaped across the Tiber and took refuge
at Veii, while a few fled to Rome with news of the disaster.

There seemed little hope that the State could survive so
crushing a blow. There was no force adequate for the defence
of the walls and the city was utterly unprepared for a siege.
Nevertheless it was resolved to make a last stand for the defence
of the Capitol, the heart and centre of Roman civic life, and a
few picked men were told off for this duty, while the rest of
the citizens, with the Vestal Virgins and the priest of Quirinus,
sought refuge in the neighbouring cities. Some, however,
who were disabled by age or sickness, remained of necessity,
and a few aged men of the highest rank chose rather to perish
on their own hearth-stones than to spend their last days as
dependents on the bounty of strangers. Putting on their
robes of state, they sat down at their doors, like Anchises
in Virgil's famous description,[2] waiting for their doom.

SACK OF ROME

These preparations occupied two days, and during the
interval the Gauls seem to have done nothing, being amazed,
according to Livy, by the suddenness of their victory, and
expecting a renewal of the battle. On the third day they

---

[1] τῇ γνώμῃ δεδουλωμένοι (Thuc. iv. 34).
[2] *Aeneid*, ii. 634 *sqq.*, perhaps in allusion to this incident.

appeared before Rome, and marched unopposed through the open gates and along the deserted streets. Only the aged patricians sat mute as statues at the doors of their houses, and the barbarians gazed in awe at these venerable figures, arrayed in a majesty which seemed to them more than human. But when one of the Gauls ventured to touch the long white beard of Marcus Papirius, and the old man smote him in anger with his ivory staff, the spell was broken and a general massacre ensued. Then, after a vain attempt to carry the Capitol by storm, they began to plunder the city, leaving a detachment to hold the fortress in blockade.

The Saving of the Capitol

We can imagine the feelings of the brave men gathered on that narrow platform of rock when they saw the flames spreading from house to house and heard the screams of the unhappy creatures who had remained behind in their helplessness, and who were now dragged from their hiding-places and butchered in cold blood. But soon their thoughts were concentrated on their own desperate situation, for they were closely blockaded, their supplies of food were scanty, and they had little prospect of any relief from without. A gleam of hope came to them when a gallant youth named Pontius succeeded in eluding the vigilance of the sentinels and, having scaled the Capitol by a precipitous path, brought news that the Roman army was reassembling at Veii, and that Camillus, who was living in exile at Ardea, had armed the citizens and inflicted a severe blow on a flying squadron of Gauls who were plundering the neighbouring fields. It was at once resolved to appoint Camillus dictator, and Pontius, having procured the necessary authority, once more managed to slip through the line of blockade, and carried the decree of the Senate back to Veii. But the marks which he had made in his passage were observed by the Gauls, and they resolved to carry the stronghold by surprise. In the dead of night a picked band of the enemy crept up the rocky ascent, and the foremost of them had already reached the top when the loud

84

cackling of some geese in the neighbouring temple of Juno caught the ear of Marcus Manlius, a valiant Roman warrior, whose lodging was close at hand. Hastily arming himself, he rushed to the spot, and was just in time to hurl back the leader of the band, who fell headlong down the cliff, carrying several of his comrades with him. The rest were dismayed by this sudden reverse, and, being assailed by numbers of the garrison, who had been awakened by the shouts of Manlius, they were easily beaten off.

But weeks lengthened into months, and the hopes of the defenders grew fainter and fainter as no sign of the promised succour appeared. Nor were the besiegers in a much better plight, for their ranks were thinned by pestilence, and they were threatened with famine, having stripped the whole surrounding country by repeated forays. And to complete their uneasiness news reached them that their own territory had been invaded by the Veneti. Both sides were therefore inclined to make terms, and after some parley it was agreed that the Gauls should leave the city on receiving a thousand pounds weight of gold in ransom. While the gold was being weighed Quintus Sulpicius, a consular tribune, who was presiding over the transaction, perceived that the weights were false and attempted to protest. Thereupon Brennus flung his sword into the scale, crying, " Woe to the vanquished ! " But at this very moment Camillus arrived on the scene with his army, drove off the Gauls, and saved Rome from the last infamy of buying her freedom from a victorious foe.

Thus for the second time within little more than a century the future arbitress of the world's destinies had been humbled to the dust by a foreign invader. Those who wish to read the story in all its power and pathos will turn to the original from which this brief sketch has been taken and indulge their literary sense with the musical cadences and the glowing fancy of Livy. But even this scanty abridgment will be sufficient to show the reader that he has been treading the path of romance, far removed from the stern realities of history. However reluctantly, we must tell the harsh truth and pronounce every detail of Livy's narrative to be a fiction, artfully dressed up to please the national vanity and cloak the ignominy of a great defeat. We see here the desire to *moralize* the facts of history, to mould them into conformity with certain preconceived ideas of justice, compensation, retribution, and the like, which is common to all the ancient historians, and has sometimes warped the judgment and clouded the vision even of so great a writer as Thucydides.

DEVELOPMENT IN THE FIFTH CENTURY

We may now cast our eyes rapidly over the wide field which we have traversed and gather up such meagre fragments of fact as remain to us from the ruins of the past. After more than a century of warfare the Roman frontier has been advanced far into Etruria, the power of the Aequians and Volscians has been broken, and a system of border fortresses has been established to secure what has been gained on that side. The Etruscans, assailed and crippled in every direction, can now hardly hold their own in the province which bears their name. For the moment the star of the Romans is in eclipse, but we shall soon find that invincible people recovering from their great reverse and asserting themselves as the dominant power in Italy. Looking toward the southern coasts of the peninsula, we find the Greek cities, with the exception of Tarentum, giving way one after another before the advance of the Lucanians, a branch of the Sabellian stock, and the aggressive policy of Dionysius, tyrant of Syracuse. And before this the Samnites have descended from their hills and usurped the place of the Etruscans in Campania.

Meanwhile a whole cycle of history had revolved in the lands washed by the eastern waters of the Mediterranean. After the final repulse of the Persians Athens rose rapidly to the highest pinnacle of power and glory, and laid the foundations of that intellectual empire which has survived the wreck of a hundred kingdoms. Then came the long agony of the Peloponnesian War, at the end of which the Athenians were left with a mere shadow of their national greatness, and their position as leaders of Greece passed to the narrow and bigoted Spartans. At the time when Rome was taken by the Gauls Sparta's supremacy was already on the decline, and the political ascendancy of Thebes was just beginning. Under the rule of Archelaus (413–399 B.C.) Macedon had begun to rise into importance, and eleven years after the date which we have reached, Philip, the future conqueror of Greece, was to be born. The huge, unwieldy mass of the Persian dominions had been rudely shaken by the assaults of Cyrus and Agesilaus, and was only waiting for the mightier arm which was to shatter it to pieces and mould it anew under Grecian influence. And all these conditions, the suicidal strife of the Greeks, the weakness of Persia, and the coming greatness of Macedon, were preparing for the day when Greece should bow her head under a Roman yoke, and the gates of the East should be thrown open to the legions of Sulla, Lucullus, and Pompeius.

CHAPTER V

THE LATIN, SAMNITE, AND ETRUSCAN WARS

A NEW century lies before us, filled, like the last, with the clash of arms and the harsh sounds of civil strife. Again and again the old war of parties breaks out within the walls, and once at least the Roman State seems on the verge of dissolution. And outside, in the lands north and south of the Tiber, Rome is engaged in a deadly struggle, which taxes her resources to the utmost. But by the beginning of the third century the long strife of parties is composed at last, and the city of Romulus, triumphant over Latins, Etruscans, Samnites, and Gauls, has extended her authority over the greater part of Italy. As the circle of dominion widens there is a corresponding expansion in the character and policy of the conquering people. The Romans have become conscious of their destiny, and in addressing the other races of Italy they begin to assume a tone of dignity and lordship. The growth of their political genius keeps pace with the advance of material power, so that every fresh need is answered by a new resource, and a vast and complicated machinery is created to keep pace with the manifold demands of a rising empire. That the Romans should have supported this enormous strain, pressing on them simultaneously from within and from without, and that every addition to their burden should have brought an access of strength, is a singular proof of their wonderful energy, hardihood, and elasticity.

REBUILDING OF THE CITY

We take up our story from the moment when, as the legend runs, Camillus had cancelled the compact with Brennus, or, to

88

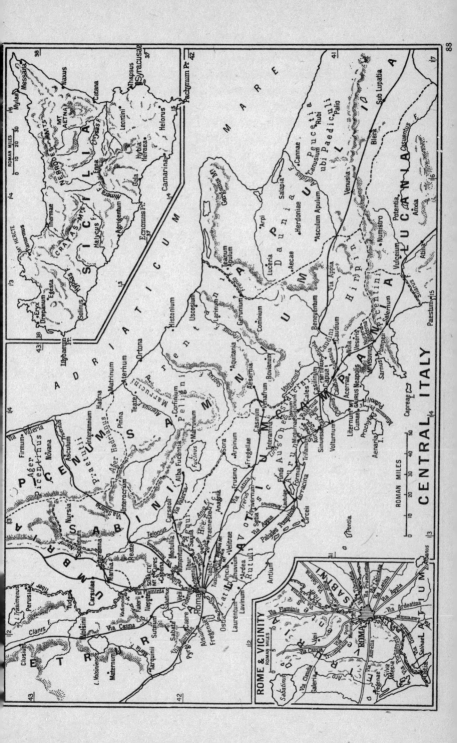

CENTRAL ITALY

ROME & VICINITY

speak the bald truth, when the Gauls had gone off with their load of gold, leaving the Romans at liberty to resume possession of their ruined city. It was a sad and dispirited host that came streaming back from various places of refuge, to bivouac among the blackened heaps which had once been the homes of Roman families and the temples of Roman gods. Never had the fortunes of the Republic sunk to so low an ebb, and for the great mass of the struggling plebeians, who had lost their all in the late invasion, the prospect seemed hopeless indeed. In this state of the public feeling the tribunes found ready hearers when they came forward with the proposal, already mooted five years before, that the more needy among the citizens should migrate to Veii, where there were houses and lands only waiting for occupation. If this fatal suggestion had been carried out the whole subsequent course of history might have been altered ; but happily it was overruled by the firmness of the patricians, with Camillus at their head. The veteran warrior discoursed with great eloquence on the ruinous consequences of such a step, which would have undone the work of four centuries. And a chance utterance, let fall shortly afterwards, when the Senate was sitting in debate, confirmed the effect which his words had produced. For while the Fathers were discussing this grave question a centurion who was passing the Senate House with a company of soldiers cried in a loud voice: " Standard-bearer, pitch your ensign on this spot, for here we had better remain." Then all agreed that the gods had declared their will by the voice of the centurion, and the work of rebuilding the city was taken up with spirit. Stones, timber, and tiles were furnished at the public expense, but each citizen had to give security that his house should be completed within the year. With such an incentive to speed, every man built wherever he could find a vacant space, without regard to the lines of the old streets, which had followed the direction of the underground canals ; and for centuries afterwards Rome retained visible evidence of the Gaulish conquest in its crooked and narrow streets and crowded, ill-ventilated dwellings.

REPUBLICAN ROME

There was, indeed, good reason why the Romans should lose no time in setting their house in order, for on all sides their enemies were arming against them, and half a century of fighting was required to secure their recent acquisitions in southern Etruria and confirm and extend their authority in Latium. Fortunately there was little union and no central directing policy to organize the efforts of these armed multitudes, so that the Romans, operating from a common centre and inspired by a common purpose, were able to overpower them one by one. We must now pass in review the military history of these fifty years, grouping the events according to the several nations who turned their arms against Rome.

WARS WITH THE GAULS

Five times, if we may trust our chief authority, the Gauls renewed their invasions, and five times they were defeated by the Romans, who were taught by familiarity to despise their once dreaded foes. The first of these attacks was happily delayed until Rome had put down some dangerous movements among the Latins, and was enjoying a respite from internal troubles, which had lamed her action for several years. A battle was fought in the neighbourhood of the Anio (367 B.C.), and the honours of the day fell to the old hero Camillus, who had been named dictator, though now approaching his eightieth year. The Gauls were routed, and the scattered remnant of their army wandered off into southern Italy. Six years later a second engagement took place, the Gauls being once more encamped at the bridge over the Anio, and it was on this occasion that Titus Manlius [1] gained immortal renown by overthrowing a gigantic Gaul in single combat and spoiling him of his gold collar, an exploit which won him the title of Torquatus. Twice during the next three years the war was renewed, and the Gauls were now in alliance with the revolted city of Tibur. To meet the crisis Sulpicius was appointed dictator, and he held his men back from fighting, thinking it more prudent to wear out the barbarians by delay. But he

[1] To be distinguished from Marcus Manlius, the saviour of the Capitol.

was compelled by the ardour of his soldiers to risk an engagement, and the Gauls were defeated with great slaughter. After an interval of ten years Lucius Furius Camillus, a son of the renowned warrior of that name, achieved a decisive victory over these persistent marauders (349 B.C.), who had encamped on the Alban Mount and were ravaging the fields of Latium. This battle was rendered memorable by a young Roman officer, Marcus Valerius, who, emulating the exploit of Manlius, accepted the challenge of a Gaulish braggart, and slew him. Valerius, so runs the story, was assisted in the duel by a crow, which perched on his helmet and harassed the Gaul by repeated assaults with its beak and claws.[1] From this incident he obtained the surname of Corvus.

During their long sojourn in Italy the Gauls had lost much of their rude vigour and had become addicted to drunken and slothful habits. Their huge, unwieldy frames, overloaded with superfluous flesh, were unequal to any prolonged exertion, and after one furious charge they were brought to a standstill, bathed in sweat and panting for breath, to be slaughtered like cattle by the agile and sinewy Romans. They were greatly inferior to the Romans also in warlike equipment, having no defensive armour except their wooden shields ; and their ponderous, ill-tempered swords, which they brandished unskilfully, like wood-cutters, as if they would cleave their opponents in two at a single stroke, after one or two heavy blows became bent and useless. The Romans, on the other hand, were thoroughly protected by corslets, helmets, and greaves, and they had been trained by Camillus to close with their gigantic enemies, advancing under the cover of their shields and avoiding the wild, sweeping blows of the Gaulish claymore. They relied chiefly on their short, two-edged swords ; and when once the Roman had got within his adversary's guard he used his keen weapon with deadly effect.

---

[1] Compare the incident in Virgil, *Aeneid*, xii. 865 *sqq.*, possibly suggested by the adventure of Valerius.

REPUBLICAN ROME

ETRUSCAN WARS

We have seen that after the fall of Veii the Romans had advanced their frontier beyond the Tiber as far as the verge of the Ciminian Forest, and had taken possession of Sutrium, which commanded the passes into northern Etruria. It was from this quarter that the first signal of danger came in the year following the battle of the Allia (389 B.C.). The Romans were still occupied with the task of rebuilding their homes when news was brought by traders that the Etruscans had seized Sutrium and were conspiring to recover all the territory which had been wrested from them by Camillus. After six years of warfare the Romans succeeded in making good their hold on southern Etruria, and Latin colonies were planted at Sutrium and Nepete. A blank of twenty years ensues in the broken and scanty annals of these wars, and we are then presented with some details which throw a curious light on the manners of the cruel and fanatical Etruscans. A Roman general, who bore the famous name of Fabius, suffered defeat from the people of Tarquinii, and three hundred Roman captives were sacrificed by the victors to their native gods. Two years later (356 B.C.) the Tarquinians, who were now joined by the Faliscans, inflicted a second defeat on a consular army, and the event of the battle was determined by the frightful appearance of their priests, who led the attack like furies, with writhing serpents in their hair and blazing torches brandished in their hands.[1] The Romans, we are assured, recovered from their panic and turned their defeat into a victory ; but this is hardly consistent with the narrative which follows. For the Etruscans were so elated by the issue of the battle that the whole nation rose in arms, and, led by the victorious Tarquinians, penetrated as far as the salt-works on the left bank of the Tiber. So grave was the outlook that Caius Marcius Rutilus was named dictator—the first plebeian ever appointed to that great office. By his vigorous

---

[1] Livy, vii. 67 ; cf. iv. 33. The 'serpents' were formed of parti-coloured ribbons (Florus, i. 6, 7).

PLATE XVIII. CERVETERI (CAERE)

PLATE XIX.   TEMPLE AT CORA   93

action the invaders were soon repelled, and, in spite of opposition from the Senate, he was awarded a triumph by a vote of the people. After another interval of two years a signal victory gained over the Tarquinians enabled the Romans to avenge the butchery of their soldiers who had been sacrificed at the Etruscan altars. Three hundred and fifty-eight prisoners were brought to Rome, and scourged and beheaded in the Forum. The Tarquinians, however, remained in arms, and a painful impression was produced at Rome by the news that the ancient city of Caere, where the Roman Vestals had found a refuge during the terror of the first Gaulish invasion, had gone over to the enemy. But the Caerites soon repented of their defection, and entered into a truce with Rome for a hundred years (353 B.C.) ; and a systematic ravage of the Tarquinian territory at length broke the resolution of these obstinate foes. Peace was concluded with Tarquinii for forty years, and at the same time the people of Caere were admitted into a limited form of Roman citizenship, which gave them the private rights of Roman citizens, but excluded them from the right of voting in the assemblies and from holding public offices.

MINOR WARS

The league with the Latins and Hernicans which had been renewed by Spurius Cassius remained unbroken for a whole century. In the course of three generations many occasions of discontent had doubtless been given to the Latins, who saw their old rivals steadily advancing in power and prosperity, while they themselves, who bore the greater part of the burden and suffered grievously from the constant raids of the Aequians and Volscians, were excluded from the best fruits of the alliance. It will be remembered that the proposal of Cassius to admit the Latins to a share in conquered territory raised a furious outcry against him at Rome, and was the immediate cause of his ruin. And doubtless many unrecorded instances of injustice occurred in the levying of troops, the appointment of officers, and the distribution of booty. One glaring example of Roman iniquity remains on record, which may serve as an illustration

of the general relations between Rome and her allies. There
had been a long-standing quarrel between the neighbouring
cities of Aricia and Ardea concerning the possession of a
piece of land, which had led to much fighting and loss of
life on both sides. At last they agreed to refer the matter to
the Roman people, and sent envoys to urge their respective
claims. While the case was under discussion a certain Scaptius,
an aged plebeian of worthless character, came forward with
pretended proofs that the land in question belonged to the
Romans. In vain the consuls tried to silence him, knowing
him to be a mere idle brawler; by appealing to the tribunes
he succeeded in getting a hearing, and his words produced such
an effect on the people that they decided the case in their
own favour and declared the land to be Roman territory.[1]
Such flagrant injustice produced a very bad impression, and
in the troubled years which followed the capture of Rome by
the Gauls this instance of fraud, together with a mass of
unrecorded grievances, was no doubt still rankling in the
minds of the Latins. Accordingly, for more than twenty
years after the return of the Romans to their city all
Latium was in a state of wild confusion and disorder. The
bonds of the old league were dissolved, and city after city
took sides with the enemies of Rome—Volscians, Aequians,
and Gauls. The hopes and the jealousies which had armed
all Latium against Rome after the fall of the kings were
rekindled with new strength. And once more they were
doomed to disappointment. The indomitable people turned
fiercely on their enemies, and a series of victories rapidly
restored the prestige of the Roman arms. The Aequians were
easily put down, and the Volscians suffered so crushing a
defeat that from this time forward they play but a little part
in Roman history. Long years of fighting and the constant
passage of barbarian hordes through their lands had brought
about a change of feeling among the Latins. The result was
a renewal of the alliance with the Latins and Hernicans,
which was effected in the third year after the third invasion of

[1] Livy, iii. 71-72.

the Gauls (358 B.C.).   Henceforth the Latins once more served
in the Roman armies; but they served as subjects, and no
longer as equal allies. Thus discontent still lingered on among
them, and one more sharp lesson was needed before the
Romans were assured of their supremacy from the Tiber to the
Liris.

THE SAMNITES

For the present, however, all was quiet in Latium, and
nearly half a century of warfare had brought a great accession
of territory to the Roman State. Rome was beginning to
attract attention in the outside world, and one consequence
of her growing importance was the arrival of an embassy from
the Samnites, who sought and obtained her friendship and
alliance. This was the first time Rome had come into contact with these hardy mountaineers, who were soon to be
arrayed against her in a long and deadly struggle for dominion
over Italy. The friendly relations thus created were cut short
eleven years later (343 B.C.), not long after the Romans had
extended their frontier toward the borders of Samnium by
the capture of Sora, on the Liris. Strangely enough, the cause
of offence was an appeal from the descendants of the Samnites
who, nearly three generations before, had seized Capua and
Cumae and expelled the Etruscans from their possessions in
Campania. Dwelling in the garden of Italy, and surrounded
by all the seductive influences of Greek and Etruscan civilization, the new conquerors had soon lost the rugged virtues
of their ancient mountain home and become soft and luxurious.
They formed a noble caste in the cities where they had settled,
living side by side with the original Oscan inhabitants. These
lowland Samnites soon learnt to look with dread and hatred
on their kinsmen of the hills, who coveted the fat things of
Campania, and sallied forth from their cold mountain valleys
to plunder the rich fields and vineyards of that favoured
land. It was one of these raids which led them to invoke the
help of Rome, and opened the long series of the Samnite wars.
On the eastern slope of the Mons Massicus, a district famous

for its generous wine, lay the Oscan town of Teanum Sidi-
cinum, commanding the route between Campania and Latium.
Being attacked by the Samnites, the people of Teanum appealed
to the Campanians [1] for help, and a force was sent by the
cities of the Campanian league to raise the siege. But the only
result of this interference was that the whole weight of the
war was directed on to the Campanians themselves. For the
Samnites, only too glad of a pretext for turning their arms
against this wealthy and effeminate people, drew off their
forces from Teanum and encamped on Mount Tifata, which
overhangs Capua, the chief city of Campania. Repulsed in
the field and confined within their walls, the Capuans turned
in their distress to the Romans, the natural champions of
lowlander against highlander.

In what follows we have a fine specimen of Roman hypocrisy.
The Campanian envoys addressed the Senate in terms of
fulsome adulation, extolling Roman valour to the skies, and
promising the most abject devotion in return for the aid and
countenance of Rome. " We ask not," they said, " that you
should fight our battles for us—that will not be necessary ;
we ask only to find shelter under the shadow of your mighty
name, and if that is vouchsafed us we shall henceforth regard
our lives, our fortunes, our very selves, as a gift of your
bounty."

The advantage of such an alliance was indeed obvious,
for the accession of Capua was an important step toward the
conquest of Campania, which would make the Romans undisputed masters of the whole lowland district from the Ciminian
Forest to the foot of Vesuvius. But the crafty Roman statesmen were not disposed to provoke the hostility of a formidable
people on the strength of mere vague professions, however
abjectly worded, and they answered that they were prevented
by their treaty with the Samnites from taking part openly with
Capua, but that they were willing to address a friendly remonstrance to their allies with regard to the recent act of aggression.

[1] The name includes the original Oscan inhabitants and their Samnite
conquerors.

LATIN AND SAMNITE WARS

Then the envoys played their last card, and declared themselves ready to surrender themselves, their city, their lands, and all that they possessed into the hands of the Romans, to be dealt with at their absolute discretion. Such an act closely resembled the mediaeval ceremony of homage, by which a man sought the protection of some great feudal lord. No sooner were the words uttered, with the accompaniment, as we are informed, of tears and prostrations, than the Romans laid aside all their scruples, forgot their obligation to the Samnites, and became convinced that it was their solemn duty to take up the cause of the distressed Campanians, who had fallen so low as to implore help upon their knees. An embassy was immediately dispatched to the Samnites, with a civil request that they would abstain from molesting those who had placed themselves under the protection of Rome. The Samnites replied by renewing their devastations in Campania, and war was then formally declared.

FIRST SAMNITE WAR

This was the First Samnite War, which lasted for two years (343–341 B.C.), and led to the establishment of Roman influence in Campania. The heroes of the campaign were Marcus Valerius Corvus, who had begun his career by his famous duel with the Gaul, and Publius Decius Mus, of whom we shall have more to tell presently, when we come to relate the history of the Latin War. Valerius gained a great victory at Mount Gaurus, between Cumae and Puteoli, and, following up the retreating Samnites, defeated them again at Suessula. Cornelius, the other consul, who had rashly allowed himself to be drawn into a dangerous position among the mountains of Samnium, was extricated from his peril by the prompt and bold action of Decius, and then, taking the enemy by surprise, he added a third victory to those gained by his colleague.

Several important results followed these brilliant successes of the Roman arms. The people of Falisci, in Etruria, concluded a treaty with the Senate, and the Latins, who were already preparing to revolt, thought better of their purpose, and were employed against the Peligni, a Sabellian people, and near kinsmen of the Samnites.[1] The fame of the Roman victories had reached even to Carthage, and an embassy arrived at Rome from that great commercial city, bringing a gold crown, weighing twenty-five pounds, and a congratulatora address.

At the request of the Campanians, Roman garrisons had

A SAMNITE WARRIOR

been stationed at Capua and Suessula, to check any hostile movement from the Samnites. Allusion has frequently been made to the voluptuous climate of Campania and the fatal spell which it exercised on one race of conquerors after another. Capua especially was notorious as a nest of debauchery and licence, and a life of indulgence in these luxurious quarters soon undermined the discipline of the Roman soldiers. "These Campanians," they whispered, "owe their pleasant home to an act of treachery;[2] it would be but just to retort on them their own crime, and thrust them from the seat which their fathers won by treason to their hosts." As the time drew near for their recall to Rome the mutinous voices grew louder and louder. Why should they leave a land of plenty to cowards incapable of defending it, and return to a life of toil and privation on the fever-haunted banks of the Tiber, or in the stifling alleys of the city, where debt grew upon them day by day like a wasting pestilence? These seditious murmurs spread from Capua to the country districts, and when Caius Marcius Rutilus arrived to take over the command in Campania he found the whole army of occupation ready to break into open mutiny. He sought to quell the

movement by granting leave of absence to the ringleaders
in the conspiracy, and sending secret instructions that they
should be detained at Rome. But his design soon leaked out,
and the disbanded soldiers, filled with alarm by the prospect
of summary punishment, gathered in great force at Lautulae,
in the neighbourhood of Tarracina, and there, throwing
off all disguise, openly raised the standard of revolt. They
found a leader in an invalided veteran, of patrician family,
named Titus Quintius, whom they dragged from his retirement at Tusculum and compelled under threats to assume the
command. Then they marched on Rome, and pitched their
camp within eight miles of the city. But the danger was
averted by timely concessions. Marcus Valerius Corvus, who
was appointed dictator to meet this great public danger, gave
a patient hearing to their grievances, and certain remedial
measures were carried with a view to improving the condition
of the Roman soldier. Henceforth it was declared unlawful
to erase the name of any soldier enrolled in the army without
his consent, or to appoint anyone who had served as military
tribune to the post of centurion. The object of this reform
was to prevent the privileged classes from keeping lucrative
appointments in the army at their disposal ; and the same
popular tendency is seen in the demand to reduce the pay of
the knights, which was three times that of the infantry. When
these points were settled the mutineers dispersed to their
homes.

But the state of disquiet resulting from so serious an outbreak, and the threatening attitude of the Latins, compelled
the Romans to make terms with the Samnites, and a peace was
patched up, from which the Latins and Campanians were
excluded. The result was a new combination among the
contending races. Rome and Samnium were once more in
alliance, while the Latins, who complained that they had been
betrayed by the selfishness of the Romans,[1] entered into a
league with the Auruncans, the Campanians, and the remnant
of the Volscians, and the war was carried on under Latin

[1] Dionysius, xv. 7.

auspices. Finding their frontier menaced by a powerful army, the Samnites called upon the Romans to interfere, but the answer they received made it only too evident how small was now the authority of Rome over her allies. The Senate, it was alleged, had no power to prevent the Latins from levying war on their own account. This was understood by the Latins as an acknowledgment of their independence, and they determined to push matters to a crisis. Two of their leaders, Lucius Annius of Setia and Lucius Numicius of Circeii, who had been summoned to Rome with eight others to give an account of their actions, were instructed to demand that the constitution should be remodelled on a new basis, one of the consulships and a due proportion of seats in the Senate being reserved for the Latins. This was equivalent to a declaration of war, as it was not to be supposed that the Romans would yield to such exorbitant demands; and the envoys, who had hardly escaped from personal violence, took their departure with words of defiance and menace (340 B.C.).

LATIN WAR

The Romans, recognizing the gravity of the crisis, had compelled the consuls to resign their office before the usual date, and replaced them by two men of tried valour and ability, Titus Manlius Torquatus, renowned for his slaughter of the Gaulish champion, and Publius Décius Mus, who had saved a consular army in the late Samnite war. The new consuls took the field together, with two powerful armies, and, marching through the territory of the Marsi and Peligni, pitched their camp in the neighbourhood of Capua, where the Latins and their allies were already assembled in full force. It was a cruel and unnatural war, in which two peoples, closely connected by blood, by language, and by common worship, and united in many cases by domestic ties, were to meet in deadly combat. To deepen the note of tragedy, says the record, the gods themselves intervened, and demanded the sacrifice of two noble lives, as if to appease their anger at the fratricidal struggle.

LATIN AND SAMNITE WARS

Strict orders had been issued that no Roman soldier should leave his station or engage in single combat with one of the enemy ; for it was desirable to prevent all intercourse, of whatever kind, with the Latins until the decisive moment arrived. But the young Titus Manlius, son of the consul, who had been sent out to reconnoitre with a troop of cavalry, accepted a challenge from a knight of Tusculum, and, having slain his opponent, brought back the blood-stained spoils and laid them at his father's feet. "Thou hast defied my commands," said the stern Roman, "and given an example of disobedience—thou, the son of a consul. Learn that the first duty of a Roman is to obey. Approach, lictor, and bind him to the stake." Then, as many times before in Roman history, a scene of horror was witnessed, and the spirit of discipline prevailed over the dearest bonds of nature. But when that young head rolled in the dust a cry of grief and execration fell upon the consul's ears, and from that day until his death he was shunned and detested by all those of the younger generation.

THE ROMAN LEGION

This incident occurred while the army lay encamped before Capua. But the battle which was to decide the issue was fought at Veseris, on the western slopes of the Apennines, opposite Vesuvius, though no reason is given for the sudden change of scene. The Latin and Roman armies were equipped and drawn up in precisely the same manner, and many of those who fought on the opposite sides were old comrades in arms. It is on this occasion that we first hear of the great change which had been brought about in Roman tactics since the days of Servius Tullius. Under the old system the Roman army was marshalled in a solid body, like the Greek phalanx, and depended mainly on the effect produced by the shock of the first charge. The wealthiest citizens, clothed in complete armour, formed the first rank, while the four inferior classes, with a gradually diminishing order of equipment, advanced in close array behind them, adding weight and momentum to the general mass. But centuries of warfare had taught the Romans to break up and reorganize this cumbrous machine, and before the middle of the fourth century an entirely new system was introduced, which is described by Livy in connexion with the Latin War.[1] This is the first detailed account of the renowned Roman legion, the greatest engine of conquest known in history. In its earliest form the legion was marshalled in three divisions, and each of these divisions contained fifteen companies, called maniples, of sixty men, with two centurions and a standard-bearer to each company. The first division, called the *hastati*, or spearmen, was composed of youths who had just attained the military age, and who served as light skirmishers. Then followed the fifteen maniples of the *principes*, men who had reached their full strength, completely armed and equipped. The third division also consisted of fifteen maniples, but each maniple was broken up into three groups of sixty men each, and these forty-five groups were drawn up in three sections. In the first section stood the *triarii*, veterans tried by long years of service ; after them came the *rorarii*, so called from the light missiles with which they sprinkled the enemy ; and last of all were the *accensi*, or supernumeraries, in whom little confidence was reposed.

The ordinary course of an engagement is clearly described by Livy. The action began with the advance of the *hastati*, and if their attack was repulsed they fell back and took up their station behind the *principes*. These in their turn advanced, supported by the *hastati* ; and meanwhile the veteran *triarii* remained at their posts, kneeling on the ground with their left foot advanced, their shields resting on their shoulders, and their spears planted in the ground. If the second attack also failed, the *hastati* and *principes* fell back behind the *triarii*, and these, closing their ranks, now led the van, backed by the whole weight of the other divisions and presenting a new and formidable front to the enemy. It will easily be seen how greatly superior was the light and flexible legion to the ponderous masses of the old citizen army. It was a living

[1] viii. 8.

organism, consisting of many parts, but animated by one spirit, and responding readily to the hand of a skilful leader, whether separate or united action was required.[1]

BATTLE OF VESERIS

The battle of Veseris, so memorable on other accounts, acquires a special and personal interest from the devotion of the consul Decius. While the army lay in camp before Capua each of the consuls had the same dream, in which a being of more than human stature and majesty appeared to him, promising victory to the army whose general offered himself as a sacrifice for his people. So when the fight was at its hottest, Decius, who was commanding on the left wing, seeing that his men were hard pressed by the enemy, summoned Marcus Valerius, the high-priest, and bade him dictate the solemn words of that awful rite. Then the priest directed him to veil his head, to set his feet on a javelin which was laid on the ground, and, raising his hand, covered by the toga, to his chin, to dedicate himself in these terms : " Janus, and Jupiter, and Mars our sire, ye guardian spirits of Rome, and ye, the spirits of the mighty dead, thou too, Bellona, and thou, Quirinus, and all ye gods, both young and old, I beseech you to give victory to the Roman arms, and strike our foes with terror, dread, and death. Herewith I devote to the infernal powers myself, the Latins, and all who are on their side, for the Republic, the army, the legions, and the allies of the Roman people." Then, robed as for sacrifice, he took his sword in hand, and, leaping on his horse, rode headlong into the thickest of the fight. The Latins drew back in terror, for he seemed to them as the red star which brings fever and pestilence in the sickly autumn season.[2] But at last he fell, pierced by a hundred wounds, and the gods accepted his sacrifice, giving new strength to the Romans, and spreading panic and dismay among the ranks of the Latins.

After their defeat at Veseris the Latins still remained in arms for two years, but their strength was broken, and at last

---

[1] Livy, ix. 19.   [2] Livy, viii. 9, from Homer, *Iliad*, xxii. 26.

they were obliged to sue for peace. The Romans were now undisputed masters of Latium, and there could be no question of equality between conquerors and conquered. The old Latin League was therefore finally dissolved (338 B.C.), and the relation which each city was to bear toward Rome was determined by a decree of the Senate, specially drawn up to meet the particular case. Some, like Tusculum, received the full Roman citizenship, but the majority were granted only the private rights of Roman citizens which had been bestowed on Caere. Above all it was the policy of Rome to isolate the several communities of Latium, by prohibiting intercourse for purposes of business and forbidding intermarriage. This led to a rapid decline of the Latin townships—Latium withered, while Rome grew and flourished. One or two towns whose conduct had been marked by implacable hostility were treated with exemplary severity. Thus the walls of Velitrae, a border town of the Volscians, were demolished and the nobles sent into banishment beyond the Tiber; and Antium, an old nest of pirates,[1] now became a citizen colony, after having been deprived of all its war-galleys, the beaks of which were set up on the speaker's platform in the Roman Forum.[2] Tibur and Praeneste, on the other hand, retained their independence, though they lost part of their territory and were obliged to furnish troops and follow the Romans in war. The conquered districts of Campania received the same rights as the less favoured among the Latin communities.

Roman Magnanimity

There is an interesting passage in Dionysius,[3] contrasting the conduct of the Greeks and Romans in their dealings with their conquered kinsmen. The Romans, he says, were a large-minded people; they never allowed themselves to be carried away by feelings of mere personal resentment, which so often led the Athenians and Spartans to inflict the most frightful cruelties upon their revolted subjects. The observation is just, and shows us one main source of Roman greatness,

[1] Strabo, v. c. 232.   [2] *Rostra*, 'beaks.'   [3] xiv. 6.

the noble qualities of patience and self-command. There was cruelty, indeed, deeply ingrained in the Roman character, but it was a cold and passionless cruelty, which was never allowed to interfere with great public aims.

Second Samnite War

The Samnites, it must be remembered, had been in alliance with Rome during the Latin War, and the presence of their army is just mentioned by Livy in his account of the battle of Veseris. But during the years which followed events tended more and more to draw the Romans and Samnites apart. For some time their attention was taken up by the affairs of southern Italy, where the Greek cities, with Tarentum at their head, had formed a league to repel the incursions of the Sabellian peoples. The Greeks found a champion in Alexander of Epirus, uncle of the great conqueror of that name, who defeated the Lucanians and Samnites in a battle fought near Paestum. Thereupon the Romans concluded a treaty with Alexander (332 B.C.), thus virtually renouncing their alliance with the Samnites. But Alexander's death, which occurred about a year later, left the Samnites free to concentrate their attention on the affairs of central Italy, where the steady advance of the Romans was enough to cause them serious disquiet. Fregellae, on the Liris, and Cales, on the border of Campania, were now Latin colonies, threatening their frontier, and the submission of the Aurunci had consolidated the recently conquered districts into one unbroken system. It wanted but a small occasion to bring on the inevitable struggle, which lasted, with a brief interval, for over thirty years (327–304 B.C., 298–290 B.C.), and finally decided whether Romans or Samnites were to be masters of Italy.

The First Proconsul

It was from a Greek city, Palaeopolis,[1] which stood side by side with the later foundation of Neapolis,[1] that the cause of offence came. After the Roman conquests in Campania

[1] ' Old Town ' and ' New Town.'

numerous settlers from Rome had established themselves
on the rich lands watered by the Volturnus and the Savo.
These colonists complained that their lands had been plundered
by the Greeks of Palaeopolis, and after a vain attempt to obtain
satisfaction war was declared on the offending city. Palaeopolis
capitulated (326 B.C.), after a siege of more than a year's duration, and obtained favourable terms, being henceforth united
with Neapolis as one city in alliance with Rome. The long
resistance offered by the garrison led to a most important
innovation, full of the gravest dangers to Roman liberty,
which were little suspected at the time. For the consul
Quintus Publilius Philo, whose term of office expired while he
was conducting the siege, was continued in his command by
a vote of the tribes, with the title of Proconsul. Such was the
beginning of that mighty proconsular power, which grew in
proportion as the circle of Roman conquests expanded, until
it overshadowed the constitution and left a corrupt Senate
and a degenerate people at the mercy of their own victorious
generals.

From the moment when the siege of Palaeopolis was undertaken it became evident that the Samnites were preparing
for war. The garrison was found to consist chiefly of Samnite
and Campanian troops, and it was proved that emissaries
from Samnium were tampering with the fidelity of Rome's
Latin allies. The Romans were deeply impressed with the
gravity of the crisis, and they discharged the customary
forms which preceded a declaration of war with more than
usual solemnity. Envoys were dispatched to protest against
the recent unfriendly acts of the Samnites, who were still
nominally their allies, and they brought back an answer
which dispelled the last hope of a peaceful solution. Far from
admitting themselves to be in the wrong, the Samnites retorted
by complaining of the occupation of Fregellae as a violation
of their territory. And when the envoys hinted at arbitration
their reply was an appeal to the God of Battles. " Let us
have no more words," they said ; " this quarrel can only be
decided by the sword, and in the fields of Campania we will

fight out the issue." Then all negotiations were broken off, and the Romans implored the favour of heaven by holding a solemn supplication, in which the images of the gods were brought forth from their shrines and laid on couches before tables furnished with a costly banquet, while the people, dressed in holiday attire, took part as silent worshippers in the mimic feast.

At the outbreak of the war the Romans were joined by the Lucanians and Apulians, but the former people were soon detached from their alliance by the intrigues of the Tarentines, who were alarmed by the fall of Palaeopolis, taking it as an omen of the fate which might be in store for themselves. In the same year a rising occurred among the Vestini, which, had it been allowed to proceed, might have led to an overpowering combination of the whole Sabellian stock against Rome. But a single campaign sufficed to put down the movement, and this danger was averted.

The narrative of these wars is full of confusions and contradictions, being greatly vitiated by the boasting fictions of the family records, from which it was largely derived.[1] The same actions are sometimes ascribed to two or three different persons, and Livy himself, who certainly does not err on the side of critical severity, confesses that he is often baffled by conflicting statements. There is every reason, therefore, to study conciseness.

The third year of the war (325 B.C.) was rendered memorable by the famous quarrel between Lucius Papirius Cursor, who was conducting the campaign in Samnium with the rank of dictator, and Quintus Fabius Maximus Rullianus, his Master of the Horse. Fabius, who had received strict orders not to engage the enemy during a temporary absence of the dictator, yielded to a moment of temptation and gained a victory over the Samnites. This breach of discipline was bitterly resented by Papirius, and he resolved to vindicate his authority by the summary execution of his subordinate. But Fabius, who had the army on his side, escaped to Rome, and the dispute was

---

[1] Livy, viii. 40.

continued in the presence of the Senate and people. Hardly could all the prayers of senators, tribunes, and Fabius's aged father prevail to turn the dictator from his purpose. But at last he gave way, and consented to spare the life of his young officer, insisting, however, that he must resign his post, confess himself in the wrong, and accept his pardon as an act of pure grace on the part of his commander. Thus, without impeachment to the majesty of a great office, a gallant life was saved for the service of the Republic.

The Caudine Forks

We read of valorous actions and prodigious slaughter wrought by the Romans, but little result seems to have been attained after six years of warfare. But in the seventh year (321 B.C.) occurred the famous incident of the Caudine Forks. The Roman consuls were encamped in full force near Calatia, on the Campanian border, and Caius Pontius, who was in command of the Samnite army, watched their movements from behind the cover of the neighbouring hills. Presently some captive Samnites were brought into the Roman camp, and, being questioned, they informed the consuls that Pontius, with his whole army, was laying siege to Luceria, a town of great strategic importance in northern Apulia. The prisoners were agents of the Samnite general, who had been directed to prowl round the Roman outposts, disguised as shepherds, and driving their flocks before them. Suspecting no guile, the consuls determined at once to break up their camp and march to the relief of Luceria. The shortest route to that city lay through a long and narrow gorge, enclosed by steep wooded sides, and opening out into a level valley of considerable extent, on the other side of which the mountains drew together again, leaving a passage still narrower and more difficult than the first. Into this deadly trap the Roman legions passed, like beasts driven into a pit for slaughter,[1] to the number of forty thousand men ; and the generals, as if blinded by fate, neglected every precaution, advancing without guides, and sending out no scouts

[1] Livy, ix. 5 ; perhaps a genuine piece of camp wit.

to guard against surprise. When they reached the mouth of the second pass they found the way blocked by a barrier of timber and stones, and, retracing their steps, they encountered a similar obstacle barring their retreat. And now the steep hill-sides enclosing the central plain resounded to the tramp of an armed multitude, and helmets and shields were seen flashing among the trees. There was doubtless a severe struggle, though Livy makes no mention of it, leaving us to infer that this mighty force surrendered without a single blow. But the position of the Romans was hopeless from the first. Nor was the situation without difficulty for the young Samnite leader, and, distrusting his own judgment, he sent to ask the advice of his father, the aged Pontius Herennius. To his question, " What shall I do with these captured thousands ? " the old man answered : " Let them all go in honour " ; and when the young general, doubting whether he was in earnest, sent the messengers to inquire again, the reply came back : " Put them all to the sword." There was real wisdom in the counsel, whichever way it was taken ; but Pontius, by choosing a middle course, threw away all the fruits of his victory. After repeated parleys it was agreed that the consuls and chief officers of the Roman army should swear to a treaty binding the Romans to withdraw from Samnium, give up Fregellae and Cales, and conclude peace on equal terms with the Samnites. Six hundred Roman knights were handed over as hostages to Pontius, and then the Roman legions, stripped and unarmed, with the consuls at their head, were passed under the yoke. Pontius had indeed let slip a golden opportunity, which gave him the choice of inflicting a deadly blow on the Romans by destroying the flower of their fighting men, or of earning a title to their lasting gratitude. As it was he gained an empty triumph, and inflicted a stain on the honour of a proud people which was not likely to be forgotten or forgiven.

When the terms of the surrender were announced at Rome there was little hesitation as to the course to be pursued. The treaty was at once repudiated by the senators, who

denied the right of their generals to accept such conditions
without sanction from the central authority. To save appear-
ances the consuls and chief officers who had signed the compact
were sent back to Pontius, to be dealt with as he pleased. But
the gallant Samnite rejected this poor evasion with contempt,
inveighing bitterly against the perfidy of the Romans. Let
them, he said, send back the forty thousand to Caudium, and
then, and not till then, he would be ready to open negotiations.
As to the consuls and their subordinates, they might go home
again and carry their burden of treason with them. There
was a strain of fantastic chivalry about the character of this
noble Samnite which must have raised a smile among the
grave statesmen who guided the counsels of Rome.

Course of the War

From the moment when the Roman and Samnite forces
first met on the battlefield there was little room for doubt
as to the ultimate issue of the contest. Though at least equal
to the Romans in personal valour and prowess, the Samnites
were far inferior in military discipline and skill, while in steadfastness, endurance, and reach of political vision the distance
between the two nations was even greater. For the next ten
years the Romans pursued their policy of shutting up these
fierce highlanders in their mountain fastnesses, by forming
alliances with the neighbouring peoples and planting military
colonies at every post of importance. And wherever they came
they came to stay. They might be expelled from their fortresses—and they were expelled, in some instances, again and
again—but they returned to the attack with dogged persistence,
and drew the net closer and closer until the system of isolation
was completed. For some years after the disaster of Caudium
progress was slow. The Samnites took Fregellae, on the
Liris (320 B.C.), and this success was followed by some dangerous
movements in Latium. But the Romans retorted by making
a bold dash into Apulia, and the capture of Luceria set free
the six hundred knights who had been given as hostages
for the fulfilment of the shameful Caudine treaty. In the

next year the upper road into Apulia was secured by the submission of the Frentani, on the Adriatic coast, and three years
later the fall of Saticula (316 B.C.) gave the Romans the
command of the western passes leading into Samnium. There
was, indeed, one moment of great peril. Much discontent
had been caused in Campania by Roman interference in the
local government of some of the cities, and the Samnites took
advantage of this feeling to throw garrisons into Nuceria and
Nola. Simultaneously the inhabitants of Sora, on the upper
Liris, between Samnium and the Hernican territory, massacred
the Roman garrison and declared for the Samnites. The
redoubted Fabius Maximus, who had been named dictator,
suffered a defeat at Lautulae in trying to check the Samnite
advance on Latium, and this was followed by the revolt of
all Campania and a general rising among the Aurunci. To
aggravate their difficulties the Romans were alarmed by
rumours of treason among their own citizens. But the storm
passed as rapidly as it had gathered. A decisive victory
restored the Roman ascendancy in Campania, while the
Aurunci were betrayed by a party among their own nobles,
and their defection was punished with such merciless severity
that the old Ausonian race was well-nigh extirpated.[1] These
successes gave a welcome respite to the Romans, and they
employed the interval in founding new colonies and strengthening the old. Within nine years after the defeat at Caudium
the system of Roman fortresses was extended along the valley
of the Liris from Sora to Suessa Aurunca, they obtained a
firm hold on the Campanian frontier toward Samnium, Luceria
was secured by a Roman colony, and the more recent acquisition
of Nola took their influence to the lowland region north of
Vesuvius. A new departure was made by the establishment
of a colony on the island of Pontia, which shows that the
Romans were beginning to awaken to the importance of protecting their commerce against pirates and providing a new
means for the transport of troops.

[1] Livy, ix. 25.

REPUBLICAN ROME

THE APPIAN WAY

Yet another momentous step was the commencement of the great Appian Road (312 B.C.), which left Rome at the Porta Capena and, passing through the pleasant valley of Egeria, made one straight leap to the Alban Lake and the ancient temple and grove of Diana at Aricia ; then, crossing the deadly Pomptine marshes, it touched the sea at Tarracina, and so ran on through the rich vineyards of the Auruncan and Campanian districts until it came to Capua, where for the present its course was ended. This was the first of those great military roads to which Rome owed the extension and the maintenance of her empire, not less than to the valour of her soldiers and the genius of her generals.

RISINGS IN ETRURIA

But while the Romans were still engaged in these important works alarming news reached them from Etruria. The forty years' truce concluded after the war with Tarquinii had now expired, and, thinking that the Romans were fully occupied elsewhere, the Etruscans raised a great force and laid siege to Sutrium. After one unsuccessful attempt had been made by a Roman consul to relieve the town, Quintus Fabius Rullianus—the same who had suffered defeat at Lautulae, and who still earlier had narrowly escaped death at the hands of Papirius—assumed the command, and by a brilliant campaign (311–310 B.C.) convinced the Etruscans that Rome was fully capable of sustaining two wars at once. Finding that his operations at Sutrium were delayed, he resolved to effect a diversion by penetrating the wilds of the Ciminian Forest and shifting the seat of war to northern Etruria. Accordingly he broke up his camp and, crossing the forest, descended into the rich country on the other side, from which he returned laden with booty. He then turned on his tracks and, facing the Etruscans, who had been dogging his footsteps, inflicted on them a severe defeat. But next year the Etruscans rallied again, and Fabius, who had been continued in his

PLATE XX. 'L'ARINGATORE'   112

PLATE XXI. THE VIA APPIA

command as proconsul, cut to pieces their finest troops, after an obstinately contested battle, which was fought on the shores of Lake Vadimo, not far from the junction of the Tiber and the Nar. Yet another rising, in which the Umbrians took part, occurred in the following year, but it was successfully put down, and after that all was quiet in Etruria for a time.

CAMPAIGN IN SAMNIUM RENEWED

Meanwhile affairs were once more assuming a serious aspect in Samnium. The consul Marcius, who had been recalled from his command in Etruria, met with a defeat, and from all their wild mountain fastnesses the Samnites were rushing to arms. It was thought expedient to appoint a dictator, and the choice fell on the aged Papirius Cursor (309 B.C.). Some interesting details are mentioned by Livy in his description of this campaign, giving a touch of romance to the story of these warlike mountaineers, who were doomed by a strange fate to waste all their splendid energies in a hopeless cause. The Samnites had raised two armies, composed of the best of their fighting men, and distinguished by the colour of their uniforms and the decoration of their shields. The right division wore tunics of white linen, and their shields were embossed with cunning work of silver, while those on the left were arrayed in tunics embroidered in gay colours and bore shields ornamented with gold. Both alike were equipped with coats of mail, and tall plumes nodded on their helmets. But all their valour and all their gay devices could not save them from utter defeat, and their golden and silver shields went to grace the triumph of the dictator.

THE SAMNITES SUBDUED

Still the indomitable people struggled on for five years longer, and kept up a resistance which taxed the energies of the Romans to the utmost. They broke repeatedly into Campania, where the Roman position had recently been strengthened by the capture of Nuceria Alfaterna. They

tried, with some success, to raise a coalition against Rome
among her old enemies, the Aequians, and her old allies, the
Hernicans, and they received some help from the Marsians
and Pelignians, who recognized, when it was too late, the
common danger of the whole Sabellian race. But all their
efforts proved unavailing. The rising among the Hernicans
was easily put down, the Marsians and Pelignians soon
retired from the field, and the Samnites, after the loss of
Bovianum and the systematic ravaging of their territory,
were at length compelled to lay down their arms. The ancient
treaty [1] with Rome was renewed, and the other Sabellian
tribes who had recently borne arms on the side of the Samnites
were included in the alliance.

COLONIES AND MILITARY ROADS

During the six years (304–298 B.C.) which intervened
between the Second and Third Samnite Wars the Romans
steadily pursued their purpose, extending their influence
by arms or by policy, and blocking all the approaches to
Samnium, where the sullen enemy lay crouching like a wounded
lion in his lair, beaten but still unsubdued. The Hernicans
were brought into the circle of their dominion, receiving
the private rights of Roman citizenship. The Aequians, who
had given a pretext by joining the Samnites toward the close
of the late war, saw their territories overrun by a Roman
army and their old mountain strongholds levelled to the
ground. After a fierce resistance, which resulted in the
destruction of their whole military force, they submitted, and
were afterwards united to Rome under the same conditions
as the Hernicans. To confirm their hold on this new conquest
the Romans planted colonies at Carseoli and Alba Fucentia,
and after a brief war with the Marsians this warlike little
people, with the neighbouring Sabellian tribes, entered into a
new alliance with Rome, which made them virtually her
subjects, with the obligation of serving in her armies. A

[1] Livy, ix. 45.

further advance was made by the reduction of Narnia (299 B.C.),
on the southern frontier of Umbria, which received a Latin
colony; and during these years two new military roads were
begun, afterwards called the Flaminian and Valerian Roads,
the former connecting Rome with Narnia, and the latter
running in a south-easterly direction to Alba in the Aequian
land. The capture of Narnia was the result of hostilities
with the Umbrians and Etruscans, and this brings us to the
brink of the final struggle with Samnium.

THIRD SAMNITE WAR

The immediate cause of the Third Samnite War (298–290 B.C.)
was an appeal which came to Rome from the Lucanians,
whose territory the Samnites had invaded. The Lucanians
had proved faithless allies in the previous war, but their
excuses were readily accepted and they were taken under
Roman protection, and on the refusal of the Samnites to
withdraw from Lucania war was immediately declared. For
the first two years operations were chiefly carried on in Samnium
itself. City after city was stormed and sacked by the Roman
armies, and the whole country was laid waste far and wide.
Driven to desperation, the Samnites, by the advice of Caius
Egnatius, their leader, made a bold resolve. The Romans
were already involved in a fresh war with Etruria, the Umbrians
had been drawn into the circle of hostilities, and these northern
enemies of Rome would hail with delight the advent of such
potent allies as the Samnites. Moreover, the ever-restless
Gauls were stirring again, and seeking new lands for the
overflow of their population. What if the Samnites should
break through the net which was being drawn closer and closer
around them, and, making common cause with Etruscans,
Umbrians, and Gauls, strike with overwhelming force against
the common oppressor of Italy? The plan was at once put
into operation, and the Samnites, leaving their wasted fields
and ruined cities behind them, marched under Egnatius into
Etruria. At first all seemed to promise well. Volunteers
flocked from Etruria and Umbria into the camp of Egnatius,

and the Gauls, lured by the hope of plunder, joined the coalition in great numbers.

But the Romans were equal to the emergency. After a brief moment of panic vigorous measures were taken to meet the new danger. Two consular armies, with a full contingent of allies, numbering in all some fifty thousand men, were dispatched to the seat of war under the command of Fabius Rullianus, who had grown old in the wars with Samnium, and Publius Decius Mus, the son of that Decius who had devoted himself in the Latin War. Two legions were appointed to invade Samnium, another force was stationed at Falerii, in southern Etruria, and a fourth army lay encamped in the Vatican Field, across the Tiber, to serve for home defence.

BATTLE OF SENTINUM

The decisive battle was fought at Sentinum (295 B.C.), in the heart of Umbria. Happily for the Romans, they had only to deal with the Gaulish and Samnite forces, for the Etruscans had marched away into their own territory, which was menaced by a forward movement of the two armies stationed at Falerii and in the Vatican district, and the Umbrians, for some unexplained reason, had also deserted their allies. But even as it was the engagement was most obstinately contested, and the issue long remained doubtful. Fabius commanded on the right wing, facing the Samnites, and the left, under Decius, encountered the Gauls. The veteran commander, setting an example which was afterwards imitated by his more famous descendant, kept his men in check and allowed the Samnites to wear themselves out by one furious assault after another, knowing that the superior discipline and the stubborn endurance of the Romans must prevail in the end. Yet the day was almost lost by the rashness of his younger colleague, who began by an impetuous charge with horse and foot, as if he would gain the victory by a single blow. His cavalry was driven back, and their hasty retreat disordered the ranks of the infantry, who began to give ground. All the terrors of the Allia seemed to be revived, and a new horror

116

was added by the scythed chariots of the Gauls, which drove the Roman horse in panic before them and began to trample down the front ranks of the foot. In this extremity Decius bethought him of his father's heroic end, and resolved to redeem his error by the sacrifice of his own life. After performing the same rites and uttering the same solemn words of dedication, he rode into the densest ranks of the enemy, and perished. His act of devotion restored the fainting courage of his soldiers, who were, moreover, now supported by reinforcements brought up from the reserve. But the Gauls, standing in close order, fought on with desperate valour, until Fabius, who had meanwhile driven back the Samnites to their camp, sent the Campanian cavalry, five hundred strong, to attack them in the rear. Then at last victory declared for the Romans. The Gauls were routed with great slaughter, and the remnant of the Samnites fled along the mountain paths to their own country.

End of the Samnite Wars

The bloody day of Sentinum completed the isolation of the Samnites and destroyed their last hope of maintaining a successful rivalry with Rome. With fanatical persistence they kept up the struggle for five years longer, fought pitched battles, and more than once obtained victories over the Roman armies. But all their gallantry availed them nothing against the iron discipline and the deep policy of Rome. Worn out by the murderous struggle, they were at length forced to sue for peace and enrol themselves among the Roman allies. The last stage in these weary wars is marked by the Roman occupation of Venusia, on the borders of Samnium, Lucania, and Apulia, which received no fewer than twenty thousand colonists, with Latin rights. Henceforward the Samnites remained locked up in their mountain valleys as in a dungeon, to which the Romans kept all the keys. Yet unquenchable rancour still smouldered in these savage hearts, and blazed up again and again, until their power for mischief was finally stamped out by the fearful massacre of Sulla.

CHAPTER VI

SETTLEMENT OF THE CONSTITUTION

AFTER the legislative reforms which followed the fall of the decemvirs a long pause ensues in the struggle for political equality, and no important measure tending to that result was carried for nearly eighty years (445–367 B.C.). This was due partly to the pressure of constant wars and partly to the clever management of the patricians, who by juggling with the constitution contrived for a long time to defeat the efforts of their opponents. But from the passing of the Canuleian Law (445 B.C.) sanctioning marriages between patricians and plebeians, the ultimate fusion of the orders became inevitable, and the way was slowly prepared for the final assault on the chief stronghold of aristocratic privilege, the consulship.

Marcus Manlius

The demand for political reform had arisen, a hundred years before, out of social distress, and in the later stage of the contest which we have now to describe the wants of impoverished citizens gave a powerful lever to the wealthy and ambitious plebeians who led the movement. For the first ten years after the retirement of the Gauls the social question held the foremost place, and claimed another victim in the person of Marcus Manlius, the saviour of the Capitol. Manlius, so far as we can gather from the partial statements of Livy, was a benevolent but weak-minded man, whose head had been turned by the fame of his great exploit. He was touched by the sufferings of the poor, who after losing their all in the terrible time of the Gaulish invasion had been com-

118

THE CONSTITUTION

pelled to contract heavy debts in rebuilding their houses and stocking their farms. Many of these unfortunates were enabled by his bounty to discharge their obligations, and he openly declared that so long as he had the means of raising money no Roman should be dragged into a debtors' dungeon. By these words and acts he aroused the jealousy of the patricians, and he was arrested and thrown into prison. But the indignant outcry which followed among the people compelled his enemies to set him at liberty. Then the infatuated man threw all prudence to the winds, and by his violent and seditious behaviour gave some colour to the charge that he was aiming at monarchy. He was brought to trial and condemned to die the death of a traitor, and among all those whom he had relieved not a voice was raised in protest when he was flung from the brow of the very hill from which he derived his name.[1]

Rome's Reform Bill

Very different was the fate of those able and crafty men who, seven years later (377 B.C.), were the authors of what may not inappropriately be called the Great Reform Bill of Rome. For generations back distinguished plebeians had held a place in the Senate, where they sat as silent members, voting in the divisions but taking no active part in the debates. Many of them had amassed great wealth, were married to patrician wives, and in political capacity and experience were equal to the best of the patricians. The time had now come when they were to stretch their hands out for the prize to which they were so fully entitled. The leaders of the reform movement were Caius Licinius Stolo and Lucius Sextius, the former of whom had married into a patrician house. If we are to believe the narrative of Livy, it was his wife's ambition which induced Licinius to bring in the famous measure which bears his name.[2] Livy's account of the transaction does little credit to his historical insight, but we may well believe that the haughty dames who were wedded to plebeians chafed under the

[1] Marcus Manlius Capitolinus.   [2] Licinian Rogations.

119

restrictions which debarred their husbands from a great political career.

Licinius and Sextius, while holding the office of tribunes, artfully worked on the minds of the needy plebeians, and used their necessities as a ladder to attain the height to which they were themselves aspiring, the ivory chair of the consul, which they pompously described in their public utterances as " the summit and citadel of liberty." Having thus prepared the way, they brought in their bill, which contained three clauses, one political, the other two economical. The first clause provided that the consular tribunate should be abolished and the consulship restored, and that one of the consuls must in future be a plebeian. The second clause aimed at the relief of debtors, by deducting from the sum of the debt interest already paid and allowing three years for the payment of what remained, which was to be made in equal yearly instalments. The third clause struck at the root of the economic grievance, forbidding anyone to occupy more than five hundred plough-gates [1] of the public land. A fourth and fifth clause are mentioned by some authorities, limiting the number of cattle which might be fed by any single owner on the public land to five hundred sheep and a hundred oxen, and compelling landlords to employ free labourers up to a certain proportion on their estates.

The bill, which seemed to undermine the three main pillars of privilege—wealth, landed property, and office—excited determined opposition, and by gaining over eight of the tribunes the patricians succeeded in getting it rejected. But they soon found that the tribunician veto was a two-edged weapon, which might equally well be employed against themselves. During five years Licinius and Sextius were re-elected to the tribunate, and by a persistent use of the dreaded formula [2] they prevented any elections from being held except those for the appointment of tribunes. It was a sort of secular papacy, similar in its political effects to the religious interdict of the

---

[1] *Jugera.* The *jugerum* was about three-fifths of an acre.
[2] *Veto*—' I forbid.'

mediaeval popes.   The mass of the plebeians began to weaken :
they were indifferent to the political side of the controversy,
and would have been well contented with the measures for
economic relief.   But Licinius and Sextius held their ground.
They on their side cared little, as events afterwards proved,
for the sufferings of the populace, which they were merely
using as a means to attain their own end.   The bill, they
declared, must be carried as a whole, or they would prevent
any part of it from being carried.   In vain some of the patricians, with Appius Claudius at their head, affecting sympathy
with the people, denounced the obstinacy of the tribunes, whom
they described as Tarquins and tyrants.   In vain they revived
the old religious scruples, alleging that a plebeian consul
could not approach the gods, or consult them by the auspices.
Licinius met this objection by adding a fresh clause to the
measure, providing that five of the keepers of the Sibylline
Books, whose number was to be raised to ten, should be
plebeians.

THE BILL CARRIED

At length (367 B.C.), after ten years of strife, matters came
to a crisis.   The Romans, under Camillus, had just gained a
victory over the Gauls, and on their return from the campaign
the plebeians, still led by Licinius and Sextius, determined
that the bill should be carried.   The fight was renewed on
both sides with more obstinacy than ever.   At length the
plebeians, strong in numbers, ably led, and elated by their
recent victory,[1] gained their end, and in the teeth of a fierce
opposition from the Senate and dictator [2] the bill became
law.   Even then the patricians would not give way, and they
refused their sanction to the act.   Then angry threats were
heard among the plebeians : some talked of a new secession,
while others hinted at open violence.   The patricians turned
once more to Camillus, the great champion of their order,
imploring him to use his authority as dictator and put down
these disturbers of the public peace.   But the veteran warrior

[1] Plutarch, *Camillus*, c. 42.   [2] Livy, vi. 42.

and statesman, now in his eightieth year, chose the better part, and ended a long career of honour by acting as mediator between the rival orders. By his advice the patricians withdrew their opposition, and the law was duly sanctioned by the Senate. As a concession to aristocratic prejudice it was agreed that two new offices should be created, to which only patricians were to be eligible. These were the office of Praetor, who took over the judicial functions of the consul, and that of two Curule Aediles, to take charge of the public games. The restriction as far as concerned the aediles was withdrawn in the next year, when the office was thrown open to plebeians ; but the praetorship remained in the hands of the patricians for thirty years. After this compromise had been arranged, Sextius, the colleague of Licinius, who had already been elected by the Parliament of the centuries, was duly confirmed in his office by the vote of the curies, and entered on his duties as the first plebeian consul.

END OF PATRICIAN PRIVILEGE

We have dwelt at some length on the fortunes of the Licinian Reform Bill because it marks the turning-point in two centuries of civil strife, and may justly be described as the deathblow to patrician privilege among the Romans. The patricians, indeed, obstinate to the last, still kept up a factious and peevish opposition, which delayed the final issue for eighty years, and in defiance of the constitution they succeeded several times in securing the election of two of their own order to the consulship. With a pretended regard for the purity of elections, they procured the passing of the first law against canvassing, the real object of which was to diminish the chances of ambitious plebeians in their candidature for the great offices of State. But in spite of all their efforts they steadily lost ground. Only eleven years after the Licinian Bill had become law they saw a plebeian dictator, Caius Marcius Rutilus, escorted through the streets of Rome, and five years later the same Marcius was invested with the purple robe of the censor. Thus two great dignities expressly created to strengthen the barrier against

PLATE XXII. SUOVETAURILIA

122

PLATE XXIII. INSULA TIBERINA

plebeian encroachment had been usurped by the despised and hated class. After the mutiny at Capua (342 B.C.) a measure was carried throwing open both consulships to the plebeians. The praetorship, resigned to the patricians as a consolation for their defeat in the crisis of the constitutional struggle, went the same way, and by the Ogulnian Law (300 B.C.), which opened the colleges of priests and augurs to the plebeians, they were driven from their last refuge, the management of the State religion. All that remained to them was the monopoly of certain minor priesthoods, the confirmation of laws, and the duty of ratifying the election of higher magistrates, which soon became a mere form, like the royal assent to an Act of Parliament in England. The command in war, the administration of justice, the taking of the census and all the vast powers associated with that function, the regal office of dictator, and the control of the national conscience through the agency of religion were now shared equally by plebeians. On the other hand, the patricians remained excluded from the tribunate, which became a factor of great importance in the new constitution.

THE NEW NOBILITY

But it would be a great mistake to suppose that the change inaugurated by the Licinian Laws was in any sense a democratic revolution. The fond hope of complete social and political equality which has always accompanied great legislative reforms was doomed, as it always must be, to disappointment. The privileges of the old noble houses had been swept away, but class privilege and class prejudice survived. Soon a new nobility, founded on office, rose on the ruins of the old, and sought to close its ranks against intrusion from without. The proud plebeian, who saw the waxen images of his ancestors, with their long list of public honours, arrayed in his hall, viewed with jealous eyes the efforts of a mere commoner to enter the charmed circle of official life. As time went on the possession of wealth became more and more essential to a political career, and when we reach the last century of the Republic corruption is widespread. Nevertheless the infusion

of newblood into the governing class which followed the triumph
of the plebeians was in its immediate effects a great blessing to
the Roman State.   Generations were to elapse before the era
of degeneracy began and the Romans lost hold on the grand
ideals of the past.   A wider prospect, with larger duties, new
interests, and new perils, opens out to the Republic after its
second birth, and the period which follows has been described
as the Golden Age of Roman history.

The Social Grievance Unhealed

It will naturally be asked how far the distress of the poor
was relieved by the economic clauses in the bill.   Speaking
generally, the old social grievance remained unhealed, and we
may add that the farther we advance the wider grows the
breach between rich and poor.   It should be borne in mind
that the great ambition of a Roman, in his private capacity,
was to become the owner of an estate, however small.   In
modern societies the poor ask for regular labour and a decent
scale of wages ; in Rome they asked for land.[1]   Hence the
constant recurrence of agrarian agitation in the annals of
ancient Rome.   " Land for the people " was the watchword
of one popular leader after another, kindling new hopes in the
poor man's heart, and arming the rich to determined and
relentless opposition.   In the end victory declared for the rich.
The small farmer, burdened with debt, and interrupted in his
labour by the obligation of military service, found it harder
and harder to hold his own against the capitalist.   Like his
modern representative in the United States he was forced
sometimes to sell his harvest before it was sown, while his
profits were swallowed by usury, until at last he became a
broken and ruined man and went to swell the great mass of
the proletariat, " the hungry and miserable mob, that leech
of the treasury," [2] which played so conspicuous and so fatal
a part in the last era of the Republic.

The mischief, of course, required time to attain its full
dimensions, and in the great epoch which succeeded to the final

[1] Duruy.   [2] Cicero, *Ad Att.*

THE CONSTITUTION

union of the orders (287 B.C.) its progress was arrested by many mitigating circumstances, by the foundation of colonies in the conquered districts, by the increase of the State revenues and consequent reduction of taxes, and by the patriotic ardour which animated all classes as the star of Rome's destiny rose higher and higher. But in the period which immediately concerns us—that is to say, the interval of eighty years which separates the Licinian from the Hortensian Laws (367–287 B.C.) —there is ample proof of constantly recurring and acute social distress. How little the authors of the bill cared for the principles which they had so loudly advocated is shown by the fact that Licinius was one of the first to be convicted of exceeding the limit proposed by himself (see p. 120). Then the plebeians saw that they had been betrayed by their leaders, and their clamours grew so loud that a series of measures was passed for their relief. The most important of these was the appointment of five banking commissioners, who placed their tables in the Forum and advanced money from the treasury on easy terms for the payment of debts, and interposed their authority to prevent the sale of a debtor's goods at a ruinous loss. Five years before this (357 B.C.) an attempt had been made to check the growth of usury by fixing the limit of interest at 10 per cent. The rate was afterwards lowered to 5 per cent., and at last, in the year of the mutiny at Capua, interest was forbidden altogether. It must be remembered that among the Romans all interest was regarded as usurious, and the usurer, according to Cato,[1] was worse than the thief. Such desperate remedies, of course, proved totally ineffectual. Usury went on in secret, and the old barbarous law allowing the insolvent debtor to be sold into slavery remained unrepealed. This great blot on the Roman statute-book was at last removed, in consequence of the shameful treatment of a youth of plebeian family who had surrendered himself as security for his father's debts. Henceforth all loans involving loss of liberty to the person were forbidden.

[1] *De R. R.*, c. 1. The same view is maintained by Dante, *Inferno*, xi. fin., *Convito*, iv. 9.

REPUBLICAN ROME

Third Secession of the Plebs

But all the efforts of statesmen could not check the growth of a social evil whose sources lay beyond the reach of any law Insolvency, distress, and discontent still went on, and rose to such a height that the Romans were brought to the verge of civil war. Once more the plebeians marched out of Rome, and pitched their camp on the Janiculum. This event is known as the Third Secession (287 B.C.), and led to the passing of the Hortensian Laws, which provided for the abolition of debts and the distribution of public land among all the citizens, and established the legislative powers of the tribal assembly by giving to its resolutions the force of law. By these measures the struggling farmers were relieved, at least for a time, and the long strife between patricians and plebeians came to an end.

The Four Parliaments

The third clause in the Hortensian Laws was the last in a long series of enactments regulating and defining the parliamentary powers of the people, assembled in their curies, their centuries, or their tribes. There were in all four of these Parliaments, and it is time to speak more particularly of their several functions. The old Parliament of the curies, representing the original Populus Romanus, had now become obsolete, and its right of confirming the election of the higher magistrates dwindled gradually to an idle ceremony, which in Cicero's time was hurriedly performed by thirty lictors. The Parliament of the centuries elected the higher magistrates, decided all cases involving a capital charge against a Roman citizen, and voted on questions of peace and war. As to the second point, it may be observed that the Romans had a jealous regard for their personal dignity, and the Valerian Law (509 B.C.), securing to every Roman citizen the right of appeal to his peers, was re-enacted again and again. The sovereignty of the people in all matters of legislation and election was distinctly affirmed by the Publilian Law (339 B.C.),

which withdrew the centuriate assembly from the direct
control of the Senate by decreeing that all measures passed
by the centuries should receive the sanction of the Fathers
beforehand. Thus the presidency of the Senate, which dates
from the time of the kings, was reduced in appearance to a
mere form.[1]

In speaking of the tribal division we have to distinguish
between two Parliaments, the Parliament of the plebs, from
which patricians were excluded, and the Parliament of the
tribes in the wider sense, which included both orders.[2] It is
to the former of these, the plebeian Parliament, that the
Hortensian Law referred, finally establishing the constitutional
position of that body. In effect the distinction between the
two Parliaments must have been nominal rather than real,
for the plebeians vastly outnumbered the remnant of the old
patrician order and could always command a voting majority.
But the plebeian Parliament could only be summoned by the
tribunes ; while the other, representing the whole Populus,
had for its presidents the higher magistrates, the consuls, the
praetors, and in some cases the curule aediles.

A Strange Constitution

The Roman constitution in its fully developed form, with its
four Parliaments and its multitude of officials, was a strange
patchwork, which had been built up by degrees, partly by a
series of compromises between the two orders and partly by
the distribution of the consular powers among a host of magistrates, with varying degrees of dignity and power. Outside
the main body of the Government stood the tribunate, originally
a militant and, strictly speaking, an unconstitutional office,
but destined in the reformed constitution to play a new part,
which will presently be described. In theory the People
were still sovereign, but in practice their influence on State
affairs becomes more and more insignificant. For as the

[1] Livy, i. 17.
[2] This distinction, which was maintained by Mommsen, is denied by Niese
(*Grundriss der römischen Geschichte*, p. 81, n. 4).

REPUBLICAN ROME

Roman territory, and with it the Roman franchise, was extended to the remoter parts of Italy, a large proportion of the citizens were practically excluded from attendance in the popular assemblies, so that the voters were drawn solely from the inhabitants of Rome and the immediate neighbourhood. Even the most advanced of the ancient thinkers had not grasped the principle of representation as we understand it, and down to the end of the Republic the constitution remained that of a city instead of that of a state.

THE SENATE

The parliamentary system was thus rendered inefficient, the regal office of the consuls was split up into departments, and the tribunes stood apart, with vast but ill-defined powers, which offered opportunities of boundless usurpation to an able and ambitious man. Rome seemed to be left without a guide, and must have fallen a prey to discord and anarchy but for the presence of a supreme directing body, which controlled every wheel of this huge, ill-organized machine, and for a century and a half filled with consummate ability the gap which had been made by the civil convulsions of two centuries. That body was the Senate, now so constituted as to draw into itself the whole wisdom and political experience of the Roman commonwealth. The duty of filling up vacancies belonged to the censors, but it was recognized that those who had held the higher magistracies had the first claim to be elected. The senators held their seat for life, and were invited by the presiding magistrate in order of seniority to express their opinion on the question before the house. All the great public officials, from the quaestors upward, had the right to sit and to speak in the Senate, but they did not become life-members until they had been duly elected by the censors. Outside of these were the silent members, men who had a place in the Senate by eminent public service, and who took part in the divisions but had no right to speak, giving their opinions, as it was quaintly expressed, by their feet, not by their voice. In this way the Senate came to represent the most

128

various forms of talent and merit, and a permanent seat on its benches was a patent of nobility. The senators were distinguished by a broad purple stripe woven into the front of their tunic or under-garment, by their red shoes, and by their gold rings; but the last-named ornament was also worn by the knights.

As the senators were mostly ex-magistrates, and these magistrates were chosen by the people, the Senate was in a certain sense a representative body. But the tendency to assume a democratic and radical character which might hence have resulted was placed under severe restrictions. For the elections were controlled by the magistrates, and the magistrates, in their turn, were under the direction of the Senate, and in this way a high standard of character was maintained in the public life of Rome. An attempt was, indeed, made by the able and eccentric Appius Claudius, during his tenure of the censorship, to lower the dignity of the Senate by inscribing on its list the sons of freedmen removed only by one generation from the taint of slavery. When this design proved abortive, he strove to pollute [1] the tribal Parliaments by giving the franchise to a motley multitude composed of freedmen, artisans, and other landless men, and distributing these new voters among all the tribes, both urban and rural. The object of this proceeding was to swamp the ascendancy of the landed proprietors, and thus render the popular assemblies more democratic. But here again the reformer was defeated by the action of Quintus Fabius Rullianus, who held the censorship eight years later, and gained the title of Maximus by collecting all this factious rabble into the four city tribes. It was a wise measure, which postponed at least, though it did not remove, a serious public danger without exciting discontent among a numerous and turbulent class of the citizens. For as the votes were counted by tribes, and not by heads, this change had the effect of destroying, to a large extent, the voting power of the new members introduced by Appius. On the other hand, the degradation of the city

[1] *Forum et campum corrupit* (Livy, ix. 46).

tribes which began with this measure was a source of endless disorder in the last age of the Republic.

It was the Senate, then, which guided the counsels of the nation in the important task of completing the conquest of Italy and organizing the various races of the peninsula under one head, in the struggle with Pyrrhus, through all the long agony of the Punic Wars, and in the period of foreign conquest which succeeded. It held in its hands all the guiding threads in the complicated tissue of government, the control of finance, the assignment of provinces, or spheres of duty,[1] to the magistrates, the revision of laws, the administration of justice, the conduct of wars and conclusion of treaties, and the prolongation of commands. The great officers of State were its obedient ministers, and the tribunes, who had formerly stood outside the constitution in a hostile and menacing attitude, were now admitted into the Senate, and became a useful instrument for coercing refractory officials and restraining the licence of the plebeian assemblies. Thus every power in the State was concentrated in this august body.

AFFAIRS IN GREECE

While the Romans were thus laying the foundations of their future greatness the course of affairs in Greece had tended more and more to produce a condition of disunion and decay. The Spartans during their brief period of empire had made themselves detested by every species of tyranny and injustice, and had crowned their iniquity by destroying the Confederacy of Olynthus (379 B.C.), which might have served as a bulwark against the growing power of Macedon. The Spartan empire was utterly broken by the victories of Epaminondas, which made Thebes the dominant power in Greece. Then followed a period of wild disorder, which exhausted still further the energies of the nation, until Greek liberty was extinguished on the fatal day of Chaeronea (338 B.C.). After the death of Philip (336 B.C.) the victories of Alexander spread the language and manners of Greece over a great part of western Asia, and

[1] The word *provincia* has in its original meaning no relation to place.

THE CONSTITUTION

out of the quarrels of his successors grew up the vast kingdom of Seleucus, and a number of minor principalities scattered over Asia Minor. Egypt flourished under the Ptolemies, and Alexandria became a famous centre of commerce and a seat of learning. But in Greece, in Egypt, and in western Asia every germ of free national development was dead or dying. Learning flourished, the arts of life were cultivated with assiduity and success, but political liberty, and with it the higher forms of creative genius, had perished. And hence it was that neither the Greeks nor any of the great potentates who reigned as the successors of Alexander were able to offer any effectual resistance when they were brought into conflict with the arms of Rome.

CHAPTER VII

THE WAR WITH PYRRHUS AND THE FINAL CONQUEST OF ITALY

AFTER two centuries of constant warfare and civil conflict the Romans had become a united people, and Rome was left without dispute as the greatest power in Italy. The Samnites were beaten into sullen submission, and the boundaries of the Roman state now included all southern Etruria, to the verge of the Ciminian Forest, the richest part of Campania, and the whole eastern district as far as the Abruzzi. In the same year which saw the submission of the Samnites (290 B.C.) Curius Dentatus celebrated a triumph over the Sabines, and these ancient kinsmen of the Roman people were forced to accept a limited form of citizenship, which was exchanged twenty-two years later for the full Roman franchise. The warlike Sabellian races of the central Apennines and the adjacent coast districts were in alliance with Rome, sending their best warriors to fight under the eagles; and a long line of forts, extending from Narnia in the north to the confines of Samnium and Campania, with outlying posts at Luceria and Venusia, formed a continuous bulwark, which was doubled in the most vital places, where an enemy might strike at the heart of the growing empire. It was now to be seen how this wonderful fabric, planned and executed with so much toil, patience, and foresight, would stand the first shock of collision with a great foreign power.

WARS WITH ETRUSCANS AND GAULS

But before the Romans were called upon to face this trial new troubles arose from the inveterate enmity of Etruria.

WAR WITH PYRRHUS

The great city of Arretium, which was in alliance with Rome, was besieged by an army of Etruscans and Senonian Gauls (284 B.C.), and a Roman general who was sent to relieve the place sustained a crushing defeat, with the loss of thirteen thousand men. But the Romans acted with characteristic promptitude and vigour. The rising in Etruria was quickly put down, and Cornelius Dolabella marched with a powerful army into the land of the Senones, cut to pieces their army, and gave up the whole district to pitiless devastation. The Gallic land, extending along the coast from the Rubicon to the Aesis, was denuded of its population, and a Roman colony was planted at Sena to occupy the conquered soil. Alarmed by the fate of their kinsmen, the Boii, who dwelt along the northern slope of the Apennines, from Parma to Bononia, descended in great force into Etruria, and, being joined by the disaffected portion of the inhabitants, met the Roman army near Lake Vadimo (283 B.C.), where twenty-seven years before Fabius Rullianus had gained a great victory over the Etruscans. Roman valour again prevailed, and the forces of the Boii and their allies were cut off almost to a man. In the next year the Boii raised another army, but after a second severe defeat they were compelled to lay down their arms and sue for peace. With the exception of some isolated movements in Etruria, all remained quiet in the north for nearly fifty years.

TROUBLE IN THE SOUTH

But no sooner had this danger been averted than an appeal came from the southern end of the peninsula, which led to most serious results. It had been the fate of those Greek cities which lined the eastern shores of Lucania and Bruttium to be ground to pieces between the tyrants of Syracuse and the Sabellian tribes who were constantly pressing southward. In their desperation they had turned for protection from one to the other, and in both they had found oppressors. One of these cities, Thurii, built near the site of the ancient Sybaris, now invoked the aid of Rome against the Lucanians, and the

consul C. Fabricius was dispatched with an army to its relief
(282 B.C.). Fabricius raised the siege of Thurii, defeated the
Lucanians and Bruttians in the field, and after a brilliant
campaign returned, laden with booty, to Rome, leaving a
garrison to guard the town.

TARENTUM

In the most sheltered recess of the broad gulf which bears
its name lay the great and wealthy city of Tarentum. Built
on a tongue of land commanding the entrance to a spacious
harbour, this famous Dorian colony offered a conspicuous
contrast to the fate which befell the other settlements of
Greater Greece. Its fine climate, and the smiling landscape
which lay beneath its walls, with rich olive-groves and vineyards, attracted the eye of Horace, who fondly hoped to spend
here the declining years of his life. The green meadows
of the Galaesus provided pasture for countless flocks of sheep,
whose wool, woven in the looms of Tarentum, was a large
source of wealth to the thriving community. Not less renowned
was the purple dye produced in the town, derived from a species
of mussel, and the great heaps of shells scattered along the
shores of the inner bay still attest the importance of this
industry in ancient times. But above all Tarentum was a
great commercial city, keeping up close relations with the
trading centres of the mother country. While the Romans
still adhered to their rude copper currency the gold coins
of Tarentum were in circulation throughout Samnium and
Apulia.[1]

This unbounded prosperity was attended by its usual
consequences, and the Tarentines were notorious for their
wanton and luxurious lives. Their public festivals, according
to Strabo,[2] were of such frequent occurrence that they exceeded
in number the days of the year. These descendants of the
Spartans had forgotten the stern discipline of their ancestors,

---

[1] For most of these details I am indebted to the valuable work of Nissen,
Italische Landeskunde (1902).

[2] vi. 4.

and the turbulence and levity of their popular assemblies rivalled the licence of the Athenian democracy at its very worst.

THE ATTACK BY TARENTUM

The Tarentines had long looked with jealous eyes upon the growing power of Rome, and had made a futile attempt to interpose as mediators during the Samnite wars. The recent successes of the Roman arms in southern Italy caused them serious alarm, and provoked them to an act which kindled the flames of a new war, and ultimately led to their own ruin. It was the joyous season of the Dionysia (282 B.C.) and the people of Tarentum were assembled in the theatre to witness the performance of tragic plays, when a Roman fleet, which had been sent to cruise in the Adriatic, was seen entering the great harbour. At the instigation of a worthless demagogue, the Tarentines rushed down to the docks, manned their ships, and, attacking the Roman squadron, sank four of the vessels and captured one with its crew. The Romans serving on board the captured galley were put to death and the rowers sold into slavery. Not content with this, the Tarentines sent a force against Thurii, which expelled the Roman garrison, plundered the town, and drove the leading citizens into exile.

THE TARENTINES AND POSTUMIUS

When the news of this outrage was brought to Rome envoys were sent to Tarentum, with Postumius at their head, to demand satisfaction. On entering the city they were at once exposed to the insults of a half-drunken rabble, who mocked their grave manners and cast ridicule on their outlandish garb ; and when they were admitted to the theatre, and Postumius preferred his remonstrance to the assembled people, the volatile multitude laughed aloud at his broken Greek. Postumius thereupon assumed a tone of menace, but this only provoked his audience to anger, and he and his companions were driven from the theatre and reviled as insolent barbarians. As they were leaving the building a drunken buffoon came reeling up and defiled the robe of Postumius, and this choice stroke of satire was applauded by a loud clapping of hands and peals of laughter from the whole theatre. Turning back and holding up his soiled robe, the Roman again addressed the crowd: "Aye, laugh, ye men of Tarentum, while ye may: ere long ye shall have cause enough to weep." And being answered by hisses and threatening gestures from those who sat nearest, he added: "Are ye angry? Then, to provoke you more, I tell you that this robe shall be washed clean with your blood."

War now appeared inevitable, but it was only after a long and anxious debate that the Senate decided on the proper course to be taken in avenging this gross insult to its representatives. For Etruria was in a state of unrest, and the Lucanians and Bruttians were in revolt and preparing to form a new coalition with the Samnites. At length it was resolved to send the consul Aemilius with an army to bring the Tarentines to reason by threatening devastation of their rich territory. The presence of an armed force before their walls sobered the fickle Greeks for a moment, and there seemed to be some prospect of a peaceful settlement. But presently the more violent party got the upper hand, and an embassy was sent from Tarentum to Pyrrhus, king of Epirus, inviting him to appear in Italy as the champion of the Greek cities against the Roman barbarian. Pyrrhus readily responded to the appeal, and having sent one of his officers, named Milo, to take the direction of affairs in Tarentum, he began to make preparations for the invasion of the peninsula.

Pyrrhus

Pyrrhus is perhaps the most interesting personality among the many able men who strove to carve out kingdoms for themselves in the dismembered empire of Alexander. Of Greek blood, he traced his descent from the great national hero, Achilles. His childhood was passed at the court of Glaucias, king of Illyria, to whose care he had been consigned by faithful domestics when the prince of Macedon, who had defeated and slain his father, was aiming at his life. At

136

PLATE XXIV. ETRUSCAN GATE, VOLTERRA   136

PLATE XXV. PYRRHUS   137

the age of twelve he was restored to his kingdom by Glaucias, but five years later a revolt of the Molossians drove him again into exile. After a wandering life he was enabled by the assistance of Ptolemy, king of Egypt, whose stepdaughter he had married, once more to recover his throne. He harboured great ambitions, and at one time it seemed as if he were destined to rule as sole monarch over the united kingdoms of Epirus and Macedon. But at the moment when the call came from Tarentum his dominions had shrunk to their original extent, and this fiery spirit, who had sought to emulate the conquests of Alexander, saw no prospect before him but a life of rude sport and revelry among the wild hills of his native Epirus. He who had fought under Demetrius, the greatest strategist of his time, and had lived in the purple at Alexandria, could ill support such a conclusion as this. And now his opportunity seemed to have arrived. He had failed in his hope of founding a great Eastern empire, but what if he should turn his arms to the West and, having conquered Italy and Sicily, should lead a great host against Carthage, the hereditary enemy of the Greeks? Here indeed was an enterprise which might rival the achievements of Alexander himself.

Pyrrhus invades Italy

With his wonted impetuosity, Pyrrhus would not wait for the return of spring, but embarked on the wild Adriatic and set sail for Tarentum. The number of his forces as given by Plutarch was twenty thousand infantry, three thousand cavalry, five hundred slingers, and twenty elephants. In the middle of the passage a violent storm burst upon his fleet, scattering the vessels, and he himself, after narrowly escaping shipwreck, arrived with a single ship on the shores of Italy (281 B.C.). Having waited until his armament, which had happily weathered the storm, was assembled at Tarentum, he at once employed himself in organizing the affairs of the city. At first the inhabitants received him gladly, being overjoyed at the advent of so great a captain to fight their battles for them. But they were soon undeceived. They had sought an ally, and they found a stern master, who put their city under severe military discipline, closed all the places of public entertainment, and kept their able-bodied men at a perpetual drill. Pyrrhus, on his side, was disappointed to find that the hopes of a general rising among the Italians which had been held out to him were not realized. The firm fabric of the Roman alliance remained unshaken at this momentous crisis, and the Romans thus gathered the first-fruits of their wise and far-seeing policy.

BATTLE OF HERACLEA

Special efforts were made at Rome to raise a force adequate to the emergency. Even the lowest class of citizens, who were generally exempt from military service, were called out, and the city was placed in a state of defence. One consular army was sent to put down a rising in Etruria, and a second, commanded by Publius Valerius Laevinus, received orders to proceed to Lucania and check the advance of Pyrrhus. Laevinus marched through Lucania, ravaging the country as he went, and having left part of his forces to overawe the Lucanians and secure his retreat, he pushed forward to meet the king. Pyrrhus, who was anxious to gain time, made an attempt to negotiate, and offered to act as arbitrator between the Romans and the Italian Greeks. But Laevinus answered that he had come to fight, not to talk, and Pyrrhus, who felt that any further hesitation would be fatal to his cause, now marched out to meet the Roman army, which was encamped on the southern bank of the Siris, in the neighbourhood of Heraclea. The engagement which followed (280 B.C.) was fought with desperate valour on both sides. The Roman cavalry at first gained an advantage, and Pyrrhus himself, whose horse was killed under him, was only saved from death by the devotion of his followers. Seven times, we are told, the Roman and Greek infantry met, and recoiled, and met again in the shock of battle. But at last the event was decided by a charge of the elephants, whose strange forms and enormous bulk scared the Roman horses and threw the cavalry back in wild disorder upon the foot. A general rout ensued, and the Romans, abandoning their camp, took refuge in one of the cities of Apulia. The total loss of the Romans was stated at fifteen thousand men, but the forces of Pyrrhus had also suffered severely, and when he read the list of the slain he is said to have remarked that another such victory would send him back to Epirus.

But although a judicious observer might already have foreseen that Pyrrhus was engaged in a vain enterprise, his victory, however hardly earned, had vastly improved his position. The Lucanians and Samnites began to send in their contingents, and the Greek cities in the south revolted from Rome. At Rhegium the Campanian legion which held the town for the Romans rose against the inhabitants, and after a general massacre kept possession of the place in their own name. For the moment Pyrrhus was master of all southern Italy, and the Romans were driven back behind their inner line of defence. On the other hand, the real strength of the Romans remained untouched. In Latium there was no sign of serious defection, the Sabellian peoples of the central peninsula did not move, and even the great fortress of Venusia, though now menaced on all sides, stood fast.

The Mission of Cineas

Pyrrhus now prepared to advance upon Rome, but before risking his fortunes in a second battle he determined to try the effect of negotiation. Accordingly he sent Cineas, a Thessalian Greek, and his favourite adviser, to offer terms of peace. Cineas was one of the most accomplished men of his day. He had listened to the eloquence of Demosthenes, and studied to rival the fame of that great orator. He was a consummate diplomatist, and had gained, it was said, more cities for Pyrrhus by his tongue than that great warrior had won by his sword. And now he came to try what Greek art and subtlety could effect against Roman sense and steadfastness. He brought with him bribes for the leading citizens, and rich presents for their wives ; for there was no shield, he was wont to say, which was proof against gold. His graceful manners, his wit, and the charm of his address were not without their effect on those with whom he conversed, and he, on his part, was profoundly impressed by the high character of the Romans and the wisdom and grandeur of their institutions. In due course he appeared before the Senate, and made known the terms offered by Pyrrhus. The king, he said, admired the Romans, and offered them his friendship and alliance if they would let the Greek cities go free and restore all the towns and lands which they had won from the Lucanians, Samnites, and Bruttians. If those conditions were accepted, he would restore without ransom all the Roman prisoners taken in the recent battle.

At first it seemed as if the mission of Cineas was to be crowned with success. A majority of the senators were disposed to make peace, and the general mass of the citizens, cowed by defeat and dreading a second encounter with Pyrrhus, inclined to their view. Happily the scale was turned the right way by the authority of one man, who, though old and blind, had a clear vision of the issues at stake. This was Appius Claudius, renowned for the deeds of his censorship. He was now living in retirement, being prevented by age and infirmity from taking an active part in public life. When he saw that the constancy of his countrymen was wavering, he asked to be carried in a litter to the Senate House, and, standing before the assembled Fathers, he addressed them in solemn words of counsel and warning.

Pyrrhus advances on Rome

Finding that he could accomplish nothing by policy, Pyrrhus at once took the field. Moving northward from Lucania and Samnium, he entered Campania, and, after making a vain attempt on Capua, he crossed the Liris, gaining Fregellae on his way, captured Anagnia in the Hernican district, and took up a position at Praeneste, within a day's march from Rome. He expected, perhaps, that his presence would lead to a general rising in central Italy, but if so his hopes were disappointed.

WAR WITH PYRRHUS

The allies of Rome remained firm, he was in the centre of a hostile district, Laevinus was watching his movements on the southern side, Coruncanius, who had put down the rising in Etruria, was advancing with another army from the north, and at Rome enlistment was rapidly going on under the direction of a dictator. In these circumstances nothing was left to him but to retreat, and he slowly retraced his steps, carrying with him a plentiful booty, and went into winter quarters at Tarentum. Thus the first year of the war came to an end.

BATTLE OF ASCULUM

During the winter ambassadors arrived at Tarentum to arrange terms for the release of the Roman prisoners. One of them was Fabricius, the type of antique Roman virtue ; and the writers of a later age, who loved to moralize on the past, told how he remained proof against all the attempts of Pyrrhus to shake his integrity by intimidation or corruption. Pyrrhus, we are assured, was so much impressed by the magnanimity of Fabricius that he allowed Roman prisoners to go home on parole for the purpose of keeping the Saturnalia, a great winter festival corresponding in some respects to our Christmas. At the beginning of spring, however, he resumed operations, and opened the campaign by laying siege to Asculum, in Apulia. The two consuls had already taken the field, and advanced to meet him with a powerful army, composed of Roman citizens and a large contingent of allies. The battle was fought in the neighbourhood of Asculum, but the details are imperfectly known, and the long fragment of Dionysius, containing an elaborate account of the engagement, does not enable us to follow the movements of the opposing armies. The numbers were the same on each side, amounting to seventy thousand infantry and eight thousand cavalry. To meet the attack of the dreaded elephants the Romans had prepared three hundred wagons, with scythes and spears projecting on all sides, and long beams armed at the end with spikes, strongly reminding us of the boarding-bridges afterwards used in the

First Punic War. But this clumsy contrivance proved use-less in the battle, for Pyrrhus kept his elephants in reserve until the oxen drawing the wagons had been hamstrung and the soldiers in charge of them had been dislodged by a shower of missiles. The nature of the ground gave full scope to the famous Macedonian phalanx, standing in dense and impenetrable array, sixteen deep, with five lines of lances, tier above tier, presented to the enemy. The Romans advanced with desperate valour to the attack, but they could make no impression on that rampart. Victory at last declared for Pyrrhus, but it was dearly purchased by the loss of his best men, and he himself received a wound in the course of the engagement. The consuls, though beaten, were able to draw off their forces, and no action of importance was attempted for the rest of the year.

PYRRHUS IN SICILY

We have seen that an essential part of Pyrrhus's scheme had been the conquest of Sicily and the invasion of Africa. The affairs of the island, long the battle-ground of Greeks and Phoenicians, were just then in such a state that they offered a fine opportunity for carrying out this part of his design. Agathocles, whose daring genius had shown the way to the future conquerors of Carthage, had now been dead for ten years, and since his death many of the Greek cities of Sicily had fallen into the hands of the Carthaginians, while the rest were torn by internal faction or oppressed by petty tyrants. A band of Campanian mercenaries who had served under Agathocles was now in possession of Messana, having butchered the inhabitants and made slaves of their wives and children, setting an example which was afterwards followed by the garrison at Rhegium. Syracuse itself, the centre of Greek life in Sicily, was blockaded by a Carthaginian fleet, and just at the moment when Pyrrhus, seeing no end to his perplexities, was looking round for a means of escape envoys arrived from that city inviting him to take up the cause of the Sicilian Greeks. Restless, impulsive, and always ready to embark on some new adventure, he grasped eagerly at the opportunity, and, leaving Milo in charge at Tarentum, he sailed with the main body of his forces for Sicily (278 B.C.). Avoiding the fleet of the Carthaginians, who had lately entered into an alliance with Rome and were waiting to intercept him in the strait, he reached Syracuse in safety, and was welcomed as a deliverer.

It was a peculiar feature in the career of this child of fortune that all his undertakings prospered at first, holding out the hope of some exalted and complete achievement which was destined never to be realized. His life is made up of a series of anticlimaxes. For a time in Sicily all went well with him and his arms prospered in every direction. He defeated the Campanian freebooters, who called themselves Mamertines, or children of Mars, and confined them within their walls, recovered Agrigentum, and then swept across Sicily, carrying all before him, until he reached Lilybaeum, at the western extremity of the island. But his fortunes were wrecked on the walls of that impregnable fortress, which defied all the efforts of the Romans in the First Punic War. Though in command of a splendid force and provided with a powerful train of siege-engines, he was baffled by the stubborn courage of the Semitic race, always most formidable when driven to bay, and after wasting much time and draining his resources he was obliged to relinquish the attempt. His failure at Lily-baeum and the arrogance and injustice of his subsequent behaviour shook his authority in Sicily and raised up numerous enemies against him. Once more he had followed a glowing vision of conquest and glory, which had only led him into new embarrassments, and at the end of two years he found himself a disappointed man, waiting, like a desperate gambler, for some turn in the game which might enable him to retrieve his fortunes. A year after his victory at Asculum he had snatched at the first excuse for leaving Tarentum, and now he was as eager to return to Italy as any shipwrecked sailor to reach the shore.[1]

[1] Plutarch, *Pyrrhus*, c. 23.

PYRRHUS RETURNS TO ITALY

Once more he found the pretext he was seeking. During his absence the Romans had recovered their footing in southern Italy and gained possession of the coast towns, with the exception of Rhegium and Tarentum. While Pyrrhus was lingering at Syracuse an urgent message reached him from the Samnites, Lucanians, and Bruttians, whose lands were being ravaged, imploring him to come to their aid, and, well pleased at the call, he embarked the remnant of his forces and set sail for Tarentum (276 B.C.). But he sighed as he looked back on the retreating shores of Sicily, remarking to those about him : " What a fine battlefield we are leaving to the Romans and Carthaginians ! " On his voyage he made a sudden descent on Locri, which was now held by the Romans, expelled the garrison, and, being in sore straits for money, plundered the rich treasure which was stored in the vaults under the temple of Demeter. From that moment, says the pious Dionysius, his fate was sealed. After a stormy voyage, during which he lost some of his ships, he reached Tarentum, and began to organize his forces for a final trial of strength with the Romans.

At this critical moment the Romans were under the influence of religious panic, and there was a general reluctance to face the dreaded Epirot in the field. One of the pestilences so frequent in the early annals of Rome had recently visited the city, and an alarming portent had occurred which seemed to threaten disaster and defeat. The statue of Jupiter which crowned his temple on the Capitol was struck by lightning and shattered to pieces, and the head was afterwards found in the bed of the Tiber. The magistrates found it necessary to adopt severe measures in order to bring the alarmed citizens to a sense of their duty. To appease the anger of the gods, one of the Vestal Virgins, who had been accused, rightly or wrongly, of unchastity, was buried alive,[1] and the heaviest penalties were declared against those who hesitated to give in

[1] Livy, Epitome xiv., places this event after the retreat of Pyrrhus.

their names for enlistment. By the latter means the consuls succeeded in making up the full complement of troops, and Curius Dentatus, taking the command of one army, marched into Samnium and occupied a position at Beneventum, while his colleague Cornelius watched the king's movements in Lucania.

BATTLE OF BENEVENTUM

The decisive battle was fought at Beneventum (275 B.C.). Pyrrhus, hoping to take the Romans by surprise, had planned a night attack, but he lost his way in the darkness and day was breaking when he came in sight of the Roman camp. Curius led out his men, and, favoured by the broken ground, attacked and drove back the troops of Pyrrhus and captured some of the elephants. Encouraged by this success, he ventured to resume the action on level ground, but here, after a severe struggle, his men were repulsed by a charge of the elephants and thrown back on their camp. Here they stood at bay, and the soldiers guarding the ramparts assailed the elephants with a shower of missiles. The huge beasts, galled by the javelins, turned and fled, carrying confusion into the ranks of their own army, and the Romans, following up this advantage, made a determined charge and gained a complete victory

PYRRHUS LEAVES ITALY

The fine scheme of conquest had ended in total failure. Foiled in Sicily and beaten in Italy, Pyrrhus had no course left but to return to his own country. He lived two years longer, and gained great victories, but fate pursued him still and his unquiet spirit would not allow him to remain constant to any single purpose. Finally he was killed by a tile thrown by a woman while fighting in the streets of Argos.

CONQUEST OF THE PENINSULA

The cloud of war which had hung over Italy for more than six years was now dispersed, and the Romans were left free to complete the task of subjugating the peninsula and organizing the scattered elements of its population under one head. Tarentum, indeed, was still held for Pyrrhus by his general Milo; but after the king's death Milo felt his position to be hopeless and was allowed to withdraw under a capitulation. The Tarentines were deprived of their ships, and compelled to pull down their walls, to pay a yearly tribute, and to enter the Roman alliance, with freedom to manage their own local affairs. The surrender of Tarentum had been accelerated by the appearance of a Carthaginian fleet, sent, as the Carthaginians asserted, to co-operate with the besieging army. Grave suspicions were entertained at Rome as to the good faith of these pretended allies, and the action of Carthage undoubtedly foreshadowed a great possible peril in the future, but no immediate breach of the treaty ensued. The Romans next turned their attention to Rhegium, where the Campanian mutineers, despairing of pardon, offered a most determined resistance, which prolonged the siege for many months. In this difficult undertaking the Romans found an ally in Hiero, who had fought under Pyrrhus in Sicily and had recently been raised to the throne of Syracuse, where he reigned for fifty-four years and revived the ancient prosperity of that famous city. Hiero sent supplies of corn to the Roman camp, and attacked the Mamertines at Messana, thus preventing them from effecting a junction with their kinsmen at Rhegium. The Romans at length succeeded in carrying the town by storm (271 B.C.), those of the mutineers who survived being sent to Rome and scourged and beheaded in the Forum. Rhegium was then repeopled by the remnant of its former inhabitants, and resumed its life as a Greek city under the protection of Rome.

Meanwhile the Roman armies had been led out, year after year, into Samnium, Lucania, and Bruttium, where the Sabellian tribes were making a last ineffectual stand for their liberty. The submission of Bruttium was secured by the capture of Rhegium, and the Romans thus came into possession of a vast tract of territory, abounding in timber and providing inexhaustible supplies of resin, which brought large sums into their treasury. The Samnites, true to their nature, kept up the struggle longest, and were hunted like brigands from one stronghold to another, until even their fierce spirit was subdued and they were compelled to acquiesce in a Roman peace. Another branch of the Sabellian stock, the natives of Picenum, were brought next year into the circle of the Roman dependencies, and part of the inhabitants were transported to the neighbourhood of Salernum. A campaign against the Sallentines in the south-eastern extremity of Italy (267 B.C.) secured the adhesion of that district, and gave the Romans command of the fine harbour of Brundisium,[1] which after the Punic wars became the chief port of departure for Greece, and rose to a position of commercial importance which it still retains, after two thousand years. The final reduction of Umbria, which falls under the same date, completed the long labour of conquest, and made the Romans masters of the whole peninsula, from the northern boundary of Etruria and the banks of the Rubicon to the southern sea.

ORGANIZATION OF ITALY

What Roman arms had conquered Roman policy organized and held together. The system which we have now to describe had grown up slowly in the course of generations, developing step by step with the victorious progress of the legions. In Italy there was no natural bond of union to overcome the barriers imposed by differences of manners, of language, and of religion. The Greeks, with all their local jealousies, were one people by blood, and they had their national festivals, which drew them together from the remotest parts of the great inland sea to join in a common worship at Olympia or at Delphi. These gatherings had a powerful influence in promoting the spiritual unity of the race and directing its energies into their proper channel, the pursuit of a high artistic and poetic ideal. But in Italy what had been denied by nature had to be induced by force. When Virgil says of the reputed ancestor of the Romans that he is destined to wage a mighty war in Italy and *weld*

---

[1] Brindisi.

together fierce peoples [1] he strikes a true note, and indicates the original basis of Rome's dominion, which depended ultimately on the power of the sword.

But mere brute force could neither have effected nor maintained so great an achievement. There were other influences at work, which, co-operating with the natural genius of the Romans, thrust them steadily forward to the proud eminence they had now attained. First there was the geographical position of Rome, at the meeting-point of three great nations, the Etruscan, the Latin, and the Sabellian. This gave the Romans an advantage which was wanting to their rivals, the possession of a strong strategic centre, and made them the champions of their Italian kinsmen, first against the Etruscans and afterwards against the Gauls. Secondly, there were standing causes of division among their opponents, of which the Romans skilfully availed themselves when the struggle for sovereignty in Italy began. In Etruria, in Campania, and at Tarentum there was a constant schism between the nobles and the commons, which the Romans carefully fostered, always taking sides with the aristocratic party; and they reaped the fruit of this policy at the great battle of Sentinum, which was largely determined by a brilliant charge of the Campanian horse. During the Samnite wars the Sabellian tribes of the central Apennines, the Marsians, Pelignians, and others, either took sides openly with Rome or remained neutral, or, at the worst, offered but a feeble resistance. This was a circumstance of the utmost importance, as it left open the passes of the Abruzzi to the march of the Roman legions when the southern approaches to Samnium were closed. The attitude of these Sabellians is explained by the peculiar position in which they were placed. As at the present day, the inhabitants of the high Apennines derived a large portion of their livelihood from cattle-breeding, and the maintenance of this industry depended on their keeping free access to the winter pastures of Apulia. After the defeat of the Romans at Caudium the Samnites, also a pastoral people, for a time obtained the upper hand in Apulia,

---

[1] *Populosque feroces contundet (Aeneid, i. 262).*

and it was their interference with the grazing rights of the central Sabellians which drove the latter to take sides with Rome.[1]

THE NEW ORDER

In speaking of the organization of Italy after the Roman conquest we are approaching a subject beset with difficulties, which have been solved in very different ways by the greatest authorities. But the main lines of the system may be laid down with tolerable certainty. We have to draw a distinction between three different classes—those who voted in the tribes as full Roman citizens, those who enjoyed a limited form of citizenship, and those who stood outside this inner and outer circle and were known under the comprehensive name of Italian Allies.

ROMAN CITIZENSHIP

As to the first class, it now included, besides the inhabitants of Rome and the immediate neighbourhood, a widely scattered population, settled in the conquered territories of Etruria and Campania, and in the Hernican, Sabine, and Volscian lands, with an outlying community at Sena Gallica, in what is now the March of Ancona. Sena was one of the maritime colonies, specially founded for the protection of the coast districts, which, beginning with Ostia in the time of the kings, gradually spread until they occupied all the important stations on both seas. These colonies were composed of full Roman citizens, who were exempted from the duty of serving in the legions, their sole function being to hold the garrisons, though to this was added at a later time the obligation of manning the Roman fleets.[2] Also there were certain Latin towns, like Tusculum, which after the loss of their independence had been admitted to the full Roman franchise. All of these were included in the tribes, which twenty-five years after the date we have reached rose to the full number of

---

[1] This is a brilliant conjecture of Nissen's (*Italische Landeskunde*, vol. ii. p. 434), which is so probable that I have not scrupled to adopt it.
[2] Beloch, *Der Italische Bund*, p. 113.

thirty-five, and the inner circle of Roman citizenship was thus made, for the present, complete.

THE LATIN CITIZENSHIP

The second circle was formed by those who possessed the private rights of Roman citizens, but had not the privilege of voting in the legislative and elective assemblies. Here again there were different degrees of independence or subjection, varying according to the circumstances which had determined their relationship to Rome. Some were allowed to appoint their own magistrates and to manage their local affairs, others lost all right of self-government and became entirely dependent on the ruling state. To provide for the administration of justice in towns of the latter class, and in the country districts occupied by Roman citizens, prefects were appointed, who acted under the Roman praetor, and were sent out every year to hold their courts in local centres, called prefectures.

THE LATIN COLONIES

Mention has been made more than once of the Latin colonies, which held a most important place in the organization of Italy and were the chief prop and stay of the Roman power. In order to understand their position it must be remembered that the term 'Latin' had now lost all connexion with the old federal league of Latium, reconstituted by Spurius Cassius in the early years of the Republic, and was applied, without respect to geographical situation, to all those military colonies which during the course of two centuries had been planted at places of strategic importance to guard the Roman frontiers and keep down the conquered population. Beginning in the time of the old struggles with the Volscians and Aequians, these outposts of empire were steadily pushed forward from the immediate neighbourhood of Rome to the line of the Liris and the frontiers of Samnium and Campania, to Etruria, Umbria, Apulia, and Picenum, until they formed a complete system of forts, holding all Italy in a grasp of iron, and connected by the great military roads. They were garrisoned by men who were Romans by birth but who had renounced some of their privileges as Roman citizens, being compensated for the loss by the solid advantages of their altered condition. Belonging to the poorer class, in Rome they had little chance of rising and could derive but little consolation for the narrowness of their lot from the privilege of voting in the assemblies. But in their new home they formed a sort of aristocracy, ruling as members of a conquering race over a subject community and reaping all the honour and profit which belong to such a position. Being endowed with a portion of the confiscated territory, they enjoyed the dignity of landed proprietors, and had many opportunities of acquiring wealth. Nor was their connexion with Rome severed by their change of residence, for they remained in a state of close dependence, and looked to the central government for continuance and support. Moreover, any Latin colonist who left a son to represent him or who had risen to the rank of a magistrate had the prospect before him of resuming his full rights of citizenship and spending his declining years in ease and honour at Rome. There was thus a true filial relation between the Latin colonies and the parent city, and any attempt to break that tie was regarded as an act of impiety.

THE ITALIAN ALLIES

Last of all we have to speak of the Italian allies, who remained outside the pale of Roman citizenship, whether in the full or in the restricted sense of that term. They were united to Rome by a federal bond, the exact nature of which was determined in each case by a special treaty concluded with the Roman Senate. How various and complicated these relations were is shown by the fact that the number of such treaties was not less than a hundred and fifty.[1] But there were certain specific obligations imposed on all the Italian allies without distinction. While retaining their own internal constitution they were bound to acknowledge the sovereignty of Rome

[1] Nissen, i. 68.

REPUBLICAN ROME

and to furnish at their own expense a fixed quota of troops, which served under their own officers, but acted under the command of the Roman general. The Greek cities on the coast, instead of military service, had the duty of equipping and manning ships for the Roman navy. Precautions were taken to isolate the several units of the Italian confederation. No member of the league was allowed to enter into a treaty with another Italian state, or with any foreign power. In all questions of international import Rome alone had the determining voice. Thus the Italian peoples, though nominally the allies, were in reality the subjects of Rome, and had to endure many galling restrictions, which clouded their prosperity and cut them off from the prospect of future development. They were, indeed, exempt from direct taxation, and were not subject, like the provinces of a later period, to the extortions of a Roman governor and his rapacious retinue. Yet in truth their general condition, with some favoured exceptions, was hard enough. Vast tracts of their land had passed into the hands of the Romans, to be portioned out among Roman settlers or leased to wealthy Roman capitalists. Their fairest cities were converted into Latin colonies, so that these former seats of their pride and power had become so many fortresses and strongholds of oppression. In every commercial enterprise they had to compete, at a great disadvantage, with Roman speculators, and they were exposed to all sorts of injury and insolence from the swarm of colonists who had come to live among them, and from civil and military officials from the ruling city. These grievances pressed hardest on the southern provinces, and especially on the Samnites and Lucanians, who had fought with the most determined obstinacy in defence of their liberty. The Sabellians of the central Apennines were, as we have seen, on the whole favourably disposed to Rome and secure of better treatment, and this explains their unshaken loyalty after the dreadful disaster at Cannae, when the southern Italians went over to the side of Hannibal.

CONQUEST OF ITALY

BENEFITS OF ROMAN RULE

The Roman conquest of Italy was a necessary step in the progress of civilization, and, like all great events in the cycle of human affairs, brought with it a mingled harvest of good and ill. On the one hand peace and order were established through the whole length of the peninsula, after the distracting conflicts of so many generations. No longer could the fierce Samnite descend from his mountain strongholds, to prey upon the rich fields or menace the prosperous cities of Campania. Without fear of molestation the Marsian or Pelignian drove his flocks and herds at the approach of winter from the cold valleys of the Apennines into the lowland pastures of Apulia. The old barbarous life of constant border warfare, of foray and counter-foray, was at an end, and Etruscan and Umbrian, Samnite and Campanian, lived side by side at peace with each other. If any disputes arose they were settled in the tribunals of the sovereign state. These were great benefits, and there were other advantages which might help to console the Italians for the loss of their independence. When the period of foreign wars began they had their share in the glory and in the spoils of conquest. And though the doors of privilege were now jealously guarded, they were not closed altogether and the Italian subject had always the hope of escaping from his depressed condition and rising to the full dignity of a Roman citizen.

WOUNDED ITALY

But on the other hand the internal warfare of the last hundred years had inflicted dreadful wounds on Italy. Whole districts which had once supported a thriving population were now turned into wastes, inhabited by a few savage herdsmen, who watched over the cattle of their wealthy masters. The system of great pasture-farms, described by Pliny as the ruin of Italy, gained ground more and more, and with it the decay of agriculture went hand in hand. Now began also the senseless destruction of the noble mountain forests which served as a natural reservoir, retaining the superfluous water after heavy rains, and thus checking the inundation of the lowlands. Large tracts of coastland, once covered with cornfields, olive-grounds, and vineyards, were thus turned into pestilent swamps.

SPREAD OF ROMAN INFLUENCE

Whether for good or for evil, however, Roman influence was now paramount in Italy, and the process had begun which by slow degrees converted the whole country into one vast suburb of Rome. Italians were gradually being fused into one people, and the outward sign of the change was the universal adoption of the toga, which became the national garb of the Italian, distinguishing him from the trousered Gaul. Local differences of manners, language, and costume fell into disuse, or lingered only in the remoter parts, and men of ability looked toward Rome as a great intellectual centre, where alone they could find a proper sphere for the display of their talents. This accounts for a certain uniformity of tone, a want of racy local flavour, which strikes us in the perusal of the Latin writers, and offers a marked contrast to the rich variety of the Greek.

FALL OF THE TOGA

With rare exceptions, the most eminent representatives of Roman culture were not Romans by birth. Yet we find in them all the true Roman spirit, and the Calabrian Ennius, the Volscian Cicero, the Sabellian Ovid, Horace, born on the confines of Apulia and Lucania, Livy and Virgil, natives of the great northern plain, and even the Spaniard Lucan, all use the same language and look to the great city as their common spiritual mother. The familiar saying that all roads lead to Rome has a deep significance, carrying us far beyond the literal meaning of the words.

Through the trials and struggles of five centuries Rome had slowly risen to take her place as the equal and possible rival of the other great Mediterranean

154

states.   After the defeat of Pyrrhus at Beneventum an embassy arrived from the Egyptian Ptolemy, the greatest potentate of his time, which led to a treaty of friendship and alliance with the Romans.   Ptolemy laid claim to sovereign rights over Cyrene, whose situation made it a sort of debatable ground between Egypt and Carthage, and the relations thus begun with Egypt, not less than the benefits recently received from the Syracusan Hiero, were significant of the course which events were about to take.   The Romans, it is true, were in formal treaty with Carthage, but the bond had already been severely strained, and a small occasion would suffice to bring on the inevitable conflict.

CHAPTER VIII
THE FIRST PUNIC WAR

WE have now emerged from the darkness which envelops the early annals of Rome and reached the beginnings of authentic history. Our principal authority for the events of the time is the Greek Polybius, who, however, is more than half a Roman in spirit, who had lived many years in Rome, and had followed the fortunes of Scipio, the conqueror of Carthage. Polybius was born toward the end of the Second Punic War, he came to Rome when men were still living who had played their part in that great historical drama, he had visited the battlefields and the cities which he describes, and he had before him the writings of contemporary witnesses. To these qualifications he added others, not less important. He was himself a soldier and a statesman, versed in great affairs, and endowed with a calm, judicial mind, generally free from small passions and local partialities. Unfortunately his works have come down to us in a fragmentary and imperfect form. But wherever we have his evidence before us we can walk with firm steps in the full light of credible history.

An Inevitable Conflict

In his first book Polybius gives an account of the First Punic War, which lasted for twenty-three years (264–241 B.C.) and ended in the cession of Sicily to Rome. The struggle between Rome and Carthage was a necessary sequel to the long series of wars which had brought all Italy under the Roman sway. To protect the coast towns of Italy and secure command of the great channels of commerce was a duty which could not

156

PLATE XXVI. A VESTAL   156

PLATE XXVII. CARTHAGE : VIEW OF BYRSA HILL

be neglected, and it led inevitably to a collision with the greatest maritime power of the Mediterranean. Already the Romans had made some half-hearted attempts to create a navy, and the same line of policy is to be traced in the foundation of burgess-colonies in the seaport towns. But it would be a mistake to suppose that in declaring war on Carthage the Romans had any clear view of the tremendous issues at stake. It was a step in the dark, forced upon a reluctant Senate by the blind enthusiasm of the people, and leading to consequences which no one could foresee.

LORDS OF THE SEA

The Carthaginians were heirs of a great tradition, and claimed, not without reason, the proud title of lords of the sea. Through their mother-city, Tyre, they could boast of a hoary antiquity, connecting them with the most ancient civilizations of the East, with Babylon, with Chaldaea, and with Egypt, compared with which Rome, Athens, and Sparta were but creations of yesterday. While Greece was still peopled with wandering tribes without settled abode or common name, before Troy had fallen or Homer sung, the great cities of Tyre and Sidon had risen to a height of power and prosperity which made them the wonder of the ancient world. Generally speaking, the seaman of antiquity was a timid being, who never, if he could help it, lost sight of land, but crept cautiously from cape to cape and from island to island, and always, if it were possible, passed the night on shore. But the Phoenician mariner put out boldly into the deep and sailed night and day, steering his course in the darkness by the polar star,[1] from Tyre to Cyprus, from Cyprus to Crete, through the long waste of waters between Crete and Malta, and onward by Sicily, Sardinia, and Minorca,[2] until he reached the distant land of Spain, the El Dorado of the ancients, from whence came those "ships of Tarshish" which brought gold and ivory to adorn the temple of Solomon. Nor did they shrink from the perils of the great unknown ocean which down to the time of Caesar

[1] Strabo, i. 3.   [2] Nissen.

remained a name of terror to the Romans. Cadiz still bears, but thinly disguised, its ancient Phoenician name,[1] and it is generally believed that the quest of wealth carried these dauntless traders as far as the coast of Britain and the Scilly Isles. Between the eleventh and the seventh centuries the Tyrian factories fringed all the coasts of the Mediterranean, from the Hellespont to the Pillars of Hercules. On the island of Thasos Herodotus [2] saw with amazement a whole mountain which had been " turned upside down " by the Phoenicians in their eager search for gold, and this is but one example of the restless avarice which pursued its end in defiance of hardship, toil, and danger.

THE CARTHAGINIAN CHARACTER

All the energy, all the adventurous daring of the Phoenicians were directed to one sole object, the acquisition of wealth. They had none of that noble curiosity which inspired the great discoverers of later times to go forth in search of new worlds. The famous voyage of exploration, which lasted for two years and established the fact that Africa is surrounded by the sea,[3] was undertaken at the command of an Egyptian king, and when Hanno early in the fifth century visited the western shores of that continent he was merely seeking to enlarge the commerce of Carthage. The Phoenicians added nothing, and sought to add nothing, to the intellectual riches of mankind. Their religion was monstrous, sensual, and cruel, and no great creative work in art, in literature, or in science bears their name. Consequently, while Rome and Athens are still living forces in the mind of Europe the ancient glory of Tyre is but dimly remembered and a few broken stones are all that remains of the brilliant city which once strove with Rome for the empire of the world.

BEGINNINGS OF CARTHAGE

Carthage, like Rome, rose to greatness from very small beginnings. Founded about the end of the ninth century

---

[1] Gadir, ' Fortress.'   [2] iv. 42.   [3] Herodotus, iv. 42.

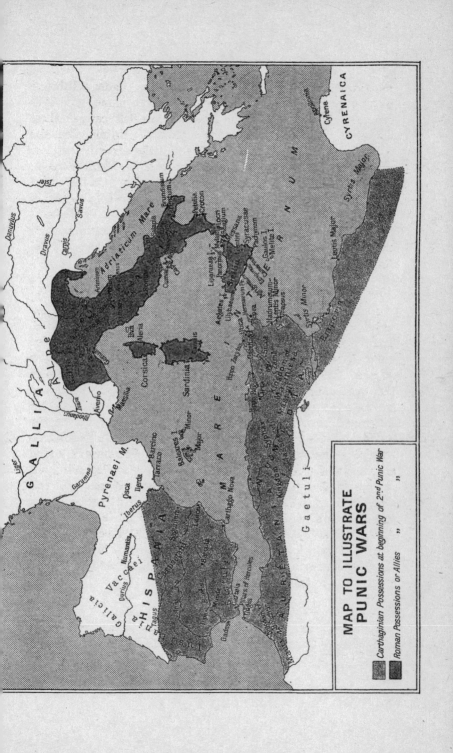

MAP TO ILLUSTRATE
PUNIC WARS

Carthaginian Possessions at beginning of 2nd Punic War
Roman Possessions or Allies

before Christ, the little colony received the modest name of Newtown, to distinguish it from the earlier Phoenician settlements at Hippo, Utica, and Hadrumetum. But the geographical position of Carthage marked her out from the first as destined to a great career. Just at this point the dull uniformity of the African coast is broken by a deep bay, and a bold cape stretches out northward, seeming to grasp like a hand at the fair island of Sicily. Within this bay is a rocky headland, facing eastward, and connected with the mainland by an isthmus three miles broad. Here, on the summit of a steep hill, the Tyrian colonists raised their Byrsa, or citadel, and from this centre the city spread on all sides, until it covered the whole surface of the peninsula, extending, with its suburbs, to a circumference of thirty miles. By degrees Carthage rose from a state of humble dependence on the native Libyans and became the metropolis of a wide empire, stretching along the northern coast of Africa from the borders of Cyrene to the western ocean. The core of this territory lay to the southwest of Carthage, taking in a large part of the modern Tunis and Algeria, but to the east and west it was a mere fringe of coastland, from twenty to fifty miles in breadth. The inhabitants of the conquered country were partly Libyans, an agricultural people, who paid tribute to Carthage, and partly a race of half-breeds, of mixed Libyan and Phoenician descent. The most favoured spots were taken by the wealthy Carthaginians for their country seats, and the whole district adjacent to Carthage wore the aspect of a garden, whose beauty and luxuriance, surpassing the most favoured parts of Italy, excited the envy and cupidity of the elder Cato. Beyond the provinces immediately subject to Carthage dwelt the Numidians or Nomads, who preserved their independence, but supplied the Carthaginians with mercenary troops.

After the decline of Tyre her wealthiest citizens migrated to Carthage, and the struggle between Greek and Semite, which in the eastern Mediterranean had been decided in favour of the former, was transferred to the west. The chief scene of this contest was the island of Sicily, which forms a sort of natural

bridge connecting Italy with Africa. For two centuries the
tide of war rolled to and fro, from the great day of Himera,
when Gelo of Syracuse overthrew the immense host of Hamilcar
(480 B.C.), to the day when the victorious progress of Pyrrhus
was brought to a close before the walls of Lilybaeum. After
the death of Pyrrhus Carthage was once more in the ascendant,
until her advance was finally checked by the intervention of
Rome.

Carthaginian Enterprise

Besides their possessions in western Sicily, the Carthaginians
had planted their foot in Sardinia, in Corsica, in Malta, and in
the sister island of Gozzo, whose name [1] still recalls the earlier
Phoenician occupation. Further west they kept their hold
on the Balearic group, the modern Majorca and Minorca, whose
hardy natives, renowned for their skill with the sling, formed an
important element among the light-armed troops of Carthage.
In Spain their factories were scattered along the coasts of
Granada and Andalusia. Beyond the Strait of Gibraltar they
knew, and had perhaps colonized, the Canary Islands, and their
fleets had explored the western coast of Africa as far as the river
Senegal. Far into the heart of the great African continent
their merchants penetrated every year with long trains of
camels, and brought back strange stories of that wonderland,
with its giants and pigmies and its mountains of gold. And
it is not improbable that in the crowded marts of Carthage
and at the tables of her merchant princes rumours were heard
of a new world beyond the western ocean.

Carthage and Rome Compared

In wealth, in external pomp and splendour, and in ancient
renown Carthage stood high above her rival Rome. But the
foundations of her power were far less broad and deep. The
Romans were still in the heyday of their youthful vigour,
they had been trained in the long contest with the warlike
races of Italy, and they were gifted with a special genius for

---

[1] From *gaulos*, a Phoenician merchant ship.

law and government, which had been sharpened by the civil strife of many generations. The Carthaginians, on the other hand, belonged to a much older civilization, which had already passed its prime and was verging on decay. Moreover, the Phoenician mind moved generally in a narrower and lower sphere, which was not favourable to the development of liberal talents or high ambition. With rare exceptions, the whole bias of the nation was in the direction of commerce and gain. The Italian subjects of Rome, also, were for the most part of the same race as their rulers, and by a gradual process of assimilation conquerors and conquered were slowly becoming one people.

COIN USED FOR PAYING CARTHAGINIAN MERCENARIES

But no such bond united the Libyan farmers to their masters at Carthage. They were aliens in blood, and suffered heavily from harsh treatment and oppressive taxation. No line of forts like the double rampart which guarded the heart of the Roman empire in Italy confronted the invader who landed on the shores of Africa, for such places of strength would have served the discontented Libyans as centres of insurrection. Not less marked was the contrast between the military organization of the two powers. The flower of Rome's armies was composed of her own citizens, men of war from their youth and inheriting the high traditions of a conquering race; and outside of these were the Italian allies, bound to the sovereign state by ties of common blood and common interests. But the Carthaginians were for the most part soft and luxurious and shrank from the hardships and perils of military service, trusting for their defence to a motley host of mercenaries, Gauls, Numidians, Iberians, and Greeks, many of the last being men of the most desperate character, escaped criminals or runaway slaves. In their dealings with this turbulent multitude the Carthaginians showed all the

cunning and perfidy which made the Punic name a byword
for broken faith. The troops were often cheated of their
pay and stinted in their supplies, and whenever it was thought
convenient whole battalions were betrayed to the enemy
or left to perish in desert places. The discontent which
resulted from such treatment led more than once to an open
mutiny which brought Carthage to the brink of ruin.

THE CARTHAGINIAN OLIGARCHY

In theory the constitution of Carthage was a mixed form of
government, in which the powers of kings, lords, and commons
were held in equal balance. But at the outbreak of the Punic
wars it had become in practice a close oligarchy, founded on
wealth. The power of the suffetes, or kings, who were two in
number and were elected by the people, had become more and
more restricted, and the supreme control of State affairs was
in the hands of a corporation called the Hundred, composed of
the wealthy merchants, who commanded the vast financial
resources of the State. Below these was the general body
of the citizens, who remained in a sort of passive attitude,
being fed by the bounty of the rich or provided for by the
foundation of colonies. In times of peace and prosperity
internal tranquillity was thus assured, but when the flow of
wealth was checked by the pressure of foreign wars the good
understanding between nobles and commons gave place to
ill-feeling and discord. The great generals, whose plans were
constantly checked and hindered by the jealous interference
of the government, leaned on the people for support, and
amid these elements of discord the trembling oligarchs were
perpetually haunted by the dreaded spectre of despotism.

EARLY RELATIONSHIP

Between Rome and Carthage friendly relations had subsisted from very early times. According to Polybius the
first treaty with Carthage was concluded in the year following
the fall of the kings, with the object of defining the commercial
relations between the two cities. The Romans bound them-

selves not to sail beyond the Fair Cape in an easterly direction,
and Carthage was pledged to respect the coast towns subject
to Rome.   Two centuries later (306 B.C.) we hear of a second
treaty, imposing further restrictions on Roman commerce,
and the general tenor of these documents points to the
rising pretensions of Carthage as queen of the western Mediterranean and the depressed condition of the Roman mercantile
marine.   A closer bond had lately been formed, resulting from
the ambitious designs of Pyrrhus; but when that danger was
removed Rome and Carthage were left face to face in scarcely
disguised hostility, and Sicily lay between as the battlefield on
which the quarrel was to be fought out and as the rich prize
of victory.

CAUSE OF THE FIRST PUNIC WAR

The immediate cause of the First Punic War came from
Messana, and some curious conclusions might be drawn from
the fact that the first step on the path of conquest was taken
by the Romans at the call of outlaws and robbers.   Some
twenty years before a band of Campanian mercenaries, known
in history as the Mamertines, had taken possession of Messana,
in circumstances which have already been described.   After
the departure of Pyrrhus from Sicily they carried their depredations far and wide, and made their name a terror throughout
the western districts of the island ; but at last they found a
leader able to cope with them in the young Hiero, who defeated
them in the field, confined them within their walls, and as a
reward for his services obtained the throne of Syracuse.
Eleven years after the defeat of Pyrrhus at Beneventum the
Mamertines were in sore straits, and an appeal was sent to
Carthage, which led to the occupation of the citadel by a Punic
garrison (264 B.C.).   But meanwhile another party among
the outlaws had sent to invoke the interference of Rome on
their behalf.   The problem involved in this application was
full of difficulty and perplexity.   If the Romans openly
espoused the cause of the Mamertines they would be entering
on a new line of policy the issue of which it was impossible

to foretell. Hiero, whose righteous arm had chastised the freebooters of Messana, was their friend and ally, and the treaty with Carthage was still nominally in force. And how could the Romans, who a few years before had taken exemplary vengeance on the mutinous garrison at Rhegium, stand forward as the defenders of men whose crimes, the same in character, were still deeper in degree ? But on the other hand the danger threatening from the Carthaginians was real and imminent. Already they held command of Corsica, of Sardinia, and of Lipara, and if Messana were added their stations would form an unbroken line fronting the whole western coast of Italy. Honour seemed to point one way, interest the other, and at last the Senate, after long deliberation, resolved to leave the decision to the people. The scruples which had weighed so heavily on the conscience of the Fathers were easily brushed aside in the popular assembly. Many of the citizens were needy, all of them were covetous, and the military spirit of the nation had been wrought to a high pitch by the conquest of Italy. By working on these feelings the ambitious leaders who desired a larger field of action easily brought the people to adopt their views, and it was resolved to admit the Mamertines into the Roman alliance.

First Hostilities

The conduct of the campaign was entrusted to Appius Claudius Caudex, and he at once began his preparations for the relief of Messana. One of his lieutenants, Caius Claudius, succeeded by an act of treachery in inducing Hanno, the Carthaginian commander, to evacuate the citadel. On his return home Hanno was crucified for his cowardice, and the Carthaginians, in concert with Hiero, pressed the siege of Messana. But Appius, skilfully eluding the enemy's fleet, carried his troops without mishap across the strait, and then, boldly engaging the besieging armies, gained a victory, first over Hiero, and afterwards over the Carthaginians. The immediate object of the expedition was thus attained. Hiero retired to Syracuse, the Carthaginian army was dispersed, and Messana was occupied by a Roman garrison.

ROME ALLIED WITH SYRACUSE

Encouraged by this success, the Romans enlarged their field of operations, and aimed at nothing less than the conquest of all Sicily. At first it seemed as if a few resolute strides would bring them within grasp of the coveted prize. In the year after the capture of Messana (263 B.C.) two consular armies landed in Sicily, and the presence of this powerful force induced many of the cities to join the side of the Romans. The prudent Hiero now became convinced that fortune had declared for Rome, and resolved to throw in his lot with the winning side. He accordingly entered into a fresh treaty with his former friends and allies, and the bond thus renewed remained unbroken till his death. The value of this alliance appeared in the following year, when the Romans, with the active co-operation of Hiero, defeated the Carthaginians before Agrigentum, and obtained possession of that city, after Syracuse the most important place in Sicily. This was a very severe blow to the Carthaginians, and they no longer attempted to dispute the superiority of the Romans in the field. But they still kept command of the sea, and their fleets hovered constantly round the shores of Sicily and Italy, carrying havoc into all the coast districts. Unless the war was to be prolonged indefinitely, it was evident that the Romans would have to meet the Punic seamen on their own element.

BEGINNINGS OF A FLEET

But in order to effect this great change it was necessary to create a navy, to train the rowers, and to accustom the fighting men to keep their footing and manage their arms on a plunging ship. At the beginning of the war the Romans had not even a single galley, and the transports which carried their troops to Sicily were convoyed by armed vessels borrowed from Tarentum and other Greek cities. To transform a great military into a great naval power, able to cope with the seasoned

REPUBLICAN ROME

mariners of Carthage, might well seem a hopeless enterprise ; and that such an undertaking should have been carried out within a few months appears almost miraculous. Yet by a happy audacity the Romans succeeded in performing this feat. In those days the ordinary line-of-battle ship was the quinquereme, a huge galley of some five hundred tons burden, propelled by ponderous oars, arranged in five lines on each side, tier above tier. The Roman shipwrights had no experience in the construction of quinqueremes, but they found a model in a Carthaginian vessel of this class which had been captured at the beginning of the war. While the building of the fleet was in progress scaffolds with rows of benches were set up on land, and on these the crews practised the motions of rowing, sitting in the order they were to occupy on the ship, and thus learning to swing their bodies together and keep time to the voice of the boatswain. Admirable timber was supplied by the forests of Latium, and by the end of the winter a hundred and twenty quinqueremes were ready to be launched.

ANCIENT NAVAL WARFARE

According to the most approved method of ancient naval warfare, the captain employed his whole art and skill in manoeuvring his vessel and using her as a projectile to sink or disable an opponent's ship. With this object each galley was provided with a beak or ram, which was aimed against the stern or side of the vessel selected for attack. But the Romans, with their raw crews and ill-furnished quinqueremes, hastily hammered together out of green timber, were in no condition to employ these delicate tactics, which required the utmost coolness, dexterity, and judgment, and a crew under perfect command. Just at the right moment some inventive genius hit upon a contrivance which was designed to frustrate the superior skill of the enemy and give full scope to the prowess of the legionary soldiers who manned the decks of the Roman ships. Each quinquereme was furnished with a wooden gangway, thirty-six feet long, and defended at the sides by a low parapet. When not in use, the gangway was stowed

166

PLATE XXVIII. COLUMNA ROSTRATA   166

PLATE XXIX.   TRAPANI (DREPANUM) AND ERYX

Photo from " Aus dem class. Süden " (published by C. Coleman, Lübeck)

[*See page 178*]

167

along the middle of the deck, and when the ship went into action it could be hauled up by means of a pulley fixed at the top of a stout mast, which was set up at the prow of the vessel. Lying close to the mast, and playing freely round it, the gangway could be dropped at any moment on the deck of the attacking ship, where it was held fast by a strong claw or grappling iron, fixed underneath at its farther end. Then the boarding-party, with two picked men at their head, rushed in a double file on to the enemy's deck, and carried all before them by sheer strength of hand and skill with the sword. The strange machine was called a 'crow,' and its effect was to change the whole character of a sea-fight and give it the aspect of a battle on land.[1]

BATTLE OF MYLAE

At the beginning of spring in the fifth year of the war (260 B.C.) the Roman fleet set sail for Sicily, commanded by Scipio, one of the consuls, while his colleague, Duilius, had charge of the land forces. Scipio was surprised and taken prisoner while making a rash attempt on the island of Lipara, and the command of the fleet, which was stationed at Messana, passed to Duilius. The Carthaginians were just then engaged in plundering the coastlands not far from Messana, and being informed of this Duilius put out to sea with his whole fleet, and fell in with the enemy in the open waters off Mylae. The Punic captains advanced gaily to the encounter, being full of contempt for the seamanship of the Romans and expecting an easy victory. They were, indeed, somewhat surprised at the appearance of the 'crows,' which were hoisted up ready for action and towered ten or twelve feet above the top of the masts, armed with their iron claws. But the sight served only to heighten their confidence, for they never suspected the purpose of these clumsy engines, and they laughed at the ungainly aspect of the Roman quinqueremes as they wallowed

---

[1] How the 'crow' was employed when a ship was charged in the stern does not appear. Perhaps it was arranged to run on wheels up and down the deck; but this is nowhere mentioned.

and yawed in the rolling seas. But they soon learnt their mistake, for as ship after ship came within range of the ' crows ' the ponderous machine crashed down on her deck, driving its iron fang deep into her timbers and holding her fast. The Carthaginian crews were totally unprepared for this sort of encounter, and they offered but a feeble resistance to the Roman boarding-parties. Whether they charged the enemy on the bow, on the quarter, or on the stern, the fatal ' crow' was ready to receive them, baffling all their skill and placing them at the mercy of the Roman swords. At last, finding that their seamanship availed them nothing, they turned and fled, leaving fifty of their ships in the hands of the enemy.

Rome takes Corsica and Sardinia

On his return to Rome Duilius celebrated the first Roman naval victory by a well-merited triumph, and a column, decorated with carvings representing the oars and beaks of vessels, was set up in the Forum. So signal a success seemed to warrant the hope that the Romans might strike with effect at the maritime possessions of Carthage, and drive their enemies from the seas as they had conquered them on land. Accordingly, in the next year Lucius Scipio, the consul, sailed to Corsica and captured Aleria, the chief town of that island, an achievement which is recorded by an inscription still preserved on his tomb. Then, proceeding to Sardinia, he defeated the Carthaginians, ravaged the island, and took many captives. But after this the Romans made no decisive progress. Scipio was unable to obtain a permanent footing in Sardinia, the war in Sicily dragged on, and though the Romans remained masters in the field the Carthaginian strongholds in the west of Sicily defied all attack.

Designs on Carthage

Finding themselves thus brought to a standstill, the Romans determined to change the field of operations and strike at the centre of the Carthaginian power. Nor was there wanting an example to show where the blow was to be struck and encourage them with a prospect of success. More than fifty years before Agathocles, hard pressed by the Punic fleet at Syracuse, had broken through the blockade with a squadron of sixty ships and made a bold dash for the African coast.   Fortune favoured his seemingly desperate enterprise, and for several years he maintained his position in a hostile country, capturing town after town and spreading havoc and terror to the very gates of Carthage. The brilliant feat of Agathocles, the very character of the Carthaginian empire, with its discontented population and its rich territory, undefended by places of strength, their own unassailable position at home, all seemed to beckon the Roman legions toward the shores of Africa. And the Romans were not slow in answering the call. Vast preparations were made for the contemplated invasion. With a fleet of three hundred and thirty ships, manned by a hundred thousand rowers, the two consuls, Manlius Atilius Regulus and Lucius Manlius Volso, passed the strait of Messana (256 B.C.), and, skirting the eastern coast of Sicily, came to anchor at Ecnomus, on the southern side of the island. Here they embarked their troops, numbering forty thousand men, and prepared to encounter the Carthaginian fleet, which was approaching from the direction of Lilybaeum. The armament of Carthage was fitted out on an even grander scale, and, judged merely by the numbers engaged, the battle which followed was the greatest ever fought in the history of naval warfare.

BATTLE OF ECNOMUS

At Ecnomus, as at Mylae, the Carthaginians had the advantage in nautical experience and in the sailing quality of their vessels. Moreover, the Roman ships were crowded with troops and embarrassed by the number of transports. In view of this the consuls adopted an order which was designed to break through the enemy's line and carry the day by mere weight and mass. Two vessels with six banks of oars, commanded by the consuls themselves, were stationed in front, so as to form the apex of a triangle, the sides of which were formed by two lines of ships, diverging to the right and left, and pointing their beaks outward. Behind these was posted a third division forming the base of the triangle, and each of the vessels in this section had a horse-transport in tow. A fourth division brought up the rear, extended at either wing beyond the extremities of the line in front. The four squadrons of the fleet were called 'legions,' and the whole disposition was modelled on the tactics of the Roman army.

The consuls hoped to break through the enemy's line by one determined charge and carry their whole fleet in safety to Africa. But these calculations were frustrated by the superior skill of the Carthaginian admirals, who drew up their fleet in one long line, outflanking the Romans on the right, and curving round to the left so as to lie parallel to the coast of Sicily. The battle began with a forward movement of the Roman consuls, who struck at the enemy's centre, leading the way in their powerful six-banked galleys and followed by the two front divisions. Hamilcar, the Carthaginian admiral who commanded at this point, retreated before their attack and drew them away from the main body. Then, having lured them to a sufficient distance, he wheeled his vessels round and attacked the two squadrons with great resolution. Meanwhile Hanno, the other admiral, whose position was on the extreme right, taking a wide curve through the open sea, fell upon the rear division of the Roman fleet, and at the same time the ships in charge of the horse-transports were compelled to cast off their tow-lines and grapple with the left wing of the enemy, which had wheeled round into the space left vacant by the rash advance of the consuls. The solid phalanx of the Roman fleet was thus broken into three separate squadrons, each engaged in a desperate battle and divided by a wide space of water from the others. At length the division under Hamilcar was overpowered and put to flight, and Regulus, seeing that his colleague was engaged in securing his prizes, went to assist the rearguard, which was encumbered by the drifting transports and hard pressed by Hanno. Hereupon the Carthaginian admiral, finding himself assailed in front and rear, was obliged to give way, and made for the open sea. Then the two consuls made a final charge on the Carthaginian left, which was driving the remaining Roman division on the shore, and, being now hemmed in on all sides, the Carthaginians here suffered very severely, so that only a few of the fastest ships succeeded in making their escape. Ninety-four of the Carthaginian vessels were taken or destroyed in the course of the action, while the Romans lost only twenty-four. As in the battle of Mylae, the 'crows' did excellent service.

ROMANS LAND IN AFRICA

The way to Africa was now open, and the consuls, after refitting their ships and taking in fresh supplies, struck across the sea and effected a landing at Clupea, on the north-eastern angle of the Hermaean Cape. The town surrendered after a short siege, and, making this their basis of operations, the Roman generals began to ravage the rich district which was covered with the villas and estates of the wealthy Carthaginians. But presently envoys arrived from the Senate with orders that Manlius was to return to Rome, bringing with him the fleet and the larger part of the army. Manlius accordingly departed, taking with him an enormous booty, and Regulus was left to continue the campaign with a force of fifteen thousand men. For a time the bold enterprise prospered in every direction, and but for the ill-advised action of the Senate and the folly of Regulus the fall of Carthage might have been anticipated by more than a century. Beaten in the field and filled with a lively terror of the Roman legions, the Carthaginians retired within their walls and remained passive spectators of the ruin and devastation, which were carried to the very gates of the city. Regulus obtained possession of Tunes, and made that town his headquarters, thus cutting off the Carthaginians from their communications with the mainland. A new terror was added by a general rising among the wild nomad tribes, who overran the country, plundering and burning whatever the Romans had left.

REPUBLICAN ROME

XANTHIPPUS

Carthage was now threatened with famine, for the population had been swelled by a multitude of fugitives who had sought shelter within the walls. In their distress the Carthaginians sent envoys to arrange terms of peace with Regulus. But the attitude of the consul was so overbearing and his demands so exorbitant that a new spirit was kindled in the elders of Carthage, and they resolved to brave the worst rather than submit to conditions which would make them the humble dependents of their ancient rival. Their stubborn courage brought its proper reward, and just at the critical moment the beleaguered citizens found what they wanted, a brave and competent leader. Shortly after the return of the envoys there arrived in Carthage a contingent of Greek mercenaries, and with them was a Spartan officer named Xanthippus, who had been trained in the ancient discipline of Lycurgus and had fought with honour against Pyrrhus when that monarch was besieging Sparta. Xanthippus soon gave evidence of conspicuous ability, and the troops of Carthage were placed at his disposal. The Greek saw the mistake which had been made by the Carthaginian leaders, who dreaded an encounter with the Roman legions in the open field and clung to the hills and high ground, where they could not use their cavalry and elephants with effect. Having spent some time in organizing and drilling his troops, he marched out of Carthage and encamped in the open plain, with a force consisting of twelve thousand infantry, four thousand cavalry, and a hundred elephants. Regulus was not slow to accept the challenge, and a battle ensued which ended in a complete victory for the Carthaginians. The Roman soldiers, indeed, fully justified their reputation and proved themselves far superior to the infantry of Carthage. But they were borne down by an overwhelming charge of the elephants and trampled to death, or cut to pieces by the horsemen, except two thousand, who succeeded in making their escape to Clupea. Only five hundred were taken alive, and among these was the consul Regulus.

FIRST PUNIC WAR

DISASTER OF CAMARINA

When the news of this disaster reached Rome a fleet of three hundred and fifty vessels was dispatched to bring off the survivors, who were closely besieged at Clupea. Having met and dispersed the Carthaginian fleet, which had been hastily equipped for the occasion, the Roman commanders sailed to Clupea, took the garrison on board, and started at once on the return voyage. In this they were doubtless acting on their instructions, for all thought of continuing the war in Africa had now been abandoned. But disaster followed on disaster. The consuls had been warned by their pilots not to linger on the harbourless coast of southern Sicily; for it was now midsummer, between the rising of two stormy constellations,[1] when the navigation of these seas is rendered peculiarly dangerous by violent gales from the south-west. But the Roman commanders, with that dogged obstinacy which was at once the strength and the weakness of their nation, cared nothing for such warnings. They had business in this part of Sicily, and the powers of sea and sky must wait on their convenience.[2] They paid dearly for their rashness. Just as the great fleet was passing Camarina it was overtaken by so terrible a storm that three-fourths of the vessels were lost. Some foundered in the open sea, but the greater number were dashed to pieces on the rockbound coast, and the shore was strewn with corpses and wreckage.

PANORMUS TAKEN

Undismayed by this heavy blow, the Romans at once set about building another fleet, and within a few months two hundred and twenty new vessels were ready to put to sea. These, with the eighty ships which had survived the storm, made a fleet of three hundred sail, and the whole force was concentrated on Panormus[3] (254 B.C.), the most important naval station held by the Carthaginians in Sicily. They soon forced an entrance into the harbour-town, and after the

[1] Orion and the Dog-star.   [2] Polybius, i. 37.   [3] Palermo.

surrender of the upper city which lay farther inland, Panormus
was occupied by a Roman garrison. But it seemed as though
fortune were determined to hold the balance even between the
two contending powers. For next year the consuls were sent
with the whole naval force of Rome to make descents on the
African coast, and after narrowly escaping destruction on the
perilous sands of the Lesser Syrtis they were caught in a storm
on the home voyage and lost more than a hundred and fifty
ships. The Carthaginians were now once more masters of the
sea, for the Romans were so disheartened by their misfortunes
that they reduced the number of their fleet to sixty vessels,
for the protection of the coasts and the transport of troops
and supplies.

VICTORY OF PANORMUS

But even on land the fortunes of the Romans seemed to be
at a low ebb. Hasdrubal, who had been sent from Carthage to
take the command in Sicily, had brought with him a hundred
and forty elephants, and the defeat of Regulus had inspired
the Romans with such terror of these huge beasts that they
shrank from meeting the enemy in the open field. Observing
their state of mind, Hasdrubal determined to strike a decisive
blow, and advanced in force upon Panormus (250 B.C.), taking
with him all his elephants, and destroying the corn-crops,
which were ripe for harvest, as he went. But in the consul
Metellus, who held command at Panormus, he found an opponent equally prudent and daring. Metellus posted his heavy
infantry near one of the gates, ready for a sally, and lined the
walls and the moat with archers, slingers, and javelin-men.
Then he sent out light skirmishers, to draw the attack of the
elephants and lure them within range of the walls. The
elephants advanced, scattering their assailants before them,
but as they drew near the moat they were met by a storm of
arrows, javelins, and stones, and driven back, bellowing with
rage and pain, on the ranks of their own army. At this moment
of panic and confusion the gate was flung open, and Metellus,
placing himself at the head of his troops, charged the enemy in

flank and gained a complete victory. Not the least part of his achievement was the capture of the whole brigade of elephants, which were brought to Rome and made a conspicuous feature in the consul's triumphal procession.

LEGEND OF REGULUS

To this date belongs the famous legend of Regulus. The Carthaginians, we are informed, were so dismayed by their defeat at Panormus that they sent ambassadors to negotiate an exchange of prisoners and arrange terms of peace. With them went Regulus, who was to use his influence in forwarding the objects of the mission, and who was bound by a solemn oath to return to Carthage if the negotiation broke down. But from the hour when he left Carthage the stern Roman had taken his resolve. Arrived at Rome, he refused to enter the walls, alleging that he had forfeited all rights as a citizen. And when the Senate came out to confer with him he used all his influence to frustrate the purposes of the embassy. He was a broken man, he said, dishonoured by defeat, and he knew that his days were numbered, for his health was undermined by a slow poison. Let the Fathers take counsel for the best interests of their country, without regard to his own worthless life, or the lives of the unworthy men who were now living in captivity at Carthage. Then, seeing that his words had prevailed, he turned away and went to meet his doom. His friends pressed round him and strove to hinder his departure, and his wife and children clung to him with sobs and pitiful cries. But he remembered his oath and put them all aside, though he knew that he was going to a cruel and lingering death. And on his return to Carthage he was handed over to the executioners and expired under horrible tortures.

The story of the ex-consul's sufferings seems to have been invented in order to palliate the atrocious treatment of two noble Carthaginian prisoners, who were kept in confinement by the relations of Regulus and subjected to such horrible barbarities that the affair became a public scandal, until it was ended by the interference of the magistrates. In later

REPUBLICAN ROME

times the tragic fate of Regulus was appropriated by the teachers of rhetoric and worked up into the form which has been made familiar by the verses of Horace. Our chief authority, Polybius, passes the incident in silence.

LAST STAGE OF THE WAR

We now enter on the last stage of this long and weary struggle, and for the remaining eight years of the war our attention is concentrated on the western district of Sicily, where the Carthaginians had mustered all their strength at Drepanum and Lilybaeum to make a final stand against the Romans. Nearly a generation before the impregnable fortress of Lilybaeum had defied all the efforts of Pyrrhus, and it was now to be seen what Roman courage and skill could effect against the stubborn energy of the Punic leaders. Built on a promontory, in the extreme west of Sicily,

RAM AND TONGS

the town was defended on the land side by strong walls and towers and by a deep moat, and an enemy approaching by sea had to steer his way through a narrow channel beset by shallows and quicksands. Himilco, the Carthaginian commander, was a man of great ability and resolution, and the garrison, consisting of mercenaries, numbered ten thousand men.

SIEGE OF LILYBAEUM

The victory of Panormus had inspired the Romans with new hope, and they resolved to strike with all their force at the

176

centre of the Carthaginian position in Sicily. Accordingly, soon after that battle a fleet of two hundred ships, with both consuls in command, was dispatched to the seat of war, and the siege of Lilybaeum began. The besieging force outnumbered the garrison by ten to one, and the town was completely invested by sea and land. Furnished with a formidable train of siege-engines,the consuls steadily advanced their lines, and then brought up their battering-rams to beat down the walls. Breach after breach was made, and the Romans penetrated farther and farther into the town; but as fast as they demolished one rampart

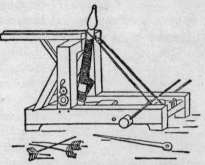

BALLISTA: AN ENGINE FOR HURLING STONES AND BLOCKS OF WOOD

Himilco threw up another. No incident of siege-warfare was omitted; there were mines and countermines, sallies and night assaults, and frequent attempts to destroy the Roman artillery by fire. Himilco was the soul of the defence, and the garrison, fired by his example, fought with desperate courage. The Romans, on their part, pushed the siege with undaunted energy, and such was the fury on both sides that the numbers slain in a single day's fighting often surpassed those of a pitched battle.

The siege had been prolonged for months and provisions began to run short in the town when unexpected succour arrived from outside. For the Carthaginians were growing anxious about the fate of Lilybaeum, and they sent an officer named Hannibal,[1] with a fleet of fifty ships and a strong force of troops, with instructions to run the blockade at all costs and carry relief to the besieged. Hannibal dropped anchor at the island of Aegusa, and having waited until the wind blew

[1] Not, of course, the great Hannibal, who was not born until three years later.

hard from the north-west, he hoisted all sail, manned his decks, and dashed boldly for the mouth of the harbour. The Romans who guarded the entrance were so surprised by his audacity that they allowed him to pass unmolested, and he brought his whole fleet safely into dock amid the shouts and

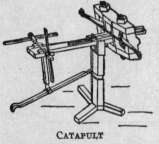

CATAPULT

clapping of the people, who had been anxiously watching his movements from the walls.

The example of Hannibal was successfully followed by several other captains, and communication was thus kept up with Carthage, and with Drepanum, which was now the chief Carthaginian naval station in Sicily. Misfortunes gathered thickly round the Romans as the first year of the siege drew toward its close. Taking advantage of a violent storm of wind, Himilco made a determined sally and set fire to the Roman siege-engines, which were completely destroyed. All hope of carrying the town by storm was now at an end, and the siege was turned into a blockade. But the ranks of the Roman army had been greatly thinned by long and severe fighting, and sickness broke out in the camp, owing to the scarcity of corn, which compelled the men to live chiefly on meat. Such a change of diet was most injurious to a native of Italy, who was nourished almost entirely on farinaceous and vegetable food. This cause of distress was, however, at length removed by the arrival of a supply of corn from Hiero.

BATTLE OF DREPANUM

Such was the state of things when Publius Claudius Pulcher, one of the new consuls, arrived at Lilybaeum to take over the command (249 B.C.). Claudius had little of the ability but more than his share of the overweening pride which distinguished his house. Despite the warnings of his staff, he prepared to attack the Carthaginian fleet, which was stationed at Drepanum under the command of Adherbal, an able and experienced officer. Just before his departure he was warned by the keepers of the sacred chickens that these birds had refused their food, a sure omen of ill-success. "If they will not eat, they shall drink," replied the impious consul, and he ordered them to be thrown into the sea. But his talents as a commander were not equal to his wit. By daybreak the Roman fleet was seen entering the long arm of the sea which forms the harbour of Drepanum. Adherbal was taken by surprise, but, acting with great promptitude and coolness, he set his fleet in motion and rowed with all speed along the opposite shore until he reached the mouth of the harbour. Then, wheeling suddenly, he fell upon the Roman ships, which were thus cut off from the open sea and thrown into confusion by the suddenness of the attack.

THE SACRED CHICKENS

The unworthy consul made his escape with twenty vessels, but all the rest, to the number of ninety-three, were captured with their crews, or run ashore and abandoned. Claudius, it seems, had neglected to supply his fleet with 'crows,' which had done such good service at Mylae and Ecnomus, and to this omission, added to his general incapacity, the Carthaginians owed the only great naval victory they could boast of in the whole course of the war.

ANOTHER DISASTER

Meanwhile another fleet was on its way from Italy, bringing supplies for the army besieging Lilybaeum. Warships and transports together, it numbered more than nine hundred vessels. The Carthaginian admiral, who was waiting for its approach on the southern side of Sicily, received warning from his pilots that a storm was brewing in the south, and by great efforts he contrived to round the headland of Pachynum and moor his ships in sheltered water. But the Romans, sailing blindly on, encountered the full fury of the tempest, and out of their vast fleet hardly a single vessel escaped destruction.

A Narrow Policy

The war had now lasted for fifteen years, and the Romans seemed to be farther from their goal than ever. Their recent heavy losses had once more disgusted them with the sea, and that part of the service was now left to the enterprise of private individuals, who fitted out galleys at their own expense to plunder the merchant ships of Carthage. But they clung doggedly to the land war, and the operations against Lilybaeum and Drepanum were still carried on, though little result was produced. On the whole, the advantage was undoubtedly on the side of the Carthaginians, and had they acted with vigour they might have brought the contest to a triumphant close. But the merchant princes who guided their fortunes were incapable of grasping any large and statesmanlike design. Their views were commercial, not military or political, and at the very crisis of the war, when the path of conquest lay open before them and a great man stood ready to lead the way, they showed the same sluggish and suspicious temper which in later times paralysed the genius of Hannibal.

Hamilcar Barca

The man of whom we speak was Hamilcar Barca, who now makes his first appearance on the stage of history. Hamilcar saw that the great need of the Carthaginians was a body of trained infantry able to meet the Roman legions on equal terms in the field. Being now appointed to the chief command in Sicily (247 B.C.), he applied himself with all his energies to supply this want. He chose as his centre of operations a lofty, isolated plateau, named Mount Hercte,[1] a few miles north of Panormus. The extensive plain which forms the top of the mountain is defended on all sides by precipitous cliffs, and commands the approach to a sheltered cove, with a convenient anchorage for ships. Here Hamilcar gathered a chosen band

[1] Monte Pellegrino.

of mercenary troops, and though encamped in the midst of
enemies he not only maintained his position, but kept his
communications open and made repeated assaults on the
Roman outposts. Nor did he confine his operations to Sicily,
but having a small fleet at his disposal he made repeated
descents on the western coast of Italy, which he plundered
as far as Cumae. After three years of incessant fighting he
succeeded in capturing the town of Eryx, which had been
occupied by the Romans shortly after the battle of Drepanum,
and here he continued the struggle for two years longer, though
the lofty hill above him was held by a Roman garrison and
another army lay encamped in the plain below.

Rome's Final Effort

Polybius, wishing to characterize the last stage of the
great duel between the rival cities, employs a homely but
striking image. He compares them to two fighting-cocks,
reduced to utter exhaustion by a long and furious battle. For
a while they stand glaring at each other, breathless and unable
to stir ; then one of them collects himself for a final effort,
leaps upon his antagonist, and dispatches him at a single
blow.[1] Thus the Romans, in the twenty-third year of the war
(242 B.C.), mustered their remaining energies for a decisive
stroke. Since the battle of Drepanum no naval operations on
a large scale had been attempted on either side. The Romans
were disgusted by their ruinous losses, and the Carthaginians,
who might have profited by their exhaustion, let the chance
slip and allowed their navy to fall into neglect. But now
Rome resolved once more to commit her fortunes to the sea.
By the patriotic efforts of the wealthier citizens, who advanced
the necessary funds out of their own private purses, a fleet of
two hundred quinqueremes was built and equipped. Early
in the year Caius Lutatius Catulus, one of the consuls, sailed
to Sicily, and, after strengthening the position at Lilybaeum,
prepared to lay siege to Drepanum. The arrival of so large
a force placed the Carthaginian garrisons at Drepanum and

[1] Polybius, i. 58.

Lilybaeum in great peril, and a fleet was hastily dispatched
from Carthage to their relief. Hanno, the commander, was
anxious to land his stores and get his ships into fighting
condition before hazarding an engagement. Accordingly he
put in at the island of Hiera, some thirty miles to the west of
Drepanum, and lay there waiting for a favourable wind. But
Lutatius was determined at all costs to bring on a battle before
the Carthaginian admiral could effect his purpose and establish communication with his friends ashore. For the terrible
Hamilcar was still at Eryx, and there was no telling what his
daring spirit might accomplish if Hanno were once allowed to
enter the harbour of Drepanum. Moreover, the Carthaginian
ships were ill-furnished and encumbered with their cargoes,
and their crews, recently enlisted, were hardly broken to the
oar, while the Roman fleet was admirably manned and served,
for Lutatius had employed the interval in carefully drilling
his men.

CARTHAGE SWEPT FROM THE SEA

Lutatius had been wounded in the fighting off Drepanum,
but he still kept the command, and gave his orders from a
sick-bed. On the evening before the tenth of March he
brought his fleet to anchor off the island of Aegusa, where he
could keep an eye on the enemy's movements. When day
broke a strong breeze was blowing from the west, raising a
heavy sea, and Hanno's fleet was sighted running before the
wind and heading straight for the harbour of Drepanum.
The weather was very unfavourable to the Romans, and for
a moment Lutatius hesitated. But the importance of bringing
on an immediate engagement overbore all other considerations,
and he gave the order to advance. In the teeth of the gale the
Roman galleys came on to the attack, and the Carthaginians,
when they saw them approaching, lowered their masts and
prepared for action. When once the squadrons had come to
close quarters the issue was not doubtful for a moment. In
nautical skill, in the quality of their fighting men, and even
in the construction of their vessels the Romans were now far

PLATE XXX. ERYX

Photo from "Aus dem class. Süden" (published by C. Coleman, Lübeck)

182

PLATE XXXI. TOMB OF SCIPIO BARBATUS

superior to their rivals, and though the Carthaginians fought bravely they were soon beaten, and a hundred and twenty of their vessels were captured or sunk.

END OF THE WAR

The last fleet of the Carthaginians had thus been swept from the seas, and their troops in Sicily were now threatened with destruction. Hamilcar, indeed, still remained in arms, and it might cost the Romans a long and exhausting campaign to bring him to submission. But Hamilcar knew that to continue the struggle under such conditions would be an act of desperation, and he was not the man to waste the resources of his country for nothing. Accordingly, when he was instructed by the home authorities to arrange terms of peace he yielded with a good grace, taking care that nothing dishonourable should be demanded from himself or his brave soldiers. Peace was finally arranged (241 B.C.) on the following terms : The Carthaginians agreed to evacuate Sicily and the Liparaean Islands, to pay an indemnity of 3200 talents (£790,000), and to restore all the Roman prisoners without ransom. The Romans, on their part, bound themselves not to meddle with the subjects of Carthage, and the independence of Hiero, whose kingdom occupied the south-eastern corner of the island, was secured. When the negotiation was completed Hamilcar laid down his command and handed over his troops to Gisco, who was commanding at Lilybaeum, for transmission to Carthage.

Thus ended the First Punic War, which, in the magnitude of the forces engaged, the losses sustained on both sides, and the length of the struggle, is the greatest naval war recorded in ancient history. The creation of a Roman navy was a gigantic effort, forced on the Romans by circumstances, and never attempted again on the same scale. That horror of the sea which is so feelingly expressed by Horace was deeply ingrained in the character of the nation, and the Romans remained to the end a land power. But though the contest extended over twenty-three years and entailed an enormous sacrifice of men and treasure, it was but a prelude to the greater struggle which was to follow. The invasion of Africa, which but for the folly of Regulus and the incompetence of Rome's advisers might have ended so differently, was a lesson not thrown away upon Hamilcar. Already, perhaps, he had conceived the bold plan of carrying the war into Italy and fighting out the quarrel before the gates of Rome. And while he was training his troops and upholding his country's cause in Sicily a child had been born to him, to be the inheritor of his designs and his rival in fame. That child was Hannibal, the Napoleon of antiquity, and a name of terror and hatred to the Romans as long as they remained a nation.

A SAILING VESSEL

CHAPTER IX

BETWEEN THE FIRST AND SECOND PUNIC WARS

A PERIOD of twenty-three years separates the First from the Second Punic War, and during this interval the Romans made steady progress in their career as a conquering and civilizing power. Three important tasks, all directed to the same end, successively claimed their attention. They had, first, to plant their feet firmly in Corsica and Sardinia, and thus secure command of the Tyrrhenian Sea. Secondly, they had to put down the pirates who infested the Adriatic, and, if possible, to establish a hold on the opposite mainland. Thirdly, they had to extend their conquest to the great northern plain, where the Gauls still dwelt unsubdued on both banks of the Po, and, in conjunction with their warlike kinsmen beyond the Alps, were a standing menace to the peace of Italy. All these enterprises were taken in hand, and almost brought to a conclusion, within the period of which we are speaking. But meanwhile a dark cloud had been gathering in the west, which suddenly burst in tempest over Italy, and for more than ten years [1] involved the Romans in a struggle for bare existence.

CARTHAGE AND THE MERCENARIES

At first, indeed, it seemed as if Carthage, humbled and weakened as she was by the recent war, must sink under the pressure of new calamities, which brought upon her sufferings far more terrible than any which the Romans had inflicted. It has already been mentioned that Hamilcar, after the

---

[1] 218–207 B.C. (defeat of Hasdrubal).

conclusion of peace, had handed over his troops to Gisco, the commander at Lilybaeum, for transmission to Carthage. Gisco well knew the danger which might arise from the presence of so large a body of these wild men in the unwarlike and wealthy city, and he therefore embarked the troops in separate detachments, according to their several nations, wishing to give the government time to pay them off separately and dismiss them to their homes. But his prudent purpose was frustrated by the folly of the home authorities, who allowed the whole army to remain in Carthage, and treated the men with unwise indulgence, in the hope of inducing them to remit a portion of their wages. The result was what Gisco had foreseen. The soldiers, growing mutinous and disorderly, began to commit outrages in the city, and in order to rid the capital of a nuisance they were sent away to Sicca, an inland town about a hundred miles from Carthage, consecrated to the worship of the Phoenician Venus. Surrounded by all the seductions of the Love City, the soldiers abandoned themselves to lawless pleasure, or employed themselves in calculating the arrears of pay due to them from Carthage, the sum of which grew from day to day. Presently Hanno, the suffete, appeared on the scene, and attempted to satisfy their claims; but he only succeeded in embroiling matters further, and the soldiers, convinced that he was trying to cheat them, broke up their camp and, marching back to the coast, took up their quarters at Tunes, within a day's march from Carthage.

The Carthaginians were now seriously alarmed, and they sent Gisco, who was popular among the mercenaries, with full authority to pay them off and disband the whole force, whose numbers amounted to more than twenty thousand. But it was too late. The long delay and the growing suspicion of bad faith had totally relaxed the bonds of discipline and kindled the worst passions in the hearts of these rude swordsmen. And meanwhile they had found two leaders who sedulously undermined the good influence of Gisco and fostered the seeds of discontent. One of these was Spendius, a runaway Cam-

186

panian slave, who was determined to effect a complete rupture with Carthage, knowing that if the troops were disbanded he would be sent back to Rome, where a death by lingering torture awaited him. He found an able ally in Mathos, leader of the Libyans, who composed the main body of the army. Mathos pointed out to his countrymen that if the foreign troops were dismissed the whole vengeance of Carthage would fall upon themselves, whose homes and families lay at the doors of their perfidious masters. Meanwhile Spendius was busy in the camp, visiting each contingent in turn, and holding out a prospect of unbounded licence if only they would throw away scruples and stretch out their hands to seize the rich booty which was offered to their grasp. These speeches, added to the natural ferocity of the soldiers, made them ready for any act of desperation, and being provoked by a hasty word from Gisco they laid hold of him and his staff and threw them into chains.

THE TRUCELESS WAR

Such were the circumstances which led to the Truceless War (241–238 B.C.), so called from the peculiar ferocity with which it was waged on both sides. The details, constituting one of the darkest chapters in ancient history, may be read in the vivid narrative of Polybius, or in the modern reproduction of Flaubert,[1] who has combined fact with fiction to exhibit a picture of exaggerated and unnatural horror. The revolt spread to all the dependent districts of Libya, and for three years the Carthaginians endured the extremities of famine, terror, and distress. At length the unrivalled patience, courage, and craft of Hamilcar succeeded in making head against the greatest peril that had ever threatened his country. Forty thousand of the mutineers were entrapped in a mountain defile, and cut off to a man. Spendius ended his days on the cross, and Mathos, who had made a last stand at Tunes, was brought in chains to Carthage, where the citizens celebrated

[1] In his *Salammbô*.

their triumph by feasting their eyes on the dying agonies of the savage but dauntless Libyan.

Rome seizes Sardinia

The most important result of the mutiny, so far as concerned the Romans, was the acquisition of Sardinia. Following the example of their kinsmen in Africa, the mercenary troops stationed in that island broke into revolt, and crucified the Carthaginian officer who was sent to bring them to obedience. But they in their turn were driven out by a rising of the natives, and took refuge in Italy. By the terms of the late peace Rome was expressly prohibited from interfering with the possessions of Carthage, but the temptation was too strong for Roman virtue, and a force was dispatched to occupy the island. A remonstrance from Carthage was met by a declaration of war, and the Carthaginians, exhausted by the recent contest in Africa, were in no condition to take up the challenge. Far from attempting to assert their claims by force of arms, they were glad to purchase peace by the cession of Sardinia and the payment of twelve hundred talents to Rome. Apart from its importance as a naval station and its abundant grain-harvests, the Romans derived little advantage from the occupation of Sardinia, for the island was notoriously unhealthy, while the character of the natives, dull, brutal, and lazy, made them useless even as slaves, so that " Sards for sale, one worse than the other," became a proverb for something worthless. Some years later (231 B.C.) Corsica and Sardinia, united as one province, were formally incorporated with the Roman dominions.

The Provincial System

It is from this period (238–227 B.C.) that we have to date the beginning of the Roman provincial system, which reached its full development under the reign of Augustus. We have already spoken of the three different degrees of relationship existing between the various communities of Italy and the central government at Rome, the full Roman citizenship, the

188

restricted or Latin citizenship, and the Italian alliance. The three political groups involved in this distinction were viewed as concentric circles, and the amount of privilege enjoyed by each depended on its degree of proximity to the common centre. To these three divisions we have now to add a fourth, the class of provincial or subject communities in Sardinia, Corsica, and Sicily. Speaking generally, the difference between the Italian allies and the inhabitants of the provinces lay in the fact that the former served Rome with their arms, the latter with their purses. The Italians sent their military contingents to fight under Roman generals, the provincials paid a fixed tribute, and were prohibited from bearing arms, except in the case of actual invasion. But here, as in Italy, the Romans remained faithful to the imperial maxim, " Divide and govern." Special privileges were conferred on some of the Sicilian cities which had adhered to Rome during the late war with Carthage, and among these communities were the bandits of Messana, who were admitted to the same position as the Italian allies. The principle of isolation, which we first noticed more than a century back, at the conclusion of the Latin War, was strictly observed in the treatment of the Sicilians. No native of Sicily could henceforth acquire property outside the territory of his own city, and the same rule was possibly extended to marriage. This cruel restriction resulted in a general crippling of native commercial enterprise, and paved the way to the fearful abuses which are described in such moving terms by Cicero.

THE PIRATES OF ILLYRIA

The annexation of Corsica and Sardinia was hardly completed when the Romans were called upon to turn their arms against the fierce tribes of Illyria,[1] whose piratical habits had long rendered them a terror to the coast towns of Epirus and western Greece. Under the rule of Agron, who was in alliance with Macedon, these vikings of the Adriatic had pursued their wild trade with unparalleled audacity, and after his death,

---

[1] Dalmatia, Montenegro, and Northern Albania.

REPUBLICAN ROME

which took place during a drunken orgy following a successful raid, his widow Teuta authorized her subjects to regard any foreign merchant ship as lawful booty. Unfortunately for her, they took this permission as extending to the trading vessels of Italy, and naturally the Romans, as a sovereign people, could not put up with a nuisance of this kind. Ambassadors were accordingly sent to Teuta to demand satisfaction for the damage inflicted on Italian commerce. They found her in her court at Scodra,[1] and made their complaint. The barbarian queen behaved with great haughtiness and insolence, disclaiming all responsibility for the outrages she had instigated, and coolly adding that she had no right to interfere with the private enterprises of her subjects. " If that be the case, madam," replied Coruncanius, one of the envoys, " we must teach you to manage your affairs better." He had, however, to pay dearly for his plain speaking, for Teuta, incensed by the taunt, caused him to be assassinated on his way home. As a further act of defiance, she recommenced her piratical operations on a larger scale, and sent out a fleet to attack the Greek towns of the eastern Adriatic. After an unsuccessful attempt on Epidamnus,[2] the Illyrians obtained possession of Corcyra,[3] which received a garrison, commanded by Demetrius of Pharos, a Greek adventurer in the service of the queen.

Illyria Subdued

But Teuta soon learnt that Roman envoys were not to be murdered or Roman dignity insulted with impunity. At the beginning of the next year (229 B.C.) the two consuls were sent with a fleet of two hundred ships and twenty thousand troops to put down the freebooters of Illyria. With so overwhelming a force at their disposal they found their task an easy one. Corcyra was promptly surrendered by Demetrius, who had fallen into disfavour with Teuta, and Epidamnus and Apollonia placed themselves under the protection of Rome. The army then marched through the interior, subduing town after town and receiving the submission of the natives, while

[1] Scutari.   [2] Dyrrachium, Durazzo.   [3] Corfu.

the fleet proceeded along the coast, driving before it the scattered remnant of the piratical galleys. Before the end of the year Teuta was shut up in her last stronghold, and at the beginning of the following spring she made peace with Rome, consenting to give up a great part of her territories, to disband her fleet, and to pay a fixed tribute. The conquered districts were placed under the government of the renegade Demetrius.

GREECE AND ROME

The Romans had thus accomplished the second of the three tasks which awaited them at the close of the First Punic War. They had asserted the cause of law and order in the Adriatic and established relations with the Greek coast towns. Corcyra, Epidamnus, and Apollonia were now formally received into alliance, and complimentary messages were exchanged with the Aetolian and Achaean Leagues, which now represented the last vestige of free political life in Greece. Accustomed for more than a century to the presence of a foreign master, the Greeks had become adepts in the servile art of flattery, and two of their most famous cities now took the lead in paying honour to these dangerous allies. At Corinth a decree was passed (228 B.C.) admitting the Romans to the Isthmian Games, and the Athenians, carrying their complaisance still farther, gave them the right of initiation into the holy mysteries of Eleusis. It was the first explicit recognition of the Romans as a genuine branch of the old Hellenic stock which was afterwards preached as an article of faith by the pious Dionysius.

Nine years later, when Rome was preparing for the great struggle with Hannibal, the fickle Demetrius transferred his allegiance to Antigonus, king of Macedon, and attacked the Roman territories in Illyria which had been entrusted to his care. But Antigonus, who had extended his dominions over a great part of Greece, died shortly afterwards, and his youthful successor Philip was embarrassed by a war with the Aetolians and their allies. The Romans were thus enabled to

deal with Demetrius alone, and one campaign sufficed to
re-establish their influence in Illyria. Demetrius was driven
into exile, and passed the rest of his life at the court of
Macedon.

NORTHERN ITALY

We must now go back a little and trace the course of events
in northern Italy since the conclusion of the First Punic War.
After the conquest of the Senones, Italy, considered as a
political unit, was bounded on the north by the rivers Rubicon
and Arno. Setting aside the Ligurians, of whom we shall
speak presently, the whole country beyond these limits was
occupied by the Gauls and their neighbours the Veneti, whose
territory, starting from the Istrian peninsula in the east, took
in a great part of the Adige valley and extended south as far
as the delta of the Po. This noble province, surpassing in
wealth and dimensions many a modern kingdom, was still
foreign soil to the Romans, on which their legions had hardly
set foot. Its unrivalled fertility, which offered a prospect of
boundless riches, excited the admiration of the historian
Polybius some fifty years later, when he passed several years
in Italy as an involuntary guest of the Romans. The vast
plain, which tires the eye of the modern visitor with a sense
of endless monotony, was still broken in many places by tracts
of primeval forest, where immense herds of swine were fattened
on the beech-mast and acorns. Where the forests had been
cleared all kinds of grain afforded a rich return to the industry
of the inhabitants, and provisions of all sorts abounded.

The Gauls who occupied this favoured land were divided
into various tribes, the chief of which were the Boii, who
dwelt on the northern edge of the Apennines, the Insubres,
whose political centre was at Mediolanum, the Lingones, along
the lower course of the Po, and the Cenomani, on the northern
skirts of the plain, from Bergamo to Verona. Of these the
Cenomani were in alliance with Rome, and their support was
to prove invaluable in the coming struggle with the three
hostile tribes. Even more important was the ready friendship

of the Veneti, a people akin to the Illyrians, whose timely invasion of the Gaulish territory had hastened the retirement of Brennus (see p. 85), and thus relieved the Romans in their direst extremity.

RISINGS AMONG THE GAULS

Since their last defeat by the Romans the Gauls had remained quiet for nearly half a century (282–238 B.C.). But in the same year which saw the cession of Sardinia they began to renew their aggressions, knowing, perhaps, that the Romans had resolved on their destruction, and wishing to strike the first blow. Several battles were fought without decisive result, and two years' later a more formidable coalition, in which the Transalpine Gauls took part, was ended by a quarrel between the Boii and these new-comers, who turned their swords against each other, and thus did the work of the Roman army which had been raised to meet their attack. After an interval of four years a general rising began (232 B.C.), which spread to all the hostile tribes between the Alps and the Apennines. The immediate cause of this outbreak was a measure carried by the tribune Flaminius, to distribute among Roman citizens the land acquired by the conquest of the Senones. The new settlement, composed of their hereditary enemies, and planted on their very borders, excited the alarm of the Boii, and, uniting with the Insubres, they prepared to make a determined stand against the usurping power of Rome. They enlisted in their service a large body of Gaulish free-lances called the Gaesatae,[1] who were drawn from their home in the Rhone valley by the offer of large pay and the prospect of a rich booty.

Knowing that they were about to enter on a struggle for life and death, the Gauls acted with great deliberation, and several years elapsed before they were ready to take the field. It was a busy and anxious time for the Romans, whose labours grew heavier as the circle of their empire expanded. The Illyrian War was in progress, the rude natives of Corsica and Sardinia had risen in revolt against their new masters, and the

[1] From *gaesum*, 'a spear.'

REPUBLICAN ROME

long contest with the Ligurians had recently begun. A more serious cause of disquiet was the advance of the Carthaginians in Spain, where Hamilcar had been building up a new empire, which seemed to threaten possibilities of boundless aggression. As was usual in times of great public excitement, rumours of dire portents and prodigies were afloat, and an oracle was in all men's mouths which foretold that the Gauls and the Greeks should one day take up their abode in the Forum at Rome. But Roman cunning found a way to evade the impending disaster, by fulfilling the letter of the oracle, and so frustrating the purposes of heaven. Two Gauls and two Greeks, a man and a woman of either race, were buried alive in the cattle-market, to dwell there for ever, as the gods had promised.

Rome's Vast Preparations

After this sacrifice to the Moloch of superstitious terror, the Romans turned to count up and organize the military resources at their disposal. And here, indeed, they had a more reasonable ground for confidence. A general call to arms was issued throughout Italy, and it was met by a ready and hearty response, for all grievances were forgotten in the face of so imminent a peril, and Umbrians and Etruscans, Samnites and Campanians, were united to defend their common country against the savage Gaul. Officers were sent round to draw up a list of the men fit for military service throughout the peninsula, and the grand total, including Romans and Italians, amounted to seven hundred thousand infantry and seventy thousand horse. Such, says Polybius, was the mighty power which Hannibal ventured to attack a few years later, with an army numbering less than twenty thousand men.[1]

The Northern Campaign

About a fourth of this vast force was called out for active service, while the rest was employed in garrison duty, or held in reserve. One of the consuls, Caius Atilius, who was fighting in Sardinia, received orders to return without delay, while the

[1] Polybius, ii. 24. In iii. 56 he gives the number as twenty-six thousand.

other, Lucius Aemilius, with a full consular army, took up
his position at Ariminum, to guard the eastern coast route.
Another army, composed of Sabines and Etruscans, and commanded by a praetor, advanced into Etruria, and it was here
that the decisive engagement took place (225 B.C.). The Gauls,
wishing to avoid an encounter with Aemilius, marched rapidly
through the central passes of the Apennines, and, entering
Etruria, passed on unopposed as far as Clusium, plundering
and burning as they went. Here they were brought to a
stand by the praetor, who had made a hasty retrograde movement on perceiving that the enemy had got between him and
Rome. The Gauls then fell back toward Faesulae, leaving
their cavalry to cover their retreat, and the Roman general,
pursuing them incautiously, allowed himself to be drawn into
an ambuscade and suffered a severe defeat. The Roman force
was only saved from total destruction by the arrival of
Aemilius, who had quitted his position at Ariminum as soon
as he learnt that the Gauls were on the march toward Rome.
Laden with spoil and anxious to secure their treasure, the
Gauls were in no mind to renew the engagement, and as the
route by which they had come was blocked by the consul's
army, they moved off toward the western coast, intending to
escape by the passes of Liguria. Aemilius, having united his
own forces with those of the praetor, followed their march,
and the two armies, pursuers and pursued, had advanced as
far as Telamon when the Gauls found their way barred by a
new and unexpected enemy. For the consul Atilius had just
landed at Pisa, bringing his troops from Sardinia, and was
marching southward by the coast route, when he fell in with
the advance-guard of the Gaulish force. In this desperate
situation the Gauls behaved with great courage and coolness,
and, forming a double front, they prepared to fight both armies
at once. All the wild valour of the Celt came out in that
terrible conflict. The fierce spearmen of the Rhone flung off
their garments and went into battle naked, and for a moment
their strange aspect and their savage yells, mixed with the
blare of innumerable horns and trumpets, shook the firm

195

courage of the Romans. But long habits of discipline soon prevailed, and the cupidity of the Roman soldiers was inflamed by the sight of the gold collars and bracelets which adorned the enemy. In spite, therefore, of the most desperate resistance the battle soon became a massacre, and when evening fell forty thousand Gaulish warriors lay dead on the field. The engagement was further signalized by the capture of one Gaulish chieftain, the suicide of another, and the death of the consul Atilius, who fell fighting among the cavalry.

Elated by this great victory, the Romans resolved to push the war with vigour, and to complete the conquest of Italy by carrying their frontier to the foot of the Alps. One campaign sufficed to secure the submission of the Boii (224 B.C.), and in the following year Flaminius, who had been elected consul by the favour of the people, crossed the Po and invaded the country of the Insubres. The narrative of this campaign seems to have been coloured by political prejudice. Flaminius had incurred the implacable hostility of the nobles by his popular measure for the distribution of the Gallic lands, and on the eve of battle he received a dispatch from the Senate ordering him and his colleague, who was acting with him, to return. For signs and wonders had recently appeared in the sky, and the augurs pretended that the consular election had been vitiated by unfavourable omens. Flaminius guessed the contents of the dispatch, and left it unopened until the battle had been fought and won. He had already, we are informed, stained the honour of a consul by breaking faith with the Insubres, who had defeated him and allowed him to retire under a truce into the country of the Cenomani. Before the armistice had expired he reinforced his army with a contingent of the friendly Gauls and fell suddenly upon the Insubres before they were prepared. Though taken by surprise, the Insubres rushed to arms with alacrity, and fought with great resolution; but the wretched quality of their broadswords, which bent at the first stroke,[1] and their want of defensive armour, placed

[1] See the curious passage in Polybius, ii. 33, who compares the weapon thus disabled to the crooked piece of metal used as a flesh-scraper after bathing.

them at a great disadvantage, and they were utterly defeated.
Next year they rallied again, and, aided by thirty thousand
mercenaries from the Rhone valley, made a last determined
stand for their liberty. The fight was long and stubborn, and
the Gauls gave much trouble to the two consuls who had been
sent against them; but after the fall of their capital, Mediolanum, they were compelled to submit. It was during this
campaign that the consul Claudius Marcellus won the *spolia
opima*[1]—the third and last time in Roman history this
honour was gained—by slaying the Gaulish king and stripping
him of his splendid armour.

One important result of these victories was to cut off the
Celtic tribes beyond the Po from their southern kinsmen.
The Transpadane district remained long unsettled, and was
exposed to constant raids from the wild natives of the Alps,
until these latter were finally subdued in the reign of Augustus.
Living thus in the midst of danger, and retaining their hardy
and simple habits, the Gauls of this region furnished splendid
material for recruiting the Roman legions in the days of the
later Republic. From them Caesar drew the flower of his
troops, and when he made his famous march on Rome it was
not without reason that he was described as a second Brennus.[2]
Very different was the fate of the southern tribes, who dwelt
between the Apennines and the Po. Here the Romans pursued
the policy that had guided them in their treatment of the
Senones, which aimed at rooting out the native population
by making large assignments of land to Roman settlers. Two
frontier fortresses, at Cremona and Placentia, were designed
to guard the line of the Po, and the latter town, with Parma,
Mutina, and Bononia, afterwards formed a continuous line
of forts, connected with Ariminum by the Aemilian Way.
These extensive works were interrupted by the invasion of
Hannibal, but the completion of the great northern road,
which had been begun during the Samnite wars, belongs to
the date which we have now reached (220 B.C.). It was now

---

[1] Plutarch, *Marcellus*, c. 7.
[2] Nissen, *Italische Landeskunde*, i. 483.

carried across the Apennines, and, descending their eastern slope along the valley of the Metaurus, followed the coast-line from the mouth of that river until it finished its course at Ariminum. The honour of naming this great military highway, which rivalled the fame of the Appian, was reserved for the champion of popular rights, Flaminius.

THE LIGURIANS

It is during this period that we begin to hear of wars with the Ligurians, whose name hardly occurs in the earlier annals of Rome. They were a very ancient people, and at a time previous to the Aryan migration their territory extended from Pisa to Marseilles. But they were gradually driven back by the advance of the Celts and confined to the barren hill-country above the Gulf of Genoa which bears their name. Here they remained unmolested for centuries, wringing from that stony and ungrateful soil a scanty subsistence, eked out by occasional hunting and fishing. The descriptions of the ancient writers enable us to form a singularly vivid picture of their physical character and manner of life. In strong contrast to the huge, brawny Celt, the Ligurian was short in stature, tough, sinewy, and active, and possessed of indomitable courage and endurance. The women had the strength and activity of men, and the men of wild beasts.[1] The Ligurians were skilled mountaineers, bold sailors, and expert in the use of the sling. Living in rude huts or mountain caves and inured to toil and privation, they clung to their wild freedom with fierce tenacity, and two centuries elapsed before they were finally subdued and brought within the pale of Roman civilization.

THE DEVELOPING EMPIRE

Looking back on the events of the last twenty years, the Romans might well view with complacency the work they had accomplished. By the acquisition of Sardinia and Corsica they had obtained command of the western sea and abolished the commercial monopoly of Carthage, and their victories over

[1] Posidonius, cited by Nissen.

the Illyrians had established their authority in the Adriatic. The Gaul was put down, and that ever-recurring terror which for generations past had haunted the slumbers of many an Italian household seemed to have been banished for ever.

CARTHAGE TAKES NEW ROOT

But this expansion of Roman power had been accompanied, step by step, by a corresponding growth in her humbled and vanquished rival. The loss of Sicily, and the cession of Sardinia, extorted from his country in the days of her weakness, had left a deep impression on the proud heart of Hamilcar, and after the successful conclusion of the war with the mercenaries, which was effected solely by his genius and prudence, he began to nourish new plans of conquest and vengeance. The events of these three terrible years had thrown into a glaring light the selfishness, cowardice, and incompetence of the Carthaginian oligarchs, and made it plain that the future of Carthage depended on the house of Barcas.[1] By the favour of the people Hamilcar was appointed to the supreme command of the army, with a commission to levy war on the free tribes of north-western Africa. But Hamilcar had far wider views, and he was resolved not to be bound by the terms of his commission. His eyes had long been turned toward the rich country of Spain, which offered a new field of enterprise, where he could develop his grand designs untrammelled by the venal multitude or the corrupt rulers of Carthage. Accordingly he shipped his troops across the strait and landed on the great peninsula, which had never yet been trodden by the foot of an invader. Partly by policy and partly by force of arms he overcame the resistance of the warlike Iberians, and at the time of his death, which occurred eight years later, the whole eastern and southern district had become a Punic province. His plans were carried on by his son-in-law Hasdrubal, who extended his conquest as far as the Ebro and founded the city of New Carthage,[2] which soon became a great strategic and commercial

---

[1] Barcas—Hebrew *barak*, ‘lightning.’   [2] Cartagena.

REPUBLICAN ROME

centre, drawing a large revenue from the tin- and silver-mines
in the neighbourhood.

ADVENT OF HANNIBAL

Hamilcar's dream had thus been realized, and the empire
of Carthage, transplanted to the West, had struck deep root
and grown with astonishing rapidity. It was a memorable
work of creative genius, and for some years the Romans,
absorbed in their own affairs, suffered it to go on unchecked.
But the foundation of New Carthage opened their eyes to the
peril threatening from Spain, and they entered into an alliance
with Saguntum, a town of supposed Greek origin, and bound
Hasdrubal by a treaty not to carry his arms beyond the Ebro.
In the years which followed their attention was fully occupied
by the Gallic war, and Hasdrubal was left to pursue his plans
unhindered, until his career was cut short by the hand of an
assassin. But this event, which seemed to promise relief to
the Romans, let loose upon them the storm which had been
slowly gathering for the last seventeen years. For by the
unanimous voice of the army the young Hannibal was appointed
to the supreme command in Spain, and he took up his father's
work with more than his father's genius, and with a hatred
which had burned with a fiercer and still fiercer heat since first
it was kindled at the altar-fire of Carthage.

CHAPTER X

THE SECOND PUNIC WAR: I. FROM THE SIEGE OF SAGUNTUM TO THE BATTLE OF CANNAE

HAMILCAR and his son-in-law Hasdrubal had founded in southern Spain a great dominion, over which they ruled with almost kingly sway, and which might in some sort be regarded as an hereditary possession of their house. This power now passed to Hannibal, and with it he inherited from his father a legacy of undying hatred toward Rome. This was the guiding motive of his life, which governed all his actions, from the day when he repeated the famous oath from his father's lips to the day when he was hunted from his last refuge by the implacable rancour of the Romans. Growing up in the camp under the eye of Hamilcar, and familiar from his earliest years with the perils and privations of a soldier's life, he learned to combine in an extraordinary degree the talents of a consummate strategist and tactician with the hardihood and endurance of a common man-at-arms. Often after a hard day's fighting he would wrap himself in his soldier's cloak and snatch a short interval of repose stretched on the ground by a picket fire, and his simple and hardy habits and his ever-ready humour made him the darling of the rude men who followed his fortunes. But apart from his military talents, in which he has been surpassed by no general of ancient or modern times, Hannibal was a profound politician, and followed with vigilant eye the progress of events in all the chief countries of the Mediterranean. He was a master of Greek, the diplomatic language of the age, and his spies kept him constantly informed of the state of

parties and the characters of the leading men in Italy and
Greece. The knowledge thus obtained enabled him to avail
himself of every turn in the political currents of the time
and to change his plan of campaign according to the temper
of the general sent against him. Above all he knew, like
Caesar, how to astonish and paralyse his opponents by the
lightning rapidity of his movements, and this gave him a
great advantage in the earlier stages of his struggle with
Rome.

PLANS FOR THE INVASION OF ITALY

Hannibal was twenty-six years of age when he was called
to the supreme command in Spain (221 B.C.). After settling
the affairs of the great Carthaginian province and establishing
his authority as far as the Ebro, he entered on the great task
of his life, and formed his plans with the comprehensive grasp
of a veteran strategist and statesman. In Spain his power
was almost unlimited, and it was to Spain, accordingly, rather
than to Carthage that he looked for constant supplies of men
and money. Italy was to be invaded, and the invasion must
be made by land, for Hannibal would not commit his fortunes
to the precarious chances of the sea, even if the Carthaginian
fleet had been in a condition to provide for the adequate
convoy of his great army. His agents had been at work
among the disaffected tribes of the Po valley, and he was assured
that when once he had the Alps behind him the Gauls would
flock in thousands to his standard, eager to share in the
conquest and plunder of Rome. But his hopes beyond the
Alps were not based only on the fickle Celt. He expected to
raise a general insurrection among the Italian allies of Rome,
who, he believed, were chafing under intolerable oppression
and ready to hail the deliverer as soon as he appeared in their
midst. Nor did his designs end here, for he hoped to enlist
a powerful ally against the Romans on the other side of the
Adriatic. The young Philip had recently ascended the throne
of Macedon, and the monarchs of that country were the hereditary enemies of Greece. The Romans, in their character as

SECOND PUNIC WAR

champions of Greek liberty, were likely to be obnoxious to
Philip, and if he could work successfully on this feeling Hannibal
might expect to see a Macedonian phalanx fighting side by
side with the armies of Africa and Spain. Effective support
from Carthage formed, perhaps, the smallest part in Hannibal's
calculations, but the home government had undertaken to
send out a fleet with orders to make descents on the coasts
of Italy and Sicily. Thus the grand scheme of conquest was
complete on every side, and the proud city which had dared
to lift its head so high was to be overwhelmed by a storm of
war gathering from all the four quarters of heaven.

Hannibal takes Saguntum

Two years were employed by Hannibal in maturing his
plans and completing his preparations, and the Romans,
though they received ample warning of their danger, suffered
him to proceed unmolested. They had yet to learn the
character of the man with whom they had to deal, and they
thought, no doubt, that when they had time they could strike
down this presumptuous youth with a single blow. Accordingly they turned their attention to Illyria, where fresh troubles
had broken out, owing to the restless ambition of the traitor
Demetrius. Nor were their eyes opened when news arrived
that Hannibal was laying siege to Saguntum. They were
indignant, indeed, and astonished at this wanton attack on
their friends and allies, and they had already warned Hannibal
not to meddle with those districts of the Spanish peninsula
which were under their protection. But while they were
protesting and negotiating Hannibal was acting. He had as
little regard for treaties as had been shown by the Romans
themselves when they had fraudulently annexed Sardinia, and
he replied with bitter scorn and anger to the peremptory
message from Rome. The capture of Saguntum was an
essential part of his plan, for the place was strongly fortified
and it would have been a fatal error to leave so important a
position in the hands of his enemies. Moreover, he wished to
replenish his coffers with the plunder of the town, which would

203

afford a rich largess for his troops and enable him to stop
the mouths of his political opponents at Carthage. The siege
was therefore pressed with desperate energy, and though the
Saguntines resisted with all the heroic valour of their race [1] they
were slowly driven inward, as line after line of their defences
was stormed and destroyed. They looked for help from Rome,
but no help came, and after a siege of eight months their last
stronghold was carried (218 B.C.). It was the first great
blunder of the Romans, who should have made the cause of
the Saguntines their own instead of wasting their energies
in Illyria. If they had struck with all their force at this
critical moment Hannibal, indeed, might never have crossed
the Pyrenees.

CARTHAGE DECLARES FOR WAR

The most difficult part of Hannibal's task was to obtain
the support of his countrymen in his own forward and aggressive policy. In this he had to a large extent succeeded, and
for the present his influence was in the ascendant at Carthage.
Accordingly, when ambassadors arrived from Rome with a
peremptory demand for the surrender of Hannibal and his
chief officers they found the Carthaginians in no mood for
listening. A long debate was held in the Carthaginian Senate,
and the speakers who stated the case for Carthage, refraining
at first from provocatory language, tried to justify the action
of Hannibal on grounds of international law. But the time
for argument and negotiation was now past, and the Roman
envoys persisted in their sharp alternative, the surrender of
Hannibal or immediate war. "Here," said Fabius, the senior
member of the embassy, holding up a fold of his gown, "I
bring you peace or war. Choose which you will have." "Let
it be war then," cried a majority of the senators, who little
guessed that with this word they were pronouncing the doom
of Carthage.

[1] The Saguntines were Iberians, not, as is commonly asserted, Greeks.
See Niese, *Grundriss der römischen Geschichte*, p. 110, n. 1.

SECOND PUNIC WAR

The Muster at New Carthage

Meanwhile Hannibal was making his last preparations for the invasion of Italy. To secure the tranquillity of Spain during his absence, a body of troops newly drafted from Africa was placed under the command of his brother Hasdrubal, while a contingent of Spanish troops was sent across the strait to act as the army of defence in Africa. The object of this exchange was to diminish the temptation to revolt, a danger never far distant in the mercenary armies of Carthage; for the soldiers when quartered in a foreign station were more amenable to discipline, and each force served in some sort as a pledge for the fidelity of the other. At the beginning of spring a grand muster of troops was held at New Carthage, and then for the first time Hannibal made known his intention of marching against Rome. He had taken pains, he said, to collect information as to the route, and was informed that it was quite possible to lead an army across the Alps. The passage, indeed, was difficult, and not free from hazard, but when once this obstacle was surmounted they would be among the friendly Gauls, who were ready to help them with heart and hand against the oppressors of their nation. He painted in vivid colours the rich and happy land of Italy, with its olive-grounds and vineyards, its corn-lands, its abundant flocks and herds, and its prosperous cities; and all these good things, he said, should be theirs if they would follow him to victory.

Hannibal's Vision

The gloomy and fanatical religion of his people had a strong hold upon Hannibal, and just before setting out on his march for Italy he made a pilgrimage to Gades, the most ancient seat of Phoenician worship in the West, to fortify himself by prayer and sacrifice at the altar of Melcarth. He returned to New Carthage with his mind full of the god, and being now on the very eve of his departure he saw a strange vision. A youth of divine beauty appeared to him in the night, and told him that

205

he had been sent by the supreme deity to guide the son of Hamilcar to Italy. " Follow me," said the ghostly visitor, " and see that thou look not behind thee." Hannibal followed, and for some time, in obedience to the command, refrained from looking back, but presently, being overpowered by curiosity, he turned his head, and saw a gigantic serpent crashing through forest and thicket, and spreading ruin as he passed, while a black tempest gathered in his rear, with lightnings and deafening peals of thunder. When Hannibal asked the meaning of this portent the god replied : " What thou beholdest is the desolation of Italy. Follow thy star, and inquire no farther into the dark counsels of heaven."

The March Begins

Then the mighty host, numbering ninety thousand infantry and twelve thousand horse, was set in motion, and the great march began (218 B.C.). After crossing the Ebro Hannibal entered a hostile country, and the subjugation of this district as far as the Pyrenees involved a heavy loss both of men and of time. But the sacrifice had to be made, for if this part of the task had been neglected a vantage-ground would have been left to the Romans, who had already formed friendly relations with some of the northern tribes, and who were known to be meditating an attack on Spain. Eleven thousand troops were left under the command of Hanno to secure the recent conquest, and the same number, selected from the Spanish veterans, were discharged from service and sent with rich presents to their homes. In acting thus Hannibal showed himself both politic and generous, for he thereby increased the number of his friends in Spain and confirmed the loyalty of those remaining with him, who might hope to end their labours with equal honour and profit. By these withdrawals and by months of severe fighting his forces were reduced to fifty thousand infantry and nine thousand horse. But they were all picked men and devoted to their great leader, and the whole army was high in heart and hope when Hannibal passed the Pyrenees and pursued his march toward the Rhone.

PLATE XXXII. PONS MILVIUS

PLATE XXXIII. LAKE TRASIMENUS (THRASYMENE)
[*See page 223*]

SECOND PUNIC WAR

ROMAN PREPARATIONS

All through the spring and summer of that year the Romans had been making their preparations, in a leisurely and deliberate manner, thinking that they could choose their own time and place to meet and crush Hannibal. One of the consuls, Tiberius Sempronius, was ordered to proceed to Sicily, where he was to fix his headquarters at Lilybaeum and watch for an opportunity of carrying the war into Africa. His colleague Publius Cornelius Scipio, was appointed to take the command in Spain. Sempronius was the first to complete his levies, and he started for his province with a fleet of a hundred and sixty quinqueremes and a full consular army. But Scipio's departure was delayed by a rising among the Insubres and Boii, who had attacked the Roman colonists at Cremona and Placentia and compelled them to seek safety behind the walls of Mutina. The praetor, Manlius, who was commanding in that district marched to their relief, but he was defeated and chased into Tanetum, a town in the country of the Boii, and was now being held in close blockade. To complete their offence, the Gauls had made prisoners of three Roman commissioners who had been sent to superintend the distribution of lands, and whom they had lured out of Mutina under pretence of a parley. The tidings of this outbreak compelled Scipio to detach one of his legions for service in the disturbed district, and much time was lost before he could complete his levy and embark his troops for Spain.

FATAL DELAY

It was the fortune of the Romans during the whole of the eventful year which preceded their first encounter with Hannibal that they always came too late. They had suffered their allies at Saguntum to be destroyed, after an heroic defence which had lasted for eight months. They never attempted to interfere when Hannibal crossed the Ebro and engaged in a fierce struggle with the brave Spanish tribes, which cost him more than twenty thousand men. Until the

REPUBLICAN ROME

last moment they seemed to have no suspicion of his real purpose, thinking that the choice of a battlefield lay with them. They had sent one consul to look for him in Spain ; they had hoped, perhaps, to draw him into Africa ; and presently they heard to their amazement that he was already knocking at the gates of Italy. These routine politicians and military formalists were slow to learn that Hannibal was made to lead, not to follow, and for the first time in their history they became acquainted with a new and startling phenomenon, the swift decision and overpowering energy of a great and original mind.

SCIPIO'S MISTAKES

Scipio embarked his troops at Pisa, and proceeding, as usual, by the coast route, put in at the friendly harbour of Massilia [1] to rest and recruit his men, who had suffered severely on the voyage. Here he learnt that Hannibal had crossed the Pyrenees and was marching toward the Rhone. He pitched his camp on the left bank and sent out a party of light horse to gather intelligence of the enemy's movements. But once more Hannibal was too quick for his opponents. The Roman horsemen rode on up the river until they met with a troop of Numidian cavalry, who had been sent out by Hannibal on a similar errand. After a sharp skirmish they drove back the Numidians, and pursued their way until they came to a wide plain, which was covered with the tents and baggage of the Carthaginian army. One glance was sufficient, and, wheeling their horses, they rode back at full speed to inform Scipio that Hannibal had crossed the Rhone. Then Scipio made another mistake. Having once let his enemy slip through his hands, his proper course was to reship his army and make all haste to meet Hannibal in Italy. There he should have concentrated the whole available force of Rome, and should have fallen on the Carthaginian army when it emerged, broken and disorganized, from the passes of the Alps. But he wasted many days in a futile march up the Rhone, and reached the site of Hannibal's camp only to find that the whole force,

[1] Marseilles.

208

cavalry, infantry, and elephants, had departed three days
before. Pursuit was out of the question, and he accordingly
returned with all speed to the coast, dispatched his army,
under the command of his brother Cnaeus, to Spain, and set
sail himself for Pisa, to take charge of the Roman forces in
northern Italy. The consul doubtless showed personal courage
in thus hurrying to the scene of danger, but in withdrawing so
many troops from the home defence he was running a fearful
risk and smoothing the way for Hannibal's victorious march
through the peninsula. But he was an official pedant, bound
by the letter of his instructions. The army had been enlisted
for service in Spain, and to Spain it had to go.[1]

HANNIBAL REACHES THE RHONE

We must now resume the narrative of Hannibal's march
from the time when he left the Pyrenees. He encountered
little opposition on his way through southern Gaul, and after
following the coast route for some distance he turned inland
and reached the Rhone at a point distant about four days'
march from its mouth. Here he at once set about preparations for transporting his men across the river. Great numbers
of rude boats, hollowed out of the trunks of trees, and other
vessels of heavier burden, were purchased from the natives,
and as these proved insufficient many of the soldiers cut down
trees and shaped them into boats with such skill as they had.
But meanwhile the Gauls had been gathering in formidable
numbers on the opposite bank, with the evident intention of
disputing the passage. The danger was serious, and time was
pressing, but Hannibal found a means of extricating himself
from his difficulty. A picked body of troops was dispatched,
with orders to march up the river, to effect a crossing with all
possible speed, and to fall upon the enemy in the rear. Some
ten miles from the camp they found a place where the stream
was divided by an island, and here they crossed on rafts hastily

---

[1] This seems to be the view of Mommsen (vol. ii. p. 257 of the English
translation). Arnold (vol. iii. c. 43) speaks of Scipio's action in terms of
high praise.

constructed from the trees which lined the banks. They met
with no opposition, and after resting awhile they marched
down the left bank of the river.

CROSSING THE RHONE

Two days after the departure of the flying column a cloud
of smoke was seen rising on the opposite shore, and Hannibal
knew that his men had taken up a position in the rear of the
Gaulish army. Everything was now ready for the crossing,
and at a given signal the first division of boats pushed out
into the stream. The larger vessels had been moored some
way up the river, in order that they might break the force of
the current, and so facilitate the passage of the lighter craft.
These put out first, each containing a detachment of heavy
cavalry and a certain number of horses, saddled and equipped
for battle, while the rest of the horses were towed astern.
Below this screen a multitude of canoes advanced into the
smoother water, and rowed a race for the farther shore, where
the Gauls were gathered in dense masses, yelling defiance and
brandishing their weapons. The progress of the flotilla was
watched with intense anxiety by those who remained behind,
for on the success of this first venture depended the fate of the
whole army. But presently the Gauls were observed to relax
their threatening attitude and to cast uneasy glances in the
direction of their camp, where flames were beginning to arise.
It was the work of the flying column, and the barbarians,
assailed on both sides, and eager to save their property, were
easily dispersed. The crossing of the Rhone was now completed without further opposition, though great difficulty was
experienced in conveying the elephants, which were carried
on huge rafts covered with earth.

PASSAGE OF THE ALPS

Thus for the fourth time[1] the Romans had allowed their
enemy to outstrip them, and Hannibal had advanced another
stage toward his goal. It was now that the encounter occurred

[1] Saguntum, Ebro, Pyrenees, Rhone.

between Hannibal's Numidians and the reconnoitring party
of Scipio, and this was the first blood shed in the war. No
other incident of importance occurred for some days, during
which the army crossed the Isère, marched through the
territory of the Allobroges, and reached the western spurs of
the Alps. And now began the famous passage of the gigantic
mountain barrier, which, more even than Hannibal's greatest
victories, roused the wonder of his contemporaries and has
fixed the attention of posterity. The question of the exact
route followed by Hannibal has led to a famous controversy,
the details of which cannot be entered upon here. The weight
of authority still favours the Little St. Bernard, and one
consideration seems to be decisive in support of that view.
This pass led into the country of the Insubres, who were ready
to welcome the invader, and Hannibal, with his famished and
exhausted army, was bound to choose a route which would
bring him among friends.

Leaving the level country, Hannibal turned his face toward
the mountains, and encamped at the mouth of the western
pass. Before him stretched a narrow and perilous track,
winding along the mountain-side, and all the heights commanding the defile were thronged by the wild tribesmen of the
Alps, prepared to attack the army as soon as the ascent began.
If they had planned an ambush skilfully, and kept their design
secret, they might easily have destroyed the whole Carthaginian host. But Hannibal selected a body of light troops,
and, stealing a march in the darkness, when the natives had
retired to their homes, he occupied all the positions which they
had left undefended. At daybreak the signal was given to
strike camp, and the vast multitude began slowly and pain-
fully to ascend the steep mountain path. For some time
the natives, finding that they had been outmanoeuvred by
Hannibal, allowed the march to proceed without attempting
any hostile movement. But soon the prospect of so much
booty fired their cupidity, and swarming down the mountain-
sides they fell upon the advancing line. Forthwith the lonely
Alpine valley became a scene of wild confusion and uproar.

Assailed by the agile mountaineers on the rugged and slippery path, with a bare wall of rock on one side and a yawning precipice on the other, Hannibal's men could offer but a feeble resistance, and as they swayed to and fro hundreds were pushed over the edge and fell crashing in their armour to the torrent below. Many of the mules lost their footing and rolled into the abyss, carrying their burdens with them, and horses, driven frantic by wounds or terror, plunged hither and thither. Then Hannibal, seeing the helpless state of his army, left his position on the heights and cleared the way by a vigorous charge, killing most of the Gauls, and putting the rest to flight. Thus, after a heavy loss of life, and with a baggage-train sorely diminished, the army emerged from the perilous defile, and came into a wide valley, situated between Lake Bourget and the Isère.[1] Here was the chief centre of population of the district, and Hannibal gained possession of a Gaulish stronghold, with outlying hamlets, well stocked with corn and cattle, which had been deserted by his late assailants.

In the Heart of the Mountains

After a day's rest the march was resumed, and for three days the army advanced through a country which grew wilder and wilder as they neared the heart of the Alps. But new mischief was brewing in the mountains beyond. The news of Hannibal's march had reached the native tribes, and they laid a plot to destroy him. They sent men with boughs and garlands in token of peace, who offered to guide him through the difficult country he was approaching and to provide food for his army. Hannibal, though he suspected treachery, thought it better to accept their help, and in two days they brought him to the mouth of a narrow gorge, through which, they assured him, lay the only possible route. The place was a very death-trap, but Hannibal had no choice but to proceed, and placing his cavalry and baggage in the van and his heavy infantry in the rear he advanced. This prudent disposition of his forces

[1] Arnold, Mommsen.

saved him from disaster. No sooner had the last man entered the ravine than the natives began a fierce attack from the surrounding cliffs. Hannibal, who was at the post of danger in the rear, fought his way step by step under a bombardment of stones and rocks, which made great breaches in his ranks, until at last shelter was found under a projecting mass known as the White Cliff, where a halt was made for the night. Meanwhile the cavalry and the baggage-train, though under great difficulties, had passed the line of peril, and in the morning the whole army was reunited at the head of the pass.

DESCENT INTO ITALY

All danger of attack from the hill tribes was now over, and the army had reached the point from which they were to begin their descent into Italy. But the situation was forlorn enough. It was late in the season,[1] and they had to make their comfortless bivouac in the deep snow. Before them towered the gigantic form of Mont Blanc, an object of horror to these children of the South, and all around them reigned the awful silence of the mountains, broken only by the scream of an eagle or the hoarse roar of a torrent. Reading despondency on the faces of his men, Hannibal employed all his eloquence to raise their spirits. They had stormed, he said, the citadel of Italy, the great barrier which nature had raised as a rampart to that favoured land. Let them look upon those rocky heights as the battlements of Rome itself, for in gaining them they had mastered by far the hardest part of their task, and what remained would be smooth and easy. In a few days they would reach the pleasant valley of the great northern river, where they could refresh themselves after their labours, and then, joining their forces with those of the friendly Gauls, strike irresistibly at the heart of Italy. His brave words and indomitable spirit kindled new hope in the weary men, and after resting two days they entered upon the descent, which led through the valley of the Dora Baltea.

[1] November 9, 218 B.C. (Polybius, iii. 54).

Already greatly diminished in numbers, the army went on dwindling day by day, for the difficulties of the route increased as they advanced, and many lost their footing on the frozen track and fell into the depths below, or sank down exhausted never to rise again. Presently they came to a place where the path had been carried away by an avalanche for a distance of two or three hundred yards, and after vainly attempting to find another track they were obliged to encamp and cut a new road along the edge of the precipice. After a day's labour the way was wide enough for the horses and mules, and these were sent on to find pasture in the first green spot. But three days more were required before the elephants could pass in safety, and meanwhile the wretched animals almost perished from hunger. At last, nearly three weeks from the time when they had begun the ascent, they left the horrors of the Alps behind them and set foot on the plains of northern Italy.

ROME'S LOST OPPORTUNITY

The great march had been accomplished, but it had cost Hannibal more than half his army, and what remained was but the wreck of the splendid force he had brought with him from Spain. Now, if ever, was the time for the Romans to strike at their enemy, while he lay, faint and exhausted, on the threshold of Italy. A twentieth part of the enormous force at their disposal would have sufficed at this moment to crush the invader and to save them and their country from years of fearful suffering. But they had acted from the first on the assumption that the seat of war would be in Spain and in Africa, and had consequently made no adequate provision for home defence. One full consular army, as we have seen, was in Sicily, under the command of Sempronius, and another had been conducted to Spain by Cnaeus Scipio, who was acting as deputy for his brother. There were, indeed, two legions, with the usual complement of Italian allies, in the Po valley, and even these small numbers, employed at the right time and in the right place, might have effected much. But the golden

opportunity was allowed to pass, and Hannibal thus gained
time to reorganize his broken army and to obtain his first
success over the Romans, which relieved the pressure on his
Gaulish allies and brought thousands of recruits to join his
standard.

BATTLE OF THE TICINUS

After allowing time for his troops to recover their strength,
Hannibal invaded the territory of the Taurini, a Ligurian
people who were at war with the Insubres, stormed their
capital, and put the garrison to the sword. Having thus
secured himself against hostility on the part of the natives,
he advanced to meet Scipio, who had already crossed the Po
and was now engaged in constructing a bridge over the
Ticinus. His bridge completed, Scipio pushed forward in a
westerly direction, and presently Hannibal found himself for
the first time face to face with a Roman army. The engagement which followed, somewhat loosely called the battle of the
Ticinus, was a mere cavalry skirmish, serving as a prelude to
the trilogy of slaughter which was afterwards enacted at the
Trebia, at Thrasymene, and at Cannae. The Romans were
defeated and driven back on the Ticinus, where they had just
time to destroy their bridge and place that river between
themselves and the enemy. They then fell back behind
the line of the Po, and took up a position near Placentia.
Scipio himself received a severe wound in his encounter with
Hannibal's cavalry, and was only saved from death by the
devotion of his youthful son, afterwards renowned as the victor
of Zama.

CAMPAIGN OF THE TREBIA

The wounded consul was now distracted by a multitude of
cares. With a weak army, composed of raw recruits and
disheartened by its recent defeat, he was encamped in the
country of the hostile Boii, who were arming on all sides and
preparing to join the enemy. His chief supply of stores was

215

at Clastidium, in a district commanded by Hannibal, who had crossed the Po by a bridge of boats shortly after the skirmish at the Ticinus. He was, moreover, anxious about the movements of his colleague Sempronius, who had been summoned from Sicily at the first news of Hannibal's approach, and might be expected to join him at any moment. It was therefore a most complicated problem which Scipio had to solve. He had to keep in touch with Clastidium, to watch the movements of Hannibal, to overawe the insurgent Gauls, and to keep open his communications with the other consul. For a time he lay encamped at some distance from Placentia, with the Trebia at his back,[1] facing Hannibal, who had taken up a position some miles to the west. But it soon became evident that to maintain his ground here was impossible. One night a contingent of two thousand Gauls who were serving under compulsion in the Roman army rose in mutiny, murdered their officers, and marched off in a body to the camp of Hannibal. Alarmed by this outrage, and fearing that a general insurrection of the Boii was impending, Scipio abandoned his present quarters, crossed the Trebia, and entrenched himself strongly on the eastern bank of that stream, so that his front was protected by the river, while his left flank rested on the northern spurs of the Apennines, and his right was extended in the direction of Placentia. Hannibal followed his movements, and pitched a new camp on the opposite side of the Trebia. One result of this retreat was that the rich magazine at Clastidium fell into the hands of Hannibal, and the Romans were compelled to depend on supplies brought up the Po. But Scipio was now in an excellent position, protecting him against the assaults of Hannibal's terrible cavalry and giving him command of the main route into central Italy. Shortly afterwards he was joined by Sempronius, and the numbers of the Roman army were thus raised to forty thousand men.

Hannibal had every reason for desiring to bring on a general

---

[1] There is a great conflict of authorities on the details of this campaign. I have followed the suggestions of Neumann, as quoted in the new edition of Arnold's *Second Punic War*.

engagement. At present he was in the position of an adventurer, engaged in a desperate enterprise against an enemy who had the whole resources of Italy at his command. Nothing but a brilliant and unbroken series of victories could confirm the loyalty of his adherents and bring over the waverers to his side. The Gauls, it is true, were supporting him heartily, but he knew that their patience would break down if the hopes of plunder and vengeance which had brought them to his standard were long deferred. On the other hand, Scipio, who had formed an accurate estimate of Hannibal's prospects, was determined to frustrate his intention, knowing that the Romans had everything to gain by delay. But he was still disabled by his wound, and obliged to delegate all the active duties of his office to his colleague Sempronius, a man of fiery and ambitious temper, who was eager to snatch a hasty laurel before his year of office had expired. It would be a disgrace, argued Sempronius, to lie there inactive while this brigand from Africa was trampling on the fields of northern Italy. The honour of Rome demanded that they should take the field at once and chastise the insolence of the invader. The censures which have been passed on Sempronius for his conduct at this crisis seem to be rather overcharged. Judged by a contemporary at this stage of the war, his reasoning may have seemed sound enough. But there was one dominant factor in the situation which the Romans too little appreciated, and this was the supreme, the overwhelming military genius of the Carthaginian commander.

The precariousness of Hannibal's position was soon proved by the action of certain Gauls who inhabited the tongue of land formed by the winding courses of the Trebia and the Po. These cautious barbarians were playing a double game, intending, when Fortune had declared herself, to throw in their lot with the winning side. They soon had reason to repent their double-dealing, for their fields were mercilessly ravaged by a detachment of Carthaginian troops, and they sent envoys to the Roman camp with a piteous tale. Sempronius dispatched a party of cavalry and light infantry to their relief, and when the contingent returned, after gaining a considerable advantage over the enemy, he was more than ever eager for a general engagement. Hannibal, who knew the temper of the man, resolved to give him the opportunity he desired. He made a careful survey of the ground between the two camps, and his quick eye soon discerned the deep bed of a stream, overgrown with bushes and weeds, which seemed designed by nature for an ambuscade. During the night he sent his brother Mago with a picked body of a thousand horse and the same number of infantry to occupy this place, instructing him to lie close and wait for a favourable moment to make his attack.

BATTLE OF THE TREBIA

The pale light of a December dawn was spreading over the waters of the Trebia when a cloud of Numidian cavalry was seen hovering on the outskirts of the Roman camp. In hot haste Sempronius dispatched his cavalry and six thousand light-armed infantry to hold the Numidians in play, and he himself followed with the main body, as soon as the men could be got under arms. But in his eagerness the consul had allowed himself to be taken by surprise. The Romans went fasting into battle, and the river being in flood, they had to wade breast-high in the icy water before they could reach the enemy. Hannibal, on the other hand, whose plans were all matured, gave his men time to make a hearty meal and to oil their bodies by the camp-fire before they put on their armour. The same features were to be repeated in the later scenes of this lamentable war. On one side there was rash confidence, followed by hurry and confusion, on the other the firm grasp and the calm precision of a master mind.

Seeing that he had achieved his object, by luring Sempronius from his entrenchments, Hannibal marched out of camp and drew up his forces in order of battle. Eight thousand light-armed troops, spearmen, and Balearic slingers formed the advance-guard, and behind this moving screen was posted the main body, with the infantry, Libyans, Spaniards, and Celts, twenty thousand strong, in the centre, and the cavalry,

218

numbering ten thousand, posted behind the elephants on
either wing. The main strength of the Romans lay, as usual,
in their infantry, which consisted of sixteen thousand citizen
soldiers and twenty thousand Italian allies. On the other hand,
Sempronius had but four thousand cavalry with which to con-
front the overwhelming numbers of the Carthaginian horse.
But his troops shared the confidence of their leader, and advanced to the attack in firm order, while the light-armed
troops skirmished in their van. These latter, however, were
already exhausted by the encounter with the Numidians, and
the rain, which had poured incessantly since daybreak, had
relaxed their bowstrings and warped the straps of their
javelins.[1] They were accordingly soon driven in, and fell
back behind the main army. The Roman cavalry shared the
same fortune, and was quickly swept from the field by the
irresistible onset of the enemy. Thus the infantry was stripped
of its defences, and Hannibal now let loose his Numidians and
spearmen, who kept up a galling attack on both flanks. Still
the Romans and their allies, though faint with hunger and half
frozen by the icy rain, held their ground gallantly, and fought
with all the stubborn valour of their race. But just at this
moment Mago, who had been watching his opportunity, rose
from his ambush and charged the consul's army in the rear,
spreading panic and disorder from rank to rank. Only the
Romans fighting in the van still kept a firm front, and, standing
shoulder to shoulder, they cut their way through the Celts and
Africans opposed to them. Then, seeing that the day was lost,
they left the battlefield behind them and marched onward,
ten thousand strong, until they found shelter in the walls of
Placentia, where they were joined on the following night by
the consul Scipio, who had succeeded in bringing off the broken
remnant of the army. The loss had been severe, and would
have been still greater but for the wild storm which raged all
through that winter day and covered the retreat of the Romans.

---

[1] This interesting detail, briefly noted by Polybius (iii. 73), is well illus-
trated by Schweighäuser. The javelin was hurled by means of a strap,
which gave it a rotatory motion, serving the same purpose as the rifling of a
gun-barrel.

REPUBLICAN ROME

Hannibal's losses were light, but many of his men died after-wards from the effects of exposure, and all the elephants except one fell victims to the severity of a northern climate.

ROME AFTER THE DEFEAT

The state of feeling produced at Rome by the news of this defeat is described by Livy in a rhetorical flourish which goes far beyond the mark. He is so lavish of his colours on this occasion, and after Thrasymene, that words fail him when he comes to Cannae, and he passes over the scenes which followed that crowning disaster in a gasp of silence. Far more impressive are the words of Polybius, who had a truer sense of Roman greatness than the patriotic historian. " The defeat of the Trebia," he says, " was met by a burst of determined energy, for the Romans are always most to be feared in the hour of danger." Without any excitement, almost without emotion, the Senate proceeded to pass measures for the conduct of the war in the ensuing year. Reinforcements were sent to Spain, Sicily, and Sardinia, Tarentum was garrisoned, and a fleet of sixty quinqueremes was got ready for sea. At the same time ample provision was made for home defence by the enlist-ment of four new legions, which were incorporated with the surviving forces of Scipio and Sempronius and appointed to guard the approaches to central Italy.

FLAMINIUS

The new consuls for the ensuing year (217 B.C.) were Cnaeus Servilius Geminus and Caius Flaminius Nepos. Flaminius has already figured prominently in the political annals of Rome. His fame rests chiefly on the great public works which bear his name, the Via Flaminia and the new circus erected under his auspices in the Field of Mars. These were the chief fruits of his censorship, and they entitle him to an eminent place among the many distinguished men who held that high office. But he had incurred the bitter hatred of the nobles by his agrarian law (see p. 193), by his rigorous collec-tion of the rents on public lands, and by a recent enactment forbidding any senator to possess a ship of more than ten tons burden. The latter restriction, which afterwards fell into disuse, was intended to preserve the Fathers of the city from the illiberal associations of commerce. By these measures and by his constant championship of the popular party Flaminius fell into very ill odour with his own class, and this feeling is reflected in the pages of Livy and Polybius, two writers who, while differing in almost all other respects, agree in their strong distaste for everything that savours of democracy. In an evil hour for the State this demagogue, this subverter of the constitution, had been carried to the supreme office on the breeze of popular favour. The gods had declared their disapproval in loud and emphatic tones, and the air was thick with portents of evil. An infant six months old had shouted " Triumph ! " in the herb-market ; a bull had of his own accord ascended to the third story of a house and flung himself out of the window ; the Temple of Hope had been struck by lightning ; a wolf had plucked the sword of a sentry from its sheath and carried it off. These alarming incidents, and many more like them, are gravely set down by Livy, who copied them from the archives of the priestly colleges. They exemplify the low credulity and superstition which were so curiously mingled with the grander traits of the Roman character. That these signs and wonders were not mere gossip of the barber's shop, as Polybius would have us believe, is proved by the fact that they were held worthy of serious attention by strong and earnest minds, that they were made matter for public debate, and were recognized as warnings of the divine displeasure, to be appeased by costly offerings, by a solemn act of purification, and by sacrifices of atonement for the sins of the people. Under such auspices and in such an atmosphere of gloomy foreboding Flaminius prepared to enter on the duties of his consulship.

HANNIBAL ENTERS ETRURIA

We must now return to Hannibal, whose victory had made him master of all northern Italy, with the exception of the military colonies at Mutina, Placentia, and Cremona. The Cenomani, also, still held out for the Romans. But though the Gauls were now joining him by thousands he knew that his position was very precarious, and he resolved, if possible, to spare his allies the burden of supporting him through the winter. Accordingly he made a determined effort to cross the Apennines and reach Etruria; but he was overtaken by a furious storm, which compelled him to retrace his steps and quarter his troops among the Gauls. He soon found new reason to distrust the fidelity of these unstable adherents. Information reached him that they had formed a plot for his assassination, in the hope, perhaps, of reconciling themselves to the Romans by ridding them of their great enemy. In order to baffle their designs, he caused a number of wigs to be made, and disguised himself so effectually that he was not to be recognized even by his most intimate friends. At the first approach of spring he set his army in motion, and, having crossed the Apennines without difficulty, entered the northern plain of Etruria. All this district, now one of the most fertile in Italy, was then a vast swamp, formed by the untamed waters of the Arno and its tributaries. During four days Hannibal's army endured the most fearful sufferings, and he lost the greater part of his baggage-train in crossing the morass. The African and Spanish troops were placed in the van, and Mago, with the whole of the cavalry, brought up the rear, driving before them the Gaulish recruits, who were thus cut off from all possibility of escape. But for this precaution the Gauls would have deserted to a man, for their huge, fleshy frames were ill fitted to bear such fatigues and privations and they murmured grievously as they struggled through the mire. Many of the horses lost their hoofs, which rotted and dropped off in consequence of their long march through the mud. Never was the army nearer to destruction. But the chief sufferer was Hannibal himself, who was enduring exquisite torture from an attack of ophthalmia, and came out of that dreadful trial with the loss of an eye.

Flaminius was stationed with his army at Arretium, and it

SECOND PUNIC WAR

was Hannibal's object to force an engagement before he was
joined by his colleague Servilius, who was approaching from
Ariminum. As soon as the condition of his troops allowed
him to move, he broke up his camp, which had been pitched
in the neighbourhood of Faesulae, and advanced into the heart
of Etruria, plundering and burning as he went. Flaminius,
he well knew, was a noisy demagogue, whose head had been
turned by the plaudits of the mob, and who was eager to fight
a battle before his colleague should arrive. So at least Polybius
would have us believe, but it is impossible to avoid the suspicion
that the historian is here repeating the slanders which he heard
at the tables of his Roman patrons. And when he adds that
Flaminius was followed on his march by a vast multitude of
traders carrying chains to bind the captives we are somewhat too strongly reminded of the fine stories with which the
Father of History is wont to embellish his narrative.[1] Moreover, the account of Polybius is hardly consistent with itself,
for he expressly informs us that Flaminius lay quiet at Arretium,
waiting for Servilius to join him, until Hannibal had marched
past his station and seemed likely to carry his ravages to the
very walls of Rome.[2] Then at last he took the field, and
followed in the track of the invader, determined at all hazards
to bring him to a stand.

LAKE THRASYMENE

Hannibal, however, had attained his object. He had drawn
Flaminius from his stronghold, and he pushed steadily onward,
leaving a track of desolation behind him. In this part of his
work he was ably assisted by the Gauls, who found here a
more congenial occupation than that of wading through the
marshes of the Arno. Meanwhile he scanned the country with
his practised glance, looking for a place where he might turn
with advantage on his unwary pursuer. And presently he

[1] Herodotus, i. 66, and elsewhere.
[2] This criticism of a writer whose reputation stands so high as that of
Polybius may perhaps be thought presumptuous. But the view here expressed
is shared, I find, by Mr. Capes. See his note on Livy, xxii. 3.

found what he wanted. The road from Cortona to Perusia,
after running for some distance in a southerly direction, turns
eastward and skirts the northern shore of Lake Thrasymene.
Just at the point where the road first touches the lake the hills
dividing the valleys of the Clanis and the Tiber send down a long
spur almost to the verge of the water, and then receding leave
an open plain of considerable extent, which is closed about four

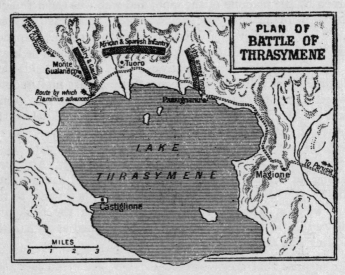

miles farther on by a second projection from the same range.
The greatest breadth of the plain is at its eastern and western
end, for the enclosing heights stoop forward in the middle,
so that the whole configuration resembles a Greek bow, with
its bridge and double curve.[1] Hannibal posted himself with
the flower of his troops on the projecting ridge which commands the centre of the plain. The Gauls and all the cavalry
held the key to his position, being stationed on the heights
overhanging the western defile, while the light-armed troops
were sent to close the eastern outlet. He had laid his net
skilfully, but would the noble quarry, who thought himself

[1] Nissen, *Italische Landeskunde*, ii. 320.

the hunter, allow himself to be caught? There can be no
doubt that Flaminius behaved on this occasion with almost
incredible rashness. His one thought was to overtake Hannibal's army, and, rushing blindly on, he arrived in the evening
at the north-western angle of the lake, and pitched his camp
almost under the shadow of the bluffs which were swarming
with his foes.

THE BATTLE

Day had hardly dawned and a dense fog was rising from the
surface of the water when Flaminius set his army in marching
order, and, without sending forward scouts or reconnoitring
the ground, entered the fatal trap. The heavy tramp of the
legions was muffled by the moist and misty air, but soon a
more fearful sound fell upon the ears of the consul, for hardly
had the last ranks of the long column crossed the defile when
the Gauls rose from their ambush and, raising their war-cry,
swept down upon the rear of the Roman army. Dim forms
were now seen moving on the hill-sides in front and to the
left, and the Romans perceived, when it was too late, that
the heights were alive with enemies. Six thousand men who
formed the vanguard broke through the light-armed troops
who were barring their way, and marched forward until they
reached the higher ground. Here they halted, and found to
their surprise that they were alone. For, being considerably
in advance of the main column, and having their eyes and ears
fully occupied in their encounter with the troops opposing
them, they had not observed what was going on in their rear,
but thought that they were engaged with the advance-guard
of Hannibal's army. As they stood irresolute, listening to the
confused uproar which filled the valley below them, the mist
rolled aside and they saw the terrible truth. Thirty thousand
Romans and Italians were standing at bay with their backs
to the lake, huddled in a confused mass, and striving in vain to
make head against a multitude of assailants, who pressed them
hard in front and on both flanks. Then their dense array
was broken to pieces, and the whole valley became a scene of

225

flight and pursuit, capture and slaughter. Many ran into the lake, and strove to escape by swimming, until they were borne down by the weight of their armour and drowned, or stood immersed up to their necks begging for quarter, only to be cut down by Hannibal's cavalry. Flaminius himself, after making frantic efforts to rally his men, was dispatched by a Gaulish horseman. Fifteen thousand were slain and as many more were made prisoners. Among the latter were the six thousand who had broken through to the hills, who were brought in the same evening by a detachment of light cavalry sent out for the purpose. In his treatment of these prisoners Hannibal made a marked distinction between the Romans and the Italian allies. The former were kept in rigorous confinement, ill fed, and loaded with chains; the Italians, after receiving the kindest attention, were dismissed without ransom to their homes, bearing with them messages of goodwill from the Carthaginian commander. He had come, he said, to put down the insolence of Rome, not to make war on Italy, and if he succeeded every Italian state should share in the fruits of his victory. This, as we have seen, was an essential part of Hannibal's policy, on which the ultimate issue of his enterprise mainly depended. He hoped, by raising the cry of " Freedom for Italy," to strip the Romans of their allies and stir up a war of independence throughout the peninsula.

THE CRISIS AFTER THRASYMENE

It was evening, and an excited multitude was gathered before the steps of the Senate House at Rome crying for news. Vague rumours were abroad of a great disaster which had befallen the Roman arms, and fearful apprehensions were burning in a thousand anxious hearts. Presently the praetor appeared at the doors of the building, clothed in his purple-bordered robe and attended by two lictors. He raised his hand to command silence, and amid the hush these words fell upon the ears of the waiting crowd : " We have been defeated in a great battle." It was a staggering blow, and many of those present were observed to recoil, as if they had seen their nearest

Plate XXXIV. Passignano, Lake Trasimenus (Thrasymene)

226

PLATE XXXV.   HANNIBAL (?)

227

SECOND PUNIC WAR

and dearest struck dead. But as yet nothing certain was known, and for some days the gates of the city were thronged by distracted women, who besieged all who entered with clamorous importunity, inquiring about the fate of brothers, husbands, and sons. Every day the Senate sat in close debate from sunrise to sunset, to concert measures of defence in the face of so imminent a peril. But even in that august assembly signs of panic appeared when three days later tidings of a second disaster were received. A body of four thousand cavalry which had been sent forward from Ariminum by the other consul was met half-way by Maharbal, one of Hannibal's officers, who cut to pieces two thousand men and made prisoners of the rest.

QUINTUS FABIUS

As the ordinary machinery of government seemed inadequate to deal with such a crisis it was decided to appoint a dictator, and the choice fell on Quintus Fabius, who has already been mentioned as the leader of the embassy which was sent to Carthage after the fall of Saguntum. His illustrious descent and a long career of honour marked Fabius out as the natural representative of the old conservative party in Rome. The singular mildness of his temper had procured him in his youth the nickname of ' the Lamb,' but under his placid exterior there lay an iron constancy of purpose, not to be daunted by any dangers or shaken by any trials. He is the type of that one quality in the Roman character, its dogged, imperturbable patience, against which all the stormy energy of Hannibal dashed itself in vain.

A SACRED SPRING

According to strict precedent, the dictator should have been nominated by one of the consuls, armed with authority for that purpose by a decree of the Senate. But of the two consuls for the year one had been slain and the other was absent from Rome. Consequently, as the occasion was pressing, Fabius was appointed to his high office by a vote of the centuries,

227

and Minucius, a popular favourite, became his Master of the Horse. The first care of the dictator was to appease the angry powers who had been flouted by Flaminius, and had taken such signal vengeance for his impiety. Every temple was full of worshippers and every altar smoked with sacrifice, and as an extraordinary means of propitiation the Romans bound themselves by a solemn oath to offer a Sacred Spring (see p. 35). " If, for the space of five years," ran the oath, " it shall please Heaven to preserve the Roman People, in the war which they are now waging against Carthage, and against the Gauls that dwell on this side the Alps, then shall the Roman People offer the firstlings of all their flocks and herds born in the spring, from the day that the Senate and the People shall appoint." It was a strictly commercial transaction, conceived in the very spirit of Roman religion, and pledging the people to make a certain payment for value received. But Fabius, though he was thus anxious to obtain the divine favour, did not neglect more obvious precautions. The fortifications of Rome were placed in a state of repair, and the bridges over the Tiber were broken down, for no one knew that Hannibal was not at that very moment on the march against the capital. Two fresh legions were enrolled, and Servilius received orders to hand over his men to the dictator and to take command of the fleet, which was prepared for immediate service, as Carthaginian vessels were now hovering off the coasts of Italy. Then Fabius, placing himself at the head of the whole military force, which numbered some sixty thousand men, marched out to take the field.

HANNIBAL'S ADVANCE

Meanwhile the victor of Thrasymene had left the scene of his triumph behind him, and, crossing the Tiber, marched on through Umbria, until he stood under the lofty towers of Spoletium, a strong fortress built on the western edge of Monte Somma, and not far from the spot where, in a grove of cypress-trees, rose the crystal source of the Clitumnus. All that rich valley, afterwards hallowed by the songs of

Virgil, now felt the heavy hand of the invader. But the stout-hearted Latin colonists who garrisoned the town looked on unmoved while their fields were laid waste, and an attempt to carry the walls by storm was repulsed with loss. Hannibal might learn from this failure, if he needed any such lesson, that the time was not yet ripe for an attack on Rome, and, turning his face eastward, he led his army into Picenum, a region abounding in corn and wine and famous for its orchards.[1] Like a pack of hungry wolves the fierce hordes of Africa and Spain fell upon the spoil, and glutted themselves with the wealth which had been heaped up during long years of peace. Hannibal put no restraint on the passions of his men, but indulged them in a holiday of pillage, to indemnify them for all the hardships they had endured. Large numbers both of the men and horses were suffering from a species of scurvy, brought on by long exposure to the wet and cold; but by bathing their sores with old wine and by rest and plentiful diet they were soon restored to perfect health. Keeping along the shore of the Adriatic, and advancing by easy stages, Hannibal arrived in the northern plain of Apulia, and took up his quarters near Arpi, the legendary seat of the Homeric hero Diomedes. The country through which he passed was thickly peopled by Roman and Latin colonists, and all such, whenever they fell into his hands, were butchered without mercy. It was during this march that Hannibal took the bold step of equipping his Libyan infantry in the Roman fashion, having ample materials for the change in the arms which he had taken at Thrasymene. But in one important respect his calculations had not been fulfilled. As yet not a single Italian city had opened its gates to the invader.

FABIAN TACTICS

Before long Hannibal's scouts brought him word that the dictator was approaching, and at nightfall innumerable twinkling lights announced that the Roman army was encamped on the neighbouring hills. Next morning Hannibal drew up

[1] Strabo, v. c. 241 ; Juvenal, *Satires*, xi.

his forces in the plain below and offered battle. But Fabius
was not to be moved. He knew that he was no match for the
Carthaginian general in the open field, for the Roman soldiers
were cowed by their defeats, and his cavalry, poor in quality
and inferior in numbers, was utterly unable to cope with the
wild riders of Africa and the heavy cuirassiers of Spain. His
plan was to dog the footsteps of Hannibal and wear him out
by delay, keeping always within the protecting circle of the
hills, and never committing himself to the hazard of a regular
engagement. His intimate knowledge of the country enabled
him to choose the strongest positions for his camps, and being
within reach of ample supplies he had no need to scatter his
troops, but held his great army together, massed like a storm-
cloud upon the heights and constantly threatening attack.
From time to time he sent out light detachments to cut off
Hannibal's followers, and as he always chose his opportunity
with judgment he inflicted no small loss on the enemy and
raised the spirits of his men. Such were the renowned Fabian
tactics, which extorted the reluctant admiration of Hannibal and
have made the name of the dictator immortal.[1] It was a long
and obstinate duel, with slow, indomitable tenacity on one side
and impetuous genius on the other. But as time went on and
the Roman arms seemed to make no progress, while the most
fertile districts of Italy were laid waste with fire and sword,
murmurs began to arise in the Roman camp, and the dictator's
own lieutenant, Minucius, made himself spokesman of the
general discontent. "Fine work our leader has found for us,"
cried the scoffers, "to sit here on the hill-sides, like spectators
in a theatre, watching the ruin of Italy!" But 'Hannibal's
lackey,' as he was impudently nicknamed by Minucius, let
them rail on, for his Roman spirit was raised above the fear of
a slanderous tongue.

HANNIBAL IN CAMPANIA

Finding that Fabius was not to be drawn into the level
country, Hannibal crossed the eastern barrier of the Apen-

---

[1] He was given the surname of ' Cunctator ' (' the Delayer ').

SECOND PUNIC WAR

nines and came down upon the rich pastures of Samnium,
which had risen to a great height of prosperity under the
Roman government. He passed the walls of Beneventum,
gathering an immense booty as he went, and then followed the
line of the Via Latina until he reached the upper waters of
the Volturnus. Crossing that stream, he descended into the
northern plain of Campania. He was now in the very garden
of Italy, the coveted possession for which Greek and Samnite,
Gaul and Etruscan, and even, as it was fabled, the gods themselves, had fought and bled. Surely, he thought, Fabius, in
very shame, would be provoked to give battle when he saw
this choice region with all its olive-grounds and vineyards
plundered and laid waste. So he let loose his Numidians,
and they spread themselves over the country, to destroy in a
few days what it had taken the labour of generations to
create. Meanwhile Fabius had been following him at a cautious
distance, and was now encamped on the eastern slopes of Mons
Massicus, looking on at the work of destruction. Paying no
heed to the clamours of his soldiers, who demanded to be led
instantly into battle, he silently proceeded to close all the
mountain passes that led out of Campania. For once, as it
seemed, the mighty hunter had allowed himself to be caught
in a trap. His only way of escape led through the mountains
on the north and east, and every outlet in this direction was
held by the men of Fabius. Hannibal saw his danger, and
resolved by a bold stroke to break through the net by which
he was surrounded. Fabius with his main army was encamped
on the hills above the Volturnus, just where that river first
enters the plain, and he had posted a body of four thousand
men to hold the gorge leading into the mountains of Samnium.
It was at this latter point that the blow was to be aimed.
At dead of night Hannibal set his army in marching order,
and sent forward a detachment of light troops, who drove
before them a herd of two thousand oxen, each with a lighted
torch bound to its horns. With loud uproar and commotion
the strange cavalcade ascended the slopes of the hills commanding the gorge, and presently the dictator's men who were

holding the pass saw a multitude of moving lights on the hill-tops above them. Thinking that Hannibal was trying to break through in this direction, they left their posts and rushed up the slope to attack the retreating column. The way was now open for Hannibal, and he marched with all his forces and with all his enormous booty through the pass. Then, making a wide *détour*, which carried him as far as the territory of the Peligni, he returned through Samnium to Apulia. Soon the two armies were confronting each other in the old fashion, that of Hannibal being quartered at the town of Gerunium, which he had taken by storm, while Fabius lay encamped on the spurs of the neighbouring hills.[1]

FABIUS AND MINUCIUS

During the autumn Fabius was summoned to Rome for the performance of certain religious ceremonies, and he left Minucius in command, with a strict charge to act purely on the defensive. When he arrived at the capital Fabius found that a strong feeling had arisen against his timid and dilatory tactics. The mutinous talk of the army found an echo in the Forum, and many voices were calling for a more vigorous and effective plan of campaign. Nor were these complaints altogether unfounded. Fabius had, indeed, lost a golden opportunity. He had let his enemy slip through the toils and allowed himself to be shamefully foiled and outwitted. His slow, plodding mind was ill fitted to cope with the daring genius of Hamilcar's mighty son. It was all very well to talk of exhausting Hannibal, but meanwhile Rome's allies were being ruined, and sooner or later their patience must be worn out, when they saw that no effort was made in their defence. The waiting game might after all prove a losing game. The popular excitement attained its climax when news arrived that Minucius, in defiance of orders, had engaged the enemy and won a brilliant victory. The report was of

---

[1] Gerunium seems to be wrongly placed in all our maps. It was on the banks of the Frento (Fortore), just on the northern edge of the Apulian plain (Nissen, *Italische Landeskunde*, ii. 785).

SECOND PUNIC WAR

course greatly exaggerated, but it found ready credence, and
by a measure unparalleled in Roman history Minucius was
appointed co-dictator with Fabius. Thus, with diminished
powers and a reputation greatly lowered, Fabius returned
to the seat of war, and the two dictators agreed to divide the
army equally between them and to occupy separate camps.
Hannibal, whose spies were everywhere, knew exactly how
matters stood, and he resolved to profit by the occasion.
The hot-headed Minucius, proud of his generalship, was easily
lured into an ambush, and but for the timely intervention of
Fabius he would have been cut off with his whole army.
Schooled by this incident, he voluntarily laid down his command
and resumed his position as lieutenant of Fabius. Winter was
now approaching and the second year of the war drew toward
its close.

DISSENSION IN ROME

Early in the spring (216 B.C.) the dictators' term of office
expired, and their place was taken by the consuls of the previous year, Cnaeus Servilius and Marcus Regulus (the successor
of Flaminius), who were invested with proconsular authority.
The feeling of irritation which had long been fermenting
among the masses broke out with uncontrollable violence
at the election of the new consuls. The nobles, it was said,
were wantonly prolonging the war, by setting mere party
motives above the interests of the State and raising one incompetent leader after another to the supreme command. New
blood must be infused into the decrepit body of the government
if any real progress was to be made. The candidate in whom
the popular hopes were centred was Caius Terentius Varro,
who, beginning life, it was said, as a butcher's apprentice,
had risen by his talents to the dignity of aedile and praetor.
He thus belonged to the class described in the political slang
of the day as New Men, meaning those who could point to no
one among their ancestors as a holder of curule office. In
the face of a strong opposition he was elected by a large
majority to the consulship, and received as his colleague

233

REPUBLICAN ROME

Lucius Aemilius Paulus, the aristocratic candidate. Thus the dissensions of the Forum were once more carried into the camp, an omen of evil for the impending struggle with Hannibal. Aemilius was a gloomy and embittered man who had narrowly escaped conviction on a charge of embezzlement in the Illyrian war. His hands were, in fact, quite innocent of such a stain, but he could not forgive even the shadow of dishonour which had been cast upon him by the people. Long and anxious was the charge delivered to Aemilius by the aged Fabius, who warned him that he would find in his colleague an enemy not less dangerous than Hannibal himself.

HANNIBAL SEIZES CANNAE

It was now midsummer, and the broad cornfields of Apulia were already whitening toward harvest. Hannibal, who wished to fix his quarters in that land of plenty, had recently broken up his camp at Gerunium, and marching southward he threw himself suddenly upon the small town of Cannae, which contained valuable stores and munitions of war for the Roman army. Tidings of this movement reached Rome on the eve of the consuls' departure, and they set out with instructions to unite their new levies with the two proconsular armies and take the first favourable opportunity for bringing on a general engagement. When the junction was effected the whole Roman force amounted to no less than eighty thousand men, or four times the force employed in an ordinary campaign. So imposing an array of troops was a striking tribute to the military genius of Hannibal.

THE POSITION BEFORE CANNAE

Before long it became known in the capital that the two armies were confronting each other on the banks of the Aufidus, that skirmishes were occurring every day, and that a decisive engagement could not long be delayed. Then a fever of anxiety took possession of the whole city. To add to the distress, superstition awoke with all its terrors, giving a dire significance to the most trivial sights and sounds. Meanwhile Hannibal had his own reasons for serious disquiet. He was encamped on the right bank of the Aufidus, a few miles west of Cannae, and behind him lay the marshes, barring all retreat. To his left was a hilly country, unsuitable for the evolutions of his cavalry; in front of him, on both sides of the river, the Romans were entrenched in overwhelming force. So far the consuls had made their dispositions wisely. Two-thirds of their army lay encamped on the right bank of the Aufidus, facing Hannibal's position, and the other third was stationed in a smaller camp on the left or northern bank, to threaten the enemy's foraging parties.[1] Hannibal was brought to bay, and nothing but a decisive and immediate victory could extricate him from the surrounding perils. But his spirits rose to the emergency, and when his men saw their great leader laughing and jesting with his staff they felt sure that all was well and prepared to do battle with cheerful hearts.

By an unhappy custom, long prevalent among the Romans, each consul held the supreme command on alternate days. Aemilius was all for delay, knowing that Hannibal's difficulties must increase as time went on. But he found himself constantly checkmated and all his prudent counsels blown to the winds by the impetuosity of his colleague. On the eve of the fatal day there was great excitement in the Roman camp, for in a few hours Varro's turn would come round again, and it was believed that he had resolved to give battle. At daybreak every man was afoot, and the crimson mantle floating over the consul's tent showed them that their expectations were fulfilled.

BATTLE OF CANNAE

The scene of the battle was on the left bank of the Aufidus. Varro crossed the river, and, uniting his main army with the troops in the smaller camp, arranged his line of battle so as to face almost southward. On the right, next to

---

[1] There is great difference of opinion as to the details of this campaign. The view I have taken is in the main that of Nissen (*Italische Landeskunde*, ii. 852–853). See the rough sketch annexed.

the river, were stationed the Roman cavalry, two thousand
in number, who were commanded by Aemilius. The whole
middle space was occupied by the dense masses of the
infantry, seventy thousand strong, and drawn up in files
of unusual depth. These were commanded by the consuls
of the previous year. Varro himself led the detachment of
six thousand Italian cavalry, whose post was on the left.
On the other side Hannibal had but forty thousand infantry
to meet the shock of the ponderous Roman column. Of these
the Gauls and Spaniards held the centre, which was thrown
forward in a crescent shape, so as to draw the first attack
of the enemy, while the Africans, armed in the Roman fashion,
were held in reserve on either wing. Hasdrubal, with the
heavy cavalry of Gaul and Spain, faced the Roman horse
nearest the river, and on the extreme left was a body of
Numidian cavalry, confronting Varro and his Italians.

According to the usual practice in ancient warfare, the main
army on either side was covered by a curtain of light-armed
troops, and these first advanced to the attack, with a shower
of javelins, stones, and arrows. Then Hasdrubal charged
down upon the Roman horse, who were quickly overpowered
and swept from the field. Having cleared the ground on
this side, he went to the help of the Numidians, who were
engaged in an indecisive struggle with the Italian cavalry.
On his approach the Italians broke their ranks and fled, and,
leaving the work of pursuit to the Numidians, Hasdrubal
turned his attention to the Roman infantry, already reduced
to sore straits by the skilful tactics of Hannibal. At first
the Roman legions, bearing down with irresistible weight on
the Spanish and Gaulish foot, had carried all before them.
But as they pressed forward, confident of victory, the Africans,
wheeling to right and left, assailed them on either flank, and
thus afforded relief to the Gauls, who rallied and returned
to the attack, while Hasdrubal, to cut off all hope of
escape, fell upon their rear. The vast numbers on which the
Romans had relied now proved their ruin, for as the ring of
iron tightened round them rank was pressed on rank and file

on file, so that they had no space to wield their weapons. Then began such a scene of carnage as never was enacted either before or since in all the cruel wars which have wasted Italy. All through that burning summer day Gaul, Libyan, and Spaniard relieved one another at the deadly work, mowing their way deeper and deeper into the helpless, shrieking multitude,

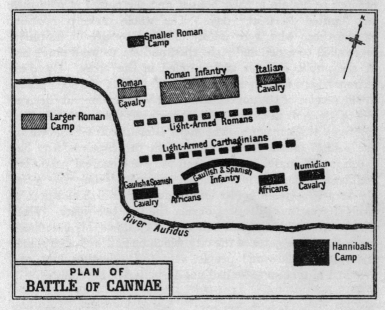

PLAN OF
BATTLE OF CANNAE

until swords were blunted and arms fell numbed with weariness. And when the stars came forth seventy thousand brave men lay cold in death, to bear witness that Hannibal had once more plotted well.

ROME'S HEROIC SPIRIT

That Rome was not utterly ruined by this crushing blow was due to the firmness of the Senate and the heroic spirit of the ruling class. The example was set by the young Scipio, who had found refuge with some thousands more at Canusium after the battle. Sword in hand, he appeared before a party of young nobles who had talked of flying the country, and compelled them under threat of instant death to resign their intention. At Rome, after the first paroxysm of grief and dismay, severe measures were taken to repress the wild agitation of the public mind and to provide against the attack on the city which now seemed inevitable. The women were ordered to remain in their houses, and the period of mourning was limited to thirty days. The whole male population, except those who were totally disabled by age or infirmity, was called to arms, and eight thousand slaves were purchased at the public expense and enrolled in the army. By these extraordinary measures a force of four legions was soon placed at the service of the government, and Varro, who had survived the battle, sent news that he had gathered ten thousand of the fugitives at Canusium. The stern Roman spirit is shown by the refusal of the Senate to ransom the captives who had fallen into Hannibal's hands, and the same exalted patriotism which could thus triumph over every private feeling now healed the breach between nobles and commoners which had been so fruitful a cause of disaster during the last two years. When Varro, who had received orders to lay down his command, approached the gates of the city which he had well-nigh ruined the whole Senate and people went forth to meet him, and thanked him because he had not despaired of his country.

CHAPTER XI

THE SECOND PUNIC WAR : II. FROM CANNAE TO ZAMA

A T Cannae the tide of Hannibal's fortunes reached its height, and for a space it might have seemed that the solid structure of Rome's dominion was to be swept away by the advancing flood. Capua, the second city of Italy, opened its gates to the invader, and Casilinum, commanding the passage over the Volturnus, was reduced by famine. In Apulia Hannibal gained possession of Arpi immediately after the battle. The Samnites, with one important exception, declared against Rome, and their example was followed by the Bruttians, and by most of the Lucanians. The slaughter of the Trebia, Thrasymene, and Cannae had made fearful gaps in the ranks of the Roman citizens, and the Senate itself was so reduced in numbers that a dictator was appointed to fill up the vacant seats. Day after day the news of some fresh disaster broke in upon the debates of the anxious and distracted Fathers. Hardly had they begun to take breath after the tremendous blow of Cannae when tidings were brought that the praetor Postumius, who had been sent to hold the Gauls in check, had been caught in an ambush and cut off with all his forces. Urgent appeals for help came from Sardinia, where the native tribes were in revolt, and from western Sicily, which was threatened with an attack by the Carthaginian fleet. Hiero, their old and faithful ally, was no more, and his place had been taken by his grandson Hieronymus, a giddy and vicious youth, who forthwith commenced to intrigue with Carthage. With so many calls on its resources. how could the Republic make head against its invincible enemy, who already had taken nearly the whole of southern Italy in his grasp?

HOPE FOR ROME

Yet even when things were at their worst a close observation would have shown that the Romans had still good ground for hope. In Italy itself the main strength of their position remained unshaken, for the Sabellians of the central Apennines, and the Latin colonies, stood fast, and the Pentrians, the most powerful branch of the Samnite nation, maintained their allegiance to Rome. The loss of Capua was indeed a heavy blow, and the fearful vengeance which was afterwards inflicted on that ill-fated city shows how deeply the Romans felt the defection of their once favoured ally. But even the Capuans, remembering, perhaps, how Pyrrhus had formerly dealt with Tarentum, insisted that Hannibal should leave them the right of self-government and that no citizen of theirs should be enlisted for military service against his will. Nola, which commanded the southern plain of Campania, was successfully defended by Marcellus, and all attempts of Hannibal to obtain command of the western sea by the capture of Cumae or Neapolis were frustrated. In southern Italy Croton, Locri, and Petelia fell into his hands, but the obstinate defence offered by the Petelians against overwhelming odds was an ominous sign of the insuperable difficulties which lay in the conqueror's way.

HANNIBAL'S DIFFICULTY

As time went on it became increasingly evident that the issue of the war depended on the progress of events outside of Italy. Great genius as he was, Hannibal could not, with the force at his disposal, subdue the Romans. In the field he was irresistible, and during the thirteen years which were to elapse before his final departure from Italy no Roman general could boast that he had defeated Hannibal.[1] But in attacking

[1] See the authorities quoted by Streit in his monograph on the Second Punic War after Cannae, p. 4.

fortified places his cavalry was useless, and he was unprovided
with those siege-engines which had been brought to such
perfection by the military genius of the Greeks. In Italy,
then, he could do little more than keep possession of what he
had won and wait for reinforcements from beyond the sea.
Anxiously he scanned every dispatch which brought news from
Spain, from Sicily, from Macedon, or from Carthage. But one
by one the hopes which he had cherished so zealously faded
and vanished. In Spain the Scipios provided ample occupation for Hasdrubal and delayed his departure for many years ;
Syracuse was struck down by the iron hand of Marcellus ;
Philip, the young king of Macedon, wasted his energies in petty
local wars, until the Romans had time to raise a coalition
against him and keep him employed at home ; from Carthage,
divided in counsels, no efficient help was sent. There was,
indeed, one terrible moment when it seemed that Rome's
worst fears would be realized, and the two sons of Hamilcar
would share between them the spoils of Italy. But that
danger passed, and the ghastly trophy which was flung into
Hannibal's camp told him that the final hope of his house
was extinguished. Even then he held his ground for four
years longer, and only left the land which he had all but conquered at the call of his country in her need.

THE WAR AFTER CANNAE

The above brief sketch may serve as a sort of plan or chart
to the wide historical tract which we have now to examine
somewhat more in detail. Down to the battle of Cannae the
narrative of the Second Punic War has a unity and consistency
which give it a peculiar and absorbing interest. Our attention
is concentrated on one great personality, and we follow his
victorious career from the walls of New Carthage to the banks
of the Aufidus, only turning aside to view the dismay of the
proud city whose armies he has scattered and whose pride he
has humbled to the dust. But after Hannibal's crowning
victory the whole character of the contest changes. The
scene shifts from Italy to Sicily, from Sicily to Spain, and from

Spain to Africa, where the final issue is decided. In Italy itself the war flags, and instead of pitched battles we have a long series of marches and counter-marches, and towns lost and recovered. Livy, indeed, knows how to embellish his narrative with the wonderful feats of his favourite heroes, but these episodes owe their origin mostly to the lively imagination of the historian, or to the untrustworthy sources from which he copied.

HANNIBAL'S POSITION

It has been a matter of wonder both in ancient and modern times why Hannibal did so little after his supreme achievement at Cannae. It was said then, and the statement has often been repeated, that he might have marched upon Rome and carried the city by assault before the Senate and people had recovered from the panic which followed that great disaster. Yet he allowed the opportunity to go by, and, after obtaining possession of Capua, did nothing of importance for the rest of the year. This supposed transition from portentous energy to apathetic negligence produced a fine crop of aphoristic reflections, such as became fashionable in the decline of literature, when the great characters and the great events of history were treated as themes for schoolmasters and schoolboys. Hannibal, we are told, knew how to conquer, but he knew not how to use his victory. Hannibal, we hear again, found his Cannae at Capua, and the discipline of his army was ruined by the seductions of that voluptuous city. But all this moralizing is shown to be futile when tested by simple fact. Hannibal's own losses at Cannae were by no means inconsiderable, amounting to some six thousand men, and of the others many must have been disabled by wounds, and all would be in need of rest after the exertions of that memorable day. Moreover, his army was mostly composed of half-savage men, accustomed after every great effort to a period of licence and indulgence. Then, too, the rising among the Italians on which he had built so many hopes fell far short of his expectations. Umbria, Etruria, and the whole of central Italy, a great part of Samnium, and most of the Greek cities on the coast remained faithful to the Romans, and even in Campania he had failed to obtain a footing in any harbour-town and was hampered by the southern fortress of Nola. Limited as his sphere of influence was, it compelled him to divide his forces, for he dared not trust his Italian allies too far, nor could he look for large reinforcements from this source. In Apulia the great fortresses of Luceria, Canusium, and Venusia fettered his movements, and in Bruttium the important town of Rhegium was held for the Romans, hindering his communications with Sicily. Even the Gauls, after the defeat of Postumius, remained quiet, being watched by two Roman officers from Ariminum and Picenum. But the circumstance most fatal to his prospects was the victorious career of the Scipios in Spain, which long prevented him from deriving any advantage from the military resources of that great peninsula. Thus the dark year of Cannae came to an end, and already the Romans might feel that the worst was over.

COURSE OF THE WAR

In the next year the position of affairs in Italy remained substantially unaltered, but the advantage remained on the whole with the Romans. By a great effort four armies were placed on foot, and the chief seat of the war was again in Campania. Hannibal, who took up his station on the heights of Tifata, overlooking Capua, was watched by the two consuls, Gracchus and the old Fabius, and a third army, under Marcellus, lay at Nola, while Valerius, the praetor, whose post was at Luceria, overran the lands of the Lucanians and the revolted Samnites. Baffled in an attempt on Cumae, and besieged by complaints from his Italian allies, Hannibal withdrew from Campania and took up his winter quarters at Arpi, in Apulia. During the summer he had received the long-looked-for reinforcements from Carthage, which landed in Bruttium under their general Hanno. Mago, Hannibal's brother, who was sent to Carthage after Cannae with news of the victory, had at first been appointed for this service, but the serious aspect of affairs in Spain compelled the home government to send him with the

greater part of his troops to augment the army of Hasdrubal.
The prospects of Rome were steadily improving. Two more
victories were announced from Spain, and the revolt in Sardinia
was put down by Manlius Torquatus, who had gathered his
first laurels in the same island twenty years before. Another
piece of good fortune was the capture of envoys from Philip
of Macedon who had been sent to arrange an alliance with
Hannibal. A second embassy succeeded in reaching Hannibal's camp, and returned in safety. But the Senate, warned in
time, sent Valerius Laevinus to command the fleet at Brundisium, with orders to forestall the threatened invasion from
Macedon by carrying the war into the enemy's country.

Events in Sicily

For the next two years (214–213 B.C.) the chief interest in
the war is found in Sicily and its capital Syracuse. That
brilliant city, which for three centuries had defied all the power
of Carthage, which had humbled the pride of Athens, Syracuse,
the bulwark and glory of western Hellenism, had fallen on
evil times and the day of her desolation was drawing near.
After a reign of little more than twelve months Hieronymus,
the grandson of Hiero, had been assassinated, and the partisans
of Rome sought to confirm their ascendancy by a general
massacre of the royal family. But all Sicily was in a state of
ferment and excitement, and there was a general belief that
the Romans could never survive their crushing defeat at
Cannae. Appius Claudius, the Roman praetor in the island,
found himself unable to cope with the growing disorder, and
the consul Marcellus was sent to take the supreme command.
Marcellus first turned his attention to Leontini, which had
become the rallying-ground for the party opposed to Rome.
Being in command of a powerful force, he speedily carried the
place by storm, and publicly scourged and beheaded two
thousand deserters from the Roman fleet, who formed part of
the garrison. This act of severity, and the cruelties which
attended the sack of Leontini, raised a cry of horror throughout
Sicily, and gave the opportunity for which Hannibal's agents

Photo from "Aus dem class. Süden" (published by C. Coleman, Lübeck)

PLATE XXXVI.   SYRACUSE

244

PLATE XXXVII. FORT EURYELUS

in Syracuse had been waiting. The chief among these were Hippocrates and Epicydes, two Greeks of Syracusan descent, but born and educated in Carthage, who had followed Hannibal to Italy, and had been sent by him after the death of Hiero to work upon the mind of the young Hieronymus. Since the arrival of Marcellus they had been lurking in the neighbourhood of Syracuse, but they now came forth from their retirement and suddenly appeared among the Syracusan troops, who were stationed in the neighbourhood of the capital. Their inflammatory speeches and the exaggerated reports of the recent atrocities at Leontini lashed the soldiers to fury, and breaking up their camp they marched back to Syracuse, with the two renegade Greeks at their head. Here they were joined by all the rabble of the city, the prisons were broken open, slaves were set at liberty, and after a general butchery of the party favourable to Rome Syracuse declared openly for Carthage, and prepared to stand a siege.

SYRACUSE

In mere extent Syracuse was the greatest city of western Europe, its walls embracing a circuit of more than twenty miles. It was divided into three main sections—the original settlement, on the island of Ortygia, connected with the mainland by a bridge; Achradina, which covered the eastern end of a triangular plateau, with its base resting on the sea; and an extensive suburb, including the whole remaining portion of the plateau, and terminating in a point called Euryelus. From the time of Dionysius the whole of this vast area had been included within the line of walls, but Achradina formed a city in itself, being isolated from the suburban quarter by a wall running north and south from sea to sea.

THE SIEGE

Uniting his forces with those of Appius Claudius, Marcellus made a vigorous attempt to carry the city by assault. But all his efforts were baffled by the genius of the famous mathematician Archimedes, who applied the principles of the science of which he was so consummate a master to provide the means of defence for his native town. Huge masses of rock hurled by his engines shattered the Roman ships at long range, or if the vessels approached nearer they were assailed by a volley of missiles from the lighter artillery,

or caught by iron grapples attached to powerful cranes, which plucked them bodily out of the water and then let them go, so that they were swamped by the fall. The whole city seemed to be converted into a vast engine of war, worked and directed by one supreme mind, and such was the terror inspired by Archimedes that Marcellus was obliged to abandon the attack and turn the siege into a blockade. But with the force at his disposal it was impossible to complete the investment of so extensive a place, and meanwhile the revolt had spread to nearly the whole of Sicily, so that his attention was diverted to other parts of the island. Urged by Hannibal, the Carthaginians acted for once with energy, and a force was sent under Himilco, which captured Agrigentum, "the second eye of Sicily," and lent active support to the revolted towns. Accordingly the siege was protracted for two years, Marcellus being continued in his command with proconsular power.

FALL OF SYRACUSE

But at last the long-looked-for opportunity arrived. It was the height of summer, and the great festival of Artemis was at hand, when the whole city would be given up to revelry. For the Syracusans, confident in the strength of their walls and wearied by their long confinement, had resolved to celebrate the feast with unusual pomp, and wine was to be distributed among the citizens without stint. Informed of their intention by deserters, Marcellus set out at nightfall with a chosen troop, and planted his ladders at the foot of the wall which ran along the northern edge of the plateau on which the outer city stood. He met with little or no opposition, for this part of Syracuse was thinly inhabited and the houses were separated by wide spaces of open ground. At daybreak the northern gate, called the Hexapylon, was forced, and Marcellus was thus master of the whole western quarter of Syracuse, with the exception of the fort at Euryelus. The hardest part of his enterprise, however, was yet to be accomplished; for though he soon obtained possession of Euryelus, and was thus secured from attack in his rear, Achradina and Ortygia still held out, and a new army had been dispatched from Carthage to the relief of Syracuse. But the deadly fevers bred by the heats of summer in the low, marshy ground of the Anapus wrought havoc in the ranks of the relieving army, and the city itself was a prey to discord and anarchy, which destroyed all hope of effectual resistance. Achradina was betrayed into the hands of Marcellus by a Spanish officer, Ortygia was carried by a sudden assault, and the whole city became a scene of pillage and slaughter. Marcellus, it would seem, did his best to check the fury of his troops, but in spite of all his efforts much blood was shed, and among the victims was the aged Archimedes, who was cut down by a rude soldier while intent on a problem in geometry.

DESOLATION OF SICILY

Marcellus left Sicily a year later, carrying with him the rich spoils of Syracuse, among which were the statues of her gods, the work of renowned artists, now destined to adorn the temples of her conqueror. But the island was still in a disturbed state, Agrigentum remained in the hands of the enemy, and Mutines, an able cavalry officer, who had been sent over by Hannibal, was scouring the country with a wild horde of Numidians. The work which Marcellus had left unfinished was taken up by M. Valerius Laevinus, who had gained distinction in the war against Philip of Macedon, and at the end of the year (210 B.C.) he was able to report to the Senate that the sacred Island of the Two Goddesses[1] was enjoying the blessing of a Roman peace. There was peace, indeed, in Sicily, but with it there came paralysis of all native energy and complete political degradation. If Theocritus could have lived again he would have seen the happy rural population of which he had sung superseded by a multitude of slaves, who tilled the fields for their rapacious masters, and eked out a scanty subsistence by robbery and violence. Not the least of the evils which were wrought by Hannibal's fatal ambition was the ruin and desolation of Sicily.

INDECISIVE WAR

The true measure of Hannibal's genius is seen in the magnitude and extent of the war which he had kindled, and the gigantic efforts made by the Romans to keep the field against a host of enemies, in Italy and in Sicily, in Sardinia, Greece, and Spain. Every year great levies of troops had to be raised, and something like a third of the whole military force of Rome and her allies was constantly under arms. The tide of war swept to and fro over all the south of Italy, but for some time no decisive progress was made on either side. Just before his departure for Sicily Marcellus had taken part with Fabius in the storming of Casilinum (214 B.C.), and this important place, commanding the bridge over the Volturnus, was recovered for the Romans. The next year is almost a blank, and the only event recorded is the recapture of Arpi by the consul Fabius, son of the famous Cunctator. But the year which followed is crowded with important events—the fall of Syracuse, the ruin of the Roman armies in Spain, the betrayal of Tarentum to Hannibal, and the investment of Capua.

[1] Demeter and Persephone

SECOND PUNIC WAR

Siege of Capua

The Romans had long been waiting for an opportunity of striking with effect at the revolted capital of Campania, and more than once great armies had been massed at convenient points ready to pounce upon the coveted prey. Hitherto these had been frustrated by the vigilance of Hannibal, and the dread inspired by his terrible cavalry. But presently Hannibal was called away to southern Italy, and the consuls, Appius Claudius and Quintus Fulvius Flaccus, were thus left at leisure to converge in overwhelming force on the doomed city. Great magazines of corn were established at Casilinum, at Puteoli, and at the mouth of the Volturnus, to provide for the victualling of the besieging army, and the blockading works were then taken in hand and carried out on a gigantic scale. A double wall and trench were drawn round the whole circuit of the city, and the space between the lines served to contain the camp and arsenals of the Roman army. The siege-works, when completed, had the appearance of a vast suburb, with a wide space of open ground between the inner line of circumvallation and the city wall. But it was a suburb peopled by sixty thousand armed men, and fortified against all assaults from within or from without.

Hannibal at Tarentum

Meanwhile Hannibal had obtained some important successes, which might compensate him in no small degree for the approaching loss of Capua. His eye had long been fixed on Tarentum, the richest and most powerful city of southern Italy, and for some time past he had been in communication with a party among the citizens who were discontented with the Roman rule. One attempt which had been made two years before had been frustrated by the precautions of the Roman commander at Brundisium, who took effectual means for the defence of the city, and sent some of the malcontents to Rome to serve as hostages for the good behaviour of the rest. These men were subsequently caught in an attempt to escape from their confinement, and the Romans, with impolitic harshness, condemned them to be scourged and flung from the Tarpeian Rock. This act removed the last scruples of the Tarentines, and they renewed their application to Hannibal, who was not slow to profit by the occasion. Marcus Livius, the governor, was a good soldier, but a man of indolent and luxurious habits, and on the night appointed for the attempt he had been feasting with his friends, and retired to rest heavy with food and wine. In the middle of the night his slumbers were rudely disturbed by the tidings that Hannibal had entered the town with ten thousand troops and that his own men were being cut down as they came out in scattered parties from their quarters. He succeeded in making his escape to the citadel, and, being joined by the remnant of his troops, maintained his position against all the assaults of the enemy. But the city itself was lost to the Romans, and all the Greek towns of southern Italy, with the exception of Rhegium, now went over to Hannibal.

Capua Relieved

The fall of Tarentum seems to have occurred at the time when the consuls were making their preparations for the siege of Capua, and Hannibal was still engaged with the affairs of southern Italy when an urgent appeal for help reached him from his Campanian allies.[1] Acting with his accustomed energy, he set his forces in motion, and in a few days was once more encamped in his old station on Mount Tifata. His sudden appearance for a moment changed the aspect of affairs, for as yet no Roman general was to be found who dared to meet the invincible Phoenician in the open field. The Roman armies fell back, and Hannibal entered Capua without opposition. The arrival of the great captain and the triumphant evidence which he had just given of his still unshaken ascendancy raised the spirits of the Capuans and nerved them for the impending struggle.

[1] The chronology of this period is in great confusion, and the placing of the events largely conjectural.

PLATE XXXVIII. THE ANAPUS

PLATE XXXIX. THE TARPEIAN ROCK   251

ROME LOSES THREE ARMIES

Hannibal, however, had to content himself with the moral effect which he had produced, for it was impossible for him to fix his quarters in Campania and there was great need for his presence in the southern provinces of Italy. On his return march he fell in with a tumultuary force which had been raised by Centenius, a brave centurion, for the defence of Lucania, where Gracchus, the proconsul, had recently been betrayed into an ambush and his army dispersed. Centenius was rash enough to measure himself with the victor of Cannae, and he paid for his folly with his own life and the loss of his whole army, amounting, it was said, to sixteen thousand men. As if this were not enough, Hannibal then attacked Fulvius, the praetor, who was encamped with two legions at Herdonea, and cut to pieces nearly the whole of his troops. Thus within a few weeks three armies had been lost to Rome, and Hannibal might well be content with his year's work when he went into winter quarters in Apulia (212 B.C.). But the material resources of Rome were immense, and her moral energy was inexhaustible. Once more the fatal lines closed round Capua, and within that circle at least Hannibal was never to set foot again.

INTERNAL AFFAIRS

We turn with relief from the endless record of battles and sieges to take a glance at the internal state of Rome during these eventful years. A series of fearful disasters and the pressure of imminent peril had allayed the strife of parties and brought harmony for a time into the complex organism of the State. The antiquated machinery of government, which had prolonged the first struggle with Carthage for twenty-three years and had recently led to the slaughter of Thrasymene and Cannae, was to a large extent set aside, and the Senate, with Fabius at its head, assumed the supreme control. If Rome was to survive this fearful visitation it was above all things necessary that none but competent men should be sent into the field against Hannibal, and that their command should be prolonged, if the occasion required it, from year to year. There must be no shifting of control from one consul to another, no more political jealousy carried from the Forum to the camp. If the people prove refractory and insist on their constitutional rights, Fabius does not scruple to override the constitution; and when the popular candidate tries to assert his claims he points significantly to the axes of his lictors and reminds the ambitious aspirant that he is in the Field of Mars and subject to the last extremity of military law.

An Empty Treasury

One of the hardest problems which the government had to face was the difficulty of providing funds for the conduct of the war. Business was at a standstill, vast tracts of land remained uncultivated, and the ordinary sources of revenue were dried up. Although the *tributum*, a war-tax levied on personal property, was doubled, the public accounts still showed a heavy balance on the wrong side. As in the First Punic War, Rome's needs were supplied by the patriotic devotion of her wealthier citizens. The great capitalists who contracted to provide food and clothing for the Roman armies renounced all claims to profit, simply stipulating for a bare return of their outlay when better times came. These contracts naturally left an opening for fraudulent practices, similar to those which have afforded a subject for legislation in our own times. Rogues were found who sent rotten ships to sea with worthless cargoes, caused them to be scuttled, and sent in a claim to the treasury for many times their value. But the villainy of these was exposed, and they were punished by the loss of citizenship and the confiscation of their property. Among other extraordinary measures to meet the drain on the public funds was the surrender of moneys held in trust for widows and orphans, which were paid over to the State, and the obligation gradually discharged by deferred bills on the exchequer.

SECOND PUNIC WAR

An Outburst of Fanaticism

The prolonged strain of peril and anxiety led to a sudden outburst of fanaticism among the people, and new and extravagant forms of worship were publicly paraded before the very eyes of the magistrates. Like men afflicted by some grievous disease, the Romans lost faith in the saving virtues of their ancestral worship and betook themselves to quacks and impostors. The city was crowded by a needy multitude, driven in from the rural districts, and many of these destitute persons sought to supply their necessities by trading on the credulity of their fellow-citizens. At every street-corner vendors of oracles and new forms of prayer might be seen, and they found eager hearers and ready purchasers. Even the Capitol and the Forum were beset by a mob of frantic women, performing strange rites to unknown gods. To make an end of these scandals an edict was issued by the urban praetor ordering all books of a religious tendency to be delivered up before a certain date, and forbidding all unauthorized forms of worship, whether public or private. And in order to allay the paroxysm of fanatical excitement a solemn service was held in the temples of the national gods.

Hannibal before Rome

The chief event of the next year (211 B.C.), and one of the most famous in the whole war, was Hannibal's march from Capua and his sudden appearance before the walls of Rome, which profoundly impressed the imagination of the Romans and was recalled with a shudder by their latest posterity. But here, as elsewhere, we have to deplore the wretched materials [1] from which ancient history is in a great part constructed; and even if the limits of the present volume allowed it we should find it impossible to give a circumstantial account of this renowned episode. The narrative of Livy is a huddle of incongruous details, such as form the common stock-in-trade of cheap romance. At one moment we hear of

[1] A complaint often raised, with good reason, by Arnold.

the wild panic caused at Rome by Hannibal's approach, of temples thronged by hysterical women, who sweep the pavement with their long hair as they lie in prostrate supplication,[1] at another of swaggering defiances, fit only for schoolboys, which are said to have been exchanged between a great man and a great people when involved in a struggle for life and death. Avoiding all such " perilous stuff," we shall confine ourselves to the barest outline.

Hannibal was in Bruttium, engaged in preparations for the capture of the citadel of Tarentum, when an imploring message reached him from the Capuans, who were beginning to feel the rigours of the siege. With a picked body of troops, mainly composed of cavalry and light infantry, he marched with all speed from Bruttium, and, taking up a position behind the sheltering heights of Tifata, opened communications with the beleaguered garrison and arranged for a combined assault on the Roman lines. Attacked simultaneously from within and from without, the Romans made a valiant defence, and Hannibal, finding that all attempts to break the blockade were fruitless, abandoned his camp on Tifata and disappeared into the highlands of Samnium. His plan was to show himself before the walls of Rome, and thus compel the proconsuls[2] to raise the siege of Capua, or at least to withdraw part of their forces for the defence of the capital, and he had contrived to apprise the Capuans of his intention, so that they might not be alarmed by his sudden departure. Keeping to the hill-country, and marching with secrecy and dispatch, he crossed the Arno, and pitched his camp within five miles of Rome. But if he had expected to take the Romans by surprise he was disappointed. With three legions, newly levied, the consuls took the field against him, and, pursuing the old Fabian tactics, watched his movements from a safe distance, while ample measures were taken for the defence of the walls. Hannibal's bold design had failed : Rome was still impregnable, and not

---

[1] This curious detail is mentioned both by Livy and Polybius.
[2] Fulvius and Appius Claudius, who were continued in their command with proconsular authority.

a man had been withdrawn from the siege of Capua.[1] With
the quick decision which inspired all his movements, he turned
his back on Rome, and, directing his course toward southern
Italy, made a rapid dash on Rhegium, at the remotest end of
the peninsula, and almost succeeded in carrying the city by
surprise.

The dreaded moment, so long awaited at Rome, had come
and gone, and young Roman mothers might tell their grand-
children in after-days that they had looked into the face of
the demon Hannibal. At the point from which his retreating
columns had last been sighted, in front of the Porta Capena,
a chapel was erected to Rediculus Tutanus, the guardian spirit
who had turned back the tide of war from the city beloved by
the gods.

Fall of Capua

Capua was now cut off from the last hope of relief, and no
course was left to the citizens but unconditional surrender or
a voluntary death. Some twenty-seven of the nobles, whose
offence was beyond forgiveness, chose the latter course, and,
having fortified themselves by a final banquet, with copious
draughts of wine, they passed round the poisoned cup. Then
the gates were opened, and the trembling Capuans waited to
receive their doom from the hands of the conqueror. Fifty-
three of the nobles, the chief authors of the revolt, were sent
to Cales and Teanum, to be kept in custody until the Senate
had pronounced on their case. Such, at least, was the intention
of Claudius,[2] but Fulvius, the other proconsul, a stern and hard
man, was resolved to make sure and speedy work, and in one
day he caused all the prisoners to be scourged and beheaded
before his own eyes.

Measures of extraordinary severity were then passed by the
Senate to determine the future condition of Capua and the
adjacent district of Campania. The whole body of the citizens

---

[1] This is the account of Polybius. According to Livy, Fulvius was recalled.
[2] According to another account, Claudius died of a wound just before the
capitulation.

was transported beyond the Volturnus, the Liris, or the Tiber, according to their varying degrees of guilt, and the city was left to be inhabited by a motley multitude of artisans and traders, who were governed as a subject community by a prefect sent yearly from Rome. The rich fields of northern Campania were added to the public lands and rented to Roman citizens, who paid a fixed charge to the State. Livy extols the clemency of the Romans, who measured out vengeance in due proportion on a rebellious people, but refrained from venting their anger on the walls and houses of the ancient city. Capua, indeed, was left standing, but it was left as a body without a soul, and another step had been taken toward the extinction of local life and manners in Italy.

THE WAR IN SPAIN

The shifting current of our narrative now carries us to Spain, where for six years (218-212 B.C.) the cause of Rome had been upheld by Cnaeus Scipio and his brother Publius, who arrived with reinforcements after the defeat of the Romans at the Trebia. Having established their headquarters at Tarraco, they crossed the Ebro, formed connexions with the Spanish tribes, and entered into communication with Syphax, a powerful Numidian chieftain, who was engaged in war with Carthage. Above all they kept Hasdrubal fully employed, and prevented him from joining his brother in Italy at a time when such a combination would have been utterly ruinous to the Romans. There was one moment when it seemed as if they were to anticipate the achievement of the younger Scipio and effect the conquest of all Spain. Hasdrubal was recalled to Africa to put down the insurrection of the Numidians, and during his absence the Scipios recovered Saguntum, and carried their arms into the southern districts of the peninsula, beyond the Guadalquivir. But the revolt of Syphax was quickly put down, and from the time of Hasdrubal's return to Spain their fortunes began to ebb. The fickle Spaniards, lured by the gold of Carthage, deserted their new allies, and the Scipios, separated from each other and attacked by overwhelming numbers, were defeated and slain (212 B.C.). The Roman cause was only saved from ruin by the spirit and ability of Lucius Marcius, a young Roman knight, who collected the broken remnant of the army and made a gallant defence on the northern side of the Ebro. The fall of Capua set free part of the immense forces which had hitherto been employed in Italy, and enabled the Romans to send considerable reinforcements to Spain. But the new commander, C. Claudius Nero, a man of harsh and arrogant temper, was ill-qualified for the task to which he had been called, and a subtler spirit was needed to restore the sinking fortunes and revive the influence of Rome among the proud and sensitive people of the Spanish peninsula.

Scipio Africanus

The Romans found what they wanted in the person of the young Scipio, the most brilliant figure that had so far appeared to adorn the annals of his country, and the first of those kingly natures who by slow degrees accustomed the Romans to the sway of one sovereign mind. Scipio was now in his twenty-seventh year,[1] and as yet he had held no higher office than that of aedile. But he had attracted attention by his gallant behaviour at the battle of the Ticinus, when he had saved his father's life, and his firm demeanour had done much to arrest the panic which followed the dreadful day of Cannae. His wonderful personal beauty and the unique charm of his address made him the darling of the people, and with that touch of charlatanism which, according to Heine, is a weapon not disdained even by the greatest men, he took pains to promote the vulgar belief in his divine origin and in the mystic tie which bound him to the supreme deity of Rome. Such was the man who now offered to take up the onerous task which all others had declined, and who was appointed by the universal vote of the centuries to take command in the distracted country in which his father and uncle had recently found a soldier's grave. By a measure unprecedented in Roman history he was invested

---

[1] According to Livy, he was twenty-four (xxvi. 18).

with full proconsular authority, and with him were associated M. Junius Silanus, who succeeded Claudius as propraetor, and Laelius, Scipio's intimate friend, who took command of the fleet.

With reinforcements consisting of ten thousand infantry, a thousand cavalry, and thirty quinqueremes, Scipio embarked at Ostia, and arrived without mishap at Tarraco, the head-quarters of the Roman army in Spain. He soon won all hearts by his gracious demeanour, and by his generous recognition of the services of Lucius Marcius, and as soon as the season permitted he crossed the Ebro (spring, 210 B.C.) with the avowed intention of seeking out the Punic forces and giving them battle. At this time there were three Carthaginian generals commanding in Spain—Hasdrubal, the son of Hamilcar, Mago, his brother, and another Hasdrubal, the son of Gisco. By repeated acts of oppression they had excited general hatred among the native Spaniards, and having no common plan of campaign they were acting independently and at wide intervals from each other. All this was known to Scipio, and he knew also that New Carthage, the grand arsenal of the Carthaginian armies, had been left with a weak garrison and that not one of the three generals was less than three days' march from the town. Accordingly he resolved on a bold stroke, and, advancing by forced marches, he swept down upon New Carthage and pitched his camp on the northern side of the wall. He had kept his design secret from all except the admiral Laelius, who was instructed to time his movements by those of the army, and the operation was so skilfully conducted that fleet and army appeared on the scene of action at the same moment.

Scipio takes New Carthage

The city of New Carthage was built on a peninsula, facing south, and on the landward side the whole line of the walls, except a narrow strip on the north-eastern side, was protected by a lagoon, which at low tide was so shallow that it might easily be forded. Scipio, who had been informed of this circumstance by native fishermen, announced to his troops

that the sea-god Poseidon had appeared to him in a dream
and promised to aid him in the approaching assault. Early
next morning the storming parties fixed their ladders, and the
attack began at the north-eastern angle of the wall. But the
fortifications were so lofty at this point and the defence was
so desperate that after many hours of severe fighting the
Romans were driven back, and the soldiers of the garrison
breathed freely, thinking that their day's work was over.
They soon found that they were mistaken. Later in the day
Scipio, whose eyes were fixed on the lagoon, observed that the
waters were sinking. Aided by a strong north wind, the out-
flow grew stronger and stronger, and at last, with a mighty
rush, a vast volume of water poured through the narrow
channel connecting the lagoon with the western end of
the harbour. This was the moment for which Scipio had
been waiting, and he at once ordered the assault to be resumed
at the eastern gate. Then, placing himself at the head of five
hundred picked men, he led them across the shallow waters of
the lagoon, bidding them be of good cheer, since Poseidon was
visibly fighting on their side. The point selected for attack
was on the northern edge of the town, where the wall was low
and left almost without defenders. Thus assailed on both
sides, and exhausted by their previous exertions, the garrison
made but a feeble resistance, and New Carthage, the centre of
the Punic power in Spain, where the house of Hamilcar had
kept almost regal state, was carried by storm. A vast treasure
fell into the hands of Scipio, and, what was of at least equal
importance, he obtained possession of three hundred Spanish
prisoners, who had been seized as hostages by the Carthaginian
commanders. He treated them with the utmost kindness, and
afterwards dismissed them to their homes, where they spread
golden opinions of his goodness among their kinsmen, who
belonged to the noblest families in Spain.

Scipio defeats Hasdrubal

The fame of this exploit made a profound impression on the
Spanish chiefs and brought numerous adherents to Scipio's

standard. No other action of importance was attempted until the following year, when Scipio marched to encounter Hasdrubal, who was stationed at Baecula, on the northern bank of the Guadalquivir. The accounts of the great victory obtained by the Roman proconsul over the son of Hamilcar are evidently exaggerated, and it is certain that Hasdrubal was able to carry off his treasure, his elephants, and the greater part of his troops. Hasdrubal had no desire to risk another engagement, as his great desire was to make his way to Italy and effect a junction with his brother Hannibal. The eastern route, which had been followed by Hannibal, was barred by a detachment of Scipio's troops, and accordingly Hasdrubal crossed the Pyrenees at the extreme west and plunged into the heart of Gaul. More than a year later he emerged from his retreat, and the Romans had to face that peril which had hitherto been held aloof by the exertions of Scipio's predecessors in Spain. Scipio was bitterly attacked for this negligence by his political opponents, and there is no doubt that his conduct deserved severe censure, but when the danger was past his one great fault was soon eclipsed by the general lustre of his achievements.

BATTLE OF ILIPA

The next two years saw the steady advance of the Roman arms in Spain, and the issue of the contest was practically decided by a great battle fought at Ilipa, on the Guadalquivir, in which Hasdrubal, the son of Gisco, was totally defeated and his army dispersed (206 B.C.). In the course of the contest Scipio obtained a new ally, whose adherence was to be of the utmost importance when the scene of the war was shifted to Africa. This was Masinissa, a young Numidian prince, who had fought for Carthage in the war against Syphax, and had subsequently served in Spain under Hasdrubal Gisco. The brilliant feats of Scipio had fired the imagination of the young warrior, and having this visible image of Roman greatness before his eyes he became convinced that Carthage was engaged in a hopeless struggle. So he sought and obtained an interview with the proconsul, and was captivated by the spell of that magic personality.

Peace in Spain

The alliance with Masinissa was almost the last, and perhaps the most important, fruit of Scipio's work in Spain. Previously to this he had tried to establish a connexion with Syphax, the old enemy of Carthage, and, with blameworthy rashness, for which he was afterwards severely reprimanded by Fabius, he had crossed the strait and visited the king of western Numidia in his capital. He was courteously received, but another influence was at work,[1] which presently drew Syphax, with all his great military resources, to the side of Carthage. On his return Scipio was confronted by a general insurrection of the Spanish tribes, which was put down with ruthless severity, and before this task was well completed a severe illness, brought on by his exertions, confined him to his quarters at New Carthage. Forthwith the flames of insurrection broke out again, and to add to his difficulties a whole battalion of his own troops rose in open mutiny. But the gods were kind to their favourite and brought him safely through the crisis. Rapidly restored to health, Scipio quelled the mutiny by a judicious mixture of sternness and indulgence, and in a single campaign stamped out the last embers of revolt. Peace was now restored throughout Spain, and by the submission of Gades the Carthaginians were deprived of their last stronghold in the peninsula. Four years had sufficed for the accomplishment of this grand enterprise, and Scipio's thoughts were now turned elsewhere. But before we accompany him on his triumphant return to Rome we must take up the main thread of our narrative and follow the course of the war in Italy, where great events had been happening since his departure for Spain.

[1] I have been compelled to omit the romantic story of Sophonisba, from considerations of space.

REPUBLICAN ROME

Rome gains Ground

During the three years which followed the fall of Capua the Romans by sheer dogged persistency steadily gained ground. Campania had already been recovered, the revolted Samnites returned to their allegiance, and Hannibal was slowly thrust back into the extreme south of Italy. Most of the hard fighting was done by the veteran Marcellus, and though the reports of his victories have doubtless been exaggerated it was much that he could meet the victor of Cannae in the field and fight action after action without incurring disastrous defeat. Laevinus, after the subjugation of Sicily, had put a thorn in Hannibal's side by conveying four thousand hardy adventurers who had hitherto disturbed the peace of the island to Rhegium, where they maintained themselves against all attacks and harassed the allies of Hannibal by making constant raids into the Bruttian territory. Assailed every year by great armies, and with his own numbers constantly diminishing, the indomitable Phoenician still upheld his superiority in the field. But he was sadly embarrassed by the want of a fixed centre for his operations, by the difficulty of providing food for his soldiers, and by the distracting nature of the war, which obliged him to hurry to and fro and tire out his troops by constant forced marches. All his attempts to reduce the citadel of Tarentum had failed, and while his attention was occupied at the extremity of Italy the town itself was betrayed to Fabius by a Bruttian who had been left in command of the garrison (209 B.C.). Thus within two

A Knight's Ring

years the two most important fruits of Hannibal's victories, Capua and Tarentum, had been torn from his grasp. It was but a slight consolation for this severe loss when, in the following year, Marcellus, consul for the fifth time, and his colleague Crispinus, lost their lives in a cavalry skirmish near Venusia. On this and other occasions Hannibal showed a chivalrous spirit which the Romans would have done well to imitate. He gazed with sorrow on his

262

fallen enemy, who at the age of sixty had acted with the heedless precipitance of a boy, and, after taking the gold ring from his finger, ordered his body to be burned, and the ashes to be conveyed in a silver urn to his son.

GENERAL DISTRESS

But though on the whole the tide was running decidedly in favour of the Romans, yet the hardships and sacrifices imposed on Rome and her allies by this cruel war were becoming almost unbearable. The general stagnation of business and industry made it increasingly difficult to meet the enormous demands on the exchequer, and it had recently been found necessary to lay hands on a reserve fund, arising from a tax on emancipated slaves, which had been put by with prudent thrift from year to year since the old days before the Samnite wars (357 B.C.). Losses on the battlefield had made fearful gaps in the muster-roll of Roman citizens, and the census returns showed that their number was reduced to little more than half. Another ominous sign of the general exhaustion was the refusal of twelve out of the thirty Latin colonies to send in further contributions of men or money.[1] The city was crowded with refugees from the rural districts, and but for the pacification of Sicily and a timely supply of corn from the king of Egypt it would hardly have been possible to find food for this helpless multitude.

HASDRUBAL IN ITALY

And now, when the pulse of the nation was beating thus low, there came a sudden call which filled every heart with anxious foreboding. The old peril which had loomed remote for more than ten years was now approaching swiftly from the north, to burst in tempest on the wasted fields of Italy. Rome was still in mourning for her stoutest champion, Marcellus, when news arrived that Hasdrubal, the son of Hamilcar, was marching toward the Alps. He had remained a whole year

[1] It may be observed that Niese, a high authority, rejects this incident, as " bearing a legendary character."

263

in Gaul, and penetrated as far as Auvergne, enlisting troops and preparing for the grand invasion which was to decide the issue of the war. He crossed the Alps early in the year (207 B.C.), without encountering any of those difficulties which caused such ruinous loss to Hannibal, and, marching along the line of the Po, halted before Placentia, which had closed its gates against him.

The imminence of the crisis roused the Romans to extraordinary exertions. They had ample cause for alarm, for the Gauls and Ligurians were joining Hasdrubal by thousands, and signs of disaffection had recently appeared in Etruria and Umbria. But with these exceptions, and leaving out of account the half-barbarous Bruttians, the general heart of the nation was on their side. Two great armies were to be stationed at the chief points of danger, one confronting Hasdrubal in the north and the other to keep Hannibal in check and prevent him from effecting a junction with his brother. Etruria, Bruttium, and the district of Tarentum were each guarded by two legions, which could unite, if necessary, with the two consular armies. Two legions formed the garrison of Rome, and a third was appointed for the defence of Capua. All Italy bristled with arms, and the number of men called out amounted to not less than a hundred and fifty thousand.

The consuls for this memorable year were C. Claudius Nero, to whose brief command in Spain we have already alluded, and Marcus Livius Salinator, the brother of that Livius whose negligence had lost Tarentum, and who had afterwards redeemed his fault by his stubborn defence of the citadel. Livius was a stern and sullen old man, embittered by an old grievance, and Nero had as yet given no proof of the brilliant qualities which he displayed at this momentous crisis. The choice of two such men at such a time is somewhat surprising, but it was amply justified by events.

Failing in his attempt on Placentia, Hasdrubal advanced upon Ariminum, where the praetor Lucius Porcius was stationed with two legions. Presently Livius, whom the lot had appointed to take command in the north, arrived at Ariminum with a full consular army, and the two Roman generals, uniting their forces, fell back upon Sena Gallica, about twelve miles to the south of the river Metaurus. Meanwhile the other consul, Nero, had been watching Hannibal in the south, and after a series of strategic movements, which we cannot now unravel,[1] we find him encamped near Canusium, where Hannibal had taken up his position, not far from the scene of his greatest victory.

March of the Seven Thousand

Hannibal's mind was torn with anxiety. His main object was to avoid an engagement until he had united his forces with those of Hasdrubal; but he knew not where his brother was, or by what route he intended to advance on central Italy. At this very moment six horsemen were riding southward with loose rein, bearing a dispatch from Hasdrubal, which he had sent off before leaving Placentia. But Hannibal was never to break the seal of that fatal missive, on which the future of two nations depended. After threading their way for hundreds of miles through the midst of enemies the horsemen lost their way in the neighbourhood of Tarentum and fell into the hands of a Roman officer, who sent them as prisoners to Nero's camp at Canusium. Informed by the dispatch that Hasdrubal intended to march from Ariminum by the Flaminian Road and wait for his brother in Umbria, Nero made a bold and resolute move. After sending the dispatch to Rome, with instructions that the southern pass into Umbria should be held by a strong force stationed at Narnia, he quickly got together a corps of seven thousand men, carefully selected for their strength and activity, and ordered them to prepare for immediate service, saying that he intended to make a sudden raid into Lucania. At nightfall he gave the signal to march, and as soon as he felt himself to be beyond the reach of pursuit he addressed his little army in a stirring speech, informing them of his real

[1] The evolutions of Hannibal as described by Livy and the counter-dance of Nero form together one of the curiosities of ancient history.

intention. He was leading them, he said, to join the other consul, that they might win an unfading wreath of glory as the conquerors of Hasdrubal and the saviours of Italy. A few days of strenuous exertion, followed by one brave effort, would win them this splendid prize and make them to be envied of all mankind. His men took fire from their leader's words, and such was their speed that, it is said, they accomplished a distance of ninety leagues in six days. Their march resembled a triumphal progress, for Nero had sent horsemen in advance to give notice of his approach, and the road was lined on both sides by an eager multitude, who brought food, wine, and all things necessary to help them on their way and invoked blessings on their heads as they passed. Timing his march so as to arrive at nightfall, Nero entered his colleague's camp in secrecy and silence, and the brave seven thousand, whose numbers had been swelled by volunteers on the road, were quartered in the tents of the elder consul's men.

DEFEAT OF HASDRUBAL

But in spite of all precautions the secret somehow leaked out. Hasdrubal was informed by his scouts that new faces, blackened by exposure, and horses lean from recent exertion had appeared in the Roman camp, and that the trumpet had been heard to sound twice in the quarters of Livius, betraying the presence of both consuls. Filled with apprehension, Hasdrubal resolved to retreat and place the Metaurus between himself and the enemy. But his guides deserted him, and, losing his way in the broken and difficult country, he was overtaken by the consuls as he wandered up and down looking for a ford. Thus driven to bay, he drew up his weary and dispirited troops and prepared to do battle. The Gauls, who were utterly disorganized by their hasty retreat, were placed in an unassailable position on the left, facing the contingent of Nero. In the centre were the Ligurians, covered by the elephants, and Hasdrubal himself, with his trusty Spaniards, occupied the right, where he was confronted by the consul Livius. Here the fighting was long and obstinate, until Nero,

who had vainly attempted to storm the height on which
the Gauls were posted, brought round his troops behind the
Roman army and assailed the division of Hasdrubal in flank
and rear. The situation of the Spaniards was now desperate,
and though they still fought on manfully they were overpowered and cut to pieces. The Gauls never came into action
at all, and many of them were found scattered about the
country, and were butchered where they lay, stupefied by
drink and fatigue. Seeing that all was lost, Hasdrubal set
spurs to his charger and, flinging himself upon a Roman cohort,
died the death of a hero. As to the numbers slain, it is
impossible to speak with certainty,[1] but the victory of the
Romans was complete and decisive, and a great treasure
which Hasdrubal was carrying to his brother came into their
possession.

REACTION IN ROME

How fearful had been the anxiety at Rome while the issue
was still pending was shown by the violence of the reaction
when the event of the battle was placed beyond doubt. There
followed a great outburst of joy, which spread like a mighty
wave from town to town and from homestead to homestead through the length and breadth of Italy, and its
echoes still ring loud and clear in the triumphant paean of
Horace.[2] The mood of dumb endurance and sullen resolution
which had lasted for so many years gave place to a general
cheerfulness, and women flocked to the temples with their
children, clad in their gayest attire, to offer up prayer and
praise to the guardian deities of Rome. Money was brought
out of secret hoards, and the throng and bustle in the centres
of business was the surest indication that the numbing spell
which had lain so long on the nation was broken at last.

---

[1] Fifty-six thousand on the side of the Carthaginians, according to Livy
(xxvii. 49); according to Polybius (xl. 3), ten thousand—a remarkable
discrepancy.

[2] *Odes*, iv. 4.

REPUBLICAN ROME

HANNIBAL'S FAILURE

Nero had returned straight from the battlefield to his army in Apulia, and the first notice which reached Hannibal of his brother's defeat was the gory head of Hasdrubal, which was flung into his camp by the consul's order. He sighed as he gazed on the pallid and distorted features, and said : " I recognize the fortune of Carthage." His cause in Italy was indeed ruined, and the sphere of his influence was now confined to a narrow corner of Bruttium. Yet here he maintained his ground for four years longer, and no one ventured to disturb the Punic lion in his lair. Even Livy pays an involuntary tribute to Rome's greatest enemy, in whose army, composed of such motley elements, the voice of mutiny was never heard, who for ten years had held a great part of Italy in fee, and who now stood, unassailed and unassailable, in his last retreat.

SCIPIO'S AFRICAN EXPEDITION

We now enter on the last act of this grand historical drama, which begins with Scipio's return from Spain (206 B.C.). All eyes were fixed on the brilliant young soldier, who by an unbroken series of victories had swept the Punic armies from the great peninsula and carried the arms of Rome to the western ocean. By an overwhelming majority he was elected consul for the next year, and before long he was busy with his preparations for the invasion of Africa. It was in vain that the aged Fabius, supported by a majority of the senators, raised his voice against the rash enterprise. Scipio openly avowed his intention of throwing himself on the support of the people if the senators persisted in their opposition, and after a warm debate the matter was compromised and he received permission to proceed to Sicily, with the liberty, if he thought fit, of carrying the war into Africa. His commission, which bore a peculiar and irregular character, was wrung from the Senate by strong political pressure and granted, as it were, under protest. His province was not to be Sicily, for the ordinary provincial governor exercised jurisdiction in the island, and he was forbidden to raise troops by the usual consular levy. But the enthusiasm of the Italian allies made amends for this factious and unworthy obstruction. From Etruria came supplies of arms and provisions and abundant materials for building a fleet; the Umbrians and Sabines, the Marsians and Pelignians, sent volunteers to serve in the army and man the ships. Within seven weeks from the time when the keels were laid Scipio set sail for Sicily with thirty vessels of war and a force of seven thousand men. But the core of the invading army was formed by two legions, the remnant of the slaughter of Cannae, who since that fatal day had been living as exiles in Sicily, excluded from all honourable service. Scipio welcomed these unfortunate men to his standard, and by a singular destiny the fugitives of Cannae became the main instruments of victory on the historic field of Zama.

First Macedonian War

The same year in which Scipio sailed for Sicily saw the conclusion of the ten years' war with Philip of Macedon. We have seen that one of the main elements in Hannibal's grand scheme of conquest was the support of the Macedonian king, and since the year after Cannae Philip had been in alliance with Carthage. But the projected invasion of Italy from the east never went farther than an idle menace, and within a few years Philip found himself involved in a harassing war which divided his energies and prevented him from lending any effectual aid to his Punic allies. By a series of politic negotiations the Romans succeeded in raising a powerful coalition against Philip, in which the Aetolians, the Illyrians, Elis, Sparta, and Messene, and Attalus, king of Pergamum, took part. The war dragged on with varying fortunes until the year of Hasdrubal's invasion, when the Romans were fully occupied in Italy, and the Aetolians, hard pressed by Philip, were compelled to sue for peace. After the defeat of Hasdrubal the Romans prepared to resume hostilities, but by the intervention of the Epirots they were induced to make terms with Philip, and the First Macedonian War came to an end. The grand fabric which had been raised by Hannibal's genius was now totally broken to pieces. In Spain, in Sicily, in Italy, the arms of Rome had triumphed ; the eastern peril had been kept at bay by a combination of valour and policy ; and before long her great enemy was summoned to fight his last fight in defence of his native land.

SCIPIO REACHES AFRICA

Scipio had spent the rest of the year in drilling his men and completing his preparations, and in the following spring he set sail from Lilybaeum with forty ships of war, four hundred transports, and thirty thousand men.[1] With him went his friend Laelius as commander of the fleet, and his quaestor was no less a person than Marcus Porcius Cato, then in his thirty-fifth year. Landing at the Fair Promontory, to the north of Utica, Scipio overran the country, and gathered a rich booty. Soon after his arrival he was joined by Masinissa, now a fugitive and an outlaw, having been expelled from his kingdom by his rival Syphax, who was now in alliance with Carthage. Presently Syphax himself appeared on the scene with a host of Numidians, and with him was Hasdrubal Gisco, who commanded the levies of Carthage. Scipio was reduced to the defensive, and months passed in fruitless negotiations with the king of Numidia, who was proud to figure as the arbiter between Carthage and Rome. Syphax, it would seem, was quite sincere in his efforts to promote peace, but Scipio was merely playing a game of diplomacy to mask a deeper design, which can hardly be reconciled with any law of military honour. Having lulled his opponent into a sense of complete security, and having fully informed himself as to the topography of the Numidian camp, he sent a curt message to Syphax announcing that the truce was broken off, and before the deluded Numidian had recovered from his

---

[1] The number of soldiers is uncertain ; according to other estimates it was under twenty thousand.

SECOND PUNIC WAR

astonishment Scipio struck a sudden blow, which involved both the armies of the enemy in utter ruin. In the dead of night, when most of the Numidians were in their beds and a few belated revellers were still carousing by the camp-fires, flames were seen rising from the light reed huts in which the men of Syphax were quartered, and soon the whole camp was wrapped in a roaring sheet of fire. It was the work of Laelius and Masinissa, who had previously taken care to beset every outlet of the camp. The surprise was complete, and the wretched Numidians, heavy with drink or dazed by sleep, were trampled to death in their efforts to escape or devoured by the flames, and if any succeeded in breaking through the struggling masses of men and beasts they were cut down as they emerged, naked and unarmed, from the zone of fire. Meanwhile a similar scene was being enacted in the camp of Hasdrubal, where Scipio himself was conducting the operations. Out of the two great armies, numbering together more than eighty thousand men, only a mere handful escaped destruction.

BATTLE OF THE GREAT PLAINS

Hasdrubal and Syphax had both succeeded in extricating themselves, with a few followers, and the arrival of four thousand mercenaries from Spain determined them to make one more effort to keep the field against Scipio. New levies were raised at Carthage and in Numidia, and they soon found themselves at the head of thirty thousand men. Scipio, whose command had been extended until the end of the war, marched from Utica to meet them, and a battle was fought at a place called the Great Plains, which resulted in the total rout of the Carthaginian army. Syphax fled to his own kingdom, but he was pursued by Laelius and Masinissa and brought back a prisoner to the Roman camp.

HANNIBAL RECALLED FROM ITALY

Scipio's triumph seemed now complete, and envoys were actually dispatched from Carthage to arrange terms of peace

271

with the Roman Senate. But the war-party at Carthage had one resource left. Their great general still held his ground in Italy, and for the past two years his brother Mago had been carrying on the war in Cisalpine Gaul. It was resolved to recall both the sons of Hamilcar, who might yet, it was hoped, retrieve the falling fortunes of Carthage, if they united their forces for one last desperate stand on their native soil of Africa. Hannibal had for some time been expecting such a call, and though he had small reason to respect his ungrateful country-men, who had shown so little sympathy with his great designs, he prepared without a murmur to leave the scene of his glory and his failure. His departure was saddened by the news of another loss which had recently fallen on the ill-fated house of Hamilcar. Mago, his younger brother, who had lately suffered a crushing defeat in the land of the Insubres, died on his voyage to Carthage of a wound received in the battle.

BATTLE OF ZAMA

The final encounter, in which the two greatest generals of the age were matched against each other, took place at Zama Regia, an inland town, five days' march to the south-west of Carthage (202 B.C.). Hannibal had with him his trusted veterans, who had shared with him all the fatigues and honours of his Italian campaigns. These were stationed in the rear, and held in reserve until the decisive moment of the action should arrive. Next in order were the Libyan and Cartha-ginian troops, and a contingent lately arrived from Macedonia, while the van was formed of twelve thousand mercenaries, Celts, Ligurians, and Balearians, covered by a formidable line of eighty elephants, and the cavalry took their station on the wings. Scipio's army was also drawn up in three lines, as was then still usual in Roman warfare,[1] but the maniples, contrary to the ordinary practice, were posted one behind the other, leaving a free passage between the several columns.[2]

[1] See p. 102.
[2] Usual order thus : ——   —— Scipio's order thus : ——   ——

SECOND PUNIC WAR

By this arrangement the charge of the elephants was rendered comparatively harmless, for the huge animals, assailed by missiles from the light-armed troops, rushed straight through to the rear, leaving the Roman order of battle unbroken. Almost at the same moment Masinissa with his Numidians and Laelius with the Italian horse made a simultaneous charge on Hannibal's wings and drove his cavalry from the field. Then the legions closed with the mercenaries, who fought with great courage, and for a long time held their ground. But they were slowly thrust back by the weight and mass of the Roman infantry, and, finding themselves left without support, they turned their swords against the Carthaginians, who had remained idle spectators of the struggle. A furious *mêlée* ensued, in which Romans, Carthaginians, and mercenaries grappled together in a confused multitude, but at length the first two divisions of Hannibal's infantry were put to utter rout, only a few remaining, who took refuge on the deserted wings. There was now a pause in the action, for Hannibal's veterans still stood grimly in their ranks, waiting for the Romans to come on, and the intermediate space was so encumbered with corpses and so slippery with blood that a direct advance was impossible. But Scipio re-formed his troops in front of that dreadful barrier and led them to the charge. Bravely did the Old Guard of Hannibal support the high name which they had won by a long career of victory. Hand to hand and knee to knee they fought, resolute to slay or to be slain. But at length the cavalry of Masinissa and Laelius, returning from the pursuit, charged them in the rear, and being now hemmed in on all sides they were cut down almost to a man, and the slaughter of Cannae was avenged.

Terms of Peace

Carthage had made her last effort and had lost, and nothing remained but to come to such terms as she could with her conqueror. There were, indeed, a few desperate men who proposed to jeopardize the very existence of their country by closing their gates and facing all the horrors of a siege.

273

But they were brought to their senses, or at any rate reduced to silence, by the stern voice of Hannibal, among whose great qualities not the least was his dignified submission to the inevitable. He bade them accept thankfully the conditions offered, which, though severe enough, still secured them immunity from the worst evils of conquest. The Carthaginians were to retain their territory in Africa, to enjoy undisturbed possession of their city, and to be governed by their own laws. On the other hand, they were to pay an indemnity of ten thousand talents (£2,400,000) in fifty yearly instalments, they were forbidden to make war in Africa without the consent of Rome, and they were to surrender all their ships of war, except ten triremes. The loudest murmurs were raised at the last two articles in the treaty, one of which left Carthage without defence against the incursions of Masinissa, who was now king of Numidia, while the other fatally crippled her great commerce. But the counsels of Hannibal prevailed, and after some demur the treaty was signed and the Second Punic War came to an end. That the terms were not harder was due to the magnanimity of Scipio, and within little more than fifty years a far heavier doom was to be dealt out to the unhappy city by the hands of his nephew and adoptive grandson.

CHAPTER XII

PROGRESS OF THE ROMAN ARMS TO THE TIME OF THE GRACCHI

THE advance of the Roman dominion is marked by a sort of logical progression, in which each successive step follows as an inevitable consequence on the last. In virtue of her geographical position Rome became the political centre of Italy, the champion of civic development against the lawless attacks of the rude highland tribes, and the bulwark of Italian nationality when threatened by the alien domination of Etruria or the wilder assaults of the savage Gauls. Two centuries of almost incessant fighting were required to put down the fierce highlanders who hovered on the flanks of Latium, to humble the power of Etruria and subdue the discontent of the Latins, and to impose the Roman yoke on Samnium. The victorious career of Rome excited the alarm of the Greeks in southern Italy, who invoked the aid of Pyrrhus to check the progress of the aggressor. But the hopes of that brilliant adventurer were extinguished on the field of Beneventum, and within ten years from the departure of Pyrrhus all Italy south of the Po valley was brought under the Roman sway. From Italy it was but a step to Sicily, which both politically and geographically is an integral part of the peninsula, and after a twenty years' struggle with Carthage that great island became incorporated in the territories of Rome. An interval of twenty-three years followed, during which the Romans were occupied by a formidable outbreak of their old enemies the Gauls, and were called upon for the first time to assert their influence on the other side of the Adriatic for the protection of Italian commerce against the Illyrian pirates. The forced cession of Sardinia and Corsica, wrung from Carthage in the time of her distress, excited the bitter hatred of the great Hamilcar, and was one of the chief causes which led to the fearful visitation of the Second Punic War. In the course of that great contest Spain was brought within the circle of the Roman dependencies, and no sooner had the Romans emerged triumphantly from the trial than they were plunged into a new war with Philip of Macedon, whose alliance with Hannibal they had neither forgotten nor forgiven, and who had lately afforded new grounds for alarm by his aggressive attitude in the east. The power of Philip was broken on the plains of Thessaly, but his ambitious designs were taken up by Antiochus, king of Syria, and the speedy overthrow of that ill-fated monarch laid the foundations of Rome's empire in Asia. One final effort was made by Philip's son and successor, Perseus, to resist the advancing tide of conquest, but after a series of blunders and mishaps the Romans put out all their strength and crushed the liberty of Macedon at a single blow. The wars with Philip, Antiochus, and Perseus, with the results which ensued to the neighbouring states, Greek or barbarian, will form the chief subject of the present chapter, and we shall also have to touch briefly on the affairs of Spain and Africa, and the final pacification of Italy, which was secured by years of fighting with the Gauls and Ligurians. It is a period of incessant activity, filled with the sound of arms and stained by one awful crime, and at its close Rome's ascendancy was established beyond dispute in all the wide circle of the Mediterranean states. The subsequent acquisitions, great and important as they were, may be regarded as a supplement to the grand scheme of conquest, which had been built up partly by happy circumstance and partly by the irresistible impulse of the Roman genius; for the main fabric of the empire was complete before the time of the Gracchi.

The Eastern World

For the space of an entire generation (200–167 B.C.) the arms and policy of Rome were chiefly directed to the affairs of

Greece, Macedon, and Asia. It will be well, therefore, to turn our eyes toward the lands of the eastern Mediterranean and try to form a general view of this strange world as it appeared at the close of the Second Punic War. It would be impossible within the compass of the few pages we can give to the subject to unravel all the tangled skein of conflicting ambitions and jarring interests which is here presented to us. But the general features of the picture may be drawn with tolerable clearness. After a long period of wild disorder three kingdoms had arisen out of the wreck of Alexander's empire. These were Macedon, Syria, and Egypt. For the last twenty years (220–200 B.C.) the throne of Macedon had been occupied by Philip, the fifth of that name. The bright hopes which attended the boy king when he first assumed the crown had long since faded, and he had made himself odious by repeated acts of cruelty, perfidy, and violence. We have seen that when Hannibal was maturing his large plans for the invasion of Italy the alliance of Macedon played an essential part in his calculations. If Philip had been other than he was, if he had been a monarch of wide and politic mind, capable of composing the petty differences which divided the states of Greece, and so of uniting the whole military force of Greece and Macedon against Rome, the course of history might have been changed, and Greek instead of Roman influence might have moulded the civilization of western Europe. But the opportunity was allowed to pass, and it never recurred. Instead of lending hearty support to Hannibal, Philip frittered away his energies at home, and meanwhile the dark days of Thrasymene and Cannae passed by and the Romans gained time to recover their strength.

MACEDON

After Rome, Macedon was still the greatest military power in Europe. Her people were brave, patriotic, and loyal to their king, and the great traditions of the age of Alexander had not yet wholly died out. Beyond his own borders Philip exercised a sort of half-acknowledged suzerainty over a great part of Greece, and his garrisons at Demetrias, Chalcis, and

Corinth gave him a strong hold on Thessaly, Euboea, and Peloponnesus. We shall presently find him seeking to extend his influence to Thrace and the coast towns of the Hellespont and Asia Minor.

SYRIA

The vast kingdom founded by Seleucus Nicator, whose career as a conqueror rivalled that of Alexander, had once extended from the confines of India to the shores of the Black Sea and the Aegaean. But it had now shrunk to a mere remnant of its former dimensions, being curtailed in the east by the rising power of the Parthians, and on the west by the principality of Pergamum, by the invading hordes of Galatia, and by the rival claims of Egypt. The present representative of the Seleucid dynasty, Antiochus III, affected to keep up the high pretensions of his predecessors, and assumed the style of King of Kings and Lord of All Asia. He had gained some credit by his campaigns against the Parthians and Bactrians, which earned him the title of ' the Great.' But all this pomp and grandeur was a hollow show, which burst like a bubble when brought into contact with the iron power of Rome.

EGYPT

Both Macedon and Syria laboured under the disadvantage of a wide and exposed frontier, which laid them open to the constant danger of invasion from the fierce peoples who hovered on their borders. Some eighty years back (278 B.C.) Macedon had been brought to the verge of ruin by an invasion of the Celts, and the boundaries of Syria were a vague and wavering line, expanding and contracting from one generation to another. But Egypt, from her peculiar position, enjoyed a degree of stability which placed her alone among the kingdoms founded by the successors of Alexander. Surrounded by seas, deserts, and impassable swamps, the land of the Pharaohs was secure against invasion, and under the wise rule of the Ptolemies Alexandria rose to a great height of wealth and prosperity. The brilliant city, hallowed by the shrine of

Alexander, became the chief emporium for East and West, and a great centre of learning, in which were gathered all the treasures of Greek wisdom and eloquence. Secure at home, the Ptolemies were left free to extend their dominions to Cyrene, Cyprus, and the Cyclades, and they were constantly at strife with the successors of Seleucus for the possession of Phoenicia and southern Syria.

PERGAMUM

Early in the third century before Christ a great movement began among the restless Gaulish tribes who roved to and fro in the vast regions watered by the Danube. One great marauding host burst through the mountain barrier protecting the northern borders of Macedon and swept on southward until it was met and repulsed by an army of confederate Greeks. Another band of these invaders penetrated into the heart of Asia Minor, and settled in the district which was afterwards known as the kingdom of Galatia. From this centre they pursued their depredations far and wide, spreading terror among the peaceful and effeminate population. This band was divided into four tribes, and parcelled out the country between them for purposes of plunder. It was to his successful campaigns against this robber-state that Attalus owed his elevation to the throne of Pergamum. That city attained great importance under the rule of Attalus and his successors, and rivalled the fame of Alexandria as a school of learning and of art. The kings of Pergamum remained faithful in their allegiance to Rome throughout the struggles of the succeeding years, while their neighbours and rivals, the kings of Bithynia, generally leaned to the side of Macedon.

RHODES

Among the Greek cities which successfully maintained their independence against Egypt, Syria, and Macedon, the noble republic of Rhodes holds the foremost place. Founded toward the end of the fifth century, by the union of three ancient cities, Rhodes soon attained a position of high political and

REPUBLICAN ROME

commercial importance. By a wise and temperate policy her rulers contrived to hold the balance between the great rival powers whose endless disputes filled the states of the eastern Mediterranean with perpetual unrest. Above all they gained a name for moderation and justice which is almost unique in the annals of Greek cities. For these reasons Rhodes became the acknowledged leader of those commercial cities on the coasts and islands of Asia Minor which still retained a precarious and uncertain freedom.

GREECE

Turning now to the mainland of Greece, we find on every side the unequivocal symptoms of weakness and decline. Athens, though still holding much of her intellectual pre-eminence, had long lost her high public spirit, and that Attic eloquence which had once been the terror of foreign oppressors was degraded into an instrument of abject flattery. Thebes had never recovered from the chastisement inflicted upon her by Alexander, and the countrymen of Pindar and Epameinondas, neglecting all higher aims, were devoted to a dull round of convivial indulgence. Corinth, the key to Peloponnesus, was held by a Macedonian garrison, and Philip's influence was paramount as far as the northern frontier of Boeotia. Epirus, after a brief interval of glory under the renowned reign of Pyrrhus, had sunk into insignificance, leaning for support on the kings of Macedon. What remnant was left of free political life was concentrated in the Aetolian and Achaean Leagues. Throughout the great period of Greek history the Aetolians had lived apart in their wild mountain valleys, clinging to their savage freedom, and despised by the more polished communities of Greece as a race of highland brigands and cattle-stealers. But in the general decline of the national life their rude vigour and effective political organization made them one of the first powers in Greece. They were united in a federal league, with a president, a general council, and a national assembly. Outside of Aetolia their influence extended to parts of Epirus, Acar-

280

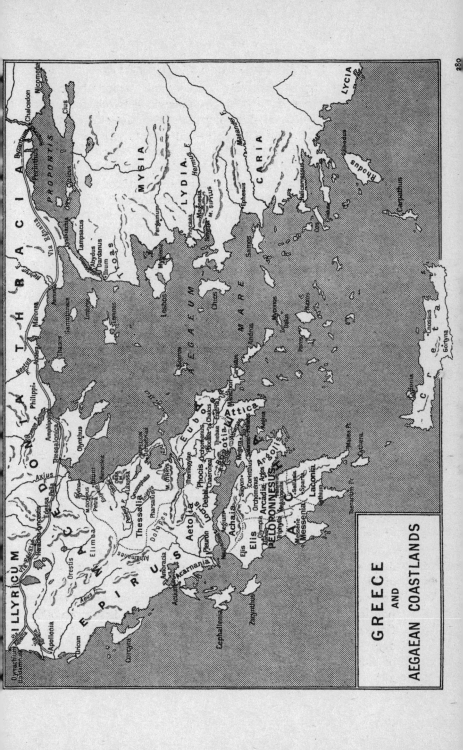

GREECE
AND
AEGAEAN COASTLANDS

nania, Thessaly, and Peloponnesus, and even to the remote regions of Thrace and Asia Minor. They had played an honourable part in the last struggle of Greece against Macedon, and to their valour was mainly due the destruction of the Celtic marauders who had dared to invade the sacred precincts of Delphi (279 B.C.). But their predatory instincts never forsook them, and they remained to the last a race of freebooters and mercenaries, ready to sell their swords to the highest bidder.

THE ACHAEAN LEAGUE

A far higher interest attaches to the Achaean League, the only example in Greek history of a serious attempt to combine the scattered elements of Greek nationality into a free and equal union. Like the Aetolians, though for different reasons, the Achaeans had lived in complete obscurity throughout the most brilliant period of Greek history. Their importance begins with the later years of the Macedonian epoch, and in the third century the Achaean League rose to great fame and influence under the masterly leadership of Aratus. At one time it seemed as if the whole of Peloponnesus was to be united under the same federal bond. But all these fair prospects were wrecked by one disastrous error, when Aratus invoked the aid of Macedon against the rising power of Sparta. At the period which we have reached the military genius of Philopoemen had restored to the League some measure of its former glory. Yet even this brief gleam of prosperity was but a prelude to a deeper fall, for it was the unhappy fate of the Greeks that their best energies were almost always turned against themselves, and the most brilliant victories of Philopoemen were gained at the expense of his own countrymen.

We may close our review of the contemporary state of Greece by a brief glance at Sparta, lately restored to something like her former eminence by the heroic Cleomenes, but now degenerated into a nest of pirates and robbers under the rule of the brutal tyrant Nabis.

REPUBLICAN ROME

PHILIP'S AGGRESSIONS

Allusion has been made in the previous chapter to the First Macedonian War, which on the part of the Romans was a defensive contest, undertaken with the purpose of keeping Philip employed at home and preventing him from joining forces with Hannibal. This object had been fully attained, and, true to their policy, the Romans, after some years of indecisive fighting, withdrew from the field, leaving their allies the Aetolians to bear the brunt of the struggle. Peace was concluded on the eve of Scipio's departure for his final campaign in Africa, and for the next four years Philip was left to pursue his career of aggression, unchecked by any interference from Rome. The opportunity thus offered was promptly seized by the ambitious monarch of Macedon, who forthwith entered into an infamous compact with Antiochus for the partition of the foreign possessions of Egypt, the throne of which was now occupied by Ptolemy Epiphanes, a child four years old. Antiochus was to take Coele-Syria, Cyrene, and part of Egypt as his share of the spoil, while Philip bargained for the islands and coast towns of the Aegaean. Philip lost no time in beginning the work of spoliation, and his high-handed proceedings soon involved him in a war with the allied forces of Pergamum, Rhodes, and Byzantium. He gained a number of successes, and incurred great odium by his barbarous treatment of Cius and Thasos, which had fallen into his hands.

SECOND MACEDONIAN WAR

These events had not passed unnoticed at Rome. Complaints came pouring in from the Greek cities which had felt the heavy hand of Philip, and at last a peremptory demand was sent by the Senate bidding him to refrain from meddling with the territorial rights of the young king of Egypt, who had recently been placed under the protection of a Roman guardian. The pert tone of Philip in replying to these remonstrances gave no hope of an amicable settlement, and the conflict which in the

282

course of the next generation was to lay all Greece and western Asia at the feet of Rome loomed nearer and nearer. The immediate pretext for hostilities was given by the Athenians, who had provoked Philip to invade their territory by the murder of two hapless Acarnanians, guilty, as it was alleged, of profaning the sacred mysteries of Demeter. The Athenians appealed to Rome, where it was generally felt that the time for this momentous decision had now arrived. Antiochus, flushed with his victories in the East, was pushing the war against Egypt, lately, as we have seen, brought under the shadow of the Roman protectorate. For the present he was suffered to have his way, that the whole energy of Rome might be brought to bear on the more immediate danger. If Philip were not crushed, these two potentates might prove a formidable obstacle to Roman interests in the East. The senators were unanimously resolved on war, but the formal decision lay with the people assembled in their centuries, and here the question assumed a very different aspect. Only a few months had elapsed since the conclusion of peace with Carthage, and the nation was exhausted by the long and murderous struggle with Hannibal. At the first meeting of the centuries the motion for war was rejected by a large majority of votes, and it was only on the urgent expostulation of the consul Sulpicius that the people were induced to alter their decision. Either, said Sulpicius, they must attack Philip in his own country or they would have to face the horrors of a second invasion of Italy. This argument turned the scale, and war was declared (200 B.C.).

In their conduct of the Second and Third Macedonian Wars the Romans showed that talent for blundering into success which is said to be characteristic of our own countrymen. For the first two or three years little is effected, one incompetent commander succeeding to another, until at last the right man is found, who ends the contest by a single blow. At the beginning of the war the Romans numbered among their allies the Illyrian prince Pleuratus, Amynander, king of the Athamanians, and the Dardanians, while on the sea they were supported by Rhodes, Pergamum, Byzantium, and other

Greek commercial cities. The Aetolians for the present remained neutral, and all the wiles of Philip could not secure the adhesion of the Achaean League. At the outset of the war Athens was relieved from siege by the allied fleet, and in the following year the consul Sulpicius gained some advantage over Philip and threatened the western borders of Macedon. It was then that the Macedonian troops observed for the first time the terrible effect of the Roman sword, a heavy, two-edged blade, which lopped off limbs at a single stroke and dealt the most appalling wounds. The advantage gained by Sulpicius, indecisive as it was, sufficed to induce the Aetolians to declare for Rome, and in concert with Amynander they overran Thessaly and threatened Demetrias. They were, indeed, driven back by Philip with great loss, and only saved from destruction by the help of Amynander, but they had shown the way to the Romans, and it was resolved in the next year to break through the mountain barrier in full force and carry the war into the north-east of Greece. But Philip, whose generals had meanwhile been successful in defending his northern frontier against the Dardanians, formed a strongly entrenched camp commanding a wild mountain-pass in Epirus, on the upper course of the Aous, and Villius, who had taken over the command toward the end of the summer, made no attempt to force the passage.

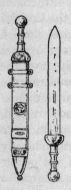

ROMAN SWORD

FLAMININUS

Such was the position of affairs when Titus Quintius Flamininus, who had been elected to the consulship at the early age of thirty, arrived at the seat of war (198 B.C.). Flamininus was one of the most remarkable men of his day. Well skilled in the language and literature of Greece, and an enthusiastic admirer of Greek culture, he is the most prominent representative of that sentimental Hellenism which had been fashionable for some time past in the more refined circles of

284

Rome. His fame as a general rests on a single victory, but that victory broke the power of Philip, and his skill as a diplomatist was proved during several years in the tortuous mazes of Greek politics. But under all this subtlety and refinement there lurked the iron nature of the Roman, crafty, relentless, and cruel, and the professed admirer of humane culture was the chosen instrument employed in hunting Hannibal to his death.

THE CAMPAIGN IN GREECE

At this moment a brief gleam of light is shed upon our narrative by the words of a contemporary witness. This was the poet Ennius, who a few years later visited the scene of the campaign in the train of Fulvius Nobilior. For six weeks Flamininus had lain encamped before the impregnable lines of the Macedonian king, and one day when he was sitting in his tent, sorely perplexed in mind, he received a visit from an Epirot shepherd, who offered to show him a circuitous mountain-path which would enable him to turn the enemy's position. The man was an emissary from Charops, a prince of Epirus, and, having assured himself of his good faith, Flamininus resolved to take advantage of the opportunity offered. Guided by the shepherd, a picked body of troops stole round to the rear of the Macedonian entrenchments, and the enemy, suddenly assaulted on both sides, were seized with panic and abandoned their camp, leaving the road open into Thessaly. Philip now took up his station at Tempe, and remained a passive spectator while Flamininus marched up and down the whole district of northern and central Greece, reducing his fortresses and calling upon the inhabitants to throw off the yoke of Macedon. At the same time the allied fleet gained possession of Eretria and Carystus and prepared to form the siege of Corinth. One most important result of these operations was the accession of the Achaean League, which now abandoned its neutrality and declared for Rome. Argos, however, still remained faithful to Macedon, and all efforts to dislodge the garrison at Corinth proved abortive.

REPUBLICAN ROME

The Macedonian Phalanx

The winter was passed in fruitless negotiations, and in the following spring Flamininus marched northward through Boeotia and Phocis to encounter the forces of Philip, who was encamped at Larissa. Constant warfare had sorely reduced the military resources of Macedon, and the king was compelled to fill up his levies by enlisting boys of sixteen and recalling discharged veterans to his standard. By these measures he had contrived to raise an army of sixteen thousand heavy-armed infantry, who formed the phalanx, seven thousand light-armed troops, and two thousand cavalry. The Roman army was about equal in number, consisting of two legions, with the usual complement of Italian allies, and eight thousand auxiliaries, mostly drawn from Aetolia. Flamininus had also at his disposal a number of elephants, sent from Africa by Rome's faithful ally Masinissa. The great strength of the Macedonian army lay in the phalanx, which was a sort of moving fortress, invincible in a frontal attack and presenting five rows of spear-points to the assailant. But this cumbrous machine required a wide space of level ground to act with effect, and if once its firm order was shaken it rapidly became demoralized and fell an easy prey to a more flexible and agile force. Nevertheless the phalanx, which had been the main instrument of Alexander's conquests, still bore a great name, and presented a truly formidable aspect, sufficient to shake the firmness even of a veteran commander.

Battle of Cynoscephalae

In wet and gloomy weather the two armies advanced to meet each other across the misty fields of Thessaly, quartering the ground, and each seeking to take the other at an advantage. For two days they moved in parallel lines, separated by a range of hills, and the action was at last brought on against the will of Philip, who was feeling his way toward Scotussa, where there was a level plain favourable to the operations of his phalanx. Before the desired position could be reached, however, an encounter took place between one of the Macedonian outposts, which had been sent to occupy the ridge of Cynoscephalae, and a reconnoitring party of the Roman army. The Roman cavalry and light infantry engaged in this service were hard pressed by the king's troops, when the Aetolians advanced gallantly to their support, and held the enemy in check until Flamininus had time to bring his main body into action. Sorely against his will Philip was compelled to form his phalanx on the hilly and broken ground. His right wing, hastily drawn up on the ridge, charged with irresistible force down the slope, carrying all before it. But Flamininus, leaving the king to pursue his advantage, concentrated his attention on the Macedonian left, which had been outpaced by the king's division and was still forming in the rear. A sudden charge of the elephants, followed by a brisk attack of the legionaries, broke the dense ranks of the Macedonians, and they turned and fled. The king's army, being thus cut in half, lost the solidity and cohesion on which its efficiency depended, and the event was determined by a brilliant manoeuvre of a young Roman officer, inspired, perhaps, by the example of Nero at the Metaurus. Leaving his comrades to follow up the pursuit, he wheeled round the maniples under his command and attacked the right wing of the Macedonians in the rear. Philip saw the destruction of his phalanx from a neighbouring height, and rode off with a handful of cavalry to Tempe, leaving the flower of his troops dead on the field.

End of the War

The war was thus brought to an end, and terms of peace were arranged in the following year (196 B.C.). Philip was compelled to give up all his recent conquests, to resign his possessions in Greece, to give hostages, among whom was his son Demetrius, and to surrender his fleet. The Aetolians, who boasted that the recent victory was won entirely by their own prowess, clamoured loudly for harder terms, and demanded nothing less than the complete destruction of the Macedon an power. But this was contrary to the policy of the Romans, who wished to preserve the integrity of Macedon as a barrier against the Celtic and Thracian barbarians. The envoys of the Aetolians were accordingly treated with scant ceremony, and, finding that their exorbitant claims were contemptuously set aside, they retired in sullen resentment, exclaiming that Greece had only exchanged one master for another. The chief gainers by the new settlement were the Achaeans, whose power was extended to the greater part of Peloponnesus, and the Athenians, who received as their share the islands of Paros, Scyros, and Imbros.

FLAMININUS AT THE ISTHMIAN GAMES

The eyes of all Greece were turned to the young victor of Cynoscephalae, and expectation rose to the highest pitch when he appeared at the Isthmian Games, accompanied by ten commissioners who had been sent from Rome to assist his deliberations. Had the Greeks indeed found a champion of their liberties, or was their long dallying with a foreign power to find its usual reward, and would Rome, as the Aetolians asserted, prove a false and treacherous ally? Such were the eager questionings which ran from lip to lip, and every ear was strained to catch the voice of the herald as he came forward to read the Roman proclamation. But when the words of the decree were heard, proclaiming liberty to all the Greeks who had hitherto been subject to Philip, there arose a tempest of applause, which filled all the sacred precinct of Poseidon, and startled the birds flying overhead. Thousands pressed forward to catch a glimpse of the young hero, who had fought, not for selfish aggrandisement, but for the rights and liberties of an oppressed people. We need not scan too closely this generous outburst of national enthusiasm, to which the events succeeding afford a melancholy comment. The Romans had not yet developed the full measure of that cynical hardness which marks their later dealings with other nations, and their admiration for Greek genius survived the age of their own worst political corruption. Nor can we demand from the
288

Greeks themselves that sad self-knowledge which might have taught them that true liberty, whether for nations or individuals, is a gift which cannot be bestowed by the hands of others.

Sparta Besieged

But the labours of Flamininus in Greece were not yet ended. At the outbreak of the war Philip had made over to Nabis the city of Argos as the price of his alliance. Nabis accepted the bribe, but betrayed the giver, and sent a force of Cretan mercenaries who fought in the Roman army at Cynoscephalae. The ruffianly leader of banditti had since then made himself odious by his cruelty and extortion, and to put down this nuisance Flamininus marched into Peloponnesus with a powerful force and laid siege to Sparta (195 B.C.). Assailed by overwhelming numbers, Nabis was obliged to submit, and his authority was henceforth confined to the inland town, Argos and the coast-cities of Laconia being united to the Achaean League. The Achaeans, indeed, urged Flamininus to complete his work and crush the robber in his den. But this would have thrown the whole power of Peloponnesus into the hands of the League, a measure inconsistent with the balancing policy of Rome. Nabis was accordingly left, crippled, but still capable of mischief, and in the following year Flamininus returned to celebrate his triumph at Rome. His last act was to withdraw the Roman garrisons from Demetrias, Chalcis, and the Corinthian citadel, thus formally redeeming the solemn pledge given at the Isthmian Games.

Designs of Antiochus

It soon appeared that in evacuating these important places, often spoken of by historians as the fetters of Greece, the Romans had acted with unwise precipitation and left open a door to a new invader. While they were still engaged in the war with Philip the proceedings of Antiochus had given them cause for serious anxiety. After successfully engaging the

Egyptian forces in Syria he had concluded an alliance with
Egypt, cemented by a marriage between his daughter Cleopatra and the young king Ptolemy. This gave a colour of
right to his designs on the cities of Asia Minor and the Hellespont which owed allegiance to the crown of Egypt. He made
terms with the Rhodians, who threatened to oppose his progress, gained possession of Ephesus, and, crossing the Hellespont, rebuilt Lysimachia, which had been destroyed by the
Thracians. It was his ambition to restore the empire of
Seleucus as it was in the days of its greatness, and he treated
with scorn the remonstrances of the Roman envoys who forbade him to meddle with the Greek cities of Asia.

HANNIBAL REAPPEARS

Embassies passed to and fro during the next three years
(196–193 B.C.), and in the meantime events had occurred
which tended to precipitate the inevitable collision. The
Aetolians were bestirring themselves to raise a national coalition against Rome, and had already entered into communication
with Antiochus, holding out hopes that Philip might be induced
to join hands with the king of Syria against his old enemies.
And there was another counsellor who now sat close to the
ear of Antiochus, trying to kindle in him something of his own
lofty and aspiring spirit. This was no other than the great
Hannibal himself, who after the defeat of Zama had been
devoting himself heart and soul to the task of rebuilding the
shattered fortunes of his country. Under his able administration Carthage soon began to recover from the wounds
inflicted in the recent war, and was rapidly rising in wealth and
prosperity. But he had bitter enemies among the old oli-
garchical party, whose corrupt administration he had successfully opposed, and they had long been labouring to bring about
his ruin. By circulating reports of his dark intrigues they
contrived to work upon the fears of the Romans, and a commission was sent to inquire into the charges against him.
Hannibal well knew that there could be but one issue to a
trial promoted by such accusers and conducted before such

judges, and that his only safety lay in flight. Taking ship at Thapsus, he sailed first to Tyre, and from thence made his way to Ephesus, where Antiochus was then residing. The illustrious fugitive was hospitably received, and he at once began to unfold an extensive plan for the invasion of Italy. But the scheme was derided as chimerical by the courtiers of Antiochus, and by their influence Hannibal was thrust into the background and employed only in subordinate commands

Antiochus joins the Aetolians

Meanwhile the ever-active Aetolians were making desperate efforts to kindle a new war in Greece. An attempt to gain possession of Sparta proved unsuccessful, and resulted only in the death of Nabis and the incorporation of Laconia into the Achaean League. But they made good their footing in Demetrias, the most important harbour-town in Thessaly, and sent urgent messengers to Antiochus, inviting him to take the command of their League, and holding out the most extravagant hopes of a general rising in Greece against the Roman oppressors. After long hesitation Antiochus decided to follow the call, and, crossing the Aegaean (192 B.C.), he landed at Demetrias and placed himself in communication with his Aetolian allies.

The Forces Opposed

The vain boasts of the Aetolians had been well matched by the lofty vaunts of Antiochus, who was coming, as he said, like a second Xerxes, to flood all Greece with the innumerable hosts of Asia. It was a fine game of bragging, in which the honours were divided between the deceiver and his dupes. The whole invading army amounted to but ten thousand men, and the great patriotic movement, which was to unite all Greece under the banner of Antiochus, began and ended in the heated imagination of the Aetolians. Some petty states, indeed, were induced to join the king, and he found an ally in Amynander, ruler of the Athamanians, whose brother-in-law

Philip had some shadowy claim to the crown of Macedon. But the chief powers of Greece remained firm in their adherence to Rome. Flamininus had been busy in Peloponnesus, counter-mining the intrigues of the Aetolians, and the Achaean League lost no time in declaring war on Antiochus. The Romans also numbered among their allies Eumenes, who had succeeded to the throne of Pergamum five years before, Prusias of Bithynia, a former adherent of Philip, Rhodes, Byzantium, and Egypt. In Athens and in Thessaly the Roman cause was in the ascendant, and Philip, who had conceived a bitter grudge against Antiochus, gave his loyal support to the Romans throughout the war. This last circumstance was of the utmost importance, for if Philip had assumed a hostile attitude the difficulties of Rome would have been enormously increased.

During the autumn Antiochus displayed some activity. Chalcis, with the whole of Euboea, fell into his hands, and he gained possession of some of the Thessalian towns. But after these exertions he lay inactive at Chalcis throughout the winter, being enslaved by a passion for a Greek lady of that town, whom he had raised to share his throne, though she had but half his years and was greatly his inferior in rank. His weak self-indulgence, exhibited on the eve of a momentous contest, had its natural effect on the minds of his troops. All discipline was relaxed, and the winter passed away in idle festivity.

The War with Antiochus

The Romans, according to their wont, hesitated long before embarking on the inevitable struggle. It seemed a great thing to make war on a monarch who was supposed to have at his back all the resources of Asia. Hannibal, too, whose very name was a terror to the Romans, was known to be in the confidence of Antiochus. The dread excited by this crisis lingered long in the national mind, and finds expression in the patriotic songs of Horace. Measures were taken to defend the eastern frontiers of Italy and guard the coast against invasion by sea. But the first fears soon passed away, and the presence of Antiochus in Greece drove the Romans to armed interference. Already in the previous year hostilities had commenced, and a detachment of Roman troops had been cut off in Boeotia. Rome now determined to put out her strength, and the consul M. Acilius Glabrio arrived at the seat of war with forty thousand troops, and, marching through Athamania, entered Thessaly (191 B.C.). At the news of his arrival Antiochus, who had been engaged in negotiations with the Acarnanians, returned in haste to Chalcis, and, setting his army in motion, entrenched himself in the renowned pass of Thermopylae. It almost seemed as if the powers which govern the destinies of nations had deliberately designed a historic parody. Antiochus, the Great King, and Lord of Asia, was holding the gates of Greece against a barbarian army, and both invader and defender posed as the champions of Greek liberty. And the parallel is continued in the details of the campaign. While the Roman army was preparing to assault the position of Antiochus at the mouth of the pass, Cato, who held a subordinate command under Glabrio, led a picked body of troops across the hills, taking the path that had been followed by the traitor Ephialtes three hundred years before, cut to pieces a detachment of Aetolians who had been sent to guard the route, and fell upon the enemy in the rear. Outnumbered and surprised, the weak army of the king made little resistance, and Antiochus, with a few followers, made his escape to Chalcis, where he took ship for Asia.

ANTIOCHUS RETREATS

But though baffled in his designs on Greece Antiochus was not yet conquered. The vast resources of his wide dominions were still at his disposal, and he at once began preparations for renewing the war by land and sea. Two fleets were equipped, one of which made its headquarters at Ephesus, while the other, composed of Phoenician ships, was placed under the command of Hannibal. But the fortune of the Romans did not desert them. Two naval victories left the seas open to their fleets, and the squadron under Hannibal was met and defeated by the Rhodians off Aspendus, in Pamphylia. Antiochus now began to falter. He had lost command of the sea, an attack on Pergamum was beaten back, and he was disappointed in his hopes of gaining Prusias of Bithynia to his side. With fatal weakness he withdrew the garrison from Lysimachia, abandoned the line of the Hellespont, and fell back upon Lydia, leaving the road into Asia open to the Romans.

SCIPIO'S MARCH TO ASIA

The formal command of the Roman army was committed to Lucius Cornelius Scipio, one of the consuls for the ensuing year. Lucius, however, was a man of no marked ability, and it was felt that a stronger hand was wanted to direct the operations of so important a campaign. And who could more worthily lead the Roman legions into Asia than the great Scipio Africanus, younger brother of Lucius, and conqueror of Hannibal ? But the victor of Zama had been consul a few years before, and could not, without violation of the laws, be re-elected to the office after so short an interval. To evade the difficulty, Lucius was thrust into the consulship, and Africanus received an extraordinary commission, with the title of proconsul, which made him virtual commander-in-chief.[1] Thus strangely associated, the two Scipios landed their forces, which constituted a full consular army, at Apollonia, and, marching across the mainland, halted on the confines of Thessaly. It was the intention of Africanus to bring the war to a speedy issue by a rapid advance on Asia. Some delay was caused by the Aetolians, who had remained in arms since the defeat of Antiochus and still kept up an obstinate resistance. But this obstacle was removed by the conclusion of a six months' armistice, and Scipio then resumed his march, directing his course toward the Hellespont. His route lay along the coast of Macedon and Thrace, and he was relieved of all anxiety by the hearty co-operation of Philip, who since his

[1] See Niese, *Grundriss der römischen Geschichte*, p. 133.

PLATE XL. M. CLAUDIUS MARCELLUS   294

SCIPIO AFRICANUS (?)

MARIUS (?)

PLATE XLI

295

defeat at Cynoscephalae had been constant in his adherence
to Rome. Roads had been set in order, bridges repaired,
magazines of stores placed at convenient intervals, and Philip
exerted his authority over the warlike Thracian tribes to secure
the consul's troops from molestation. Accordingly the long
and arduous march was completed without mishap, and,
crossing the Hellespont unopposed, the Roman legions set
foot for the first time on the shores of Asia.

ROME'S TERMS

As the peril drew nearer the courage of Antiochus sank
lower and lower, and he tried once more to make terms with
the Roman commanders. But the consul's answer was brief
and stern. If Antochus would have peace he must pay the
whole cost of the war and resign all his dominions on this side
of Mount Taurus. Nor did he fare better with the younger
Scipio, though the latter was bound to him by a personal
obligation, having received back his son, who had been taken
prisoner some months before, without ransom or express
stipulation. Africanus acknowledged the favour in suitable
terms, but seasoned his thanks with a piece of unpalatable
advice. The king, he said, had admitted his inferiority by
abandoning his frontier to the Romans. Having yielded
thus far, he had better give up the contest and accept the
terms offered. He had taken the bit, and must submit his
will to the rider. But Antiochus had not yet fallen so low as
to give up half his kingdom at a word. "What more could
they ask," he exclaimed indignantly, "if they had scattered
my armies and left me defenceless?" And so he resolved to
try his fortunes in a pitched battle.

BATTLE OF MAGNESIA

It was at Magnesia, on the plains of Lydia, near Mount
Sipylus, and between that mountain and the river Hermus,
that the battle was fought which decided the fate of western
Asia for centuries to come (190 B.C.). Antiochus had assembled
a motley host, drawn from all parts of his extensive kingdom,

and numbering in all seventy thousand foot and twelve thousand horse. The main strength of his army lay in the phalanx, drawn up and equipped on the Macedonian model, but distributed into ten columns, each having a front of fifty and a depth of thirty-two men. In the several intervals between the columns towered the gigantic bulk of two Asiatic elephants, larger and more formidable than the African species, their lofty foreheads protected by armour and surmounted by nodding plumes, and on the back of each elephant was a turret, manned by four soldiers. On either wing, extending to a great distance, was ranged a mixed multitude, gathered from many nations—the wild Celts of Galatia, drawn from their homes by the hope of plunder, horsemen from Media, Scythians from the eastern shore of the Caspian, bowmen and slingers from distant Elam. In the van was posted a long line of four-horsed chariots, armed with scythes, and intermingled with these was a troop of Arabian archers, mounted on drome-daries, and wielding thin-bladed swords, six feet in length. All the pomp and pageantry of the East seemed to have been mustered on the shores of that famous river, with every circumstance which could captivate the imagination and strike terror into an unpractised mind. But it was a hollow show, fit only to take the eye. On the other side stood the two Roman legions, with their Italian allies, some twenty thousand men, drawn up, as usual, in three divisions, and supported by a force of seven thousand auxiliaries. Scipio Africanus, who should have taken the command, was confined to his bed by sickness, and his place was taken by Cnaeus Domitius Ahenobarbus.

On the morning of the battle a thick mist rose from the valley of the Hermus, enveloping the dense masses of the king's army, so that the wings were invisible to those who fought in the centre. All concerted action was thus rendered impossible, and the confusion was increased by the babel of tongues and a divided command. The engagement began with an attack on the left wing of Antiochus, which was conducted with great spirit and judgment by Eumenes, king

296

of Pergamum. He sent forward a detachment of light troops
and cavalry to harass the chariots in the van, which made a
terrible show with their bristling spears attached to the yokes
and their whirling scythe-blades. These clumsy engines were
soon dispersed and flung back upon the main army, and a
charge of the Roman cavalry completed the discomfiture of
the Syrian left. Disorder now began to spread to the phalanx
in the centre, which was embarrassed by the huge, unwieldy
Macedonian spear and hampered in its movements by the
crowd of fugitives who sought shelter within its ranks. Meanwhile Antiochus, who commanded on the other wing, advanced
impetuously against the Roman left, and, sweeping horse and
foot before him, penetrated as far as the consul's camp. But
Marcus Aemilius Lepidus, who was in command of the camp,
exerted himself to rally the flying troops, and they turned on
their pursuers, while at the same moment Attalus, the brother
of Eumenes, arrived with a body of two hundred horse and
charged the enemy in the rear. The Romans were thus victorious on both wings, and soon the Syrian phalanx, stripped
of its defences and assailed on all sides, broke and fled, and the
battle ended with a general assault on the king's camp, which
was taken and pillaged with great slaughter. Fifty thousand
of the troops of Antiochus are said to have fallen, while the
losses of the Romans and their allies amounted only to a few
hundred men.

DIVISION OF SYRIA

Thus the pride of Antiochus had been humbled at a blow,
and all his cherished hopes of restoring the empire of the
Seleucids to its former splendour melted away like a dream.
By the terms of peace settled in the following year Antiochus
agreed to give up all his possessions in Europe, and the western
frontier of his kingdom was fixed at the river Halys and the
Taurus Mountains. To the east of this limit a huge slice was
cut out of his hereditary dominions by raising Cappadocia
and the two Armenias to the position of independent kingdoms.
Other conditions were added which tended further to cripple

and impoverish the Syrian monarch. He was to surrender all his warships except two, to keep no more war-elephants, and to pay an indemnity of fifteen thousand talents (£3,600,000). In the disposal of the wide territories between the Halys and the Aegaean the Romans pursued their accustomed policy of balance and division. The Gaulish tribes who were settled on the western bank of the Halys received a severe chastisement from the consul Manlius Volso in the year after the battle of Magnesia. They were now suffered to retain their independence, and, being received into the Roman alliance, constituted a permanent garrison on the frontier of the protected district. Prusias of Bithynia was left undisturbed in possession of his kingdom. The greatest gainer in the new distribution of lands was Eumenes of Pergamum, who was rewarded for his high services by the gift of the Chersonese and an immense tract of territory in Asia Minor. Rhodes, whose merits were second only to those of Eumenes, received Caria and Lycia, and the Greek towns, except those which owed tribute to Pergamum, were declared free. The friends of Rome were to be made strong, but not too strong, and all of them were to be educated in the belief that they owed their prosperity, and their very existence, to the same mighty hand. It soon, however, became clear that between protection and annexation there was but a step.

The Aetolians Submit

It remained to deal with the Aetolians, who had been directly instrumental in stirring up the war with Antiochus, and who were now in arms against Rome's ally, Philip of Macedon. Assailed on all sides by the forces of Achaea, Rome, and Macedon, the Aetolians were obliged to submit, and henceforth remained in a state of dependency on Rome. The fruits of this campaign were seen in a cargo of statues and pictures which was carried off from Ambracia, now detached from the Aetolian League, and in the acquisition of the islands of Cephallenia and Zacynthus, places of great strategic importance in the western waters of Greece. The Achaeans laid claim to

Zacynthus as a possession of their own, acquired by purchase, but Flamininus bade them confine themselves to Greece, comparing them with the tortoise, which was only safe when it kept its head within its own shell.

PHILIP'S DISCONTENT

Rome might now abstain for a time from interference in the affairs of Greece, for her people, with their "strange alacrity in sinking," were sure to take the path which led downward to dissolution and decay. The Achaeans wore themselves out in endless brawls with Messene and Sparta, and Rome had her spies and creatures everywhere, who studiously fostered the elements of discord. Meanwhile a new storm was brewing on the northern borders of Greece, for Philip, whose recent services had been poorly requited, and who viewed with bitter jealousy the elevation of his old enemy the king of Pergamum, was quietly nursing the resources of his kingdom and brooding over plans of vengeance. " Do they think that the sun has set for ever on Macedon ? " he was heard to mutter when the Thessalians, made bold by the countenance of the Senate, assailed him with open abuse ; and the taunt was construed as a direct menace against Rome.

PHILOPOEMEN

If we may rely upon the received chronology of this period, the same year (183 B.C.) was rendered memorable by the deaths of three men, each of whom had played a foremost part in the history of his country—Philopoemen, Hannibal, and Scipio. Philopoemen has been called the last of the Greeks, and his name closes the long list of those Greek worthies who live for ever in Plutarch's great gallery of historical portraits. His ruling passion was military glory, and if his lot had been cast in an earlier and better age he might have taken rank with the great patriot soldiers of Greece, with Leonidas, Miltiades, and Cimon. Under his inspiring influence a fever of warlike enthusiasm spread among the rising generation, and the Achaean League became supreme in Peloponnesus. But he was checked and harassed by the petty spirits around him, and several years of his life were wasted in inglorious warfare among the half-savage Greeks of Crete. When he once more assumed the lead in Peloponnesus his efforts were thwarted by the intrigues of the Romans, and at the age of seventy he fell into the hands of the Messenians, who were at war with the League, and perished miserably by poison.

Last Days of Scipio

If Philopoemen may be said to have been born too late, the opposite statement may be applied with some reason to the brilliant and magnificent Scipio. The growth of individualism, which is the dominant note in the last century of the Republic, had as yet hardly begun, and his high personal pretensions constantly brought him into collision with the rigid forms of constitutional usage. In later years his eminent achievements were in some degree overshadowed by the claims of younger competitors, and his pride and arrogance made him unpopular among those of his own class. At the close of the campaign against Antiochus both he and his brother Lucius were brought to trial on a charge of peculation. He indeed achieved a momentary triumph over his opponents, for it happened that the day of the trial was the anniversary of the battle of Zama, and the people were so struck by the coincidence that at a word from Scipio they broke up the meeting and followed him to the Capitol, to commemorate that great national deliverance by prayer and sacrifice. But he could not save his brother from conviction and punishment, and he himself only escaped further persecution by retiring to his private estate at Liternum, and there his haughty spirit consumed itself in solitude for the few remaining years of his life.

Death of Hannibal

While Scipio was devouring his heart in voluntary exile the career of his great antagonist drew toward its tragic close. Among the conditions imposed on Antiochus after his defeat at Magnesia the Romans stipulated for the surrender of his too illustrious guest. For the memories of Thrasymene and Cannae were still fresh in their minds, and they could not feel secure while their dreaded enemy was still at large. Warned in time, Hannibal fled to the court of Prusias, king of Bithynia, who was at that time engaged in a war with Eumenes of Pergamum. Old as he was, the great captain infused new spirit into the king's forces and gained some important successes against Eumenes. Just at this time it happened that Flamininus was engaged in diplomatic business which required his presence in the neighbourhood, and the victor of Cynoscephalae was not ashamed to act as the bloodhound of Rome's implacable resentment. Prusias received a peremptory order to surrender the person of his guest, and, not daring to refuse, he sent soldiers to surround the house where Hannibal was residing. The fate which afterwards befell Jugurtha and Vercingetorix now stared Hannibal in the face—to be dragged in chains to Rome, and there to be strangled like a malefactor, or to die in lingering agony in the vaults of the State dungeon. But the Romans were saved from this infamy by the free act of their intended victim. Fearing such a catastrophe, Hannibal had provided himself with a powerful poison, which he carried in the hollow of a ring, and when his pursuers broke into the inner chambers of the house that proud and magnificent soul had fled to its last retreat.

DEATH OF PHILIP

By the death of Hannibal an old terror had been laid to rest which had caused many an unquiet hour to the Romans. But presently they began to fear that some portion of his restless spirit had passed to his old ally, Philip of Macedon. Bitterly must that monarch have reproached himself when he thought of Hannibal's grand scheme of conquest, the ruin of which was largely due to his own irresolution and faint-heartedness. Since that day he had seen his phalanx shattered on the fields of Thessaly and himself reduced to become the humble vassal of Rome. He had stooped to play a menial part, serving his masters faithfully and well, and he had not even a servant's wages, but was stinted in his scanty reward, and his own subjects, who had been used to tremble at his frown, were set on to inform against him. Embittered by these reflections, the fierce old man nursed his anger in secret and waited for the day of revenge. The army of Macedon was carefully recruited and reorganized, stores of arms and provisions were established, and by an act of tyrannical rigour the inhabitants of the coast towns, whose loyalty he suspected, were compelled to remove inland, and their place was supplied by Thracian immigrants. What date Philip had fixed for an open defiance of Rome, or what issue he anticipated for so desperate a step, does not appear. Whenever he put out his hand toward the coveted towns of Thrace he was met by a peremptory order to draw back, which he did not see fit to refuse. But the life of the unhappy king, whose early promise had been so fair, was now rapidly approaching its end. His last hours were darkened by a domestic tragedy, which was brought on by his own jealous and suspicious temper. Demetrius, his younger son, had lived for some years as a hostage at Rome, and had won the friendship of Flamininus and other eminent men. It was by his mediation that a direct collison with Rome was averted during his father's life. But he had a bitter enemy in Perseus, his half-brother, the offspring of a left-handed marriage, who feared in him a possible rival in the succession, and on his return to Macedon a plot was laid for his destruction. Accused of a treasonable correspondence with the Romans and of designs against his father's life, he was secretly dispatched by poison. On his death-bed Philip learned that he had been deceived, and endeavoured in vain to repair his error. Then, broken by disappointment and worn out by gross indulgence, the king of Macedon sank into his grave, and the sceptre passed into the hands of Perseus (179 B.C.).

PHILIP'S SUCCESSOR

In some respects the new sovereign was well qualified by nature for his high position. His grave and stately presence and severe manners offered a striking contrast to the rude bearing and debauched life of his father Philip. He entered upon his reign with a full exchequer, a well-organized kingdom, and a powerful army, trained to a high state of efficiency. But all these advantages were neutralized by a strain of weakness and vacillation in his character, which always caused him to draw back when the moment for decisive action came, and by his sordid avarice, which drove from his side more than one able ally. At first, indeed, he displayed considerable activity, and it may have appeared to some that the Romans were to find a new Hannibal in the successor of Philip. In Greece there was a widespread discontent, and many were inclined to hail the accession of Perseus as the beginning of a new era of liberty. His proclamations, inviting all who were dissatisfied with the existing state of things to repair to the court of Macedon, were eagerly read by thousands of bankrupt and broken men, ready to grasp at any hope of restoring their ruined fortunes. And when the king passed through the towns of Thessaly and made a State visit to the temple of Delphi the old hopes revived in many hearts and the old vain cries were repeated. Perseus also looked for support from Syria and Bithynia, having formed marriage alliances with both of these kingdoms. Genthius, a prince of Illyria, was on his side, and Cotys, a powerful prince of Thrace, promised succour. The attitude of Rhodes was not unfriendly, and his agents were at work in Epirus, Boeotia, Aetolia, and Peloponnesus. With such prospects and with such resources, Perseus prepared to match himself against the usurping power of Rome.

ROMAN DIPLOMACY

For some years the alarming development of Macedon had been watched with anxiety by the Roman Senate, and embassies had crossed and recrossed between the two powers for remonstrance or exculpation. Rumours were afloat of great movements impending among the wandering hordes of central Europe, instigated, it was believed, by Philip, and the foundation of Aquileia, the last of the Latin colonies, was designed to check any attempt at invasion through the eastern passes of the Alps. Still the Romans, whose attention was engaged with the affairs of Italy and Spain, were loath to take upon themselves the burden of another war. But when report after report, disclosing the wide intrigues of Perseus, reached the ears of the Senate, when Eumenes, Rome's firmest ally, came on a special mission to Rome and bore emphatic testimony to the impending danger, and when that prince was waylaid on his return journey and left for dead by the hired assassins of Perseus, it was felt that any further hesitation would be construed as weakness, and active preparations were made for landing a Roman army at Apollonia in the spring of the following year (171 B.C.). Meanwhile Quintus Marcius Philippus was sent to negotiate with Perseus and hold out elusive hopes of peace until the Roman legions were ready to take the field, a piece of double-dealing which was extolled by some as a master-stroke of policy, though a few, whose standard of public virtue was higher, condemned the proceeding as unworthy of the majesty of Rome.

THIRD MACEDONIAN WAR

The diplomacy of Philippus, however, served its purpose, and the Romans gained time to mobilize their troops and secure their position in Greece before coming to blows with Perseus. A movement in Aetolia was suppressed, with the help of its president Lyciscus, a creature of the Romans, and Boeotia was kept quiet by the presence of a powerful Roman fleet. Not a hand stirred in Greece to aid the cause of the king, and after all his high hopes he went into the war almost alone. Yet all these advantages were frittered away by the incompetence of the Roman commanders, and for three years no progress was made. Several minor engagements were fought, which ended in favour of Macedon, and if Perseus had displayed vigour and resolution he might have raised an insurrection among the Greeks, who were bitterly provoked by the violence and cruelty of the Roman officers. Several towns in Boeotia were sacked, the allied contingents were treated with great harshness, and the conduct of officers and men alike made the name of the Romans odious throughout Greece.

ROME'S PRESTIGE FALLS

The prospects of Rome seemed to be steadily darkening. Her armies were demoralized, her generals corrupt, and Perseus, with unwonted energy, had even ventured to launch a fleet, which threatened the Roman supremacy in the eastern waters. Genthius the Illyrian was beginning to stir actively on behalf of Macedon, and swarms of warlike Germans [1] from the district between the Dnieper and the Dniester were ready at a word from Perseus to throw their rude valour into the scale against Rome. Even Rome's warmest friends began to waver, and her loss of prestige is shown by the attitude of certain Rhodian envoys, who took upon themselves to lecture the Senate in a tone of lofty superiority, which cost their city dear a few years later. Matters were brought to a crisis by the rash action of Quintus Marcius Philippus, the same man who had been so successful in hoodwinking Perseus at the beginning of the war. With a heedless neglect of precaution he forced his way through the passes of Olympus and entered Macedon, where he found himself cut off from his supplies and confronted by the army of Perseus. But the recklessness of Philippus was only equalled by the timid apathy of the king, and the two armies sat facing each other until the arrival of a new commander changed the whole aspect of affairs and brought the war to a speedy conclusion.

AEMILIUS PAULUS

General indignation had been excited at Rome by the depravity and incompetence hitherto displayed in the operations against Perseus, and it was resolved to appoint a man of tried character and ability to take the place of Philippus. The general selected was Lucius Aemilius Paulus, who at the

[1] The Bastarnae. According to other accounts, they were Celts.

mature age of sixty was raised for a second time to the consulship, and charged with the weighty task of restoring honour
to the Roman arms. Paulus combined the austere virtue of
an antique Roman with the taste for Greek art and learning
which had taken deep root among his countrymen during the
last two generations. He had gained some distinction in
the Ligurian and Spanish wars, and in an age of growing
corruption he was conspicuous as one whose hands had never
been soiled by unlawful gain. In the customary harangue
addressed to the people after his election Paulus asked for
their hearty co-operation and sympathy in the conduct of
his campaign. "If anyone," he said, "thinks himself competent to advise me, let him come with me to Macedon.
He shall be furnished with a ship, a horse, and a tent, and the
whole cost of his journey shall be defrayed at my expense.
But let those who sit safe at home have the grace to keep
silent, or exercise their tongues with their own affairs. We
have had enough of these land-pilots, who pretend to steer
the ship from the shore." After this significant hint addressed
to the busybodies of the Forum Paulus embarked his fresh
levies and set out for the seat of war (168 B.C.).

PERSEUS DRIVEN TO BAY

The first task of the new general was to restore the relaxed
discipline of the troops taken over from his predecessor, who
were encamped at Heraclea, on the narrow strip of coast which
lies between the eastern spurs of Mount Olympus and the sea.
Some weeks elapsed before he felt himself in a position to take
the offensive ; and when his authority over his men was completely established there was still considerable doubt as to the
method of attack. To assail the lines of Perseus in front seemed
too hazardous, for the king had entrenched himself on the
farther side of the river Enipeus, whose deep bed and precipitous sides offered a formidable obstacle. But Paulus was
relieved from his embarrassment by the gallantry of Scipio
Nasica, who made his way with eight thousand troops through
the western passes of Olympus, and, having overpowered a

body of the enemy which had been sent forward to bar his approach, appeared in the rear of the Macedonian camp. Finding himself outmanoeuvred, Perseus abandoned his position and fell back upon Pydna, and there, being now fairly driven to bay, he resolved to give battle. Paulus, with the detachment of Nasica, had pressed hard in pursuit, and when he came upon the enemy his soldiers, though full of ardour, were worn out by their forced march under the burning sun. By a clever artifice the veteran general repressed their impetuosity and gave the order to pitch a camp. On the night which followed the moon was in eclipse, and wild cries were heard from the Macedonian lines as the dark shadow crept across her face, " with fear of change perplexing monarchs." But among the Romans the phenomenon was viewed with indifference, for it had been predicted and explained by one of the military tribunes, who was a learned astronomer. Then the words which Philip had uttered in scorn were fulfilled in very truth, and the sun rose for the last time on the free kingdom of Macedon.

BATTLE OF PYDNA

The battle, which in its results may be reckoned among the most important in history, was brought on prematurely and against the desire of both leaders, for Paulus wished to gain time until he had completed the fortification of his camp, and Perseus was seized with one of his cold fits when the moment came for throwing his final stake. The outposts of the Roman army came into collision with those of the enemy as they were watering their horses in a little stream, and as fresh troops came hurrying up on either side to the support of their comrades a general engagement ensued. Paulus, compelled to fight against his better judgment, flung himself bare-headed into the van, and strove to steady his ranks against the first shock of the phalanx. But even the iron heart of the consul failed him for a moment as that living fortress came on with its dense array of mail-clad warriors and bristling spear-points, line above line. With the force of a battering-ram the massive column hurled itself on the Roman front, bearing down all opposition, and swept forward through the breach, leaving the ground behind strewn with trampled corpses. But this brief flush of success was followed by a speedy downfall, and the superiority of the Roman tactics soon appeared. For as the phalanx advanced it came upon broken and uneven ground, and its ranks were thrown into disorder. The Romans, on the other hand, with their open and elastic formation, soon rallied from their reverse, and, hovering round the huge, disorganized mass, assailed it in detail, rushing boldly into every gap, like the Swiss at Sempach and Morgarten. At close quarters the Macedonians were no match for the Romans, being encumbered by their ponderous lances, and having in their daggers but a poor defence against the terrible Spanish sword. The phalanx, the most famous engine of conquest which the world had hitherto seen, fell before the legion, and the power which it had created fell with it

Perseus Surrenders

The wretched Perseus, who had been one of the first to leave the field, fled with a handful of horsemen to Pella, the royal seat of the second Philip. Thence, after spending a few hours in his empty palace halls, he made his way to Amphipolis. Here also there was neither countenance nor comfort for the fallen king, and seeing nothing but cold looks or averted faces on all sides he took ship for Samothrace, thinking to find safety in the ancient shrine of the mystical Cabiri. But the slayer of his brother, the would-be assassin of Eumenes, had lost all claim to the divine favour, and after stooping to the basest shifts and equivocations he was compelled to surrender himself to Octavius, the commander of the Roman fleet, who handed him over to the custody of Paulus. Broken in spirit and lost to every sense of manly dignity, the last in the line of Alexander was kept to make a public show at the triumph of his conqueror, and survived for some years to eat the bitter bread of captivity in the bleak Marsian hills.

ROME'S VENGEANCE

The sovereign power of Rome, which for a moment had seemed to be tottering, was now re-established on a firmer basis than ever, and a heavy reckoning was prepared for all who had wavered or had appeared to be wavering in their allegiance. In the first year of the war, when the star of Perseus was in the ascendant, the Epirots had thrown in their lot with Macedon. It was Epirus, accordingly, which felt the first and keenest edge of Rome's resentment. The decree went forth, and in a single day seventy cities were given up to military licence, and a hundred and fifty thousand of the inhabitants were sold into slavery. This fearful visitation was carried out under the eye of Paulus, who was conspicuous among his countrymen for his mild and humane temper, and who had lately been gazing in rapt contemplation on the artistic glories of Athens and Olympia. Elsewhere the Romans were generally content to have their work done for them by the informers and pick-thanks who swarmed in every city of Greece. Judicial murders or wholesale massacres became the order of the day, and were winked at or openly abetted by Roman officers. At last, from weariness of bloodshed, or perhaps from some impulse of pity, an order was issued for the wholesale deportation of all disaffected persons to Italy, and by this act of mercy a multitude of Greeks from Boeotia, Aetolia, and Acarnania were doomed to a life of hopeless exile. The sentence, however, fell hardest on the cities of the Achaean League. The members of that renowned federal body had given no just cause for suspicion. During all the recent convulsions they had remained unshaken in their loyalty to Rome, and the only crime which could be charged against them was that in the midst of the national degradation some sparks of public spirit still survived among them. But in the eyes of their oppressors this was enough, and by an act of high-handed tyranny a thousand of their most distinguished citizens were carried off to Italy, and quartered in the cities of Etruria, where most of them succumbed to the hardships of their lot.

One bright exception was the historian Polybius, who was fortunate enough to find protectors in the great house of Aemilius Paulus, and devoted his leisure to the collection of materials for his monumental work.

Such, then, was the sad sequel to that memorable day when Flamininus was greeted with a storm of jubilation as the liberator of Greece. And outside of the Greek peninsula there were others who felt how bitterly they had been deceived. For nearly two centuries Rhodes had held a high position as the honoured ally of the Roman Republic. But all her merits were forgotten when weighed against the arrogant words which had been addressed by her representatives to the Senate in a time of anxiety and peril. The sword was sharpened against her, and she only escaped the last extremity of vengeance by the most abject and degrading submission. Finally the tears and prostrations of her envoys were allowed to prevail, and the proud city which had held its head so high through many a dark year was graciously permitted to exist. The jealous eyes of the Senate were then turned upon Eumenes, who was suspected of having entered into treasonable correspondence with Perseus and his father Philip. He boldly resolved to plead his cause in person and meet his accusers face to face, but on landing in Italy he received a cold intimation that his presence was not desired at Rome, and during the rest of his reign he was harassed by constant inroads of the Gauls, and by the hostility of his neighbour Prusias, who had contrived by the most slavish self-abasement to gain favour with the sovereign Republic. How mighty and far-reaching was now the terror of the Roman name is seen by the behaviour of Antiochus Epiphanes, son of Antiochus the Great, who had succeeded his brother Seleucus on the throne of Syria. This able and ambitious prince had a dispute of long standing with the two Ptolemies, who were then reigning as joint sovereigns of Egypt, and shortly after the battle of Pydna he was preparing to lay siege to Alexandria, when he was confronted by the Roman legate Popilius, who peremptorily bade him to retire. The king said that he would take time to consider the matter, but Popilius, drawing a circle with his staff round the spot where Antiochus and his suite were standing, forbade him to cross that line until he had made his choice between peace and war, and Antiochus was so much cowed by the resolute bearing of the rude Roman that he signified his submission to the will of the Senate.

HOMAGE TO ROME

Rome was now the centre to which all eyes were turned, and a kind of fever of adulation came upon all the peoples, Greek, African, or Asiatic, who had watched the irresistible progress of the victorious Republic. Princes and ambassadors vied with one another in an exaggerated display of homage and devotion. The Rhodian envoys lay prostrate on the floor of the Senate House, begging with sighs and tears that the name of Rhodes might not be blotted out of the list of Greek cities. Prusias, king of Bithynia, shaved his head and put on the cap of liberty, in token that he had received his freedom as a gift of the Roman people. Even the powerful Masinissa, ablest and most fortunate among the allies of Rome, trembled for his kingdom and abased himself before the sovereign state to which he owed his elevation. In a tone of subtle flattery, disguised as friendly remonstrance, he gently rebuked the senators for requesting those services which they had a right to command, and begged permission to present himself at Rome that he might offer his congratulations in person for the recent glorious victory. These are only a few examples of the obsequious addresses which poured into Rome after the downfall of the Macedonian monarchy. If the Romans became arrogant and overbearing it must be admitted that they were not altogether without excuse.

DISMEMBERMENT OF MACEDON

In settling the affairs of Macedon the Romans tried to effect a compromise, which only served to show that they were still novices in the art of imperial government. Instead of organizing

the country as a province under the strong grip of a central
administration, they adopted a plan which tended at once
to impoverish and distract the conquered people. Macedon
was divided into four separate districts, each of which was
carefully isolated from the others by the prohibition of intermarriage and commercial intercourse. The right of bearing
arms was restricted to the inhabitants on the exposed frontiers,
always threatened by the surrounding barbarians, and half
the taxes formerly levied by the kings of Macedon were now
to be paid into the Roman exchequer. The same treatment
was extended to the Illyrian kingdom of Genthius, which in
the year of the battle of Pydna had been overrun and subdued
by the praetor Anicius, and was now cut up into three
separate republics, each paying tribute to Rome. Such a
system was evidently not destined to be permanent, and the
sequel, so far as it concerns us at present, may be briefly
related.

RISING UNDER ANDRISCUS

The dismemberment of Macedon and the crippling of her
commercial enterprise bred poverty, poverty bred discontent,
and discontent, after the lapse of some twenty years, broke
out into open insurrection. The movement was headed by
a certain Andriscus, a low-born pretender, who gave himself
out to be a son of Perseus, and found a large following among
the ruined and desperate population of Macedon. He obtained
some considerable successes in the field, and defied all the efforts
of the Romans for a whole year, but at last he was beaten
and taken prisoner by Quintus Caecilius Metellus, and Macedon,
now deprived of the last shadow of liberty, was formally constituted a Roman province and incorporated as one subject
state with southern Illyria and Epirus. At the same time a
new military road, the Via Egnatia, was carried across the
whole breadth of the peninsula, from Apollonia to Thessa-
lonica, to facilitate the passage of troops and keep open
communications between the Adriatic and the Aegaean.[1]

[1] The Via Egnatia was at a later date extended to Byzantium.

PROGRESS OF ROMAN ARMS

War in Greece

It had been the deliberate aim of the Romans for many years past to weaken, distract, and provoke the unhappy states which had fallen into their power, and they were now to reap the fruits of their insidious policy in Greece. The final catastrophe was brought on by the old feud between the Achaean League and Sparta, which in the days of Aratus had led to the fatal interference of Macedon, and had drawn a long train of disasters on the nation. The moment seemed favourable for asserting the independence of the League, for just at this time the Romans were about to enter on the Third Punic War (149 B.C.), Spain was in open revolt, and Andriscus, the Macedonian pretender, was not yet subdued. In an evil hour the Achaeans resolved to take advantage of Rome's embarrassments, and war was declared against Sparta. A battle was fought, which ended in the total defeat of the Spartans, and the League was about to make unsparing use of its success when its proceedings were interrupted by the arrival of a Roman embassy at Corinth bearing a summary order from the Senate. The rising in Macedon had by this time been put down, and the Romans, who had hitherto confined themselves to warning and remonstrance, were resolved to make an end of the miserable quarrels which had so long embroiled the affairs of Greece. Ignoring the high claims of the League altogether, the commissioners summoned an irregular meeting, composed of the local magistrates from the several cities,[1] to Corinth, and announced that the Senate had seen fit to separate Sparta, Argos, and the Arcadian Orchomenus from the League. Then all the elements of disorder broke loose, and the Greeks, throwing prudence to the winds, rushed with the frenzy of impotence into war with Rome. In vain Metellus, who was watching the course of events from Macedon, repeated his warnings ; in vain the Senate, still holding its hand, made yet another attempt to settle the dispute by friendly negotiation. Roman envoys were threatened with personal violence, riots broke

[1] Freeman, *History of Federal Government*, p. 541.

out in Corinth, and at last it became evident that harsher methods were needed to make an end of these wretched broils.

DESTRUCTION OF CORINTH

Metellus now marched into Thessaly, routed the army of the Achaeans at Thermopylae, and then, advancing southward, laid siege to Corinth. But the completion of his ungrateful and inglorious task was reserved for a ruder hand. At the beginning of spring (146 B.C.) Lucius Mummius, the consul, arrived from Rome with reinforcements, and Metellus went back to his province. Mummius was not the man to be perplexed by any sentimental scruples in the work which lay before him. Eagerly accepting battle, he had little difficulty in routing the ill-disciplined forces of the League, which were largely composed of manumitted slaves, and after his victory he marched without resistance into Corinth. The beautiful city, already famed for its wealth in the days of Homer, commanding the traffic of East and West, renowned among the foremost in arts and in arms, now fell a prey to the spoiler, and for a whole century its blackened ruins bore witness to the folly of the Greeks and the savage vengeance of Rome.

SETTLEMENT OF GREECE

The settlement of Greece was entrusted to Mummius, who was assisted by ten commissioners from Rome. The first step was to break up all the old federal unions, and the Achaean League, long the hope of Greek patriots, and in our own days the cherished darling of political philosophers, came to an end. The territory of those cities which had played a leading part in the recent outbreak was confiscated to the Roman State, and in all the other communities the constitution was carefully modelled in the interests of Rome. But Greece, though now tributary and dependent, was not yet formally made a province, and the department of Achaea belongs to a much later date. So far as there was any central administration

PLATE XLII. SITE OF CORINTH AND THE ACROCORINTHUS

314

Photo from " Aus dem class. Süden " (published by G. Coleman, Lübeck)

PLATE XLIII. SITE OF CARTHAGE

315

it was vested in the hands of the governor of Macedonia,
while the management of local affairs was left to the native
magistrates.

ROME'S ENMITY TO CARTHAGE

From the sack of Corinth and the degradation of Greece
we are summoned to witness a deeper tragedy and contemplate
the dying agony of Carthage. In no other instance was the
cynical and pitiless policy of Rome carried to such a length
as in her dealings with her beaten but still dreaded rival.
Along with the other fruits of their conquest the Romans
took up that legacy of fierce hatred which was bequeathed
by Hamilcar to his son and had been the ruling passion
in the grand but disastrous career of Hannibal. In the
arrangements which followed the battle of Zama and in the
whole play of Roman diplomacy for two generations we can
read the same dark and insidious design. Stripped of her
fleet, curtailed in her territory, and exposed without defence to
the assaults of her bitter enemy Masinissa, Carthage seemed
doomed to a death by slow torture. But the wonderful
toughness and vitality of the Punic race frustrated that cruel
and treacherous purpose, and in spite of snares and impedi-
ments the city throve apace. Jealous watchers, however,
were observing her growing prosperity, and by degrees the
sullen rancour of the Romans gave place to a sharper and
more deadly enmity. If slower methods would not avail,
then Rome must put out her strength and crush the detested
rival who had dared once more to lift her head. These new
counsels found their most unblushing exponent in the aged
Cato, a typical Roman of the old school, whose homespun
virtues were crossed by the darker threads of cruelty, craft,
and avarice. While employed on a public mission to Africa
he had seen the whole country round Carthage teeming with
wealth and plenty, and the sight had stirred him to envious
greed. Henceforth whenever he had occasion to speak in
the Senate he always concluded with the monotonous refrain,
" *But my opinion is that Carthage must be destroyed.*"

REPUBLICAN ROME

MASINISSA'S DESIGN

By dexterous management and supple compliance under every humiliation the Punic traders contrived for more than half a century to disappoint the hopes of their cunning and jealous enemy. To an ordinary observer it might have seemed that the ghost of national hatred was laid and that Carthage would be suffered to exist in a state of humble dependence on Rome. Her harbours were thronged with shipping, her treasury was full, her men fought under the standards of the Republic in the Eastern wars, and Roman and Carthaginian consorted together in the busy haunts of commerce. But beneath this smooth surface the old wounds were still festering and eating deeper and deeper into the vitals of the State. For meanwhile Masinissa, the chosen instrument of Rome's malice, was pursuing his designs unchecked, which aimed at nothing less than the extirpation of the Punic name and the establishment of a Numidian kingdom from the borders of Cyrene to the Pillars of Hercules. Disarmed and helpless, the Carthaginians had to look on in passive submission while province after province was torn from their grasp and the circuit of their territory grew narrower and narrower. In vain their bitter cry was carried to Rome, imploring the Senate to fix some limit to these aggressions, that they might know at least what they could call their own. They were met by hypocritical evasions and excuses, and the encroachments of Masinissa went on as before.

PANIC IN CARTHAGE

By the terms of the peace concluded after the battle of Zama the Carthaginians were forbidden to levy war without the permission of Rome, and both Masinissa and the Romans had their parties in Carthage, who crippled the action of the patriotic party. But even Punic patience had its limits, and at last the popular leaders, abandoning their attitude of humble obedience, banished the adherents of Masinissa and declared war on their persecutor. The veteran warrior,

now nearing his ninetieth year, showed all his old energy,
and cut to pieces the Carthaginian army, which numbered
fifty thousand men. The Romans had now obtained the
pretext for which they had been waiting so long. Carthage
had broken the terms of the treaty, and unless they wished to
see the rich prize snatched from them by their too powerful
ally it was time for them to intervene. The Carthaginians,
seeing themselves menaced by a new war, were seized with
panic, and attempted by the most abject concessions to avert
the wrath of the Senate. Hasdrubal, who had commanded
their forces in the recent battle, was condemned to death,
but he escaped, and mustered a new army in the neighbourhood
of Carthage. Then the envoys who had been sent to Rome,
and empowered to accept almost any conditions, humbly
requested to know what was required of them. But it was some
time before the whole purpose of the Senate was revealed.
For meanwhile the Roman consuls, Manilius and Censorinus,
had set sail for Sicily (150 B.C.), and, crossing the narrow sea,
quartered their army at Utica, which had gone over to Rome
on the first hint of hostilities. The people of Carthage, now
reduced to the extremity of terror, waited with sinking hearts
to learn their fate. The sentence was delivered with lingering
cruelty, so as to prolong the agony of suspense to the very
last moment. While the fleet was still lying at Lilybaeum
a pretended ultimatum had been dispatched to Carthage :
" We grant you your liberty, your laws, and your territory,
on condition that you send three hundred noble boys as
hostages to Lilybaeum." There was a fearful ambiguity in
the wording of this demand, which deepened the anxiety of
the Carthaginians, but nevertheless they complied, and the
boys were sent. Having thus obtained security for the passage
of their fleet and established themselves at Utica, the Roman
commanders sent a second requisition demanding the surrender
of all arms and engines of war. Once more the Carthaginians
obeyed, thinking that now at any rate they had learnt the
worst, and a long train of vehicles made its way slowly to the
Roman headquarters, laden with two hundred thousand suits

of armour and three thousand siege-engines. Then the consul Censorinus dropped the mask altogether, and the Carthaginian envoys were summoned once more into his presence, to learn the final decision of the Roman Senate. It was held expedient, he said, with a hypocritical assumption of good-will, that the Carthaginians should abandon their city and choose a new site ten miles inland, where they would be removed from the temptations and allurements of a seafaring life.

Carthage resolves on War

With pale lips and trembling knees the envoys appeared before the Senate at Carthage and delivered their message, which meant nothing less than utter ruin to their country. The news soon spread throughout the city, and when the whole extent of Roman cruelty and perfidy was made manifest a paroxysm of grief and horror took possession of the population. But a sterner and more dangerous mood succeeded. All the latent ferocity of the Semitic race, repressed so long by the habitual caution and timidity of a nation of shop-keepers, blazed out with uncontrollable violence, and men, women, and children became united in one deep and desperate resolve. Rather than quit the sacred soil of Carthage, the tombs of their ancestors, and the hallowed seats of their country's gods, they would resist to their last breath and find in the ruins of their city a common grave. Having taken their resolution, the Carthaginians proceeded to act with great coolness and prudence. It was absolutely necessary to gain time, for the Roman consuls were at hand with an army of eighty thousand men, and they could not defend the vast circuit of their walls with their naked hands. By feigning submission they succeeded in obtaining a few weeks' respite, and meanwhile the whole population worked with frantic energy to place the city in a state of defence. Every temple was turned into a workshop and rang with the sound of the armourer's hammer. Swords, shields, and spears were fashioned by thousands, and the women even cut off their hair to make cords for the catapults. Accordingly, when the Roman army and fleet appeared before the walls of Carthage a month later everything was prepared for a desperate defence.

SCIPIO AEMILIANUS

The consuls, who had anticipated an easy and bloodless victory, were most disagreeably surprised by the formidable

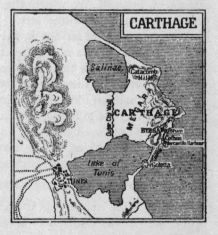

preparations which had been made for their reception, and in their manner of conducting the siege, which had resulted solely from their own remissness, they showed no likelihood of repairing their error. Hasdrubal, who had been reconciled to his countrymen, succeeded in keeping the field against them, and they failed in all their attempts to carry the walls by assault. The prospects of the Romans grew steadily worse, and things would have worn a still darker aspect but for the presence in the camp of a young officer who held a subordinate command under the consul Manilius. This was Scipio Aemilianus, the son of Aemilius Paulus, who had been adopted into the family of the great Africanus and had already gained distinction in the Spanish and Macedonian wars. With the stern virtues of a Cato Scipio united the culture and finer graces of character which belonged to the best of the Greeks, and his mind had been carefully trained by the historian Polybius and the Stoic philosopher Panaetius. Such was the man who, by a strange destiny, was called upon to be Rome's instrument in an act of atrocious vengeance which violated every principle of public right.

REPUBLICAN ROME

Scipio takes Command

The most noteworthy event in the first year of the siege was the death of Masinissa, who kept unimpaired to the last all his wonderful faculties of body and mind. He had been profoundly impressed by the eminent qualities of Scipio, and assigned to him the responsible duty of executing the provisions of his will, by which the kingdom of Numidia was divided between his three sons. Among the Romans also, both those who were serving in the camp and those who were watching affairs from home, the fame of Scipio rose higher and higher. On more than one occasion his courage and foresight had averted an imminent disaster, and one of the ablest of the Carthaginian officers, Himilco, a commander of cavalry, was induced by his influence to join the Romans. The general opinion was expressed by Cato, now on the extreme verge of old age, who, speaking of the Roman officers serving before Carthage, said, in the words of Homer :

He alone hath understanding—all the rest are flitting shades.[1]

At last, after another year had been wasted in fruitless operations, it was resolved to break through the forms of the constitution and appoint Scipio to the supreme command, with the full dignity of consul (147 B.C.). A special decree was required for this purpose, for Scipio, who had come home to stand for the office of aedile, had not yet reached the age required by law for the consulship. When all formalities had been complied with he set out from Rome with reinforcements, and on his arrival at the seat of war the siege was taken up with new vigour. A wall and a trench were drawn across the isthmus, cutting off the city on the land side, and a huge mole constructed of solid masonry blocked the entrance to the outer harbour. Though hard beset, the Carthaginian garrison, which was now commanded by Hasdrubal, still kept up a desperate defence, and while the construction of the mole was in progress they cut a new outlet from the Cothon,

[1] *Odyssey*, x. 495.

or inner harbour, and launched a new fleet of fifty vessels, which they had hastily put together from such materials as they could collect. The Romans, who were totally unprepared for such a movement, were seized with astonishment, but they soon rallied from their alarm and drove the Carthaginians back within their defences.

CARTHAGE FALLS

The siege had entered upon its fourth year, and famine was making fearful havoc in the ranks of the garrison, when Scipio resolved to shorten his labours by one vigorous effort. The inner harbour was carried by assault, and the Romans then found themselves involved in a labyrinth of streets, where every house was a fortress that had to be stormed and cleared of its defenders. For six days the carnage went on, and Scipio's men fought their way doggedly, step by step, until they reached the Byrsa, or citadel, in the very heart of Carthage. Here the remnant of the inhabitants, to the number of fifty thousand, had taken refuge, and they surrendered on receiving a promise that their lives would be spared. The last stand was made by a handful of desperate men, chiefly deserters, who threw themselves into the temple of Aesculapius, and finally, despairing of mercy, set fire to the building and perished in the flames. Fire, famine, and the sword had done their work, and out of all the population of the great city not a tenth part survived. Among those who refused to accept quarter was Hasdrubal's wife, who flung herself and her children into the burning temple, after heaping scorn on her miserable husband, who had stooped to receive his life from the hands of his enemies.

Carthage had fallen, and the few who remained from her teeming multitudes were henceforth doomed to a life of slavery. But even now the bitter hatred of the Romans was not appeased, and they pursued their vengeance against the broken fragments of her temples, and the very soil on which she had stood. The plough was passed over the site of the city, and the most awful curses were invoked on anyone

who should make that unhallowed ground the seat of human
habitation. The territory of Carthage then became the new
province of Africa, with Utica as its capital city.

SPAIN

The peninsula of Spain, which is interposed as a natural
barrier between the stormy Atlantic and the calm waters of
the inland sea, holds in ancient history the place which was
afterwards taken by the continent of America. It was the
land of the West, the El Dorado of antiquity, to which Phoenician, Greek, and Roman were drawn by the hope of boundless
wealth. This vast tract of territory had been added to the
dominions of Rome by the triumphant issue of the war with
Hannibal. But for many years the coveted possession brought
far more of burden than of benefit. Sicily, the prize of the
First Punic War, sank, after one sharp lesson, into a state of
apathy, which lasted until the outbreak of the Servile War.
But Spain was the scene of almost incessant fighting, and was
not finally reduced to subjection until the time of Augustus.
The details of these endless campaigns are tedious and obscure,
but it is important to observe the general features of the contest,
intimately connected as they are with the change which was
gradually coming over the Roman character and institutions.
The remote situation of Spain and the length and danger of
the voyage from Italy tended more and more to protract the
term of service required from the levies which were raised for
these wars. The result was to widen the breach between
citizen and soldier and give prominence to the rude and unsocial
habits of a military class. This was an ominous sign for the
future, pointing to the day when Rome would be at the mercy
of her own armies. Nor was the conduct of the generals
commanding in Spain calculated to relieve these misgivings.
Employed in a distant and perilous service, and far removed
from the controlling eye of the Senate, the Roman proconsul
or propraetor was but too apt to forget the claims of public
duty and to assume the character of a military adventurer.
The tie between soldier and commander was drawn closer

322

in proportion as the sense of civil obligation was relaxed and the day was approaching when the central authority, weakened and demoralized, was to bow to the will of its own servants.

For administrative purposes Spain was divided into two provinces, the northern or Hither province, comprising the districts later known as Aragon and Catalonia, and the southern or Farther province, corresponding to the modern Andalusia, Murcia, and Valencia. All the eastern and southern coast from the Pyrenees to Gades was fringed with prosperous and thriving cities, and the district south of the Baetis,[1] which had long been in contact with foreign influence, had attained some degree of civilization. But on the great central plateau, watered by the streams of the Douro, the Tagus, and the Guadiana, wandered the fierce native tribes, Celtic, Iberian, and Celtiberian; and the Lusitanians, in what is now the kingdom of Portugal, still clung to the independence which they had successfully maintained against the conquering arms of Hamilcar.

CHARACTER OF THE SPANIARDS

In the manners of the native Spaniards as described by the ancient writers we can already trace the leading characteristics which, after the lapse of ages and the infusion of new racial elements, marked their descendants in the age of Spain's greatness. We see the high courage and heroic endurance which carried the followers of Cortés and Pizarro through incredible perils and privations to their goal of conquest, and the fantastic spirit of chivalry which still lends so strange a fascination to the immortal pages of Cervantes. Inured to war from his youth, hardened to the extremes of heat and cold, equally at home on horseback or on foot, wielding with matchless force and precision his terrible weapon, which he had learnt to temper by a peculiar process,[2] the Spaniard was

[1] Guadalquivir.
[2] The blade of the Spanish sword was buried in the ground until the metal was purged of all impurities by the action of rust (Diodorus, v. 33).

perhaps the most formidable opponent whom the Romans ever had to encounter, and but for the fickleness of his character and his utter want of political genius he might have upheld his freedom to the last.

RISINGS IN SPAIN

At the close of the Second Punic War the Spanish possessions of Carthage, with the districts conquered by Scipio, passed to Rome, and within a few years the newly acquired territory was regularly organized into the Hither and Farther provinces, each governed by a praetor, with full consular power. But sixty years had to elapse before the Roman authority was established on a firm foundation. The warlike tribes of the interior were not at all disposed to acquiesce in the rule of their new masters, and seven years after the battle of Zama a general insurrection broke out among the Celtiberians, whose home was in the bleak upland region which forms the watershed between the southern feeders of the Ebro and the great rivers flowing from east to west. The movement was so serious that Cato, who had just been raised to the consulship, was sent to take the supreme command in Spain. He put down the revolt with unsparing rigour, and took measures to secure the peace of the country by destroying the fortified places which served as centres of disaffection. A new outbreak, which occurred sixteen years later (179 B.C.), introduces to us the famous name of Tiberius Sempronius Gracchus, the father of the two great patriots with whose tribuneship begins the era of revolution. Successful in the field, Gracchus gained a higher and purer fame by his upright dealings with the native population, and his laws were quoted as an ideal of justice by the Spaniards of a later age.

OFFICIAL OPPRESSION

Cato and Gracchus were bright exceptions to the general rule of conduct observed by Roman officials in Spain, whose career was marked for the most part by cruelty, extortion, and a shameless repudiation of their sworn pledges. Now began the plunder and oppression of the subject communities which afterwards rose to such a scandalous height, and the bitter cry of the outraged peoples is heard from time to time in the Roman Senate. An attempt was made to check the growth of this abuse by the establishment of a special commission for the trial of provincial governors who had been guilty of extortion. But laws and tribunals could effect little against the fever of avarice which was yearly gaining ground among the Romans, and the guilty magistrate, gorged with the plunder of a province, could generally secure acquittal by surrendering a portion of his ill-gotten wealth.

VIRIATHUS

Two episodes stand out in bright relief to illumine the obscure and sordid annals of the Spanish wars—the career of Viriathus and the heroic defence of Numantia. The name of Viriathus first occurs in connexion with an act of atrocious perfidy committed by Sulpicius Galba (150 B.C.), who nearly twenty years before had won an evil notoriety by opposing the claims of Paulus, the conqueror of Perseus, to the honours of a triumph. Galba decoyed several thousands of the Lusitanians into his power, and, having induced them to lay down their arms, caused them to be massacred in cold blood. Among those who escaped was Viriathus, a Lusitanian shepherd, who had already made himself conspicuous among his countrymen by his extraordinary strength, courage, and intelligence. His daring exploits have earned him a place among the national heroes of Portugal. Surrounded by a band of desperate men, he carried on an irregular warfare against the Romans for several years, gained victory after victory, and crowned his achievements by entrapping a Roman consular army into a mountain gorge and compelling its commander to sue for a dishonourable peace. The treaty was formally ratified by the Roman assembly, but the standard of public honour had now sunk so low that Caepio, the consul for the ensuing year, had no scruple in repudiating the terms which his own brother had made. With the connivance of the Senate he

REPUBLICAN ROME

invaded Lusitania, and Viriathus, attacked at the same time
by the commander of the northern province, was forced to
make submission. In the course of the negotiations which
followed the Lusitanian patriot was murdered while asleep by
three of his most intimate associates, who had been instigated
to the deed by the Roman consul (140 B.C.). After the fall
of their leader the Lusitanians still kept up a desultory warfare,
but the force of the insurrection was broken, and Decimus
Junius Brutus, the successor of Caepio, had a comparatively
easy task. Supported in his operations by a fleet, he overran
the whole country, and even carried on a successful campaign
in the remote district of Galicia.

The Siege of Numantia

The subjugation of the northern or Hither province was
only completed after twenty years of continuous fighting,
marked by the same traits of perfidy, rapacity, and incompetence which generally appear in the conduct of the Roman
generals through the whole course of these wars. The career
of Viriathus had kindled new hopes among the Celtiberians,
and three years before the death of that chieftain a serious
rising among these tribes led to the appointment of Caecilius
Metellus, the second conqueror of Macedon, in Hither Spain.
Metellus was an able officer, and when the year of his office had
expired most of the revolted tribesmen had laid down their
arms. But a core of resistance was left in the little town of
Numantia, situated in an almost impregnable position on the
upper course of the Douro. One Roman general after another
exhausted himself in his efforts to reduce the last stronghold
of Spanish liberty, and the disgrace of the Roman arms reached
a climax when the consul Mancinus, after a shameful defeat,
was forced to purchase a retreat for his army by humiliating
concessions. Then the old farce of Caudium was repeated,
and the Senate, refusing to ratify the sworn compact of its
officer, surrendered the consul to the vengeance of the enemy.
Stripped of his insignia and loaded with chains, the wretched
Mancinus was left standing before the walls of the town;
326

but the Numant nes disdained to wreak their malice on a
defenceless man, and he lived to incur a new mark of infamy
at the hands of his own countrymen.[1] Another year passed,
and another consul carried his rods and axes to Spain, but still
the heroic garrison remained unsubdued.

SCIPIO AND NUMANTIA

To Scipio, the destroyer of Carthage, belongs the dubious
honour of crushing the Spanish patriots by sheer weight of
numbers. Elected for a second time to the consulship by
the favour of the people (134 B.C.), he was prevented by the
factious jealousy of his political opponents from raising a
regular force, but the authority of his name enabled him to
supply the deficiency, and he took with him a volunteer army
and was attended by a large following of personal friends.
We are impressed by the rapid march of events, and note the
approach of what in some sense may be called the modern
period of Roman history, when we read that among those
who accompanied him to Spain were Jugurtha, the grandson
of Masinissa, and Caius Marius, whose soldierlike qualities
and strict attention to his duties soon attracted the notice
of his high-born commander. On landing in Spain Scipio
found that the bonds of discipline had been utterly relaxed by
the scandalous remissness of his predecessors. The Roman
camp was a scene of revel and disorder, filled with a rabble
of mummers, jugglers, and courtesans, and by habitual indulgence the soldiers had been rendered lazy and insubordinate.
After driving out the dissolute train of camp-followers Scipio
took steps to harden the bodies and brace the minds of his men.
" If they will not fight they shall dig," he said, with bitter
contempt, and the debauched legionary was set to work all
day with the mattock and spade. And it was the spade, not
the sword, which was the instrument of victory in that inglorious
contest. Having at his disposal a force of sixty thousand men,
Scipio threw a double line of walls round the doomed city,

[1] His name was expunged by the censors from the list of senators.

whose defenders numbered no more than eight thousand. An attempt to bring succour from without was repulsed ; and finding that supplies were still brought into the town by the river, Scipio cut off this last means of relief by building a barrier, armed with sword-blades and javelins, from shore to shore. For more than a year the blockade was kept up, and at last the Numantines, reduced to extremity by famine, tried to make terms with the Roman consul. When they found that they had no prospect but unconditional surrender most of those who survived perished by their own hands. Then the gates were opened, and a little train of living skeletons crept slowly from the town, moving even the iron hearts of their con-querors by their squalid and emaciated appearance. Thus fell Numantia, after a siege which had lasted altogether for more than ten years and had taxed the mighty power of Rome to the utmost. But the heroic spirit of its defenders still lives in the fervent verse of Cervantes, who, besides his supreme achieve-ment in the vein of comedy, has won a place by the side of Aeschylus by his patriotic drama *Numancia*. When the French artillery was battering the walls of Saragossa it was the performance of this noble play which gave new courage to the garrison and enabled its handful of men to prevail against overwhelming odds.

With the destruction of Numantia the last spark of national resistance was trampled out, and from this time forward a new era begins in the history of Spain. Roman influence gained ground steadily throughout the peninsula, subduing the fierce spirit of the inhabitants and quickening that natural genius which in later times gave to literature the distinguished names of Martial, the two Senecas, and Lucan.

Conquest of Northern Italy

To complete our survey of military events we must retrace our steps for a moment and follow the progress of the Roman arms in Italy since the end of the Second Punic War. At the close of that struggle the conquest of the great northern plain, which had been interrupted for seventeen years, was resumed, and Rome's vengeance fell heavy on the Gaulish tribes who had joined the side of Hannibal. After ten years of warfare a great victory gained by the consul Scipio Nasica crushed the last national rising of the Boii, and the whole of their territory between the Po and the Apennines was finally brought under Roman influence (191 B.C.). A new military road, whose name still survives in the department of Emilia, was carried from Ariminum to Placentia, and Parma and Mutina, peopled by full Roman citizens, with the Latin colony of Bononia, became centres of the new civic life, and formed at the same time a continuous chain of fortresses from the upper valley of the Po to the sea. The submission of the Cenomani, who had played a double part in the later stages of the contest, established the authority of Rome in the territory of Verona and Mantua, and beyond this lay the country of the friendly Veneti, which was secured by the foundation of Aquileia, the last of the Latin colonies (181 B.C.). Steadily the tide of conquest rolled eastward, overflowing the peninsula of Istria, with its piratical population, and carrying the terror of the Roman name into Dalmatia, another nest of pirates and robbers, whose insolence was chastised by the Roman consuls in two successive years. The fall of Comum, which earned a triumph for another Roman consul, broke the last resistance of the Insubres, and they, with the Cenomani, were left in a position of nominal independence, to serve as a barrier against the Alpine tribes.

More resolute was the stand made by the Ligurians, whose home was in that wild mountain region where the Apennines, sweeping round from east to west, form a mighty arch enclosing the Gulf of Genoa. In the heart of this arid and savage region towers the huge bastion of the Pania della Croce, confronting the great marble mountain which now affords a mine of wealth to the fortunate citizens of Carrara. Here dwelt the Apuani,[1] a powerful Ligurian tribe, who distinguished themselves by their fierce and obstinate defence of their liberty, until they

[1] The name still survives in the designation Alpi Apuane, a beautiful mountain district in north-east Tuscany.

were torn from their native seat and transplanted to the
neighbourhood of Beneventum, in Samnium. Slowly Roman
science and discipline made their way against the savage
valour of the natives, and the great fortress of Luna, celebrated
by Ennius for the beauty of its site, served as a permanent curb
on any future outbreaks.

A Decrepit Constitution

Thus amid crimes and blunders innumerable, but with
tremendous and relentless energy, the people of Romulus
was pressing steadily forward toward its destined goal, and the
day was not far distant when all the states of the Mediterranean
were to be brought under the gigantic shadow of Rome. But
meanwhile that unique constitution which had survived so
many shocks from within and from without, which had grown
with the growth of the people and expanded with its needs,
was beginning to show unmistakable signs of decrepitude and
decay. We must now, therefore, turn our eyes to the internal
history of the Romans, and trace the course of those changes,
social and political, which, after a century of civil convulsion,
threw the whole machinery of government into one directing
hand.

CHAPTER XIII

ON THE EVE OF REVOLUTION

SEVENTY years of constant warfare had decided the fate of the Romans as a conquering and civilizing power and raised Rome to a position of undisputed pre-eminence in the ancient world. In Italy Roman authority had been carried to the foot of the Alps. The last national rising had been stamped out in Spain, and that great peninsula was in course of time to become thoroughly Romanized in language, in manners, and in laws. The great military monarchy of Macedon had been humbled to the dust, and was never to raise its head again among the nations. All the pomp and pride of the East, arrayed under the banner of Antiochus, had been shattered by the Roman legions on the plains of Magnesia. Carthage was now but a name, and even Roman hatred might be appeased by the utter ruin of that hapless rival. The fickle and passionate Greeks, after many a bitter lesson, had at last become convinced that their only hope lay in submission and obedience. It may well have seemed to contemporary observers that the political system under which the Romans had achieved such triumphs must be possessed of some peculiar virtue which would preserve its integrity for ages to come, and Polybius, in his elaborate account of Roman institutions written at the close of the foreign wars, hardly betrays by a hint that he was conscious of the momentous changes which were preparing for the State. The admiration which he entertained for the Roman manners and character was, indeed, well founded ; but if he anticipated long permanence for the outward forms of the constitution which he described he was strangely deceived. Even as he wrote the State was tottering on the brink of revolution, and a whole century of civil strife and bloodshed was to ensue before a new system emerged out of the ruins of the old. But the genius of Rome, like a fine essence, was destined to survive all vicissitudes and to enter as a lasting element into the spiritual heritage of mankind.

GROWTH AND CHANGE

The anomalous constitution of Rome had grown up by a series of compromises, and the exact distribution of powers between the three estates had never been determined with legal precision. After the expulsion of the kings the regal power passed unimpaired to the two consuls, balanced, however, and checked by the substitution of two sovereigns for one, by the yearly change of the supreme magistrates, and by the limitation of their prerogatives as long as they remained within the city walls. One cherished privilege of the monarch, the right of deciding all matters relating to the life and freedom of a Roman citizen, was left in the hands of the people, and was jealously maintained down to the latest age of the Republic. A new feature appeared with the institution of the tribunate, which was designed to protect the plebeians against the tyrannical abuse of consular power. One by one the royal attributes of the consulate were torn away, until it remained with greatly diminished dignity and prestige. The administration of finance was transferred to the quaestors, the duty of revising and filling up the list of the Senate passed to the censors, and the judicial functions of the consuls were made over to the praetor. As the pressure of judicial business increased and Rome began to assume something of a cosmopolitan aspect the praetorship in its turn was divided, and a second praetor now held his court to decide all suits affecting the interests of foreigners. When Sicily and Sardinia came into the possession of Rome two more praetors were appointed, to administer the affairs of these provinces, and later still the number of praetors was raised to six, to provide for the annual rotation of governors in Hither and Farther Spain. By the time which we have reached

ON THE EVE OF REVOLUTION

the original functions of the consuls were distributed among more than twenty magistrates, with varying degrees of rank and authority. Yet with all these restrictions the consulship still remained the highest office in the State, and the conduct of important wars was generally entrusted to one of its holders.

THE NEW POPULUS

From the earliest days of the Republic, when the consuls governed with almost kingly sway, the people, gathered in their assemblies, claimed to be the supreme power in the State. It was by the voice of the people that the magistrates were elected, laws enacted or repealed, sentences passed affecting the life or rights of a Roman citizen, and questions of peace or war decided. In theory the people remained sovereign, and long after the fall of the Republic this shadowy title lingered on, lending a keener edge to the bitter taunts of Juvenal. But between theory and practice there was already, in the period of which we are speaking, a very wide gulf. After the conquest of Italy the electoral body was scattered over a vast extent of territory, and it became a physical impossibility for a large proportion of the Roman citizens to exercise their political rights. It would have taken weeks or months to collect a truly representative meeting from the remoter districts of the peninsula, and meanwhile public business would have been at a standstill. And, setting aside this material difficulty, there were formal restrictions on the parliamentary machinery of the Romans which seriously impaired its effective working. The two Parliaments, that of the centuries and that of the tribes, had no fixed days for meeting, and they could only be brought together by the summons of a magistrate. When convened they had no power of initiative and no liberty of debate, but were strictly confined to the question proposed by the presiding official. Gagged by constitutional forms, they were left with the bare right of accepting or rejecting the measure proposed. In addition the more respectable members of the body were for the most part away serving in the wars or engaged on their farms many

333

REPUBLICAN ROME

days' journey from Rome. The result was that the sovereign Populus became reduced to a mere rabble, made up of bankrupt and broken men, ruined farmers, discharged soldiers, dependents of the great houses, and adventurers of all sorts, who had been drawn to the capital by the prospect of an idle and easy life.

REPRESENTATION THE NECESSITY

It will be seen, then, that the Roman constitution was crumbling away at its very basis. Party leaders might aim at a temporary advantage by readjusting the electoral and legislative machinery ; but such expedients could not avert, they could not even arrest, the process of decay. The system itself was worn out, and the only way to renew its vitality was to broaden the foundations of government and give room for the influence of new and healthy elements from outside. There were still ample materials for such a reform in the provincial districts of Italy, whose inhabitants formed the third or outer circle of the old Roman polity (see p. 151). But the whole tendency of the age was to depress the status of the Italian allies, and the principle of representation, which alone could have given practical efficiency to an extended franchise, had hardly entered into the vision of the most enlightened among the ancient legislators.

POWER OF THE SENATE

Thus dissipated and weakened in its outer defences by the degradation of the commons and the partition of the executive, the whole force of the government had taken refuge in its central fortress, the Senate. Here at least there was a consistent and well-organized body, always at hand, prompt to answer every summons, animated by one spirit, and representing in its three hundred members the collective wisdom and experience of the State. As the sphere of Rome's influence enlarged new and complicated problems of international policy arose which were entirely beyond the grasp of the noisy multitude calling itself the Populus Romanus. Unversed in

PLATE XLIV. VIEW FROM THE TEMPLE OF CASTOR   334

Plate XLV. The Palatine from the South

335

public business and preoccupied by personal cares, the average commoner stood toward the senator in the relation of an ignorant layman to a trained expert. Moreover, the control of the finances and the assignment of public contracts placed a vast patronage in the hands of the Senate, and there was hardly a man in Rome who was not in some degree dependent on that patronage for his living. Accordingly we find that throughout the long struggle with Carthage and during all the period of the foreign wars the Senate was the central force in the administration, holding all the guiding threads in the complicated tissue of government. A reactionary tendency appeared in the interval between the First and Second Punic Wars, when the popular leader Flaminius succeeded in extorting some measures of a democratic character from the ruling caste. But the ascendancy of the Senate was restored and confirmed in the fearful years which followed, when Rome was fighting for bare existence against her great enemy Hannibal. And well it was for the Romans that they were content to follow that clear and steady guidance in the crisis of their fortunes. Whenever they succeeded in breaking away from control and assuming the direction themselves some crushing disaster, like those of Thrasymene and Cannae, was sure to follow. The warlike and aggressive policy which began after the battle of Zama was initiated and carried out by the resolute attitude of the Senate, and we have seen with what reluctance the people were forced into that path at the outbreak of the Second Macedonian War. But the supremacy of the Senate, though it was sanctioned by prescription, and though on the whole it was salutary in its results, was in its essence a usurpation, and as soon as the pressure of foreign wars was released the strife of parties broke out afresh, and never ceased until the whole system of republican government was swept away for ever.

CHANGE IN THE NATIONAL TEMPER

The long strain of the Hannibalic war had left deep marks on the national mind and settled the direction of its future

development. From the capital of Italy Rome grew into a
great world-power, and in proportion as she rose the political
horizon expanded, opening out new fields of activity to able
and aspiring men. It was not for nothing that the Romans
had measured their strength for seventeen years against the
greatest military genius of antiquity. Under that stern master
they had made great progress in the art of war, and the old
citizen-levies and farmer-generals were rapidly becoming a
thing of the past. But if they had gained much under that
fiery ordeal their loss was not less conspicuous. When they
emerged from the trial the Romans had left their youth
behind them, and as we advance in our narrative the instances
of generous impulse and disinterested devotion such as brighten
their earlier annals will grow rarer and rarer. Their natural
hardness becomes exaggerated into insensibility, and by
degrees a sort of ferocious cynicism takes possession of all
classes. But in growing harder they gained nothing in self-
restraint. A long period of unnatural repression produced a
reaction similar to that which followed the rule of the Puritans
in England, and an unbounded appetite for pleasure succeeded
to the grand simplicity of antique Roman life. As the circle
of the State grew wider social and political ties were loosened
and that fervent patriotism which marks the days of the
early Republic gave place to a grasping selfishness, setting
citizen against citizen and governors against governed. Thus
at the very time when a large and generous policy was needed
to weld together the multitudinous elements of a growing
empire a pernicious tendency had appeared, which led directly
to anarchy and disintegration. We must now proceed to
consider how this force operated on the privileged body which
controlled the fortunes of Rome.

THE PLEBEIAN NOBILITY

Allusion has been made in a former chapter to the great
change which came into the constitution of parties at the close
of the long struggle between patricians and plebeians. What
happened in England during the Tudor period, when a nobility

of office succeeded to the nobility of birth, was brought about in Rome, though with very different results, by the Licinian legislation. And as time went on the new nobles developed the same tenacity of their privileges and the same jealous exclusiveness as had led to the downfall of the old hereditary houses. The patrician noble could point to a long line of ancestors, reaching back into immemorial antiquity, and connecting him with the divine or heroic personages who figure in the early annals of Rome. The plebeian noble, wanting this venerable sanction to his dignity, strove to build up a pedigree by attaching a factitious importance to the outward signs of rank—the gold ring, the broad purple stripe, the waxen portrait-masks of those among his ancestors who had held any of the higher offices of State. The possession of one such mask was equivalent to a patent of nobility, and as the line of ancestral effigies grew longer the family rose in dignity and estimation. Pericles, in his great funeral speech,[1] dwells upon the spiritual continuity of the race which preserves an immortal record of the great men who have passed away, not in pompous epitaphs or monumental marble, but in the living hearts of each succeeding generation. But the grosser perceptions of the Roman required some more concrete stimulus to awaken the memories of the past, and he found it in the waxen features of consuls, censors, and senators who had served their country in council or in war, and who now gazed upon him with deathless eyes from the walls of his palace. And when his turn came to join that illustrious company a sort of formal resurrection was arranged, that he might be escorted to his last resting-place by those whose deeds he had striven to emulate. A long train of men, each chosen for his personal likeness to one of these departed worthies, marched solemnly in the funeral procession, wearing the masks of the dead, and clothed in the dress appropriate to their office. There might be seen the toga of the consul or praetor, with its broad purple border, the crimson robe of the censor, and the gorgeous vestments, stiff with embroidery

[1] Thucydides, ii. 43.

and gold, which glittered in the triumph of a victorious general. The cold fancy of Polybius, whose sympathies were Roman rather than Greek, kindles into a sort of mild rapture as he recites the details of this strange masquerade.

A STRONGHOLD OF ARISTOCRACY

Exhibitions like these, however questionable in taste they may seem, served to nourish the pride of the nobles and to mark them off as a distinct caste, separated by an ever-widening gulf from the unprivileged many. And with that genius for statecraft which was ingrained in the Roman character they knew how to utilize every power in the government as a means for confirming their monopoly and keeping out intruders. The tribunate, originally created as a counterpoise to patrician privilege, was now a useful instrument which enabled them to check the turbulence of the popular assemblies. The Senate, which in its original intention had been merely an advisory body, attached to the person of the king, and afterwards to the consuls, became by the same process of silent revolution the stronghold of the new oligarchy and the very focus and centre of aristocratic prejudice. The censors, indeed, were allowed a certain discretion in filling up vacancies, and in expelling those senators who were notorious for their scandalous lives ; but by the time of the Second Punic War the principle was firmly established that those had the first claim to the vacant seats who had held the higher offices of State, from the quaestorship upward. The Senate, by the exercise of every art, lawful or unlawful, knew how to maintain its influence on the electors so as to secure the monopoly of the higher magistracies to men of noble birth. Thus the Senate controlled the appointment of the magistrates, and the magistrates, in due course, took their seat in the Senate, and the whole body of the nobles, united by common interest, formed a compact phalanx, presenting an almost impenetrable barrier to the low-born aspirant who strove to enter the charmed circle. Well might the commons exclaim against the more than patrician pride of their new masters and clamour

for the election of New Men as the only true representatives
of the cheated and forsaken Populus. How bitter was the
feeling of the nobles against such unauthorized intruders,
even though they might be men of the highest talents, will be
seen in the careers of Marius and Cicero.

Moreover, this jealous spirit which guarded the ranks of
the nobles against all invasion from without was not less
vigilant against the pretensions of those high-born and
ambitious men who strove to raise themselves above the
level of their own order. High and commanding talent is
always viewed with suspicion by the members of a usurping
oligarchy,[1] whose cohesion depends on the maintenance of a
safe and tame mediocrity. It was this feeling which afflicted
the last years of the elder Africanus, and in a later age pointed
the dagger of the assassin against the great Julius.

A Vast Corruption

It will now be understood how far the Romans had travelled
from the wise and liberal policy which had made their city
great, that of gradually extending the privilege of citizenship
and opening the avenues of political distinction to able and
deserving men. Office had now virtually become hereditary,
and the Senate, which in the days of its glory had defied the
power of Pyrrhus and stood fast against all the assaults of
Hannibal, was sunk into a close corporation, the organ of a
party. The wisdom of ages, the resources of a wide empire,
the sanctions of law and religion, were all abused to uphold
the cause of unlawful privilege. The Senate held a monopoly
of the judicature, and the new standing commissions which
had recently been established for the trial of powerful offenders
were composed of senators, who were not likely to view with
severity crimes committed by men of their own order. Decrees
passed in the Senate House had come to have the binding
force of law, and in cases of necessity the Senate claimed a
dispensing power which enabled it to override the constitution.
In the office of tribune, which was now regularly held by men

[1] *Cf.* Thucydides, viii. 89.

of noble birth, the Senate had a ready means of controlling
the popular assemblies. If that proved insufficient they could
work on the religious fears of the masses and overawe opposition by reporting unfavourable omens. A recent enactment
had empowered any higher magistrate to suspend all parliamentary business by simply announcing his intention of watching
the sky until he had obtained a decisive token of the divine
will.[1] Finally, the nobles held in their hands the greatest
power of all, the power of the purse Direct bribery of the
voters had not yet reached the height which it afterwards
attained ; but a more insidious form of corruption had already
become widely prevalent, in the games, gladiatorial shows,
and theatrical exhibitions, which were the direct price paid
for popularity by those who aimed at the highest offices of
State. The taint of greed, which was rapidly infecting all the
relations of public and private life, spread from the city to
the armies, and the victorious general who had added a new
province to the empire scattered his gold among the soldiers
to secure their votes when he returned to claim the honours
of a triumph. It was his refusal to comply with the exorbitant
demands of his troops which almost deprived the high-minded
Paulus of the coveted distinction.

EXTORTION IN THE PROVINCES

The possession of wealth had, accordingly, become indis-
pensable to all who aspired to a public career. The means of
raising a large fortune were at hand in the vast territories
which in the course of the last century had been conquered
and annexed—Sicily, with its broad corn-lands and famous
cities, Spain and Macedonia, with their mineral wealth, and the
fertile district of Carthage, whose farms and gardens with
their teeming produce had excited the cupidity of the aged
Cato. To these we have to add the kingdom of Pergamum,
which at the close of this period (133 B.C.) was bequeathed by
Attalus III to the Roman people, and was henceforth incorporated as a province with the richest and most populous portions

[1] Lex Aelia Fufia (156 B.C.).

of Asia Minor. Such was the immense heritage which now
passed to the sovereign Populus, or rather to the corrupt and
selfish oligarchs who held the reins of government. And those
who in their home policy paid so little heed to the rights of
their fellow-citizens were not likely to be over-scrupulous in
their dealings with conquered and subject nations. In Italy
itself we may observe a sharp and distinct descent from
noble to citizen, and from citizen to Italian ally, and in this
severance of interests lay the seeds of much future evil to the
State. Outside of these three grades lay the great mass of the
provincials, who, with a few privileged exceptions, were hardly
held to possess rights at all. Each province was like an immense
estate left by its owner to an unprincipled agent, who abused
his position to enrich himself and his followers, flinging a
small portion of his gains to his careless and indolent master.
As yet the evil was only in its infancy, but it grew apace, and
reached its climax two generations later, when it was said
that a province had to yield three fortunes to its governor,
one to pay his debts, one to bribe his judges, and one to recompense him for his arduous and disinterested labours. The
earlier Roman satraps were but novices in extortion, and
many years of licence were required to produce such a monster
as Verres. But that the grievance was already a very real
one is proved by the loud complaints of the Spaniards and
the measures taken for their relief, and by the temporary
closing of the mines in Macedonia, to prevent them from
becoming a prey to the greed of Roman speculators.

THE PROCONSULAR POWER

Side by side with the advance of Roman arms and the development of the provincial system there had grown up a practice
of extending the command of the consuls and praetors when
their year of office had expired. In adopting this expedient
to meet a temporary emergency (see p. 106) the Romans had un-
wittingly called into existence a power which was destined to
absorb every other element in the constitution and swallow
up their liberties. About the middle of the second century

before Christ it was found that the praetors, to whom the administration of the provinces had hitherto been assigned, were sufficiently occupied by the affairs of Italy, and from this time forward it became the regular practice to leave this department in the hands of the proconsuls and propraetors. The deputed command was at first limited to one year, but the term was gradually extended, and the possibilities of mischief involved in this viceregal office were proportionately increased. At the close of his year of office in Rome the provincial governor joyfully turned his back on the capital, where he was watched by jealous eyes and hampered at every step by the rigid formalism of official life, to indemnify himself for his long restraint by the exercise of almost unlimited power. With him went a hungry cohort of friends and adherents, who had backed him in the keen race for promotion, and who now looked for their reward in a share of the rich prize which they had helped him to win. These were the first claimants whose demands he had to satisfy. Another greedy multitude brought up the rear, like the camp-followers of an invading army— farmers of the taxes, with all their dependents, small and great, and Roman speculators, whose high privileges as citizens gave them endless opportunities of overreaching the helpless foreigner in every field of commercial enterprise. Like a swarm of locusts the motley host descended on the unhappy province, and the work of spoliation began. It should be repeated that the state of things which we are describing did not reach its full development until a later age. And of course, even when things were at their worst there were always to be found honourable Romans whose treatment of the subject communities left nothing to be desired. But these were isolated exceptions. Speaking generally, the attitude of the Romans toward Spaniard, Greek, or Asiatic was the same from the first, and evidences the depths of sordid selfishness to which the conquering race of Italy had already sunk. It was not until the time of the Empire that the provincial administration was regularly organized, and vigilantly watched by the eye of the reigning sovereign.

ON THE EVE OF REVOLUTION

DESPOTIC RULE

Nothing contributed so much to determine the course of the great constitutional changes which were impending over Rome as the vast powers of the provincial governors. Surrounded by devoted adherents, removed from all the restraints of the capital, and living among cringing Orientals, effeminate Greeks, or half-savage races who had to be kept down by the sword, the ruler of a Roman province wielded an authority which was virtually despotic, and his return to Italy became a sort of exile, not unlike that of a monarch banished from his hereditary kingdom. In the letters of Cicero we have several allusions to the haughty manners and almost regal condescension affected by Pompeius on his return from the East. He is the " three-tailed Bashaw " who has forgotten the noble simplicity of Roman ways. Something of the same sort, though on a much smaller scale, was seen in the England of the eighteenth century, when the wealthy nabob came home from India and settled down to the life of an English country gentleman. The appetite for power grows by indulgence, and it is hard for any man who has tasted of the intoxicating cup to resume the sober habit, of a private citizen. The Roman provinces thus became the nursery of empire, and fed the spirit of absolutism, until the day when the forces of East and West were arrayed against each other under the banners of Pompeius and Caesar.

OMINOUS CHANGE

We have taken a brief survey of the ancient world so far as it had come under Roman sway, and on all sides we have observed the signs of discord and division, full of evil omen for the future. As yet we can perceive no principle of cohesion, no strong central policy to bring all these jarring elements into harmony. In the provinces we have seen a vast subject population, held down by force, with many burdens and hardly any rights. And the same hard selfishness which set a gulf between governors and governed had widened the

343

breach between the two great divisions of the conquering race, the Romans and their Italian allies. The old graduated scale of privilege had now disappeared, and was merged into one broad distinction between those who held and those who did not hold the franchise. In the growing distaste of the Romans for military service the armies of the Republic were mainly recruited from the Italians, who thus found themselves exposed to all the perils and hardships of a soldier's life, while the fruit of their labours was reaped by others. It is true that the possession of the franchise had to a large extent lost its political value, and that those who voted in the assemblies were but a small minority of the whole voting body. But since the establishment of Rome's influence throughout the Mediterranean states the Roman citizen stood in a position of proud eminence, and he alone could be called in the full sense of the term a free man. The law, which to others was a terror and an instrument of oppression, was to him a sure guarantee of comfort and security, protecting his person from violence and upholding his claims, just or unjust, against any unprivileged suitor. We can see, then, that it was for no visionary advantage that the Italians fought when they plunged into the murderous struggle with Rome which is known as the Social War.

The Slaves

There remains, however, one large class of the population to be mentioned, the great toiling, suffering multitude of the

A SLAVE'S COLLAR

unfree, on whose cheerless and colourless lives was raised the splendid but half-barbarous edifice of ancient civilization. In the early days of Rome the number of slaves had been few, and as far as we can judge from the scanty evidence remaining they were treated with comparative mildness. We

344

know, at least, from the poems of Homer that the condition of the slave in a similar state of society was mitigated by many gentle observances. But in the period of conquest which we have just been surveying slavery had risen to gigantic proportions, and before the close of the second century the number of these hapless creatures must have far exceeded that of the free population. After the sack of an enemy's town, after every victory in the field, thousands of captives were brought under the hammer, and henceforth became the living chattels of their purchasers. And as the standard of living rose and the race for wealth became keener all these unnamed millions, who had to bear the brunt of life's battle, were handled with increasing harshness and severity. The Romans, as we have seen, had grown harder and more cruel in their life-and-death grapple with Hannibal and in the long wars which followed, and the full rigour of their temper was naturally visited on those unfortunates whom the chances of war or the accident of birth had left at their mercy.

The vast slave population of Rome formed a state in itself, with many grades of rank and privilege, from the confidential secretary, often a man of learning and refinement and a humble friend of the family, to the branded and proscribed outcast, who was condemned to work in chains on the fields and confined at night in an underground dungeon among a gang of wretches as miserable and as ferocious as himself. A distinguished example of the former class is Cicero's friend and freedman Tiro, who survived his master, and published an edition of the great orator's letters and speeches after his death. But speaking generally the sternness and coarseness of the national character made the lot of a slave one of peculiar

A SLAVE WORKING
IN FETTERS

hardship, and those who worked on the fields or served as shepherds and herdsmen were commonly treated with atrocious severity. As the practice of farming on a large scale came more and more into fashion the numbers thus employed rose to hundreds of thousands, and became a standing menace to the public safety. The fierce Illyrian, the warlike Celt, or the stubborn Sardinian who had exchanged a life of wild liberty for one of hard fare and hopeless toil nourished a deep and deadly hatred against his oppressor, and was ready to face any hazard if he could gain a brief period of licence and satisfy his thirst for revenge. The natural resentment which rankled in the heart of a slave was often heightened by a special sense of personal injury, for as the demand for slave-labour increased the supply of captives taken in war proved insufficient, and many a free man was torn from his home and exposed for sale in the great market of Delos which had become the centre for this infamous traffic. The pirates who infested the eastern waters of the Mediterranean derived a large part of their gains from this source, and Roman traders made no scruple of sharing the profits from human merchandise.

SLAVE OUTBREAK IN SICILY

Isolated outbreaks which occurred in Italy, at Athens, and at Delos toward the close of this epoch showed how widespread was the discontent which was fermenting below the surface, and at length the long peace of Sicily was broken by a general insurrection of the slaves, which lasted for seven years (139–132 B.C.), and served incidentally to illustrate the growing feebleness of the central government. When the revolt was at its height two hundred thousand slaves are said to have taken the field, and under the leadership of Eunus, a Syrian, and Cleon, a Cilician, they captured several fortified cities, gained victories over Roman consuls and praetors, and established a reign of terror throughout the island. The movement was ultimately suppressed by the consul Publius Rupilius, and no further outbreak occurred for thirty years. But the Romans failed to profit by this terrible lesson. The worst abuses of slavery went on unchecked, and led two generations later to the rising under Spartacus, which for a time seemed likely to endanger the very existence of the State.

THE ANCIENT ROMAN DISCIPLINE

With this brief account of slave-life we may conclude our general view of the outward aspect of society and of the relations which subsisted between conquerors and conquered at the close of the foreign wars. We must now look a little closer and examine the deeper causes of that silent revolution which had wrought such important changes in the mind and character of the Roman people. And we shall best appreciate the meaning of that revolution if we fix our attention on the three cardinal features of the ancient Roman discipline, its lively faith, its preoccupation with agriculture, and the purity of its domestic manners. These three together made the mould in which was shaped the mighty Roman spirit.

THE OLD RELIGION DEBASED

In the heart of the antique Roman there was a large portion of that earnest natural piety which, under whatever forms, is the true source of all healthy national life. But the mind of the nation, naturally cold and unimaginative, failed to create any system of worship capable of satisfying its higher religious aspirations, which, wanting a firm centre, gradually withered away. Left without a guide, the general mass of the people took refuge in the gross superstition of Etruria or the voluptuous religion of the Greeks. By the time of the Punic Wars the orthodox State ritual had sunk into a barren formalism, void of all spiritual content, which was worked for political purposes by the ruling class. Even Cato, the staunch conservative and rigid upholder of ancient manners, wondered that one augur could look another in the face. The same cynical view appears again and again in the writings of Polybius.

IMPORTED GODS

All forms of polytheism have this much in common, that they extend a ready hospitality to foreign modes of worship.

REPUBLICAN ROME

This readiness of assimilation was peculiarly characteristic of the Romans. The old pastoral divinities of Rome early gave place to the usurping potentates of the Greek pantheon, and at times of public distress a formal embassy was sometimes sent to invite one of these complaisant powers to take up his residence at Rome. Thus Aesculapius, the god of healing, became domiciled on the banks of the Tiber in consequence of an order issued by the keepers of the Sibylline Books at a time when Italy was desolated by a pestilence (293 B.C.). The cult of this god was on the whole humane and refined, but a different character attaches to the rites of Cybele, which were introduced from Asia toward the close of the Second Punic War. Cybele represents the principle of fertility, the perpetuation of life from age to age, a great mystery, which lies at the root of all religious faith. But as practised at Pessinus, the chief seat of this goddess, her worship had become grossly materialized, and was conducted with an orgiastic frenzy which encouraged every kind of extravagance and excess. The old gods of Rome may well have averted their faces when this strange guest first set foot within their confines, bringing with her a troop of effeminate priests, and attended by the loud strains of barbaric music. It was the vanguard of an invading army, to be followed in due course by fresh hordes from Syria, Egypt, and Chaldaea, who took by storm the temples of Rome and filled the sacred city with all the pollutions of the East.

FANATICISM AND CRIME

The worship of Bacchus, like that of Cybele, was strongly tinged with Oriental influence, and had a strange power over its devotees, sometimes raising them to a high mood of mystical contemplation, but more frequently degenerating into gross and brutal licence. Its worst tendencies are displayed in the wild outburst of fanaticism which is so vividly described by Livy. Not long after the conclusion of the war with Antiochus one of the consuls received information from a private source that nocturnal gatherings were being held at Rome for the

348

purpose of celebrating the rites of Bacchus, which were made a pretext for shameless debauchery. These orgies had begun in Etruria, where they were introduced by a low-born Greek, and from thence they had been brought to Rome, and had spread to all the provincial districts of Italy. Under the mask of religion the most atrocious crimes were committed, and murder, forgery, and the wholesale corruption of youth had become a regular part of the business planned or executed at the secret gatherings. When these facts were made generally known something like a panic took possession of the public mind. For some time past sudden deaths had occurred in circumstances which led to a strong suspicion of poisoning, and many persons had mysteriously disappeared. The general apprehension was increased by the discovery of a plot for the subversion of law and order. A searching inquisition was immediately set on foot, and seven thousand persons were arrested and condemned to death or imprisonment. Steps were then taken to prevent a renewal of the secret practices, and a decree of the Senate is still extant setting severe restrictions on all private meetings held for purposes of worship.

Ruin of Agriculture

From these instances of fanaticism we turn to consider the national decadence in another aspect. Since the early days of the Republic many causes had been at work to ruin the class of small farmers, who formed the backbone of the ancient Roman commonwealth. All legislation proved impotent to cope with this evil, and the growth of large estates went steadily on, promoted by the greed of the rich and the necessities of the poor. The long occupation of Hannibal had desolated vast tracts of land in Italy, and many a small homestead was thrown into the market by the death of its owner and his male heirs. Patriotic statesmen might try to restore the old state of things by the foundation of colonies and the assignment of lands. But the disbanded soldier who had acquired the restless habits of camp-life during long years of foreign service would not settle down to the monotonous routine of

349

rural pursuits. He sold his allotment, squandered the pur-
chase-money, and then drifted to Rome, where he joined the
needy and profligate rabble and lost the last remnant of his
self-respect. Or if he clung to his holding and tried to live
by the labour of his hands he soon found that farming on a
small scale would not pay. Conveyance was costly, country
roads were bad, and when he brought his produce to the
market he was forced to sell it at a price which left hardly
any margin of profit. For corn was now imported in immense
quantities from abroad, and this foreign competition was one
of the chief causes which contributed to the ruin of Italian
agriculture. Olive-grounds and vineyards were more profitable, but these forms of rural industry required a good deal of
capital, and the owner had to wait for years before he could
expect a return for his outlay. As if all this were not enough,
the struggling farmer who toiled with plough and mattock to
provide bread for his little ones was watched with jealous eyes
by his wealthy neighbours, whose cattle broke down his fences
and trampled on his crops. Sooner or later he was obliged to
give up the struggle, and his scanty acres were swallowed up
to round off a corner of some rich man's estate. The cheerful
farmhouse gave place to the hideous barrack, into which chained
and branded slaves were driven like beasts at nightfall.

Decay of Family Life

The same causes which led to the ruin of agriculture acted
with fatal effect on the third main pillar of Roman society,
a pure, vigorous, and hearty family life. Thousands of families
were broken up by the loss of the head of the household, who
had gone to the wars and never returned, and the younger men,
in the rude licence of camps, had acquired a distaste for the
tame uniformity and humble joys of home. New fields of
enterprise were opening beyond the seas, and few were disposed
to encumber themselves with domestic ties, which would confine them to one spot, or at least diminish their chances in
the race for wealth. Even among the rich and high-born
there was a general disinclination to assume the duties and

burdens of the married state. A significant symptom of decadence was the growing facility afforded for divorce, the earliest recorded instance of which occurred between the First and Second Punic Wars, more than five centuries from the date assigned for the foundation of the city. But when once the first step had been taken the descent was rapid, and the ancient form of marriage, which was a solemn religious ceremony, was largely superseded by a mere civil contract, lightly taken up and easily set aside.

The New Woman

Women, too, had begun to rebel against the severe decorum imposed on them by time-honoured custom, which restricted them to a life of domestic seclusion. Under the old *régime* a woman was kept in a state of perpetual pupillage. In the eyes of the law she had no personal identity, but was subjected to the will of her husband or male relations, and she could hold no property of her own. But now these severe restraints had been swept away, and in the later days of the Roman Republic, as in the times of the Spartan decadence, large estates were held and administered by women. The emancipated Roman lady no longer shunned the glare of publicity, but, if she conceived herself injured, carried her grievance to the very doors of the Senate House and assailed the ears of the Fathers with indignant clamour. One such incident may be briefly described. In a time of great financial distress, at the beginning of the Second Punic War, a law had been passed to restrain the luxury of women and limit the use of gold for personal adornment. Some twenty years later, when the need for such austerity had abated, it was proposed to repeal the law, and a lively debate ensued, which is described by Livy with his usual graphic power. When the day for the voting came on an excited throng of women beset all the approaches to the Forum, prepared to do battle for their earrings and necklaces. Cato, a professed woman-hater and a stern upholder of the ancient discipline, stood out bluffly for the law, as a wholesome curb on the extravagance

351

of a vain and giddy sex. Valerius, true to the liberal policy of his house, spoke strongly for repeal, and his eloquence, backed by the importunate outcry of the women, won the day.

Nor was it only in matters which immediately concerned themselves that women claimed the right of intervention, but they presently began to meddle with larger questions of State, and for good or for evil feminine influence was to become a force in Roman politics.

FATHER AND SON

In the general loosening of family ties the intimate relationship between father and son which had been so characteristic of primitive Roman manners had almost entirely died out. A few Romans of the old school, like Paulus and Cato, might still pride themselves on being companions and teachers to their sons and take delight in watching the gradual development of a young mind. But these were rare exceptions, and for the most part the education of Roman boys was left to Greek tutors, men of servile condition, who could neither claim authority nor command respect. And this leads us to another part of our subject, the profound influence which was exercised on the Roman mind and character by the art, the literature, and the manners of conquered Greece.

THE GRECIAN MOULD

The whole nation had put itself to school, as if resolved to obliterate the antique Roman type and reshape itself in a Grecian mould. The intellectual conquest of the Romans by a people whose liberties they had destroyed, and the alacrity with which the victors submitted to that yoke, present to us the highest example afforded by history of the triumph of mind over material power. An obvious comparison is suggested by the enthusiasm for Greek learning which arose in the schools of Western Europe at the time of the Renaissance. A further illustration may be drawn from modern Germany, where the passion for foreign books and foreign tongues

prejudices the vernacular literature. These instances, however, offer but an imperfect parallel to the complete self-
abandonment with which the Romans resigned themselves to
the loss of their own intellectual identity. The ground had
been prepared by the total effacement of local life and manners
which went on step by step with the conquest of Italy. The
germs of native genius had everywhere been stamped out,
and the national mind lay like a fallow field ready to receive
the new seed.

When a fresh enthusiasm takes possession of a people it
is commonly carried to extravagance. What happened in
England at the revival of learning was seen, though on a
far larger scale, among the Romans of the third and second
centuries. A flood of Greek words poured into the language
and threatened to swamp the native idiom of Latium. The
vast treasure of Greek poetry was to be appropriated to Roman
use by means of wholesale translation and adaptation. Then
the divine steed Pegasus, yoked to a Roman car, moved
awkwardly to the measure of tuneless saturnians and lurching
hexameters. The satirist Lucilius, a contemporary and friend
of the younger Africanus, employed a sort of mongrel dialect,
half Greek, half Latin, in the composition of his voluminous
works. But in spirit he was thoroughly Roman, and he
exerted all the vigour of his genius to lash the strange frenzy
which had come over his countrymen. The Roman exquisite
as exhibited by this writer seems determined to strip off the
last trace of his nationality. He dines on Greek dishes, wears
Greek clothing, salutes his friends in Greek, and distorts the
manly and robust language of his native country by a fantastic
euphuism borrowed from the school of Isocrates. It was long
before this foolish mimicry wore itself out and the Romans
returned to a sense of national dignity and self-respect. Then
it was recognized that the first exponents of Hellenism, in
their fervour, had taken a false direction, and the whole
mass of the hybrid literature which had shot up with such
rank luxuriance in Italy sank into general neglect. The highest
creations of Greek genius, the tragedies of Aeschylus, the epic

song of Homer, were beyond the reach of Roman rivalry. But by following their great models at a due distance the Romans were able to create fresh shapes of beauty, and a new literature arose, Greek in form but Roman in spirit, which attained great heights of excellence in the luminous prose of Cicero, the polished lyrics of Horace, and the stately cadences of Virgil.

DEGENERATE TENDENCIES

But what concerns us more immediately is the moral effect which was produced on the Romans by their preoccupation with Greek thought and manners. In this respect the consequences, for a long time at least, were almost wholly bad. At the time when a free intercourse began between the two nations the Greeks had long been sunk deep in corruption. In the general stagnation of political life the descendants of Pericles and Sophocles exhausted their energies in a round of loose pleasures and elegant dilettantism. The field of literature, cut off from every vigorous and fertilizing influence, was held by a mob of grammarians, commentators, and poetasters. There was, indeed, one exception. The New Comedy, which dates from the time of Alexander, was a genuine expression of contemporary Greek manners, and in the grace and beauty of its external form it might vie with the greatest masterpieces of Greek literature. But the prevailing tone of thought and sentiment was pitched in a low key, suited to the temper of a soft and effeminate age. And Plautus, who appropriated the whole of this dramatic material and transferred it bodily to the Roman stage, while falling far behind his originals in wit and elegance, greatly surpassed them in the open display of profligacy and indecency. Certain types of character—the young rake whose sole occupation is intrigue, the doting father, his dupe and victim, the knavish servant deeply versed in the arts of cheating and lying, the courtesan whose snares are spread for young and old—are presented over and over again with wearisome iteration, and the cynical treatment of the relation between the sexes recalls the worst features of the Restoration drama.

ON THE EVE OF REVOLUTION

THE NEW PHILOSOPHY

Such was the entertainment offered to the Romans in their lighter hours, but little calculated, as we may easily perceive, to refine the manners or elevate the taste. The new philosophy, too, which attracted more thoughtful minds, could ill supply the void which had been left by the general decay of religious faith. The theories of Epicurus, even in their original purity, encouraged an attitude of selfish indifference, which tended to make those who adopted them deaf to the claims of public duty ; and by holding up pleasure as the chief end and final good the founder of this sect had opened a door to the grossest forms of sensual indulgence. At the opposite pole of thought were the grand ideals of the Stoics, which had always a strong fascination for men of loftier temper, and, in the later days of tyranny, had power to arm the heart against the worst that could befall. But both of these rival schools, which had grown up in the decline of Greek liberty, had this in common, that the virtues which they aimed at were passive rather than active. Neither the Porch [1] nor the Garden [2] could provide any potent, creative principle to serve as a guide in the great process of demolition and reconstruction which began with the era of the Gracchi. The easy Epicurean, when the evil days came, saw the storm pass by with a smile and a shrug, and turned for solace to his studies or his pleasures. The rigid Stoic, rapt in the pursuit of unattainable perfection, drove sober patriots to despair by his iron bigotry and his intolerance of all compromise. There were always, of course, minds of a more elastic fibre, which could wear their convictions lightly and shun the perilous issues of a logical conclusion. But for most men philosophy is a dangerous ally, throwing them into discord with themselves or their surroundings.

A CITY OF PLEASURE

These heights of thought, however, could be reached only by a few select spirits; and even the comic drama, depraved

[1] Stoicism.　　　　　　　　[2] Epicureanism.

355

as it was, might in some sense be called an intellectual pastime, implying a certain degree of refinement. For the mass of the people other and grosser means were provided to satisfy the craving for excitement which had taken possession of all classes. Of these some were of native growth, others had been imported from abroad. The triumph, once a rare and coveted honour, was now demanded after every petty campaign, to feed the vanity of the vulgar great, and the fashion of adding titles to the family name, which had been begun by the elder Africanus, was carried to the point of absurdity. And that many-headed monster the sovereign mob, on whose voice depended the bestowal of consulships, praetorships, and triumphs, sought and obtained the price of its favours in the games of the circus and the bloody contests of the arena. Rome was become a gay metropolitan city, and the ministers of pleasure flocked thither from East and West to pamper the inordinate craving for amusement, which bade fair to supplant the gravity and austerity of ancient Roman manners.

Cato

Amid the deluge of foreign influence which was rapidly sweeping away the old landmarks one massive figure stands prominently out, opposing a stubborn barrier to the rising tide of innovation. For more than half a century [1] Marcus Porcius Cato pursued his strenuous career, holding up an example of rigid Roman virtue, and we will conclude this chapter with a brief sketch of his life and character, as they serve to illustrate by contrast the prevailing tendencies of the age. Born at Tusculum, seven years after the close of the First Punic War, and descended from a race of sturdy yeomen, he passed his early years in the cultivation of a small estate in the Sabine country, which he had inherited from his father. His vigorous and upright character attracted the attention of Valerius Flaccus, a powerful noble, who encouraged him to seek a wider scope for his talents in the arena of public life. His uncouth appearance, his red hair, green eyes, and huge,

[1] 204 (quaestor under Scipio) to 149 B.C. He was born in 234 B.C.

tusk-like teeth, made him the butt of small contemporary wits; but, combined with his extraordinary gifts, these peculiarities served to fix the attention of his countrymen, and when once he had set foot on the ladder of promotion his rise was rapid. He ran through all the stages of a political career, winning golden opinions by his close application to business and by the severe simplicity of his personal habits. In politics he was attached to the party of Fabius, who sought to merge the individual in the State, and was the sworn enemy of those high personal pretensions which seemed inconsistent with the traditions of a free Republic. Such principles marked him out as the natural opponent of the brilliant and stately Scipio, and from the time when he served as quaestor under that leader in Sicily he led the outcry which finally drove the victor of Zama to the seclusion of his villa at Liternum. In 198 B.C. he became governor of Sardinia, with the rank of praetor, and gained general applause by his impartial administration of justice and by the strict discipline which he maintained among his subordinates. The events of his consulship, which were transacted in Spain, have already been referred to.

When the war broke out with Antiochus, Cato, still in the full vigour of his powers, served as a subordinate under Glabrio, and after the battle of Thermopylae he had the honour of conveying the news of the victory to Rome. From this time onward his energies were chiefly devoted to the affairs of civil life. The stout old warrior, who from the age of seventeen had borne arms against his country's enemies, and whose body was covered with honourable scars, was not less formidable in the Forum than in the field. His robust eloquence, mordant wit, and dauntless courage, backed by all the weight of his character, made him the terror of evildoers. A born fighter, he was ever ready to engage in the war of words, and down to the extreme limit of old age he was involved in almost constant litigation. But his fame rests chiefly on the iron firmness with which he performed the duties of the censorship, when he was appointed to that high office at the age of fifty, with his friend and former patron, Valerius Flaccus. In the exercise of his large inquisitorial powers he was no respecter of persons, and the wealthy noble whose life was a scandal to public decency not less than the meanest plebeian felt the weight of his hand All who sought to set private interest against public right— the landowner who bored an aqueduct to convey water to his orchard or garden, contractors who cheated the treasury, builders detected in encroaching on the common highways— received prompt and stern warning that their day of licence was past. Nor was he less resolved to root out the taste for extravagance which had been imported into Rome from Greece and Asia, and ladies who loved jewels and rich attire or epicures devoted to the pleasures of the table found that they would have to reduce their style of living or pay an exorbitant price for their luxuries.

Toward the close of his life Cato yielded so far to the current fashion as to apply himself to the study of Greek and to relax somewhat from the severity of his private habits. He loved to unbend his mind in the circle of his intimate friends, and when mellowed with wine he would pour out a rich store of anecdote, seasoned with keen observation and caustic wit. But he maintained his vigour unimpaired to the end, and at the age of eighty-five he took a leading part in the prosecution of Sulpicius Galba, who had been guilty of gross cruelty toward the Lusitanians.

Cato was a typical Roman of the old school, and he exhibits that character in all its strength, and in all its limitations. His versatile talents enabled him to serve his country in many fields, and gained him high distinction as an orator, as a general, and as a statesman. Seen at his best, he may be thought to deserve the high place which he holds among the worthies of Greece and Rome. But there were dark shades in his character, such as might almost make virtue hideous and zeal contemptible. The advocate of a wise and liberal economy degraded his own precepts by the meanest avarice. For the sake of a paltry sum of money he sent to the hammer the old horse which had carried him through a long campaign, the old slave who had served him faithfully from childhood. The stern censor of morals dishonoured his grey hairs by a low intrigue. The Roman Aristides, renowned for his justice, instigated his countrymen, almost with his dying breath, to one of the greatest crimes recorded in history. His measures of reform, which were largely dictated by private prejudice, show the same narrow and persecuting spirit. He kept his eye fixed on the past, and utterly failed to grasp the nature of the change which had raised Rome from the position of capital of Italy to that of the centre of a great empire.

CHAPTER XIV
THE GRACCHI AND MARIUS

WE are now entering on the last century of the Roman Republic, a period unequalled, perhaps, in interest and importance, filled with great events, and thronged by illustrious men, whose features have been preserved for us in the vast historical gallery of Plutarch. In the long struggle which ended in the establishment of a monarchy we may distinguish three principal stages. First we have the attempt made by the Gracchi to remodel the constitution on a popular basis, and in connexion with this the career of Marius and the efforts of the Italians to obtain admission to the Roman citizenship. Then comes the reaction which was led by Sulla, the object of which was to restore the ascendancy of the Senate. In the third and last stage the personal element becomes supreme, and the struggle between Senate and people is merged in the ambition of the great military leaders. It is the first of these stages which will form the subject of the present chapter.

TIBERIUS GRACCHUS

Among those of the younger generation who came into notice at the beginning of this epoch there was none who seemed more clearly marked out for safe and easy distinction than Tiberius Sempronius Gracchus. His father, of the same name, had filled the highest offices of State, and had gained general applause by his justice and moderation in dealing with the native Spaniards. His mother, Cornelia, a high-minded and accomplished woman, was a daughter of the elder Africanus. Educated under the eye of this noble lady, he and his brother

360

THE GRACCHI

Caius grew up in the highest traditions of antique Roman virtue, tempered by all that was best in the learning and discipline of the Greeks. Scipio, the destroyer of Carthage, and the foremost man of his day, was his brother-in-law and adoptive cousin, and he himself had married a daughter of the proud Claudian line. Thus connected by birth and by marriage with the greatest houses in Rome, Tiberius might have mounted to political eminence by a smooth and easy ascent. But the mind of the young enthusiast, fired by Greek ideals, disdained the common avenues to renown, and carried him into a rugged and perilous path, which led him and his brother to an invidious height and a tragic fall.

A Young Enthusiast

The main root of all the evils which brought upon Rome a century of civil strife was the want of a strong central authority to bring order and harmony into that huge, disorganized body, composed of conquerors and conquered, which called itself the Roman State. The old Republican constitution had proved itself utterly incompetent to deal with the task. The Senate, which for many glorious years had guided the destinies of the nation, had now become a corrupt and selfish oligarchy. The executive, split up into a multitude of co-ordinate magistracies, was feeble and insubordinate, while the sovereign rights of the old Populus Romanus were now wielded by a hungry and ignorant mob. Outside of these were the Italians, who had long been chafing against their exclusion from political privileges, and the oppressed and downtrodden provincials. To reconcile all these jarring interests was a problem requiring a mind of the most comprehensive grasp, and a calm, judicial temper, free from all passion and prejudice. The elder Gracchus, though of a high and generous character, was something of a dreamer, whose aim was to restore a state of things which had long since passed away and could not be revived. While passing through Etruria on his way to Spain, where he served as quaestor in the disastrous expedition of Mancinus, he had seen with sorrow the desolation of that once populous and fertile district, and on inquiring he found that the same decay of rural industry was now but too general in the greater part of Italy. On his return from Spain he was elected to the office of tribune (133 B.C.), and forthwith threw himself with all his energy into the question of agrarian reform. To revive an interest in agriculture, to repeople the desert places of Italy with a race of sturdy yeomen like those who had fought under Curius and Cincinnatus, such was the grand design of this young enthusiast. With indignant eloquence he declaimed against the selfish greed of the noble and wealthy few who had robbed the Roman people of their lawful heritage and left them not a foot of land in all the wide realm of Italy. " The wild beasts," he would say, " have their dens and lairs, but you, the conquerors and lords of the earth, have not a clod of soil to call your own." But for the undoubted sincerity of the orator, it would be hard to defend this famous outburst from the charge of cant. The decline of agriculture in Italy was due to a complication of causes, and was now really past remedy ; and those whom he addresses as conquerors and lords of the earth were for the most part a rabble of dissolute idlers, whom he proposed to convert, as if by magic, into sober and industrious farmers. But for the moment his passionate zeal carried all before it and he had his way.

Gracchus's Land Bill

By the law of Licinius, passed before the middle of the fourth century (367 B.C.), no citizen had been allowed to occupy more than five hundred ploughgates [1] of the public land. But no precaution had been taken to ensure the observance of the act, which was a mere mask to disguise the ambition of powerful plebeians, and it had long been suffered to fall into abeyance. For more than two centuries the appropriation of domain-lands by private individuals had been tacitly suffered to proceed, and estates thus unlawfully acquired had passed from father to son, or changed hands by regular purchase. Nevertheless these estates, according to law, were still public

---

[1] The Latin word is *jugerum*—about half an acre.

PLATE XLVI. THE PALATINE FROM THE NORTH

PLATE XLVII. THE AVENTINE

363

lands, for by a principle of Roman jurisprudence no length
of prescription was allowed to override the original right of
ownership, which lay with the State. Availing himself of this
principle, Gracchus now proposed to revive the provisions of
the Licinian law, with due safeguards to prevent their infringe-
ment in the future. Accordingly he brought in a bill to
enforce the limit of five hundred ploughgates, with an addition
of two hundred and fifty ploughgates each for two grown-up
sons. Estates thus assigned were henceforth to be regarded
as private property, and all further occupation was forbidden.
The rest of the public land was to be resumed by the State
and parcelled out in small holdings to the poorer citizens, and
these holdings were to be permanent, inalienable leaseholds, for
which a small rent was to be paid. Compensation was to be
allowed to the evicted occupants for buildings and improvements.

OUTCRY AGAINST THE BILL

It will easily be understood that the measure proposed by
Gracchus was nothing less than an act of wholesale confiscation, involving great hardship, and in some cases downright
ruin, to a large class of the community. In the long lapse of
ages the distinction between public and private lands must
to a large extent have been obliterated, and the attempt to
reconstruct the map of Italy as it had been two centuries back
was an absurdity. Title-deeds had been lost, boundary-marks
removed, and many a landowner whose right went back to
the days of the infant Republic saw himself threatened with
summary eviction. Hardly less was the injustice inflicted on
those occupants of public lands whose claim rested on tacit
prescription and seemed sanctioned by the long apathy of
the government. It is no wonder, therefore, that the bill of
Gracchus caused a loud and vehement outcry, and we are
somewhat surprised to hear that the hot-headed young reformer
was at first supported in his proceedings by such men as
Appius Claudius, a haughty aristocrat, and Mucius Scaevola,
the famous jurist.

REPUBLICAN ROME

The Reformer's Mistake

Hardened by opposition, and spurred on by the clamours of the populace, Gracchus began to assume a more determined and militant attitude. The provisions of the land bill were made more stringent, and the clause allowing compensation for improvement was withdrawn. The breach between the two contending parties was thus widened, and Gracchus, in whose character there was a good deal of the fanatic, was now betrayed into an act which placed him clearly in the wrong. The nobles had secured the co-operation of Octavius, a rival tribune, who placed his veto on the bill. Gracchus, who was a personal friend of Octavius, implored him with tears to withdraw his opposition. But finding him deaf to remonstrance he appealed to the people, and called upon them to depose the refractory tribune. In acting thus Gracchus was committing a direct breach of the constitution. Octavius was a lawfully elected magistrate, whose proceedings could not be called into question until his term of office had expired, and, moreover, the person of a tribune was invested with a peculiar sanctity. But Gracchus for the moment was all-powerful with the masses, and a vote of deposition was carried against Octavius, who was ignominiously dragged from the speakers' platform and compelled to resign his office to a more popular candidate. Feeling that he had exceeded his powers, Gracchus tried by a tissue of cunning sophistries to defend the violent expulsion of his colleague, but all his eloquence failed to palliate the gross breach of privilege of which he had been guilty.

Tiberius goes to Extremes

The way was now cleared for the land bill, which was carried without further opposition, and a commission, consisting of Tiberius and his brother Caius, and Appius Claudius, the father-in-law of Tiberius, was appointed to carry out the provisions of the act. Here again Tiberius laid himself open to invidious construction, by keeping so important a transaction in the hands of a family coterie. His opponents, who had been temporarily paralysed by his impetuosity, rallied their forces, and the struggle was renewed with increased bitterness on both sides. Tiberius, wishing to strengthen his hold on the popular favour, brought in new measures, more and more radical in character. Attalus, the last king of Pergamum, had recently died, bequeathing his kingdom and his treasure to the Roman people. According to long constitutional usage, this heritage should have been disposed of by the Senate. But Tiberius, in a measure brought before the assembly, proposed to distribute the wealth of Attalus among the holders of the new allotments, in order to provide them with the means of stocking their farms. And the prerogatives of the usurping oligarchy were to be further curtailed by extending the right of appeal, and by transferring the judicial functions of the senators to the knights.

DEATH OF TIBERIUS

The conduct of Tiberius during the last months of his tribunate reminds us of a desperate gambler who stakes his all on one cast of the die. His brief term of power was now rapidly drawing toward its close, and very soon he would be reduced to the status of a private citizen, left without defence to the malice of his enemies. The only hope of escape from the perils which surrounded him lay in his re-election to the tribunate for the following year. But the legality of such re-election was more than doubtful, and the nobles were straining every nerve to defeat his candidature. There was, besides, another circumstance which was highly unfavourable to his chances of success : it was now midsummer, and most of his adherents, who were drawn from the country tribes, had gone back to their work in the fields. When the day for the voting arrived the partisans of Tiberius assembled on the Capitol, while the Senate held its session in the Temple of Fides, near at hand. It was commonly believed that the proceedings would be interrupted by some act of violence on the part of the nobles. The consul, it was said, had refused to

interfere, but the extreme party in the Senate was determined
at any cost to stop the election. Presently Tiberius was seen
ascending the slope of the Capitol, and to those who trembled
for his safety it seemed that his brow was already darkened
by the shadow of death. It was not without warning from
heaven that he had set out on that fatal errand. From the
moment when he had crossed the threshold of his house evil
omens had appeared at every step to admonish him of his
danger. Then amid a scene of riot and confusion the voting
began. The younger nobles, mingling with the crowd, jostled
the adherents of Tiberius as they came up to record their
votes, and the presiding magistrate tried in vain to maintain
his authority. Suddenly Tiberius, who had received private
warning from a friendly senator, raised his hand to his head,
to signify that his life was in danger. " He claims the crown ! "
shouted those among his enemies who had observed the
gesture ; and the cry was heard in the Temple of Fides, where
Scipio Nasica, one of the most violent of the nobles, was
trying in vain to invoke the interference of Mucius Scaevola,
the consul. But Scaevola, though he had withdrawn his
support from the party of Gracchus, refused to take action,
except by regular process of law. Thereupon Scipio, exclaiming that Rome was betrayed by her consul, sprang from his
seat and, calling upon all who loved the cause of justice to
follow him, rushed out of the temple. The call was obeyed
by many of the senators, who armed themselves with pieces
of broken benches and tables and made their way with loud
cries and menacing gestures to the scene of the election. All
who attempted resistance were clubbed to death, and Tiberius
himself, while trying to make his escape, stumbled over a
prostrate body, and was instantly struck down by the hand
of one of his own colleagues. It was the first time since the
days of the kings that Roman blood had been shed by open
violence in civil strife, and this outrage was the prelude to
a murderous struggle which swept away untold thousands of
citizens, and only ceased when the fleets of Antony and
Octavian met to decide the issue in the bay of Actium,

366

THE GRACCHI

The ten years (133–123 B.C.) which separate the tribunate
of Tiberius Gracchus from that of his brother form a sort of
twilight interval, such as sometimes separates two important
periods of history, full of half-articulate cries, broken lights,
and shadows of great events to come.   Much is begun, nothing
ended, and the course of events seems to hang in suspense, as
if waiting for some master-hand to give the decisive impulse.
Having destroyed their opponent and proscribed his adherents,
the extreme section of the nobles drew back for a time, as if
dismayed by their own violence, and room being thus left for
the moderate reformers the land act was allowed to proceed.
At first all went smoothly, and a vast number of allotments
were made, with the result that within a few years some
eighty thousand names were added to the list of citizens qualified
to serve in the legions.   But when the commissioners began
to meddle with land belonging to the Italian allies a loud outcry
arose, and the aggrieved Italians found a champion in Scipio,
who had recently returned from Spain and was now the foremost man in Rome.   By his influence the judicial powers of
the commission were transferred to the consul, and the distribution of land was thus brought to a standstill.   Other causes
had contributed to accumulate a mass of odium against
Rome's most illustrious citizen.   He had openly expressed his
approval of the murder of Tiberius Gracchus, and his own
haughty and imperious manners had given great offence to
the pampered multitude which still called itself the Sovereign
People.   " Peace, ye bastard children of Rome ! " he would
exclaim, when assailed with groans and hisses by the popular
assembly ; and when the clamour grew louder he added :
" What, do ye think that I shall be cowed by the voice of men
whom I myself brought in chains to Italy ? "   The description
of Scipio was, indeed, but too true, and that mighty third
estate which was once so august, and still dispensed consulships, praetorships, and triumphs was now largely composed
of liberated slaves, drawn from the dregs of conquered nations.

REPUBLICAN ROME

DEATH OF SCIPIO

But the lofty demeanour of Scipio, better befitting an autocrat than the citizen of a free republic, was not likely to conciliate affection, even among those of his own class, and his open patronage of the Italians brought to a head the hatred which had been slowly gathering volume against him. The circumstances of his death were mysterious, though it is almost certain that he was the victim of foul play. He retired to rest one evening, after having been escorted to his house by a great crowd of friends and admirers, and in the morning he was found dead in his chamber. No marks of violence were to be seen on his person, and we are left to suppose that he was smothered in his sleep.

POPULAR MEASURES

One or two popular measures which were passed or proposed during this interval may be briefly mentioned. An attempt had been made some years before (139 B.C.) to secure the purity of elections by introducing the ballot. Two years later the ballot was extended to criminal trials conducted before the people, and a tribune, Papirius Carbo, now carried a law by which the secret method of voting was employed in matters of legislation. It was a futile attempt to protect the independence of the voters and maintain the purity of popular government. For, ballot or no ballot, every species of bribery, direct and indirect, continued to be practised, and twenty years afterwards the half-savage Jugurtha could declare that every Roman had his price. Another measure which was proposed at the same time, but not carried until some years later, gave legal sanction to the re-election of a tribune. But in passing this bill the people, all unknown to themselves, were taking a long step toward monarchical rule. For a perpetual tribunate meant a perpetual despotism, and the tribunician power was to become one of the mightiest weapons in the hands of those who founded the Empire.

THE GRACCHI

Position of the Italians

Yet another reform which pressed with growing insistence on more thoughtful minds was the extension of the full franchise to the Italian allies. The Italians were closely related to the ancient Roman stock, and had a far better right to call themselves the true children of Rome than the mongrel crew who filled the Forum with tumult and disorder. All those of the great Sabellian race, inhabiting central Italy, could point to a record of unshaken loyalty which had stood fast even in the most terrible days of the Hannibalic war, while in the long period of foreign conquest which followed the fall of Carthage the main burden of military service had rested on the Italians. Yet with all these claims on the gratitude of their countrymen the allies were in a position little better than that of Helots, exposed to every kind of injury and outrage. An Italian peasant, for some paltry affront offered to a young Roman noble, was seized and beaten to death on the high-road. The chief magistrates of a Campanian town, who had offended the morbid delicacy of a consul's wife, paid the penalty by a public scourging in the market-place. The wrongs of the Italians and the means of their redress had engaged the earnest attention of the younger Africanus, and four years after his death (125 B.C.) Marcus Fulvius Flaccus, a partisan of the Gracchi, boldly proposed to raise them to the status of full Roman citizens. But Senate and people united against him, and he was obliged to withdraw the measure. The hopes of the Italians had been raised to a high pitch, and in the first bitterness of their disappointment the people of Asculum and Fregellae broke into open revolt. But the movement, being unsupported by other Italians, was easily put down, and the much-coveted privilege was dearly purchased a generation later at the cost of war.

The Younger Gracchus

Out of this darkness and confusion emerges at last the brilliant figure of Caius Sempronius Gracchus. Younger than

his brother by nine years, Caius far surpassed him in energy.
eloquence, and statesmanlike breadth of view. Tiberius had
confined himself to a single abuse, the monopoly of land, but
the reforms of Caius were of a wide and comprehensive
character, embracing every section of the Roman State and
every branch of the administration. Side by side with the
loftier aims of a great patriot there burned in his heart an
unquenchable desire for revenge, the spirit of *vendetta*, which
belonged, and still belongs, to every true child of the South.
For some years he had been content to play a subordinate
part, feeling that he was too young to act with effect. But
after his return from Sardinia, where he had served as quaestor
under the proconsul Orestes, he saw that his opportunity had
arrived, and he became a candidate for the office of tribune.
Being elected in the face of a strong opposition (123 B.C.), he
plunged heart and soul into the work of reform, postponing the
satisfaction of his private revenge until he had established his
power on a broad and solid basis. His commanding presence,
fiery eloquence, and far-reaching projects soon made him the
most conspicuous figure in Rome. His hand was everywhere, his voice was never silent. He was the first of those
great imperial administrators, such as Caesar, Napoleon, and
Frederick the Great, whose untiring energy and sleepless
vigilance enabled them to keep hold of all the complicated
threads of government.

GRACCHAN REFORM

It was the aim of the younger Gracchus to remodel the whole
constitution, by putting down the usurpation of the Senate
and giving reality to the sovereign rights of the people. But
where was he to find the materials from which he might build
up this new democracy? Not, assuredly, in the motley
multitude of the Forum, that many-headed monster, without
ideals, without political principles, which hung like a mill-
stone round the neck of the government down to the latest
times of the Empire. Yet the clamour of these hungry mouths
could not be ignored, and one of his earliest acts was to provide

for this need by a new corn law, appointing regular distributions of grain to the people at a nominal price. This measure was justified by the theory that every Roman citizen was a landowner, and therefore entitled to his share in the produce of conquered territory. But it was a pernicious law, establishing a constant drain on the treasury and perpetuating the cancer which had fastened on the body of the Roman State. To get rid of this mock Populus, or at any rate to lop its rotten members and replace them by new and healthy elements from outside, would have been an achievement worthy of the highest political genius. Gracchus perceived, with true insight, that the materials for such a reform were at hand in the towns and rural districts of Italy, which were still untouched by the corruptions of the capital. One of his latest proposals was designed to make use of this material by conferring the full Roman citizenship on the Latins, and giving Latin rights to the Italians, as a preliminary step to their complete enfranchisement. But he was defeated by the bigoted jealousy of the commons, who united with the nobles to frustrate the measure ; and in any case the reform would have been void of political effect unless accompanied by some scheme of representation.

The problem, therefore, of finding a counterpoise to the Senate had to be solved in some other way, and Gracchus sought to accomplish his object by breaking down the old alliance between the Senate and the Equites, and giving new powers to the latter, which made them an independent and a formidable factor in the government. The order of Equites, or Knights, had long lost all military significance, and now constituted a sort of financial aristocracy, existing side by side with the landed aristocracy of the Senate. To sever the interests of these two powerful bodies, Gracchus enacted that henceforth no senator should take his seat among the eighteen centuries of the Knights. And he placed a terrible weapon in the hands of the Equestrian Order by withdrawing from the senators their judicial powers and filling up the jury-lists from the ranks of the Equites. The chief importance of this

change lies in its connexion with the administration of the
provinces, and with the treatment of those conquered nations
whose lives and property now lay at the mercy of Rome.
This part of the Gracchan legislation was again, like his corn
law, most pernicious in tendency, and its evil effect was greatly
heightened by another innovation in the method of raising the
taxes in the province of Asia. Henceforth this great department of the public revenue was let out on contract to the
capitalists of the Equestrian Order, who paid a fixed sum to
the treasury for the right of collecting the tax. The same
plan was afterwards extended to the other Roman provinces.
The mischief involved in such a system is sufficiently obvious.
The conduct of the high-born nobles, who ruled with almost
regal power over the subject communities, was often violent
and unscrupulous, but at least they were the inheritors of
great traditions which were not always forgotten. But the
wealthy knight who farmed the revenues was under no such
restraint. His life had been spent in the mean calculations of
loss and gain, and his energies were devoted to extracting the
uttermost farthing of profit from his bargain with the State.
Nor was this the whole extent of the evil. A conscientious
provincial governor who took a high view of his duties found
himself surrounded by a thousand jealous eyes, and if he
refused to connive at the extortions of the revenue-farmers
he knew that when he returned to Rome he would be dragged
before the bar of the Equites, whose new judicial powers gave
them an easy means of working his ruin. The result, in most
cases, was a vile collusion between the governor and the tax-
gatherers. Thus Gracchus, in his desire to lower the power of
the Senate, had fashioned a double scourge for the unhappy
subjects of Rome.

Among the measures aimed at the Senate was a regulation
for assigning the consular provinces before election, by which
Gracchus thought to set up a barrier against jobbery and
favouritism. Then, having clipped the wings of the oligarchs,
and created a powerful rival to their usurped ascendancy in
the reformed Equestrian Order, Gracchus applied himself to the

other part of his work, the enlargement and elevation of the masses. Like Pericles, he sought to rule as a prince of democracy, and when he spoke from the Rostra his face was turned to the multitude which thronged the Forum, not, as was the usual custom, toward the Senate House. To him the people were to look for protection against official tyranny, for power, for privilege, for the very means of living. He provided occupation for the poorer citizens by employing them on large public works, the construction of granaries, the building of bridges, and the laying down of new roads. To lighten the military burdens of the commons he shortened the term of service, provided free clothing for the soldiers, and limited the authority of commanders in the field.

In all this Gracchus had his eye on Greek models, and especially on the golden days of the Athenian democracy. But there was one fatal defect in the analogy, and by this defect the whole of his fine scheme was frustrated. The Athenian democracy, with all its faults, had been a reality, and every Athenian had a real voice in the control of public affairs. But in Rome there was not, and never had been, even potentially, any system of popular government. Even in its best days the Roman Parliament had been a passive assembly, dependent on the presiding magistrate, without initiative, without power of debate. Consequently the legislation of Gracchus fell with its author. He crippled the machinery of government, but he created no new system to take its place. Nevertheless he supplied fruitful lessons to the statesmen who came after him, and pointed the way to what was perhaps the only remedy for the ills of a diseased and decrepit republic, the concentration of all the powers of government in a single hand.

GRACCHUS DEPOSED

Gracchus was assisted in his schemes of reform by Marcus Fulvius Flaccus, who had been on the side of his brother, and by Rubrius, one of his colleagues in the tribunate, to whom he owed the suggestion of founding a colony of Roman citizens beyond the seas. Citizen colonies in Italy formed a part of the Gracchan legislation, and two such settlements were actually established, one at Tarentum, and the other at Scylacium, on the east coast of Bruttium. But to repeople the deserted sites of Corinth and Carthage was a noble and liberal design, which, if carried out, might have led to grand results and gone far to regenerate the decaying energies of the Roman State. Gracchus himself, who had been re-elected tribune (122 B.C.), was appointed by lot to lead the new colony to Carthage, and during his absence the conduct of the reform movement was left to Fulvius. This was unfortunate, for Fulvius was noisy and injudicious, and the opponents of Gracchus seized the opportunity to undermine his influence by setting up a rival candidate to the popular favour. Their agent was Livius Drusus, one of the colleagues of Gracchus in the second year of his tribunate, and, acting on his instructions, he pursued the familiar tactics of political chicanery. The plan was to outbid the offers of Gracchus by proposing measures still more tempting to the people. Twelve new colonies were to be founded in Italy, the rent on the allotments already granted was to be remitted, and the right of sale, which had been expressly denied by Gracchus, was to be conceded. No one explained where the land for the new colonies was to be found, and the insincerity of the whole bill was only too obvious. But the fickle multitude caught eagerly at the proffered bait, and on his return from Carthage Gracchus found that his day of power was past. He failed to obtain the tribuneship for the third time, and the attitude of the senatorial party grew every day more threatening. At last all the forms of constitutional procedure were laid aside, the consuls were invested with dictatorial power,[1] and the two parties stood arrayed against each other in armed hostility. The Gracchans pitched their camp on the Aventine, which by immemorial tradition was the stronghold of the popular party. Some attempts were made

---

[1] This was a substitute for the dictatorship, which had now fallen out of use.

to effect a reconciliation, but without success.   Then Opimius,
one of the consuls, and a bitter enemy of Gracchus, led a body
of armed men to storm the Aventine, and the followers of
Gracchus, after a feeble resistance, were slain or dispersed
(121 B.C.).   Fulvius, who had fled with the rest, was hunted
out of his hiding-place and dispatched.   Gracchus himself,
lately the arbiter of Rome's destiny, now an outlaw and
a fugitive, fled across the Tiber, accompanied by a single
slave.   But seeing that his pursuers were gaining on him
he turned aside into the grove of the Furies and ordered
the slave to give him his death-blow.   His adherents were
afterwards prosecuted, and three thousand are said to have
perished by the hand of the executioner.

HASTY REFORMERS

A certain air of romance lingers round the figures of the
Gracchi, and it is impossible to withhold our sympathy from
the young idealists, who fought almost single-handed against
the crying evils of their time.   But their proceedings were
marked by a sort of haste and fury, which offers a striking
contrast to the patience and quiet pertinacity of the early
legislators.   The elder brother ran his impetuous course in a
single year, and two years sufficed for the sweeping measures
of the younger, by which he hoped to pull down and build
up again the whole constitution.   Caius was undoubtedly by
far the abler man, and he left a mark on the history of his
country which was never effaced.

A LEGACY OF ILL

By the fall of Gracchus the Optimates,[1] as they had now
come to be called, gained a few years of precarious ascendancy,
and the popular party, left without a head and cowed by the
ferocity of their opponents, fell into the background.   But
Gracchus had sown a seed in the hearts of his countrymen

[1] The party of the nobles, who called themselves the 'Best Men' in the
State.   The use of Good and Bad in a political sense is as old as Theognis
(c. 540–500 B.C.).

which was destined to bear bitter fruit before many years
were past. What was really salutary and judicious in his
legislation was thrown aside, while that which was of evil
tendency remained. His admirable scheme of foreign colonization came to nothing, and the grievances of the Italian allies
were left unredressed. But the mob of Rome was still fed
by cheap foreign corn, and the province of Asia still groaned
under the burden of taxation and the extortions of the revenue-
farmers. By allowing the right of sale the party opposed to
reform had frustrated the intention of his agrarian laws,
and the process of absorption began afresh, the small allotments disappearing into the broad estates of the nobles. All
that survived from the patriotic labours of the Gracchi was a
legacy of hatred, and a method of working the State machine
for party ends.

JUGURTHA

For a period of fifteen years (116–101 B.C.) our attention is
chiefly occupied by the history of two wars, which threw a
glaring light on the incompetence and corruption of the
ruling caste and raised a man of the people to the highest
pitch of glory and power. In itself the war with Jugurtha
was but an obscure episode, of no greater importance than the
endless border fighting which forms so familiar a feature in
the annals of India under British rule. But it attained a
momentous significance from the repeated disasters inflicted
on the Roman arms, and from the corrupt trafficking of
high-born leaders with the enemy. The state of Africa at the
time which we have reached may be described in a few words.
On the death of Micipsa (118 B.C.), the son of Masinissa, the
kingdom of Numidia had passed to his two sons, Adherbal
and Hiempsal, and his nephew Jugurtha, a base-born youth,
whom he had raised to equal dignity with his lawful offspring.
By the provisions of Micipsa's will the two brothers and their
cousin were to share between them the government of Numidia.
In any circumstances such an attempt to balance a single
crown between three heads must have led to collision and

disaster; and Jugurtha, who inherited all the ability and ambition of his renowned grandfather, was not likely to rest until he had thrust out his young kinsmen from the throne. His brilliant gifts and varied experience peculiarly fitted him for the perilous part which he aspired to play. Under the feeble rule of his uncle Micipsa he had gained great credit by his skilful conduct of State affairs, and his matchless skill and courage made him the foremost figure in a nation of riders and hunters. It was not enough, however, to win the affections of his own wild countrymen. The kings of Numidia held their power by the sufferance of the Romans, and unless he could procure the connivance of the Senate his ambitious plans would be nipped in the bud. But there was a ready and easy way—so, at least, he believed—out of this difficulty; for while serving at Numantia under Scipio he had formed intimacies among the dissolute Roman nobles, and from them he had learnt the valuable secret that in Rome all things were to be bought for gold.

Conflict with Jugurtha

It soon became evident that Jugurtha would be satisfied with nothing less than the sovereignty of all Numidia. Hiempsal was got rid of by assassination, and Adherbal fled to Rome, where he invoked the interference of the Senate. A commission was sent out to settle the claims of the two rival princes (116 B.C.), and by means of bribes Jugurtha obtained the better part of the kingdom for himself. No sooner had the Roman commissioners departed, however, than the quarrel broke out afresh, and Adherbal was obliged to shut himself up in Cirta,[1] his capital, where he was held by Jugurtha in close siege. A second embassy, headed by Aemilius Scaurus, one of the proudest of the nobles, was sent out to Africa, and after a few empty menaces the representatives of the Senate returned to Rome, bringing with them nothing but heavy purses and damaged reputations. Cirta was now reduced by famine (112 B.C.), and the wretched

[1] Constantine.

REPUBLICAN ROME

Adherbal was put to death under torture. To aggravate the outrage, a large number of Italian traders who were residing in the town shared his fate. A violent outcry, headed by the tribune Memmius, now arose against the feeble and corrupt government, and the Senate was compelled to consent to an immediate declaration of war against Jugurtha. The campaign was conducted by Lucius Calpurnius Bestia, one of the consuls, and among those who attended him was Scaurus, who longed, perhaps, for another taste of Numidian gold. If so, he was not disappointed. The old farce was repeated, and the consul, after some show of hostilities, concluded a disgraceful peace, for which he and his staff received, of course, a handsome consideration. When the news of the bargain was brought to Rome it led to a fresh outburst of popular indignation. The treaty with Jugurtha was instantly repudiated, and on the motion of Memmius it was resolved that the perfidious prince should be summoned to Rome to answer for his crimes before the people. Attired as a suppliant, and composing his features to an expression of feigned humility, the crafty Numidian stood up before the assembled commons and listened to the harangue of Memmius, in which the long list of his crimes was recited. But when he was called upon to reply to his accuser, a tribune, whom he had taken into his pay, interposed his veto, forbidding him to speak, and by this contrivance the inquiry was quashed.

Jugurtha's Audacity

Not many days after the Romans had new reason to admire the audacity of their dangerous guest. There was residing at Rome a certain grandson of Masinissa's named Massiva, who had been encouraged to set up a rival claim to the Numidian throne. This was more than enough to bring down upon him the deadly resentment of Jugurtha. He gave the order to Bomilcar, one of his suite, and the unfortunate prince was waylaid by assassins and dispatched. So little precaution had been taken to preserve secrecy that there was no doubt on whom the guilt rested. Even then the Senate took no

378

MARIUS

action against Jugurtha, beyond issuing a peremptory order
that he and his train should at once leave Italy. As he passed
the gates he lingered awhile, and, fixing his eyes on the towers
and temples of the capital, uttered his famous farewell : " O
venal city, and destined soon to perish, if only it can find a
purchaser ! "[1]

Marius

Another year of mock hostilities ensued, with a new harvest
of infamy to the Roman name. By direct collusion with the
enemy, obtained at the usual price, a Roman army was defeated,
disarmed, and passed under the yoke, and another treaty
was concluded, giving formal sanction to all the claims of
the usurper. But the scandal had now become too flagrant
to be tolerated any longer. On the motion of a tribune a
judicial commissioner was appointed to take proceedings
against all those who had betrayed the interests of the Republic
for foreign gold. Five Romans of the highest rank, among whom
was a pontiff, were arraigned and found guilty, but Scaurus,
one of the worst offenders, adroitly evaded the danger by
getting himself nominated as a member of the commission.
Then the Romans looked round for a leader of tried ability
who was known to be proof against the bribes of Jugurtha.
They found him in Quintus Caecilius Metellus, of an illustrious
plebeian family, which had played no small part in building
up the Roman empire. Among those who attended Metellus
was a low-born officer, little known as yet, but destined in a
few years to rise to the highest pinnacle of fame and power.
This was Caius Marius, whom we have seen more than twenty
years back serving his apprenticeship as a soldier in the
trenches before Numantia. Sprung from a hardy peasant
stock, Marius had been bred in the primitive school of rugged
Roman manhood. Rude in aspect and uncouth in manners,
with virtues exclusively military, he seemed set apart as the
natural antagonist of the polished and degenerate nobles. A
strange portent, it was said, had appeared to him in his youth,

[1] Sallust, *Jugurtha*, c. 35.

foretelling his future greatness. While he was sleeping under
a tree an eagle's nest, with seven eaglets,[1] fell into his lap.
Yet the fulfilment of the divine promise was long delayed.
He had, indeed, risen to the office of praetor, and his marriage
with Julia [2] had brought him into connexion with the proudest
patrician house in Rome. But at the age of forty-seven he
remained a New Man, shut out from the charmed circle of that
high nobility which held in fee the most coveted honours of
the State. Metellus little guessed the boundless ambition
which was burning in the heart of that moody and discontented man, who was so sharp and cynical of speech, and yet
so punctual in the performance of all his military duties.

Marius gains Command

For two years (109–107 B.C.) Metellus prosecuted the war
with vigour, defeated Jugurtha in the field, hunted him from
one refuge to another, and gained possession of Cirta, the
Numidian capital. It was to no purpose that Jugurtha, who
perceived that his old tactics were unavailing, offered to make
submission. The Romans were resolved to put an end to
the nuisance by the complete destruction of this faithless
enemy. But the task was by no means easy. Driven from
his kingdom, Jugurtha found new allies among the wild
Gaetulians,[3] and Bocchus, his father-in-law, king of Mauretania, was now induced openly to espouse his cause. An
attempt to get rid of him by assassination was detected, and
Bomilcar, who had undertaken to perform the vile service
for the Romans, paid the penalty of his treachery with his
life. The allied kings now advanced with a large force upon
Cirta, and a decisive action seemed to be impending, when
Metellus received the unwelcome news that he had been superseded in his command. The long delay of the operations in
Africa had given new matter for invective against the ruling
oligarchy, and the people, now fully roused from their long
apathy, were looking for a leader. Availing himself of this

[1] Symbolizing his seven consulships.　　[2] Aunt of C. Julius Caesar.
[3] Inhabiting southern Morocco and the western Sahara.

380

change in the political current, Marius, who had with difficulty obtained leave of absence from his commander, appeared in Rome on the very eve of the consular elections, and, putting himself forward as the representative of the commons, was carried triumphantly to the head of the poll and appointed to take over the command in Africa.

SULLA

Metellus returned in high dudgeon to Rome (107 B.C.), where he was consoled by a triumph and by the title of Numidicus. Meanwhile Marius had set sail with large reinforcements, promising to bring the war to a speedy end. And the people were not disappointed in their hero, though the real glory of the achievement lay, not with Marius, but with Lucius Cornelius Sulla, who served under him as quaestor and held a command of cavalry. Not only did Sulla distinguish himself highly in the field, but to him belonged the merit of capturing Jugurtha, which was the main object of the expedition. The methods, indeed, which were employed for attaining this end would have revolted the conscience of the Romans of a better and simpler age, but Sulla's performance may well have seemed to his contemporaries a masterpiece of diplomacy. Defeated in two engagements, Bocchus had grown weary of the struggle, and was ready to purchase peace with Rome by betraying his guest and relative. The negotiations naturally required nice and skilful management, and Sulla offered himself as an agent for concluding the nefarious bargain. Taking his life in his hand, he went almost unattended to the camp of Bocchus, and his mingled coolness and resolution so impressed the Mauretanian king, who was still wavering in his purpose, that he resolved to throw in his lot with the Romans. Jugurtha was invited to a conference, and on his appearance he was seized and handed over to the quaestor. The last days of the fierce Numidian were a fit ending to his career. After gracing the triumph of Marius, he was flung into the Mamertine dungeon, a horrible pit hewn in the side of the Capitoline Hill, where many a nobler enemy of the Romans found a living grave. There, after six days of agony, the savage prince breathed out his life.

The Northern Peril

The war with Jugurtha was a mere incident in Roman history, important only from the light which it throws on contemporary politics in Rome, and from the fact that it raised a man of the people to the highest office in the State. Very different in character was the tremendous struggle with the Cimbri and Teutones, which called up again the old spectre of the Gallic terror and taxed the vast resources of Rome to their uttermost. In order to understand the circumstances which led to this contest we must take a brief view of the political map of Europe as it appeared toward the close of the second century before Christ. The conquests of the Romans had carried them to the foot of the huge mountain barrier which stretches like a natural fortress from Nice to Vienna, and is continued in the wild and irregular ranges of the Balkan peninsula. We are impressed with a profound sense of Rome's power and greatness when we reflect that this immense region, beset with the terrors and hardships of Alpine travel and inhabited by warlike tribes, was conquered by the Romans with thrust of lance and stroke of sword. This great achievement, however, was reserved for a later age, and down to the time of the Empire the Alpine districts remained unsubdued. But beyond the western passes of the Alps, in the fertile Rhone valley, lay a favoured land, famed in after-times as the home of mirth and song, and now the playground of Europe, the happy realm of Provence. Here was situated the rich and prosperous city of Massilia, founded at the beginning of the sixth century by Greek refugees from Phocaea, and long united in firm alliance with Rome. It was the necessity of protecting their allies from the raids of the Ligurians that led the Romans to extend their territory in this district, and another important motive was the maintenance of easy communication between Italy and Spain. They pushed their conquests to the frontier of the modern Auvergne, and formed friendly relations with

382

PLATE XLVIII. THE TULLIANUM

PLATE XLIX.   JUTURNA ALTAR

the Aedui, who dwelt between the Upper Loire and the Saone. The new possession was secured by the foundation of fortresses at Aquae Sextiae[1] and Narbo,[2] the latter of which became the capital of this important province. It was in the neighbourhood of Aquae Sextiae that the battle was fought which saved Italy from the peril of invasion from the north for generations to come.

THE CIMBRI

Beyond the mountain rampart lay the plains of central and northern Europe, a region of forest, river, and swamp, the rude cradle of young nations whose day of glory was yet to be. Here roamed the wild hordes of the Celts and Teutones, driven hither and thither with their wives, their cattle, and their little ones as the pressure of material want or the impact of new invaders directed their course. They came like the wind, and like the wind they went, and their path was marked by desolation and ruin. Foremost among these marauders were the Cimbri, whose original seat seems to have been in Jutland, called after them the Cimbric Chersonese. Whether they belonged to the Celtic or Germanic stock is a point still disputed among historians. Seven years before the capture of Jugurtha they suddenly appeared on the confines of the eastern Alps, in the country now called Styria, where they were confronted by the consul Papirius Carbo, and peremptorily ordered to retire (113 B.C.). The Cimbri, who knew something of the fame and might of Rome, seemed inclined to obey, but being treacherously attacked by Carbo before the parley was ended, they turned fiercely upon him, and defeated his forces with great slaughter. Italy was only saved from invasion by the fickleness of these wild people, who neglected their opportunity and marched away westward in search of new adventure. Uniting with the Teutones, Tigurini, and Ambrones, they crossed the Rhine and passed on into Gaul. Here they again came into collision with the Romans, and one commander after another suffered defeat at their hands. Matters came to a

[1] Aix. [2] Narbonne.

climax in the year after the conclusion of the Jugurthine war
(105 B.C.), when two Roman armies were utterly defeated at
Arausio, on the Rhone, with a loss of eighty thousand men.
Great was now the terror at Rome, for all Italy seemed to lie
at the mercy of the barbarians. But the peril was once more
averted by the characteristic weakness of this savage host,
whose designs, planned without forethought and abandoned
without reason, resembled the fitful working of some elemental
force. The Cimbri forsook their allies and turned toward
Spain, while the rest of the multitude dispersed, we cannot say
whither.

A Momentous Change

The Romans thus gained time to breathe and rally their
strength before these dreaded enemies should reunite their
forces and make a fresh assault on the barriers of the empire.
It was generally felt that there was one man only who could
save the State, and that man was Caius Marius. Before he
left Africa he was elected a second time to the consulship, and
on his return to Rome he applied himself to the task of forming
a new army. In the enlistment of troops for the war against
Jugurtha he had already introduced a change, which led to
the most momentous consequences in the later history of the
Republic. Hitherto the legions had been recruited from the
five classes of the Servian constitution, while the great Un-
classed, or Proletariat, were exempt from military service,
except in extraordinary emergencies; for it was thought
dangerous to place arms in the hands of those who, having no
share in the national wealth, might be supposed to harbour
a standing grudge against their more fortunate fellow-citizens.
But in the long foreign wars the numbers of those qualified for
service in the legions had steadily diminished, and there was a
growing disinclination among the propertied classes to face
the perils and hardships of war. Marius now threw open the
military career to the penniless multitude, thus creating a
new precedent for his successors, and a new peril to the State.
The gulf which separated citizen from soldier henceforth grew

wider and wider, and, conversely, the tie between general and soldier was drawn ever closer. Needy and desperate men looked to their commander as a patron, from whose hand they might obtain the means of licence and a provision for their old age. When he made this innovation Marius was unconsciously following the lead of Caius Gracchus and taking a long step in the direction of a military despotism.

GALLIC PLAN OF INVASION

The army of Marius consisted largely of raw recruits, and after taking up a position at the mouth of the Rhone (104 B.C.) he employed the respite afforded him by the dispersion of the barbarians in training their minds and bodies for the coming struggle. In ancient warfare the issue depended to a large extent on the personal skill and prowess of the soldiers, and Marius accordingly drilled his men assiduously in every martial exercise. When not otherwise employed, he made them toil with the spade, knowing the high moral value of long and patient labour; and one of his works, a great canal drawn through the Rhone delta, remained in use for ages after, under the name of the Marian Dyke. Two years passed away in these labours, and Marius, contrary to all constitutional usage, was elected consul a third and fourth time. Meanwhile the clouds of war had been gathering again, and were soon to burst in tempest on the outposts of the Roman empire. The Cimbri, repulsed from their attempt on Spain, came surging back into Gaul, and, uniting with their allies, held their muster on the banks of the Rhone. It was then agreed that an invasion of Italy should be made simultaneously from two different points. The Cimbri and the Tigurini, a Helvetian tribe, were to make a wide circuit along the northern spurs of the Alps and descend into Italy by the Brenner Pass and the valley of the Adige. The Teutones and Ambrones were directed to take the shorter route, by the coast-line of Liguria, and the two hosts, joining hands, would then pour into the heart of Italy.

REPUBLICAN ROME

BATTLE OF AQUAE SEXTIAE

Marius, who had gone to Rome for the elections, hastened back to his army and prepared to meet the first shock of invasion, while his colleague in the consulship, Quintus Lutatius Catulus, was entrusted with the defence of north-eastern Italy. From his fortified camp on the Rhone Marius watched the Teutones and Ambrones as they defiled past. For six days, we are assured, the strange procession continued, and the Roman general had some difficulty in restraining the impetuosity of his men, who were provoked by the bitter taunts and derisive gestures of the barbarians and demanded loudly to be led out against them. At last, when the rear of the long train had disappeared in a cloud of dust, Marius gave the order to strike camp, and followed cautiously on their footsteps. He came up with them in the neighbourhood of Aquae Sextiae, and chose for the site of his camp a bare and waterless hill. When some of his officers protested against his apparent want of common prudence he pointed to a stream skirting the huge laager of the barbarians, whose wild cries could be distinctly heard, and remarked grimly : " You must get your water there." On going to the stream with their vessels the Roman camp-followers were assailed by the Ambrones, who were, however, driven back with great loss. After a pause of two days the whole savage host advanced with desperate valour to assault the Roman lines. But the trained legions of Marius met their onset with determined resolution and compelled them to fall back to the level ground, and their discomfiture was completed by a sudden charge in the rear, led by Marcellus, one of the consul's lieutenants. The number of those killed or taken prisoners was computed at a hundred thousand, and the soil of the battlefield is said to have been so fertilized by the torrent of blood that it became famous for its abundant harvests. Marius was preparing to celebrate his victory by a solemn offering of the captured arms to the gods when a horseman rode up bringing him the news that he had been elected consul for the fifth time.

MARIUS

BATTLE OF VERCELLAE

As yet, however, the great soldier's work was but half done, for meanwhile the Cimbri had made their way through the eastern pass and taken up their quarters in northern Italy to await the arrival of their allies, whom they supposed to be still on the road. Catulus, thinking himself not strong enough to meet them in the field without further supports, fell back before them, and remained an idle spectator while the great northern province was harried and plundered. The arrival of Marius (101 B.C.), who had paid a brief visit to Rome after his victory, at once changed the aspect of affairs. He summoned his troops from Gaul and effected a junction with Catulus, who had retired behind the line of the Po. The combined Roman armies then crossed the river and advanced to meet the enemy, who were encamped near Vercellae. The Cimbri, glutted with booty and rendered insolent by high living, were full of riotous confidence, and they sent a message to the consul demanding lands for themselves and their brethren. " Your brethren have all the land they want," replied Marius, and ordered the captive chieftains of the Teutones to be exhibited in chains before the Roman lines. But the news of their comrades' defeat only served to inflame the native ferocity of the Cimbri, and they forthwith prepared for battle. Formed in a solid square, they bore down upon the Romans, whom they outnumbered by three to one, thinking to crush them by the sheer weight of their impact. But they were blinded by the July sun, which shone full in their faces, and choked by the dense clouds of dust raised by the trampling feet of so many thousands, and when once their front rank was broken the fight became a mere carnage. The Romans gained a complete and easy victory, and the greatest danger that had threatened Italy since the day of Cannae was thus averted.

MARIUS IN POLITICS

The honours of the day were claimed by both generals, but the united voice of the people hailed Marius for the second

time as the saviour of his country, and even the nobles were
shamed into a reluctant acquiescence. For the moment Marius
was by far the greatest figure in Rome. Had he been a man
of marked political ability he might now have led the opposition against the nobles and gained a decisive triumph for the
popular party. The scandalous conduct of the Jugurthine
war and the long series of defeats in the contest with the
northern barbarians had brought the credit of the usurping
oligarchs to the lowest ebb, and filled the courts of justice with
high-born criminals, many of whom were broken in fortune
and reputation by the trial. All eyes were turned upon
Marius, who seemed pointed out by destiny as the natural
successor of the Gracchi, charged with the task of rebuilding
the constitution and restoring the sovereign rights of the
people. But those who cherished these hopes were soon to
find that their champion was, politically speaking, a mere
man of straw, as feeble and helpless in the Forum as he had
been strong and resourceful in the field. Marius the soldier
and Marius the statesman were two very different men. The
veteran warrior who had faced death a hundred times in
battle against Rome's enemies was reduced to speechless
terror by the stir and bustle of the assembly ; the great captain
who could govern ten thousand fierce swordsmen by his nod
became an image of imbecility in the face of a political crisis.
With no higher principle than a dull rancour against his social
superiors, with no better motive than childish vanity, he tried
to balance between two parties, and won the contempt of
both.

THE APPULEIAN LAWS

These weaknesses, however, could only be revealed by time,
and Marius, by a strange freak of fortune, was thrust into the
position of a great party leader. With the flush of his triumph
still upon him, he entered on his sixth consulship (100 B.C.),
and, joining hands with the chief opponents of the Senate,
concerted with them a plan of campaign. The issue of the
contest might have been foretold from the character of his

associates, and the scenes of violence which inaugurated their brief term of power. His principal advisers were Saturninus, who had a personal grudge against the Senate, and Glaucia, a low-born demagogue, whose only gifts were a talent for low buffoonery and a matchless impudence. Saturninus held the office of tribune, which he had obtained by the assassination of the rival candidate, and Glaucia had been raised by the popular favour to the praetorship. It was a difficult and complicated problem which the strange triumvirate had to solve. The mob was to be flattered and fed, provision was to be made for the discharged soldiers of Marius, the Italians were to be conciliated, the Senate was to be weakened, and the alliance between the Equites and the popular party was to be confirmed. To meet these manifold necessities, Saturninus proposed a series of measures, named after him the Appuleian Laws.[1] The first clause in the bill provided for the distribution of conquered lands, especially those of southern Gaul, among the poorer citizens, and the Italian allies, who thereby became tacitly admitted to the Roman franchise. The second revived the scheme of foreign colonization which had been projected by Caius Gracchus, with especial mention of Achaea, Sicily, and Macedonia as the field for the new settlements. The third satisfied the claims of the hungry multitude by a still further reduction in the price of grain. A special feature in the bill was an order directing the senators to give it their assent within five days after it had been passed. This injunction struck at the very root of the Senate's authority, reducing it to its original position as a mere advisory and deliberative body.

Marius Changes Front

When the day for the voting came on the Optimates mustered their forces and tried to stop the proceedings by force. But they were overpowered and driven off by the veterans of Marius, and the bill became law. It remained to procure the sanction of the Senate, and the Fathers, cowed by the ferocity

[1] From Appuleius, his gentile name.

REPUBLICAN ROME

of their opponents and bewildered by the double-dealing of
Marius, took the oath required of them. There was, however,
one honourable exception. Metellus declined to stultify himself, and went into voluntary exile. But the triumph of the
demagogues was of brief duration. It was one thing to carry
the bill, but to give it practical effect was quite another.
Saturninus, indeed, took the first step toward this end, by
securing his re-election to the tribunate, and Glaucia, who was
a candidate for the consulship, procured the removal of a rival
candidate by assassination. But the violence of these unprincipled men had now overreached itself, and all who had
anything to lose united with the Senate to put them down.
To complete their ruin, Marius, who for some time had been
playing a double game, now openly changed sides and stooped
to become the tool of the faction which he hated. Abandoned
by their leader, the demagogues took refuge in the Capitol,
where they were held in close siege, until they surrendered
under a promise that their lives should be spared. Marius,
who had not yet lost all sense of honour, caused them to be
confined in the Curia Hostilia,[1] hoping thus to preserve them
from the fury of their enemies. But his day of authority was
past, and he had the mortification of seeing his recent adherents
stoned to death before his eyes.

Shadows of the Imperium

Glaucia and Saturninus were a pair of political pretenders
who, while assuming the *rôle* of reformers, acted on merely
personal motives and pursued their aims without a vestige of
true public spirit. Viewed outwardly, their brief career looks
like a fantastic caricature of the Gracchan tragedy. Nevertheless this episode forms a landmark in the party strife of Rome,
showing the steady growth of the personal factor in Roman
politics and the hollowness of the names which were invoked
by the leaders of the opposing factions. Gracchus had failed
because he was not backed by the element of material force,
on which the ultimate issue depended. But the coalition

[1] The old Senate House.

formed between Marius, Saturninus, and Glaucia, though it
ended in utter and ignominious failure, was full of ominous
presage for the future. The three men so strangely associated
flit across the stage of history like shadows, but shadows
which forerun a tremendous reality. There was yet to arise
a leader of true imperial mind who, uniting in himself the
political genius of Gracchus and the soldierly qualities of
Marius, and far surpassing each in his own sphere, should
teach both Senate and people to bow beneath the hand of a
master.

Two Urgent Questions

For a short time the victory of the Senate seemed to be
complete. The alliance instituted by Caius Gracchus between
the popular party and the wealthy capitalists of the Equestrian
Order was broken by the violence of Saturninus and his crew,
which seemed to threaten a reign of anarchy and confiscation,
and the shifting of the political balance is indicated by the
return of Metellus from exile and the abrupt departure of
Marius, who went away to Asia on a diplomatic mission.
Some successes gained by Roman arms abroad shed a faint
lustre on the ruling faction, and lent colour to the common
boast of aristocratic governments, a vigorous foreign policy.
But this brief respite was only a prelude to new civil commotions.
Two questions urged their claim for immediate settlement,
the reconstitution of the jury-courts and the grievances of the
Italian allies. For the Equites soon forgot the panic which
had thrown them into the arms of the Senate, and abused
their judicial powers more shamelessly than ever. The scandal
reached a climax when Publius Rutilius Rufus, a man of the
highest character, was brought to trial and condemned on a
charge of extortion simply because he had refused to connive
at the malpractices of the revenue-farmers in Asia. The hand
of the murdered Gracchus was still doing its work. He had
thrown down a dagger between the two orders, and thirty
years after his fall the fatal weapon was being used with deadly
effect. And the question of admitting the Italians to the

Roman franchise could not be much longer postponed. Three times they had been deluded by false hopes, and three times their demands had been thrust aside. It was clear that there could be no peace for Italy until they had received full recognition of their rights.

Drusus

To redress the wrongs of the Italians and reform the corrupt jury-courts were the main objects aimed at in the legislation of Marcus Livius Drusus, the last of the great tribunes (91 B.C.). He was the son of that Drusus who had been set up by the nobles to outbid the popular measures of Caius Gracchus, and by birth, character, and talents was one of the most eminent men of his time. Drusus thought to end the strife of parties by a system of balance and compromise. The Senate was to be recruited by three hundred new members, chosen from the Equestrian Order, and the judicial powers conferred by Gracchus on the Knights were to be restored to the senators. At the same time severe penalties were imposed on any juryman who should be convicted of selling justice for a bribe, and a special commission was appointed for the trial of such offenders. To secure the support of the poorer classes, Drusus added other clauses, providing for a free distribution of grain and the assignment of lands in Italy and Sicily. Lastly, he proposed to make an end of the injustice which had so long estranged the Italian allies, by conferring on them the full Roman franchise.

Futile Reform

Drusus was undoubtedly an earnest and high-minded patriot, but he had undertaken a task far beyond his powers, and by attempting to reconcile so many clashing interests he only succeeded in uniting all classes against himself. The Knights were provoked by the proposed diminution of their prestige. Many of the senators were content to leave the jury-courts in the hands of the financial aristocracy, on condition of sharing with them the plunder of the provinces.

The people viewed with jealousy the large extension of the franchise involved in his measures. Even among the Italians there were wealthy landowners whose estates were threatened with curtailment by the new agrarian law. He succeeded, indeed, in carrying the bill, with the help of some of the nobles who sympathized with his ideas. But he had been guilty of an informality in compelling the people to vote on a number of different measures together, and his opponents, availing themselves of this technical flaw, succeeded in getting the law annulled by the Senate. Moreover, insidious whispers were afloat which accused him of conspiring with the Italian allies for the overthrow of the constitution. These reports were industriously circulated by his enemies, and the dreaded name of king, which had proved fatal to many a patriot, was brought up against him. The Italians, it was said, were in a state of wild excitement—they were taking up arms—they were marching on Rome. In the midst of the alarm caused by these rumours, which, though greatly exaggerated, were not wholly without foundation, Drusus was struck down by the hand of an assassin. He fell unwept and unavenged, and a cruel persecution was immediately set on foot against all who had taken part in his scheme of reform.

THE SOCIAL WAR

Then the storm which for many years had been gathering over Rome broke at last, and the Italians, exasperated by so many disappointments, flew to arms (91 B.C.). The revolt began with the massacre of the Roman residents at Asculum, in the March of Ancona, and thence spread rapidly to all the Sabellians of central Italy, who were joined by the Samnites and Lucanians. It was no longer a question of union with Rome or an equal participation in the rights of her citizens. It was a grand secession, which, if successful, would have torn all Italy asunder and altered the whole course of history by leaving the Romans in a state of weakness and isolation. After a last appeal to Rome, which was contemptuously rejected, the Italians solemnly renounced their allegiance, and

393

formed themselves into a great confederate state, with its capital at Corfinium, in the Pelignian highlands, which received the new name of Italica. To commemorate the league coins were struck, bearing the image of the Sabellian bull trampling on the Roman wolf, and a ready-made constitution was provided for the new state, closely modelled on that of Rome, with a Senate of five hundred, two consuls, twelve praetors, and a popular assembly, open to all the members of the league. The work which seemed to have been completed two centuries before was to be undone, by renewing the old strife between highlanders and lowlanders and shifting the political centre to the heart of the peninsula. Such was the peril brought upon the Romans by their narrow and selfish policy and their obstinate refusal to recognize the just claims of their kinsmen and allies.

THE ADVANTAGE WITH ROME

In numbers, in personal courage, and in warlike training the two sides were fairly matched, and among the Italian commanders there were men who might challenge comparison with the ablest of the Roman generals. But the Romans had the great advantage of a single strategic base, connected by the military roads with the Latin and Roman colonies, which formed a chain of fortresses planted in all the strong places of Italy. In case of a protracted struggle, also, the prospects of the Romans were far better. Their fleet enabled them to command the vast resources of the provinces, with their inexhaustible supplies of men and money; while the Italians, unless they could bring the contest to a speedy and successful issue, would be fatally crippled by want of the sinews of war. Then again the different states of the league were separated by huge mountain barriers, which made it difficult for them to act in concert, and their lines were cut in all directions by the great military settlements. Moreover, a large part of Italy had taken no part in the insurrection. Umbria and Etruria as yet stood fast, the Gauls of the Po valley, broken by a long series of disasters, made no sign of rising, and the Greek cities of southern Italy were united by close ties to Rome.

MARIUS RETIRES

In spite, however, of all these advantages, the result of the first year's fighting was decidedly unfavourable to the Romans. One of the consuls, Lucius Julius Caesar, sustained a defeat in Samnium, and was obliged to fall back, leaving Campania to be overrun by the insurgents. In Apulia and Lucania the Italians were gaining ground, and the important cities of Venusia and Canusium fell into their hands. Meanwhile the other consul, Rutilius Lupus, who was defending the eastern approaches to Latium, had been defeated and slain, and though Marius, who held a subordinate command, subsequently engaged the enemy and gained a decisive victory, he did not follow up his success, but soon afterwards threw up his commission and retired to his villa at Misenum. Some scruples of conscience may perhaps have deterred the veteran general from pressing the war against the Italians, who had once looked to him as their champion and friend ; or perhaps his action may be ascribed to the apathy and disgust of a disappointed man, now far advanced in years, suspected by all parties and bankrupt in reputation. Whatever the cause, his retirement made room for his rival Sulla, who was young, bold, and utterly unscrupulous, and whose rapid rise to power dates from this moment.

ROME GIVES WAY

An important success was gained before the end of the year by Pompeius Strabo, who beat the Picentines in several engagements and laid siege to Asculum. Nevertheless the prospects of Rome were so dark that the Umbrians and Etruscans prepared to join the insurrection. In the face of this new danger the Romans at last gave way, and fear wrung from them the concession which they would never have made to justice. Three laws were brought in and passed in rapid succession (90–89 B.C.), granting to the Italians the long-

coveted privilege.   The first of these, called after its author the
Julian Law, gave the full Roman franchise to all those among
the allies who had not borne arms against Rome.   Early in
the next year a second law, proposed by the tribunes Plautius
and Papirius, extended the boon to all the Italians south of
the Po, on condition that they reported themselves in Rome
within sixty days.   In the same year the consul Pompeius
Strabo added a supplement to these two measures, bestowing
the restricted or Latin franchise on the cities and village
communities between the Po and the Alps.   The new citizens
were to be enrolled in eight of the thirty-five tribes, or, according to another account, ten new tribes were added to the old ;
but if this latter arrangement was really made it was soon
afterwards set aside.[1]

FIGHTING CONTINUES

The allies had obtained what they wanted, and it might
be supposed that the contest, which is known in history as
the Marsic or Social War, would thereby have been brought
to an end.   But war kindles passions which often carry the
combatants far beyond the issues immediately involved.   Old
grudges are revived, old hatreds fanned into a blaze, and the
cruel game goes on even though the stake may have been
lost and won.   Moreover, the condition appended to the
Papirian Law ordering the applicants for citizenship to present
themselves at Rome within two months rendered it impossible
for many of the Italians to claim the benefit offered.   All the
lawless elements of society had been set loose by the bitter
feud, the country was in a ferment, and armed bands infested
the roads, so that it was highly dangerous to travel without
a powerful escort.   For these reasons a large number of the
Italians still kept the field, and the war was protracted into
the following year.   But the main strength of the league was
now broken, and the Roman arms made steady progress.   The
fall of Asculum, which was taken after an obstinate resistance

---

[1] Niese, *Grundriss der römischen Geschichte*, p. 190.

by Pompeius Strabo, decided the fate of the rebellion in the
north, most of the Campanian towns were recovered by Sulla,
the warlike Marsians sustained a crushing defeat, and the
fortress-towns of Samnium and Apulia were retaken one by
one. In Lucania the war still lingered on, and the fierce
Samnites, nursing an inveterate grudge against their old
enemies, remained irreconcilable. Their obstinacy was even-
tually to bring on them a signal and bloody vengeance at the
hands of Sulla. But meanwhile a civil war had broken out
in Rome itself, which delayed the work of pacification in Italy
for several years.

DISSENSIONS WITHIN

Many causes had lately contributed to hasten the process
of dissolution which had long been going on in the Roman
State. The Social War had devastated large tracts of land in
the peninsula and deprived many of their means of living.
The great province of Asia was in open revolt, and the Romans
were thus cut off from their richest source of revenue, while
thousands of families were reduced to beggary. The old feud
between rich and poor, so familiar in the annals of the early
Republic, was revived in its acutest form, and one of the
praetors who intervened for the relief of the debtors was
publicly murdered by the enraged capitalists. The tardy
boon of the franchise, grudgingly bestowed on the Italians
under pressure of necessity, had been hampered by vexatious
restrictions, which deprived it of half its value. The ruling
class was divided by rivalries and jealousies, and those moderate politicians who had been driven into exile after the fall
of Drusus were still living under the ban of an unrighteous
persecution. And beneath all these elements of disorder
lurked another peril, in the fanatical ambition of the disgraced and neglected Marius. He had recently emerged from
his retirement, and was watching with jealous eyes the rapid
progress of his rival Sulla, who had just been raised to the
consulship and appointed to take the command against
Mithradates,

397

REPUBLICAN ROME

Civil War

Such was the position of affairs when one of the tribunes, Sulpicius Rufus, a famous orator, essayed to heal the diseased body of the State by the old remedy of a reform bill (88 B.C.). He proposed to distribute the new citizens and the freedmen among all the tribes, a measure which would greatly enhance their voting power, to reform the Senate by excluding all insolvent members, and to recall those who had been banished by the judicial persecution which followed the death of Drusus. The bill encountered fierce opposition, and scenes of violence ensued, in the course of which the son of Pompeius Rufus, Sulla's colleague in the consulship, was murdered. Sulla himself, who had hardly escaped with his life, fled to his legions in Campania, and by dint of armed force the bill was then carried. But the position of Sulpicius was highly dangerous, for Sulla was now at the head of thirty-five thousand men, devoted to his person, and he was known to be restrained by no scruples. In this emergency Sulpicius conceived the desperate design of deposing Sulla from his command and appointing Marius in his place to conduct the war against Mithradates. A measure to that effect was carried through the assembly, and two tribunes were dispatched with an official order requiring Sulla to lay down his commission. In thus playing off one famous commander against another Sulpicius deliberately provoked an appeal to arms and gave the signal for civil war. And Sulla was not slow to take up the challenge. The wretched tribunes were torn to pieces by his infuriated soldiers, and the consul, who was shortly afterwards joined by his colleague, marched with his whole army upon Rome. The forms of the constitution, so often strained to the breaking-point, had parted at last. The day of legal authority was over ; the reign of the military despot had begun.

Sulla Triumphs

The sudden advance of Sulla filled Marius and his party with dismay. They had no regular forces at their disposal,

398

MARIUS

their disorderly bands were easily dispersed, and Sulla entered
Rome as a conqueror. Sulpicius was dragged from his hiding-
place and put to death, and his head was displayed on the
Rostra, which had so often resounded with his vivid, copious,
and sonorous eloquence. It was the first of those hideous
trophies which afterwards became so familiar to Roman eyes.
Marius, after a series of hairbreadth escapes, succeeded in
reaching Africa, where he remained nursing his vengeance and
waiting for a turn in the tide. Thus left master of the situation,
Sulla set himself to undo the work of Sulpicius and restore the
ascendancy of the nobles. To check the licence of the tribunes
and raise a barrier against hasty and ill-considered legislation
he enacted that henceforth no measure should be proposed to
the people without the previous sanction of the Senate. In
addition he altered the democratic character of the centuriate
assembly by restoring the ancient organization of Servius
Tullius, which gave the preponderance in voting to the propertied classes. For the present, however, a complete reform
of the constitution was out of the question. The aspect of
affairs in Asia was growing darker and darker, and the whole
fabric of Roman power beyond the Adriatic seemed in danger
of falling to pieces. In the same year in which Sulla made
his victorious entry into Rome (88 B.C.) the Asiatics, instigated by Mithradates, rose against their oppressors, and eighty
thousand Romans were put to the sword.

SULLA'S ALTERNATIVE

It was indeed a terrible alternative which was offered to
Sulla—the choice, as it were, between one sinking ship and
another. Of the two consuls for the following year, Octavius,
though a staunch partisan of the Senate, was not strong
enough to stand alone, while Cinna, the other, was a notorious
partisan of Marius. How little confidence could be placed in
the Senate's own officers was shown by the conduct of Pompeius
Strabo, who had distinguished himself in the Social War, and
still held command of an army in Picenum. Being ordered to
hand over his troops to Quintus Pompeius, Sulla's colleague in

399

the consulship, he set on his mutinous troops to murder the consul, and retained his command in defiance of the government. Nor were there wanting other grounds for disquiet. In Rome the elements of disorder were only kept down by Sulla's presence. In Italy the embers of the Social War were still smouldering, and the implacable Samnites remained unsubdued. Whichever way he turned Sulla saw himself faced by a fearful hazard. But that iron soul never hesitated for a moment. Above all the clamour of faction and the loud voice of rebellion he heard one peremptory summons, calling him to chastise the insolent foe who had flouted the sovereign power of Rome. Thus, leaving his country in the throes of a new revolution, he embarked his troops and set sail for Greece.

CINNA MARCHES ON ROME

In order to guard against a reaction Sulla had exacted a solemn oath from Cinna binding him to make no change in the constitution. But no sooner was the pressure of that powerful hand removed than Cinna, repudiating his sworn engagement, began to move for a revival of the Sulpician laws and the complete enfranchisement of the Italians (87 B.C.). Thereupon the strife of parties broke out again with greater fury than ever, and after a sanguinary encounter, in which thousands lost their lives, Cinna was driven from the city and formally deposed from his office. He fled to the legions stationed before Nola, which was still held by a garrison of the insurgent Samnites, and here he was joined by many of the party opposed to the Senate. With them came one who was destined to a romantic career and a tragic end, and who now found himself in strange company, the gentle, the chivalrous, the high-minded Sertorius. In the guise of a suppliant Cinna threw himself on the compassion of the legions, and called upon them to vindicate the majesty of the people violated in the person of their chief magistrate. His tale of wrong found ready sympathy, and the men swore to follow him as their lawful leader. His forces were soon swelled by large numbers of discontented Italians, and by numerous

400

PLATE L. OSTIA

CATO OF UTICA (?)

PLATE LI

MARIUS

exiles of the Marian faction, and the army of invasion, formed into three separate divisions, set out for its march on Rome.

BATTLE BEFORE ROME

Meanwhile another enemy, more terrible than Cinna, had appeared on the scene to complete the dismay of the affrighted Senate. Hunted from one place of refuge to another, Marius had contrived to keep himself informed of the course of events, and perceiving now that the favourable moment had come, he set sail from Africa, and landed at Telamon, on the coast of Etruria. Here he raised a band of fugitive slaves, entered into communication with Cinna, and by making a sudden descent got possession of Ostia, thus cutting off the capital from its sole source of supplies. Threatened with attack on four sides at once, the Senate sent an urgent message to Pompeius Strabo, and directed Metellus, who was commanding against the Samnites, to make what terms he could with the enemy and return to Rome. But the demands of the Samnites were so exorbitant that Metellus refused to accept them, and in consequence of his ill-timed scruples thousands of these fierce swordsmen went over to the side of Marius, who readily granted what they asked. The last hopes of the Senate were now centred in the army of Strabo, which presently appeared before Rome and engaged the division under Sertorius near the Colline Gate. The battle was indecisive, and soon afterwards Strabo himself was cut off, killed, as it was said, by a flash of lightning. Meanwhile thousands of the citizens were perishing by famine and pestilence, and the cowed and dispirited Senate had no course left but submission.

MARIUS'S REVENGE

So the scale had turned again, and the moment for which Marius had waited so long was come at last. Through all the weary months of exile, in the swamps of the Liris, in the dungeon of Minturnae, among the ruins of Carthage, he had clung with desperate tenacity to one sole hope, the hope of a full and signal revenge. All the hoarded venom of years,

401

fed by a thousand taunts and indignities, was working in that diseased and disordered mind ; and as he stood by the chair of Cinna, unshorn and unwashed, like one bound by a vow, the envoys of the Senate might read their doom on that terrible face.

MASSACRE IN ROME

After playing with their victims for a while, by making some show of a parley, Cinna and Marius led their troops into the city and the work of vengeance began. For several days the carnage went on unchecked, and all who had favoured the party of Sulla were involved in a general massacre. Among the most illustrious victims were Catulus, who had shared with Marius the honours of the Cimbric campaign, and the famous orator Marcus Antonius, whose eloquence moved compassion even in the rude soldiers sent to dispatch him, so that the fatal blow had to be struck by their officer. A row of ghastly heads soon decorated the Rostra, the senators being reserved for this unenvied distinction. At length the foul work was stopped by Cinna and Sertorius, who led their troops against the ruffians of Marius and put some thousands of them to the sword. But this act of retribution does not seem to have taken place until after the death of Marius (86 B.C.).

DEATH OF MARIUS

The days of the fierce old man were now drawing rapidly to a close. After suffering every extremity of fortune he had attained the summit of his ambition and seen the fulfilment of the prophecy which foretold that he should be seven times consul. He had triumphed over his enemies and paid back scorn with blood. He had now to learn that the cup which he had deemed so sweet is the bitterest of all. Tortured by remorse, and haunted in his dreams by the angry face of his great rival, he sought oblivion in deep draughts of wine. But his health, weakened by the toils and hardships of seventy years, was broken by these excesses, and after a brief sickness he sank into his grave.

CHAPTER XV

THE WAR WITH MITHRADATES AND THE DICTATORSHIP OF SULLA

WHILE the Romans were absorbed in the suicidal struggles of faction and the rivalries of party leaders great things had been happening in the East, and a new power had grown up on the southern shores of the Euxine which for a brief period seemed destined to rob them of the fairest portion of their empire. The kingdom of Pontus, named after the great inland sea [1] which forms its northern boundary, dates its rise from the confused and troubled time which followed the death of Alexander. Originally a part of the satrapy of Cappadocia, it was formed into an independent state by Mithradates I, who traced his descent from the ancient kings of Persia. In its eastern and southern part it was a rugged and mountainous land, inhabited by wild highland tribes, who gave much trouble to the Ten Thousand in their famous retreat from the interior of Asia. But the coast districts were level and fertile, rich in grain, timber, and olives; and here lay a number of Greek cities, the most important of which were Sinope and its yet more famous colony Trapezus.[2]

MITHRADATES

In the year following the fall of Caius Gracchus (120 B.C.) the throne of Pontus was left vacant by the death of Mithradates V, an able and ambitious prince, who had entertained large designs for the extension of his hereditary dominions.

[1] Pontus Euxinus, or Black Sea.   [2] Trebizond.

He was murdered in his palace at Sinope, which had become the royal seat of the Pontic kings, and the crime was believed to have been instigated by his wife Laodice, who aspired to rule the kingdom in her own name. His son, afterwards famed in history as Mithradates the Great, then a lad of thirteen years, was only saved from sharing his father's fate by the devotion of his attendants. With a few faithful followers he escaped

MITHRADATES

into the mountains, and there for seven years he lived the wild life of a hunter, acquiring in that arduous school an extraordinary degree of endurance, dexterity, and strength. In later years, when his name had become famous, wonderful stories were current about the great Pontic king. He could ride, it was said, forty leagues at a stretch, changing from one horse to another.

He astonished all who lived with him by his heroic appetite, consuming vast quantities of food and wine. By the habitual use of antidotes he had so hardened his constitution against every species of poison that he was proof against that most insidious form of assassination. Nor were his mental gifts less remarkable. He was skilled in Greek learning, was an eloquent speaker and a keen judge of men, and his prodigious memory enabled him to master the languages of more than twenty nations who peopled his wide dominions. But with all his wonderful powers he remained at heart an Asiatic, with the worst vices of the Oriental tyrant. He was cruel, sensual, and superstitious, a prey to dark suspicions, which the utmost degree of devotion could not subdue, and given to fits of brutal fury, which did him fatal injury at the most critical moments of his career. Born in an earlier age, he might have become, like Cyrus, the founder of a great empire. But all his schemes were shattered to pieces when he came into collision with the unrivalled political genius and the organized civilization of Rome.

WAR WITH MITHRADATES

AMBITION OF MITHRADATES

At the age of twenty Mithradates emerged from his retreat, overthrew the tyranny of the queen-mother, and established himself firmly on the throne of Pontus. But his designs went far beyond the narrow limits of his hereditary dominions. On the opposite shores of the Euxine lay the Greek kingdom of Bosporus, situated on the Tauric Chersonese,[1] which in earlier times had attained a high degree of wealth and prosperity, but whose very existence was now endangered by the advancing tide of barbarism. An appeal from the Greeks of this district, who were attacked by a host of invading Scythians, gave Mithradates the opportunity he wanted. His armies, trained on the Greek model and led by Greek captains, drove back the Scythian marauders, and within a few years he had established a sort of suzerainty over all the coast districts of the Euxine as far as the Danube. He then thought of extending his frontier southward, and aimed at nothing less than the conquest of all Asia Minor. We catch the strong flavour of Oriental romance when we read that the young monarch disappeared from view for two whole years, and that during this time he was wandering in disguise from land to land to make himself acquainted with the political and social conditions of Roman Asia. On his reappearance he resumed his career of conquest and aggression. He found an ally in Tigranes II, king of Armenia, under whose rule that kingdom was rapidly rising in power and importance. The designs of Mithradates were first aimed at the acquisition of Bithynia and Cappadocia, and it was by his persistent meddling in these directions that he drew upon himself the attention of the Romans, whose interests in Asia demanded that the integrity of these states should be respected. In playing the game of diplomacy which arose out of this dispute Mithradates showed that he was as crafty as he was bold. Whenever the attitude of the Senate became threatening he drew back, pretending to concede everything that was demanded, but as

[1] The Crimea

soon as the pressure was removed he put out his hand again
to seize the coveted prize.

THE FIRST ENCOUNTER

It was in the course of these intrigues that Sulla, who was
then governor of Pamphylia, was sent on a mission to Cappadocia (92 B.C.), which, though its results were almost immediately cancelled, contributed in no small degree to raise his
reputation as a soldier and a statesman. Ariobarzanes, a
creature of the Romans, had recently been driven by the
machinations of Mithradates from the throne of Cappadocia,
and Sulla received an order from the Senate to restore him.
After a brief campaign he dispersed the forces sent against
him, brought back Ariobarzanes to his kingdom, and, marching through Cappadocia, encamped on the banks of the upper
Euphrates. It was the farthest point eastward that had been
reached by the Romans, and here for the first time they came
into contact with the great Parthian power, which for ages
afterwards was to dispute with them the empire of the East.
Mounted on a lofty seat, with the king of Cappadocia on one
side and the Parthian envoy on the other, Sulla showed that
he knew well how to maintain the sovereign majesty of Rome.

MITHRADATES MAKES WAR

No sooner, however, had Sulla departed than Mithradates
resumed his aggressive policy, drove out Ariobarzanes again,
invaded Bithynia, and compelled the reigning king, Nicomedes III, to make room for one of his satellites. Again the
Senate interfered, and again Mithradates gave way to direct
pressure from Rome. But the crisis was precipitated by the
folly of Manius Aquillius, who had been sent out at the head of
a commission to adjust the affairs of Asia. At his prompting
Nicomedes, the newly restored king of Bithynia, committed
an act of unprovoked aggression by invading the territories of
Mithradates after that monarch had yielded to all the demands
of the commission. Then Mithradates, whose long double-
dealing might have earned him the title of the fox, showed that

he could play the lion's part when the time for action arrived. The moment for which he had plotted and schemed during twenty years was come at last. He had at his disposal an immense force of cavalry and infantry, and his powerful fleet gave him command of the sea. The fortunes of the Romans, on the other hand, seemed to be at the lowest ebb. In Italy the Social War was still raging, and numbers of the discontented Italians escaped to Asia and took service in the king's army. All Roman Asia, provoked beyond endurance by years of extortion and tyranny, was in a ferment of discontent and awaiting the signal to break out into open revolt. With such guarantees of success and with a fair pretext for commencing hostilities, Mithradates struck, and struck with overwhelming effect. Cappadocia and Bithynia were invaded, the ill-disciplined levies hastily raised for the defence of the province were everywhere defeated, and within a year (89–88 B.C.) Mithradates found himself master of all western Asia, except some isolated places in Caria and Lycia, which still held out for Rome. The operations of his fleet were equally successful, and Rhodes alone, true to the far-sighted policy which had always characterized that great merchant-city, remained faithful to her old allies and resisted all the efforts of his admirals. But in the high tide of his fortunes Mithradates gave signal proof of that wild and ferocious temper which ultimately estranged his warmest adherents and brought him to a dishonoured old age and a miserable death. The wretched Aquillius, who had been betrayed into his hands, was paraded in mock triumph through the cities of Asia, bound to the back of an ass, and killed by having molten gold poured down his throat. And the cruelty evinced in this treatment of a single enemy was soon afterwards displayed on a gigantic scale. Secret instructions were issued to all the governors in the towns of western Asia appointing a day for a general massacre of the Italian residents. The order was carried out only too faithfully, and on the lowest computation eighty thousand Italians perished on this occasion (88 B.C.). The brutality of the act was only equalled by its impolicy, for many of those slain were the king's friends and well-wishers.

GREECE JOINS MITHRADATES

For some time previously the agents of Mithradates had been at work on the mainland of Greece, and a ready opening had been afforded him by the restless vanity and giddy ambition of the Athenians. In the midst of their degradation the countrymen of Pericles had never forgotten the ancient glories of their city, and they retained in full measure that dreaming and fantastic temper [1] which had hurried Athens to ruin in the days of her pride. Accordingly they listened with eagerness to the harangues of Aristion, a low-born rhetorician, who was in the pay of Mithradates, and who inflamed their minds with glowing descriptions of the pomp and wealth which he had seen displayed at the court of the Great King. Mithradates, he averred, was the Athenians' best friend, and by his aid Athens might once more become the Queen of the Aegaean and the first city in Greece. Three centuries before the same hopes had been held out by Alcibiades, and had been swallowed with the same greedy credulity. It was resolved to renounce all relations with Rome and share the fortunes of the Pontic king. The example of Athens was widely followed, and soon all Greece, except Aetolia and Thessaly, was ripe for revolt.

THE EASTERN PERIL

After his victories over the Romans Mithradates had removed his royal residence to Pergamum, from which place he could exercise a more immediate control over the affairs of Greece. The tide of invasion, which had been thrust back after the overthrow of Antiochus, was once more running westward, and that Eastern peril which has haunted the mind of Europe in all ages began to assume alarming dimensions. One great army, commanded by a son of Mithradates, was directed to

---

[1] How persistent was this fatal weakness may be seen by a comparison of the following passages : Herodotus, v. 97 ; Thucydides, iii. 38 ; Aristophanes, *Aves, passim* ; Demosthenes, *Philippics*, i. 44 ; Acts of the Apostles, xvii. 21.

march along the coast of Thrace and invade the Roman province of Macedonia, while another was entrusted to Archelaus, a native of Cappadocia, to be conveyed across the Aegaean and carry on the war in central Greece. Archelaus paused in his voyage to make a descent on Delos, which since the war with Perseus had been the most important commercial station in the eastern Mediterranean. The garrison was easily overpowered, and the little island, which was crowded with Roman and Italian traders, was given up to rapine and slaughter. Arrived at Athens, Archelaus found the way prepared for him by the demagogue Aristion, who was left in command of the upper city, while Peiraeus was occupied by the king's troops. The presence of Archelaus with a powerful force completed the work which had been begun by the king's agents. All central and southern Greece declared for Mithradates. In Macedonia, overrun by hordes of Thracians and threatened by a second Pontic army, the governor was powerless to move, and the fleets of Mithradates held the sea, unopposed by a single Roman galley.

Sulla besieges Athens

In the spring of the year following his consulship (87 B.C.) Sulla landed in Epirus, marched across the mainland of Greece, and, after defeating the forces of the king in Boeotia, laid siege to Athens. His vigorous action and known ability soon brought about a change of feeling in Greece, and most of the revolted cities returned to their allegiance. Nevertheless his position was highly difficult, and for a time seemed desperate. He had but thirty thousand men at his disposal to meet the immense forces of Mithradates. He had brought with him no funds from Italy, and was compelled to supply his needs by plundering the treasuries of the Greek temples. The siege of Athens was prolonged for many months, and by this harassing delay his career received a dangerous check at a time when it appeared that nothing but prompt and decisive victory could save him from ruin. For already, before he set sail for Greece, Cinna and Marius had entered Rome in triumph,

and at every stage on his march he was overtaken by fugitive
nobles bearing news of the defeat of his party and the wholesale
massacre of his friends. Yet, though surrounded by perplexities
and terrors, he never looked back, but went grimly on with the
work he had taken in hand. There are few grander figures
in history than this man of firm and resolute spirit, who, with
nothing to lean on but the devotion of his soldiers, remained
faithful to his great trust and fought the battles of the country
which had disowned him. He is the real image of Roman
greatness, and it may be said with truth that through all
this fearful crisis of his people's history Sulla himself was
Rome.

LUCULLUS AND HIS EXPEDITION

Sulla was greatly hampered in his operations by the want
of a fleet, which compelled him to remain an idle spectator
while the king's ships brought abundant supplies into the
harbour of Peiraeus. It is on this occasion that we first
catch sight of another famous personage in the later history
of the Republic, the brilliant and magnificent Lucullus. Born
about 110 B.C., Lucullus was still a mere youth, but his rare
talents had already attracted the notice of his commander,
and he now received the commission, equally hazardous and
important, to raise a fleet which might be able to hold the
sea against the admirals of Mithradates. With a feeble
squadron of six small vessels he set sail in the depth of
winter, and after touching at Crete passed on to Cyrene,
which had been bequeathed by its last prince [1] to the Romans.
He then steered his course for Egypt, and, having lost most
of his ships in an encounter with pirates, reached Alexandria,
where he remained for some time as the honoured guest of
the Egyptian king. But the cautious monarch, dreading to
provoke the hostility of Mithradates, refused to supply him
with ships, and he was compelled once more to commit his
slender fortunes to the sea, which was swarming with the

---

[1] Ptolemy Apion ; died 96 B.C.

WAR WITH MITHRADATES

king's galleys and infested by pirates, who had long been the scourge of the eastern Mediterranean. For two years, counting from the time when he left Athens, he pursued his adventurous career, escaping from a thousand hazards, and gradually collecting a fleet, which was to do good service when the crisis of the war arrived.

ATHENS SACKED

After the departure of his lieutenant Sulla's progress was delayed for many months by the obstinate resistance of Athens. Under that name we have to understand two distinct cities, the upper town, or Athens proper, contained within its own walls, and the harbour-town of Peiraeus. In the days of the Athenian Empire the two had formed one metropolis, being connected by the Long Walls, but this famous structure had long since fallen into decay. Sulla had therefore to conduct two sieges together, and the immense strength of the wall protecting Peiraeus rendered this part of his task peculiarly difficult. To provide timber for his siege-engines he was compelled to strip the whole surrounding country of trees, and even the sacred grove of Academus, long considered inviolable, fell beneath the axes of his men. At length, when spring was approaching, a breach was made in the wall of the upper city, and Sulla, placing himself at the head of the storming party, advanced to the assault. The garrison, which had long been suffering from the extremity of famine, offered little resistance, and for many hours the ancient city, so often spared for the sake of its past, was left a prey to the fury of the Roman soldiers. Sulla had a personal grudge against the Athenians, who had taunted him with his blotched and discoloured face, which bore too plainly the marks of dissolute living. He therefore made no attempt to check the passions of his men, but seemed determined to devote the whole population to indiscriminate massacre. At last, however, he yielded to the entreaty of two Athenian citizens, partisans of the Romans, and gave the order that there should be no further bloodshed.

411

REPUBLICAN ROME

FALL OF PEIRAEUS

By the fall of Athens Sulla was enabled to concentrate his whole force on the siege of Peiraeus, and after a desperate struggle the great fortress-city, with its mighty walls, its arsenals, and its dockyards, was carried by assault. Archelaus, who had conducted the defence with singular energy and ability, retired into the impregnable citadel of Munychia, but the rest of the fortifications were systematically demolished by order of Sulla. Forty years later, when Sulpicius, the eloquent friend of Cicero, sailed along these historic shores, he saw the whole coast-line strewn with the tragic ruins of the past, and sighed over the desolation that Roman hands had made.

SULLA MARCHES NORTH

But Sulla, though a man of learning and deeply versed in Greek letters, had no time for sentimental regret. For while he had been battering the walls of Athens all Macedonia had been brought under the power of Mithradates, and a great army was now advancing southward, commanded by Taxiles, one of the king's generals. Finding that he was too late to raise the siege of Athens, Taxiles took up a position at Thermopylae, where he was presently joined by Archelaus, who had evacuated Munychia on learning that the main Pontic army was approaching. A decisive battle could not long be delayed, and Sulla had more than one weighty reason for wishing to hasten the issue. Marius had died at the beginning of the year, and his successor in the consulship, Lucius Valerius Flaccus, was now on his way with a new army, having been appointed to supersede Sulla in the chief command against Mithradates. Moreover, Hortensius, one of Sulla's lieutenants, was bringing reinforcements from Thessaly, and unless Sulla came speedily to his support he was in great danger of being crushed by the overwhelming numbers of the enemy. Wishing, therefore, to effect a junction with Hortensius, and determined that his hard-earned laurels should not be snatched from him by a political opponent, Sulla left his quarters at Athens and, marching swiftly northward, joined his officer at Elatea, in the district of Phocis.

BATTLE OF CHAERONEA

Appian in his narrative of the Mithradatic War estimates the numbers of the Pontic army at a hundred and twenty thousand, while Plutarch, copying from the memoirs of Sulla, who was not likely to underrate the forces of the enemy, gives a somewhat lower figure. It is certain, at any rate, that the Romans were vastly outnumbered, and the king's troops were armed and equipped with all the lavish magnificence usual in Oriental warfare. The incidents of the campaign had a peculiar interest for Plutarch, a native of Chaeronea, and his description abounds in graphic detail. The mighty host, he says, in true Homeric vein, rolled along the plain like a sea of fire, and the air was aflame with the light and colour of gorgeous uniforms and burnished armour. The battle was brought on by a rash forward movement of the Pontic generals, who were encamped at Elatea, in a position which would have given full scope to their powerful cavalry. Leaving the level country, they advanced southward, hoping by their sudden appearance to surprise the town of Chaeronea, which commanded the entrance into Boeotia. But they arrived only in time to find the town occupied by a Roman garrison, and simultaneously Sulla sent forward a troop to seize a rocky hill which commanded their line of retreat. Thus completely outmanoeuvred, Taxiles and Archelaus were compelled to give battle in a confined space, which neutralized the advantage of their superior numbers. The action began with a charge of the scythed chariots, which only served to show the futility of these dreaded but clumsy engines ; for the Romans were protected by a palisade, and when the chariots, having no space to gather momentum, came up at a feeble trot they greeted the display with shouts and clapping of hands, like spectators in the circus. Thus openly derided, and assailed by a shower of missiles, the drivers were compelled to wheel their cars, and fell back spreading confusion in the ranks of their friends.

REPUBLICAN ROME

Archelaus then tried to crush the little Roman army by
throwing the dense masses of his cavalry simultaneously on
both wings. But the Romans, though shaken for a moment,
quickly rallied, and Sulla at the same time effected a diversion
by a flank attack on the enemy's infantry. The close array
of the phalanx was pierced and broken, the cavalry, flung back
from the firm Roman front, completed the disorder, and soon
the whole host, composed of twenty different nations, became
a disorganized rabble, flying in headlong rout to the shelter
of their camp. Pursuers and pursued poured through the gates
pell-mell together, and the slaughter was continued until the
great force was almost annihilated. Only ten thousand men
were brought off in safety by Archelaus, and these were conveyed by sea to Chalcis.

Reaction in Asia

The fall of Athens and the victory of Chaeronea had the effect
of hastening a reaction which had for some time been in progress among the Roman subjects in Asia. From the first
there had been a minority, composed of wealthy and influential
men, who discountenanced the revolt from Rome, and many
of those who favoured the cause of Mithradates had soon
reason to feel that they had gained nothing by the change
of masters. The Romans, though sunk deep in corruption,
were still a civilized people, who stood for the cause of law and
order, while Mithradates represented Oriental tyranny in its
very worst aspect. The feeling of discontent, fomented by
many acts of cruelty, spread from city to city, and after the
battle of Chaeronea it blazed up in rebellion. The great city
of Ephesus led the way, and other towns of Asia which had
felt the heavy hand of the king were not slow to follow. To
check the movement Mithradates had recourse to measures of
the most atrocious severity, aiming his blows exclusively at
men of rank and wealth, who formed the strength of the Roman
party; and at last, playing the part of the unprincipled demagogue, he published a decree proclaiming freedom to the
slaves and a general abolition of debts. It was the policy

414

regularly pursued by the old Greek tyrants, striking down the noble and paying court to the mob ; and for the present it succeeded. Having arrested the spread of defection, Mithradates prepared to raise another great army, with the intention of renewing the war in Greece.

ROMAN ARMIES OPPOSED

Meanwhile it seemed probable that the work would be taken out of the king's hands, and that the Romans, anticipating the course of history by some forty years, would fight out their quarrel now on the fields of Thessaly. For while Sulla was engaged in adjusting the affairs of Greece he learnt that Flaccus had landed with two legions in Epirus, and was marching southward fast to take over the command. Sulla turned to meet this new danger with all his wonted resolution, and for a brief space the two rival generals stood confronting each other on the slopes of Mount Othrys. But Flaccus, who could not trust the temper of his troops, declined an encounter, and marched away in the direction of the Hellespont, hoping to find an easier and more profitable task in attacking the enemies of Rome. Sulla was still hesitating whether he should follow or retire when his doubts were resolved by the news that a new Pontic army had landed in Boeotia. Under the urgent orders of Mithradates a great force had been assembled, and Dorylaus, the king's general, having joined Archelaus and taken up the remnant of the defeated army, was pillaging the country and calling the towns to revolt.

BATTLE OF ORCHOMENUS

These tidings caused Sulla to retrace his steps with all speed, and, entering Boeotia, he came up with the enemy on the northern spurs of Mount Helicon. Dorylaus was eager to bring on an immediate engagement, but his ardour was somewhat cooled by a preliminary skirmish with the Romans, which ended in the discomfiture of his troops, and, falling back on Orchomenus, he pitched his camp in a position highly favourable to the operations of cavalry. Sulla brought up

his army, and set the men to work on a system of entrenchments, designed to embarrass the movements of the enemy's
horse. Dorylaus, however, made repeated sallies, dispersed
the diggers, and inflicted considerable loss on Sulla's troops.
The Romans were dismayed by the numbers and impetuosity
of their assailants, and at one moment the danger was so
imminent that Sulla sprang from his horse and, seizing a standard, advanced alone against the enemy, crying to his troops,
" Remember Orchomenus, where you left your general to die ! "
Roused by this heroic example, the men hastened to his support,
and the barbarians were thrust back. The battle was resumed
on the following day, and after severe fighting the Pontic
camp was carried, and the butchery of Chaeronea repeated.
The waters of Lake Copaïs were dyed with blood, and two
hundred years afterwards rusty helmets, arrow-heads, and
swords were found embedded in the mud and rushes of these
marshy shores.

DIVIDED ROME

The attempt of Mithradates to found a Pontic empire in
Europe had ended in total disaster, and every day his prospects
grew darker. At the time when Sulla was restoring the honour
of Roman arms in Boeotia, Flaccus, though quite against his
intention, was doing his work for him in the north and preparing
the way for his triumphant return to Italy. Marching through
Thessaly, Flaccus entered Macedonia, and, having brought
that province back to obedience and fought his way through
Thrace, reached the shore of the Bosporus. Here, however,
his career was cut short by the treason of Fimbria, one of his
lieutenants, a daring and unscrupulous ruffian, who had earned
an evil notoriety in the recent massacres at Rome. Flaccus,
though he set no bounds to his own rapacity, was a rigid
martinet, and had made himself unpopular by sternly repressing
the licence of his troops, who now broke out into mutiny.
Compelled to fly for his life, Flaccus escaped to Nicomedia,
but he was soon afterwards dragged from his hiding-place
and slain (85 B.C.). Fimbria, who had taken an active part

in this outrage, assumed command of the army, and proved
himself a bold and able leader. He defeated the king's
troops in the field, drove Mithradates out of Pergamum, and
overran the whole Hellespontine district, plundering and
ravaging as he went. It was at this moment that Lucullus,
who had succeeded in getting together a fleet and had recovered
several of the island and coast towns, appeared off the neighbouring shore, and but for his refusal to co-operate with
Fimbria Mithradates would certainly have fallen into the
hands of the Romans. It is curious to observe the blind party
spirit which had now usurped the place of all high and patriotic
aims in Roman public life. Fimbria, whose proceedings are
those of a bandit, is allowed to keep the command which he
has obtained by the murder of his general. Lucullus, out of
mere party bias, allows Rome's greatest enemy to escape,
and thus brings upon his country another costly and tedious
war. Sulla, the foremost man of his day, who has just performed the most eminent services, is branded as an outlaw,
his property is confiscated, and his family are driven into exile.

PEACE WITH MITHRADATES

But, though thus divided in their counsels, the Romans
were everywhere victorious, and after some negotiation terms
of peace were arranged (84 B.C.). Mithradates agreed to resign
all his conquests, to pay an indemnity of three thousand
talents, and to surrender a part of his fleet, which was to be used
by Sulla for the conveyance of his troops to Italy. While
the treaty was still under discussion Sulla marched to the
Hellespont, where Lucullus was waiting for him with his fleet,
and crossed over into Asia. At Dardanus, in the Troad,
Mithradates and his conqueror met face to face, and there
the king set his name to the treaty. Ariobarzanes and Nicomedes presently resumed their precarious sovereignty in
Cappadocia and Bithynia respectively, and the territories of
the king of Pontus shrank to their original dimensions. About
the same time another obstacle was removed from Sulla's
path by the death of Fimbria, whose army lay encamped at

Thyatira.   After a futile attempt to procure the assassination
of his rival Fimbria had put an end to his own life, and his
troops were then quietly incorporated with the army of Sulla.
It remained to settle the affairs of Asia, and in carrying out
this part of his work Sulla had an eye to the necessities of his
own position.   He was presently to return to Italy, and he
was to return as an invader and as the avowed enemy of the
existing government.   To ensure the success of this dreadful
enterprise he required a great fleet, a powerful army, and unlimited supplies of money.   The last of these was obtained by
heavy contributions laid on the unhappy province of Asia.
The taxes, which had fallen into arrear for the last five years,
were ordered to be paid up in full, and, as if this were not
enough, an additional payment of twenty thousand talents
(nearly £5,000,000) was demanded.   The grievous burden
imposed by Sulla lay heavy on the province for many years,
and was the cause of widespread misery and distress.   Hardly
less deplorable was the condition of Greece, which had been
cruelly ravaged and plundered in the recent war.   Now, as
ever, appeared the truth of the Horatian maxim, that the
quarrels of the mighty are atoned for by the blood and groans
of the people.[1]

AFFAIRS IN ITALY

During the whole time of Sulla's absence the government at
Rome remained in the hands of his opponents.   The Senate,
deprived of its leading members by flight or massacre, was
passive and helpless, and Cinna obtained the consulship in
four successive years (87–84 B.C.).   To secure the adhesion of
the Italians the new voters were distributed among the thirty-
five tribes, and Cinna sought to strengthen his party at Rome
by an extensive enfranchisement of freedmen, by the cancelling
of debts, and by the lavish distribution of corn.   The western
provinces remained loyal to the government, in Italy all was
quiet, and when news arrived that the war was concluded
Cinna made ready to cross the Adriatic and meet the conqueror

[1] *Quidquid delirant reges, plectuntur Achivi (Epistles, I, ii. 14)*

of Mithradates on the fields of Macedonia. But in the midst of his preparations he was murdered by his own troops at Ancona, and Carbo, his colleague in the consulship, then abandoned the expedition and remained in Italy. The death of Cinna and the news of Sulla's approach kindled new hopes in the party opposed to the government. Chief among these was the young Pompeius, the son of that Pompeius Strabo who had been the main hope of the Senate when Rome was invaded by the armies of Marius. After the victory of the Marians he had known how to make peace with the dominant party, and had married the daughter of Antistius, a political opponent. But now that the tide was turning he threw himself heart and soul on tle side of Sulla, and began to enlist troops in Picenum, where he had great estates, inherited from his father. Thus early had this famous man given proof of that strain of insincerity and duplicity which underlay the grander features of his character.

SULLA RETURNS TO ITALY

In his dispatches addressed to the Senate after the conclusion of the war Sulla's tone had been moderate, and negotiations were set on foot which gave some prospect of an amicable conclusion. But the desperate men who now swayed the counsels of Rome knew that they had sinned too deeply for pardon, and the attempted compromise was frustrated by their violence. In the spring of the year (83 B.C.) Sulla landed at Brundisium, bringing with him an army of forty thousand veterans, and accompanied by numbers of his own party who had fled from the tyranny of Cinna. Here he was joined by Pompeius, who brought with him two legions, by Metellus, son of the conqueror of Jugurtha, and by Crassus, the future triumvir, whose father had perished in the Marian massacres, and who had himself evaded his pursuers by hiding for eight months in a cave.[1] It was no easy task that Sulla had undertaken, for all the weight of authority which belongs to an

[1] This adventure, the scene of which was in Spain, is described with great humour by Plutarch (*Crassus*, c. 4–5).

established government was on the side of his enemies, while he himself was a proscribed outlaw, entering his country as an invader. Moreover, public opinion in Italy was generally against him, and the Samnites especially were implacable in their hostility to himself and his class. To weaken the influence of his opponents and bring over the waverers to his side, he had issued a manifesto promising a complete amnesty to all who laid down their arms, and solemnly confirming the political rights of the Italians. The effect of this moderation was seen on his first landing in Italy. Brundisium opened its gates and hailed him as a deliverer, and all Apulia declared for his cause. Then, having given strict orders to his soldiers to respect the rights of property in the districts through which they passed, he left his quarters at Brundisium and, advancing along the Appian Way, entered Campania. The first encounter took place at Mount Tifata, renowned as the scene of some of Hannibal's exploits, where Norbanus, one of the consuls for the year, was waiting to oppose his progress. The consul was totally defeated and compelled to take refuge in Capua, and Sulla, having crushed one opponent, prepared to meet another with the weapons of intrigue. Scipio, the colleague of Norbanus, was waiting with another army at Teanum, which commanded the route into Latium, and being a man of feeble character he was persuaded by Sulla to conclude an armistice, with a view to discussing the terms of peace. Sulla made use of the opportunity to tamper with the consul's men, and while Scipio parleyed and hesitated he found himself deserted by his whole army, which went over to swell the forces of his antagonist. Among the officers serving under Scipio was the gallant Sertorius, who had vainly warned his general against the machinations of Sulla, and of whom we shall presently hear more, as the last upholder of the democratic party in the remote province of Spain.

CIVIL WAR CONTINUES

During the summer, and at the very moment when the Romans were preparing to plunge again into civil war, a strange portent occurred. The great temple on the Capitol, the seat of Rome's guardian gods, the shrine of her sacred books, and the symbol of her empire, was consumed by fire. No man could point to the author of this sacrilege, and it seemed as if the gods themselves were wroth at the suicidal frenzy which had taken possession of their chosen people. The warning, however, was unheeded, and at the beginning of the next year both sides prepared to renew the struggle with increased bitterness. Carbo, the former colleague of Cinna, caused himself to be elected consul, and the other chair was filled by Caius Marius, nephew and adopted son of his great namesake. Carbo undertook the conduct of the war in the north, where he was confronted by Pompeius, Metellus, and the two Luculli, while Marius marched southward to meet Sulla, who was advancing from Campania on Rome. In the old Volscian land,[1] the scene of so many fierce struggles in the past, the two armies met, and the raw levies of Marius were soon scattered by Sulla's veterans and compelled to take refuge behind the impregnable walls of Praeneste. Leaving one of his lieutenants to invest the town, Sulla hastened on to Rome, but he arrived too late to prevent a last massacre of the nobles, in which Mucius Scaevola, great lawyer and upright judge, was the most illustrious victim. After remaining a few days at Rome, Sulla advanced into Etruria, and fought an indecisive battle with Carbo, who was encamped at Clusium. But Carbo was presently compelled to fall back on the Po district, where Metellus was making rapid progress. He marched to the support of Norbanus, who was holding this district for the Marians, and, having effected a junction with his lieutenant, engaged the forces of Metellus at Faventia, where the roads from Ariminum and Ravenna converge. The battle ended in a complete victory for Metellus, and this blow decided the issue of the war in the north. One by one the leaders of the Marians fell away, or were reduced by Sulla's subordinates, and Carbo himself, after struggling on for some time, gave up the cause as lost and embarked for Africa.

[1] The place, which was called Sacriportus, has not been identified.

BATTLE OF THE COLLINE GATE

Meanwhile Sulla had been recalled from Etruria by the news that the Samnites and Lucanians, seventy thousand strong, were marching to the relief of Praeneste. He arrived in time to save the town, and for some days the two armies lay facing each other. Then Pontius, the Samnite who was in command of the relieving army, made a sudden resolve. His position was growing daily more dangerous, for the whole of the Sullan forces were now concentrating on Praeneste, and if he remained in his present position he would be surrounded. What if he were to march upon Rome itself, which was left for the moment undefended, and take up his quarters within the walls where the wolves of Italy had made their lair? Pontius issued his orders rapidly and secretly, and, taking a wide circuit, before daybreak he halted before the Colline Gate, at the northern angle of the wall, and just at the point where the rampart of Servius Tullius begins. A sally made by the slender garrison was easily repulsed, and but for the timely arrival of Sulla, who had received early notice of the enemy's movements, the design would have been successful. Then began one of the most deadly and desperate struggles recorded in ancient history. It was no longer a question of Marian and Sullan, but the old racial feud between Oscan and Latin, revived after a lapse of two centuries, and embittered by long memories of humiliation and defeat. All night the battle continued, and for a long time the issue remained doubtful. At last Sulla's left wing, where he was commanding, was put to flight, and Sulla himself, who had only been saved from death by the devotion of his groom, was carried with the fugitives back to his camp. But in the morning he received the welcome news that Crassus, who led the right wing, had gained a complete victory, and was now lying at Antemnae, waiting for instructions. He then united his beaten troops with the division of Crassus, and the contest was decided by the defection of three thousand of the enemy, who turned their weapons against their own side.

DICTATORSHIP OF SULLA

LAST OF THE SAMNITES

A few days later Sulla was seated in the temple of Bellona, explaining his views to the awed and obsequious senators, when his speech was interrupted by a hideous uproar which suddenly arose outside the doors. " Be not alarmed, Conscript Fathers," said Sulla coolly. " What you hear is but the voice of certain traitors, who are receiving the penalty due to their misdeeds." It was, in fact, the death-cry of six thousand Samnites, who were butchered by Sulla's orders in the neighbouring circus. Having thus destroyed the last remnant of an ill-fated race, Sulla completed his work by turning their country into a desert, and the curse of his name has rested on the land until this day. Two years elapsed before the last embers of resistance were stamped out in Italy, and in the meantime Sicily and Africa had been rapidly reduced to obedience by Pompeius, who returned to claim a triumph, and to be greeted by his leader with the title of Magnus. In Spain Sertorius had not yet begun the career which was to make his name famous, and in Asia, where new troubles had arisen through the indiscretion of Sulla's lieutenant Murena,[1] tranquillity was restored by the authority of the all-powerful Sulla. After ten years of foreign war and civil commotion peace reigned once more throughout the Roman world.

GROWTH OF VIOLENCE

The earlier stages of party warfare in Rome had been singularly free from those scenes of violence and civil bloodshed which are so familiar to the student of Greek history. For two hundred years patricians and plebeians had striven together, slowly working out a peaceful revolution, which had hardly cost the life of a single citizen. But the bitter struggle with Carthage and the long wars of conquest which followed

---

[1] The squabble between Mithradates and Murena is commonly dignified with the name of the Second Mithradatic War, but that designation is better reserved for the last struggle with Mithradates.

brought out the latent cruelty of the Roman character, and this feature was encouraged and sharpened by the bloody contests of the arena, which came more and more into fashion from the close of the third century. In thus trampling on the claims of humanity the Romans had forged a weapon against their own peace which brought infinite misery on themselves and on their children. From the time of the Gracchi each stage in the revolution has its death-roll of Roman citizens, and each successive massacre leads to a more savage reprisal.

SULLA'S PROSCRIPTIONS

We have now to record a new butchery, surpassing in cold-blooded wickedness all those which had preceded. The vengeance of Marius had spent itself in a sort of blind and brute fury, which excited horror even in his own associates. But Sulla, more cruel, because more dispassionate, dealt out murder with the calmness of an inquisitor. He was resolved, if possible, to bar the way against reaction by pursuing a steady policy of extermination. At first he contented himself with issuing a general order condemning to death all who had borne arms against him in the civil war or who had taken sides openly with the Marian party. A thousand willing hands were ready to carry out the fatal decree, and among those who distinguished themselves by their zeal in the cause was a dissolute young noble named Catiline, whose later exploits are recorded in the pages of Cicero and Sallust. Many victims had already fallen, and all Rome was filled with a vague terror, when a young senator ventured to ask Sulla to relieve the public anxiety by saying to whom his vengeance was to apply. "Let the Romans know," he said, "who is to be counted innocent and who are the guilty." Sulla promised to comply, and presently a list was posted in a public place containing the names of eighty persons who were condemned to death (82 B.C.). Such was the origin of the famous proscriptions which henceforth become a regular feature in the annals of party strife at Rome. Anyone whose name appeared on the list became an outlaw, deprived of all civil rights, to

424

be hunted down and slain wherever he was found. Large rewards were set on the heads of the proscribed persons, and the penalty of death was denounced against all who gave them shelter. Nor was the general sense of insecurity in any way diminished by the publication of this register of murder, for within a short time a second and a third list appeared, and no one could say when the proscription would cease. The property of the proscribed was confiscated, and Sulla's favourites obtained an opportunity of enriching themselves by purchasing the forfeited estates at a nominal price. It was thus that Crassus laid the foundation of the enormous fortune which earned him the title of Dives. But avarice was not satisfied with the plunder of those who had been marked down as the victims of political hatred. Many a quiet citizen who had held aloof from all civil broils found that his cautious neutrality availed him nothing in those days of terror. A well-stocked farm, a fine orchard, or a luxurious villa was a sufficient passport to a place on the proscription list and a violent death. An instance recorded by Plutarch will serve as an example of the fate which overtook hundreds of Romans who had given no offence to either party. Quintus Aurelius, a good, harmless man, who deemed himself safe in his obscurity, was walking one day in the Forum, when, happening to glance at the list, he found to his horror that his own name was among the number of the proscribed. "Alas!" he cried, as he tottered away with unsteady feet, "it is my Alban farm which has undone me." He had not gone many steps when he was struck down by an assassin, and his farm passed to another owner.

But the terrible man who now controlled the destinies of Rome was not content with taking the lives of his enemies and reducing their families to ruin. He sought to fix a stigma on their race by ordaining that their sons and grandsons should be disqualified for any public office. In acting thus he poured new venom into the exhausted veins of the State and gave permanence to the blood-feud which had begun with the murder of the elder Gracchus. The spirit of hatred and revenge which he had invoked haunted his countrymen long after his death, following the Pompeians to their camp in Epirus, presiding at the council-board of the second triumvirs, and breeding distrust and suspicion to embarrass the humaner policy of Caesar.

The number of those who perished in the proscriptions is stated at five thousand, and the loss fell heaviest on the Equestrian Order, which was peculiarly obnoxious to Sulla and his party. But to these we have to add a multitude of unnamed victims who were sacrificed to private malice or greed. From Rome the persecution spread to Italy and the provinces, where Sulla's spies and informers were busy tracking down the fugitives to their hiding-places. Carbo was caught in the island of Cossyra, and put to death by order of Pompeius, who sent the head of his victim as an acceptable offering to his patron Sulla. Norbanus, who had escaped to Rhodes, finding the pursuers hot on his track, put an end to his own life. Of the other democratic leaders, Pontius had been cut down on the battlefield after the final victory of Sulla, Marius had fallen by his own hand after the capitulation of Praeneste, and Sertorius alone survived, to keep up a hopeless struggle for ten years longer.

CAESAR

The voice of Sulla now gave laws to the Roman world, and the most stubborn spirits bowed in submission to the uncrowned king. Even the haughty Pompeius, who for a moment had attempted to assert his independence, refusing to disband his troops at his leader's command, soon proved himself compliant, and put away his wife Antistia to make room for a mate of Sulla's own choosing. But while friends and foes were thus bending to the will of the conqueror there was one, a mere stripling of eighteen, who showed that he had a spirit which would endure dictation from no man. This was the young Caius Julius Caesar, whose family connexions[1] made

---

[1] His aunt, Julia, was the wife of Marius, and he himself had married Cornelia, a daughter of Cinna.

him an object of suspicion to Sulla and his party. Being ordered by Sulla to divorce his wife, he boldly refused, and but for the intervention of powerful friends he would have paid for his defiance with his life. The keen eye of Sulla, which had detected the latent weakness in the character of Pompeius, saw the vast powers which were disguised by Caesar under an affectation of careless profligacy. "Let him go, then," he said, when importuned by many voices to spare the life of an idle boy. "But mark my words, in that boy you will find more than one Marius."

THE DESOLATION OF ITALY

The extensive confiscations of land which accompanied the Sullan proscriptions completed the desolation of Italy, which had been steadily promoted by centuries of warfare. Agriculture, revived to some extent by the reforms of the Gracchi and their imitators, fell into almost total decay, and gangs of slaves, half shepherds, half brigands, took the place of the free cultivators. Sulla, indeed, strove to repeople the deserted countryside by a wholesale allotment of lands to his disbanded veterans. No fewer than a hundred and fifty thousand soldiers were provided with farms, chiefly in the districts of Etruria and Campania. But this short and easy way of restoring agricultural prosperity was soon shown to be futile. The soldiers, in spite of all prohibitions, parted with their allotments and resumed their wandering life, ready to sell their swords to any turbulent agitator. Thousands, moreover, had sought refuge in desert places from the myrmidons of Sulla, and every mountain retreat had its band of robbers, who infested the roads and avenged their private wrongs by making war on society.

SULLA AS DICTATOR

We have spoken of Sulla as an uncrowned king, and the powers which he wielded during his brief career as a ruler were, in fact, those of an unlimited monarchy. In order to give a sort of constitutional sanction to his proceedings, he

427

caused one of his creatures, Lucius Valerius Flaccus, to propose his appointment as dictator (82 B.C.). The office had
originally been instituted in the early days of the Republic
as a weapon held in reserve by the nobles, to be brought forth
in times of emergency for the intimidation of the commons.
But it had long fallen into disrepute, and more than a century
had elapsed since the last dictator had held office. In its
revived form the dictatorship differed in character from its
ancient prototype, and was nothing less than a thinly disguised
despotism. No limitation as to time was imposed, and Sulla
was invested with absolute authority over the lives and property of the citizens, with freedom to propose new laws and
reorganize the State.

CONSERVATIVE REFORM

Armed with these great powers, Sulla applied himself to the
task of rebuilding the shattered edifice of the constitution.
Being a man of thoroughly conservative mind, his aim was
not to create, but to restore. And being by birth and by
instinct an aristocrat, he naturally desired to aggrandize and
elevate the order to which he belonged. The long usurpation
of the Senate had been rudely shaken by the encroachments
of the commons, who claimed to be the sovereign power in the
State, by the ambition of the great military leaders, and by
the rise of the Equites, who had been brought by Caius
Gracchus into sharp antagonism with the official nobility.
Accordingly Sulla's first object was to cut down the rival
growths which had overshadowed the pretensions of the
Senate, and thus prepare the way for a complete restoration.
The stronghold of the popular party was the Parliament of
the tribes, which had been raised by the Hortensian Law to
a co-ordinate position with the centuriate assembly and had
become a recognized organ of the Populus Romanus. Sulla
withdrew from this body the greater part of its powers, and
crippled its action by restoring to the Senate the right of
initiative in matters of legislation, and by degrading the office
of tribune, which had proved so dreaded an instrument in the

hands of democratic leaders. The tribunes were forbidden to bring any measure before the people without the previous sanction of the Senate, their right of veto was curtailed, and in order further to discredit the office all who had held the tribuneship were disqualified for admission to the higher magistracies.

The Cornelii

Twenty years before, when the cause of the democrats was in the ascendant, a law had been passed [1] conferring on the people assembled in their tribes the right of filling up vacancies in the priestly colleges. This was now repealed, and the old method of co-optation was restored, leaving the election to the votes of the surviving members. But Sulla was not satisfied with clipping the prerogatives of the people and fettering the free action of their official leaders. Wishing to secure a direct personal influence in the popular assembly, he by one bold stroke conferred the franchise on ten thousand emancipated slaves whose masters had fallen in the civil war or in the proscriptions, and enrolled these new-made Romans in the city tribes. The enfranchised freedmen received the name of Cornelii, derived from the great house to which Sulla himself belonged, and formed a compact body pledged to the support of the new order established by their patron. They served further as a sort of police, to keep down the licence of the mob, and Sulla was thus enabled to abolish the corn largess, which had so long been recognized as a necessary part of popular legislation.

Checks on Ambition

In the age of the Senate's greatness the powers of the executive were held in strict subordination, and the high officers of State yielded implicit obedience to the central authority at Rome. But the growth of Rome's dominions and the habit of prolonged command had given a dangerous stimulus to the ambition of powerful and aspiring men, and

[1] Lex Domitia (104 B.C.).

loosened the tie which bound the commander of an army and the governor of a province to the government. Even before the end of the Second Punic War the irregular command of Scipio was a significant proof how far the individual might set himself above the constitution. In quite recent times Marius had only been prevented by political incapacity from making himself an autocrat, and his seven consulships were a flagrant violation of constitutional usage. But the most glaring example was Sulla himself, who, after being formally deposed from his command, had brought an important war to a successful conclusion, had made a treaty with Rome's greatest enemy on his own sole authority, and had invaded his country at the head of a victorious army. What Sulla had done himself he was determined, if possible, to prevent others from doing, and with this purpose he brought in a series of enactments intended to limit the powers of the great public officials and bring them into strict subordination to the Senate. There were statutes already in existence providing for a regular gradation from the lower to the higher magistracies, fixing the age of eligibility to each, and ordaining that an interval of ten years must elapse before anyone could become a candidate for an office which he had already held. These restrictions were now revived, and at the same time a clear division was made between the civil and military duties of the consuls and praetors. Henceforth these great functionaries were to remain at home and exercise their civil powers during their year of office, and in the year following they were to proceed to their provinces, with the title of proconsul or propraetor and armed with full military authority. Further, in order to deter anyone from walking in his own footsteps, Sulla confined the powers of the provincial governors within strict limits, which they were forbidden to exceed on pain of a prosecution for treason.

CHANGES IN THE SENATE

Having lowered the prestige of the great curule magistracies, disarmed the tribunate, and bridled the popular assembly,

DICTATORSHIP OF SULLA

Sulla turned to the constructive part of his work, the reconstitution of that body in which all the powers of government
were once more to be centred. The numbers of the Senate
had been much reduced in the late civil wars, and Sulla filled
up the vacant benches by raising three hundred citizens,
selected from the wealthier class, to senatorial rank. In order,
also, to ensure a regular supply of new members, he enacted
that the quaestors, whose number was increased to twenty,
should in due course take their seat in the Senate. One result
of this reform was that the censors, whose duty of revising the
list of senators was now rendered superfluous, suffered a great
loss of dignity, and that high office, which had once been the
final goal of political ambition, never recovered its former
position in the State.

LEGAL REFORMS

There was still another class to be humbled and another
privilege to be recovered for the restored oligarchy. Some
forty years back Caius Gracchus had dealt a heavy blow at
the nobles and created a sort of permanent opposition to the
government by forming an alliance with the great capitalists
of the Equestrian Order and placing in their hands the judicial
powers which had previously been held by the Senate. Sulla
gave back this formidable weapon to its original owners, and
took other means to degrade and weaken the Equites, whose
ranks had already been greatly thinned by the proscriptions.
One important feature in Sulla's legislation was the improvement and multiplication of standing commissions for the trial
of special offences, and the clear distinction which now began
to be drawn between civil and criminal jurisdiction. By these
reforms Sulla left a permanent mark on the Roman penal
code, and prepared the way for the great jurists of the Empire.

SULLA RETIRES

Within less than two years Sulla had finished his gigantic
task and given his countrymen a new constitution, put together
out of the fragments of the old. The edifice was now complete,

431

REPUBLICAN ROME

and the architect, oppressed by age and infirmities, was longing
for his rest.   Looking back on a career of thirty years, he could
boast that Fortune, whom he worshipped as his patron goddess,
had never forsaken him in any of his enterprises.   Beginning
as the penniless son of a noble but impoverished house, he had
risen by the favour of that fickle deity to the highest pinnacle
of fame and power.   It remained to apply the supreme test,
by descending from his lofty eminence and mingling as an
equal with his fellow-citizens, whom he had ruled as a master.
Few indeed in the whole course of history are the names of
those who have had the courage to take this step, for the
position of a retired despot is generally not less undignified
than unsafe.   It is a signal proof of Sulla's self-command that
at the moment of his highest power, when the whole Roman
world lay at his feet, he put aside all the dignities of his great
office and withdrew into the retirement and obscurity of private
life.   The peril of assassination, which has shaken even the
strongest spirits, had no terrors for him, and he had taken
means to guard against any general movement in the party
which he had defeated and oppressed. His ten thousand
Cornelii were a guarantee for peace at Rome, and his legions,
scattered over the whole length of Italy, were ready to muster
at a sign from him.   Like Pompeius thirty years later, he had
only to stamp his foot and a hundred thousand veterans
would spring to arms.   Thus fortified within and without
against all chances, he resigned the dictatorship and withdrew
to his villa at Cumae.   He survived his abdication only one
year, however, and died suddenly at the age of sixty from the
rupture of a blood-vessel, said to have been caused by a violent
fit of anger (78 B.C.).   The loathsome disease which is described
with unnecessary detail by Plutarch seems to have been an
invention of political hatred, or of that desire for poetical
justice which haunts the popular imagination.

CHARACTER AND ACHIEVEMENTS OF SULLA

Sulla is the typical aristocrat, with the vices and the virtues
of his class and of his age.   Sprung from a ruling order, he was

432

endowed with gifts of mind and character which carried him, whenever he chose to exert himself, to the summit of affairs. Born in a time of profound decadence, he astonished the most corrupt of his contemporaries by his extravagant sensuality. A certain note of insincerity runs through all his actions. The burden of high office which he seemed to bear so lightly was assumed with reluctance and abandoned with relief. He laboured for two years to rebuild the constitution, yet probably none knew better than he that when his hand was removed the work of demolition would begin anew. Yet, with all his flippant cynicism and callous disregard of human life, he performed services to his country which it is hard to over-estimate. By his capture of Jugurtha he put an end to a scandal which had brought disgrace and contempt on the Roman name. His victories at Chaeronea and Orchomenus arrested the ambitious designs of Mithradates and gave back to the Romans the fairer half of their empire, and by defeating the Samnite army he averted a deadly blow aimed at the very heart of the State. His reform of the penal code was a work of lasting value, and marks a definite step in the development of Roman jurisprudence ; while his new model of a constitution, though not destined to long continuance, helped to check the progress of decay until a great creative genius should arise to rebuild the whole structure on a more solid foundation.

CHAPTER XVI

FROM THE DEATH OF SULLA TO THE RETURN OF POMPEIUS FROM THE EAST

THE great man was dead, and Rome, deprived of his guiding hand, was once more face to face with her destiny. He had left his countrymen a constitution, remodelled on the old lines, and he had left them an example. Within ten years of his death the constitution had fallen to pieces, but the example remained, and was soon to find eager imitators. And so we pass to the final act in the great drama of revolution, in which constitutional forms are a mere empty show [1] and the personal element has become all in all. We still hear the old party cries, Senate and people, knight and noble, but these are mere watchwords under which powerful leaders rally their partisans, and the only question remaining is whose shall be the strong and daring hand to grasp the prize of sovereignty. The tribunate, that Proteus of Roman politics, which we have seen in so many shapes—as the shield of the poor, the instrument of constitutional reform, the obedient tool of the Senate, and the mighty lever of revolution—has now entered on its last phase as the sharpest weapon in the armoury of individual ambition. The Senate, after a few years of precarious rule, during which it gives final proof of its incompetence, lapses into utter imbecility and resigns the reins of power, which it has no longer strength to hold. Among all classes a greedy and selfish spirit has usurped the place of public and patriotic aims. The soldier, like a true hireling, asks for nothing better than a rich booty and a speedy discharge. The general who overthrows kingdoms and adds

---

[1] See the instructive passage in Sallust, *Catiline*, 38.

434

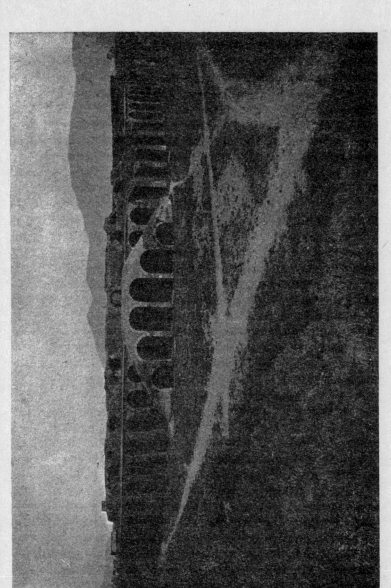

PLATE LII. THE AMPHITHEATRE, POMPEII

434

PLATE LIII. · THE BASILICA, POMPEII

435

new provinces to the empire seeks first of all to enrich or glorify himself. The knight lives for his money-bags, the luxurious senator for his fish-ponds, his garden, and his palace. The mob of Rome, degenerate heir of a great tradition, while still dispensing the highest honours of State, claims no other price for its favours than a full meal and a happy day in the circus. If there are any exceptions to the general self-seeking they are to be found in Cato, a fantastic idealist, and in Cicero, the only man of his day who, without overstepping the bounds of the constitution, can be said to have had a policy.

Last Era of the Republic

Looking at the Roman world as it appeared in the years following Sulla's death, we find the Republic threatened by perils of every kind, within and without. Spain is in open revolt, Macedonia is assailed by the wild tribes on its borders, Mithradates is arming for a new struggle, and the sea swarms with pirates, who pursue their depredations unchecked, paralysing commerce and terrorizing the whole seaboard of the Mediterranean. In Italy itself there are elements of disorder, which will presently culminate in the desperate enterprise of Catiline, and for two years all the energies of the government are employed in putting down a slave insurrection. When these troubles have been surmounted we pass on to the coalition known as the First Triumvirate, and the career of Caesar in Gaul, arriving then at the final and tremendous catastrophe which is to decide the fate of the Roman world. But before we proceed to the detailed narrative of these great events it will be well to bestow a glance on some of the leading features in this the last era in the history of Republican Rome. At first sight it would appear to be a wild and mad age, marked by nothing so much as its transcendent and enormous depravity. We need not credit the monstrous libels which were heaped upon Caesar himself, the greatest figure in history, which were eagerly caught up by the gossip-mongers of the Empire; but, making all deductions, enough remains to

435

show that the great general and statesman ranks very low in the scale of private morality. Cicero himself, the pattern of public and private virtue, habitually uses language which would hardly be tolerated in the loosest society of modern times. The revelations which were made after the acquittal of Clodius show a degree of shameless profligacy almost surpassing belief. Indeed, we want no further proof of the callous indifference to character which prevailed in the highest circles in Rome than the fact that a miscreant like Catiline could take his place unrebuked in the Senate, could be heard with respect, or at least with tolerance, on the greatest public questions, and could presume to offer himself as a candidate for the consulship.

DECAY OF THE NATIONAL CHARACTER

We have spoken in a former chapter of the gradual decay which had undermined the three corner-stones of the ancient Roman polity, its piety, its domestic purity, and its devotion to rural pursuits. That process of internal destruction had now reached its climax. Sulla and Caesar, the foremost men of their time, were avowed atheists, yet their unbelief did not save them from lapsing at times into the most childish superstition. Pontiff and augur laughed in their sleeves at the forms of State religion as a solemn farce in which no educated man could believe, useful only as a means of working on the mind of the vulgar. It may be argued that this degradation of a barren and tedious ritual was little to be regretted, bringing gain rather than loss to the spiritual life of the nation. But the habitual observance of religious forms which have become a hollow mockery argues an unwholesome state of mind. Accordingly we find the same want of reverence infecting every relation of public and private life among the Romans of the later Republic. Patriotism has become a mere empty name, or survives as a living reality only in a chosen few. The marriage tie, which for many centuries had been invested with peculiar sanctity, is formed or dissolved with the most cynical levity. The land, once the kindly nurse of Roman

436

manhood, is turned into a desert, or encumbered by luxurious palaces, the home of riotous indulgence. To complete the tale of the nation's decadence we have but to refer to its ferocious cruelty and indifference to human suffering. A traveller passing along the road between Capua and Rome after the suppression of the slave revolt (73–71 B.C.) could have counted six thousand blackening corpses nailed to the cross and planted at intervals along the roadside, as a warning to the millions who toiled in darkness to hold up the fabric of society. The savage sports of the arena, that blackest reproach of the Roman name, had now become a national pastime, and great nobles and high-born ladies looked on with complacency while men and beasts were slaughtered by hundreds to make a festival for the licentious mob.

A Brilliant Age

If, then, we confined ourselves to this side of the picture we should have to conclude that the Romans in the age of Cicero were brutal, callous, and depraved, and that the light of the nation had set for ever. But in drawing this conclusion we should be straying very far from the truth. There is an inconsistency in human nature which allows the most contradictory qualities to exist side by side in the same people or the same individual. And, in fact, if we view the subject from another standpoint we shall find abundant materials for admiration and applause. What seemed an age of hopeless decadence will then appear rather an age of transition, in which great forces were at work, giving fair prospect of high achievement in the future. Indeed, it might be asserted that this was the greatest, or at any rate the most brilliant, age of Roman history. Certainly there is no period which exhibits so striking a variety of human interest. It is especially rich in manifold types of character, which have afforded a theme for poet, biographer, and historian and become a permanent possession to all the literatures of Europe. Here we can only afford room for a few of the most prominent figures in the long procession. There is first the lordly Pompeius, surrounded by the halo of his Eastern conquests, great soldier but unstable politician, haunted by the fleeting vision of a throne which he had not the resolution to convert into a reality. Less imposing, but higher and purer in character, is the fame of Sertorius, the dreamer, the mystic, whose noble energies were wasted in a hopeless struggle. Among the martyrs to lost causes and forsaken ideals there is no grander figure than that of Cato, though the gross pen of caricature portrays him as an incarnate anachronism, with a mind stubbornly closed against facts and a finger pointing to the past. Not far removed stands the gentle Cicero, and seems to smile at his sublime extravagance, while he holds out a hand as if to guide that too lofty spirit into a lower but more useful path. We may wonder at the strange vanity which still makes him a laughing-stock to schoolboys, but, judging his life as a whole, we can find few who have left a fairer or a brighter record. Passing over many of lesser note who have earned a place in that illustrious group, we come to the imperial image of Caesar, towering high above them all, the Roman Alexander, whose career forms a new epoch in the history of the world.

Development Abroad

It would be easy to swell the list with names scarcely less memorable, but those we have cited may serve as typical examples, and it will readily be admitted that the age which produced such men must have retained many potent germs of growth and development. And if we turn to the foreign history of this period we shall find ample proof that the Romans, even when they had forgotten how to govern themselves, still possessed in an eminent degree the art of conquering and governing others. The campaigns of Lucullus and Pompeius confirmed Rome in the possession of the richest part of her dominions, added new provinces of vast extent, and advanced the eastern frontier of the empire. The conquest of Gaul was an achievement unequalled in the previous history of the Republic, and of far-reaching influence upon the future of Europe.

LAST ERA OF THE REPUBLIC

LITERATURE: LUCRETIUS

Nor were the energies of the nation wholly absorbed in the extension of its material power. It is usual to speak of the Augustan era as the golden age of Roman literature, so far at least as concerns poetical creation and if Latin poetry reached its high-water mark in the songs of Horace and Virgil. The statement may be allowed to pass if we look only to perfection of form, though even here it requires considerable modification. But having regard to the deeper qualities of poetry, the prize must be given to the two great masters whose genius sheds lustre on the last days of the Republic. If we consider the work of Lucretius as a mere intellectual feat, we must admire his athletic vigour of mind and the skill which he displays in bending a stubborn subject to his purpose. If we regard him as a moral teacher we may pay homage to the grandeur of that Stoic [1] soul, who traversed the whole compass of the universe and brought back the old dragon of superstition bound captive to his car. We may exult in the force of his satire, far subtler and more searching than that of Juvenal, which plays like lightning round the lowest depths of human folly and ignorance. Or, confining ourselves to a strictly poetical standpoint, we shall find that he satisfies the test here also, by the power of his imagination, the quick play of his fancy, his keen eye for every natural beauty, and the rich melody of his verse, which alone in Latin poetry emulates the free, bounding movement of the Homeric hexameter.

CATULLUS

Catullus, in his shorter poems, on which his fame chiefly rests, strikes a softer and more tender note. After listening in awe to the lofty 'Dorian mood' of Lucretius we hear the melting cadence which floated round the shores of Ionia when Greece was still young. He is the poet of love and joy, whose nimble and airy verse moves as blithely as the winged Cupids

---

[1] Lucretius was an avowed disciple of Epicurus, but in mind and temper he was a true Stoic.

on the frescoes of Pompeii. We cannot but marvel at the plastic touch which moulded into such delicate forms of beauty the stern language of warriors, lawgivers, and statesmen. He has all the grace and charm which we find in the choicest work of the Greek Anthology, with the racy flavour of the Italian soil, and an added witchery of his own. That the same age should have produced two poets so opposite in character, each supreme in his own sphere, is a singular proof how powerful was the creative energy which still lingered in the national mind.

CICERO'S PROSE

Among all the great masters of Latin prose—that " other harmony," as it is happily termed by Dryden—there are none to dispute the supreme excellence of Cicero. In the range and variety of his accomplishments and in the complete mastery of his instrument he stands above all other prose-writers, ancient or modern. In his hands the noble language of Latium became a perfect vehicle for the expression of every shade of thought and feeling, from the most familiar to the most exalted. As an orator he rivals the fame of Demosthenes, and as an interpreter between the mind of Greece and Rome he created a complete vocabulary of abstract terms, a gift of no mean value to the student of philosophy. His letters, extending over a period of more than twenty years, form in themselves a unique body of literature, which presents us with a full-length portrait of a most remarkable character, exhibits a rich variety of prose composition, and illustrates every aspect of contemporary life and manners. It should be observed, too, that the long series of his writings was not the product of lettered retirement, but the fruit of scanty leisure, snatched at rare intervals by a man who during most of his life was plunged in the turmoil of affairs.

LEPIDUS AND HIS REBELLION

We may now return to the main course of events, taking up our narrative from the death of Sulla. No sooner was the terror of that all-powerful presence removed than the strife of parties broke out again. Lepidus, who had been elected to the consulship by the influence of Pompeius, was a violent Marian, and began at once to agitate for the reversal of all Sulla's measures. He succeeded in carrying a new corn law, but his proposals to restore the tribunician power, to recall the exiles, and to reinstate the dispossessed landowners were frustrated. The old feud, however, was reopened, and noted Marians began to show their faces in Rome. Among these was Caesar, who after his breach with Sulla had retired from Italy, and had been leading a life of hazard and adventure in the province of Asia. Though his sympathies were wholly on the side of the democratic party, he held aloof from the designs of Lepidus, having no confidence in such a leader, and perceiving that the movement was premature. Pompeius, too, who had been warned by Sulla against the dangerous tendencies of Lepidus, withdrew his countenance from the demagogue and gave his whole support to the other consul, Catulus, who was a strong Optimate. But Lepidus, an obstinate and head-strong man, was only waiting for an opportunity to declare open war on the State, and presently the folly or blindness of the Senate gave him the chance which he wanted. Having been sent with his colleague Catulus to put down an insurrection in Etruria, where widespread distress had been caused by the Sullan confiscations, he kept his troops under arms after his year of office had expired, and dispatched one of his lieutenants, Marcus Brutus (father of the notorious Brutus), to raise the standard of revolt in Cisalpine Gaul. Then he sent to demand his re-election to the consulship and the cancelling of all Sulla's reforms, and as the Senate naturally refused compliance he broke up his camp and marched against Catulus, who was covering the approaches to Rome. The encounter took place under the very walls of the city, and resulted in the total defeat of Lepidus, who escaped to Sardinia, and died shortly afterwards. Meanwhile the movement in northern Italy had been put down by Pompeius, and Brutus, who had been taken prisoner, was put to death by his orders. The remnant of the

REPUBLICAN ROME

revolutionary army was conveyed by Perperna, one of the
Marian leaders, to Spain.

SERTORIUS IN SPAIN

The history of Rome during the last era of the Republic
resolves itself into a series of biographies. The personal note,
which is heard but faintly in grander and simpler times,
becomes louder and more insistent as we approach the final
collapse of the ancient Roman discipline. And we have now
to follow the career of one of Rome's noblest sons, who by the
sad exigence of the times was converted into an outlaw and
a rebel. The scene of his exploits was that great peninsula
whose very atmosphere seems charged with high hopes and
daring enterprises. It was in Spain that Hamilcar thought
to rebuild the fortunes of his country, brought low by the
untoward issue of the First Punic War, and in Spain the great
Scipio had gathered his earliest laurels. To Spain, therefore,
Sertorius looked as a new field of enterprise after the triumph
of Sulla and the overthrow of the Marians in Italy. Before,
however, he had time to make good his footing he was driven
out by Sulla's lieutenants, and compelled to seek refuge on
the opposite shores of Africa. For one brief moment his
thoughts turned toward the Islands of the Blest,[1] the fabled
land of innocence and peace, which in the last agony of the
civil war drew from the young Horace a rare strain of in-
spiration ;[2] but, abandoning this wild dream, he landed in
Mauretania, and, joining the native tribes, who had rebelled
against their king, gained possession of the city of Tingis.[3]
While he was considering what should be his next step he
received an invitation from the Lusitanians, who were once
more in arms, to come over and be their leader, and he was not
slow to obey the call. His soldierly qualities and rare tact in
dealing with the natives soon won him a large following, and
before long he was joined by numbers of the banished Marians.
His design was to make his position so strong that he might
be able to dictate terms to the dominant party in Rome. He

[1] The Canary Islands. [2] *Epodes*, xvi. 41 *sqq.* [3] Tangier.

442

organized a large military force, trained, and equipped after the Roman fashion, surrounded himself with a bodyguard of Spanish nobles, and set up a little Senate of his own, chosen from the most distinguished of the refugees, which gave a semblance of constitutional sanction to his proceedings. His conduct toward the native Spaniards showed a true statesman-like spirit, recalling the best features in the Gracchan legislation, and anticipating the policy which was pursued by the most enlightened of the emperors. His aim was to Romanize Spain, and with this purpose he founded a sort of university at Osca,[1] where Spanish children of noble family were taught the Latin and Greek tongues, wore the Roman dress, and were trained to become citizens of a larger Rome. Nor did he disdain humbler expedients in his efforts to gain the attachment of the simple and credulous natives. A white fawn which he had received as a present from some hunters was trained to follow his footsteps and feed from his hand, and he encouraged the belief that the creature was a familiar spirit, which imparted to him the counsels of heaven when his own judgment was at fault.

Campaign against Sertorius

The Roman officers who held Spain for the government proved quite unequal to cope with Sertorius, and his progress grew so alarming that Quintus Caecilius Metellus, one of the ablest of the Senate's generals, was sent to take the command in Farther Spain (80 B.C.). He gained some successes, and carried his arms into Lusitania, the original seat of the revolt, but his slow and cumbrous tactics made him no match for the agile Sertorius, whose forces gathered and dispersed like the storm-cloud, now melting out of view as the pursuit became hotter, and now mustering in tens of thousands to harass the march of the heavy Roman columns. After two years of inconclusive fighting it was found necessary to reinforce the army of Metellus, and Pompeius, whose credit had been raised by his services in the contest with Lepidus, was invested with

[1] Huesca, in Aragon.

443

proconsular powers in Hither Spain and commissioned to carry on the war in concert with Metellus. The appointment was a direct violation of Sulla's arrangements, for Pompeius, who was then in his twenty-ninth year, had not even held the office of quaestor, which was the lowest step in the ladder of official promotion. The concession was, in fact, wrung from the Senate at the point of the sword, for Pompeius was at the head of a victorious army and the civil authority had no means of resisting his unauthorized demands. But the performance of the young proconsul, who brought with him forty thousand troops, fell far short of his reputation Sertorius who had meanwhile been reinforced by the arrival of Perperna, laughed at the boastful language of Sulla's pupil, frustrated his attempt to raise the siege of Lauron, and in the following year taught him a severe lesson when he ventured to engage the enemy single-handed on the Sucro Pompeius nearly paid for his presumption with his life ; his horse, with its sumptuous furniture, was taken by the Sertorians, and he himself was swept from the field among his flying troops, until he fell into the arms of Metellus, who was hastening to his relief. " If the old woman had not come up," remarked Sertorius, " I would have given this boy such a whipping that he would have been glad to go back to Rome."

PRETENSIONS OF SERTORIUS

Notwithstanding some minor mishaps, which fell chiefly on his subordinates, Sertorius steadily gained ground, and after five years of fighting the Romans seemed on the point of being thrust out of Spain. Pompeius was compelled to winter in southern Gaul, and from there he sent an urgent dispatch to the Senate, describing the woeful condition of his troops, and hinting that unless he obtained speedy relief the war would be transferred to Italy. The prospect, indeed, was sufficiently disquieting, for Sertorius, inspired, perhaps, by the example of Sulla, was beginning to act as if his country's fate rested in his own hands. His relations with the great pirate state of Cilicia gave him command of the sea, and he entered into a formal treaty with Mithradates, settling, in grand imperial style, the limits which were to be assigned to that potentate's dominions when the war should have been carried to a successful issue. Mithradates, on his part, agreed to support the rebel cause with money and ships, and Marcus Marius, one of the Roman refugees, was sent to represent the interests of Sertorius in Asia.

SERTORIUS ASSASSINATED

Alarmed by the attitude of Sertorius, and urged to vigorous action by Lucullus, one of the consuls for the year (74 B.C.), who desired to keep Pompeius occupied in Spain, the Senate at last consented to send the required reinforcements. The war was now resumed with increased bitterness on both sides, and from this time the fortunes of Sertorius took a turn for the worse. His Spanish allies began to fall away, and he was embarrassed by the disloyalty and the petty jealousies of the Romans who formed his staff. His temper, naturally gentle and humane, became hardened under the pressure of misfortune, and he was betrayed into some acts of impolitic severity,[1] which still further weakened his influence among the native Spaniards. Even his personal habits deteriorated as the shadows grew darker around him, and he sought to drown his cares in wine and loose indulgence. He was now a marked man, with a price on his head, for Pompeius, little to his credit, had offered a reward for his assassination. But the deed of blood which cut short his career was prompted by envy, and not by avarice. Perperna had always been jealous of his leader, whom he despised for his humble birth, and now that the star of Sertorius was on the wane he resolved, like Fimbria, to clear the way for his own promotion by murder. The unsuspecting Sertorius was invited to a banquet, and at a given signal Perperna and his fellow-conspirators set upon him and stabbed him to death with their daggers (72 B.C.).

---

[1] According to Plutarch (*Sertorius*, c. 25), he put to death the Spanish children who were being educated at Osca, an act of senseless barbarity which is hardly to be credited.

445

It was not long before the assassin received the proper reward
of his perfidy, for, having engaged the forces of Pompeius, he
was defeated and made prisoner, and, after stooping to the
basest supplication, was put to death.

The Gladiators

Before the conclusion of the Spanish war the Romans at
home were confronted by a peril which, arising in the lowest
depths of the population, for two years filled all Italy with
tumult and alarm. The passion for gladiatorial shows
attained a great height in the last age of the Republic, and
the provision of such exhibitions, organized on a lavish scale,
was a recognized means of courting popularity and paving
the way to political promotion. The gladiators were mostly
captives taken in war, chosen for their physical strength and
courage, and exercised in their dreadful art under the eye of a
professional trainer. They were kept on a strict diet, had their
own peculiar code of honour, and practised a sort of ascetic
discipline, calculated to harden body and mind against fatigue,
pain, and danger. Not unfrequently a troop of these bravoes
was maintained in the service of some powerful noble, to be
employed, like prize-fighters at an election riot, in times of
political disturbance. Those destined for the more ordinary
purpose lived apart in barracks, which were called schools,
and most of these seminaries were to be found in Campania,
where the pastime had first been introduced by the gross and
savage Etruscans. As yet no permanent buildings had been
erected for the combats of gladiators, for the colossal stone
amphitheatres that we know belong to the times of the
Empire.

War of the Gladiators

Just after the outbreak of the second [1] war with Mithradates, when the best troops of the Republic were absent on
foreign service, a band of eighty gladiators broke out of their

[1] See p. 423, and below, p. 458.

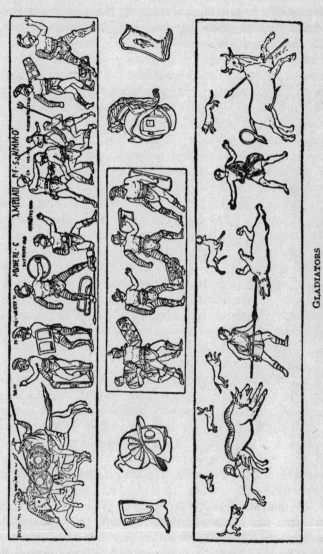

GLADIATORS

From a stucco relief at Pompeii

confinement in Capua, and, arming themselves with spits and knives stolen from a tavern, made for the open country. They had not gone far when they met and plundered a wagon laden with the weapons of their craft, and, having thus equipped themselves, they sought a temporary refuge in the crater of Vesuvius, then an extinct volcano. The leader of the band was a Thracian named Spartacus, a man of great courage and strength, who in the lowest depths of degradation had preserved many high and heroic qualities. Having scattered the first hasty levy which was sent against them, the gladiators arrayed themselves in complete warlike panoply, stripped from the slain, and as their numbers were daily increasing they now ventured to take the field. The praetor Claudius Pulcher, who was sent against them from Rome with three thousand men, suffered a total defeat, and the insurgents, who by this time formed a regular army, overran Campania and penetrated into Apulia, where they found many recruits among the wild upland shepherds. A second victory gained over a Roman praetor spread their fame throughout the peninsula, and in the course of the winter Spartacus found himself at the head of seventy thousand men, a mingled host of Thracians, Gauls, and Germans. But the command was now disputed by another leader, Crixus, and this division of authority proved in the end fatal to the enterprise.

For the present, however, all Italy lay at the mercy of the marauders, who roved up and down the country, sacking cities, and retaliating their wrongs by fearful outrages on the persons of their captives. At the beginning of the following year the position was so serious that both consuls were sent to take the field. Crixus was beaten and slain in the district of Mount Garganus, but when the consuls tried to bar the road of Spartacus, who was on his way to the north, they sustained an ignominious defeat. In spite of these repeated victories, Spartacus was in no wise deceived as to the ultimate issue of the contest. He well knew that his rude bands must in the end be crushed by the overwhelming power of the government, and his design was to force the passes of the Alps and disband

448

his army as soon as he was beyond the reach of pursuit. But the fierce hordes who followed him so readily to battle would not listen to these prudent counsels, preferring a brief period of rapine and plunder to the distant prospect of returning to their homes. Spartacus, accordingly, was compelled to remain in Italy, and his predictions were soon to be justified. The war had now lasted for two years, and the Senate, disgusted with the incompetence of its own officers, placed the conduct of the ensuing campaign in the hands of Marcus Crassus (71 B.C.), who had given signal proof of his capacity at the great battle of the Colline Gate. Crassus showed himself to be fully worthy of his charge. By a timely act of severity he inspired his troops with a wholesome terror of their commander, and then advanced against Spartacus, whom he compelled to draw back to the southern extremity of Italy. Spartacus now thought of carrying the war into Sicily, and made a bargain with the captains of a pirate fleet which was cruising off the coast to convey his troops across the strait. But the pirates took the price and sailed away without performing the service. Thus baffled in his intention, Spartacus turned fiercely on his pursuer, broke through the lines which Crassus had drawn across the isthmus, and soon afterwards gained another victory over one of the Roman general's lieutenants. But his forces were weakened by division, and after the destruction of one large contingent, which was attacked separately and cut to pieces by Crassus, he fell back into Apulia and prepared for a last desperate stand. The struggle was long and obstinate, but the victory remained with the Romans, and Spartacus himself was slain, after fighting like a hero. Five thousand of the insurgents who fled from the battlefield succeeded in making their way into northern Italy, but they fell into the hands of Pompeius, who was then on his return from Spain, and were cut off to a man. It was characteristic of Pompeius that on the strength of this easy exploit he set down to his own credit the whole honours of the campaign, declaring that Crassus, indeed, had routed the slaves, but that he himself had plucked up the war by the roots.

REPUBLICAN ROME

Pompeius demands the Consulship

In spite, however, of this affront, the two men, so different
in mind and temper, were soon drawn together in a close,
though brief, alliance. Pompeius required lands for his soldiers,
claimed a triumph for his successes in Spain, and demanded
election to the consulship. His eye had long since been turned
to the East, and he viewed with envy the laurels of Lucullus,
who was now at the height of his victorious career in Asia.
Legally his position was quite untenable, for he was not yet
qualified by age to stand for the consulship, nor had he held
any of the intermediate offices. But his whole career had
been irregular, and he who had triumphed at twenty-four and
held proconsular rank for six years in succession might well
think lightly of the rules which had so often been violated
in his person. Crassus also, though for very different reasons,
was in a somewhat equivocal position. Though a great noble
and a member of the famous Licinian house, his immense
financial transactions connected him rather with the Equestrian
Order. Though an able general, he had gained all his victories
in civil war or in conflict with revolted slaves, and could
not build any great hopes on distinctions so invidious as
these.

Sulla's Work Undone

If the nobles had been wise they would have thrown their
scruples overboard and attached Pompeius firmly to their
cause by a frank concession of his claims. But they were
jealous and suspicious, and while they were wavering the
opportunity was lost. Ever since the death of Sulla the
popular leaders had been working for the restoration of their
defeated and degraded party. But the ill-advised attempt
of Lepidus and its speedy overthrow had strengthened the
hands of the Senate, and as yet little progress had been made.
They now turned to the two victorious generals whose armies
lay encamped before the walls of Rome, and offered to satisfy
all their demands on condition that they would accept the

democratic programme. The Knights, who had suffered equally with the commons under the oppressions of Sulla, became parties to the compact, and the moneyed interest, the populace, and the military power were thus united in an overwhelming coalition. The Senate, left helpless and alone, had no means of resistance, and Pompeius and Crassus, elected by the unanimous voice of the people, took their seats on the curule chairs as consuls for the ensuing year (70 B.C.). They had now to fulfil their part of the agreement, which pledged them to a series of reactionary measures reversing the whole system which had been set up by Sulla The tribunes received back all their old rights, the most important of which was the power of initiating legislation. The jury-courts, which for ten years had been a monopoly of the Senate, were reconstructed on a new plan, which gave the preponderance to the great financiers and men of business. Henceforth only a third of the jurors was to consist of senators, the other two-thirds being chosen equally from the Knights and the tribunes of the treasury,[1] who formed an order by themselves, taking rank just below the Knights. At the same time the capitalists of the Equestrian Order recovered their cherished privilege of collecting the taxes in Asia, which had been given them by Caius Gracchus and taken away by Sulla. Lastly, the censorship, originally created as the shield of patrician privilege, and lately abolished as obsolete in Sulla's dictatorship, was now reinstated under the auspices of the popular leaders, and used as a means for completing the discomfiture of their opponents. The new censors proved ready instruments in the hands of those to whom they owed their promotion, and in making their revision of the Senate they struck the names of seventy-four members off the list.

A Withered Constitution

So the wheel had turned again, and within ten years from his death the work of Sulla was almost completely undone. But if anyone was so simple as to imagine that popular

---

[1] *Tribuni aerarii.* The exact meaning of the term has been much disputed.

government had been restored he was greatly deceived. There were still popular leaders, who raised the old party cries, but there was, properly speaking, no people—unless we can apply that name to the needy rabble who shouted at the games and hung like a leech on the exchequer. Rome had, in fact, outgrown her constitution, and after all the fostering and pruning of the last century the ancient civic government stood like a withered trunk waiting for the axe which was to hew it down. The liberal policy of expansion which had made Rome great had long since been abandoned, and, indeed, there was no method of adjustment which could have been successfully applied to adapt the existing constitutional machinery to the new needs of the time.

CICERO

There was, however, one man, of the highest character and ability, who clung fast to the old forms and centred all his hopes for the future in a revived and regenerated Republic. This was Marcus Tullius Cicero, of whose general character and policy we shall speak more in detail when we come to his consulship. Born at Arpinum, in the old Volscian land, in 106 B.C., he was of the same age as Pompeius, and was old enough to have witnessed the Cimbric triumph of his illustrious fellow-townsman, Caius Marius. Like Marius, too, he belonged to the class of New Men, whose efforts to enter the arena of public life were viewed with distrust and suspicion by the privileged order of nobles. There were two ways in which such a man might hope to break down the barriers of class prejudice and rise to the highest offices in the State. He might command attention by eminent military services, or, if he were a man of high forensic ability, he might gain a large following by successful pleading in the law-courts.[1] Being a man of peace, and gifted with extraordinary eloquence, Cicero naturally chose the latter course, and at the time which we have reached he had outstripped all competitors at the

[1] It must be observed that the services of a pleader were at this time, and for long afterwards, given gratuitously.

452

LAST ERA OF THE REPUBLIC

Roman bar, with the single exception of Hortensius, the great orator of the senatorial faction.

CICERO AND VERRES

As a member of the middle class, whose core and centre lay in the Equestrian Order, Cicero was deeply interested in the proposed reform of the jury-courts The most notorious abuse of the time was the misconduct of the provincial governors, and as long as these high-born offenders were tried by men of their own order there could be no hope of redress. The cause of reform received a new impulse from the revelations which came out at the trial of Verres (70 B.C.), who had been guilty of the most atrocious cruelty and extortion in the province of Sicily. Cicero was the leading counsel for the prosecution, and the evidence was so clear that Hortensius, who conducted the defence, threw up his brief, and Verres retired into exile. Cicero afterwards published the material which he had collected for this occasion, and the five speeches against Verres exhibit a complete picture of provincial misgovernment in its very worst aspect.

POMPEIUS IN RETIREMENT

There were certain points in Sulla's legislation which it was deemed either unwise or unsafe to meddle with.   The soundness of his reforms in the penal code was generally acknowledged, and these, accordingly, remained untouched.   Both Pompeius and Crassus, also, had been deeply implicated in the violent acts of confiscation and bloodshed which followed the civil war, so that they could not without danger to themselves offer any redress to those who had been robbed of their property or remove the ban which had been placed on the children of the proscribed. The two consuls, who had been brought together by a common ambition, drifted farther and farther apart as their year of office wore away, and an open rupture, threatening disastrous consequences to the State, was only averted by the intercession of the democratic leaders. Crassus set the example by disbanding his troops, which had been kept all the time under arms, and Pompeius had no alternative but to follow his lead. Pompeius, whose talents were exclusively military, was unfitted for the peaceful contests of the Forum and the Senate, and he was totally destitute of those graces and accomplishments by which Caesar was enabled to retain his hold on the popular affections. Accordingly, after laying down his consulship, he withdrew himself from the public gaze and lived in retirement, veiling his impatience under a haughty reserve, until an opportunity occurred which gave new lustre to his reputation and lifted him to a towering pre-eminence among his fellow-citizens.

THE CILICIAN PIRATES

For many years the whole Mediterranean seaboard had been terrorized by the daring depredations of pirates, who, issuing from their rocky strongholds in Cilicia, pursued their lawless trade from the coasts of Palestine to the Straits of Gibraltar. It was no ordinary piracy, carried on by stealth and hiding its head in terror at the approach of a single armed vessel, but an extensive organization had grown up, assuming the dignity of a sovereign state, and concluding regular treaties with great potentates on the mainland. Sertorius, when at the height of his power, thought it not beneath his dignity to solicit the aid of the freebooters, they are found commanding the passage to Sicily when Spartacus is hemmed in by the army of Crassus, and we shall see them in alliance with Mithradates when we come to speak of his last struggle with Rome. Their vessels numbered a thousand, and were equipped, in a foppery of military pride, with sails dyed in Tyrian purple and silver-plated oars. Famous cities were stormed and sacked, or forced to pay blackmail, and the very sanctuaries of the gods had to yield their treasures to the robbers. Even Italy was not safe from their incursions. They burnt a Roman fleet which was riding in the harbour of Ostia, carried off two praetors who were on the way to their provinces, with their fasces and lictors, and kidnapped the travellers who passed to and fro along the Appian Way. Meanwhile commerce was at a

454

standstill, provisions rose alarmingly in price, and the capital was threatened with famine

THE GABINIAN LAW

For nearly twenty years this strange tyranny of the sea had been spreading and growing, until it reached the vast dimensions which have been briefly described. It may well be believed that the pirates could not have risen to such power unless there had been a certain public favour on their side. They were, in fact, highly popular, being generous and free-handed outlaws, and the professed enemies of the Romans, who had set the world a fine example of lawless outrage. Several attempts had been made to deal with the evil, and Metellus,[1] who had been consul in the year after Pompeius, was now engaged in a war of extermination against the Cretans, with whom the pirates were in alliance (68 B.C.). But the mischief grew rather than abated, and meanwhile the mob of Rome was clamouring for bread. Finally, in the third year after the retirement of Pompeius the tribune Gabinius came forward with a proposal that one man should be invested with the supreme command against the marauders, that his powers should extend over the whole Mediterranean and over all the coast districts for fifty miles inland, and that he should be authorized to appoint twenty-five officers, with praetorian rank, to act under him. A fleet of five hundred vessels and an immense military force were to be placed at his disposal, and he was empowered to levy contributions in all the provinces for the support of the war. No man was mentioned, but it was clearly understood that the new office, so formidable in aspect, was designed for Pompeius. The senators stood out against the proposal of the audacious tribune, which brought before their fancy the hateful image of monarchy. But they were powerless to resist the tide of popular enthusiasm. Pompeius was the hero of the hour, and in spite of the protests of Catulus the bill was carried.

[1] Afterwards surnamed Creticus; to be distinguished from the Metellus who fought against Sertorius.

REPUBLICAN ROME

The Pirates Put Down

Pompeius used his great powers with equal energy and discretion. He divided the whole Mediterranean into thirteen districts, assigning a separate command and fleet to each, with directions that the pirates should be chased and captured wherever they were found. So efficiently were his orders carried out that before six weeks had elapsed not a pirate vessel was to be seen in the western waters of the great inland sea. Then Pompeius followed the hurrying remnant of the robbers to their headquarters in Cilicia, drove their vessels ashore, and, landing his troops, stormed and captured their strongholds one after another. When all opposition had ceased the surviving pirates were settled with their families in various cities of Asia, Greece, and Italy, and encouraged to begin life anew as peaceful and industrious citizens.

Pompeius and Metellus

A space of but three months had sufficed for this achievement. By a series of rapid and skilful operations Pompeius had dispelled the terror which lurked in every creek and bay of the Mediterranean The merchant might resume his business, the noble in his seaside villa could sleep secure, and the multitude of Rome had bread. It is to be regretted that Pompeius should have stooped from the height of success to an unworthy display of his arbitrary temper. The Cretans, hard pressed by Metellus, who was determined to give them a severe lesson, applied to Pompeius, begging him to interpose his authority, and Pompeius, as his superior officer, ordered Metellus at once to suspend hostilities. Metellus, who had received his commission before the appointment of Pompeius, refused obedience, and an armed collision between the two generals seemed to be imminent. Happily this danger was averted by a new turn of affairs, which opened up a boundless prospect to the great soldier and left Metellus to finish his work in Crete. To understand how this came about we must glance briefly at the course of events in Asia from the close of the First Mithradatic War.

LOWER ASIA

FOR CAMPAIGNS OF

LUCULLUS & POMPEIUS

THRACIA

PONTUS EUXINUS

COLCHIS

Phasis F.

Artaxata

ARMENIA

Tigranocerta

SOPHENE

Nisibis

MESOPOTAMIA

Euphrates F.

ARMENIA MINOR

Nicopolis

PONTUS

Cabeira

Themiscyra

Iris F.

Comana

Zela

Amisus

Halys F.

Sinope

PAPHLAGONIA

CAPPADOCIA

COMMAGENE

Comana

Halys F.

SYRIA

Antioch

Issus

Tarsus

Pompeiopolis (Soli)

Issus

COELE-SYRIA

PHOENICIA

Tyre

GALATIA

Sangarius F.

BITHYNIA

Nicomedia

Chalcedon

Bosporus

Byzantium

PROPONTIS

Cyzicus

Halys F.

LYCAONIA

Iconium

Tatta

ISAURIA

Coralis

CILICIA

Seleucia

Coracesium

CYPRUS

Salamis

PHRYGIA

PISIDIA

Aspendus

PAMPHYLIA

Pamphylium Mare

MYSIA

Pergamum

Mitylene

Lesbos

Hermus F.

Magnesia

Smyrna

Ephesus

Chios

Samos

Icaria

Abydus

Dardanus

Ilium Novum

Lampsacus

Lamnos

Thasos

Maeander F.

LYDIA

CARIA

Halicarnassus

LYCIA

Rhodus

Naxos

AEGAEUM MARE

CRETA

Carpathus

MARE INTERNUM

ROMAN MILES

0   50   100   150

LAST ERA OF THE REPUBLIC

Tigranes

At this time the greatest potentate in the East was Tigranes, king of Armenia, who for many years past had been pursuing a policy of aggression, and had greatly enlarged his dominions at the expense of the surrounding peoples. Toward the east his territories extended over a great part of Mesopotamia, which he had won from the Parthians, he had availed himself of the distracted state of Syria to annex most of what remained from the ancient Seleucid empire, and at the instigation of Mithradates, his father-in-law, he invaded Cappadocia and carved himself a large portion out of this protected district. In the true style of an Oriental despot he transported a vast multitude from the conquered cities to form the population of a new capital, which he built in Upper Mesopotamia, and named after himself Tigranocerta. Here he established himself in royal state, exacting the obsequious homage of subject princes and assuming the proud title of King of Kings. How frail were the foundations of his power was presently to be seen, when his slavish hordes were matched against the free legions of the Republic.

Mithradates seeks a Quarrel

But the attention of the Romans was first called to Mithradates, who seized the opportunity while Sertorius was at the height of his fortunes to take up his quarrel afresh with his old enemies (74 B.C.). The centre of his power had been left untouched by the treaty which concluded his first encounter with Rome, and he had employed the intervening years in developing his resources and building up a coalition which on the surface looked very formidable. The kingdom of Bosporus was held for him by his son Macares, he had established his influence over the warlike tribes on the northern and eastern coasts of the Euxine, and he was in alliance with Sertorius, with the Thracians, and with the pirates of Cilicia. The Romans, he now thought, had already enough to do, and would be unable to act with effect if he struck boldly and at once. For

457

more than ten years Macedonia had been continually exposed
to the incursions of the neighbouring Thracian and Celtic
tribes, and as yet the generals of Rome had been unable to
secure the borders of that province. The whole Mediterranean
was held in fee by the pirates. Pompeius and Metellus, with
the flower of the Roman soldiery, were fighting in Spain.
With three wars on their hands, how could the Romans
expect to cope successfully with the armies of the great Pontic
king ?

Second Mithradatic War

A pretext for hostilities was not wanting. The last king of
Bithynia, Nicomedes III, had recently died, and had left a
will bequeathing his kingdom to the Romans. Taking up the
cause of the disappointed heir, Mithradates invaded Bithynia,
where he was welcomed by the inhabitants, who were groan-
ing under the oppressions of the Roman tax-gatherers. The
Senate, apprised of his intentions, had sent both consuls of the
year to oppose him, and Marcus Cotta, who held the command
in Bithynia, received the first shock of the invasion. Cotta,
a feeble and incompetent general, was completely worsted, and
compelled to seek refuge behind the walls of Chalcedon. But
Mithradates soon found himself confronted by a far abler man.
This was Lucius Lucullus, whose services under Sulla have
already been mentioned. He had been appointed to the province of Cilicia, and when he heard of his colleague's distress
he advanced to his support. On the approach of Lucullus
Mithradates shifted his position to Cyzicus, hoping to take
that important city by surprise. Failing in this attempt, he
laid formal siege to the place, but presently found himself
blockaded by Lucullus, who had followed his movements and
had encamped in the rear of the royal army, cutting off its communications with the mainland. Winter was now approaching,
and the vast multitude serving under Mithradates soon began
to suffer from famine. The king's siege-engines were destroyed
by a tempest, the garrison, encouraged by the presence of
Lucullus, resisted all assaults, and at last Mithradates, whose

troops were perishing by thousands, was forced to retire. The greater part of his army was cut off by Lucullus on its retreat, and the king himself, who had fled by sea, escaped with a single vessel to Sinope. Lucullus, taking to the sea, crowned his success by the capture of thirteen great war-vessels which were cruising in the Aegaean.

THE KING IN FLIGHT

The rest of the year was passed in the occupation of Pontus, and in forming the siege of the fortified cities which still held out for Mithradates. In the following spring Lucullus marched into the interior, and came up with the king, who had mean-while got together a new army, at Cabira, on the frontiers of Pontus and Armenia. After losing the greater part of his cavalry, which was destroyed in attempting to intercept a Roman foraging party, Mithradates determined to retire. While he was making his arrangements for an orderly retreat, however, his troops, seized with a sudden panic, fled in wild disorder, and but for the negligence of the Roman soldiers, who lingered to secure the booty, the whole army would have been cut off to a man. Mithradates himself narrowly escaped capture, and sought refuge in the kingdom of his son-in-law Tigranes, who received him coldly, and assigned him a place of residence in an unhealthy district, where he was kept as a State prisoner for the next two years.

LUCULLUS AND THE DEBTORS

After the second defeat of Mithradates Lucullus occupied himself with completing the conquest of Pontus and in regulating the affairs of the Roman province, which were in great disorder. The source of the mischief was the heavy war-indemnity imposed by Sulla. The State debtors, compelled to borrow money at usurious interest, had increased their obligations to six times the original amount, and many of them, to meet the claims of their merciless creditors, were reduced to selling their sons and daughters. By lowering the rate of interest and cancelling a large portion of the arrears

459

Lucullus saved the province from imminent bankruptcy and earned the name of a benefactor in all the cities of western Asia. But his high-handed proceedings caused a loud outcry among the moneylenders, which was taken up by the whole Equestrian Order, and helped to swell the ill-feeling which was slowly gathering against him in Rome. Heedless of the unpopularity which he was incurring, Lucullus now prepared for a bold enterprise, which, though it was crowned with brilliant success, gave a new handle to his political opponents. He felt that the position of the Romans in Asia would never be secure as long as the overgrown power of Tigranes hung threatening on the borders of the province. His commission, indeed, only empowered him to make war on Mithradates, but as that monarch was now under the protection of Tigranes he had a fair pretext for extending his operations to Armenia.

TIGRANES INTERFERES

The fortunes of the king of Pontus seemed to be broken beyond hope of repair. He was a fugitive, without a foot of land to call his own, dependent for the means of living on the grudging bounty of his son-in-law; and his own son Macares, whom he had appointed viceroy in the kingdom of Bosporus, had recently sent a crown of gold to Lucullus, with a humble petition to be numbered among the friends and allies of Rome. But at the very moment when his prospects seemed at the darkest he received a letter from Tigranes, written in terms of the warmest affection, and inviting him to take up his residence at the Armenian court. Tigranes had been provoked to this step by the bold language of Appius Clodius, a brother-in-law of Lucullus, who had been sent to demand the surrender of Mithradates, and had carried out his commission with all the haughtiness of his race.[1] Enraged by the tone of the Roman envoy, which seemed to him mere insolence, Tigranes determined, when it was too late, to take up the cause of his father-in-law, and began to assemble

[1] Clodius is another spelling of Claudius, a famous patrician name.

a great army with the intention of invading the Roman province.

LUCULLUS INVADES ARMENIA

But his purpose was anticipated by the prompt action of Lucullus. With a picked force of twelve thousand infantry and three thousand horse, the Roman general advanced by rapid marches through the heart of Asia Minor, crossed the Euphrates, and pressed on toward the new capital of the Armenian kingdom (69 B.C.). Tigranes, whose aggressive designs were thus abruptly checked, at first refused to believe that the Romans had invaded his dominions, but being at length convinced of the unwelcome fact he sent out a strong force with orders to trample the audacious intruders under foot and bring Lucullus alive into his presence.[1] He was somewhat shaken when he learnt that his soldiers had been utterly beaten in the first encounter, and, retiring into the mountains, he gave orders for a general muster of troops from all parts of his kingdom. Before long a vast army, drawn from many nations, was assembled under his command, and, rejecting the counsel of Mithradates, who advised him to starve out the invader, he advanced to the relief of Tigranocerta, now held in close siege by the Romans.

DEFEAT OF TIGRANES

Plutarch, in a striking passage, compares the huge armies of the East, so imposing to the eye and so ineffective in the field, to the pompous harangues of the Greek Sophists, in which poverty of thought is mantled by the exuberance of a splendid diction.[2] The comparison is just, and goes to the very root of the difference between the Oriental and the Western character. Tigranes, moreover, like Xerxes and Antiochus before him, was now to learn how vast is the difference between men who fight for a principle and armed slaves who fight for

[1] So, at least, says Plutarch; but he seems to have been writing with one eye on the facts and the other on his master, Herodotus. See Herodotus, vii. 210.
[2] Plutarch, *Lucullus*, c. 7, and the remarkable parallel in Longinus, c. 7.

a master. Informed of the king's approach, Lucullus advanced
to meet him with two-thirds of his troops, leaving one of his
lieutenants to conduct the siege and check any movement in
his rear. When Tigranes saw the scanty numbers of the
Romans, amounting to hardly a twentieth part of his own
levies, he laughed, and said : " If they come as envoys they are
too many, if as soldiers they are too few." Lucullus directed
the chief weight of his attack on a squadron of heavy cavalry,
clothed in complete armour and many thousands strong, who
were the pride of the king's army. These heroes, commonly
believed to be invincible, did not even stand to receive the
charge of the Romans, but wheeled their horses and bore down
at full gallop on their own infantry, which was thrown into
confusion by this unexpected manoeuvre. The host of Tigranes
was thus totally demoralized, and Lucullus gained a brilliant
victory, almost without the loss of a man. The capitulation
of Tigranocerta followed immediately afterwards, and the
spoil was so plentiful that Lucullus was able to give a bounty
of eight hundred *denarii* (£33) to each of his men. The great
city, which had sprung up as if by magic at the word of a
despot, was dismantled by order of Lucullus, and all those who
had been forcibly settled there by Tigranes were sent back to
their homes.

Lucullus's Fortunes Change

Early in the following summer Lucullus marched into
northern Armenia, and gained a victory over the combined
forces of the two kings, who had been drawn into battle by a
threatened attack on Artaxata, the older capital of Armenia,
which lay within sight of Mount Ararat. But when he prepared to lay siege to the city, said to have been founded by
Hannibal, he was compelled by the murmurs of his weary
and mutinous troops to desist. Winter, which begins early in
those highland regions, was fast approaching, and the Romans
were appalled by the rigours of that terrible climate, which had
caused such severe suffering to Xenophon and his comrades
on their march to Trapezus. Lucullus accordingly retired

PLATE LIV. THE ROUND TEMPLE

PLATE LV. THE TIBUR TEMPLE   463

from Armenia, and led his troops back into northern Mesopotamia, where he effected the capture of Nisibis, an ancient
city whose fame goes back to the days of the Assyrians. This
was the extreme eastern limit of Lucullus's campaigns, and
with it he reached the turning-point of his fortunes. His
progress for six years had been chequered by no serious failure.
With resources which seemed ludicrously inadequate he had
scattered all the hosts of western Asia, he had conquered two
kingdoms, and was now meditating the invasion of Parthia.
But he had not understood the art, which the greatest commanders cannot afford to despise, of attaching his soldiers to
his fortunes by the tie of personal affection. His manners
were cold, haughty, and repellent, and though he had himself
accumulated immense riches he strictly repressed the rapacity
of his troops. The best part of his army was composed of the
veterans who had fought under Fimbria, and who had long
since earned their discharge, having served without inter-
ruption for nearly twenty years. The general discontent
found a voice in the young Publius Clodius, a brother of that
Appius whose bold language had affronted Tigranes. Having
been disappointed in his hopes of promotion, he had his own
private grudge against Lucullus, and his seditious speeches
still further inflamed the feelings of the soldiers. Meanwhile
the proconsul's enemies in Rome, who were numerous and
powerful, had long been agitating for his recall. His measures
for the relief of the distressed provincials had made him
detested by the whole body of the Knights, and as a great
noble, attached to the party of the Senate, he was cordially
disliked by the commons. In the year following the capture
of Nisibis (67 B.C.) these two parties, uniting their forces,
succeeded in passing a measure granting a discharge to the
Fimbrian veterans and superseding Lucullus in his command.
The news reached him in Pontus, where fresh disturbances
had broken out during his absence. Mithradates had once
more assumed the offensive, and had inflicted a severe defeat
on one of Lucullus's lieutenants, who had been left in charge
of the district. Lucullus had with difficulty induced his troops

to follow him, and though Mithradates retired on his approach
he was able to effect nothing further. His commission was
now formally cancelled, most of his men deserted him, and he
was compelled to look on idly while all his work was undone.
Mithradates recovered possession of his kingdom, and Tigranes
renewed his aggressions in Cappadocia.

THE MANILIAN LAW

It seemed as if Fortune had purposely ordered affairs to
prepare new honours and triumphs for her favourite Pompeius.
The commanders sent out to succeed Lucullus were mere men
of straw, whose duty was to fill up a gap while the popular
hero was engaged in putting down the pirates. That task
was completed toward the end of the year, and Pompeius,
having made his last arrangements, was preparing to leave
Cilicia when a new commission was placed in his hands invest-
ing him with the supreme command in the East and adding
extensive powers for settling the affairs of Asia. The bill
(66 B.C.), which was named after its proposer, the tribune
Manilius, was backed by all the eloquence of Cicero, and supported by Caesar, who was serving his own purposes by
creating a precedent for such vast and irregular promotion.
The Knights had an eye to their interests in Asia, the people
thought nothing too good for the idol of their worship, and in
the face of this powerful combination all the protests of the
nobles could effect nothing. It was indeed a strange pass to
which things had been brought, twelve years after the death
of Sulla. On one side was the disgraced and discredited
Senate, clamouring in noisy and impotent opposition; on
the other side were arrayed all the talents and all the free
institutions of the Republic, united to carry a measure which
raised one man, for the second time, to a position of despotic
power.

POMPEIUS AND LUCULLUS

Pompeius affected great reluctance to enter on his new
office, and complained that his countrymen would not allow

him to lead his own life in peace. But this hypocritical behaviour deceived no one, and disgusted even his friends. And he soon gave evidence of his arbitrary and ungenerous temper by annulling all the acts of Lucullus and belittling his achievements. The two famous generals met in the course of the same year, when Lucullus was on his way down to the coast and Pompeius was marching to meet Mithradates. The interview took place in Galatia, and ended in bitter recriminations, in which Lucullus at least succeeded in showing that he had the sharper wit; for when Pompeius indulged in some tasteless and clumsy ridicule of his exploits Lucullus replied with great keenness, likening Sulla's favourite to the carrion bird which feeds on the carcass when the battle has been lost and won. The taunts of Lucullus were substantially true, and his military career, though prematurely cut short, had smoothed the way for his successor.

END OF MITHRADATES' POWER

The power of Mithradates was now thoroughly broken, and after trying for some time to evade an encounter with the overwhelming forces of Pompeius he was driven to bay and defeated in western Armenia, at a place where the city of Nicopolis afterwards rose to commemorate the Roman victory. Stripped of his last means of defence, and disowned by Tigranes, he made his escape to Colchis, and from there he crossed a year later to the kingdom of Bosporus. Here the stubborn old despot, now nearing his seventieth year, but still untaught by experience, began to brood on new schemes of aggression, and conceived the design of raising the wild tribes of Scythia and Thrace and descending like a second Hannibal on Italy. But what might have been politic boldness in Hannibal was folly in Mithradates, and the Romans had nothing more to fear from this inveterate enemy, who had given so much work to her armies and engaged the attention of her ablest generals for a whole generation.

465

Tigranes Submits

In the same year which witnessed the overthrow of Mithradates (66 B.C.) Pompeius obtained a bloodless triumph over
the king of Armenia. Tigranes was just then engaged in a
war with his own son, of the same name, who had formed an
alliance with Phraates, king of Parthia, and had invaded his
father's kingdom at the head of a Parthian army. Repulsed
in an attempt on Artaxata, the young prince sought refuge in
the Roman camp, and Pompeius, taking the pretender with
him, advanced upon the Armenian capital. But Tigranes,
warned by his previous experience, had no intention of trying
issues again with the legions of Rome, and he hastened to
make submission. Mounting his horse, he rode up, with a
few attendants, to the camp of Pompeius, and asked for an
interview with the Roman general. The lictors ordered him
to dismount, and, immediately obeying, he was led on foot,
like a captive, into the presence of Pompeius. Then, taking
off his diadem, he laid it at the conqueror's feet, and prostrated
himself, as if imploring pardon for his misdeeds. He was
graciously received, and allowed to retain his title of king, but
all the territories which he had acquired by conquest were
taken from him, and he was compelled to pay an indemnity
of six thousand talents (£1,400,000). As a further humiliation
he was directed to assign an apanage in the heart of his kingdom
to his rebellious son ; but the young Tigranes, proving refractory, was soon after deprived of his principality, and reserved
for the fate which awaited all those who rebelled against the
authority of Rome.[1]

Campaign in the Caucasus

The next year was spent in a campaign against the Iberians
and Albanians, who dwelt on the southern side of the Caucasus,
between the Euxine and the Caspian. These wild people,
who had never owned submission to a conqueror, were in

---

[1] He was led in the procession of captives at the triumph of Pompeius, and
then put to death.

alliance with Mithradates, and the proximity of a Roman army, which threatened their independence, was in itself sufficient to excite their hostility. But their rude weapons and disorderly manner of fighting were no match for the valour and skill of the legions, and after two severe defeats they were glad to sue for peace. During the year Pompeius penetrated to the river Phasis, in the remote land of Colchis, renowned in Greek legend as the scene of Jason's exploits when he went in quest of the Golden Fleece. After these labours Pompeius retired into winter quarters at Amisus, a Greek city on the southern shores of the Euxine, where he lived in great pomp, receiving embassies, concluding treaties, and distributing favours in imperial style.

POMPEIUS IN JUDAEA

Pompeius had next to decide on a plan of action for the immediate future. The pursuit of Mithradates, which was urged on him by some advisers, was a barren labour, beset with difficulties and promising neither honour nor profit. But southward, beyond the Taurus, lay the favoured lands which had been left at his disposal by the submission of Tigranes. Thither, accordingly, he turned his steps, and entered Syria, where the remnants of the Seleucid kingdom were disputed between a number of petty princes, while the country was overrun by the Arabs of the surrounding desert. Pompeius restored order, and formally annexed Syria as a Roman province (64 B.C.). From this time we have to date those close relations between Rome and the Chosen People which are invested with such peculiar interest, and furnished so many dramatic incidents in the times of the Empire. Under the heroic leaders of the Asmonaean house Judaea had recovered a great part of its ancient glory, and asserted its independence against all the power of the Syrian kings. The later descendants of that family, however, had greatly fallen off in character, and two rival brothers, Aristobulus and Hyrcanus, were now quarrelling over their inheritance. Pompeius decided in favour of Hyrcanus, who was supported by the faction of the Pharisees,

and after some hesitation Aristobulus surrendered himself to
the Roman general. But the more desperate of the prince's
adherents shut themselves up in Jerusalem, and when the city
was stormed by the legions they made their last stand in the
great temple-fortress, where they were cut to pieces, mingling
their blood with the very fires of the altar. To the horror of
the pious Jews, Pompeius profaned by his presence the Holy
of Holies, and gazed on the mysterious cherubim whose wings
overshadowed the Ark. But he respected the Temple treasures,
and left the Jews in the enjoyment of their national worship
and customs, under the suzerainty of Rome.

DEATH OF MITHRADATES

While Pompeius was still occupied with the affairs of Judaea
he received tidings of the death of Mithradates (63 B.C.).
For two years the king had maintained himself in Bosporus,
where his first act had been to put to death his son Macares,
for his treasonable correspondence with Lucullus. He succeeded in getting together another army, but his subjects,
oppressed by taxation and harassed by the attacks of the
Roman fleet, grew more and more restive, city after city fell
away, and at last his favourite son Pharnaces turned against
him. His repeated cruelties had made him detested even
among his intimates, and finding himself utterly forsaken he
resolved to cut short his life by poison. But his iron constitution held out against the working of the drug, and the last
service had to be performed by the hand of a slave. His body,
hastily embalmed, was dispatched by Pharnaces as a peace-
offering to Pompeius.

POMPEIUS'S WORK IN THE EAST

In the splendid triumph which dazzled the eyes of his
countrymen two years later Pompeius vaunted himself before
the world as the conqueror of all western Asia, and an imposing list was paraded exhibiting the names of sixteen countries
alleged to have been added to the dominions of the Republic
by his arms. The hollowness of these pretensions is obvious,

468

and must have been patent to the acuter minds of his own time. By the general mass of his countrymen, however, Pompeius was regarded as a mighty conqueror, and his name was henceforth associated in the popular imagination with all the glamour and splendour of the East. His real merit lies in the wisdom and moderation he displayed in organizing the immense range of territory now finally brought under the influence of Rome. In carrying out this difficult task he showed himself to possess no small portion of that political genius which contributed at least as much as their warlike prowess to make the Romans masters of the ancient world. The system of graduated dependence which had proved so effective after the conquest of Italy was now adopted in the government of Asia. Along the eastern frontier, guarding the line of the Euphrates, a number of Arab chieftains held the outposts of the empire, as friends and allies of Rome. Special mention is made of a certain Sampsiceramus, whose chief claim to be remembered is that he furnished Cicero with a nickname for the lordly Pompeius. Armenia, where Tigranes was left in possession, had shrunk to its original dimensions, and was hemmed in on all sides by the territories of vassal princes, who held their position by favour of the Senate. Ariobarzanes might now sit secure on the throne of Cappadocia, from which he had so often been thrust by the terrible king of Pontus. In Galatia the interests of Rome were watched by Deiotarus, a native chieftain, who had done good service in the recent war, and who was now rewarded by a valuable accession of territory and by the title of king. Judaea, reduced to an inland district by the loss of its coast towns, was governed by Hyrcanus, who held the office of High Priest and paid tribute to Rome. Two new provinces were created by the annexation of Pontus and Syria, and the old province of Cilicia was reconstituted and enlarged. Above all Pompeius exerted himself to promote the growth of city life, and to heal the deep wounds left by the iron hand of Sulla. Many new cities were founded under his direction, and large privileges and immunities were granted to those already existing. The one questionable point in the policy of Pompeius

469

was his attitude toward Parthia, now the only power in the East from which the Romans had anything to fear. Phraates claimed that the Euphrates should be recognized as the frontier between the Roman and Parthian dominions, but his request was refused, and the relations of the two sovereign states were left in a position of uncertainty, which led to terrible mischief not many years later.

CAESAR AS DEMOCRAT

For the sake of exhibiting in one view the Roman conquests in the East we have anticipated the course of events by some years, and we must now resume the main thread of our narrative, from the time when Pompeius laid down his consulship. Two names, representing two totally opposite tendencies, claim our chief attention, those of Caesar and Cicero. Caius Julius Caesar was allied by birth with the oldest patrician blood of Rome, but his marriage connexions brought him into relation with the Marian party, and drew upon him, as we have seen, the animosity of Sulla. After the death of the dictator he returned to Rome, and soon gave proof of the policy which he intended to pursue. Gifted with extraordinary eloquence, which caused him to be hailed by Cicero as the greatest living master of the language, he employed his talents in the prosecution of high-born criminals, and thus became known as the declared opponent of the Sullan oligarchy. On the return of Pompeius from Spain he exerted himself to draw that leader to the side of the popular party, and to bring about the coalition which led to the restoration of the tribunate and the overthrow of Sulla's legislation. His graceful manners and great personal beauty made him the darling of the commons, and he sought every opportunity to exalt the merits of the great popular hero Marius. In two funeral orations, delivered in honour of Julia, the widow of Marius, and his own wife, Cornelia, daughter of Cinna, who died in the same year, he extolled the virtues of the democratic consuls to the skies, and on attaining the rank of aedile he exhibited the triumphal insignia of Marius, which Sulla had removed, in the Capitol, to the delight of the populace and the consternation of the nobles. The magnificence of his public shows [1] surpassed all that had yet been attempted in this form of display, and plunged him deeper and deeper into debt, until, as he said, he wanted several millions to be worth nothing. The fickle multitude would deny nothing to their new favourite. At a word from him they were ready to condemn to a frightful death an aged senator whom he had dragged up on a charge of participation in the murder of Saturninus, committed thirty-seven years back, and for whose benefit the ancient blood-tribunal had been set up again in all its grisly terrors.[2] And when, by his contrivance, they recovered the right of filling up vacancies in the priestly colleges, they elected him, the notorious profligate, the declared atheist, to the venerable office of Supreme Pontiff. Whether he had as yet conceived the design of setting himself above the constitution and destroying the Republic may well be doubted. Rather, perhaps, we should regard him as the final representative of a tendency which had been slowly gathering strength for many generations, as a man with a supreme genius for command, who was carried, first by irresistible impulse and then with deliberate intention, to the inevitable goal of monarchy.

CICERO

As Caesar, with a pedigree which went back to Olympus,[3] had, for his own purposes, adopted the radical programme, so, in this age of paradox, the constitutional principle found its staunchest champion in the humble knight of Arpinum. Cicero's character presents a highly complex and difficult problem, and the judgments passed upon him exhibit every degree of praise and blame, according to the taste and mental bias of his critics. In one aspect he may be regarded as an extreme example of the literary temperament, with its shrinking

---

[1] These exhibitions were the peculiar province of the aedile.

[2] The prosecution, however, was allowed to drop, and was doubtless never intended seriously.

[3] He traced his descent from the line of Alban kings, and through them to Aeneas, who was the son of Venus and the grandson of Jupiter.

timidity, due to an over-active imagination, its haunting self-consciousness, its anxious inward strivings, its agonies, its raptures, its despairs. His vanity is so colossal that it amounts almost to monomania. He contemplates the image of his own perfections with a sort of dainty and dandified virtuosity, like a self-conscious artist lost in rapt contemplation of a finished masterpiece, the work of his own hands. But Cicero, as we have already hinted, was very far from being a mere man of letters. He was a keen politician and a devoted patriot, ready to stake his life in the cause of that constitution of whose saving virtues he was convinced, in spite of all warnings and in defiance of all evidence. To the advocates of the 'blood and iron' theory of government he appears to be a mere political parasite, attaching himself to one faction or one party leader after another. But in fact he stood alone among his contemporaries as the exponent of a clear, a consistent, and at the same time a constitutional policy. In the centre of his ideal system stood the Senate—not that group of jaded voluptuaries and selfish place-hunters at whom he aimed the keenest shafts of his satire, but a new and reformed Senate, regenerated by the best blood of Italy and representing the highest traditions of Rome's ancient polity. With the Senate was to be associated the Equestrian Order, to which he himself belonged, and which had been largely recruited from the country districts by the tardy enfranchisement of the Italians. Last in order of dignity came the Free Parliament of Rome, purged of its baser parts, and renewed, like the Senate, by sound elements from outside. But there was yet another force with which he had to reckon, and it was here that the weakness of his whole system chiefly appeared. In the ultimate issue Rome's fate depended on the disposition of her armies and the power of the sword. Cicero was fully alive to this danger, and in his desire to provide a safeguard against lawless ambition he attached himself closely to the fortunes of Pompeius, in whom he hoped to find a loyal defender of constitutional right. How bitterly he was deceived will be seen in the sequel; and, indeed, his whole scheme of a model republic was based on self-delusion. But by his lifelong devotion to a principle, chequered though it was by many traits of human weakness, he created a noble precedent whose lustre can never fade, and his public career earned him no mean place among the statesmen of all ages. When raised to the high dignity of consul he saved Rome from a fearful peril, and in the last two years of his life he reached a heroic grandeur, fighting with the weapons of intellect and eloquence against the brute power of Antony.

Social Unrest

Cicero had passed with credit through the successive stages of quaestor, aedile, and praetor, and now (64 B.C.) all his efforts were directed toward the supreme goal of political ambition, the consulship. To overcome the obstinate prejudice which hedged that office against the ambition of a New Man was no light matter. But affairs were so ordered that the nobles withdrew their opposition, and were ready to welcome into their ranks a man who was the avowed champion of the existing order of things, and whose eloquence might be counted on as a defence against all assaults on the constitution. The hands of the democratic leaders were just then weakened by a division in their own camp. On one side stood Caesar and Crassus, who used the democratic machinery as a means to forward their own designs, to bring discredit on the conservative party, and to create a counterpoise to the formidable power of Pompeius.[1] On the other side were those who may be called the anarchists, men bankrupt in character and estate, who were ready to repair their broken fortunes by the most violent and desperate methods. For some years past rumours had been afloat of a dark conspiracy, aimed, it was believed, against all the safeguards of society. There was, in fact, both in Rome and in Italy a mass of inflammable material, which only needed a spark to kindle a general conflagration. There were, first, the dissolute veterans of Sulla, who had

---

[1] This was the aim of the agrarian law of Rullus (63 B.C.), defeated by Cicero during his consulship.

squandered their means and were willing to follow any leader
who held out a prospect of licence and pillage. Secondly,
there were the children of the proscribed, who had been robbed
of their patrimony, and were still living under the cruel ban
which debarred them from all honourable promotion. To
these elements of disorder we have to add the mob of the
capital, pauperized by free distributions of corn, debauched
by the inhuman pastimes of the arena, hating all honest
labour, and always ripe for mischief. Lastly, among the nobles
themselves there were thousands of ruined men who had
everything to gain and nothing to lose in a reign of terror and
anarchy.

CATILINE

Foremost in the class just mentioned stands the name of
Lucius Sergius Catilina, a man who united in his own person
all the blackest iniquities of that evil time. Sprung from a
great patrician house, in his early manhood he had made
himself conspicuous as one of the chief agents in carrying out
the savage decrees of Sulla. Men still in the prime of life
had seen him as he stalked through the streets of Rome
carrying on a spear the severed head of Marius Gratianus, a
kinsman of Sulla's great rival, whom he had put to death
with cruel tortures. He murdered his own brother, and afterwards got his name inscribed on the proscription lists to secure
immunity for the crime. He was accused of an intrigue with
one of the Vestal Virgins, and being captivated by the charms
of a noble Roman lady he removed her objections to a grown-up
stepson by a second domestic murder. His vast powers of
body and mind and his dexterity in all manly exercises made
him the acknowledged leader of the dissolute young nobles,
and he possessed a sort of fearful fascination which drew even
the better disposed into the vortex of crime and wickedness.
Catiline was now in his forty-fourth year, and his figure was
one of the most familiar among the motley multitudes who
thronged the thoroughfares of the capital. His portrait, drawn
in a few powerful strokes by Sallust, enables us to call up

LAST ERA OF THE REPUBLIC

without an effort that ghastly face, those wild, staring eyes, his gait, like that of a madman, now rapid, now slow, his herculean frame, which no toils could weary and no excesses could weaken. That such a monster of wickedness could mingle unrebuked in the highest social circles and offer himself as a candidate for the most important offices of State speaks volumes for the character of the age. It should be remarked, however, that, besides his other accomplishments, he was a profound master of dissimulation, which enabled him to assume any character and deceive all but the sharpest eyes.

CATILINE AND THE CONSULSHIP

Catiline had been brought to trial on a charge of extortion in Africa, which he had governed as propraetor, and had obtained an acquittal by lavish bribery of the jury, which exhausted his ill-gotten gains and left him a bankrupt. He was now standing a second time for the consulship, having failed in a previous candidature, and his pretensions were supported by Crassus and Caesar. The motives of these two eminent men in lending their countenance to such a ruffian are easily discerned. Catiline was the recognized head of the extreme section of the democrats, a numerous and powerful body, who aimed, as we have seen, at the overthrow of all social order. A consulship, followed in due course by the plunder of a rich province, would render this dangerous man harmless, by satisfying his inordinate appetites, and would thus leave his party without a leader. That such men as Crassus and Caesar should have favoured the later designs of Catiline, when he threw off the mask and appeared as the furious anarchist, is clearly out of the question. What had Crassus, the great millionaire, to hope from a crew of desperate bandits, whose programme was summed up in the pithy phrase *New title-deeds and a clean slate*? [1] Caesar, again, rested all his hopes on keeping up the credit of democratic institutions, which would have been utterly ruined by the success of the anarchists. If Catiline had carried his mad enterprise to the desired

[1] The redivision of lands and the cancelling of debts.

475

conclusion the only result would have been that, after a brief
orgy of licence and murder, he and his associates would have
been swept from the field by the legions of Pompeius, who had
now finished his victorious career in Asia, and was ready at a
word from the Senate to cross the sea and restore order in
Italy. Catiline destroyed and the democratic party broken
up, Pompeius would have reigned like a second Sulla, and all
the horrors of the proscription would have been re-enacted at
Rome. We can see, therefore, that neither Crassus nor Caesar
would have dreamed for a moment of embarking their fortunes
in a scheme of wholesale robbery and murder.

CATILINE DEFEATED

But the character of Catiline was too notorious to give him
any hope of election to the supreme magistracy. He had
already, two years before, been implicated in a scheme for the
murder of the consuls-elect, and when it became known that
he was once more standing for the consulship all the friends of
law and order united their forces to defeat him. The prejudices
of the nobles were overcome in the face of such a prospect,
the Knights rallied round the chief representative and friend
of their order, from every borough in Italy thousands of sober
citizens flocked to record their votes, and amid a scene of unparalleled enthusiasm Cicero was carried triumphantly to the
head of the poll. It was a proud moment for the plain country
gentleman who had thus risen by sheer force of talents and
character to the highest office in the State. For one brief hour
all his dreams seemed to be realized. Senate and Knights
were drawn together by the common danger, Italy had spoken
with a decisive voice, the mob of Rome was acquiescent, and
he, so lately decried as an upstart, was taking his seat on the
curule chair as the first citizen of a free Republic.

CATILINE'S CONSPIRACIES

Though foiled for a second time in his candidature, Catiline
resolved to make one more desperate effort to obtain the consulship, by means of open violence. But his designs were frustrated

by the vigilance of Cicero. The consul had secured the neutrality of his colleague Antonius, a man of low character, who was known to favour the cause of the anarchists, by yielding to him the rich province of Macedonia, and he was kept informed of all Catiline's movements by a certain Fulvia, who was the mistress of one of the conspirators. On the day of the elections he went down to the Campus Martius attended by a strong guard and armed as for battle, and the friends of order presented so determined a front that Catiline made no attempt to break the peace. Rejected for the third time, Catiline now prepared to push matters to extremities and declare open war on the State. He chose as his military centre the town of Faesulae, which still looks down from its rocky height on the valley of the Arno and the fair city of Florence. Here Manlius, one of Sulla's veterans, began to enlist troops and lay up stores of arms and money, and a day was appointed on which he was to march on Rome and co-operate with the conspirators in the capital. Every detail of the plot was betrayed to Cicero by Fulvia, and a week before the day fixed for the rising he laid his report before the Senate. Moved by the gravity of the crisis, the Fathers proceeded to pass the Ultimate Decree, which was couched in the simple formula, " Let the consuls see that the State suffers no harm." The effect of this resolution was to invest the consuls with dictatorial power and with authority to declare war on the enemies of the State. But the measure, though often resorted to, was in its essence unconstitutional, and left the whole burden of responsibility on the consuls. Cicero knew this, and he knew also that the present emergency demanded especial caution. With extraordinary cunning Catiline had given himself out as the champion of the poor against the rich. The government, he said, was held by a ring of selfish monopolists, who kept in their hands all the good things of the State and condemned the whole body of their fellow-citizens to a life of misery and privation. His sympathizers were counted by tens of thousands in all parts of Italy, and if Cicero anticipated his movements by any act of violence he would be decried as a tyrant and a persecutor.

REPUBLICAN ROME

The great object was to compel the anarchist to show his hand and force him into open and undisguised rebellion.

Cicero denounces Catiline

On the eighth of November Cicero convoked the Senate in the temple of Jupiter Stator, which was built under the northern brow of the Palatine, overlooking the Forum. Catiline, whose plans were now almost ripe, had the incredible effrontery to be present. Only the day before two of his adherents had made an attempt to assassinate Cicero in his own house, which was defeated by the precautions of the ever-watchful consul. Now he was compelled to sit, an object of abhorrence to the whole Senate, while his nefarious schemes were laid bare in every detail by the greatest master of Roman eloquence. In that fervid harangue which is known as the First Oration against Catiline, Cicero dragged the wretched man through the whole catalogue of his wickedness, challenged him to refute a word of the indictment, and concluded by ordering him peremptorily to leave Rome. " Go to the camp of Manlius," he said, " call up your assassins, raise the standard of revolt. Why delay any longer ? We all know that this is your purpose. Relieve the anxiety of your fellow-citizens by bringing matters to a speedy issue." With faltering tones and downcast face the arch-dissembler tried to deprecate the animosity of the senators, and spoke of his illustrious ancestors and his blameless life. But, being provoked by cries of anger and derision, he lost command of himself, broke out in wild abuse of the consul, that " low-born denizen of Rome," [1] and finally, raising his voice above the tumult, shouted in defiance : " Driven to bay by the machinations of my enemies, I will break through the toils and extinguish the flames of my house in the general ruin of society." With this characteristic piece of bombast he rushed out of the temple, and the same night he started for the camp of Manlius. Cicero had succeeded in his purpose. The villain was completely unmasked, and compelled to take up arms against his country.

[1] *Inquilinus urbis Romanae* (Sallust, *Catiline*, 31).

THE SCHEME FAILS

The final crisis was now approaching. In Etruria recruits were daily flocking to join Catiline, and the forces of the government were converging on the rebel position from both sides of the Apennines. Before Catiline's departure it had been arranged that on a certain day his confederates in Rome should set fire to the city in twelve different places, murder Cicero and his chief supporters, and then break out and join the insurgents. All this had been duly reported to Cicero. He knew the day appointed for the outbreak, and the very names of the men who were to conduct the work of massacre and robbery, the chief among whom were Lentulus and Cethegus, both members of the great Cornelian house. Yet still he hesitated to take any decisive step against the conspirators. To arrest these powerful nobles on the evidence of a courtesan would have been a most hazardous proceeding, and if he failed to secure their conviction he would only strengthen the cause of the rebels and involve both himself and his country in deadly peril. He waited, therefore, to obtain such proof of their guilt as should preclude all hope of evasion, and their folly presently gave him what he wanted. It happened that just at this time there were present in Rome certain envoys from the Allobroges, a Gaulish people inhabiting the district now called Savoy, whose state was reduced to bankruptcy by the extortions of the Roman usurers. Their petition had been repeatedly rejected by the Senate, and one day when they were wandering disconsolately about the Forum they were accosted by one of Catiline's followers, who promised to show them a speedy way of getting redress for their grievances. They were then introduced to the leaders of the conspiracy, and formally invited to throw in their lot with Catiline. But the envoys, oppressed by the weight of their terrible secret, laid the whole matter before Fabius Sanga, who represented the interests of their people in Rome, and by him the information was conveyed to Cicero. Acting on the consul's instructions, the Allobroges pretended to join

REPUBLICAN ROME

heart and soul in the plot, but insisted on receiving written documents to be shown to their countrymen at home. With incredible stupidity three of the leaders, Lentulus, Cethegus, and Statilius, gave them the required letters, delivered under their own hand and seal, little dreaming that they were signing their death-warrant. Then the envoys, still acting under Cicero's directions, set out on their return journey, and on reaching the Milvian Bridge, two miles from the city, they were waylaid by the consul's officers and carried back to Rome.

ARREST OF THE CONSPIRATORS

Armed with the documents which had been found on the envoys, Cicero could now strike with effect. Four of the conspirators were at once placed under arrest, and examined next day in the presence of the Senate. Confronted by their own handwriting, Lentulus, Cethegus, and Statilius confessed their guilt by their silence, and Gabinius, another leading partisan of Catiline, was convicted by the evidence of the envoys. Then Cicero addressed a meeting of the citizens in the Forum, and even those who had hitherto sympathized with the designs of Catiline were filled with indignation when the whole plot was unfolded to them, with all its contemplated horrors, the burning of the city, the arming of slaves,[1] and the proposed alliance with Rome's inveterate enemies, the Gauls. Two days later the Senate met to decide the fate of the prisoners, whose number had now been increased to five by the capture of a certain Caeparius. The scene of this famous debate was the Temple of Concord, traces of which are still to be seen under the eastern face of the Capitoline Hill. All the adjacent Forum was thronged by an eager crowd, and the approaches to the temple were guarded by a strong body of the Knights, among whom Cicero could recognize the face of his beloved Atticus, the lifelong friend whose sympathy never failed him in all the dark days which were to come.

[1] This suggestion was made by Lentulus in a private letter to Catiline, which was given to the envoys for delivery.

480

LAST ERA OF THE REPUBLIC

CAESAR'S ATTITUDE

When the senators of consular rank had given their opinions, all inclining to the extreme penalty, Caesar, who was then praetor-elect, rose to address the house. His position was extremely delicate, for he was strongly suspected of having favoured the conspiracy. But his thoughts went beyond the immediate issue, and he foresaw that public feeling, though now highly incensed against the conspirators, would presently veer round to the opposite extreme if any irreparable step were taken. He took his stand, therefore, on the ground of constitutional law and the indefeasible right of the people, who alone had the power of passing capital sentence on a Roman citizen, and proposed that Lentulus and his associates should be punished by imprisonment for life and the confiscation of their property. His argument was, in truth, quite unsound, for the penalty which he indicated was just as much beyond the competence of the Senate as the other; but he had succeeded in arousing the fears of his audience and turning the balance to the side of mercy.

CATO RALLIES THE SENATE

There was, however, one man present whose blunt common sense was not to be diverted from the issue by all the sophistries of Caesar. That man was Cato, who as tribune-elect was called upon to speak toward the end of the debate. After some bitter reflections on the conduct of Caesar he went straight to the point and brought his hearers back to the realities of their position. It was no time, he said, to weigh nice questions of constitutional law. Their own lives, and the lives of their fellow-citizens, were at stake. How would Catiline and his men, how would all the ill-affected in Rome and in Italy exult if they, the supreme representatives of law and order, were seen to flinch at this critical moment! But if they did their duty the blow which ended the lives of the traitors would strike at the very roots of the conspiracy.

481

REPUBLICAN ROME

END OF THE CONSPIRATORS

The austerity of Cato's life and his known disinterestedness made him a sort of oracle in the Senate, and when the house divided it was found that he had carried a large majority of his hearers with him. A decree was passed, framed in the very words of his speech, and Cicero proceeded at once to carry out the fatal sentence. One by one the five conspirators were conducted to the Tullianum, an underground dungeon not far from the Temple of Concord, and strangled by the hands of the public executioner. And when the consul passed through the multitude which stood waiting in the Forum a single word [1] from his lips announced that the act of justice was completed.

DEATH OF CATILINE

Opinion is still divided on the conduct of Cicero and the Senate at this momentous crisis in their country's history. By some critics the execution of the prisoners is condemned as a deed of lawless cruelty. Others regard it as an act of timely severity which was forced upon the government by the circumstances of the case. According to the strict letter of the law, it cannot be denied that both consul and Senate were in the wrong. But there are occasions on which the ordinary forms of the constitution have to be set aside and the State is compelled to take summary measures of self-defence. The right conceded to every individual of defending his person against violence cannot be denied to the community, and the law of every nation has provided for the exercise of that right in times of great public peril. The only question, therefore, to be considered is whether the peril in which Rome was placed was sufficient to justify Cicero's action, and, incidentally, whether the violent death of Lentulus and his fellows produced the desired result. As to the danger, few will deny that it was great and imminent. All Italy was waiting to hear the decision, and if the government had betrayed any weakness

---

[1] *Vixerunt,* ' They have lived.'

tens of thousands would have declared openly for Catiline. As to the result there is even 'less room for doubt. The sentence executed on these high-born felons struck terror into the hearts of all the evil-disposed and cut the sinews of the conspiracy. Catiline, deserted by a great part of his army, was soon afterwards hemmed in and slain, with the remnant of his followers, and the cloud which had so long hung over Rome was thus finally dispersed. Crassus only gave voice to the general sentiment when he declared that he owed his fortune, his liberty, and his life to Cicero, and on the day when the patriot consul laid down his office he was hailed by Cato as the saviour and father of his country.

CHAPTER XVII

FROM THE RETURN OF POMPEIUS
TO THE DEATH OF CAESAR

THE triumph of the constitutional party and of their leader Cicero seemed to be complete. Nobles, Knights, and commons had been drawn together by the common danger, and the vigorous action of their chosen magistrate had asserted the cause of law and order. Caesar, the arch-democrat, who was commonly regarded as the accomplice of Catiline, had lost credit by his supposed trafficking with the anarchists, and after the expiration of his praetorship he withdrew to his province in Farther Spain. If only Pompeius could be won to the side of the Senate the ideal policy of Cicero would be realized in every detail. But these fair hopes were shattered by the blindness of the nobles, and the strange talent for blundering which marked all the political dealings of the famous soldier. Already, before the final overthrow of Catiline, he had dispatched his agent, Metellus Nepos, to represent his interests in Rome (63 B.C.). Nepos, after obtaining his own election to the tribunate, proposed that Pompeius should be called in to take the command against the rebels and should be nominated consul for the ensuing year. The demand, however, raised such an outcry that he was driven from the field, and compelled to take refuge in the camp of his master. All the conditions which afterwards led to the civil war were now present—a fugitive and insulted tribune, a Senate refractory and aggressive, and a victorious general with a plausible pretext for drawing his sword against the government. But the hour had not yet come, nor was Pompeius the man, to take that step which was taken by

484

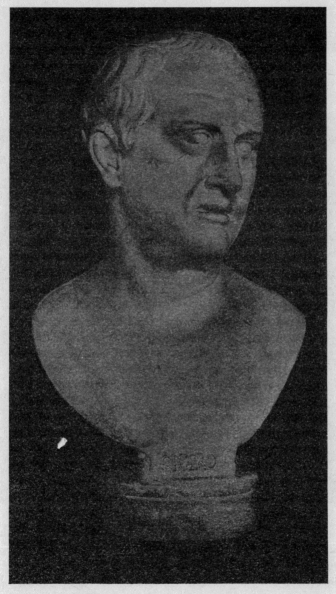

PLATE LVI. CICERO (APSLEY HOUSE)   484

PLATE LVII. PONS FABRICIUS   485

Caesar some thirteen years later, and gave a new character to the history of Europe. It required another spirit, more lofty and perhaps more unscrupulous than his, to perpetrate that glorious treason. Some moments of inward conflict he doubtless had while the glittering image of a crown floated before his eyes. Then, averting, his thoughts from the insidious temptation, he disbanded his troops and set out for Rome.

POMPEIUS NEGLECTED

Before long it became apparent that his great act of renunciation had been made in vain. Supreme in the camp, Pompeius was helpless as a child in the field of politics. Like Marius, he was abashed and disconcerted by the clamours of a popular audience, and his training, which was exclusively military, unfitted him to mingle in the polished circles of which Cicero was the brightest ornament. If he turned to the nobles he encountered the envenomed hatred of Lucullus and Metellus,[1] each of whom had a personal grudge against him, or the dogged integrity of Cato, who repelled his clumsy advances with scorn. The commons, who had formerly made him their idol, had transferred all their affections to Caesar, and Cicero, once his warmest supporter, was now seriously affronted by his cold arrogance. Two questions were pressing for immediate solution, both deeply affecting his dignity and honour. He had to make provision for his disbanded veterans and to obtain the ratification of his acts in Asia. But whenever he put forward these claims he was met by factious opposition. His vanity was doubtless soothed by the splendid pageant of his triumph, which dazzled the eyes of his countrymen for two whole days. But after this childish gratification he found himself alone, and was reduced to his old attitude of sullen and powerless resentment.

TRIAL OF CLODIUS

Meanwhile the dissolution of parties went steadily on, and the inevitable issue drew nearer and nearer. The corruption

---

[1] Caecilius Metellus Creticus. See p. 455.

of public men and the impotence of the Senate were glaringly
manifested in the trial of Publius Clodius (61 B.C.), whom we
have already seen playing the part of a mutineer in the camp
of Lucullus. Clodius had been detected in an attempt to
violate the mysteries of Bona Dea, which were performed by
women alone, all males being rigidly excluded. Disguised in
female attire, he had obtained admission to Caesar's house,
where the mysterious rites were to take place ; but he was
betrayed by a domestic, and the affair caused great scandal
to pious minds. In order to ensure the condemnation of
Clodius, concerning whose guilt there was no shadow of doubt,
the Senate proposed that he should be tried by a special jury,
chosen by the praetor. But this suggestion caused a violent
commotion among the people, who regarded it as an un-
warranted usurpation on the part of the Senate, and the jury
was selected in the ordinary way. Clodius rested his defence
on an alibi, but this plea was set aside by Cicero, who swore
that he had seen the accused man in Rome on the day when
the sacrilege was committed. In spite, however, of overwhelming evidence a majority of the jury pronounced in his
favour, and this dangerous man was let loose on society, to
work infinite mischief in the near future. The acquittal was
obtained by the gold of Crassus, who had bribed a sufficient
number of the jury ; and we are assured that other gratifica-
tions, yet more infamous, were added to the stipulated price.
In acting thus Crassus was carrying out a private understanding
with Caesar, who wished to secure the services of Clodius in
the capacity of a daring and unscrupulous demagogue. Cicero,
as we shall presently see, had more than one reason to deplore
this " debauched and venal verdict," which had widened the
breach between Senate and people.

THE STATE AT A DEADLOCK

It seemed, indeed, as if fortune had determined to use the
worst and the best man in Rome to break up that union of
orders which the patriot orator so ardently desired. Just at
this time (60 B.C.) the Knights were petitioning to be relieved

of their contract for farming the taxes of Asia, which had
been concluded on terms very disadvantageous to themselves.
But their request was rejected, chiefly owing to the uncompromising attitude of Cato, who was deaf to all pleas of
expediency and resolved to hold them strictly to their bargain.
" He was right, of course, in theory," remarks Cicero, with a
sort of comic despair ; " but he talks as if he were living in
Plato's ideal republic, and not among the dregs of Rome."
Thus, by a mixture of blundering and villainy the State machine
had been brought once more to a deadlock.   The four estates,
as they may be termed, in the Roman political world—the
lords, the commons, the financial aristocracy, and the military power, as represented by Pompeius—were torn violently
asunder, and the times called aloud for some new and imperious
force to carry on the work of government.

The First Triumvirate

That force was now at hand in the person of the extraordinary
man whose career was henceforth bound up with the fate of
his country.   For the next sixteen years to write the life of
Caesar is to write the history of Rome.   Whenever we find him
at the head of affairs we see the order, the consistency, the
resolute purpose of a great and luminous mind.   When his
hand is removed the State lapses at once into total anarchy
and hideous confusion.   During the brief period of his command
in Spain (61 B.C.) Caesar had found time to display his unrivalled talents as an administrator, to accumulate a treasure
which relieved him from all financial embarrassment, and to
give the first proof of that high military genius which places
him by the side of Hannibal and Alexander.   He was now
(60 B.C.) before the gates of Rome, with a reputation established
on a solid basis and a plan of action fully matured.   Waiving
the empty honour of a triumph, which would have interfered
with his further designs, he entered at once into communication with Pompeius and Crassus, and succeeded in effecting
a reconciliation between these two rival leaders.   Then was
formed that famous Triple Alliance, uniting the wealth of

REPUBLICAN ROME

Crassus, the genius of Caesar, and the mighty prestige of Pompeius, which is known in history as the First Triumvirate. Caesar undertook to secure for Pompeius the ratification of his acts in Asia and to provide lands for his veterans, and in return Pompeius was to exert all his influence to procure Caesar's election to the consulship. We are not informed what was to be the share of Crassus in the profits of this political partnership, but he had long been in intimate relations with Caesar and he had no distinct policy of his own. So the bargain was struck, and the threefold tyranny emerged, in which Pompeius was the nominal head, but Caesar the dominant and informing spirit.

CAESAR'S FIRST MEASURES

Against such a combination of wealth, talent, and prestige the nobles were powerless, and the utmost they could do was to carry the election of Bibulus, an obstinate and incorrigible aristocrat, as Caesar's colleague in the consulship. As soon as Caesar found himself firmly seated on the curule chair (59 B.C.) he brought in a land bill providing allotments for the soldiers of Pompeius and the more needy citizens, and appropriating for this purpose the rich Campanian territory, which since the fall of Capua (211 B.C.) had been a State domain, bringing in a large revenue to the exchequer.[1] A second measure confirmed the arrangements of Pompeius for the settlement of Asia, and a third relieved the tax-farmers of the Equestrian Order from their Asiatic contract. Another enactment of far-reaching consequences, which foreshadowed the Imperial legislation, was a law regulating the administration of the provinces and setting strict bounds to the powers of the Roman magistrates abroad. To provide themselves with money the triumvirs agreed to recognize the claims of Ptolemy Auletes, whose title was defective,[2] to the crown of

---

[1] In the first draft of the bill this territory had been specially exempted.

[2] Egypt had been bequeathed to Rome by Alexander II, who died in 81 B.C., but the Romans had not taken advantage of the bequest, and the reigning king was Ptolemy Auletes ('the Piper'), a natural son of Ptolemy Lathyrus.

Egypt, and Ptolemy undertook to pay for their support by a bribe of six thousand talents.

ILLEGAL LEGISLATION

All these measures were passed by Caesar through the popular assembly in the teeth of a violent opposition from the Senate and from his colleague Bibulus. His proceedings were entirely unconstitutional, for by immemorial right the initiative in legislation lay with the Senate, and Bibulus again and again interposed his veto, which rendered the action of Caesar null and void. But the battered machinery of the constitution had long proved itself unworkable ; nor was Caesar likely to be intimidated by the religious menaces of his colleague, who finally shut himself up in his house and spent the rest of his year of office in watching the sky. The effect of this pious preoccupation was to stop all parliamentary action in Rome, for according to a law passed about a century before,[1] no bill could be proposed to the assembly if one of the higher magistrates had announced his intention of watching the heavens for a token of the divine will. On technical grounds, therefore, Caesar's acts were trebly illegal, being against the prescriptive right of the Senate, against the veto, and against the sanctions of the State religion, which really formed a part of constitutional law, having been erected as a barrier to check hasty and ill-considered legislation. But these forms, once the safeguards of the State, were become, in Caesar's eyes at least, a mere incubus, blocking the way to wholesome reform, and he had accordingly no scruple in setting them aside.

THE TRIUMVIRATE STRENGTHENED

Having amply redeemed his pledges to Pompeius, Caesar proceeded to carry out those measures which immediately concerned his own interest. This was effected through the agency of the tribune Vatinius, who brought in a bill conferring on Caesar the provinces of Illyria and Cisalpine Gaul for five

[1] Lex Aelia Fufia (156 B.C.).

years, and to these was afterwards added the Transalpine province, or Gaul beyond the Alps. Still further to confirm their position, the triumvirs arranged that the consulship for the following year should be bestowed on Gabinius, one of the creatures of Pompeius, and Piso, whose daughter Calpurnia Caesar had recently married. The tie between the two chief triumvirs was drawn yet closer by the marriage of Pompeius with Julia, Caesar's daughter, who inherited much of her father's personal charm.

CATO DISPOSED OF

At the end of the year Caesar laid down his office and began to enlist his soldiers and prepare for the great task which lay before him. But there was still something more to be done before he could leave the capital behind him and enter on that career of conquest which was to raise him to the highest pinnacle of fame and power. Cato, the stoutest champion of the old constitution, had taken the lead in the opposition to Caesar's enactments, and Cicero, Rome's greatest orator, had recently let fall some bitter words reflecting on the tyranny of the triumvirs. It would be highly impolitic to leave these two eminent men to work their will unhindered in his absence. Some means had to be devised to render them harmless, and a ready instrument for this purpose was found in Publius Clodius. In order to qualify him for election to the tribunate, Clodius was hastily adopted into a plebeian family, and Caesar and Pompeius stood godfathers to the transaction. Then, armed with the terrible powers of that much-abused office, he at once set about the execution of his master's orders. To get rid of Cato, that model of ancient integrity was appointed to the invidious task of annexing Cyprus, which was then governed as a separate kingdom by another Ptolemy, brother to the king of Egypt. In spite of his repugnance, Cato felt himself bound to take up the hateful commission, and the triumvirs thus rid themselves, for a time at least, of their most obstinate enemy.

PERSECUTION OF CICERO

Cicero remained to be dealt with, and in carrying out this part of his work Clodius acted with exulting and relentless rigour. Caesar would fain have spared the great orator and patriot, for whom he felt a peculiar tenderness, and he exerted all his powers of persuasion to win him to his side. But finding his overtures rejected he gave the signal to his agent, and the blow fell. On the motion of Clodius a measure was passed in the assembly condemning to banishment anyone who had executed a Roman citizen without a trial. No name was mentioned, but it was well understood that the law was aimed at Cicero and the famous acts of his consulship, his chief glory and pride. Cicero had long anticipated the attack, and had thought to repel it by the force of his genius and his high public merits. But finding only cold looks and evasive answers in those to whom he appealed for help, he lost heart altogether, and went into voluntary exile. Clodius pursued him with a second decree, declaring him an outlaw, and imposing pains and penalties on all who gave him shelter. Cicero never recovered altogether from this heavy blow. He had set his feebler nature against the iron will of Caesar, and henceforth he was a broken man, knowing the right, but often choosing the wrong, and never rising to the full height of his better genius until the closing months of his life.

CAESAR AND THE HELVETII

But other and far graver cares, deeply concerning the fate of Rome and the future of mankind, now claimed the attention of the great proconsul. For some years past there had been a general forward movement among the tribes of western Germany, which tended to push back the frontier of Gaul, and threatened the whole of that country with the terrors of a German invasion. Among those who were immediately affected by this disturbance were the Helvetii, a Gaulish people whose home was in what is now north-western Switzerland. Chafing against the narrow bounds which confined them, and urged

491

by the imminence of the German peril, they had resolved to abandon their country and seek a new abode in western Gaul, on the shores of the Atlantic. They had now (58 B.C.) completed their arrangements, and, having burnt all their towns and villages, they were preparing to enter on their march, which would lead them through the heart of the Roman province in southern Gaul. The irruption of this vast multitude, numbering nearly four hundred thousand souls, would have endangered the peace of the whole country, and Caesar was determined at all costs to prevent it. Acting with his accustomed rapidity, he set out from Rome, and arrived with a single legion at Geneva, where he was met by envoys from the Helvetii, who asked permission to march through the province. Having promised to consider their request, and a day being appointed for a conference, he employed the interval in fortifying the southern bank of the Rhone, and sent round orders for a general muster of troops. When the Helvetii appeared again they found their way barred by a long line of entrenchments, extending for ten miles from Geneva to the Jura ; and after an attempt to break through, which was easily repulsed, they were compelled to fall back.

THE HELVETII SUBDUED

But the Helvetii were not to be so easily deterred from their purpose. Foiled in their effort to force the passage of the Rhone, they turned in a northerly direction, and, threading the defiles of the Jura, arrived on the left bank of the Saône. Once more Caesar was too quick for them. Before they had conveyed their whole force over the river he came upon them at the head of five legions, cut to pieces their rearguard, threw a bridge in one day across the Saône, and pursued the main body to the neighbourhood of Bibracte,[1] where they were brought to bay and defeated with immense loss. The survivors were sent back to their old home in Helvetia, to serve as a bulwark against the tide of German invasion.

[1] Near Autun.

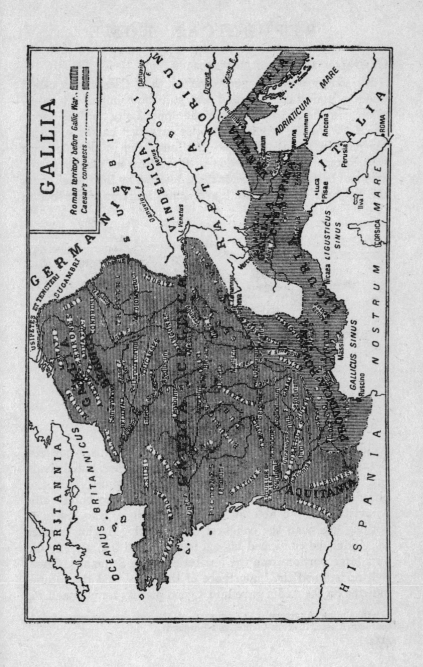

GALLIA

Roman territory before Gallic War..
Caesar's conquests...........

Campaign against Ariovistus

No sooner was this peril averted than Caesar was called
upon to undertake a second and still more important enterprise. In the district between the upper Loire and the Saône
dwelt the Aedui, whose territories extended as far south as
the modern Lyons, and who had long been in close alliance
with Rome. Their connexion with the Romans and their own
arrogant behaviour had made them detested by their neighbours
the Sequani and Arverni,[1] and some fourteen years before

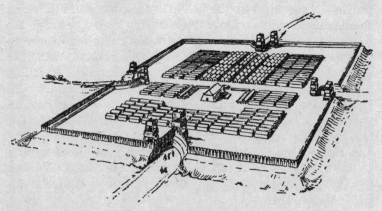

ROMAN CAMP

these two peoples had called in the aid of Ariovistus, a powerful
German prince, to put down the insolence of their hated rivals.
But the Sequani, like the Britons in after-times, had soon
bitter reason to rue the interference of their too potent ally.
Ariovistus was an able and ambitious prince, who aimed at
nothing less than the conquest of all Gaul. Having crushed
the Aedui, he continued his aggressions, and had already cut
off a large portion from the territories of the Sequani. Caesar
well understood the importance of the crisis, and the injuries
inflicted on the Aedui gave him a good pretext for commencing

[1] Inhabiting Auvergne. The country of the Sequani corresponded to
southern Alsace, Franche-Comté, and Burgundy.

hostilities. He accordingly sent envoys to Ariovistus, requesting an interview to discuss the state of affairs, and meanwhile advanced in an easterly direction through the level country between the Vosges and the Jura. Ariovistus sent a haughty answer demanding to be told what business had brought the Romans into the territory which he had made his own by right of arms. When it became evident that an encounter with the Germans was not to be avoided, a general panic fell upon the Roman soldiers, who had heard alarming reports of the gigantic stature and superhuman strength of this savage people.[1] It required all the weight of the proconsul's influence to allay these childish terrors, but having at last restored the confidence of his troops he continued his march, and came up with the enemy not far from the spot where now stands the town of Mülhausen. As if determined to atone for their late display of cowardice, the Romans advanced to the attack with great resolution, and, being seconded by a spirited cavalry charge, which was led by the young Crassus, son of the triumvir, they gained a brilliant victory, and drove the remnant of the great host in headlong flight toward the Rhine. In the course of one summer Caesar, to use his own words, had ended two mighty wars, and had trodden worthily in the footsteps of his great relative Marius.

WAR WITH THE BELGAE

The events just related had not escaped the notice of the Belgae, the bravest of all the Gaulish peoples, whose territory extended from the Rhine to the Seine. Alarmed by the rapid progress of Caesar, whose designs on the liberty of Gaul were no secret, they assembled a great army in the following spring and prepared to resist any act of aggression. Caesar, who had gained the alliance of the Remi, a Belgic tribe inhabiting the modern district of Rheims, found their forces, which numbered three hundred thousand men, encamped on the banks

---

[1] It must be remembered that Caesar's army was chiefly composed of raw recruits, and had not yet attained that perfection of training and discipline which afterwards made it so formidable an engine of war.

of the Aisne. Though now in command of eight legions, he hesitated to attack a force which outnumbered his own by six to one, and for some time the two armies lay watching each other's movements. But the attention of the Belgae was distracted by a movement of the Aedui, who made a sudden attack on one of their most powerful cantons, in the district of Beauvais. Their army dispersed, each contingent hastening to the defence of its own fields, and one by one these divisions were subdued by the Roman arms, the most obstinate resistance being offered by the Nervii, in the modern Hainault. The legions were quartered for the winter in the central region of the

COMMANDER-IN-CHIEF

Loire, and Caesar had a brief respite, which he employed among the affairs of his Illyrian province.

WAR WITH THE VENETI

In the next year (56 B.C.) Caesar was chiefly employed in the subjugation of the Veneti, a hardy seafaring folk whose home was on the rock-bound coast of southern Brittany. The Veneti had been guilty of an act of treachery, having seized certain Roman envoys who were sent to obtain supplies, and Caesar was determined to teach them a severe lesson. But the enterprise, as he himself confesses, was one of the most arduous in which he was ever engaged. The light Roman galleys were ill fitted to cope with the powerful vessels of the enemy, which were designed to buffet the stormy waves of

COMMANDER OF A
LEGION

496

the Atlantic and carried stout sails of untanned hide. But the Romans once more showed that ready invention which

CENTURION

had baffled the skill of the Punic mariners two hundred years before. Each galley was armed with a number of keen, sickle-like blades, attached to long poles, and thus equipped the Romans engaged the whole fleet of the Veneti in Quiberon Bay. Caesar and his army watched the battle from the shore, while the naval operations were conducted by Decimus Brutus, one of the ablest of his lieutenants. Avoiding the use of the ram, which would have been powerless against the ponderous oak timbers of the Venetian ships, the Roman captains laid their galleys alongside the enemy, and at the word of command the halyards were severed by the sharp sickles, and the huge mainsails toppled down on the deck, half burying the crew in their heavy folds. In hand-to-hand conflict the Veneti were no match for the practised Roman swordsmen, and one after another their vessels were laid aboard and captured. A fearful vengeance now fell upon this brave little people, which had dared to defy the majesty of Rome. All the members of its senate were put to death by Caesar's orders, and the captives were sold as slaves. At the conclusion of this laborious campaign Caesar had the satisfaction of learning that the whole of Aquitaine had submitted to his lieutenant Publius Crassus. Then, as if he had not done enough for one year, the unwearied

LEGIONARY

497

proconsul spent the rest of the season in a sort of man-hunt, conducted against the Menapii and Morini, a semi-amphibious race who dwelt among the swamps and forests of the Scheldt and the lower Rhine.

INVASION OF GERMANY

By an arrangement with his fellow-triumvirs, of which we shall speak more in detail presently (see p. 507), Caesar had contrived to get his period of command prolonged for five years, and at the opening of the following season he was called to the north by a new movement among the German tribes. Two of these, the Usipetes and Tencteri, had crossed the Rhine and effected a forcible occupation in the land of the Menapii. They had been driven to take this step by pressure from the great Suevic nation, of which Ariovistus was king, and their presence in Gaul caused much excitement among the fickle and volatile natives, who were as yet only half subdued. It was imperative, therefore, to expel them, and Caesar, setting his legions in motion earlier than usual, and marching swiftly northward, confronted the intruders at the confluence of the Rhine and the Meuse. The Germans affected a submissive tone and requested time for a parley, but as Caesar had reason to suspect their good faith he seized their envoys and gave the word for a general advance. Taken by surprise, the Germans were totally defeated, and those who escaped the sword of the Romans perished in the waters of the Rhine. In one day a whole nation, numbering, with the women and children, more than four hundred thousand, was exterminated. Caesar's conduct on this occasion and his severe treatment of the Veneti were bitterly denounced by his political opponents in Rome, and the cry was led by Cato, who demanded that the victorious general should be surrendered to the enemy. Unmoved by these clamours, Caesar proceeded calmly on his course. His immediate duty was to teach the Germans respect for the Gaulish frontier and to guard against any violation of territory in the future. With this object he determined to cross the Rhine and wipe out this dangerous enemy on his own ground. Any design of conquering Germany was of course far from his thoughts. He merely wished to make an imposing demonstration and impress the barbarian mind with a sense of irresistible power. Choosing a spot somewhat north of the modern Coblenz, he threw a wooden bridge across the river, and for eighteen days he led his legions up and down the country, finding none to oppose his progress. The inhabitants fled in terror at his approach, and even the powerful Suevi withdrew into the impenetrable forests of the interior. Then, having achieved his purpose, Caesar recrossed the Rhine, broke down the bridge, and returned into northwestern Gaul. Brief as it had been, this invasion of Germany, combined with the previous defeat of Ariovistus, effectively checked the advance of the Teutonic tribes.

CAESAR IN BRITAIN

The season was now far advanced, but Caesar had yet another task to perform before he could dismiss his legions into winter quarters. The Britons had given active support to their countrymen on the mainland in the struggle with Rome, and the great island afforded a convenient asylum to fugitive patriots, in which they could hatch new plots against their conqueror and oppressor. Resolved to show these fierce islanders that he would brook no interference with his plans, Caesar collected a small fleet, and, placing on board two legions, on a calm day toward the end of August he set sail across the Channel, and early the next morning his ships were descried from the white cliffs near the modern Dover. Where the town now stands the sea then formed a deep bay running far inland, and all the heights commanding the entrance were thronged with armed men. Moving, therefore, slowly along the coast, he came to anchor where the shore levels near Romney, and after an obstinate struggle succeeded in effecting a landing, and threw up entrenchments close to the sea. But the force he had brought with him was totally inadequate, and the reckless enterprise nearly brought his career to an untimely end. His ships were shattered by a storm, the Britons, rallying after their first panic, assailed him fiercely, and he was thankful to steal away in the night and put twenty miles of sea between himself and these formidable enemies.

BRITAIN AGAIN INVADED

Both honour and expediency demanded that Caesar should wipe out the stain of this hasty retreat, and during the winter preparations for a second expedition were made on an imposing scale. In the following summer he set sail with five legions and eight hundred vessels, and, landing unopposed, marched into the interior. He crossed the Thames, defeated the native levies under their king Cassivellaunus, and stormed their stronghold, on the site of the modern St. Albans. But his ships had again suffered severely in a heavy gale, the season of the equinox was approaching, and he had never seriously contemplated the conquest of Britain. He contented himself, therefore, with imposing a tribute, which was never paid, and at the beginning of autumn carried his legions back to Gaul. Scanty as had been the results of these two invasions, they had served their purpose, by impressing the minds of the Britons with a sense of Roman power and by raising the proconsul's reputation to the highest pitch among his own countrymen. Among all Caesar's achievements there was none which struck the imagination of the Romans so strongly as this adventure into the great unknown sea and his victorious march into Britain, the land of mystery and terror. More than a hundred years were to elapse before the work which he had hardly attempted was taken up again and Britain became incorporated into the Roman empire.

NEW RISINGS IN GAUL

The pressure of the Roman occupation had begun to weigh upon the spirit of a brave and sensitive people, and it soon became evident that the work of conquering Gaul was only half done. Owing to the scarcity of supplies Caesar was compelled to divide his forces, and quarter them for the winter in separate camps, remote from each other. This gave the opportunity for which the Gauls were waiting. One whole legion which was stationed near the site of the modern Liége was treacherously lured from its camp by the Eburones and cut to pieces. Another, commanded by Quintus Cicero, brother of the orator, was only saved from destruction by the prompt action of Caesar, who, hearing of its distress, hurried to the rescue. These troubles compelled Caesar to remain in Gaul throughout the winter, and the next year (53 B.C.) was employed in restoring order in the disturbed districts. A movement among the Treveri in the valley of the Moselle had been put down by Labienus, the ablest of Caesar's lieutenants, and as the insurgents had been helped by the Germans beyond the Rhine Caesar again crossed the river and made an armed demonstration in the territory of the Suevi. The whole weight of his anger then fell upon the Eburones, whose country was harried with fire and sword, while those who escaped the general massacre were hunted like beasts in the Forest of Ardennes. At the close of the campaign Caesar held a general assembly of the Gauls at Rheims, and a popular chieftain named Acco, who had raised a revolt in the district of Champagne, was solemnly condemned, scourged, and executed. Believing that the insurrection was now stamped out, Caesar sent his legions into winter quarters, and crossed the Alps to administer the affairs of the Cisalpine province.

VERCINGETORIX

But his departure gave the signal for another rising, which for the first time assumed a truly national character. The soul of the movement was Vercingetorix, a young prince of Auvergne, who has earned a place by the side of Arminius as the champion of his country's liberty, though, unlike the great German patriot, he was foredoomed to tragic failure. His design was to strike with all his force against the main Roman army, which was quartered in northern Gaul, while another attack, directed against the Roman province in the south, was to engage Caesar's attention and prevent him from joining his veteran legions. But he had not calculated on the extraordinary rapidity which so often enabled Caesar to astound and paralyse his enemies. With such troops as he had at his disposal, Caesar entered the Narbonese province, forced his way through the deep snows of the Cevennes, and descended into Auvergne. Then, having made provision for the defence of the southern province, he marched with all speed up the valleys of the Rhone and Saône, and reached his faithful legions in the district of Langres. The arrival of Caesar compelled Vercingetorix to adopt a new plan of campaign. He knew that the Roman veterans, under their great leader, were a match for almost any odds, and he accordingly resolved to avoid encounters in the open field and starve out the enemy by turning the whole country into a waste. The work of devastation began, but Avaricum,[1] the capital of the Bituriges, was spared, and after a desperate resistance the beautiful city, with all its rich stores, fell into the conqueror's hands.

A PERILOUS POSITION

At the approach of spring Caesar sent Labienus with four legions to carry on operations in the north, while he himself marched with the remainder of his troops into the country of the Arverni. But this division of his forces nearly proved his ruin. The impregnable city of Gergovia resisted all assaults, and at the news of this reverse the Aedui, who had for some time been wavering in their allegiance, joined the insurrection. Caesar was now in great peril, and many of his officers advised him to fall back on the Roman province. But he well knew that a retreat would mean utter ruin to his fortunes, for if he returned to Rome with the mark of failure upon him he would fall a victim to the malice of his enemies. At all costs he must find a way through the hostile country and effect a junction with Labienus. He therefore turned his face northward, crossed the swollen waters of the Loire, and reached his lieutenant in the country of the Senones.[2]

[1] Now Bourges.
[2] Ile-de-France and Champagne.

LAST ERA OF THE REPUBLIC

CAESAR'S GERMAN ALLIES

Nearly the whole of Gaul was now in revolt, and a general attack was planned on the Roman province, while Vercingetorix, who had been elected commander-in-chief, lay in wait with a powerful army to intercept the march of Caesar, who was hastening with all his forces to its defence. The encounter took place in eastern Gaul, on the borders of the country of the Sequani and Lingones, and resulted in a victory for the Romans, which was chiefly due to the valour of the German horsemen who had recently been enrolled by Caesar.

SIEGE OF ALESIA

Vercingetorix now threw himself with all his forces into the strong city of Alesia,[1] and round this famous fortress the last struggle for the liberty of Gaul was fought out. Caesar enclosed the place in an immense system of circumvallation, ten miles in circuit, and outside this he drew a second line of works, knowing that he would have to play the part both of besieger and besieged. Five weeks and the labour of sixty thousand men were required to effect the investment of the city, but before the blockade was completed Vercingetorix sent out his cavalry with orders to scour the country and bring the whole fighting force of the Gauls to his relief. Thirty days passed, and the supplies of the garrison, which numbered eighty thousand men, were almost exhausted. Between the walls of the town and the Roman lines wandered a multitude of helpless wretches, old men, women, and children, thrust out of their homes by the stern necessity of war, to perish miserably by hunger and exposure. In this extremity the anxious watchers on the city walls saw the glint of armour on the wooded heights which skirted the town on its western side. The horsemen sent out by Vercingetorix had done their work well, and help was at hand. On the next morning the great assault began, and the swarming hosts of the Gauls flung them-

---

[1] Alise-Ste.-Reine, in the department Côte-d'Or.

REPUBLICAN ROME

selves like the waves of the sea on the outer Roman lines, seconded by the desperate efforts of the garrison, who strove to force the entrenchments immediately enclosing the town. On the third day, after a last grand attack, which was within an ace of succeeding, the Gauls fell back and dispersed to their homes, leaving the besieged army to its fate.

DEVOTION OF VERCINGETORIX

Vercingetorix had fought nobly, and he now thought to save his countrymen from the worst consequences of defeat by an act of sublime self-sacrifice. Clothed in complete armour, he mounted his horse, and, riding at full gallop into the Roman camp, surrendered himself as a prisoner to his great enemy. But his chivalrous self-devotion had no power to move the cold heart of the Roman. In Caesar's eyes the hero of Auvergne was simply a rebel who had committed an act of high treason against the sovereign power of Rome. He was reserved to grace the triumph of his conqueror, and to die the death of a malefactor in the foul dungeon which had witnessed the last agonies of Jugurtha.

GAUL CONQUERED

The fall of Alesia and the loss of their leader broke the spirit of the Gauls, and no further attempt at a national rising was made. Much hard fighting had, however, yet to be done, and it was not until the end of the next year (51 B.C.) that the conquest of Gaul could be regarded as complete. In all the annals of Roman warfare there is no achievement to compare with what Caesar accomplished in the eight years following his consulship. He made an end of a great national contest which had lasted for three centuries and a half. He added to the Roman dominions a vast extent of territory, corresponding to the whole of modern France, with Alsace and Lorraine, Belgium, and part of Holland, and thereby gave a new impulse to the development of a gifted people.

PLATE LVIII. TOMB OF CAECILIA METELLA   504

PLATE LIX: POSIDONIUS

505

LAST ERA OF THE REPUBLIC

EVENTS IN ROME

The close of Caesar's Gallic campaigns and his return to the capital brings us to the eve of that tremendous convulsion which shook three continents, and still sends its echoes to our ears, after the lapse of twenty centuries. But before we enter on the narrative of the civil war it is necessary to sketch briefly the course of events in Rome from the time when Cicero went into exile (58 B.C.).

The absence of Caesar left Clodius for a time virtually master of Rome. The whole rabble of the capital obeyed his nod, and scenes of riot and violence were of daily occurrence. This lord of misrule affected to play the part of a second Gracchus, and passed laws which were designed to break down the last remnant of aristocratic privilege. The Senate was powerless ; the great Pompeius himself was openly insulted, and at last shut himself up in his house, declaring that his life was in danger. Amid this anarchy the thoughts of all sober citizens turned to the patriot orator who had saved his country from still worse disorders, and whose banishment had been a scandal to public justice. Pompeius himself felt that he had played but a sorry part in abandoning the man who had ever been his warmest supporter. The recall of Cicero began to be openly mooted. But as long as Clodius retained his office of tribune nothing could be done, and it was necessary to secure the consent of Caesar, who even in his absence exercised a powerful influence over the feebler spirit of Pompeius. After some negotiations this difficulty was removed, and on the retirement of Clodius from the tribunate the measure for Cicero's recall was brought forward a second time. Clodius, though now in a private station, still ruled the rabble, but he had a formidable rival in Titus Annius Milo, a friend of Cicero's, who collected a band of gladiators and opposed violence with violence. Milo was now tribune, and after a series of street-fights, in which blood was shed freely on both sides, the bill was carried, and Cicero returned to Rome, having been absent from the capital for a year and a half The orator's journey

REPUBLICAN ROME

from Brundisium resembled a triumphal progress, and he was carried back to Rome, as he said himself, on the shoulders of Italy. But it was a fact full of significance, showing the utter impotence of the government, that the professed champion of law and order could only be restored by the intervention of the strong hand.

CICERO'S NEW HOPE

Cicero, however, with his sanguine and impulsive temperament, was highly elated by this brief gleam of prosperity. All his hopes revived, and the vision of a restored constitution, with a united Senate, a middle class reconciled and loyal, and Pompeius as the strong shield of the Republic against military aggression, once more rose before his fancy. But once more these fine dreams were to end in bitter disillusionment. The distrust which the nobles had always felt toward Pompeius had been deepened by his alliance with Caesar, and they were less inclined than ever to second his designs. The great object of Pompeius was to obtain some important command which would enable him to balance the rising power of Caesar, whose brilliant victories in Gaul had filled him with envy and anxiety. But the plan was frustrated by the persistent opposition of the Senate. He obtained, indeed, an appointment which gave him the control of the corn-supply for five years, but the bill conferring this office was clipped of its most important clause, which would have bestowed on him the disposition of funds and the command of legions. Crossed in this attempt, he tried next year to obtain a commission to restore Ptolemy, king of Egypt, who had been driven out by a rebellion of his subjects, but he was again thwarted by the obstinate prejudice of the Senate. Thus the course of events was steadily forcing him into a closer connexion with Caesar, and this result was precipitated by the action of Cicero, who, untaught by the past and blind to the present, remained rapt in his favourite illusion. Thinking himself strong enough to assume an independent attitude, the orator had recently indulged in bitter invective against Vatinius, one of Caesar's followers, and he

506

was now about to call in question the law passed in the first year of the Triumvirate, for distributing the Campanian land among the poorer citizens. It was the second time that he had crossed the path of Caesar, and he was soon to learn how grievously he had miscalculated his own strength.

CONFERENCE OF THE TRIUMVIRS

It was the usual practice of Caesar, during the time of his Gallic wars, to pass the winter in Cisalpine Gaul, where he could watch the affairs of the capital and keep in touch with his adherents. Just before departing for his campaign against the Veneti he took up his quarters at Luca, on the south-western confines of his province, and there was held that famous conference which renewed the bond between the triumvirs and shattered all the recently formed hopes of Cicero. The three powerful men who held the fate of Rome in their hands entered into an agreement by which Caesar's command in Gaul was to be extended for five years, while Pompeius and Crassus were to hold the consulship in the ensuing year (55 B.C.). At the expiration of their year of office Pompeius was to have the province of Spain and Crassus that of Syria. The threefold tyranny had thus once more raised its head, and the dream of a free Republic seemed farther from realization than ever.

CICERO RECANTS

Cicero now received clear intimation that he would have to lower his tone, unless he wished to see Clodius let loose upon him again, backed by all the power of the triumvirs. It was a bitter moment for that eager and aspiring spirit, who had thought to guide the destinies of his country, when he found that he would henceforth have to play a subordinate part and submit to complete political extinction. It would have been better for his dignity, and better for his fame, if he had chosen the latter course, or if he had retired, for a time at least, from public life. But he could not forsake the scenes in which he had lately been so prominent a figure, and after some inward struggle he chose the less worthy part. In his speech *On the Consular Provinces* he made a public recantation of his recent line of policy and pronounced a magnificent eulogy on the victorious career of Caesar. " The gods," he said, in a famous passage, " raised the bulwark of the Alps for the defence of Italy against barbarian invasion. But now let the Alps sink into the earth, for Caesar has made an end of that peril and there is no enemy left for us to fear." Two years later, as if determined to make perfect his self-effacement, he undertook the defence of Vatinius, whom he had lately assailed with the most furious abuse ; and when Gabinius, a creature of Pompeius who had done him more than one ill turn, was brought to trial on a charge of extortion it was Cicero who appeared as his advocate. In a later age such conduct might have been extolled as the height of Christian charity, but Cicero has to be judged on other grounds, and his conduct on this occasion helps to explain, though not to justify, the contempt which has been poured upon his memory.

Caesar and Pompeius Estranged

Meanwhile the arrangements concluded at Luca had been carried out. By the use of open intimidation Pompeius and Crassus secured their election to the consulship, and the partition of provinces according to Caesar's stipulation followed in due course. But the events of the next few years tended more and more to isolate the position of Caesar and draw Pompeius over to the side of the Senate. In Rome the two triumvirs showed themselves utterly unable to maintain order, and the old scenes of tumult and riot were renewed. In one of these street-fights an untoward incident occurred whose historical importance has perhaps been exaggerated. At the election of aediles the partisans of the rival candidates came to blows, and a man who was standing near Pompeius was wounded, and fell, sprinkling the consul's gown with his blood. Pompeius dispatched an attendant to his house to bring a change of raiment, and Julia, meeting the man as he entered, fell fainting to the ground at the sight of the blood-stained robe. The shock so undermined the constitution of the young and tender wife that she died in the following year. We need not believe, as some writers seem to imply, that the fate of Rome hung upon the life of a feeble woman, but with Julia's death a coldness sprang up between Caesar and Pompeius, and from this time they drifted farther and farther apart.

A FATAL EXPEDITION

Crassus had followed the military successes of Caesar with a growing envy, and he now thought to emulate the victorious general's achievements by a career of conquest in the East. Evil omens attended him on his departure for his province, and Ateius, one of the tribunes, taking his stand at the gates, solemnly devoted him to the infernal gods. These forebodings seemed to be justified by the fearful disaster which followed. On his arrival in Syria Crassus made preparations on a great scale for the invasion of Parthia, whose king, Orodes, had been guilty of hostile acts against the king of Armenia, a dependent and ally of Rome. Deaf to all warnings, the infatuated man advanced with a splendid force into the waterless desert of Mesopotamia, where his men soon began to suffer severely from thirst and fatigue. In this plight he was attacked by swarms of mounted bowmen, the chief strength of the Parthian army, and after a vain attempt to cut his way through, which resulted in the death of his son, the gallant Publius Crassus,

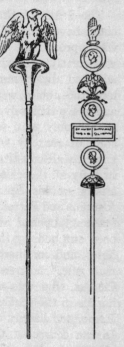

AN EAGLE   STANDARD

he was compelled to fall back. Overtaken on the outskirts of Armenia, he was lured into a parley, and treacherously murdered, with the chief members of his staff (53 B.C.). Half of his great army had perished in the desert or fallen by the arrows of the Parthians, and ten thousand prisoners were carried away, with the Roman eagles, into the heart of Parthia, where they were settled by the Parthian king, married native wives, and passed the rest of their days in ignoble servitude. The remnant of the Roman force was led back to Syria by Caius Cassius,[1] whose prompt action, aided by domestic dissensions in the royal house of Parthia, averted the worst consequences of the defeat.

ROME UNDER MOB RULE

The death of Crassus was a serious blow to Caesar, who could have counted on his co-operation in the struggle which was approaching. On the other hand, the position of Pompeius was greatly strengthened by the removal of the third triumvir, who had always nursed a secret enmity against him, and before long the nobles were compelled to lay aside their prejudices and place themselves unreservedly in the hands of Pompeius, as the only man who could put an end to the intolerable state of anarchy which had long prevailed in Rome. Contrary to all constitutional precedent, Pompeius had remained in Italy at the close of his consulship, and administered the affairs of his Spanish provinces through his lieutenants, Afranius and Petreius. The year following the death of Crassus (52 B.C.) opened without any consuls, as the elections had been stopped by the riotous proceedings of the rival candidates, and for many months Rome was left at the mercy of mob rule. Matters were brought to a crisis by the death of Clodius, who was met by Milo on the Appian Way, and lost his life in the scuffle which ensued. The body was brought to Rome, and hastily burnt on a pyre constructed in the Forum. In the course of these proceedings the Curia Hostilia, the old Senate House of Rome, took fire, and was burnt to the ground. Highly incensed by the death of their favourite, the rabble paraded the streets, to the terror of peaceful citizens;

[1] Afterwards notorious as the leader of the conspiracy which led to the assassination of Caesar.

and at last the Senate, powerless to cope with the disturbance, called upon Pompeius to restore order. By a sort of compromise, in order to avoid the use of the hateful name of dictator, he was invested with the office of sole consul, and he at once began to enlist troops and take steps to assert the authority of the government. Milo was brought to trial, condemned, and sent into banishment. Cicero, who owed him a deep debt of gratitude, had undertaken his defence, but his nerve failed him at the critical moment, and the eloquent harangue which he afterwards published was read by his benefactor when in exile at Massilia.

CIVIL WAR

While the drift of events had thus been promoting his rival's ascendancy, Caesar's whole energy had been absorbed in putting down the national rising under Vercingetorix. The following year (51 B.C.) was occupied in destroying the last remnants of the insurrection, and when that task was completed he remained still for twelve months in Gaul, exerting himself to win the affections of the inhabitants and reconcile them to the Roman yoke. Meanwhile his adherents in Rome had been working hard in his interests, and chief among those who figured in the events to be described was Scribonius Curio, a dissolute young noble, who had been won over to his cause by an enormous bribe. It was of the utmost importance to Caesar that he should retain his province until he had secured his election to the consulship, for if he appeared in Rome as a private citizen he would be left to the mercy of his opponents, who were bent on his ruin. Cato especially had openly avowed his intention of bringing him to trial as soon as he had laid down his proconsulship. It was further necessary that he should be allowed to stand for the consulship during his absence, and with the sanction of Pompeius a law had been passed to this effect. But Pompeius, with characteristic duplicity, doubled and shuffled, reversing his own acts and supporting contradictory measures. Clearly he was not to be trusted; and still less could Caesar throw himself on the good faith of the extreme section among the nobles, who were ready for any act of treachery if only they could compass his downfall. A long negotiation ensued, each party trying to gain a technical advantage, and matters approached a climax, when Curio, as tribune, came forward with a proposal that both Caesar and Pompeius should resign their provinces and disband their armies. The proposal was rejected, but Caesar, who was sincerely anxious to maintain peace, preserved a strictly moderate tone. Earlier in the year he had shown his pacific intention by resigning two legions, one of which had been lent him by Pompeius, at the demand of the government. These legions were ostensibly required for service in the Parthian war, but they were in fact retained in Italy. Such a breach of faith was an ominous sign of the rupture which was imminent. At the close of the year (50 B.C.) Caesar moved into the Cisalpine province, and took up his station at Ravenna, on the frontiers of Italy.[1] The suspense was growing intolerable. A large majority of the Senate and all reasonable citizens inclined strongly to peace. But the crisis was precipitated by the action of the consuls, Caius Claudius Marcellus and Lucius Cornelius Lentulus, two furious aristocrats, who entered on their office at the beginning of the following year. Determined to push matters to extremes, and supported by the military power of Pompeius, they forced a decree through the Senate ordering Caesar to disband his army and resign his provinces to the successors appointed by the government. The tribunes, in Caesar's interest, interposed their veto, but they were obliged to fly for their lives, and their appearance in Caesar's camp gave the signal for civil war.

POMPEIUS RETREATS

In his own narrative of these events Caesar says nothing of the famous incident of crossing the Rubicon, nor is it to be supposed that he would give any hint of that fearful inward conflict which is described in such moving terms by Plutarch

---

[1] Cisalpine Gaul (Lombardy and Piedmont) was not reckoned as part of Italy until the time of Augustus.

and Lucan. His resolve once taken, there was no room for doubt or wavering in that high and serene intelligence. At the outset, however, his prospects seemed dark enough. All the resources of the empire, outside of the Gaulish provinces, the mighty prestige of an established government, and the whole weight of public opinion were on the side of his adversaries. In the eyes of the world Pompeius was the lawful champion of constitutional order, while Caesar was descending, like a second Brennus, to carry war and havoc into Italy. But Caesar had two advantages on his side which justified him in defying these seemingly overwhelming odds. He knew his own mind, and he had at his back a veteran army utterly devoted to his service. It was therefore with full confidence in the issue and a just estimate of his opponent's chances that he made that tiger's spring from Ravenna. He had only one legion, with some auxiliary troops, at his immediate disposal, as the rest of his forces were quartered in Gaul. But he hoped to confound his enemies by the suddenness of the blow and by the mere terror of his name. His calculations were fully borne out by the event. Pompeius, with his usual apathy, had neglected to assemble a force for the defence of Italy, and with the exception of the two legions which he had received from Caesar, and whose fidelity was more than doubtful, he had no troops ready to take the field. When, therefore, it became known that Caesar had occupied all the towns in the March of Ancona and had thrown a garrison into Arretium, thus making himself master of the approaches to central Italy, a wild panic arose, and the whole body of the magistrates abandoned Rome, even forgetting in their haste to carry the State treasure with them. Pompeius now resolved to abandon Italy and carry on the war from the other side of the Adriatic. In the East his influence was still supreme, and he hoped to raise a vast army and crush his enemy by mere weight of numbers. But his plan was almost wrecked by the obstinacy of one of his subordinates, Lucius Domitius Ahenobarbus, who occupied Corfinium with a body of troops and stubbornly refused to obey when ordered to join his leader in Apulia. He was compelled, however, by the mutinous disposition of his men to take to flight, and the town, with all its garrison, fell into the hands of Caesar. Pompeius then resumed his retreat, and after frustrating an attempt to shut him up in Brundisium he embarked his troops and set sail for the opposite coast.

CAESAR'S ADVANTAGE

In little more than two months the position of affairs had been wholly reversed. The politic moderation of Caesar, whose troops were under strict control, had gone far to allay the terrors of the Italians, who had expected a repetition of the horrors which had accompanied the victories of Marius and Sulla. The withdrawal of Pompeius, also, though a strategic necessity, had the unfortunate effect of making him appear the invader of Italy, while Caesar now assumed the character of its defender.[1] Moreover, the furious language of the Pompeians, threatening a new reign of terror, served to emphasize by contrast the studied forbearance of Caesar. Italy, therefore, was already half won, and thousands of recruits flocked to the conqueror's standard; and among all his officers not one faltered in his allegiance, with the single exception of Labienus, who went over to the enemy at the first outbreak of the war.

THE WAR IN SPAIN

Caesar's position, however, was still highly critical. Pompeius held the sea with a powerful fleet, threatening to cut off supplies from the capital, all the vast resources of the East were at his back, and Spain was held for him by his trusted lieutenants Petreius, Afranius, and Varro, with seven legions, trained in long conflicts with the warlike natives. It was from this side that danger seemed first to threaten, for the Spanish army was ready to take the field, while Pompeius was notoriously slow in his movements and it would take him many months to train and mobilize an adequate force.

[1] Pelham, *Outlines of Roman History*, p. 235 and n.

LAST ERA OF THE REPUBLIC

To Spain, therefore, Caesar directed his course, after a few days passed in Rome, during which he was compelled by his necessities to lay violent hands on the State treasure, which the tribune, Lucius Metellus, in vain tried to defend. To provide against a famine, two of Caesar's officers were sent to occupy Sardinia and Sicily; and Curio, to whom the task in the latter was assigned, had orders to proceed from Sicily to Africa, where the Numidian king Juba had taken up arms for the Pompeians.

Having made his arrangements for the administration of affairs in Rome and Italy during his absence, Caesar set out for Spain, where six of his legions were already assembled near Ilerda, confronting the Pompeian army under Petreius and Afranius. His journey was delayed by the resistance of the Massiliots, who were encouraged by the presence of Domitius, Caesar's inveterate enemy, to close their gates against him. Having formed the siege of Massilia, he left the further operations to be conducted by his lieutenants Trebonius and Decimus Brutus, and hastened on to the scene of war in the peninsula. Presently startling rumours began to be heard in Rome, which raised the hopes of the Pompeians, and induced many of the waverers to join what seemed to be the winning side. Caesar, it was asserted, had met with a crushing disaster, and the day of liberty, as Cicero would have said, had once more dawned on the Republic. The report, though greatly exaggerated, was not without foundation, and, in fact, Caesar for one brief moment had been on the verge of ruin. An attempt to seize a strong position between Ilerda and the Pompeian camp was repulsed with heavy loss to his army, and presently he found himself penned up between two flooded rivers and cut off from his supplies. But his ready resource enabled him to extricate himself from this perilous position. During his stay in Britain he had observed with wonder the daring feats which were performed by the natives in their frail coracles, constructed of skins stretched over a wooden framework. A number of these light vessels were hastily put together under his orders, and used to convey a portion of his troops across

the river and re-establish communication with his convoys
from Gaul.

' VICTORY ' OF ILERDA

The native tribes, who had hitherto favoured the Pompeians,
now began to go over to Caesar, and Petreius and Afranius,
finding that the tide had turned against them, determined to
fall back behind the line of the Ebro. But they were not to
escape so easily. Caesar, divining their intention, set off in
hot pursuit. Then, finding themselves outpaced, they doubled
back on Ilerda, but they were brought to bay, and compelled to surrender at discretion. Acting with his accustomed
clemency, Caesar dismissed the officers unharmed, while many
of the ordinary soldiers passed over to his side. By this
brilliant though bloodless victory Caesar had within a few
weeks made himself master of all Spain, for Varro, who commanded in the southern province, immediately sent in his
submission. The capitulation of Massilia followed shortly
afterwards, and the close of the year saw Caesar's supremacy
acknowledged by half the Roman world. In Africa alone the
success of his arms had been chequered by a serious reverse,
which resulted in the death of Curio and the destruction of his
army.

CAESAR FOLLOWS POMPEIUS

Caesar had been appointed dictator in his absence, and his
second visit to the capital, which lasted only for eleven days,
was marked by some important measures, of which it will
be convenient to speak when we take a general view of his
legislation. He had work before him which admitted of no
delay, for the name of Pompeius was still all-powerful in the
East, and at his command an immense force was assembling,
drawn from all the kingdoms and dependencies of Lower Asia.
Besides these auxiliary troops Pompeius had a force of nine
Roman legions, mostly composed of raw recruits, and he
worked night and day, toiling like a common drill-sergeant,

to train and discipline his unpractised levies. Caesar's men, on the other hand, were all seasoned veterans, and the sooner he could bring on the decisive struggle the better were his chances of success. At the beginning of the year (48 B.C.) [1] he embarked with half his troops from Brundisium, and, landing without mishap on the opposite coast, occupied the towns of Oricum and Apollonia. He had run a fearful risk, for the fleet of Pompeius lay close at hand, and was strong enough to send his whole squadron to the bottom. But Caesar was once more saved by the rapidity of his movements, which baffled all the calculations of his adversaries. His position, however, was highly precarious, for Pompeius, at the news of his approach, had hurried up with his whole force from his headquarters in Macedonia, and forestalled his opponent in an attempt to seize Dyrrachium, which was full of stores and munitions collected for the use of the Pompeian army. Half of the dictator's forces still lay at Brundisium, and the admirals of Pompeius, once warned, were all on the alert to prevent them from crossing. Fortune, however, did not desert her favourite. Antonius, who had been left in charge of the second division, crossed the sea in a heavy gale, and, eluding the enemy's vessels, landed on the coast a long way north of Caesar's position, and succeeded in effecting a junction with his commander. By a rapid movement Caesar threw himself between Dyrrachium and the camp of Pompeius, which was situated at Petra, some miles farther south, and he now conceived the daring design of blockading the vastly superior forces of the enemy in their entrenchments. For this purpose he threw up a system of works, many miles in extent, starting from his own camp, and carried along the hills until they met the sea at a point south of Petra. But the rash attempt nearly ended in total disaster. Pompeius succeeded in turning his enemy's lines, and in the engagement which ensued Caesar's troops were severely beaten, and driven from the field in disorder. But for the hesitation of Pompeius,

---

[1] By the unreformed calendar. The real date was November 6, 49 B.C. See below. p. 529.

who neglected to push the pursuit, that day would have ended Caesar's career. As it was, he obtained time to rally his broken legions and make his escape to Apollonia. Thence he marched into Thessaly, and there, in the course of the summer, was fought the great battle which decided the long quarrel between the rivals.

POMPEIUS CLINGS TO THE EAST

After the retreat of Caesar Pompeius was strongly urged to carry the war into Italy, and there is little doubt that this would have been his wisest course, for the recovery of the capital would have given him an enormous political advantage. Moreover, his fleets held command of the sea, and Caesar, left alone in a country where he was comparatively unknown, would have been surrounded by difficulties. But Pompeius was reluctant to abandon the East, which he regarded as his true field of operations, and he was anxious to join his father-in-law, Scipio,[1] who was bringing up reinforcements from Syria and Asia Minor. Accordingly he directed his march upon Macedonia, effected the desired junction with Scipio, and, descending into Thessaly, took up his station at Larissa, some distance to the north of Pharsalus, where Caesar lay encamped. He still wished to put off a general engagement, but his judgment was overruled by the importunate clamour of the nobles in his suite, whose perpetual wrangling filled his camp with disorder and silenced the voice of sane counsel. " They were so eager," says Caesar, " to divide the spoils of victory that they took no time to consider how the victory was to be won." At last, wearied out by the contention, Pompeius broke up his camp and advanced upon Pharsalus.

BATTLE OF PHARSALUS

Caesar's infantry amounted to but twenty-two thousand men, less than half the number of the Pompeians, while he had only a mere handful of cavalry to oppose to the dense

[1] He had married Scipio's daughter Cornelia after the death of Julia.

squadrons of the enemy. His left, looking eastward, was covered by the river Enipeus, but his right, extending toward the open plain, was in serious danger of being outflanked, for Pompeius, with this very intention, had concentrated the whole body of his cavalry on his own left. Here, therefore, Caesar stationed his Gallic and German horse, supported by a picked troop of veteran legionaries, who had orders to strike at the faces of the enemy, as their bodies and limbs were sheathed in armour.[1] This skilful disposition decided the issue of the day. While the Pompeian infantry sustained with firmness the charge of Caesar's men on their left, the cavalry, after driving back the Gauls and Germans opposed to them, were thrown into confusion by the veteran troops stationed in reserve, and fell back in disorder, leaving the left wing of their own army exposed. Caesar then gave the order for a general advance, and the Pompeians, breaking their ranks, retreated in panic upon their camp. Pompeius had been one of the first to leave the field, and he retired moodily to his tent. But when he heard the shouts of the Caesarians advancing to the assault he mounted his horse and galloped away with one or two companions toward the coast. Meanwhile Caesar had followed up the pursuit with vigour, and on the next day the remnant of the Pompeian army, numbering twenty-four thousand men, surrendered at discretion.

DEATH OF POMPEIUS

So far Caesar, though often running desperate risks, had acted consistently in the character of a great soldier and statesman, but for nearly a year after the battle of Pharsalus we find him engaged in a series of wild adventures, which seem strangely at variance with the general tenor of his life. Taking with him a small body of troops, he set off in pursuit of Pompeius, who, after long hesitation, had decided to make Egypt the

[1] Plutarch gives a comic turn to this famous order, as if the intention were to 'spoil the beauty' of the Roman exquisites who fought on the side of Pompeius (*Caesar*, c. 45).

519

refuge of his broken fortunes. But when Caesar entered
Alexandria the first object that met his eyes was the severed
head of his great rival, which was brought him by Theodotus,
the tutor of the young king Ptolemy. By the will of Ptolemy
Auletes, who had died three years previously, the crown of
Egypt had been left to his son and namesake and his daughter
Cleopatra, who were to reign as joint sovereigns. But the
brother and sister had quarrelled over their inheritance,
and Cleopatra was driven to take refuge in Syria. At the
time when Pompeius arrived in Egypt the king's army was
encamped at Pelusium, to repel an invasion which had been
undertaken on behalf of the banished queen. There had
been some doubt as to the reception which ought to be given
to the famous fugitive, but by the advice of Theodotus he
was set upon at the moment of landing and murdered. Such
was the end of the great Pompeius, after a career which
had brought him more than once within reach of an imperial
crown.

CAESAR IN EGYPT

The taste for romantic and amorous adventure which
characterizes the dotage of literature has given undue prominence to a discreditable episode in Caesar's career. Captivated by the charms of Cleopatra, whose cause he had espoused,
he soon found that he had plunged unwarily into a hotbed of
sedition. The mob of Alexandria, always famous for its ferocious and unruly temper, rose in insurrection, and for many
months Caesar was blockaded in the royal palace, adjoining the
eastern harbour. In order to keep open his communications
with the sea, he caused the Egyptian fleet and dock-buildings
to be set on fire, and it was on this occasion that the renowned
Alexandrian library, with all its treasure of ancient learning,
was burnt to the ground. At length Caesar was set free
from his precarious and humiliating position by the arrival
of a relieving army, commanded by Mithradates of Pergamum,
a member of the royal house of Galatia.[1] Caesar now broke

[1] Niese, p. 249.

PLATE LX. Cn. Pompeius Magnus (?)   520

PLATE LXI. CAIUS JULIUS CAESAR (NAPLES)   521

out of his confinement, and, joining the army of Mithradates, met and defeated the Egyptian forces on the banks of the Nile. The young Ptolemy was swept among the fugitives into the river and drowned, and Caesar, now master of Egypt, appointed Cleopatra and a younger brother joint sovereigns. He spent the rest of the winter at Alexandria, " in dalliance with his fair Egyptian spouse," and she afterwards bore him a son, the unhappy Caesarion, who met his fate seventeen years later at the hands of Octavian.[1] Then, throwing off the spell which had so long held him captive, he turned his back on Egypt, and emerged once more as the conqueror and ruler of men.

Caesar Moves Again

It was time, indeed, for him to bestir himself, for during his long absence serious disorders had broken out in Italy, the Pompeians were flocking in thousands to their new head-quarters in Africa, Spain was in revolt, and Pharnaces, the son of Mithradates the Great, had availed himself of the opportunity to recover his ancestral dominions in Pontus. Caesar's first task was to put down the presumption of this rash pretender. He found time on his way to settle the affairs of Syria and Judaea, and then, marching into Pontus, he scattered the forces of Pharnaces at the battle of Zela,[2] and compelled him to fly for refuge to the kingdom of Bosporus, where he was shortly afterwards murdered by one of his own subjects. It was on this occasion that Caesar made a satirical comment on the exploits of Pompeius, who had won his fame so cheaply by triumphs obtained over effeminate Orientals. In the autumn he returned to Italy, after an absence of nearly two years. While in Alexandria he had been appointed dictator for the second time.

[1] It is possible that Virgil was thinking of Caesar's intrigue with Cleopatra when he spoke of Aeneas and Dido as *regnorum immemores, turpique cupidine captos* (*Aeneid*, iv. 194).
[2] *Veni, vidi, vici.*

REPUBLICAN ROME

THE MILITARY SENTIMENT

Soon after Caesar's arrival in Italy a memorable incident occurred which was full of evil omen for the future of Rome. It had been the dictator's policy to foster the military sentiment among his troops and to promote a feeling of emulation in the different divisions by conferring special marks of distinction on those who had attracted his favourable notice. On the other hand, he demanded the most unstinting devotion from those who followed his fortunes, and for many years the fidelity and endurance of his men had been taxed to the utmost. The time had now come when his unique personal influence was to be put to a severe test. A new cloud of war was gathering in Africa, and the legions destined for this service were mustered in Campania. But their loyalty broke down under the pressure of this fresh burden, and they demanded their discharge. Caesar summoned the grumblers into his presence, and reduced them to obedience by a single word : " I grant what you desire," he said. " *Citizens*, you may go." At the sound of that peaceful title, which seemed to them a bitter humiliation, the soldiers repented of their rebellious mood and begged to be received back into their commander's favour. This mutiny, and the manner in which it was quelled, was a significant symptom of the ascendancy which the sword had obtained over the gown.[1] The tendency went on gaining strength, until, five generations later, the empire was actually put up to auction by a Roman army and sold to the highest bidder.[2]

BATTLE OF THAPSUS

Caesar's long absence had given time for the Republicans to rally their forces, and they had made their headquarters at Utica, not far from the site of ancient Carthage. Hither had come Scipio, the father-in-law of Pompeius, who was appointed

[1] *Cedant arma togae*, says Cicero, in the line singled out for ridicule by Antony.

[2] Gibbon, c. 5.

to the chief command, the two sons of Pompeius, Cnaeus and Sextus, Petreius, a hardy veteran, who had been let go by Caesar after his defeat in Spain, the renegade Labienus, and the great patriot Cato. Caesar, acting with his usual vigour, crossed from Sicily in midwinter (47 B.C.); but his fleet was dispersed during the passage, and for some time he was in great danger, clinging for bare life to a strip of hostile coast with a mere handful of men. But his troops came in by degrees, and after some months he found himself in a position to assume the offensive. By a threatened attack on Thapsus he induced Scipio to risk a general engagement, which ended in the total destruction of the Pompeian army. It was a soldiers' battle, for Caesar's men, who were in a bitter and revengeful mood, rushed on the Pompeians with one mad impulse, drove them back on their camp, and butchered them in multitudes, refusing all quarter. Two incidents which followed the battle may be briefly described, as they typify the spirit of Caesar's adversaries at its worst and at its best. Juba, the fierce king of Numidia, had brought a swarm of his wild riders to the help of Scipio, and when all was lost he fled from the battlefield, accompanied by Petreius, and escaped to Zama. Being refused admission by the inhabitants, the fugitives repaired to one of Juba's country houses, and there, after filling themselves with meat and wine, they engaged in single combat. Juba, who was young and vigorous, slew his antagonist, and then received his death-blow by the hand of a slave.

CATO'S DEATH

It is with far different feelings that we are called to attend the dying hours of Cato. That pure and noble spirit had watched with bitter sorrow the suicidal struggle in which his countrymen were engaged, and he had been revolted by the savage temper which was displayed by the leaders of his party. But his high sense of duty kept him faithful to his post as long as the struggle could be maintained with any hope of success.

The news of defeat reached him at Utica, where he had been left in command at an early stage of the campaign, and his first thought was to provide for the safety of those who had most reason to fear Caesar's resentment. For himself there was only one way of escape left. The gulf between him and Caesar was too wide to be bridged by any compromise. To have accepted his life from the conqueror would have been to give the lie to his whole career. So, with a calm dignity, in strange contrast with the scene of drunken passion which we have just witnessed, he prepared to meet his end. Having supped in the society of his friends, he retired to his chamber, and spent most of the night in studying Plato's dialogue on the immortality of the soul. Then, after a brief but sound slumber, he rose from his couch in the still hours of the morning, and, plunging his sword into his side, expired after a painful struggle. By his voluntary death he achieved a terrible revenge over his enemies, and earned an immortality of fame as the great martyr of republican liberty. It is not without reason that Dante in his great poem [1] assigns an especial place of honour to the man who, in a cruel age, never forgot his humanity, and who trod the path of rectitude from the beginning to the end.

Last Stand of the Pompeians

The butchery of Thapsus was repeated a year later at Munda, in southern Spain, where the Pompeians had rallied their forces for a last desperate stand. The movement was so serious that Caesar was obliged to suspend his labours in Rome and hurry to the seat of war. After some months of desultory fighting the rebels were brought to bay in the neighbourhood of Cordova, and their forces, amounting to thirteen legions, were utterly destroyed. Among the slain was Labienus, Caesar's old lieutenant, who had distinguished himself by his barbarous treatment of the prisoners who fell into his hands. Before leaving Spain Caesar was joined by the young Caius Octavius, his grand-nephew and adopted heir,

[1] *Purgatorio*, i. 31 ff.

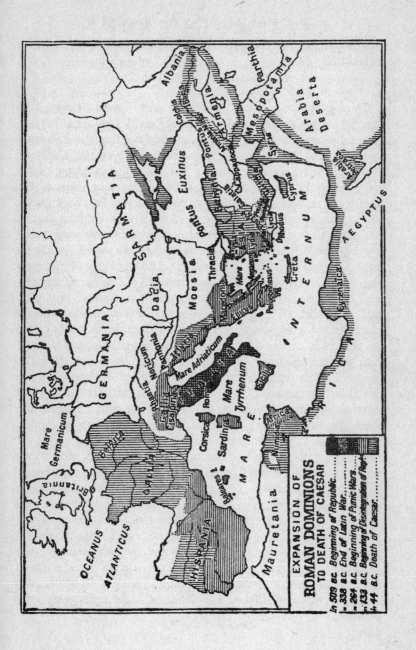

EXPANSION OF
ROMAN DOMINIONS
TO DEATH OF CAESAR

In 509 B.C. Beginning of Republic......
" 338 B.C. End of Latin War...........
" 264 B.C. Beginning of Punic Wars....
" 133 B.C. Beginning of Disintegration of Rep.
" 44 B.C. Death of Caesar............

afterwards known in history under the renowned name of Augustus.

CAESAR AS LEGISLATOR

During fourteen years we have seen Caesar involved in almost constant warfare. He had fought countless battles, generally against heavy odds, and many a time he had been in great peril, but he had always known how to pluck victory from the very jaws of defeat. Beginning his military career comparatively late in life, the sudden transformation of the profligate man of fashion and expert political intriguer into a mighty conqueror must have seemed to his contemporaries little less than a miracle. His almost superhuman energy and the lightning rapidity of his movements are noted by Cicero with a sort of horrified admiration. In the course of the civil war he twice traversed the whole breadth of the Roman world, and shattered the armies of the Republic in Greece, in Africa, and in Spain. We have now to consider him in the peaceful character of a legislator, employed in founding a new system on the ruins of the old. Short indeed was the space allotted him for this gigantic task, which might have absorbed the energies of a long lifetime. His schemes embraced every detail of government, from the largest problems of imperial administration to the humble duties of an urban magistrate. The title under which he ruled was that of dictator, which was several times renewed, and finally conferred on him for life. But the odious associations connected with that name were softened by the mildness and moderation of his measures. No act of proscription, no cancelling of debts or wholesale confiscation of property marked his accession to power. In the severe financial crisis which occurred at the outbreak of the civil war he took a middle course which showed a due regard to the distress of the debtor and the just claims of the creditor. This was a severe disappointment to the more desperate among his followers, and led to more than one serious outbreak which disturbed the peace of Italy during his long absence.

LAST ERA OF THE REPUBLIC

Social Reconstruction

One of the most difficult questions with which Caesar had to deal was the old feud between rich and poor. The same glaring contrast which meets us in Europe and America to-day was present in the Roman world of Caesar's time. On one side stood the wealthy few, who lavished their millions in tasteless luxury, and on the other side were the helpless and destitute many. The sources of the evil lay beyond the reach of reform, and Caesar, like all other statesmen, had to content himself with palliatives. He began by instituting a strict inquiry into the method of administering public relief by free distributions of grain, and a hundred and seventy thousand citizens hitherto registered as paupers were struck off the list as disqualified. Following in the steps of Caius Gracchus, he provided for many thousands of the poor by founding colonies across the sea and repeopling the sites of Corinth and Carthage ; and the desolation of Italy, which had stirred the heart of the elder Gracchus, drew from him some measures for the restoration of rural industry, and the infusion of new life into the country towns, which had been drained of their population by the general exodus to the capital. Other grand designs for the improvement of Rome and the promotion of trade and commerce were the construction of a new channel for the Tiber, embracing the whole area of the Ager Vaticanus, the draining of the Pomptine marshes and the Fucine Lake, and the cutting of a canal through the Isthmus of Corinth, which would have shortened the trade route between East and West and avoided the dangerous passage by Cape Matapan.

Caesar's Absolutism

The government of Caesar, more especially after his second Spanish campaign, tended more and more to become an absolutism. He felt that he had no equal or second in the Roman State, and it was not in his nature to study that timid and cautious policy which enabled his successor to disguise the substance of monarchy under the forms of republican

527

REPUBLICAN ROME

liberty. The world, which had owned him as master, was to
be animated by one spirit and guided by one will, the will and
the spirit of Caesar. The old constitution was not, indeed,
abolished, but it was remodelled after a fashion which caused
grave concern to orthodox statesmen of the old school. The
Senate, raised in numbers to nine hundred members, was
recruited by his nominees, chosen without respect to rank or
nationality, and the election of magistrates in the popular
assemblies was carried out under his direction. It seemed,
indeed, as if it was his deliberate purpose to throw contempt
on the most time-honoured institutions of the Republic. At
the very close of the year 45 B.C., when the chief magistracy
had been left vacant by the death of one of the consuls, he
appointed a successor to hold office for the few remaining
hours of the year, a proceeding which called forth some bitter
jests from the wits of Rome. In acting thus Caesar gave just
ground for offence, and his conduct on this occasion cannot
be excused. His temper, naturally mild and humane, had
been somewhat embittered by the long and fierce opposition he had encountered, and he was thus led into a course
which proved ruinous to himself and brought thirteen years of
anarchy and misery on his country.

Consolidation of the Empire

In one respect the new system of government inaugurated
by Caesar was productive of unmixed benefit. The old method
of applying the municipal machinery of Rome to the needs of
a vast empire, which had led to such fearful mischief, vanished
for ever. Henceforth no Roman magistrate could look forward
at the end of his year of office to the prospect of enriching
himself by the plunder of a fat province. He went forth as
the agent of a jealous sovereign, who would call him severely
to account if he made any attempt to exceed his powers. At
the same time the process was begun by which the vast
dominions of Rome were gradually welded into a great whole,
peopled by one nation and owning allegiance to one ruler.
By the enfranchisement of the Transpadane Gauls, who had

528

adhered faithfully to Caesar throughout the long struggle, the union of Italy was completed, and the extension of the same rights to distant communities like that of Gades gave promise of a new future to millions who had groaned under the Roman yoke.   One consequence of this policy was the diminished importance, politically speaking, of Rome.   The city of the Tiber was still, indeed, nominally the queen of Italy and the mistress of the world ; but the powers of the Roman magistrates were now strictly confined to the city, and Rome became simply one political unit among the municipal corporations of Italy.

Reform of the Calendar

An important reform of this time has maintained its ground to the present day.   Hitherto it had been the custom to rectify the difference between the solar and lunar year by the insertion from time to time of an intercalary month, which was left to the discretion of the Pontifical College.   But this privilege had been grossly abused for political purposes, and when Caesar became dictator for the second time there was an error of two months in the calendar.   Thus the date of Caesar's landing in Epirus, which is commonly given as January 4, 48 B.C., was, properly speaking, November 6, 49 B.C.[1]   To remedy this state of things, Caesar lengthened the old Roman year by ten days and instituted the system of leap-years still in use.   The change, of course, was derided by his political opponents, who cried out that the autocrat in thus meddling with times and seasons was usurping the functions of Jove himself.

Caesar-worship

The vast form of monarchy was, indeed, assuming gigantic proportions and throwing its shadow over the whole Roman world.   Now began the strange fashion of Caesar-worship, which in due time was adopted as an orthodox article in the

[1] Niese, p. 247.

national faith, and in after-days came to a second birth in the
high spiritual pretensions of the mediaeval popes. It seemed
as if the new monarch, not content with founding an earthly
dynasty, was determined to rival the majesty of heaven.
Caesar, too, like the gods of Olympus, must have his altar and
his priest, his burnt-offering and his throng of worshippers.
All the insignia of royalty, the golden throne, the purple robe,
the diadem,[1] and the sceptre, were flaunted before the eyes of
the Roman people. What were Caesar's motives in assuming
these outward signs of absolute power is a point which has
been much disputed. According to one view, he acted thus
from deliberate policy, wishing to accustom his countrymen
to the very form and feature of despotism. Others would
have us believe that his mind, strong as it was, had been
somewhat unhinged by the giddy height to which he had
risen, and others, again, suppose that he was urged on by
the flattery of false friends, who wished to drive him to his
ruin

THE IDES OF MARCH

But the reconstruction of an empire was not sufficient to
absorb all the energies of that great and comprehensive mind.
The work of legislation was completed, at least in outline, and
Caesar, we may imagine, was weary of the pomp of sovereignty
and sighed for the freedom and simplicity of a camp. One
great task which he had set himself was the extension of the
Roman frontier to the Danube and the Euphrates. The recent
defeat of Crassus and the loss of the Roman eagles naturally
led him to give precedence to the Eastern campaign, and he
began to make preparations for an expedition against Parthia.
But all his grand designs were cut short by the rash deed which
ended his career on the fatal Ides of March. Among the mis-
guided men who shared the infamy of that day were Marcus
Junius Brutus, whom he had taken to his very heart, Trebonius
and Decimus Brutus, his old companions in arms, and Cassius,

---

[1] The diadem, however, as is well known, though repeatedly offered to
Caesar, was always refused.

a former enemy, whom he had pardoned and loaded with benefits. Caesar had received repeated warnings of the conspiracy hatching against him, but neither fear nor suspicion could find a place in that truly imperial soul and he steadily refused to take any precautions. Nature, in raising him to a stature almost beyond mortal limits, had left him without defence against the treachery of a friend.

CAESAR THE LIBERATOR

We must now endeavour, in as few words as possible, to indicate the essential character of the work which was accomplished by Caesar. It is a common charge against him that he destroyed the liberty of Rome, and thereby committed an act of treason against his country and against mankind. But, looking at the Roman world as it appeared in the last age of the Republic, we may well ask what was the nature of the liberty destroyed by Caesar. If liberty means an unbounded freedom for plunder and outrage it was certainly enjoyed in ample measure by the narrow clique of nobles who divided among themselves the spoils of empire. There was a kind of liberty, too, in the reign of riot and bloodshed which prevailed for years in the streets of the capital. But of true liberty, whether in Italy or the provinces, we can find no trace, save in the minds of a few exalted thinkers. The Senate had long ago proved false to its great traditions and entered on a path which led straight to ruin. Unless this process had been arrested the whole State would have fallen to pieces, and the best fruits of civilization would have been swept away in a deluge of barbarism. This catastrophe Caesar averted, first by his conquest of Gaul, which checked the advance of the Germans, and secondly by the establishment of a new system of government, which brought the whole empire under the control of one supreme will. It was, in truth, a fearful remedy, involving the sacrifice of many cherished ideals; but as far as we can judge there was no other way. Caesar marked out the main lines of the system which held together the fabric of empire for nearly four centuries, and preserved those vital germs of development which, after ages of darkness, have borne splendid fruit in the larger and freer growth of modern Europe. It will be fitting, therefore, to conclude this slight and imperfect survey of Roman history with a tribute of gratitude and reverence to the memory of that illustrious man, to whose labours we owe in no small degree the measure of spiritual enfranchisement which we enjoy.

ROMAN COINS[1]

(DOWN TO 38 B.C.)

ASIA MINOR, Crete, Greece, Sicily, and the Greek cities of southern Italy, such as Taras (Tarentum), Poseidonia (Paestum), Croton, and Neapolis, had coinage, and many coins of exquisite beauty, before Rome had given up barter and had adopted at all generally her first rude metal media of exchange, her unstamped lumps and her cast bricks of bronze, and it was not till about 268 B.C., more than three centuries after the first use of the engraved die in Hellas, that the Romans began to *strike* money. The steps by which they finally attained real coinage may be intimated as follows :

(1) AES RUDE or INFECTUM, *i.e.* lumps of bronze, varying in weight and value, with no design and generally of no definite form, though sometimes roughly brick-shaped. Many specimens were found in 1828 at Vulci, in the Roman Maremma, where also such innumerable ' Etruscan ' vases were discovered. Rude lumps of metal, valued by weight, were, of course, used as media of exchange from very early times contemporaneously with barter by means of cattle, weapons, implements, cauldrons, etc.

(2) AES SIGNATUM, *i.e.* bronze cast into a quadrilateral piece weighing about four or five pounds and bearing some design, sometimes that of a weapon or implement, such as a spear or anchor, but generally that of some animal much used for barter, such as a bull, sheep, or pig (Pegasus also occurs !). The presence of such animals on *aes signatum* perhaps originated the common Latin word for ' money,' viz.

[1] In the selection of coins and preparation of casts I had the valuable aid of Mr. J. Allan, of the Department of Coins and Medals at the British Museum. The following annotations are drawn mainly from *Coins of the Roman Republic*, a fine three-volume work recently edited for the Museum authorities by H. A. Grueber.—H. B. COTTERILL.

533

pecunia. These large bronzen bricks, of which many fragments have been found (*e.g.* at Vulci, together with *aes rude*), were evidently often broken into bits corresponding roughly to divisions of the Roman pound (*libra*). Pliny tells us that Livy asserted (in one of his lost Books ?) that Servius Tullius *primus signavit aes* ; but the oldest extant specimens of *aes signatum* are evidently Umbrian or Etruscan, and the earliest Roman specimens show such skill in design (as in the *Quincussis*, or ' Five-pounder,' of Plate 62) that some writers are unwilling to date them earlier than about 350 B.C. If, however, we regard the designs as the work of Etruscan or Greek artists, they may be considerably older, and in the Twelve Tables (450 B.C.) it is ordered that certain fines be paid in *aes*, and there is no mention of cattle as a medium of payment; so it seems reasonable to speak of *aes signatum* as having existed at least from 450 B.C.

(3) The next step was the introduction of a heavy, round bronze coinage—the AES GRAVE, as it was later called, in order to distinguish it from the lighter new coinage. The *As* was now first accepted as the monetary unit, and the well-known duodecimal system of the twelve *unciae*, with the *semis*, the *triens*, and other divisions of the *As*, was introduced. At first the *As* weighed a pound (*as libralis*), but its weight rapidly declined, so that when, in 268 B.C., the new triental (4-ounce) unit was initiated, the old and new units were practically of the same weight. It was formerly believed (by Mommsen and his school) that the *aes grave* and the *As* dated from the time of the Decemvirs (*c.* 450 B.C.), but it seems certain, from the style of the Janus heads and from the form of the prows that invariably adorn these early heavy coins, that they were first cast about the year 338 B.C. The Janus design evidently alludes to the close of the great Latin War, and the prows are still more evidently the celebrated prows of the warships of Antium which were set up in the Forum at Rome and gave the name to the Rostra (see p. 104)

(4) Soon after the conquest by Rome of the greater part of the peninsula, in 268 B.C., Roman money—not only bronze,

Plate LXII. Aes Signatum (from 450 b.c.)   534

PLATE LXIII. DECUSSIS AND AS (*c.* 268 B.C.) 535

ROMAN COINS

but silver and gold, and mostly *struck*, not *cast*—began to permeate Italy, though for a long time it did not banish all the local money of the southern cities. The subject of later Republican coinages is far too large to treat here. It will be noted that many of the later pieces bear the name, or symbol, of the ' moneyer,' *i.e.* the master of the mint, or official who issued the coins. This custom began about 240 B.C.

Plate 62. *Aes signatum.* The reverse of a *Quincussis* (Five-pounder). The obverse has a similar design. Date any time after about 450 B.C.

Pl. 63. 1. A heavy bronze *Decussis* (nominally a ' Ten-pounder,' but considerably less). Head of Roma with helmet adorned with gryphon, etc. Behind, X (= 10 *Asses*). Date about 268 B.C. or later, the *aes grave* type having survived for a considerable period.

2. An *As* (cast) of same type and period. Obverse, the usual Janus design ; reverse, a prow ; above, I (= 1 *As*).

Pl. 64. 1. Earliest *Denarius.* Obverse, Roma in helmet ; reverse, the Dioscuri (Castor and Pollux), and legend ' Roma.' Date *c.* 268.

2. Earliest *Semis* (half-*As*). Obverse, head of Jupiter ; reverse, Roma and prow and S (= *Semis*).

3. Earliest gold coin ; toward end of First Punic War ; issued for funds to build a fleet. Obverse, Mars in a Corinthian helmet.

4. *Electrum* coin struck by Hannibal at Capua, *c.* 215. Obverse, Punic Persephone in Capuan janiform type ; reverse, Jupiter in chariot driven by Victory (type of Roman *quadrigatus*).

5. *Denarius* minted by the ' moneyer ' L. Saufeius (of noble Praenestan family). Victory in chariot ; alluding to Roman successes of 172–151 B.C

6. *Denarius* of C. Minucius Augurinus (150–125 B.C.), with statue of L. M. Augurinus, who was *prae-*

fectus annonae in 439 B.C., during the famine
(Livy, x. 9).

Pl. 64. 7. *Denarius* of A. Albinus (89 B.C.) ; alluding to the
battle of Lake Regillus (496 B.C.).

8. *Denarius* of M. Aemilius Lepidus (65 B.C.) ; city
of Alexandria (turreted) and his ancestor as
Tutor regis crowning (?) Ptolemy V of Egypt,
about 196 B.C. A decree issued at the coro-
nation (*Anacleteria*) is given on the Rosetta
Stone. See Hill's *Hist. Coins*, p. 52.

9. *Denarius* of C. Cassius Longinus (124–103 B.C.),
son of the Longinus Ravilla who passed the Lex
Tabellaria (Ballot Law ; see p. 368). This law
is alluded to by the voting-urn and the Liberty
in chariot. (C. Cassius Longinus, the conspirator, was of the same family, the great ancestor
of which was Spurius Cassius ; see pp. 52, 68.)

10. *Denarius* of Q. Cassius Longinus (58 B.C.). Types :
Vesta and her temple, with voting-urn and
tablet, alluding to the re-trial of the Vestals,
at which Ravilla, his ancestor, presided. See
No. 9.

11. *Denarius* of Faustus Cornelius Sulla (62 B.C.), son
of the Dictator. It depicts the surrender of
Jugurtha by Bocchus. Sulla is seated ; Bocchus
kneels, and behind kneels Jugurtha, with hands
tied behind his back. See p. 381.

12 *Denarius* of Piso and Caepio (100 B.C.). Obverse,
Saturn (as god of harvest) ; reverse, Piso and
Caepio seated ; ears of corn ; allusion to the
corn law (Lex Frumentaria) of Saturninus.

13. *Quinarius* (half-*denarius*) of C. Egnatuleius (101
B.C.). Victory and Gaulish trophy. Allusion
to victory of Marius at Aquae Sextiae.

14. Social War. Warriors taking oath on a pig.

15 Social War. Successes of the confederates.

16. *Aureus* of Sulla in Greece (87–84 B.C.). Venus

PLATE LXIV. COINS OF 268 TO 61 B.C.

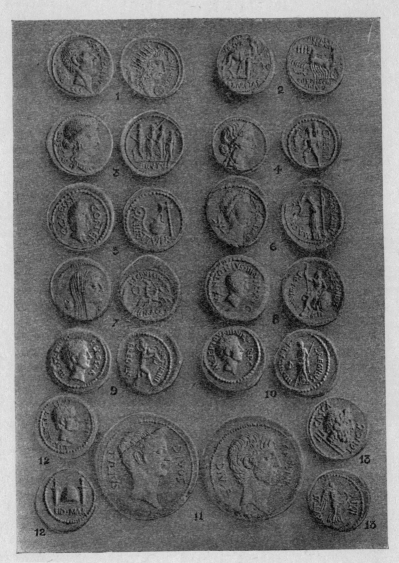

PLATE LXV. COINS OF 60 TO 38 B.C. 537

and Cupid; sacrificial ewer and *lituus* between trophies. An *aureus* is of about the same value as a guinea according to the present worth of gold.

Pl. 64. 17. *Aureus* of Pompeius. Obverse, Africa, wearing elephant-skin. Legend, ' Magnus.' The *lituus* and *capis* (jug) symbolize membership of the College of Augurs. Reverse, Pompeius in triumphal quadriga; a youth riding nearest horse. Legend, ' pro cos ' (*proconsul*). A very rare and very perplexing coin. Pompeius was propraetor in Africa in 81 B.C. On his return he was greeted by Sulla with the title ' Magnus,' which he seems to have assumed first in 75 B.C. He gained triumphs in all three continents (in 81, 71, and 61 B.C.). If the youth is his son Cnaeus (born probably about 77 B.C.), the coin must date from about 61 B.C., after the Mithradatic War, but has reference also to his earlier African triumph. See B. Mus. Cat. *Coins of Roman Rep.*, ii. p. 464.

Pl. 65. 1. *Denarius* of C. Coelius Caldus (60 B.C.) commemorating his grandfather of same name (107–94 B.C.), who was connected with the Lex Tabellaria.

2. *Denarius* of Scaurus and Hypsaeus. M. Aem. Scaurus was stepson of Sulla and served under Pompey in the East. He was curule aedile in 58 B.C. This represents the surrender of Aretas, king of Arabia Petraea.

3. *Denarius* of Q. Caepio Brutus (59 B.C.), better known as M. Junius Brutus. Reverse, his ancestor Lucius Junius Brutus (consul 509 B.C.) walking between two lictors and preceded by an *accensus* (usher or tipstaff); obverse, the head of Liberty. Note that there are also *aurei* with the head of L. J. Brutus, and it is these portraits that have led to the identification of the bust given at p. 40.

Pl. 65.

4. *Denarius* of Julius Caesar. Obverse. Venus; reverse, Aeneas, naked, with the Palladium in his right hand and carrying on his left arm his father Anchises clothed in tunic and hood. Legend, ' Caesar.'

5. *Aureus* of A. Hirtius on the third consulship of Caesar, 46 B.C. Obverse, Pietas.

6. *Denarius* of M. Mettius (44 B.C.) on the death of Caesar. Obverse, *Caesar Imperator*, with sacrificial bowl and *lituus* (pontifical symbols); reverse, Venus Victrix holding a Victory. Moneyer's mark, Mettius.

7. *Denarius* of P. Sepullius Macer on the death of Caesar. Obverse, head of M. Antonius, veiled, and a handled jug (*capis*); reverse, a rider, wreath and palm-branch.

8. *Aureus* of L. Regulus. Obverse, M. Antonius and legend ' iii Vir. R.P.C. ' (*Triumvir reipublicae constituendae*) ; reverse, the hero Anton, son of Hercules, seated on a rock with shield, spear, and parazonion (girdle). Legend, ' L. Regulus iiii Vir. A.P.F. ' (*Quatuorvir auro publico feriundo*).

9. *Aureus* of Regulus. Obverse, portrait of Octavius (C. Caesar) and legend as before ; reverse, Aeneas carrying Anchises.

10. *Aureus* of Regulus. Obverse, Octavius, as before ; reverse, Victory and moneyer's name. The date of these *aurei* is 39 B.C.

11. Bronze coin of Octavius (38 B.C.) with his portrait and that of the deified Julius Caesar. Struck in Gaul during the Triumvirate.

12. *Denarius* of M. Jun. Brutus (43 B.C.). Obverse, Brutus and legend ' Imp[erator],' his title as commander-in-chief ; reverse, cap of Liberty, two daggers, and ' Eid. Mart. ' (*Idibus Martiis*). Dion Cassius tells us that Brutus struck coins on which were two daggers and a *pileus* (felt

hat), to show that he and Cassius had given liberty to the fatherland. The moneyer's name is Cestianus. He was probably a quaestor of Brutus in Greece.

Pl. 65. 13. *Denarius* of Brutus and Casca (43 B.C.). Obverse, the head of Neptune. The moneyer's name is Casca Longus, probably the same as P. Serv. Casca, the conspirator, at this time in command of the fleet of Brutus. On reverse Victory is holding a broken diadem and treading on a (broken?) sceptre, symbolizing release from tyranny. The legend is again 'Brutus Imp.'

LIST OF IMPORTANT DATES

'B.C.' is omitted for convenience.   The dates
to about 390 B.C. are traditional.

753. Foundation of the city.

753–717. Reign of Romulus.

715–673. Reign of Numa Pompilius.

673–642. Reign of Tullus Hostilius.   Destruction of Alba.

642–617. Reign of Ancus Martius.

616–579. Reign of L. Tarquinius Priscus.

578–535. Reign of Servius Tullius.   Alliance with the Latins

534–510. Reign of L. Tarquinius Superbus.

509. Foundation of the Republic.

508. Etruscans under Lars Porsena capture Rome.

504. Appius Claudius and the Sabines migrate to Rome.

501. Latin War.   First dictator.

496. Battle of Lake Regillus.

494. First Secession of the Plebs.   Institution of the Tribunate.

493. War with Volscians.

491. Famine in Rome.

489. Wars with Aequians and Volscians begin.

485. Spurius Cassius condemned.

477. Destruction of the Fabii.

474. Ten years' peace with Veii.

458. Cincinnatus saves the Roman army at Mount Algidus.

457. Tribunes raised in number from five to ten.

451. Appointment of Decemviri.

451–450. The Twelve Tables formed.

449. Second Secession of the Plebs.   Valerio-Horatian Laws.

445. Canuleian Law.   Appointment of 'military tribunes with
      consular power.'

443. Censors appointed.

REPUBLICAN ROME

438. War with Veii renewed.

431. Battle at Mount Algidus.

406. War with Veii. First payment of the army.

396. Fall of Veii.

390. Sack of Rome by the Gauls. Manlius saves the Capitol

385. Restriction of the Latin League.

377. Licinian Rogations introduced.

367. Camillus defeats the Gauls. Licinian Rogations passed. Temple of Concord built. Praetorship and Curule Aedileship established.

366. First plebeian consul.

361. War with the Gauls.

358. Treaty with the Latins renewed.

356–351. War with the Etruscans.

356. First plebeian dictator.

354. Treaty with the Samnites.

351. First plebeian censor.

348. Commercial treaty with Carthage.

343–341. First Samnite War.

343. Battle of Mount Gaurus.

342. Mutiny of the army at Capua.

341. Treaty with the Samnites.

340–338. Latin War. Battle of Veseris.

339. Publilian Laws.

338. End of Latin War. Latin League dissolved

337. First plebeian praetor.

327–304. Second Samnite War.

326. First proconsul. Papirian Law

321. The Caudine Forks.

312. Via Appia begun.

311–308. War with the Etruscans.

310. Battle of Lake Vadimo

306. New commercial treaty with Carthage

305. Fall of Bovianum.

304. Treaty with the Samnites.

303. Via Flaminia and Via Valeria begun.

300. Ogulnian Law

542

IMPORTANT DATES

298–290. Third Samnite War.

295. Battle of Sentinum.

287. Third Secession of the Plebs. Hortensian Laws.

284. Battle of Arretium.

283. Boii and Etruscans defeated at Lake Vadimo.

281. War with Tarentum and with Pyrrhus.

280. Battle of Heraclea.

279. Battle of Asculum.

278. Alliance with Carthage.

275. Battle of Beneventum. Pyrrhus returns to Epirus.

273. Treaty with Egypt.

272. Tarentum surrenders.

271. Fall of Rhegium.

267. Campaign against the Sallentines. Brundisium taken.

266. Conquest of Italy completed.

264–241. First Punic War.

264. Siege of Messana.

263. Hiero allied with Rome.

262. Agrigentum taken.

260. Battle of Mylae.

259. Corsica and Sardinia ravaged.

256. Battle of Ecnomus. Romans land in Africa.

255. Regulus defeated before Carthage. Battle off the Hermaean Cape.

254. Romans take Panormus.

250. Great victory at Panormus. Siege of Lilybaeum begun.

249. Battle of Drepanum.

244. Hamilcar takes Eryx.

242. Battle off Aegates Islands.

241. Peace with Carthage.

241–238. Carthaginian war with mercenaries

238. War with Gauls renewed. Rome threatens Carthage and she submits.

232. Lex Flaminia.

231. Sardinia and Corsica constituted a province.

230–229. Illyrian War.

228. Romans admitted to Isthmian Games.

543

REPUBLICAN ROME

226. Rising among the Gauls.
225. Battles of Faesulae and Telamon.
222. All Gaul south of the Alps subdued.
221. Hannibal succeeds Hasdrubal in Spain.
219. War in Illyria.
218–201. Second Punic War.
218. Hannibal takes Saguntum.   Battles of the Ticinus and
      the Trebia.
217. Battle of Lake Thrasymene.
216. Battle of Cannae.
214. Syracuse besieged by Marcellus.
214–205. First Macedonian War.
212. Fall of Syracuse.
211. Hannibal before Rome.   Fall of Capua.   Scipio in Spain
210. All Sicily under Rome.   Scipio takes New Carthage.
209. Fall of Tarentum.
207. Death of Hasdrubal at the Metaurus.
206. Battle of Ilipa (or Baecula).   Scipio returns to Rome.
204. Scipio in Africa.
203. Battle of the Great Plains.
202. Battle of Zama.
200–196. Second Macedonian War   Rising of the Gauls.
198. Flamininus in Greece.
197. Battle of Cynoscephalae.   War in Gaul.
196. Flamininus at the Olympic Games.   Settlement of Greece.
195. Sparta besieged by Flamininus.
192–190. War with Antiochus.
191. Antiochus defeated at Thermopylae.   Final defeat of the
      Boii.
190. Battle of Magnesia.
189. Settlement of Asia.   Aetolians finally subdued.
187. Via Aemilia begun.   Trial of the Scipios.
186. Fanatical worship of Bacchus.
185. Ligurian War begins
184. Cato's censorship.
183. Death of Hannibal and of Scipio.
181. Aquileia founded.

544

IMPORTANT DATES

179. Death of Philip of Macedon. Tiberius Gracchus the elder in Spain.
172. Both consuls plebeian for the first time.
171–168. Third Macedonian War.
168. Battle of Pydna. Roman protectorate over Egypt.
167. Settlement of Macedon.
165. Greek patriots exiled.
156. Lex Aelia Fufia.
155. Campaign against the Dalmatians.
153–133. Celtiberian War.
150. Galba massacres the Lusitanians.
149. Death of Cato.
149–146. Third Punic War.
148. Macedonia becomes a province.
147. Scipio appointed to command in Africa.
146. Destruction of Carthage. Province of Africa formed. Destruction of Corinth.
143. Viriathus triumphant in Spain.
140. Murder of Viriathus.
139. Ballot introduced in elections. End of the war in Lusitania.
139–132. Slave war in Sicily.
133. Tribunate and death of Tiberius Gracchus. Fall of Numantia. Rome supreme in Spain. Attalus bequeaths his kingdom to Rome.
131. Both censors plebeian for the first time.
129. Assassination of Scipio.
125. Flaccus and the Italian franchise. Revolt of Fregellae.
123–122. Tribunate of Caius Gracchus.
123. The Equites become a new order.
122. Drusus outbids Gracchus.
121. Death of Caius Gracchus, and of Fulvius. Southern Gaul conquered.
113–101. Wars with the Cimbri and Gauls.
112–106. Jugurthine War.
107. Marius (consul for the first time) commands in Africa and introduces changes in the army.

545

REPUBLICAN ROME

105. Battle of Arausio.
104. Lex Domitia.
103–99. Sicilian slave war.
102. Battle of Aquae Sextiae.
101. Battle of Vercellae (Raudine Plain).
100. Appuleian Laws. Death of Saturninus and Glaucia. Birth of Julius Caesar.
96. Cyrene bequeathed to Rome.
95. Lex Licinia et Mucia alienates the Italians.
91. Tribunate and murder of Drusus.
91–88. Social War.
90. Julian Law.
89. Lex Plautia Papiria.
88. Sulpician Laws. Sulla takes Rome. Massacre of 80,000 Romans in Asia.
88–84. First Mithradatic War.
87. Sulla in Greece. Athens besieged. Cinnan revolution.
86. Sulla takes Athens. Battle of Chaeronea. Death of Marius.
85. Battle of Orchomenus. Assassination of Flaccus.
84. Death of Cinna, and of Fimbria.
83. Sulla returns to Italy. Civil War. Sertorius goes to Spain.
82. Massacre of Optimates in Rome. Sulla occupies the city. Battle of the Colline Gate. Sulla dictator. Sullan proscriptions.
81. Cornelian Laws. Egypt bequeathed to Rome.
79. Sulla resigns the dictatorship. Sertorius triumphant in Spain.
78. Death of Sulla. Lepidus's rebellion.
78–76. War with the Cilician pirates.
77. Pompeius goes to Spain.
75. Bithynia bequeathed to Rome.
74–65. Second Mithradatic War.
73–71. War of the Gladiators.
72. Sertorius assassinated. End of Sertorian War. Reforms of Lucullus in Asia.

IMPORTANT DATES

71. Great development of piracy.
70. Pompeius and Crassus consuls. Trial of Verres. Pompeius retires at end of the year.
69. Siege of Tigranocerta. Treaty with Parthia.
68. Lucullus marches on Artaxata.
68–67. Metellus in Crete.
67. Gabinian Law. Pompeius subdues the pirates.
66. Manilian Law. Pompeius goes to the East. Battle of Nicopolis. First Catilinian conspiracy.
65. Pompeius in the Caucasus. Caesar curule aedile.
64. Catiline's conspiracies. Cicero consul. Pompeius in Syria. Syria made a province.
63. Rullan Law. Caesar Pontifex Maximus. Cicero denounces Catiline ; execution of the conspirators. Pompeius in Judaea ; fall of Jerusalem. Birth of C. Octavius (Augustus). Settlement of the East.
62. Death of Catiline. Pompeius returns to Italy.
61. Trial of Clodius. Caesar praetor in Spain.
60. First Triumvirate.
59. Caesar's first consulship.
58–50. Caesar in Gaul.
58. Tribunate of Clodius. Cicero exiled.
57. Cicero recalled. Submission of the Nervii.
56. Conference of the Triumvirs. War with Veneti in Gaul.
55. Pompeius and Crassus get five-year commands, and Caesar's command is prolonged. Caesar across the Rhine and in Britain.
54. Crassus in Syria. Caesar's second expedition to Britain. Cicero submits to the Triumvirs.
53. Battle of Carrhae. Death of Crassus. Caesar again crosses the Rhine.
52. Death of Clodius. Pompeius sole consul. Caesar against Vercingetorix. Siege of Alesia.
51. Cato denounces Caesar. Organization of Gaul.
50. Pompeius leaves Rome. Caesar at Ravenna.
49. Caesar crosses the Rubicon. Pompeius leaves Italy. Surrender of Pompeians at Ilerda. Caesar dictator

REPUBLICAN ROME

48. Caesar goes to Greece. Battle of Pharsalus. Death of
Pompeius.

48–47. Caesar in Egypt.

47. Caesar in Asia. Battle of Zela. Caesar returns to Rome,
and afterwards goes to Africa.

46. Battle of Thapsus. Caesar given dictatorship for ten years.

45. Battle of Munda. Caesar awarded perpetual dictatorship.

44. Assassination of Caesar.

INDEX

ABORIGINES, in legend of origin of the Romans, 1, 2
Acca Laurentia, 4
Acco, 501
Achaea, 314; Appuleian Laws and, 389
Achaean League, 191, 280, 281, 291, 298, 299; in Second Macedonian War, 284, 285, 288, 289; joins Rome against Antiochus, 292; leading citizens of, exiled, 309; war with Sparta, and with Rome, 313–314
Achradina, 245, 247
Acilius Glabrio, Manius, 293
Acrocorinthus, xviii
Adherbal, Carthaginian officer, 178, 179
Adherbal, Numidian prince, 376, 377, 378
Aediles, 60; curule, 122
Aedui, 383, 494, 496, 502
Aegates Islands, battle off, 182
Aegusa, 177, 182
Aemilian Way, 197, 329
Aemilius Barbula, L., 136
Aemilius Lepidus, M. (consul 187 B.C.), 297, 536
Aemilius Lepidus, M. (consul 78 B.C.), 441
Aemilius Lepidus, M. (triumvir), x, 536
Aemilius Papus, L., 195
Aemilius Paulus, L., conqueror of Perseus, 305–310, 325, 340
Aemilius Paulus, L., general at Cannae, 234–236
Aemilius Scaurus, M., xvi, 377, 378, 379
Aeneas, in legend of origin of the Romans, 2; depicted on coins, 538
Aequians, 22, 66, 69, 114
Aes grave, 534, 535
Aes rude, or infectum, 533
Aes signatum, 533–534, 535
Aesculapius, Roman cult of, xiv, 348

Aetolian League, 191, 280; and Philip of Macedon, 269; in Second Macedonian War, 284, 287–288; and the war with Antiochus, 290, 291, 292, 294; submission of, 298
Aetolians, 280–281
Afranius, L., 510, 514, 515, 516
Africa, Scipio Africanus invades, 270; province of, constituted, 322
Agger of Servius Tullius, xi
Agriculture, the Romans and, 23–24; decay of, 48, 124, 349–350, 427; Tiberius Gracchus and the decline of, 362; Sulla and the decline of, 427; Caesar and the revival of, 527
Agrigentum, 143, 165, 246, 247
Agron, 189–190
Aius Locutius, 8
Alba Fucentia, 114, 115
Alba Longa, 3; destruction of, 11
Alban Lake, 77, 78, 112
Alban Mount, 3, 91
Albanians, 466–467
Aleria, 168
Alesia, 503–504
Alexandria, Caesar at, 520–521
Algidus, Mount, 69, 74, 75, 78
Allia, 82; battle of the, 83
Allies, Italian, 149, 151–152, 189, 334, 344; Hannibal and, 226; and the land bill of Tiberius Gracchus, 367; Scipio Africanus and, 367–368; and the franchise, 369, 389, 391–392, 396, 400; Caius Gracchus and, 371; Appuleian Laws and, 389; Drusus and, 392, 393; revolt of (Social War), 393–397; concessions to, 395–396; Cinna and, 400; Sulla and, 420
Allobroges, 479–480
Ambrones, 385, 386
Amisus, 467
Amphipolis, 308
Amynander, 283, 284, 291
Anagnia, 140
Anapus, xvii, 247

549

INDEX

INDEX

INDEX

INDEX

Cornelius Cossus, A., 76

Cornelius Dolabella, P., 133

Cornelius Lentulus, L. (consul 275 B.C.), 145

Cornelius Lentulus, L. (consul 49 B.C.), 512

Cornelius Lentulus, P., 479, 480, 481

Cornelius Scipio, P., appointed to command against Hannibal, 207 ; and Hannibal's crossing of the Rhone, 208–209 ; at battle of the Ticinus, 215 ; in campaign of the Trebia, 215–220 ; in Spain, 241, 243, 256–257

Cornelius Scipio Aemilianus Africanus, P., at siege of Carthage, 319–321 ; in Spain, 327–328 ; related to the Gracchi, 361 ; champions the Italian allies, 367 ; and the Populus, 367 ; death, 368

Cornelius Scipio Africanus, P., xvi, xvii ; at battle of the Ticinus, 215 ; in crisis after Cannae, 238 ; in Spain, 257–261 ; his African expedition, 268–269, 270–274 ; at Zama, 272–273 ; in war with Antiochus, 294, 295, 296 ; last days, and death, 299, 300 ; Cato and, 357

Cornelius Scipio Asiaticus, L. (consul 190 B.C.), 294, 300

Cornelius Scipio Asiaticus, L. (consul 83 B.C.), 420

Cornelius Scipio Asina, Cn., 167

Cornelius Scipio Barbatus, L., xvi

Cornelius Scipio Calvus, Cn., 209, 214, 241, 243, 256–257

Cornelius Scipio Nasica, P., 329

Cornelius Scipio Nasica Corculum, P., 306–307

Cornelius Scipio Nasica Serapio, P., 366

Cornelius Sulla Felix, L., xi, xx ; in Jugurthine war, 381 ; in Social War, 395, 397 ; in civil war, 398–400 ; reforms of, 399 ; sails for Greece, 400 ; campaign in Cappadocia, 406 ; besieges and sacks Athens, 409–412 ; at battle of Chaeronea, 413–414 ; and Flaccus, 415 ; at battle of Orchomenus, 415–416 ; makes peace with Mithradates, 417 ; and taxation of Asia, 418 ; returns to Italy, 419 ; in civil war, 419–423 ; proscriptions of, 424–426 ; Julius Caesar and, 426–427 ; becomes dictator, 427–428 ; reforms of, 428–431, 453 ; death, 432 ;

character and achievements, 432–433 ; Lepidus and the reforms of, 441 ; Pompeius and Crassus and the reforms of, 451, 453 ; depicted on coin, 536 ; coins of, 536 ; and Pompeius, 537

Corsica, in First Punic War, 168 ; becomes, with Sardinia, a Roman province, 188

Coruncanius, L., 190

Coruncanius, T., 141

Cothon, at Carthage, xviii, 320

Cotta, M., 458

Cotys, 303

Crassus—see Licinius

Cremona, 197, 207, 222

Cretans, Metellus Creticus and, 455, 456

Crispinus—see Quinctius

Crixus, 448

Croton, 240, 533

Cumae, 36, 65, 66, 181, 240, 243, 432

Cunctator—see Fabius

Cures, 67

Curia Hostilia, 11, 390, 510

Curiate assembly, 40, 126

Curiatii and Horatii, x, xiii, 11

Curies, 15

Curio—see Scribonius

Curius Dentatus, M., 132, 145

Cybele, Roman cult of, 348

Cynoscephalae, 286–287, 289

Cyprus, Cato sent to, 490

Cyzicus, 458

DALMATIA, 329

Dante, on Cato, 524

Dardanians, 283, 284

Debt, law as to, 30, 56–58, 125 ; Licinian Rogations and, 120 ; Hortensian Laws and, 126

Decemvirs, 54–55, 534

Decius Mus, P., 97, 100, 103

Decius Mus, P., the younger, 116, 117

Decussis, 535

Deiotarus, 469

Delos, and slave traffic, 346 ; in war with Mithradates, 409

Demaratus, 13

Demetrias, 284, 289, 291

Demetrius of Pharos, 190, 191, 192, 203

Demetrius, son of Philip V, 287, 302

Denarius, 535–539

Dentatus, centurion, 55

553

INDEX

554

INDEX

Furius Camillus, M., xiii, 78–80, 84, 85, 88, 89, 90, 121–122
Fustuarium, 71 *n.*

GABINIAN Law, 455
Gabinius, A., 455, 490, 508
Gabinius, P., 480
Gades, 205, 261, 529
Gaesatae, 193
Gaul, conquest of, 438, 504 ; Cisalpine and Transalpine, assigned to Caesar, 489 ; threatened by Germans, 491 ; campaigns of Caesar in, 492–498, 500–504, 511 ; effect of Caesar's conquest of, 531
Gauls, 80–85, 192–193 ; wars with, 81–85, 90–91, 133, 193–197, 329 ; Rome sacked by, 83–84 ; in Third Samnite War, 115–117 ; their country, 192 ; Roman legions recruited from, 197 ; in Hasdrubal's last battle, 266, 267 ; Transpadane, enfranchised by Caesar, 528–529
Gaurus, Mount, 97
Genthius, 303, 305
Genucius, Cn., 50
Gergovia, 502
Germans, 491, 495 ; Roman terror of, 495
Gerunium, 232 *and n.*, 234
Gisco, 183, 186, 187
Gladiatorial shows, Etruscan origin of, 34, 446 ; development of, 446
Gladiators, 446 ; War of the, 446–449
Glaucia—*see* Servilius
Gods, transformation of, 9
Gracchus—*see* Sempronius
Great Harbour, Syracuse, xvii
Great Plains, battle of the, 271
Greece, political decay of, 130–131 ; Rome and, 191, 288 ; war with, 313–314 ; settlement of, 314–315 ; joins Mithradates, 408, 409
Greek colonies in Italy, 36–37
Greeks, deportation of, 309

HAMILCAR, Carthaginian admiral, 170
Hamilcar Barca, 180–181, 182, 183, 184, 187, 199, 200, 201
Hannibal, xvi, 184, 197, 285 ; appointed to command in Spain, 200, 201, 202 ; in Second Punic War, 201–274 ; after Second Punic War, 290–291 ; at the court of Antiochus, 290, 291, 292 ; commands a fleet for Antiochus, and is defeated, 293–294 ; death, 299, 300–301 ; coin of, 535

Hannibal Rhodius, 177, 178
Hanno, and the mercenaries, 186
Hanno, at Drepanum, 182
Hanno, at Ecnomus, 170
Hanno, at Messana, 164
Hanno, brings reinforcements to Hannibal, 243
Hanno, Hannibal's general in Spain, 206
Hasdrubal, brother of Hannibal, 205, 241, 244, 256, 258, 260, 263–267, 268
Hasdrubal, Carthaginian general at Panormus, 174
Hasdrubal, Carthaginian general in Third Punic War, 317, 319, 320, 321
Hasdrubal, Hannibal's officer at Cannae, 236
Hasdrubal, son of Gisco, 258, 260, 270, 271
Hasdrubal, son-in-law of Hamilcar, 199, 200, 201
Hellenic and Roman affinity, 1–2, 191
Hellenism, Rome and, 352–355 ; Cato's attitude to, 358
Helvetii, Caesar's campaign against, 491–492
Heraclea, battle of, 138–139
Heraclea, in Macedonia, 306
Heracles, in legend of origin of the Romans, 2
Hercte, Mount, 180
Herculaneum, xiv
Herdonea, 251
Herdonius, Appius, 49
Hernicans, 66, 68, 114
Hexapylon, Syracuse, 247
Hiempsal, 376, 377
Hiera, 182
Hiero I, 65
Hiero II, 65, 146, 163, 164, 165, 178, 183, 239
Hieronymus, 239, 244, 245
Himilco, Carthaginian commander at Lilybaeum, 176, 177, 178
Himilco, Carthaginian officer, 320
Himilco, commander in Second Punic War, 246
Hippocrates, 245
Hope, Temple of, 221
Horace, 354
Horatii and Curiatii, supposed tombs of, x, xiii ; the legend of, 11
Horatius Cocles, x, 20
Horatius, M., 58
Hortensian Laws, 126

555

INDEX

INDEX

INDEX

INDEX

INDEX

INDEX

INDEX

INDEX

INDEX